THE PRACTICAL
PARALEGAL

THE PRACTICAL PARALEGAL

STRATEGIES FOR SUCCESS

DEBORAH E. BOUCHOUX

Georgetown University
Member, District of Columbia and California (inactive) Bars

ASPEN

PUBLISHERS

111 Eighth Avenue, New York, NY 10011
www.aspenpublishers.com

© 2006 Aspen Publishers, Inc.
a Wolters Kluwer business
www.aspenpublishers.com

Aspen Publishers
Attn: Permissions Department
111 Eighth Avenue, 7th Floor
New York, NY 10011-5201

Printed in the United States of America.

1 2 3 4 5 6 7 8 9 0

ISBN 0-7355-5083-2

Library of Congress Cataloging-in-Publication Data

Bouchoux, Deborah E., 1950-
    The practical paralegal : strategies for success / by Deborah E. Bouchoux.—1st ed.
     p. cm.
    Includes index.
    ISBN 0-7355-5083-2 (alk. paper)
  1. Legal assistants—United States. 2. Legal assistants—Vocational guidance—United States.
I. Title.

KF320. L4B68 2006
340'.023'73—dc22

                               2005011583

About Aspen Publishers

Aspen Publishers, headquartered in New York City, is a leading information provider for attorneys, business professionals, and law students. Written by preeminent authorities, our products consist of analytical and practical information covering both U.S. and international topics. We publish in the full range of formats, including updated manuals, books, periodicals, CDs, and online products.

Our proprietary content is complemented by 2,500 legal databases, containing over 11 million documents, available through our Loislaw division. Aspen Publishers also offers a wide range of topical legal and business databases linked to Loislaw's primary material. Our mission is to provide accurate, timely, and authoritative content in easily accessible formats, supported by unmatched customer care.

To order any Aspen Publishers title, go to *www.aspenpublishers.com* or call 1-800-638-8437.

To reinstate your manual update service, call 1-800-638-8437.

For more information on Loislaw products, go to *www.loislaw.com* or call 1-800-364-2512.

For Customer Care issues, e-mail *CustomerCare@aspenpublishers.com*; call 1-800-234-1660; or fax 1-800-901-9075.

ASPEN PUBLISHERS
a Wolters Kluwer business

TO MY BROTHERS AND SISTER, FOR THEIR LOVE AND SUPPORT.
THANK YOU TO JIM, MICHAEL, MARY KAY, AND RICK.

SUMMARY OF CONTENTS

Appendices

CONTENTS

PART I: FUNDAMENTALS FOR SUCCESS IN THE PARALEGAL PROFESSION AND THE AMERICAN LEGAL SYSTEM

PART II: PARALEGAL SKILLS

PART III: PARALEGALS IN THE WORKPLACE

CHAPTER 11: THE LAW OFFICE ENVIRONMENT   305

CHAPTER 12: PUTTING IT TOGETHER: STRATEGIES FOR SUCCESS IN THE WORKPLACE   325

Appendices

LIST OF FIGURES

PREFACE

INTRODUCTION

The paralegal field continues its rapid growth, with the Department of Labor predicting that the profession is expected to grow faster than the average for all occupations through 2102. Moreover, the value of paralegals to the legal profession is universally recognized. Consider the following statement by the American Bar Association: "The utilization of paralegals improves the efficiency, economy, and availability of legal services." Not only the American Bar Association but also a number of court decisions have endorsed the use of paralegals to make legal services more affordable and accessible.

With that growth and recognition come additional responsibilities. Today's paralegals are expected to perform a wide variety of tasks, including legal research, legal writing, interviewing, and investigating. Additionally, paralegals are expected to know substantive areas of law, such as civil procedure, litigation, and corporate law.

Graduates of paralegal programs are expected "to hit the ground running" when they get a job, yet there is a significant gap between what is learned in the classroom and the way to apply this knowledge in the real world of a law office environment. *The Practical Paralegal: Strategies for Success* is meant to bridge this gap by combining a thorough grounding in the paralegal profession with a pragmatic overview of what paralegals are expected to know and do in the workplace.

The text is divided into three main sections: The first section begins with a review of study skills and then discusses the paralegal profession and the U.S. legal system; the second section covers the paralegal skills of research, analysis, writing, interviewing, and investigating; and the final section discusses the workplace, covering what paralegals do in "real life," the various types of law practice, law office environments, career strategies, and techniques for success in the workplace.

Each chapter and section builds on the previous one. For example, once you read Chapter Four and understand the differences between trial and appellate courts, you will be ready for the discussion in Chapter Five about how to locate appellate court cases. Similarly, once you read Chapter Six's information about writing, you will understand how to prepare a memorandum or an executive summary setting forth the results of a client interview, which is discussed in Chapter Seven. Chapters Eight and Nine discuss the practice areas in which paralegals work. The text concludes with the most pragmatic information of all: how to get a job, keep a job, and quit a job and how to be successful in a law office environment.

A REAL-WORLD APPROACH

The text provides pragmatic and realistic information covering situations that occur in the real world of a law office. For example, the following topics are covered:

■ Effective ways to improve note taking and to study for exams;
■ What to do if you observe ethical misconduct in the workplace;
■ Using the Internet to impress clients;
■ Common blunders when using e-mail;
■ Cultivating listening skills;
■ Best practices for timekeeping and billing;
■ Advocating for yourself in salary negotiations;
■ How and when to quit a job;
■ What to do when you receive an assignment at work; and
■ Time-management techniques to improve job performance.

FEATURES OF THE TEXT

The text includes a number of features to enhance learning. Each chapter includes the following features:

■ **Chapter overview.** Each chapter begins with a preview of the material that will be presented in the chapter.
■ **Key terms.** The key terms and concepts used in the chapter are presented in boldface type and are defined in the margin near where the material is discussed. All of the key terms are listed at the end of each chapter so you can test your comprehension of these terms.
■ **Net results.** Each chapter provides references to websites where you can locate additional information on the topics covered in the chapter.
■ **Case illustration.** A case that illustrates one of the core concepts discussed in the chapter is presented at the end of each chapter.
■ **Chapter summary.** Each chapter's substantive discussion concludes with a review of the key presented in the Cornell Note-Taking System (as described in Chapter One).
■ **Trivia.** The Trivia section provides fun and interesting facts about some of the topics covered in the chapter.
■ **Discussion questions.** Questions to challenge comprehension of the text material and stimulate class or study group discussion are presented.
■ **Closing arguments.** Each chapter includes a series of practical questions that require readers to locate information pertinent to the chapter by accessing well-known legal or general interest Internet sites.

Each chapter also includes charts, graphs, sample forms, and other instructional aids, as needed. For example, Chapter Six includes a tip box on avoiding plagiarism in legal writing, and Chapter Ten includes a sample resignation letter.

Although every effort has been made to refer to useful websites, those sites can change both their content and addresses without notice. References to websites are not endorsements of those sites. On a final note, the eighteenth edition of *The Bluebook* was released in June 2005. The new eighteenth edition retains the same basic approach to citation form as earlier editions; however, it includes a new section called the Bluepages, which is a how-to guide offering many examples for the common citation needs of legal professionals.

FINAL THOUGHTS

Paralegals play a critical role in helping clients. Be excited about the challenges and opportunities that your new profession provides. Commit yourself to excellence both as a student and as a practicing paralegal. You will be rewarded not only monetarily but also by knowing that you have performed your job to the best of your abilities. Welcome!

Deborah E. Bouchoux
July 2005

ACKNOWLEDGMENTS

I would like to express my sincere appreciation to the many individuals who contributed to the development of this text. First, as always, I would like to thank Susan M. Sullivan, Program Director at the University of San Diego Paralegal Program. Sue gave me my first teaching position many years ago, and I value and respect her many contributions to the paralegal profession. Second, my current Program Director, Gloria Silvers of Georgetown University's Paralegal Studies Program, has been unflagging in her enthusiasm and support of both my career and the careers of all of the paralegal students who have graduated from her program.

I would like to thank Brian Yeary for providing me with some forms. Many thanks also to the various reviewers who reviewed the manuscript on behalf of the publisher. Their comments and advice were instructive and insightful. Throughout the more than 20 years I have been involved in teaching paralegals, I have received valuable comments and feedback from my students on the paralegal profession, strategies for success as students and as practicing paralegals, and the skills and attributes paralegals need to be valued members of the legal team.

Finally, my sincere appreciation to my copyeditor, Barbara Rappaport, and to the following individuals at Aspen Publishing: Melody Davies, Editorial Director; Sarah Hains, Editorial Services Manager; Laurel Ibey, Senior Manuscript Editor; and Betsy Kenny, Developmental Editor. A special thank you to Carol McGeehan, Publisher, and Richard Mixter, Senior Acquisitions Editor, who suggested this text and worked with me on its development. All members of the Aspen Publishing team offered encouragement and support throughout the writing and production phases of this text. Their thoughtful comments and suggestions were much appreciated and greatly contributed to the text.

I would like to acknowledge the following publishers and legal associations for granting me permission to reproduce copyrighted material for this text.

Figure 4-2: Map of the Thirteen Federal Judicial Courts, reprinted from West's Law Finder, copyright 1988 Thompson/West.

Figure 5-3: Reprinted with permission from Thompson/West.

Figure 5-4: Reprinted with permission from Thompson/West.

Figure 5-5: Reprinted with permission from Thompson/West.

Figure 7-1: Reprinted from the website of The Lawyer Assistant (*www.lawyerassistant.com*).

Figure 10-3: Reprinted with permission. Copyright National Federation of Paralegal Associations, Inc.

Figure 11-2: Reprinted with permission. Timeslips® is a registered trademark of Best Software SB, Inc.

Appendix C: "Model Guidelines for the Utilization of Legal Assistant Services," published online at *www.abanet.org/legalassts/modguide.html.*
© 1991 by the American Bar Association. Reprinted by permission.

Appendix D: Reprinted with permission from National Association of Legal Assistants.

Appendix E: Reprinted with permission from National Association of Legal Assistants.

Appendix F: Reprinted with permission. Copyright National Federation of Paralegal Associations, Inc. 1993.

THE PRACTICAL PARALEGAL

PART
I

FUNDAMENTALS FOR SUCCESS IN THE PARALEGAL PROFESSION AND THE AMERICAN LEGAL SYSTEM

CHAPTER 1

STUDENT SURVIVAL GUIDE: LEARNING TO LEARN

G OLD HAS A PRICE, BUT LEARNING IS PRICELESS.
—CHINESE PROVERB

CHAPTER OVERVIEW

This chapter focuses on the skills you will need to be successful in the classroom. A variety of study skills are discussed, including techniques on how to master your reading assignments and remember them, tips on note taking, and strategies to help you prepare for and take examinations. These study skills are useful not only in the classroom but also on the job, because working paralegals routinely read a great deal of material and are required to take notes for a variety of work-related tasks.

A. SUCCESS AS A STUDENT

A successful student is someone who leaves the classroom understanding the material covered and knowing how to put this knowledge to use in the real world. The only way teachers can measure whether students understand the topics covered in class is to give projects, homework, or tests, and then assign a grade based on the student's performance. While these methods may be accurate gauges of comprehension in some cases, in other cases, perhaps due to a student's test anxiety or personal problems, the grade is not reflective of the student's mastery of the material. Nevertheless, because grades are assigned in most paralegal education programs and because an employer later may rely on a student's grades as one measure of ability, it is important to be a successful student.

Students who have been highly successful at the secondary or undergraduate levels may struggle a bit in their paralegal classes. The techniques that were successful in

3

other classes and schools may not work in law-related classes. Why? Because in much undergraduate work, the focus is on getting the "right answer." In the law, however, the right answer is not always easy to spot. Issues are murky. There may well be more than one right answer. Moreover, the process of analyzing the law is as important as finding the right answer. Add in an entirely new vocabulary, a new way of writing, and rigid time constraints, and it is easy to see why new paralegal students often feel overwhelmed.

Successful students share several things in common: They do the work assigned, they come to class prepared, and they persistently work until they have mastered the material. Even more important than being a successful student and earning a good grade is being a successful learner, because learning is not something you leave behind in the classroom. You will need to learn throughout your life.

B. READING THE MATERIAL

1. Read to Remember

Legal professionals spend a great deal of time reading. They read statutes, cases, correspondence, briefs filed by adverse counsel, and so forth. To prepare you for this fact of life, your paralegal instructors will likely require a great deal of reading from you. You will take several different classes, each with at least one textbook and likely a packet of ancillary materials. The pace is nearly relentless. In some cases, the material is dry; in nearly all cases, the material is difficult. There is no plot to hold your interest. Thus, reading is a difficult assignment in and of itself. Consequently, it is critical to understand how to read the material in a way that will aid comprehension. Follow these five tips to master the reading material assigned in your courses.

- **Read before class.** First, unless instructed otherwise, read the material before attending class. You will understand the concepts discussed in class better if you have a framework in which to put them.
- **Preview for five minutes.** You will be greatly tempted to rush into the material and start reading. Don't. Invest five minutes before you begin any reading assignment by reviewing the table of contents relevant to the reading assignment. For example, if you are assigned to read Chapter Three of this text, a review of the table of contents discloses that you are given introductory material relating to ethics and responsibility, that the next topic discussed is the codes governing attorneys and paralegals, and then the chapter addresses nine specific ethical duties imposed on paralegals. Just as you cannot put together a puzzle without first seeing the complete picture, you should first understand the "big picture" of your assignment before trying to fit in the little pieces. Mark your table of contents with a sticky flag for easy reference. After reading the table of contents, read any chapter overview or chapter summary. Do not make the mistake of thinking these parts of a chapter are fluff. Generally, they are carefully constructed by the text's author to preview and then summarize the most important concepts covered. Similarly, key terms or margin notes are placed there for a reason: to reinforce learning. Don't ignore these helpful tools.

- **Divide and conquer.** Once you have completed your preview, break your reading into manageable parts. Unless your assignment is very short, it is unrealistic to think you can read all of the material in one sitting. Review the chapter headings and decide which sections you will read, how many pages you plan to read, or how much time you will read. Take frequent short breaks if needed. Set small goals for yourself. For example, decide to read the first section of a chapter. When you finish that section, reward yourself with a small break.

- **Take your text to class.** Bring your text with you to class and follow along as the instructor discusses the material. The instructor will likely explain difficult concepts and terms. Having your text in front of you will help you remember the material. Similarly, if you found a concept confusing, place a question mark or write the actual question in your text margin. When the instructor discusses this section, ask for clarification.

- **Read after class.** After the class discusses the reading material, invest another five minutes and review the text. It may be sufficient to review merely the chapter overview or the chapter summary. A quick review of the key terms may remind you of some of the material covered. Develop a habit of reviewing the material as soon after class as you can. Consider remaining in your seat for three to five minutes after class to review the material one more time and imprint it in your memory.

2. The SQ3R Method of Reading

One very popular method of reading material is the **SQ3R method**. There are five steps in this method, which is designed to improve reading comprehension.

SQ3R method
A method of reading designed to improve comprehension; its five components are surveying the material, questioning the material, reading, reciting, and reviewing the material

- **Survey the material.** Quickly scan titles, key terms, headings, introduction, and so forth within a section of your assigned reading.
- **Question.** As you survey, think of questions to ask yourself about the material. Use the titles and headings to formulate questions.
- **Read.** Read the material at your normal reading speed.
- **Recite.** Repeat from memory out loud the section you have read and formulate the answers to your questions. Summarize the material you read.
- **Review.** At the end of a chapter, review the material you read by highlighting key terms and concepts.

3. Techniques to Remember the Material

Studies show that most of us forget nearly half of what we read within fifteen minutes after reading it. Thus, we need to work to retain material. Reading a novel for pleasure is a passive activity. In contrast, reading a text to master its materials requires active work on your part. There are four ways to help you remember the materials you have read.

- **Mark your text.** Marking or writing in your textbook is an excellent way of helping you remember critical concepts. You may ignore the rule you heard all through grade school and secondary school that you may not write in your books. The books you purchased for your program are yours. Go ahead and mark them to your heart's delight. If you wish to sell your books at the end of a semester, those that are highly marked may be worth less money; however, the value to you of understanding the material is worth far more than the few dollars' reduction in resale price a marked book garners. Moreover, you may decide to keep your textbook, or a new edition may render your textbook out of date. The physical act of highlighting engages you more fully in the reading process and forces you to focus on the material. Consider skimming a section before you mark it. This approach will tell you what is important so you can mark it during your actual reading. There are different ways to mark your text to make it helpful to you:

☐ Underscoring. Underscoring is a common method of marking a text. It will enable you to find important issues and key terms at a glance.

☐ Highlighting. Many readers like to use felt-tipped markers to highlight critical issues. Consider using different colors for different issues. Highlighting important topics makes it easy to review these areas when preparing outlines or reviewing for tests. Resist the temptation to highlight nearly everything. Highlight only the core concepts.

☐ Making margin notes. Placing arrows, notes, or key terms in the margin is an effective way to help you retrieve important information when studying for tests. This technique is effective if you need to memorize certain information. For example, if you are expected to know the elements of a cause of action for fraud, use a different colored pen or symbol so that you can easily find this information when you prepare for your exams. Place question marks next to the sections you have difficulty with, so you can spend extra time on them or ask the instructor to clarify these sections in class.

■ **Challenge your understanding.** When you reach the end of a section, stop for a minute and review out loud what you have just finished. Reciting the material aloud will help you remember it. Review any discussion questions at the end of a section or chapter and challenge yourself to answer these. Write encapsulations of your answers to the discussion questions on an index card and place it at this page, so you are ready to participate if the instructor reviews these questions in class.

■ **Take notes.** After reading the assigned material, consider preparing a brief overview or outline. Use the table of contents as your guide to the key topics discussed in a chapter and prepare notes on the reading. You may wish to delay taking notes until after the class session, when you can then integrate notes on the text with notes from the class, using different colored paper so you can easily determine the source of the information.

■ **Control your environment.** Make sure that you read in an environment that is conducive to learning. Sit in a comfortable chair; make sure the lighting is adequate; and, most important, eliminate distractions, particularly television. While some activities can be multi-tasked with others, reading cannot. It requires your full attention. Try to notice when your energy levels are higher. For example, if you are more alert in the morning, schedule your reading for that time.

C. CLASSROOM ACTIVITIES TO ENHANCE LEARNING

1. Preliminary Guidelines

The classroom is the center of your learning activity. Classroom activity is meant to guide you to mastery of the subject matter, clarify any difficult material, and answer any questions you may have. Five very simple preliminary rules will greatly enhance your learning in the classroom:

- **Attend class.** Attend all classes. You paid for them, so make sure you get value for your dollars. If you are sick or cannot attend class, ask another student to take notes for you and pick up any handouts. Be responsible for your own learning.
- **Be on time.** Entering a class late is disrespectful to the instructor and other students. Other students are distracted while you search for a seat, remove your coat, locate your notebook and pens, and settle into your seat. Moreover, your ability to ask questions is compromised because it is possible the instructor has already covered certain material before you arrived. Asking the instructor to repeat instructions or material already covered is unprofessional.
- **Sit in front.** You probably search for the best seat in a movie theatre or at a concert, yet you may be opting for the worst seat in a classroom: at the back. It is harder to see the board and any displays from the back. Additionally, distraction levels are higher because you will be distracted by all the movements and activities of the students in front of you. Sitting in the front forces you to focus on what the instructor is saying because there's no place to hide.
- **Review the syllabus before class.** Your class syllabus provides an excellent overview of what material will be covered for each class and what is expected of you. Review the syllabus to make sure you will bring the required texts, notes, or other materials to the class.
- **Avoid distractions.** You will not only distract others but also yourself if you eat or drink in the class or if you try surreptitiously to open a package or a beverage can. Similarly, turn your cell phone off and do not look at it during class. Reviewing your calls or messages during class tells your instructor you don't care about the material.

2. Active Listening

Active listening, discussed further in Chapter Seven, is a method of communication in which the listener is actively engaged in the discussion. Sitting in the classroom and hearing a lecture is easy; listening is far more difficult. Consider the following to enhance your listening skills so you get the most out of your classroom experience:

- **Be attentive.** You will need to make a good faith effort to concentrate on what is being said. Try not to let your mind wander. Keep your textbook open and be ready to take notes. Avoid places in the classroom (near hallways and doors) that are distracting.

Active listening
Communication technique that lets speaker know that listener is attentive

- **Listen and watch for cues.** In many instances, instructors give cues as to what is critical. Thus, expressions such as "in sum," or "to prevail," or "there are three factors," are signals that the words to follow are important. Similarly, copy down what the instructor puts on the board or displays in any visual projection. An instructor does not go to the effort of putting information on the board or preparing a visual display if he or she doesn't think the information is important.
- **Anticipate and participate.** Think ahead to see if you can guess what will be discussed next. Such an exercise will engage you more fully in the lecture and will test your comprehension of the reading you did before class. Listen for the main idea the instructor is making. You do not need to write down every word the way a court reporter would. Focus on understanding the information being conveyed to you rather than on each word uttered. Be ready to participate. Many students are uncomfortable volunteering to answer questions posed in class. Don't be shy. Go ahead and take a chance. If something is unclear, ask for clarification. Thinking of questions will also help you understand how the material being discussed relates to material previously discussed or presented in the text. If the instructor does not provide time for questions or there is no natural "break" in the class to ask questions, talk to the instructor after class. Prepare a "to do" list or list of action items that need to be completed before the next class session.
- **Don't be judgmental.** Effective listeners avoid mentally arguing with speakers; they listen fully. Ignore a speaker's mannerisms, tone of voice, appearance, and so forth. Every minute you spend judging how a speaker looks, acts, or talks is a minute that you are not focusing on the material being presented.

3. Note Taking

a. General Comments

Taking notes is an excellent way to force yourself to be attentive during a lecture. If you are note taking you cannot be daydreaming because you will have to focus on what is being said. You will also need to take notes on the job—for example, when you are given a new work assignment or are interviewing a witness. Taking notes in class is good preparation for this skill you will need in the workplace. No matter which method you use, there are some strategies to follow to help you take notes that enhance your understanding of the material:

- Write legibly.
- Write on one side of the paper only.
- Consider using a looseleaf binder so you can add pages or shuffle sections around.
- Use a separate binder or section for each class.
- Use labels and tabs to divide your notes into meaningful sections.
- Develop a system of abbreviations (see Figure 1-1).
- Do not worry about transcribing every word. Focus on the main ideas and concepts. Fill in gaps during class breaks.
- Write verbatim notes when identifying lists, such as the elements of a valid contract. Mark this section of your notes in some way, perhaps by using colored pens

---

FIGURE 1-1
NOTE-TAKING ABBREVIATIONS

Because instructors and supervisors can speak faster than you can write, you need to develop a system of abbreviations for taking notes in class or on the job. Although there are some common legal and general symbols, any symbol or abbreviation will be satisfactory as long as you understand it.

LEGAL ABBREVIATIONS AND SYMBOLS

Π	plaintiff	JNOV	judgment notwithstanding the verdict
Δ	defendant		
§	section	Re:	regarding
K	contract	SJ	summary judgment
atty	attorney	S/F	statute of frauds
cert	certiorari	S/L	statute of limitations
dep	deposition, deponent	v., vs.	versus, as opposed to
J, J'ment	judgment		

GENERAL ABBREVIATIONS AND SYMBOLS

→	produces, causes	x	times
←	comes from, results from	#	number
≈	equivalent to, similar to, approximately	A.	answer
		b/c, bec.	because
+	in addition to, also	b/f	before
<	less than	c.	circa, about, approximately
>	more than	e.g.	for example
\	per	p., pp., pg.	page, pages
=	equal to, the same as	Q. or ?	question
≠	not equal to	.:	therefore
$	money	w/	with
&	and	w/in	within
@	at		

or placing a large "M" (for "memorize") in the margin, so you can easily find this important information, especially if you are required to memorize it.

■ Skip lines or move to a new paragraph when a new topic is introduced. Highlight new topics by underlining them, by using a different colored pen, or marking them in some way.

■ Annotate or mark your notes by circling or underlining important dates and issues. Highlight critical concepts.

■ Review your notes immediately after class and at least once before the next class session.

Don't agonize over the final appearance of your notes. They may appear to others to be awash in color and odd abbreviations. If the system works for you, stick with it. The goal is not to have the prettiest notes but to have the most effective ones for you.

b. The Cornell Note-Taking System

Although there are a number of different approaches to note taking, one of the best-known systems is called the **Cornell Note-Taking System**. The Cornell technique was devised more than 40 years ago and has been successfully used by thousands of students. First, prepare your notebook. Use a notebook with lined paper. Draw a line vertically down the page about 2-½ inches from the left side, thus dividing your paper into two columns, the narrower one on the left side, and a wider column (about 6 inches) on the right. Draw a horizontal line either at the bottom of each page or at the end of your notes for each class session, leaving a 2-inch "box" at the bottom of the page for notes. After you prepare your notebook, follow these six steps:

- **Record.** During the lecture, record general ideas in the right column. Focus on the main ideas rather than attempting to write down every word. Skip lines between topics.
- **Reduce.** After the lecture, reduce the main topics and facts to key words and phrases and place these in the left column. These will serve as cues to refresh your memory about the class presentation.
- **Recite.** After the lecture, cover up the information in the right-hand column and, looking only at the key words in the left column, recite the main ideas from the lecture. Do not reread your notes. Use your own words to express the ideas covered in class.
- **Reflect.** Think about the information. Test your memory by asking yourself questions about the topics discussed and providing your own answers to these questions.
- **Review.** Review your notes (avoiding rote rereading) at least once each week (or before the next class meeting) to help you remember the material.
- **Recapitulate.** Draft a summary of your notes in your own words at the end of each page or each lecture. Use complete sentences and summarize the material in the 2-inch box you prepared at the bottom of each page or section.

See Figure 1-2 for a sample page showing a format for note taking using the Cornell System. The chapter summaries in this text are presented according to the Cornell technique.

c. Preparing Review Outlines

A quick revision of your notes shortly after a class is probably very valuable, especially to clarify any confusing issues and to clean up illegible notes. Merely rewriting your notes word for word into a different notebook is probably less valuable because you will likely put your brain "on hold" and daydream while you rewrite. There are, however, three techniques you may wish to consider to further aid your comprehension and retention of the material.

- **Outlining.** Consider distilling your notes into a coherent outline of the class. Integrate both your class notes and your textbook information into an outline. Use your text's table of contents for the relevant chapters as a guide. Do not worry about the appearance of the outline or that each item is numbered consecutively. Incorporate the main elements of the material you will be expected

FIGURE 1-2	
CORNELL NOTE-TAKING SYSTEM	
Place key words and phrases in this section to serve as memory cues.	Place major ideas and topics in this section.
Summarize or recapitulate your notes in this section.	

to know. Use colored paper for your outline that is different from your class notes so you can easily distinguish which is which. Note that this is also a good approach if you develop notes from text readings. Use colored paper for reading notes that is different from lecture note pages so you will be able to tell the source of the information you have recorded.

■ **Using index cards.** Many students like to use index cards to review material. Each index card usually has a key term or concept written on one side and a definition or explanation on the other. Students can then easily use these like flash cards to test their knowledge. Using index cards is an effective way of mastering the material because you will need to review the information to prepare each card and you will write the information on the card (once again, reinforcing learning). Index cards are highly portable and easy to review. As you read your text or take notes in class, consider highlighting certain terms or concepts with a different colored marker to flag the items for which you will prepare index cards.

■ **Using a computer.** Many students use computers in the classroom to take notes, and there are several specialized software packages to help students organize these notes. Some students prefer to take notes on a laptop because they can type faster than they can write. Also, cutting and pasting on the computer makes organizing notes easy. Moreover, making sections of the notes more prominent through boldfacing, underscoring, and increasing the font size is readily done. Many students are becoming increasingly creative by using hyperlinks in their notes—for example, to link directly to a pertinent statute or case. Remember two critical items before you use a laptop to take notes: Ask your instructor for permission first (many teachers dislike the clicking noise produced by typing) and remember to create a backup of any notes. If you are not permitted to use a laptop during class or prefer not to, you may always use your home computer later to outline or organize your in-class notes.

4. Your Classroom Network and Study Groups

Get to know your fellow students and your instructors. Not only will making acquaintances make your school experience more pleasant, but you will also be widening your network of possible references and job resources. If your instructors do not know you, they will be unable to comment on your abilities and strengths when asked for references by potential employers. If your classmates do not know you, they will be unable to recommend you for a position with their employers. You also need a backup plan: If you are sick or cannot attend a class, you need a colleague to take notes for you and to pick up any handouts. It's a good idea to bounce ideas off your classmates. Develop a buddy system for these very practical reasons and for the emotional support your classmates can offer.

Study group
A small group of students who work together to study class material

Many students find it helpful to join a **study group**, a small group of students who work together to study the material and function as a support group for each other. Study groups not only help you as a student but also serve as models for working collaboratively in a law firm. The following are some general guidelines for forming and operating study groups:

- **Size matters.** Most experts recommend that the study group be between three and six people. If the group is too large, it may be difficult to organize and keep on track; and if it is too small, the absence of a member or two will render the group ineffective.
- **Composition matters.** Because members of the group will work closely with each other under stressful conditions, respect and collegiality are critical. If one member dominates and the others never participate, the group will fail. Similarly, try to organize a group whose members have different strengths and skills so they provide meaningful assistance to each other.
- **Organization matters.** The group must be organized and disciplined. Meeting times and dates must be scheduled and followed. Do not allow excessive socializing. Stay on task. Your library may provide meeting rooms for group study. Working in the library will remind everyone of the serious nature of the work at hand. Appoint a group leader or assign leadership on a rotating basis. Consider preparing an agenda for each session.
- **Responsibility matters.** Each member will usually be assigned to report on a particular topic or assignment, to outline a chapter, or prepare for an exam. If a member is consistently unprepared, you may need to cut the slacker loose. Remember that the point of the group is to help you learn, not to provide free tutoring for those who do not perform.
- **Making changes matters.** If the study group does not work for you, don't be afraid to leave it. However, bailing out of the group when everyone counted on you to prepare the pre-exam outline for Chapter Ten is disrespectful and unprofessional.

D. EXAMINATIONS AND CLASS PROJECTS

1. Introduction

There is no secret to what you will be expected to know on examinations. You will be tested on material from your assigned readings and from class lectures. Like

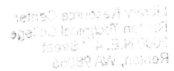

nearly every other facet of student success, the key is advance preparation. If you have been reading your assignments, taking good notes in class, and then routinely reviewing your notes, your job is nearly done. One study has reported that at the end of nine weeks (roughly one semester), students who reviewed their notes after class each day recalled about 75 percent of the material covered. Conversely, those who did not review their notes were able to recall only about 20 percent of the material at the end of nine weeks. Thus, if you consistently dedicate time to your studies during the course of your semester, you will not have to dedicate as much time at the end to prepare for your exams.

2. Strategies to Prepare for Examinations

Whether or not you have been consistently reviewing your notes throughout the semester, there are nine strategies you can adopt to improve your performance on examinations.

- **Get information about the examination.** Your syllabus will clearly indicate when your examinations will be held, allowing you to do some advance planning. If your instructor does not indicate the type of examination, ask what the exam format will be: essay, short answer, multiple choice, or some other format. If you know the exam will be in essay format and there will be four questions for you to answer in two hours, you can practice writing timed answers to questions you make up yourself or that appear in the textbook. While there is nothing wrong in asking about the structure of an examination, avoid questions such as, "Will this be on the test?" Such questions signal to your instructor that you care only about the grade and not about learning the material.
- **Pay attention to the instructor's comments.** Listen for any clues an instructor may provide, such as introducing a topic with the phrase, "it is critical to understand that. . . ." Similarly, if the instructor has repeated certain points on several occasions or put information on the board, these are tips that the material is important enough to be covered on the exam. Don't skip classes before an exam. The instructor may provide a review session or indicate exam topics.
- **Study old exams and quizzes.** Many instructors place copies of their old exams on reserve in the library. Review any such exams because they will give you an idea about the instructor's approach to tests. Determine whether most questions derive from the text or from class notes. If you have had quizzes or been assigned projects in the class, review any comments the instructor made to determine the instructor's style and preferences. Note that quiz questions sometimes have a way of reappearing in modified form on a later exam.
- **Manage your time.** Integrate all of your exam schedules into one master calendar so you can see at a glance when exams will occur, how many days you have between each exam, and so forth. Then set up a study schedule for yourself and stick to it. Break up the material into manageable chunks. Some experts suggest learning the hardest concepts or most troublesome material first and switching between topics if you become bored. Many students, however, prefer to learn the material in the order presented in the text and in the class lectures, because this approach places the material into a unified whole. See the discussion in Chapter Twelve on time-management techniques.

TIPS

Use a master calendar for each semester and enter due dates for exams, projects, and other class-related work. Use different colored pens for different classes so you can see at a glance when the "crunches" will occur during the semester. Keep your calendar handy and continually update it. Use it to plan and chart your progress on projects that you have chunked or broken into parts.

While commercial calendars or desktop calendars are fine, there are also a number of calendars you can access on the Internet and print for free. See the site *www.timeanddate.com* for monthly and customizable calendars.

- **Review notes.** One or two weeks before the exam, review all of your notes. This will bring the entire class into focus and will let you know which material you have mastered and which material is proving difficult. Annotate areas of concern in your notes with question marks or sticky flags.
- **Prepare outlines or flash cards.** If you haven't already done so, prepare outlines or flash cards. The index cards you prepared earlier serve as excellent flash cards to test your comprehension of the material. Use your highlighted text and highlighted class notes as guides to what should be included. Your outline may be a traditional outline, or it may be a paper chart taped to your wall. The format is not important. The very act of preparing an outline or flash cards will serve as a thorough review of the material.
- **Prepare a review sheet.** Based on your outline or flash cards, prepare a one-page review sheet that covers the major topics in the class. Mark the areas that need additional study so you can devote extra time to these.
- **Review the material.** Keep reviewing and re-reading the outlines, flash cards, and review sheet. Some experts suggest reviewing these materials three times each day for several days preceding the exam. Learning is accomplished through repetition, not through cramming. It is not possible to learn a semester's worth of material in one evening. Each time you start a study session, do a ten-minute review of the material you studied in your previous session. If lists need to be memorized, use mnemonic devices. For example, to remember the elements of adverse possession, a real property concept, one student developed the phrase "on a peach," which represented the required elements that possession of land be open, notorious, adverse, public, exclusive, adverse (again), continuous, and hostile.
- **Take advantage of resources.** Your program may offer a learning center, study skills workshops, computer labs, and other resources to help you achieve your goals as a student. Similarly, your instructors want you to succeed. Ask for help. Take advantage of any resources your program or school offers. Go online and enter "Study Skills" into a general search engine, such as Google (*www.google.com*). You will be directed to numerous sites, many of which are provided by colleges, to help with taking notes, studying, and preparing for exams.

3. Taking the Examination

Although you have probably heard this advice numerous times, remember to get a good night's sleep and have some food before any examination. Think of the way athletes prepare and train for events. You are in training too. Pay attention to the details. Leave plenty of time so you don't arrive at the exam late or stressed. Moreover, you will want to get a good seat with a view of the clock and away from any distractions, such as students who are fidgety or have distracting coughs. Make sure you have any needed materials, including pens, pencils, liquid paper to eliminate messy cross outs, exam bluebooks, and so forth.

While many experts suggest that the last hour or so before an exam should be spent relaxing, most students find this advice difficult to follow and prefer to review their notes or flash cards until the minute the examination is distributed. You may, however, wish to avoid discussing the test with other students because this may increase your level of anxiety.

Follow these tips to maximize your performance on the test:

- Skim the entire test as soon as it is given to you. Get an idea as to its length and structure. Make sure you have all of the pages and determine whether the exam questions are on both sides of the pages.
- Read the instructions twice. If the instructor has requested that answers be in complete sentences, write complete sentences. Students are often in such a panic at the beginning of an exam that they do not read the instructions or the questions. They are "racehorses" at the gate and seem to think that if they don't immediately start answering questions, their knowledge will drift away. Students would be surprised to learn how many times they lose points by failing to follow instructions, to answer the particular question asked, or to respond to all parts of a multi-part question.
- Pay attention to the words used in questions. Watch for modifying words such as *exclusively* or *solely*. These are often tips that help you formulate answers. Read questions all the way through before starting your answer. Then re-read the question, perhaps highlighting or underscoring critical components. If you are asked to identify three elements, make sure your answer includes three components.
- For true-false questions:
  - ☐ Watch for words such as *all, always, never,* and *only.* These words are often signals that suggest the appropriate answer.
  - ☐ If the statement is only partly correct, mark it "false."
  - ☐ If the statement has two clauses connected with the word *and*, both clauses must be true for the statement to be true.
  - ☐ If the statement has two clauses connected with the word *or*, only one clause needs to be true for the statement to be true.
  - ☐ Do not write explanatory language to support your true-false answer. You may explain yourself out of a point. If a question is confusing, ask for clarification from the instructor or proctor.
- For multiple-choice questions:
  - ☐ Read all choices before responding.
  - ☐ Eliminate the clearly incorrect choices.
  - ☐ If two answers seem appropriate, select the better choice or the more specific one.

- For essay questions:
  - ☐ Focus on the "call" of the question—namely, what you are asked to address. This is the most important part of the question. For example, if a question asks about assignments of leases, you need not discuss other real property concepts, such as easements or evictions. Do not include information that does not directly respond to the question.
  - ☐ Focus on the wording of the instructions. If a question asks you to "define," or "summarize," there is no need to write a detailed answer. Conversely, if you are asked to "discuss" or "analyze," you must provide a more thorough explanation.
  - ☐ Highlight or underscore important terms or concepts in the question.
  - ☐ Jot down a brief outline on the back of the exam and plan your answer. This is not a waste of time. It will help you develop a logical answer and eliminate the true exam time-wasters: erasing incorrect answers and including irrelevant information. Moreover, at a glance your outline will reveal whether your answer is balanced so that you don't spend too much effort on one section and too little effort on another.
  - ☐ List your mnemonic devices on the back of the page.
  - ☐ If the question has several parts, number each one (1, 2, 3, and so forth) and make sure your answer responds to each component part. Consider numbering your response as well.
  - ☐ Use standard paragraphing style. Start with an introduction or thesis statement, explain your answer, and end with a summary. Write in complete sentences.
- Consider answering questions you know or easier questions first. This will build confidence and help you get into the swing of the exam. Moreover, you don't want to miss points on things you know.
- Mark troublesome questions in pencil with an "X" or "?" in the margin to remind you to return to these questions. When you have finished these questions, erase your marks.
- Be a savvy test taker. Spend more time on questions that are weighted more heavily. A question that is worth ten points must be answered in more detail than one that is worth three points.
- Watch the clock. Some teachers recommend that students scan a test as soon as they receive it and mark its halfway point. The student should reach this part of the test halfway through the exam period.
- If you get stuck on a question or draw a blank, move to another section of the test and return to the troublesome question later. Don't waste valuable time staring at the test, waiting for the answer to come. Another question later in the test may suggest an approach or jog your memory.
- Write legibly.
- Take a chance. If you don't know something, go ahead and guess (unless there's a point penalty for incorrect answers). Fill in all blanks. You may get partial credit.
- Check to make sure your name is on the exam (and consider placing your initials on each page).
- Give the exam one more run-through before you turn it in to be sure that you have answered each and every question.

4. After the Examination

You may find that you need to decompress after an exam. Congratulate yourself for finishing the exam. Reward yourself.

Consider whether you will benefit by discussing the exam in detail with other students. Many students find that hearing remarks such as, "You saw the promissory estoppel issue in question four, didn't you?" increases anxiety.

When the examination is returned to you, quickly review the math to make sure the point calculations are accurate. Your instructor grades many papers, and it is possible that an error in calculating the points has occurred.

If the instructor reviews answers in class, take notes and consider the instructor's comments. View the exam as a learning experience. If you have questions about the test, approach your instructor but do so respectfully, showing that you care about the answer and the reasoning, not just about the points. If the instructor does not return tests, see if you can arrange to review the exam in your program office.

5. Managing Test Anxiety

It is perfectly normal to have some anxiety about a test. In fact, a little bit of anxiety may motivate you and sharpen your focus. Too much anxiety, however, might cause you to blank out on information or become physically ill. The best way to reduce anxiety is to prepare thoroughly for the exam such that you have confidence in your understanding of the material. If you are sufficiently prepared, you will likely recall the material even if you have some test anxiety. In many cases, anxiety is caused because students know they haven't prepared enough or have procrastinated. If this is the case, you can eliminate anxiety by solving its cause. Begin preparing for exams early.

One student reported to me that she and her roommate scheduled "worry time" each day. They allowed themselves 20 minutes every day to complain, panic, worry, and vent about their classes and their workload. Once the 20 minutes were over, they moved on and continued their work. The students conscientiously avoided any negative thoughts or worrying outside of the allocated schedule. When negative thoughts intruded, they shoved them aside and told themselves, "That's for worry time."

Don't think of the exam as a test of your character. It's just an exam. You've had others before and you will have more in the future. Remember that you have had many successes in the past. Complete your answer to this statement: "The worst thing that will happen to me if I do not do well in this class is _____." You can readily see that the test is not a matter of life or death. It is, however, an opportunity to show your instructor that you know the material and the core class concepts.

Don't compare yourself to others or measure your worth by how others are doing. Try to determine which students and situations create anxiety for you and avoid them. Remember that there will always be a student who finishes the test far in advance of the others. Finishing early does not necessarily correlate to superior performance.

Don't forget that being in good physical condition can reduce many of the symptoms of anxiety. Eat right. Exercise. If caffeine makes you jumpy, avoid it on exam day. Eat something so that you aren't light-headed.

During the exam, if you find yourself drawing a blank, do the following:

■ **Move on to an easier question.** Build confidence by taking small steps. Once you respond to a few questions, you will discover your own rhythm and will realize you know more than you think you do. Additionally, as noted earlier, a later question may provide you with an idea for answering an earlier question.

■ **Focus on one question at a time.** Don't think ahead to the fact that an upcoming question is difficult. Put all your efforts into the question you are currently answering.

■ **Underscore key words.** When you are faced with a difficult question or you draw a blank, underscore the key words in the question. See if these give you a hint on how to structure your answer or jog your memory.

■ **Try relaxation techniques.** Take a minute or two to close your eyes and take a few deep breaths. Clear your mind. Take a three-minute mental vacation.

■ **Do something.** Write something. Write anything. You can always erase it later. Ask the instructor if you can stretch your legs in the hallway. Move to the front of the room if seeing other students writing furiously panics you.

Finally, remember why you are taking the class. You are there to learn. Although everyone wants to get good grades, the advantage of being an adult learner is understanding that good grades are not necessarily a predictor of future success. Keep your eyes on the prize: comprehension of the material.

6. Class Projects

Nearly all of the preceding discussion about study skills and examinations applies to class projects. Carefully review the instructions for any project assigned in class. Follow the instructions to the letter. Do not lose the easy points by single-spacing when the instructions state the project must be double-spaced. Review your syllabus and mark on your master calendar the due date for any project. Set up a timetable, working backwards from the due date. Once again, chunk your project into manageable and realistic tasks. For example, mark the dates that you will allocate to research, your first draft, second draft, cite-checking, and so forth. Allow at least one extra day for emergencies, such as illness or equipment malfunctions, that might cause delays in your timetable. Don't be hesitant to check with your instructor to make sure you're on the right track. If you are working with a group, consider the suggestions given above relating to study groups.

NET RESULTS

www.uni.edu/walsh/linda7.html

This site, provided by the University of Northern Iowa, provides links to more than 30 sites offering information relating to study skills, achieving academic success, taking examinations, and other school-related topics.

www.ucc.vt.edu/stdysk/ stdyhlp.html	Virginia Polytechnic Institute's site offers a variety of articles relating to study skills.
www.byu.edu/ccc/learning/ note-tak.shtml	The Cornell Note-Taking System is fully explained at this site maintained by Brigham Young University.
www.timeanddate.com	Free monthly and customizable calendars are provided for planning projects and calendaring due dates.

CASE ILLUSTRATION

Necessity of Attention to Detail

Case: *Lloyd's Underwriters of London v. Ruby, Inc.*, 801 So. 2d 138 (Fla. Dist. Ct. App. 2001)

Facts: Ruby, Inc. filed a lawsuit against Lloyd's and served the summons and complaint on the state insurance commissioner, who then forwarded the papers to the law firm representing Lloyd's. A paralegal mislaid the papers for a significant period of time. When the law firm found the papers and forwarded them to Lloyd's, it did not disclose that the deadline to answer the complaint was imminent. A default was entered against Lloyd's. Lloyd's filed a motion to set aside the default, which was denied. Lloyd's appealed.

Holding: The appellate court reversed, holding that public policy favors setting aside default judgments so that matters may proceed to trial on their merits. In this case, excusable neglect justified setting aside the default so that Lloyd's could defend itself at trial.

Dissent: A strong dissent urged that the neglect was not excusable and that the trial court's decision of entering judgment against Lloyd's for its failure to answer should stand.

KEY TERMS

SQ3R method   Cornell Note-Taking System
Active listening   Study group

CHAPTER SUMMARY

Student Success and Reading the Material	Success as a student requires that you do the work assigned, come to class prepared, and persistently work to master the material. Consider using the SQ3R method of reading to enhance remembering: Survey the material, question the concepts, read the material, recite key points aloud, and review the material. Other techniques that will aid comprehension are marking your text and taking notes on the reading material.
Note Taking	The Cornell Note-Taking System is a well-known method for recording class information. Use paper divided into two columns, a narrow left column and a wide right column. When taking notes, record main concepts and ideas in the right column, reduce main concepts and place key words in the left column, recite the information, reflect on it, review it, and then recapitulate it in a summary.
Networking	Network with other students to have a backup if you miss classes or are sick. Join a study group to help you master class material.
Success on Examinations	To succeed on examinations, get as much information about the exam as possible, study old exams, prepare outlines and flash cards, review your notes, and prepare study review sheets. When you take examinations, skim the entire exam first and read instructions completely. Understand the different techniques that can be used in objective tests and essay exams to ensure your answers respond to the questions asked. Complete all answers and manage both your time and your stress level.

TRIVIA

- Taking verbatim notes is impossible because most individuals speak at a rate of 125-140 words per minute while the average note taker is able to write only about 25 words per minute. Thus, be selective when taking notes.

- Studies have demonstrated that unless a student reviews class notes within 24 hours or before the next class, retention drops, and the student will be re-learning the material rather than reviewing it.
- Neatness counts. Research shows that when the same paper is written neatly and messily, on average, a grader will give the neat paper a letter grade higher than the messy paper.
- Sweet Briar College's Academic Resource Center states that the best results on examinations occur when test takers get at least four hours of sleep and a protein meal before an examination.

DISCUSSION QUESTIONS

1. Pete, one of your study group members, is consistently unprepared at group meetings. He was assigned to prepare a review sheet for Chapter Ten of your text but forgot to do so. How should you handle the problem with Pete?
2. You have determined that your study group is not working for you and you would like to leave. How should you handle your departure?
3. What are some of the advantages of using index cards or flash cards to test your knowledge of class material?
4. Discuss the advantages of sitting near the front of the classroom and taking good notes during class.

CLOSING ARGUMENTS

1. Access the University of Northern Iowa's site providing links to sites offering study skills information and review the article "Remembering What You Read." What are the three processes that increase your ability to remember?
2. Access Brigham Young University's site relating to the Cornell Note-Taking System.
   a. Who developed the System?
   b. When recording facts and ideas, is it necessary to ensure notes are grammatically correct?
3. Access Virginia Polytechnic Institute's site for study skills.
   a. Review the article on the SQ3R method of reading. What are the five steps in the initial survey of material?
   b. Review the article relating to control of the study environment. What should you do if you find your mind wanders when you are reading?

CHAPTER 2

THE PARALEGAL PROFESSION

T HE AMERICAN BAR ASSOCIATION . . . HAS PROMOTED THE ROLE OF THE PARALEGAL AS A VITAL MEMBER OF THE LEGAL SERVICES DELIVERY TEAM FOR OVER THIRTY YEARS.

—AMERICAN BAR ASSOCIATION GUIDELINES FOR THE APPROVAL OF PARALEGAL EDUCATION PROGRAMS

CHAPTER OVERVIEW

To be an effective paralegal, you need to know about your profession. This chapter provides an overview of the "nuts and bolts" of the paralegal profession. The chapter begins by discussing the various definitions of the term *paralegal* and reviewing the history of the profession. The various types of paralegal education programs will be examined as well as the role of the American Bar Association in approving paralegal education programs. You will be introduced to the various paralegal associations that serve as advocates for paralegals and the profession. The chapter will then discuss the most critical issues facing the profession: regulation, licensing, and certification of paralegals. The chapter will conclude by discussing what paralegals do, where they are typically employed, their compensation and benefits, and the future of this dynamic and vital profession.

A. DEFINITIONS AND TITLES

When an individual introduces himself or herself as a doctor or a lawyer, the listener immediately knows something about the individual. For example, a listener would know that a lawyer is someone who graduated from college, attended law school, took certain required courses in law school, passed a bar examination, and is licensed to practice law in the state where he or she works. When an individual is introduced as a paralegal, however, the listener may not immediately understand the background and training of the individual. A person may become a paralegal by taking courses at a variety of different types of educational institutions, by on-the-job training in a law office or other legal environment, or by some other method of gaining experience in the profession. Through education, the paralegal may have received a certificate, an associate degree, or a bachelor degree in paralegal studies. Many of these educational programs are approved by the **American Bar Association** (ABA), which is a voluntary association of attorneys.

American Bar Association
A voluntary professional association for attorneys

Alternatively, a paralegal may have gained valuable experience while working closely with attorneys in a law firm. At present, there are no formal legal requirements that must be satisfied before a person can be called a paralegal. Similarly, there are no uniform standards followed by attorneys who hire paralegals. Some hire graduates of paralegal programs, some hire recent college graduates, some promote and train from within, and others merely gratuitously bestow the title of paralegal on various employees, whether experienced or not.

Just as there are a variety of ways by which one may become a paralegal, there are several ways of identifying those in the profession. The ABA uses the term **paralegal** (until late 2003, it used the term **legal assistant**) and provides the following definition:

Paralegal
Generally defined as a person qualified by experience or education to perform substantive legal work and who is usually employed by an attorney or law firm; often synonymous with *legal assistant*

> A . . . paralegal is a person qualified by education, training or work experience who is employed or retained by a lawyer, law office, corporation, governmental agency or other entity who performs specifically delegated substantive legal work for which a lawyer is responsible (adopted by the ABA in 1997).

In fact, the Greek prefix *para* literally means *beside, almost,* or *resembling.* Thus, the very term *paralegal* suggests an individual working closely with and assisting an attorney.

In 2001, the National Association of Legal Assistants (NALA), one of the two major paralegal associations, adopted the ABA definition of *paralegal* in order to promote uniformity in the profession (previously, NALA had its own definition of *legal assistant*).

While the ABA definition of *paralegal* is one of the most widely used, other definitions exist as well. Probably the other most prominent definition is that used by the other major paralegal association, the National Federation of Paralegal Associations (NFPA). NFPA also prefers the term *paralegal* to *legal assistant,* and its definition is slightly different from that of the ABA:

> A paralegal is a person qualified through education, training or work experience to perform substantive legal work that requires knowledge of legal concepts and is customarily, but not exclusively, performed by a lawyer. This person may be retained or employed by a lawyer, law office, governmental agency or other entity or may be authorized by administrative, statutory or court authority to perform this work.

The terms *paralegal* and *legal assistant* are the most frequently encountered and are often used interchangeably; some parts of the country have a preference for one term over another. Recently, however, *paralegal* seems to be gaining ground because many paralegals have found that *legal assistant* has been used in a vague and broad manner to include almost anyone who helps provide legal services, including paralegals, law clerks, and legal secretaries. Some theorize that the term *legal assistant* gradually evolved to refer to legal secretaries so that attorneys may bill for the secretaries' time and to reward and recognize these secretaries. A number of paralegal education programs are changing their program names to replace the term *legal assistant* with *paralegal*. Similarly, in January 2005, the Legal Assistant Management Association changed its name to the International Paralegal Management Association after 75 percent of its members indicated they preferred *paralegal* to *legal assistant*. This text will follow the current ABA approach and use *paralegal*. Nevertheless, you may well see other labels used to describe an individual who assists lawyers in providing legal services, including lay advocate, legal technician, case assistant, project assistant, and research assistant. No matter what label or what definition is used, however, a paralegal is a nonlawyer who performs substantive legal work, almost always under the direction of an attorney, and who is qualified by education, training, or experience. Just as most people are not confused by the coexistence of the terms *attorney* and *lawyer* don't be confused by the numerous terms used to describe paralegals and the various definitions of those terms.

B. HISTORY OF THE PARALEGAL PROFESSION

Many paraprofessional careers are well recognized and well established. For example, the first nursing schools in the United States were established in the 1870s. Most individuals are familiar with the wide array of paramedical titles, including registered nurse, occupational therapist, licensed vocational nurse, radiology technician, and physician's assistant. In contrast, the paralegal profession is relatively new, and the first paralegals probably entered the profession in the 1960s, when individuals were trained to help attorneys providing legal services to the poor during the War on Poverty. Even before that, however, it is likely that experienced legal secretaries began performing paralegal tasks.

As attorneys began to understand the value and benefit in using paralegals and as litigation continued to increase in the United States, the paralegal profession grew. Attorneys quickly came to understand that paralegals could perform numerous legal tasks efficiently and cost-effectively, freeing up the attorneys' time for other work. Law firms intuitively grasped that paying a paralegal to draft a will, form a corporation, or file a complaint was far less expensive than paying a new attorney to do the same tasks. This enhanced revenue for the firm, and the decreased labor costs could then be passed along to clients as well. Today, most of the marketing brochures used by large firms prominently note that to keep a client's costs low, paralegals are used to perform as much of a client's work as possible. The use of paralegals is thus proudly promoted by the nation's elite law firms.

In 1968, the ABA established a committee to study how attorneys could more effectively use nonlawyers. The results of the committee report clearly disclosed that the effective use of paralegals would greatly assist both attorneys and clients, primarily because clients could receive high-quality legal services at a reduced cost if paralegals were employed to assist attorneys. The ABA committee, now called the **Standing Committee on Paralegals**, continues to advocate for low-cost, efficient delivery of legal services through the use of paralegals and has established educational requirements and standards for its approved paralegal educational programs throughout the country.

ABA Standing Committee on Paralegals
An ABA committee that approves paralegal education programs and supports utilization of paralegals

The first paralegal schools began offering specialized educational programs in the 1960s; before that time, entry into the field was through on-the-job training. The creation of professional associations for paralegals, primarily NALA and NFPA, further enhanced the credibility of the profession. As will be discussed below, these national associations promote the interests of the paralegal profession and provide valuable resources for paralegals.

While few attorneys employed paralegals just 20 or 30 years ago, most would now agree that it would be nearly impossible to practice without them. Certain areas of law, such as large-scale litigation, would be cost-prohibitive for most law firms without the teams of paralegals employed to review documents, assemble exhibits, and prepare for trial. The cost savings can then be passed along to clients, making legal services both more accessible and more affordable. The complexity of modern-day litigation and corporate law makes hiring paralegals imperative. Thus, in just one generation paralegals have gone from being unknown and underutilized to becoming valued and critical members of the legal team, and the future is no less bright.

C. PARALEGAL EDUCATION

1. Types of Paralegal Programs

Until the advent of formal paralegal education programs in the 1960s, paralegals learned their skills on the job. As the legal profession became more complex and as greater demands were made for affordable legal services, it became clear that there was a need for formal paralegal education. Although education for paralegals is relatively new, there is no shortage of choices to be made when deciding what type of classes to take or school to attend. While many attorneys and law firms continue to "train from within" by hiring smart and competent individuals and teaching them paralegal skills, others prefer to hire individuals who have already received training and education from a paralegal program and who are thus "ready to hit the ground running" upon hiring.

The ABA has identified more than 800 institutions in the United States that offer formal paralegal education and that lead either to a degree or to a certificate of completion. The institutions vary markedly in their approach, quality, curricula, and standards. Generally, however, there are four types of programs offered for paralegal education. All of them offer either a degree, a certificate, or both.

- **Associate degree programs.** Community or junior college programs (and some four-year institutions) may offer an associate of science degree in paralegal studies. Students usually take a variety of general education courses and then several legal specialty courses, such as introduction to law, litigation, business organizations, legal research and writing, and real property law. Approximately 60 semester credits are required. Many community colleges offer both an associate degree (for those without any post-high school education or experience) and a certificate program, which is usually designed for individuals who have an associate or baccalaureate degree (or perhaps a certain level of experience). Individuals who complete an associate degree often later obtain a bachelor's degree. Many community college programs are approved by the ABA's Standing Committee on Paralegals.

- **Bachelor's degree programs.** There are numerous programs that offer a four-year bachelor's degree with either a major or minor in paralegal studies. These programs usually require approximately 120 credit hours. A variety of general education requirements, such as English, science, and foreign language must be fulfilled. Students then take numerous law-related classes, including legal research and writing, criminal law, civil litigation, and wills and estates. Paralegal programs in four-year colleges and universities may be offered by different schools within the college. For example, some programs are offered by a school of business while others are offered by a school of education. Some lead to a bachelor of arts degree while others lead to a bachelor of science degree. A newer trend is to require students to complete an internship or to provide a certain number of service hours pro bono publico (literally, "for the public good," meaning providing free legal services to indigents or the needy).

- **Certificate programs.** Certificate programs are offered by two-year, four-year, and proprietary institutions. These institutions award a paralegal certificate (rather than a degree) upon the completion of various required law-related courses. All courses relate to the law; no general education classes are offered. These programs vary in length from three months (if students attend full-time) to two years.

- **Post-baccalaureate certificate programs.** A number of colleges offer a paralegal certificate to individuals who have already obtained a bachelor's degree. These post-baccalaureate programs are often offered through a college's extension program or its school for continuing education. Because students have already received a college degree, these programs are shorter in length (usually three months for full-time students and one year for part-time or evening students) and provide legal training and education exclusively. No general education courses are required.

A few institutions have begun offering a master's degree in paralegal studies. Other institutions offer advanced degrees in various law-related fields, such as legal administration, paralegal management, and legal studies.

In addition to the programs described, other programs are offered by business and proprietary schools, many of which are freestanding institutions. A newer trend is to offer paralegal education through online courses. The ABA notes, however, that no matter which paralegal program is chosen, and no matter how rigorous its course of study, it is not the equivalent of a law degree, and credits awarded for paralegal studies are not transferable for advanced standing in any law school.

The choice of which type of program to attend varies greatly depending on the individual's background, specific career goals, and the relevant job market. Some law firms and attorneys prefer that paralegals have a college degree combined with a paralegal certificate; others are satisfied with an associate degree combined with experience. As is the case with nearly all professional careers, obtaining more education is never a mistake. NFPA's 2003 annual compensation and benefits survey revealed that nearly 55 percent of all paralegals surveyed hold a bachelor's degree and 70 percent have formal education in paralegal studies.

Moreover, some of the various paralegal associations have taken the position that a college degree is a minimum requirement for paralegals. For example, the International Paralegal Management Association's website at *www.paralegalmanagement. org* notes that "the requirement of a four-year degree is strengthening among employers." Similarly, NFPA recommends that paralegals have a four-year degree.

This preference for a college degree is likely based on the fact that most colleges require extensive writing, a skill that is required of all paralegals.

2. The Role of the ABA in Paralegal Education

In recognition of the ABA's commitment to promote high standards and encourage consistency in paralegal education, in 1974 the ABA adopted a set of standards, called the Guidelines for the Approval of Paralegal Education Programs, for approving programs that offer paralegal training and education. In 1975, the ABA approved the first group of paralegal education programs. Note that the ABA "approves" programs that are in compliance with its Guidelines; it does not "accredit" the programs. **Approval** means that the program has met various standards established by the ABA, including those relating to library facilities, curricula, qualified program staff and faculty, and job placement services.

Programs that have been in operation for at least two years may apply for ABA approval. The program must provide a report to the ABA that thoroughly describes its administration, curriculum, staff, faculty, library, and other program elements. The ABA then schedules an on-site visit to meet with the program's administrative staff, faculty, and students and to review various records and documents. To obtain ABA approval, a program must meet certain requirements, including those pertaining to curricula and courses, having an advisory board to consult on program issues, assisting in job placement, having an adequate library available to students, maintaining certain requirements for student admission, and having a program director and faculty that are knowledgeable about the paralegal field and the subject matter of courses taught in the program. The ABA approves programs offered by two-year community colleges, four-year colleges, and proprietary institutions such as technical or vocational schools.

Once a program is approved, it goes through the full evaluation process every seven years and submits various interim reports to the ABA. Paralegal programs are not required to obtain ABA approval and many elect not to do so. Thus, the fact that a school or program does not have ABA approval is not necessarily a reflection of its quality. Nevertheless, because attorneys are familiar with the ABA and its policy of encouraging the employment and effective use of paralegals, a paralegal whose résumé indicates an education from an ABA-approved institution often has an advantage. In fact, many attorneys know that ABA approval signifies that the job applicant has taken a variety of relevant courses offered by qualified faculty and is ready to join the legal team and immediately start providing high-quality legal services. The ABA does not approve any correspondence or home study paralegal programs. It does, however, allow its approved programs to offer some courses online through distance learning.

Of the approximately 800 paralegal programs in existence, only 258 are presently approved by the ABA. A list of the ABA-approved paralegal programs is available on the ABA's website at *www.abanet.org*.

3. The Role of the American Association for Paralegal Education

The American Association for Paralegal Education (AAfPE) was established in 1981 to promote and encourage high standards for paralegal education. It also provides a forum for professional training and improvement for paralegal educators.

Approval
The designation by the ABA that a paralegal education program meets ABA Guidelines; approval is not accreditation

Membership in AAfPE is available to schools offering paralegal education that are either approved by the ABA or that are in substantial compliance with the ABA's Guidelines and are accredited by a nationally recognized accrediting agency. Membership is also available to individual paralegal educators and leaders in the field of paralegal training. AAfPE offers sample syllabi and various resources to its members and holds an annual conference to promote the improvement of the paralegal profession. AAfPE is headquartered in Mt. Royal, New Jersey, and its website is *www.aafpe.org*.

D. PARALEGAL ASSOCIATIONS

Just as there are professional organizations devoted to attorneys, doctors, and architects, there are professional organizations dedicated to meeting the needs of paralegals. The two major paralegal associations (discussed in alphabetical order) are the National Association of Legal Assistants and the National Federation of Paralegal Associations.

1. National Association of Legal Assistants

The **National Association of Legal Assistants (NALA)** is headquartered in Tulsa, Oklahoma. NALA, formed in 1975, is an organization whose members are individual paralegals. Nevertheless, paralegal associations may affiliate with NALA to receive NALA's assistance in promoting the paralegal profession within their geographic areas. (See Appendix A for an identification of associations that are affiliated with NALA.) NALA provides continuing education and professional development to its more than 18,000 members and offers a code of ethics for paralegals and standards for the utilization of paralegals. (See Chapter Three and Appendices D and E.) NALA also publishes a journal, *Facts & Findings,* which is issued quarterly to NALA members. Some issues are available at NALA's website at *www.nala.org.*

In 1976, NALA established a testing and certification program for paralegals. Since its inception, more than 12,000 paralegals have earned the right to use NALA's designation of **Certified Legal Assistant** or its abbreviation, CLA (or, alternatively, Certified Paralegal or its abbreviation, CP). In order to take NALA's exam, an individual must meet various requirements, including education, experience, or both. For example, any high school graduate with more than seven years of paralegal experience may take the exam. Similarly, any graduate of an ABA-approved paralegal program may take the test, which is a two-day comprehensive examination on a variety of legal topics, including ethics, legal research, and other law-related topics. NALA also requires those who have passed its examination to complete various continuing education courses in order to maintain their designations as Certified Legal Assistants (or Certified Paralegals).

2. National Federation of Paralegal Associations

The **National Federation of Paralegal Associations, Inc. (NFPA)** is headquartered in Seattle, Washington, and was formed in 1974 to provide a communications network for paralegals and to expand the role of the paralegal profession. It is the largest and oldest national paralegal association in the United States and refers

National Association of Legal Assistants (NALA)
A professional organization for individual paralegals

Certified Legal Assistant
The designation offered by NALA to those individuals who pass its examination testing paralegal competency

National Federation of Paralegal Associations, Inc. (NFPA)
A professional organization for state and local paralegal associations

to itself as the "voice of paralegals." Its members are state and local paralegal associations. For example, the National Capital Paralegal Association, located in Washington, D.C., and the Oregon Paralegal Association, located in Portland, Oregon, are members of NFPA. There are more than 60 such associations that are members of NFPA. (See Appendix A for an identification of the associations that are NFPA members.) Additionally, more than 17,000 individual paralegals are members of NFPA. NFPA offers a suggested curriculum for paralegal studies and encourages selection of an ABA-approved paralegal program. NFPA also offers ethical guidelines for paralegals. (See Chapter Three and Appendix F.) NFPA publishes a bi-monthly magazine, *The Paralegal Reporter*, to provide information of interest to its members. Some of the magazine issues are available at NFPA's website at *www.paralegals.org*.

Paralegal Advanced Competency Exam (PACE)
A voluntary examination offered by NFPA; individuals who pass the examination are referred to as "registered" paralegals

A grass-roots organization, NFPA is directed by its membership; each member association has one vote on NFPA matters and the profession. To encourage skill and competency, in 1994 NFPA's membership voted to develop an examination to test the competency of experienced paralegals. Thereafter, NFPA developed the **Paralegal Advanced Competency Exam**, known as **PACE**. In order to take the PACE exam, typically a paralegal must have some amount of higher education and a certain number of years of experience as a paralegal. For example, an individual who has an associate degree in paralegal studies and six years of experience as a paralegal or a bachelor's degree and three years of experience is eligible to take the PACE exam. Alternatively, an individual who had four years of substantive experience as a paralegal prior to 2001 may also take the exam.

The exam tests a variety of core competencies that paralegals should understand, including topics on ethics and tasks such as how to perform legal research, how to conduct a check for a conflict of interest, how to draft documents, and how to prepare a witness for examination under oath. Individuals who pass the exam may use the designation PACE-Registered Paralegal or R.P. These individuals must also complete 12 hours of continuing legal education every two years to maintain their status as a PACE-Registered Paralegal.

3. Other Paralegal Associations

While NALA and NFPA are the major national organizations devoted to maintaining the professionalism of paralegals, other organizations exist as well. For example, the American Alliance of Paralegals, Inc., promotes the paralegal profession, provides networking opportunities, holds seminars, and advocates minimum educational criteria for paralegals. This organization recently established a voluntary program for certification of paralegals, leading to a designation of American Alliance Certified Paralegal. The Alliance's website is *www.aapipara.org*. NALS (formerly called the National Association for Legal Secretaries) is a national organization for a wide group of legal professionals, including paralegals, legal administrators, and office managers. It provides continuing education, certifications, and information and training to its members. Its website is *www.nals.org*.

In addition, most larger metropolitan areas have their own paralegal associations, which are dedicated to serving the needs of their members. For example, the Central Pennsylvania Paralegal Association and the San Francisco Paralegal Association are devoted to enhancing the paralegal profession in their respective communities. These local or state associations often conduct compensation surveys, maintain job banks for their members looking for a new job, offer seminars and continuing education, and advocate for the effective use of paralegals in their communities.

One international organization, the **International Paralegal Management Association** (**IPMA**, but formerly known as the Legal Assistant Management Association), headquartered in Avondale Estates, Georgia, promotes the development of paralegal managers. Most of its members are paralegal managers or coordinators at larger law firms and companies. IPMA maintains a job bank, provides industry reports, and provides compensation surveys to its members. Its website is *www.paralegalmanagement.org*.

Many paralegal schools and programs offer their own associations for their students, some of which are affiliated with a state or national association. For example, Montclair State University in New Jersey offers its Student Paralegal Association to provide information to paralegal students and serve as a liaison between students and working paralegals and attorneys.

Finally, paralegals may become associate members of the ABA, which enables them to obtain a number of benefits, such as belonging to sections or forums devoted to various areas of legal interest and obtaining discounts on a variety of services and products. Moreover, a number of state bar associations, including those of Michigan, New Mexico, North Carolina, and Texas maintain separate divisions for paralegals and allow associate membership by paralegals. Appendix A provides an identification of national, state, and local paralegal associations, and Appendix B lists the state and national bar associations.

International Paralegal Management Association (IPMA)
An international organization for paralegal managers

4. Summary of Paralegal Associations

The number of paralegal associations, some of which compete with each other, is likely a sign of vigor and vitality in the paralegal profession. On the other hand, because the two major organizations, NALA and NFPA, take positions on critical issues facing the profession, such as ethics, certification, and continuing legal education, it is arguable that there is no one unified organization acting on behalf of the profession.

At a minimum, you should join the local paralegal association in your area. It will likely provide career assistance, seminars, and networking opportunities, and will enhance your competency as a paralegal. Most associations provide a lower dues schedule for students, so consider joining an association now to begin meeting working paralegals and obtaining membership benefits. Also, you are wise to join any paralegal association offered by your school or program.

E. REGULATION OF PARALEGALS

Just as there are no formal requirements to be met before one may be called a paralegal, with the exception of California, there is no regulation of paralegals by any governmental entity. A number of states, however, are considering regulating paralegals and the paralegal profession, primarily in response to concerns that some paralegals might be engaged in the unauthorized practice of law. As discussed above, private associations such as NALA and NFPA offer voluntary examinations by which individuals may be "certified" as paralegals, meaning that the individual has met certain qualifications and standards imposed by the respective association. Many paralegals themselves advocate some form of certification or licensing to distinguish them from other individuals who may not be qualified to perform paralegal services.

While most paralegals work in law offices or for companies, some prefer to be self-employed and offer their services to various attorneys for specific legal projects. For example, a paralegal might be hired to work on a specific case; when the case concludes, the paralegal's engagement with the hiring attorney or firm ceases. Paralegals engaged in providing such services as independent contractors are usually called **freelance paralegals** or **contract paralegals**.

Regulation is the general term that encompasses a variety of approaches for controlling the development of the paralegal profession, including registration, licensing, and certification.

1. California Regulation

In 2001, California implemented California Business and Professions Code Section 6450, making it the only state in the nation that statutorily regulates the paralegal profession. New statutes in California define the term *paralegal*, impose educational requirements for paralegals, and identify the services that paralegals may perform. Under the new laws, *paralegal* is defined as a person who holds himself or herself out to be a paralegal, who is qualified by education, training, or work experience; who either contracts with or is employed by an attorney, law firm, corporation, governmental agency, or other entity; and who performs substantial legal work under the direction and supervision of an active member of the State Bar of California, or an attorney practicing law in the federal courts in California.

Under the statutory scheme, paralegals may contract only with attorneys to perform services; they cannot deal directly with consumers. The statute provides that the terms *legal assistant, attorney assistant, freelance paralegal, independent paralegal,* and *contract paralegal* are synonymous with the term *paralegal*.

Earlier legislation in California had imposed registration requirements on **legal document assistants,** who register with county authorities and directly assist members of the public in completing various forms, such as wills and divorce petitions. Thus, in California, paralegals work under the direction of attorneys, and legal document assistants work directly for the public in preparing certain legal documents.

California's new law provides that paralegals may not provide legal advice, represent a client in court, or engage in any conduct that constitutes the unlawful practice of law. As to requirements to be a paralegal, generally the individual must possess one of the following: a certificate of completion or a degree from an ABA-approved paralegal program or from a post-secondary institution; a baccalaureate degree, together with one year of paralegal experience; or a high school diploma together with three years of paralegal experience, which experience must have been completed by the end of 2003. To maintain their standing, paralegals must complete four hours of ethics education every three years and four hours in other legal topics every two years. A first violation of the law subjects the paralegal to a fine of up to $2,500 as to each consumer to whom a violation occurs; subsequent violations subject the paralegal to additional fines or imprisonment, or both. An injured consumer may file a lawsuit against a paralegal.

Freelance paralegal
A paralegal who is self-employed and works on a case-by-case basis as an independent contractor; also called *contract paralegal*

Regulation
The process by which development of the paralegal profession is controlled; includes registration, licensing, and certification

Legal document assistant
In California, a registered individual who provides legal document drafting services to members of the public

A number of questions and concerns have arisen about the California regulations. First, there is no means of state enforcement; the consumer must enforce the law by bringing a lawsuit against the paralegal. In contrast, a consumer injured by an attorney in California may bring a lawsuit or may make a complaint to the California State Bar. Moreover, while paralegals are required to complete continuing education courses in California, there is no mechanism to record attendance at classes, and paralegals are required to maintain their own records. Paralegals are regulated by law in California and may be subject to both civil and criminal causes of action for violations. Because the law establishes no governing body for the profession, many paralegals have voiced their opposition to the new law.

2. Registration

One means of regulation proposed by various groups is the registration of paralegals. **Registration** is a process by which paralegals would have their names maintained on a register or list so that consumers would be able to readily identify and locate individuals qualified to perform paralegal services. Many registration proposals contemplate voluntary registration. However, as noted above, in California, individuals called legal document assistants are subject to mandatory registration requirements and register with their applicable county clerk or country recorder's office. They are also required to post a $25,000 bond, the proceeds of which may be used to compensate consumers harmed by their acts.

Registration
A method of regulation of paralegals by which paralegals' names would be maintained on a register or list for consumer identification

3. Licensing

Licensing refers to the process by which a governmental entity, usually a state or state licensing board, would grant permission and issue a license to an individual to practice as a paralegal, much the same way attorneys are licensed by the state bar of the state in which they practice. Most licensing schemes contemplate certain minimum educational requirements coupled with qualifying examinations.

Licensing
The process by which a governmental entity grants permission and issues a license to individuals to practice a profession, such as the paralegal profession

New Jersey has struggled with the issue of licensing of paralegals for years. In mid-2000, after years of debate, the New Jersey Supreme Court specifically declined to establish a licensing scheme for paralegals and concluded that direct oversight of paralegals is best accomplished through supervision by attorneys rather than through a court-directed licensing system.

While licensing would afford consumers the benefit of knowing which paralegals are licensed to perform services in a state, questions as to the requirements to obtain a license, the territorial effect of a state's license for an individual who moves to another state, and eligibility requirements remain. While various states have contemplated licensing of paralegals (much the way nurses are licensed differently from doctors), at the time of writing of this text, no state has yet enacted a compulsory licensing scheme for paralegals.

NALA opposes mandatory licensing and regulation systems and advocates voluntary certification of paralegals. In contrast, NFPA generally supports the concept of regulating the paralegal profession through a licensing program. In fact, NFPA has drafted a Model Act for Paralegal Licensure, which is intended to serve as guidance for various states if they elect to develop and draft licensing schemes. The Model Act is available on NFPA's website at *www.paralegals.org*.

4. Certification

Certification
The process by which a
nongovernmental entity
identifies that an individual
has met its standards

Certification refers to the process by which a nongovernmental entity—for example, a private association—certifies that an individual has met certain standards imposed by the association. The process of certification is voluntary; the certificate provides a uniform professional credential to those individuals who hold the certificate. Thus, while no paralegal is required to achieve certification, it is a signal to employers and others that the paralegal has demonstrated advanced skills and knowledge, which can translate into enhanced career opportunities for the certified paralegal.

Certification involves demonstrating professional competency as a paralegal through meeting various educational and training requirements and successfully completing an examination designed to test knowledge and skill.

As discussed earlier, both NALA and NFPA offer certification to paralegals who elect to take the associations' examinations. An individual who passes NALA's examination may refer to himself or herself as a Certified Legal Assistant, CLA, Certified Paralegal, or CP. Similarly, an individual who passes NFPA's PACE examination may use the designation PACE Registered Paralegal or RP. These designations instantly communicate to others in the legal profession and to clients that the individual has demonstrated competence in the field. The NALA and NFPA examinations are national in scope; they do not test state-specific legal information. Also, as mentioned earlier, the American Alliance of Paralegals now offers certification to paralegals.

NALS, the national association for legal professionals, offers three certification examinations, one specifically designed for paralegals, who may use the designation Professional Paralegal (or PP) upon passing the NALS examination.

While certification is offered by these national organizations, local paralegal organizations also offer certification. For example, the Louisiana State Paralegal Association offers an examination to qualified paralegals who demonstrate knowledge and competence in Louisiana law. An individual who passes the examination is designated as a Louisiana Certified Paralegal. Similarly, the Commission for Advanced California Paralegal Specialization offers a California Advanced Specialist credential to California paralegals who have first taken and passed NALA's examination (verifying they have acquired the Certified Legal Assistant credential) and who then pass the Commission's specialist examination, demonstrating competency and advanced knowledge of California business organizations, estates and trusts, family law, civil litigation, or real estate law. These individuals are not only certified by NALA but have taken the extra step to become certified in a specialized area of California law. The Paralegal Association of Florida, Inc. also has a program that tests knowledge of Florida law for those paralegals who already hold the Certified Legal Assistant credential from NALA.

Most certification programs include an examination coupled with continuing education requirements, which also include an ethics component.

5. Regulation by Other States

While legislation has been introduced in various states to regulate the paralegal profession, to date, California is the only state that has done so. Nevertheless, a number of states continue to struggle with balancing two delicate issues: helping consumers obtain affordable legal services and yet ensuring that the services are provided only by competent individuals who do not engage in the unauthorized practice of law. As a result, various states have established procedures that allow nonlawyers to prepare basic legal documents and to provide general legal information to consumers. In some states, such as North Carolina, Texas, and Missouri, rules relating to the use of nonlawyers are promulgated and supervised by the state bar. In other states, certification and supervision is under the auspices of the state supreme court. Following are summaries (current as of the date of writing of this text) of the efforts of some states to regulate paralegals:

- **Arizona.** The Arizona Supreme Court has adopted various court rules to allow certified Legal Document Preparers to provide basic legal information and prepare documents. The Arizona State Bar is responsible for investigating and prosecuting nonlawyers who are not Legal Document Preparers who engage in the unauthorized practice of law.
- **Hawaii.** The Hawaii State Bar Association has proposed amending its Rules of Professional Conduct to regulate paralegals in the state.
- **Indiana.** Indiana's State Bar Association has promulgated guidelines for the use of paralegals and allows paralegals to become affiliate members of the State Bar Association.
- **Maryland.** The Maryland State Bar Association offers associate membership to paralegals.
- **Michigan.** The State Bar of Michigan allows paralegals to join its Legal Assistants Section.
- **New Mexico.** New Mexico's Bar Association offers a Paralegal Division to serve the needs of paralegals in the state.
- **North Carolina.** The North Carolina Bar Association allows paralegals to join its Legal Assistants Division. Also, in late 2004, the North Carolina State Bar adopted rules for a plan for certification of paralegals in the state.
- **Texas.** The State Bar of Texas has approved general guidelines for the utilization of the services of paralegals by attorneys in Texas and encourages paralegals to join its Legal Assistant Division. Texas was the first bar association in the United States to create a separate division for paralegals.
- **Washington.** In 2001, the Washington Supreme Court established a Practice of Law Board to allow nonlawyers to practice a limited form of law. Specifically, individuals would be licensed to engage in the closing of various real estate and property transactions. The board continues to review the issue.
- **Wisconsin.** The Wisconsin State Bar recently approved a Paralegal Task Force Report that recommended licensure of paralegals. The report establishes criteria for licensing Wisconsin paralegals as well as standards for training, education, and qualifications of paralegals in the state.

6. Closing Comments on Regulation of the Paralegal Profession

Nearly all consumers, attorneys, state bar associations, and judges agree that there is a need for greater consumer access to affordable legal services. Qualified paralegals can perform substantive, high-quality legal work for consumers while allowing lawyers to work on more complex legal issues, thus providing significant savings to clients. Many paralegals note that beauticians, contractors, and real estate agents are regulated through licensing schemes—why should paralegals be different? The regulation of paralegals is likely the most critical issue facing the paralegal profession today. The issue is complicated by the fact that there are no national standards for the education of paralegals.

While many paralegals have formal education and training, a number of highly qualified individuals are paralegals solely by virtue of their on-the-job experience. Ensuring that these individuals be allowed to continue in their profession is critical.

Regulation can take the form of registration, certification, or licensure. NALA opposes mandatory regulation and licensing of paralegals and advocates voluntary certification. NFPA recommends licensing, which would require passing a competency examination, adhering to a code of ethics, and mandatory continuing education. A "grandfather" clause would allow paralegals currently working in the field to become licensed.

Regulation of paralegals would provide enhanced recognition of the profession by the bench, the bar, and the general public. Moreover, the continuing education standards contemplated by most regulation schemes would ensure that the public receives competent, professional, and ethical services. Nevertheless, continuing education is expensive, and many law firms might object to paying the costs of continuing education and association dues for their paralegals.

In sum, there is clearly a need for increased access to affordable legal services, and paralegals are well qualified to fill that need. There is also a need to ensure that unqualified individuals do not harm the public by engaging in the unauthorized practice of law. Regulation of paralegals would seem to be the ideal way to balance these two goals. Unfortunately, at present there is no consensus as to the most effective way of regulating paralegals to ensure the competency and integrity of the profession.

F. WHERE PARALEGALS WORK

Because of the crisis in cost-effective legal services, the paralegal profession has steadily grown since its inception. Thus, there are a variety of employment opportunities for paralegals in both the private and public sectors. Most paralegals work in law firms. In fact, NALA's 2004 compensation and utilization survey reported that nearly three-fourths of the nation's paralegals work in law firms. Most of the remainder work for corporate legal departments and various government agencies. Within the federal government, the U.S. Department of Justice is the biggest employer of paralegals, but paralegals are also employed by the U.S. Departments of Treasury and Defense, the Federal Deposit Insurance Corporation, the U.S. Patent and Trademark Office, the Central Intelligence Agency, and the Federal Bureau of Investigation.

As will be discussed in detail in later chapters, there are a number of other employment opportunities for paralegals, including at banks and trust companies, insurance companies, real estate and title companies, public utilities, trade associations, alternative dispute resolution groups, legal aid clinics, and court systems. Thus, the variety of employment opportunities for paralegals is extensive.

According to NFPA, there are three general categories of paralegal practice:

Traditional paralegal
A paralegal who works under the supervision of an attorney, usually in a law firm, corporate law department, or governmental agency

■ **Traditional paralegal. A traditional paralegal** is one who works under the supervision of an attorney, usually in a law firm, corporate law department, or governmental agency. Most paralegals are traditional paralegals.

- **Freelance or contract paralegal.** As discussed earlier, a freelance paralegal (sometimes called a contract paralegal) is a self-employed paralegal working as an independent contractor who hires himself or herself out to attorneys for specific projects or tasks—for example, to coordinate discovery for a large class action suit. When the project or case is finished, the freelance paralegal moves on to another contract situation. Freelance paralegals provide assistance to attorneys on an as-needed basis, so the attorney does not need to hire a full-time employee. In all instances, the paralegal is supervised by an attorney.
- **Independent paralegal.** An **independent paralegal** works directly for consumers without supervision by an attorney. Generally, these paralegals complete forms and agreements and participate in real estate closings. Consumers and members of the bar are concerned that independent paralegals may engage in the unauthorized practice of law, and thus regulation of independent paralegals is a key issue facing the paralegal profession.

Independent paralegal
A paralegal who works directly for consumers without supervision by an attorney

In addition to the more traditional employers of paralegals, there are a number of other employers and employment opportunities for paralegals. For example, paralegals may be employed by legal clinics. Some legal clinics are private firms that offer affordable legal services. Many advertise and depend on a high volume of cases, often personal injury and family law cases. Other legal clinics are operated by governmental agencies or communities and offer legal services to the poor, elderly, or handicapped. Paralegals often work at these legal aid clinics on a pro bono basis to engage in meaningful work and to obtain experience.

In larger law firms, experienced paralegals often become **paralegal managers** or **paralegal coordinators**, managing the other paralegals, overseeing their work flow, coordinating their training and education, and serving as a communications link between the paralegals and the attorneys in the firm.

Paralegal manager
A paralegal who manages other paralegals; also called a *paralegal coordinator*

Just as in many other fields, paralegals are becoming highly specialized. For example, several institutions now offer certificates in legal nurse consulting (also called nurse paralegal programs). These programs are offered to registered nurses who then apply their nursing knowledge to legal services. Required courses include medical and legal malpractice, health care administration, and worker's compensation. **Nurse paralegals** are often employed by large law firms with sophisticated injury or illness practices. These highly specialized paralegals provide expert in-house assistance, including review of doctors' charts, nurses' notes, and medical testimony.

Nurse paralegal
A registered nurse who is trained as a paralegal; also called a *legal nurse consultant*

Similarly, a few institutions offer master's degrees in paralegal studies, legal studies, and legal administration. Graduates usually manage law offices or paralegal departments within large law offices. They recruit, hire, supervise, and terminate paralegals, coordinate work flow, prepare annual budgets for their departments, establish paralegal salaries and billing rates, monitor billable hours, and coordinate training and education for the group.

One of the newest trends in the provision of services by paralegals is that offered by "We the People," a franchise offering computerized legal document preparation services. We the People has approximately 120 franchised offices in more than 20 states staffed by paralegals. The organization compares its services to those offered by H&R Block, the preparer of tax forms for consumers, in that it offers affordable services to people who need help with their legal documents (especially in the area of divorce, business incorporations, and bankruptcies). In 2003, We the People processed 20,000 bankruptcy petitions throughout the

United States. Although We the People has been challenged in a number of law-suits and has been accused of engaging in the unauthorized practice of law, it is advocating for state or federal legislation, or both, that would permit it to operate without continual legal challenges. Its website is *www.wethepeople.com*.

G. PARALEGAL DUTIES

As will be discussed thoroughly in Chapter Three, paralegals may generally engage in any role that attorneys may, with just three exceptions: Paralegals may not accept clients or set legal fees, may not give legal advice, and may not represent a party in court. Thus, there is a vast array of duties and tasks in which paralegals may engage. In fact, Justice Brennan noted the following in *Missouri v. Jenkins*, 491 U.S. 274, 288 n.10 (1989):

> It has frequently been recognized in the lower courts that paralegals are capable of carrying out many tasks, under the supervision of an attorney, that might otherwise be performed by a lawyer and billed at a higher rate. Such work might include, for example, factual investigation, including locating and interviewing witnesses; assistance with depositions, interrogatories, and document production; compilation of statistical and financial data; checking legal citations; and drafting correspondence.

Although the size and nature of the employer dictate the specific employment tasks paralegals provide, the following are some of the most common. (Note that these tasks will be discussed in depth in later chapters.)

- **Interviewing and meeting with clients.** Paralegals often conduct initial interviews with clients, much the way that a nurse meets with a patient before a doctor does. Paralegals can explain the nature and background of the firm, discuss the scope of the first meeting, and obtain some factual information from the client. Later, paralegals often act as a liaison between the attorney and the client, keeping the client informed as the case progresses and maintaining the lines of communication.
- **Conducting legal research.** Conducting legal research is one of the most common tasks of paralegals. Paralegals locate and analyze relevant cases, statutes, and other legal authorities. They then cite those legal authorities using proper citation form and ensure the authorities are "still good law" by either Shepardizing or KeyCiting the authorities.
- **Drafting documents, agreements, and pleadings.** The average law practice produces reams of paper, including contracts, wills, settlement agreements, complaints, answers, motions, and other documents. Paralegals often prepare the initial drafts of these documents, which are then given to the attorney to review and finalize. Paralegals also prepare internal office memoranda reporting the results of their legal or factual research.
- **Investigating factual matters.** Paralegals perform a variety of investigative tasks, including locating witnesses and documents, reviewing public records (such as motor vehicle records, corporate filings, and real estate records), interviewing witnesses, photographing property or accident sites, tracking legislation, and so forth. Much investigative work is done in the office using computerized databases and computer searching techniques. Other investigations are conducted "in the field."

- **Assisting in litigation matters.** Paralegals are highly valued in litigation matters. They are involved in the entire litigation life cycle, from the drafting of the complaint or answer, through discovery and motion practice, to trial and appeal. They meet with clients, review and draft pleadings and motions, participate in discovery, assist with jury instructions, and help enforce a judgment or prepare various appellate documents. Large-scale litigation matters, such as class actions, require significant organizational skills to manage masses of paperwork and juggle a variety of tasks. Some paralegals are specialists in the field of large-case management.

- **Maintaining dockets and calendars.** Many aspects of law practice are time-sensitive. For example, a party usually has only 30 days to respond to a litigation complaint, or a default judgment will be entered against the party. Similarly, a trademark applicant has only six months to respond to objections to the application made by the U.S. Patent and Trademark Office or the application may be deemed abandoned. Paralegals play a pivotal role in docketing and calendaring these deadlines. Although there are several software packages that assist in the docketing function, most attorneys insist that computer systems be supplemented by a "human component." Thus, paralegals often maintain various law firm dockets and provide reminders to those in the firm of upcoming deadlines.

- **Corresponding with clients and others.** Paralegals prepare a variety of correspondence, including status letters to clients, demand or collection letters to adverse parties, and so forth. Thus, excellent communication and writing skills are required.

- **Representing clients at administrative hearings.** When authorized by law, paralegals may represent clients at both federal and state administrative hearings such as hearings relating to Social Security benefits, workers compensation benefits, unemployment benefits, and so forth. For example, the Veterans Administration, the Social Security Administration, and the Occupational Safety and Health Administration all allow nonlawyer representation. Ten states allow nonlawyers to appear before various state administrative agencies. California allows paralegals to represent clients in workers' compensation matters if the client consents and the paralegal is supervised by an attorney. These paralegals make opening statements, question witnesses, and introduce evidence at agency hearings.

Finally, a few states allow nonlawyers to appear in court to present certain orders that have been previously agreed to by the litigants in a proceeding. Such court appearances do not involve the unauthorized practice of law and save clients a great deal of money because the billing rates for paralegals are significantly lower than those for attorneys.

The most common practice area for paralegals is in litigation, but paralegals are employed in nearly every legal practice area, including appellate work, bankruptcy, corporate and business organizations, criminal prosecution and defense, environmental law, family law, immigration, intellectual property, labor and employment, personal injury, probate and estate administration, real property, securities, and tax law.

H. PARALEGAL COMPENSATION

Compensation for paralegals varies greatly, depending on experience, education, type and size of the employer, and location of the job. Generally, paralegals who work for large law firms or in large metropolitan areas earn more than those who work for smaller firms or in less populated areas.

1. Average Annual Compensation for Paralegals

The ABA does not maintain information on the starting salaries of paralegals in different regions of the United States; however, many paralegal associations conduct annual surveys to gather compensation information and publish the results for their members. Both NALA and NFPA conduct compensation surveys.

NALA's 2004 compensation and utilization survey discloses that the average paralegal salary is $44,373, with an average bonus of $3,393, for a total average annual compensation of $46,862. Of course, starting salaries are lower. NALA reported that the average total compensation for paralegals with one to five years of experience is $33,770. Salaries are higher in the far west and eastern regions of the United States and lower in the Rocky Mountains area and Plains states. The specialty areas with the highest average compensation were intellectual property, mergers and acquisitions, securities, general corporate, employee benefits, and employment law. For example, the average annual compensation for intellectual property paralegals (those engaged in trademark, copyright, or patent work) was $51,447.

NFPA's 2003 compensation and benefits report discloses the following information about the paralegal profession:

- Nearly 70 percent of the survey respondents had some specific paralegal education.
- The average salary for paralegals was reported as $44,347.
- 60 percent of paralegals received an annual bonus, and the average bonus was $2,165.
- With regard to benefits, 84 percent received paid vacation, 65 percent received life insurance, and 40 percent received fully paid employee medical insurance.

The 2001 salary survey of *Legal Assistant Today*, a paralegal magazine, reported that paralegals who work for corporate law departments were paid an average salary of $45,974 (compared to an average of $40,293 reported by those who work in law firms and government employees who were paid an average salary of $40,413).

Paralegal managers earn significantly more than paralegals. According to a 2004 survey conducted for IPMA, the association for paralegal managers, the average compensation in 2004 for a paralegal manager was $88,781.

2. Overtime Compensation

One of the most difficult issues facing the paralegal profession today is that of overtime compensation. NFPA estimates that about half of all employers pay paralegals for overtime (hours worked in excess of a 40-hour workweek). In many cases, overtime compensation is significant. For example, IPMA's 2003 survey reported that paralegal managers averaged overtime compensation of $17,736 (on top of their base salaries), while paralegals averaged nearly $6,000 in annual overtime pay.

In August 2004, new Department of Labor regulations went into effect eliminating overtime pay for "learned professionals." Generally, overtime compensation need not be paid if all of the following are met:

- The employee is compensated on a salary or fee basis at a rate of more than $455 per week;
- The employee's primary duty is performing work that is predominantly intellectual in character;

- The work requires the consistent exercise of judgment and discretion; and
- The work requires advanced knowledge in a field of science or learning that is customarily acquired by a prolonged course of specialized intellectual instruction.

Because most paralegals earn more than $455 per week and much of the work performed by them is primarily intellectual work that requires the exercise of discretion and judgment and paralegals' advanced knowledge is acquired by specialized instruction, a few experts believe that many paralegals will now be ineligible for overtime compensation under the new regulations. On the other hand, if a law firm classifies certain paralegal duties as more routine and administrative, then the paralegal performing such tasks may be eligible for overtime pay. In fact, the Department of Labor's traditional position has been that paralegals are entitled to overtime compensation. The Department's final rule expressly stated that paralegals do not generally qualify as exempt learned professionals; however, paralegals who have specialized degrees may qualify. For example, a paralegal who is trained as an engineer and who assists a patent attorney would be an exempt learned professional and thus not entitled to overtime pay.

Many paralegals are concerned that the new regulations will encourage the exploitation of paralegals. For example, if a paralegal is required to work ten hours extra during a week to ensure a client's transaction closes, the law firm would receive fees from the client for the excess hours billed by the paralegal but might not be required to pay overtime to the paralegal. Other paralegals believe that as long as paralegals accept overtime pay, they will not be considered true professionals like attorneys and doctors; the paralegals will be thought to be akin to clerical workers. A late 2003 article in *Legal Assistant Today*, a magazine for paralegals, reasoned that eventually there will be mandatory paralegal regulation, which will lead to the establishment of higher compensation for paralegals. Until that time arrives, however, the author believes that withdrawal of overtime pay for paralegals will lead to abuses in the workplace, and the new Department of Labor regulations do not change the traditional view that paralegals are generally entitled to overtime compensation.

See Figure 2-1 for paralegal salary information reported by the Bureau of Labor Statistics.

FIGURE 2-1

PARALEGAL COMPENSATION

In 2002, the Bureau of Labor Statistics reported the following:

- The middle 50 percent of paralegals earned between $30,020 and $48,760.
- The top 10 percent of paralegals earned more than $61,150, while the bottom 10 percent earned less than $24,470.
- Median annual earnings in the industries employing the largest number of paralegals in 2002 were as follows:
  - ☐ Federal government $53,770
  - ☐ Legal services $36,780
  - ☐ Local government $36,030
  - ☐ State government $34,750

I. THE FUTURE OF THE PARALEGAL PROFESSION

Nearly all firms have recognized the benefits of using paralegals. Because a paralegal's time is billed at a lower hourly rate than the time of an attorney, knowledgeable paralegals can perform a number of tasks for the client, who will reap the benefit of lower fees and have a liaison for communication with the firm. A number of courts have awarded fees for paralegal services and routinely note that if the work had not been done by paralegals, charging fees based on the higher rates of attorneys would have resulted. Moreover, delegating tasks to paralegals allows attorneys to devote their time to other matters.

According to the Department of Labor's Bureau of Labor and Statistics, paralegals and other related legal assistants held about 200,000 jobs in 2002. The field is projected to grow faster than the average for all occupations through 2012. The Bureau projects that the number of paralegal positions will increase 21 to 35 percent by 2012.

The Bureau has noted that demand for paralegals is expected to grow as our increasing population requires additional legal services, especially in areas such as intellectual property, healthcare, elder law, and environmental law. The Bureau has stated that law firms and other employers with legal staffs are increasingly hiring paralegals to lower the cost and increase the efficiency and availability of legal services to their clients. Career opportunities for paralegals will expand in the public sector as well. Agencies and programs that provide assistance to the poor, elderly, and minorities will employ additional paralegals to reduce costs and provide legal services to more people. The Bureau noted that the profession is, of course, affected by the economy, but commented that "paralegals, who provide many of the same legal services as lawyers at a lower cost, tend to fare relatively better in difficult economic conditions."

More and more firms are requiring paralegals to have formal training and education. As the quality of education improves and as uniform standards for regulation evolve, the salaries and status of paralegals should continue to increase. Thus, the demand for paralegals will continue to rise and paralegals will continue to expand their roles in delivering legal services. Paralegals will likely continue the trend of specializing in certain fields of practice, such as patent law, environmental law, and securities law. The challenges facing the profession relate to regulation of paralegals to ensure that members of the public receive high-quality legal services from trained legal professionals. Paralegals must continue to develop their skills and knowledge and become technically proficient in computer use. Computer software packages and the Internet are increasingly used to conduct investigations in law firms and legal departments, and sophisticated computer programs are used in many firms to scan documents directly into databases, catalog and index documents, and track billing of legal fees.

In sum, the paralegal profession is vital and dynamic and affords a challenging and satisfying career to those individuals who desire to be part of a legal team providing valuable and needed services to others.

NET RESULTS

www.bls.gov	The Bureau of Labor Statistics offers information about the paralegal profession, including material relating to working conditions, earnings, and employment.
www.abanet.org/legalservices/paralegals	The American Bar Association's Standing Committee on Paralegals provides information about the paralegal profession, regulation, and the ABA approval process for institutions offering formal paralegal education.
www.nala.org	The National Association of Legal Assistants offers information on its CLA exam, training programs, and standards and guidelines for paralegals.
www.paralegals.org	The National Federation of Paralegal Associations provides information on paralegal careers, schools that offer training, job postings, the PACE exam, ethics information, and current issues facing the profession.
www.aafpe.org	The American Association for Paralegal Education site provides information on paralegal training programs and education-related issues.
www.aapipara.org	The American Alliance of Paralegals, Inc. site offers valuable information for paralegals.
www.paralegalmanagement.org	The site of the International Paralegal Management Association provides information on issues relating to paralegal management.
www.paralegalgateway.com	This commercial website is targeted to paralegals and provides links to nearly all paralegal associations in the nation.

CASE ILLUSTRATION

Recovery of Paralegal Fees

Case: *Missouri v. Jenkins*, 491 U.S. 274, 288 (1989)

Facts: In a school desegregation case, the plaintiff's attorney requested attorneys' fees at market rates for his own work and that of numerous paralegals and law clerks, under a statute that provided that the court could allow "a reasonable attorney's fee."

Holding: A "reasonable attorney's fee" does not refer only to work performed personally by members of the bar. The Court noted that the practice in most communities is to bill separately for paralegal services. The Court therefore approved compensation of the paralegals and law clerks at market rates. The Court specifically noted that the use of lower-cost paralegals rather than attorneys whenever possible, encourages "cost-effective delivery of legal services, and by reducing the spiraling cost of civil rights litigation, furthers the policies underlying civil rights statutes."

KEY TERMS

American Bar Association
Paralegal, legal assistant
ABA Standing Committee on
    Paralegals
Approval
National Association of Legal Assistants
    (NALA)
Certified Legal Assistant
National Federation of Paralegal
    Associations, Inc. (NFPA)
Paralegal Advanced Competency
    Exam (PACE)

International Paralegal Management
    Association (IPMA)
Freelance paralegal, contract paralegal
Regulation
Legal document assistant
Registration
Licensing
Certification
Traditional paralegal
Independent paralegal
Paralegal manager
Nurse paralegal

CHAPTER SUMMARY

Definitions and History	Paralegals are individuals qualified through education or experience to perform substantive legal work and who usually work under the

	supervision of an attorney. Generally, the terms "paralegal" and "legal assistant" are interchangeable, but "paralegal" is likely the preferred term. The paralegal profession is relatively new and can be traced to the 1960s. The use of paralegals has been shown to improve the affordability and availability of legal services.
Paralegal Education	There are a variety of educational programs for paralegals, including two-year, four-year, and post-baccalaureate programs. Many paralegal associations and attorneys prefer that paralegals have a college degree combined with some formal education. The ABA approves various paralegal programs that comply with its guidelines and standards.
Paralegal Associations	A number of paralegal associations exist to further the development of the paralegal profession. NALA is an association whose members are individual paralegals. Generally, NFPA's members are state and local paralegal associations.
Regulation and Certification of Paralegals	The only state that presently regulates paralegals directly is California, which requires paralegals to meet certain education and experience requirements and to obtain continuing education. NALA offers a Certified Legal Assistant examination to its members who demonstrate knowledge and competency and certifies those who pass the examination as "Certified Legal Assistants." NFPA offers its Paralegal Advanced Competency Examination and certifies those individuals who pass the examination as "Registered Paralegals."
Work Environment and Duties	Most paralegals work in law firms, but a number of paralegals work in corporate law departments, for courts, and for government agencies. Paralegals can perform a wide variety of duties and can do nearly anything an attorney can do; however, they cannot set legal fees, give legal advice, or appear in court on behalf of a client.
Compensation	The average annual compensation for paralegals varies with the type and location of work, but NALA's 2004 survey noted that the average

	paralegal salary is more than $44,000. About one-half of all firms pay overtime to paralegals. In fact, the Department of Labor's new regulations likely affirm its traditional position that paralegals are generally entitled to overtime compensation.
Growth of Profession	The Bureau of Labor Statistics has projected continued and accelerated growth in the paralegal profession.

TRIVIA

- The Department of Labor's Bureau of Labor Statistics projects paralegal employment to increase 21 percent to 35 percent between 2002 and 2012.
- NALA's 2004 survey disclosed that 62 percent of the respondents have the job title "paralegal" and only 30 percent have the job title "legal assistant." The remainder have various titles.
- According to NALA's 2004 salary survey, paralegals who specialize in intellectual property reported the highest average salary: $51,417.
- NFPA's 2001 compensation survey reported that paralegals found their areas of greatest satisfaction in attorney contact and responsibility and their areas of least satisfaction in bonuses and secretarial support.
- The majority of paralegals receive life and health insurance benefits and reimbursement for dues paid by them to belong to professional associations.

DISCUSSION QUESTIONS

1. What is the difference between a paralegal and a legal assistant?
2. Give some reasons why clients like working with paralegals.
3. Identify some types of employers for whom paralegals work (other than traditional law firms).
4. What are some of the functions of paralegal associations such as NALA and NFPA?
5. What is the difference between certification and licensure of paralegals?
6. Identify some of the advantages and disadvantages of overtime compensation for paralegals.
7. What is the advantage to a paralegal of receiving some formal paralegal education?
8. Identify the pros and cons of mandatory regulation of traditional paralegals, namely, those who work under the supervision of attorneys.

CLOSING ARGUMENTS

1. Access the Department of Labor's Bureau of Labor Statistics information relating to paralegals and legal assistants. How many jobs were held by paralegals in 2002?
2. Access the website of the ABA's Standing Committee on Paralegals.
   a. What is the mission of the Standing Committee?
   b. Review the ABA's Guidelines for the Approval of Paralegal Education Programs. Describe the general composition of an approved program's advisory board.
   c. Identify the ABA-approved paralegal education programs in Georgia.
3. Access NALA's website. How many Certified Legal Assistants were there in the United States as of January 2004?
4. Access NFPA's website.
   a. Select "Consumer Education." Identify some of the benefits to attorneys who utilize paralegals.
   b. Select "Professional Development" and review the information relating to NFPA's definition of paralegal. Why did NFPA determine that the term "paralegal" should be preferred to "legal assistant"? [Note: This determination was made by a 2002 NFPA Resolution.]

CHAPTER

3

ETHICS AND PROFESSIONAL RESPONSIBILITY

I N CIVILIZED LIFE, LAW FLOATS IN A SEA OF ETHICS.
—U.S. SUPREME COURT CHIEF JUSTICE EARL WARREN (1962)

CHAPTER OVERVIEW

Clients and the public must have confidence in the legal system. Thus, it is critical that attorneys and paralegals adhere to the highest ethical principles. This chapter will discuss the ethical duties imposed on attorneys and paralegals and examine some of the ways by which these rules are commonly violated. Clients have a right to expect that those who represent them will be competent, will honor their confidences, will refrain from conflicts of interest, and will safeguard their money and property. After an examination of the specific ethical duties imposed on paralegals, the chapter will conclude with a discussion of the consequences of ethics violations.

If you do not have the opportunity to take an ethics class, consider purchasing a book on paralegal ethics. Two of the best are by well-known paralegal educator Therese A. Cannon and are titled *Concise Guide to Paralegal Ethics* (2001) and *Ethics and Professional Responsibility for Paralegals* (4th ed. 2003). Both are available from Aspen Publishers at *www.aspenpublishers.com*.

A. INTRODUCTION TO ETHICAL STANDARDS FOR PARALEGALS

Just as there are no established standards for paralegal education or for the regulation of paralegals, there are no nationwide uniform ethics codes or established guidelines for professional responsibility that govern paralegals. The conduct of paralegals is governed more indirectly. First, each state has adopted its own manda-tory ethics rules that govern attorney conduct. These rules are generally enforced by the state bar association or the state supreme court. Attorneys who employ para-legals are required under their state codes of ethics to supervise those paralegals. Thus, paralegals are governed indirectly by the rules adopted by their state that gov-ern attorney conduct. Second, a paralegal who joins a paralegal association such as NALA or NFPA agrees to be bound by the ethical rules of the association. Finally, the conduct of paralegals is governed by statutes that impose liability on persons who engage in the unauthorized practice of law and by general tort law, which imposes liability on any person whose negligence proximately causes injury to another.

B. CODES OF ETHICS AND GUIDELINES FOR ATTORNEYS AND PARALEGALS

1. Ethical Rules for Attorneys

Model Rules of Professional Conduct ABA rules that govern attorney standards of professionalism and ethics; adopted in some form by almost all states

The American Bar Association (ABA) has provided guidance and leadership on ethics and professional responsibility for nearly one hundred years. In 1908, the ABA adopted its original Canons of Professional Ethics. Numerous amendments were thereafter made to these Canons. In 1969 the ABA's Committee on Ethics and Professional Responsibility produced the Model Code of Professional Responsibility, which was thereafter adopted by nearly all 50 states and federal juris-dictions. After a comprehensive study in the 1970s, the ABA produced its **Model Rules of Professional Conduct** (Model Rules) in 1983, which replaced the ear-lier Model Code of Professional Responsibility. All but eight states have adopted professional standards based on the Model Rules. Thus, the ABA's Model Rules are followed in whole or in part by nearly all jurisdictions. There are nearly 60 model rules governing a variety of matters, including the attorney-client relationship, transactions with persons other than clients, and the integrity of the profession. The Model Rules are available at the ABA website, at *www.abanet.org/cpr/mrpc/mrpc_home.html.*

Although membership in the ABA is voluntary for attorneys and the ABA's various ethical codes have never been binding on all attorneys throughout the country, the ABA's authoritative Model Rules served as models for most states in drafting their own codes of professional conduct governing attorneys. Consequently, attorneys are not bound by the ABA's rules, but they are bound by their state's ethics codes, most of which are based on the Model Rules. Thus, vio-lation of any ABA rule will not result in any sanctions or discipline against an attor-ney (although the ABA could terminate the attorney's membership in the ABA) but an attorney's violation of a state-adopted rule will result in some punishment or dis-cipline, which might range from a reprimand to disbarment.

The ABA does not address any of its rules directly to paralegals. Nevertheless, Model Rule 5.3, titled "Responsibilities Regarding Nonlawyer Assistants," provides that with respect to nonlawyers employed or retained by attorneys, attorneys must ensure that the person's conduct is compatible with the professional obligations of the attorney. The rule further provides that attorneys may be responsible for the wrongful conduct of such nonlawyers. Most state codes are similar: They impose a duty upon attorneys to supervise nonlawyer assistants such as paralegals and provide that attorneys are liable for the wrongful acts of those persons they supervise.

There are two other ways by which the ABA promotes ethical responsibilities for paralegals. In 1991, the ABA adopted ten **Model Guidelines for the Utilization of Legal Assistant Services** (Guidelines). These Guidelines are directed to attorneys and are intended to expand on Model Rule 5.3 and to assist attorneys who employ paralegals. For example, the Guidelines specify that it is the attorney's responsibility to ensure that all client confidences are preserved by paralegals. The Guidelines further provide that while an attorney may delegate to a paralegal tasks that would normally be performed by the attorney, the attorney may not delegate to a paralegal the responsibility for establishing client fees or rendering a legal opinion to the client. See Appendix C for the ABA Guidelines. The ABA also promotes ethical conduct by paralegals through its approval of paralegal programs: The ABA requires that any paralegal education program that it approves have a curriculum that covers the full range of professional responsibility and ethics concerns applicable to paralegals.

Model Guidelines for the Utilization of Legal Assistant Services
ABA guidelines directed to attorneys to assist attorneys who employ paralegals

2. Ethical Rules for Paralegals

The two major paralegal associations, the National Association of Legal Assistants (NALA) and the National Federation of Paralegal Associations (NFPA) each have ethical guidelines, rules, or codes. Members of these associations voluntarily agree to abide by the terms of these various rules.

a. NALA's Code of Ethics and Professional Responsibility

NALA has adopted a **Code of Ethics and Professional Responsibility** (Code of Ethics) to serve as a guide for the proper conduct of paralegals.

The Code of Ethics is divided into nine canons and includes the following duties:

Code of Ethics and Professional Responsibility
NALA's guide for paralegal ethical conduct

- A paralegal must not perform any duties that attorneys only may perform.
- A paralegal may not engage in the unauthorized practice of law.
- A paralegal must strive to maintain integrity and a high degree of competency.
- A paralegal must protect client confidences.
- A paralegal must use discretion and professional judgment commensurate with his or her experience and knowledge.

Violation of any of the canons may result in cancellation of membership in NALA. NALA has also adopted **Model Standards and Guidelines for Utilization of Legal Assistants** to assist attorneys and others who employ paralegals to ensure delivery of high-quality paralegal services. These guidelines establish minimum standards that paralegals should meet, specify a variety of definitive tasks that paralegals may undertake, and provide that ultimate responsibility for the work product of a paralegal lies with the attorney. NALA's Code of Ethics and Guidelines are found at Appendices D and E, respectively.

Model Standards and Guidelines for Utilization of Legal Assistants
NALA's guidelines to assist attorneys and others who employ paralegals

b. NFPA's Model Code of Ethics and Professional Responsibility

In 1993 NFPA adopted its **Model Code of Ethics and Professional Responsibility** (the Model Code) to establish standards for professional responsibility

Model Code of Ethics and Professional Responsibility
NFPA's standards for professional responsibility for paralegals

to which every paralegal should aspire. The Model Code consists of eight rules and a variety of "ethical considerations" that expand upon and elaborate upon the rules. After NFPA adopted its Model Code, many paralegal associations throughout the United States adopted similar codes.

Some of the key provisions of NFPA's Model Code are as follows:

- A paralegal must achieve and maintain a high level of competence.
- A paralegal must maintain a high level of personal and professional integrity.
- A paralegal must serve the public interest by contributing to the improvement of the legal system.
- A paralegal must preserve all confidential information.
- A paralegal must avoid conflicts of interest.
- A paralegal must not engage in the unauthorized practice of law.

NFPA has established a disciplinary committee to conduct investigations and proceedings and to enforce its Model Rules. Upon a finding that a violation has occurred, NFPA may impose a variety of sanctions against the offending party, including writing a letter of reprimand, ordering attendance at an ethics course, imposing a fine, or referring the paralegal to the appropriate authority for criminal prosecution. NFPA's Model Code is found at Appendix F.

c. Other Paralegal Association Codes

Other associations, such as the American Alliance of Paralegals, Inc., maintain their own codes of ethics. Similarly, most local paralegal associations require their members to adhere to their ethics codes or rules. As discussed above, in many instances, these local associations have adopted NFPA's Model Code in whole or in part. Many local associations post their ethical codes on their websites.

C. ETHICAL RESPONSIBILITIES

Although they use different terminology, NALA, NFPA, and local associations agree on the fundamental rules governing paralegal behavior. The following are some of the most important ethical standards governing paralegals.

1. Duty of Competence

Perhaps the most fundamental aspect of the attorney-client relationship is the client's absolute trust and confidence in the competence of the attorney. This duty of competence is shared by paralegals, who are required to exercise the ordinary skill and knowledge that would be expected of similar paralegals in similar circumstances. In fact, Guideline 1 of the ABA's Model Guidelines for the Utilization of Legal Assistant Services specifically requires that attorneys take reasonable measures to ensure that a paralegal's conduct is consistent with the attorney's obligations, meaning that obligations imposed on attorneys are likewise imposed on paralegals. Thus, attorneys are responsible for ensuring that their paralegals are competent to perform assigned work.

The duty of competence is so critical that it is the first substantive statement promulgated by the ABA's Model Rules. Rule 1.1 provides that competent representation requires the legal knowledge, skill, thoroughness, and preparation necessary for the representation of a client. In addition, attorneys and their paralegals are expected to provide zealous representation for clients.

Attorneys and paralegals are not expected to know all of the law; they are, however, expected to know how to find the law and to know when they need to ask for further help for a client. Similarly, they are expected to educate themselves about their practice areas by taking appropriate classes, engaging in research and reading, and keeping up with recent developments in the law. The following are three of the most common pitfalls relating to the competency required of paralegals.

- **Failure to be thorough.** Most law firms handle a wide variety of cases involving several different issues. The constant pressure of juggling such different types of cases often tempts legal professionals to devote only cursory attention to a case and to "put out the closest fire" before rushing off to work on another matter. The duty of competence requires that paralegals devote their best efforts to every case. If a firm is handling so many cases that it cannot possibly provide competent legal service to its clients, it is only a matter of time until the duty of competency will be breached. You should tell your supervisor that you need additional help. Don't wait until a problem arises. Take the initiative and ask for increased supervision.

- **Failure to complete work on time.** Closely related to the failure to provide thorough representation is the failure to provide timely service. Clients routinely complain that it takes too long for a will to be drafted, a complaint to be filed, or a simple document to be reviewed. In some instances, clients do not understand the complexity of the tasks the firm has been engaged to handle. In other instances, a delay is caused by matters outside the firm's control, such as a crowded court docket or delays by the opposing attorney. Many times, however, the criticism is justified. The worst-case scenario is that a delay leads to a missed deadline and the imposition of sanctions or a malpractice action against the attorney and the firm. Paralegals are often required to maintain the firm's calendars and dockets. While most firms and companies now use computer software tracking systems to maintain their calendars (and their malpractice insurers usually require such computerized systems), you should use a backup "tickler" system, such as a desktop calendar or the old-fashioned method of writing deadlines on index cards or paper slips and then organizing these by date. Review your calendar every morning and report upcoming deadlines to the appropriate individuals. If clients routinely complain about the length of time a project takes, investigate whether the firm's internal organization and structure contribute to the problem. Perhaps the office is understaffed. Perhaps one department causes a bottleneck. Perhaps more modern equipment and software is needed. Rather than just complain, try to find a solution to the problem. Develop your own methods to streamline office procedures and share these with others. Help a disorganized attorney organize his or her files and office. Set up special color-coded bins and in-boxes for critical documents. If your lack of organizational skills causes delays, take a time-and-management course to improve. Similarly, take some computer training classes to make sure you work as efficiently as possible and learn which computer applications best serve the clients' needs. Finally, in many instances, complaints about delays can be minimized by communication. Be sure to keep the client informed of the progress of a case or transaction. Even a quick call to let the client know that you are still waiting for the court to schedule a trial date or that the opposing attorney has not yet reviewed a document because he or she is on vacation will go a long way toward improving client relationships and letting clients know that delays are not being caused by your firm. Be sure that such communications with clients do not cross over into giving legal advice, which would constitute the unauthorized practice of law (see discussion below).

■ **Errors related to carelessness.** Paralegals who are too busy often make careless errors in drafting documents. A letter addressed to one client is mailed to another. A communication or document is inadvertently faxed to the wrong party. In nearly all cases, these types of errors are caused by the pressure of being too busy. Remember that it is more important to be right than to be fast. Slow down and take the time to proofread documents. Pay special attention to names, dates, and money amounts and check these items twice. Enlist the help of a colleague to review documents for accuracy. For anything but the most routine type of correspondence, ask the supervising attorney to review the document before it is sent. Clients pay a great deal of money for legal services, and they are rightly upset by errors and mishaps such as when a document does not include its exhibits, when the client's name is misspelled, or when dates are inaccurate.

2. Duty of Integrity

Many paralegal association codes require that paralegals maintain a high level of personal and professional integrity. NFPA's Model Code provides several examples of conduct that would breach the duty of integrity, including the following:

■ Engaging in an ex parte (literally, "on one side only") communication with a court in an effort to obtain some advantage;
■ Communicating without prior consent with a party the paralegal knows to be represented by counsel;
■ Preparing inaccurate or dishonest time and billing records;
■ Inflating hours billed to a client or employer or misrepresenting the nature of work performed;
■ Failing to be honest and scrupulous in maintaining all funds or other client assets; and
■ Failing to report dishonest or fraudulent acts by any person relating to the handling of client funds or assets.

3. Duty of Confidentiality

It is a bedrock principle that attorneys must preserve the confidentiality of client information. This duty is sacrosanct because a client will not confide in an attorney if the client believes matters discussed may be disclosed to others. Thus, the attorney cannot effectively represent a client and determine the best course of action for a client unless the attorney knows all of the facts about a case, even those that are damaging to the client. Ensuring the client's information is maintained in confidence fosters this goal. The duty of confidentiality imposed on attorneys is also imposed on paralegals. In fact, ABA Guideline 6 provides that it is the attorney's responsibility to take reasonable measures to ensure that all client confidences are preserved by a paralegal. Many law firms require all employees to sign confidentiality agreements that preserve in writing the duty not to disclose confidential client information. The duty of confidentiality extends not only to a firm's current clients but also to all former and potential clients.

ABA Model Rule 1.6 is extraordinarily broad: It requires that attorneys not reveal information relating to the representation of a client unless the client provides informed consent, the disclosure is impliedly authorized, or disclosure is necessary to prevent certain death or substantial bodily harm to another or to prevent the client from committing a crime or fraud. The concept of **informed consent** means that consent is given only after a full explanation of risks, responsibilities, potential liabilities, and possible alternatives.

Informed consent
Consent provided by a party only after full disclosure of all information and risks

Thus, the scope of what is considered confidential covers nearly all information that affects the representation of a client, including the fact of the representation itself. Thus, it would be a violation of the duty of confidentiality to tell your friends or family that your firm represents a certain client (unless the fact is publicly known or the client has consented to such a disclosure). Disclosure may be made to others for the client's benefit (for example, to accountants and bankers), provided they are informed that the information must be kept confidential.

Closely related to the issue of preserving client confidences is the **attorney-client privilege**, which is a rule of evidence that prevents an attorney or paralegal (or other law firm staff) from being forced to testify about confidential client information. Other evidentiary privileges include the doctor-patient privilege (which prevents doctors from being compelled to testify about their patients' confidential medical information) and the spousal privilege, which ensures that one spouse is not forced to testify about another. The attorney-client privilege can last indefinitely, even after the client is no longer represented by the attorney. The attorney-client privilege is more limited than the far-sweeping obligation to maintain the confidences and secrets of the client, which obligation applies to material disclosed by potential clients even when no actual attorney-client relationship has yet arisen.

Attorney-client privilege
Rule of evidence that prevents an attorney or a paralegal from being forced to testify about confidential client information

In addition, the attorney's work product is viewed as privileged and need not be disclosed. **Work product** covers all notes, memoranda, or other documents prepared by the attorney or paralegals relating to mental impressions, conclusions, or strategies regarding the client's case. Of course, a client may always consent to disclosure of the work product or waive the attorney-client privilege. Moreover, the privilege is generally lost if there is disclosure (whether intentional or inadvertent) of confidential information to a third person who does not need to know the information. Thus, disclosures to others within a firm or to co-counsel are appropriate and do not destroy the confidential nature of information. See Figure 3-1 for information about inadvertent disclosures.

Work product
Notes and documents prepared by an attorney or paralegal and that need not be disclosed to adverse party

A number of individuals have considered whether sending unencrypted e-mail over the Internet violates a client's right to confidentiality. In 1999, the ABA resolved the issue in its Formal Opinion 99-413, which concluded that e-mail communications pose no greater risk of interception or disclosure than other methods of communication (such as regular mail) commonly relied upon as having a reasonable expectation of privacy. Thus, sending client material by e-mail does not violate the duty to maintain a client's information in confidence.

4. Duty to Avoid Conflicts of Interest

Attorneys must devote their best efforts to a client. Thus, generally they cannot represent adverse parties in a transaction or a case. Such would violate their duty to

FIGURE 3-1

INADVERTENT DISCLOSURES

A client's information must be maintained in confidence in order to be considered "confidential" under ethics rules and in order for the attorney-client privilege to apply. Even accidental disclosures will result in a waiver of the privilege. Thus, consider the following tips to ensure that confidential information is not inadvertently disclosed:

- Do not leave client files and materials where third parties might see them.
- Do not discuss a client's case outside the office or in front of strangers or bystanders, such as in an elevator, taxi, restaurant, at a party, with friends or family, or at a paralegal association meeting or conference.
- Do not discuss a client's case on a cell phone or other nonsecure method of communication.
- Make sure your computer screen is placed in such a way that it cannot be viewed by others.
- Make sure your office door is closed when meeting with clients and do not allow others to listen to your voice mail messages.
- Do not discuss a client's case or information at a job interview to impress a prospective employer with the work you have been performing (although you will need to identify the names of clients so that a conflict check can be conducted).
- Double check mailing and e-mail addresses and facsimile numbers before you send documents (especially when sending documents to adverse parties). Once sent, these documents cannot be retrieved, and a click of your computer mouse or push of a button can result in an ethics violation.
- Mark confidential materials "privileged" or "attorney work product."
- Do not use confidential client materials as writing samples to show prospective employers.
- Use a shredder to dispose of confidential documents.
- Be careful with confidential information stored on easily stolen laptop computers.

Conflict of interest
Situation that would involve competing duties to clients and breach the duty of undivided loyalty owed to clients

give clients their undivided loyalty and would constitute a **conflict of interest**. Attorneys and paralegals have a duty to avoid conflicts not only with regard to current clients but also to former clients.

a. Duties to Current Clients

ABA Model Rule 1.7 provides that an attorney shall not represent a client if the representation involves a concurrent conflict of interest in that the representation of one client will be directly adverse to another or there is a significant risk that the representation of one or more clients will be affected by the attorney's responsibilities to another client or third person.

There are, however, exceptions to the rules prohibiting attorneys from working for opposing parties. Thus, if the attorney reasonably believes he or she will be able to provide competent representation to all parties and each client consents in writing (after being fully informed of the possible risks and consequences of the dual representation), the conflict of interest is waived and the attorney may then represent two clients whose interest may conflict. For example, in some states an attorney may represent both a husband and a wife in an amicable divorce proceeding if there are no children and few marital assets to divide. Many states, however, would forbid such dual representation, and most attorneys would avoid taking such a case with its potential for later disputes. If the parties' interests become directly adverse, the attorney should withdraw from representing either party.

Remember that not all conflicts can be waived. For example, if representation would involve the assertion of a claim by one client against another in the same lawsuit, such as would occur if an attorney attempted to represent both the plaintiff and the defendant in a case, it would be impossible for the attorney to devote his or her best efforts to either client. In such cases, the attorney must disqualify himself or herself from representation. Client consent is then irrelevant.

b. Duties to Former Clients

Some of the most difficult conflicts questions arise when an attorney is asked to represent a party whose interests might conflict with interests of a former client. For example, assume that three years ago your firm represented ABC Inc. in a case brought against it by Paul Lyons for age discrimination. If a new client, Ted Davis, now wants to sue ABC Inc. for breach of contract, the law firm usually may not take the case because it might harm its former client, ABC Inc. ABA Model Rule 1.9, which discusses duties to former clients, provides that an attorney who previously represented a client may not later represent another person in the same or a substantially related matter if that person's interests are materially adverse to the interests of the former client, unless the former client, after being fully informed, consents in writing.

Moreover, an attorney may not use any information he or she acquired in the course of representing a former client to the disadvantage of that client. Thus, even if the second case is unrelated to the first, if representation would require the attorney to use information learned in the first case to the injury of the former client, the representation must be declined. This rule is closely related to the rules concerning protection of confidential client information: Once an attorney learns confidential information about a client, that information may not later be used in any way that would harm the client.

c. Other Conflict Situations

Model Rule 1.8 sets forth several specific rules relating to other situations that may give rise to conflicts of interest. Some of the situations that may cause conflicts include the following:

- **Business transactions.** An attorney may not enter into a business transaction with a client unless the transaction is fair and the client gives written consent after being fully informed of the terms of the transaction.
- **Gifts.** An attorney may not solicit any substantial gift from a client and may not prepare a document or will that gives the attorney a substantial gift unless the attorney is related to the client.
- **Media rights.** An attorney may not enter into any agreement that would give the attorney literary or media rights to an account based on representation of a client before representation of the client ends.

- **Financial assistance.** An attorney may not provide financial assistance to a client in connection with the client's litigation except that an attorney may generally advance court costs and litigation expenses.
- **Payment by others.** An attorney may not accept payment for representing a client from someone other than the client unless the client provides informed consent.

d. Scope of Conflict and Career Mobility

Imputed conflict
A conflict of interest involving one individual that affects others associated with the individual; a conflict that taints all attorneys in a firm when one is tainted; also called *imputed disqualification*

Under the doctrine of **imputed conflict** or **imputed disqualification**, if an attorney is disqualified from representing a client because of a conflict of interest, all attorneys in the firm are likewise disqualified. The complicated rules relating to conflicts of interest are of special interest when attorneys and paralegals desire to switch employers and go to a new firm. If Jill, an attorney with Old Firm, is disqualified from representing Charles, a client, all attorneys employed by Old Firm are disqualified. Assume Jill switches jobs and is now employed by New Firm. Does Jill carry her conflict with her so that all attorneys at New Firm are prohibited from representing Charles? If so, attorneys and paralegals would be greatly restricted in their job mobility because most law firms do not want to hire individuals who bring with them conflicts that would require the firm to either turn down business or withdraw from representing established clients. Thus, courts have taken a fairly pragmatic approach. Generally, New Firm may represent Charles so long as Jill is screened off from any involvement with Charles's case. New Firm must erect an ethical barrier, often called an **Ethical Wall** or **Chinese Wall**, to ensure that Jill has no association with Charles's matter and the firm thereby is able to protect Charles's confidences and secrets.

Ethical Wall
A means used by lawyers to isolate attorneys or paralegals who have a conflict of interest and thereby protect a client's confidential information; also called a *Chinese Wall*

There are a variety of methods that New Firm can employ to erect an Ethical Wall to isolate or effectively quarantine Jill from involvement with Charles's case:

- Inform all individuals in the firm in writing that Jill should have no access to any files or documents relating to the sensitive client matter and ask all employees, including Jill, to sign a written statement acknowledging this policy;
- Install password-protected computer systems to ensure Jill cannot retrieve or review information electronically stored;
- Maintain separate offices and use separate employees to work on Charles's case; and
- Keep all documents and files in secure locations or specially marked offices and conference rooms and flag all documents with warning labels.

In addition to erecting an Ethical Wall, New Firm should obtain Charles's informed written consent to the representation. The same conflict check and consent and screening procedures should be followed if any of Jill's former clients from Old Firm have interests that might be adverse to those of New Firm's clients.

Generally, the hiring of a paralegal will not disqualify a firm so long as the firm takes reasonable measures to safeguard client confidences and ensures that effective screening measures are implemented. Although courts have concluded that paralegals clearly obtain confidential information during employment, any presumption that the paralegal will then share this information with a new employer can be overcome by showing that reasonable steps were taken to protect the information. (See

Case Illustration, this chapter.) Note, however, that if the paralegal actually shares information with the new firm, the new firm will be required to withdraw from representation of the shared client. An Ethical Wall is intended to prevent disclosure; it cannot cure disclosure that has already occurred. See Figure 3-2 for a summary of conflicts rules.

These conflicts issues pose serious obstacles for paralegals who desire to switch jobs. Although it is clear that a firm is not required to withdraw from representation if it promptly erects an Ethical Wall, many firms do not wish to go to this trouble. The firm will simply decline to hire the affected paralegal or terminate the paralegal's employment once a conflict is discovered.

e. Determining the Existence of Conflicts: Conflicts Checks

While it might be relatively easy for a small law firm in a small community to determine if a conflict exists when a new client seeks representation (or an existing client seeks representation on a new matter) because those in the firm will know and remember cases they have worked on and parties they have represented, in a large law firm in a large city, there is only one way to ensure that a conflict does not exist: by performing a conflict of interest check.

Before accepting a new client a law firm will thus conduct **conflicts checks** to determine whether representing the potential client will conflict with the firm's existing or former clients. Paralegals often conduct conflicts checks. While a small law firm can perform the conflicts checks manually, larger law firms use specialized software to conduct checks. Most law firms require the attorney who desires to represent the client to complete a form that provides some basic information about the potential client, such as the name of the client, the names of the client's relatives and employees, identification of related companies, and so forth. This list of names is

Conflict check
Method used by law firms and attorneys to determine if a conflict of interest exists; often performed by paralegals using specialized software

---

FIGURE 3-2

SUMMARY OF CONFLICTS RULES GOVERNING PARALEGALS

Although the rules governing conflicts of interest are complicated, they can be generally summarized as follows:

- Attorneys must screen for possible conflicts of interest of their paralegals.
- If the conflicts check discloses a fatal conflict of interest (for example, the assertion of a claim by one client against another in the same litigation matter), the attorney must decline representation. Client consent is irrelevant.
- If the check discloses a conflict relating to a former client, the attorney must determine whether the two matters are the same or substantially related and whether the new client's interests will be materially adverse to those of the former client. If so, representation must be declined unless the informed consent, in writing, of the former client is obtained. In all instances, the attorney must ensure that information will not be used to the disadvantage of the former client.
- If a conflict arises out of a paralegal's job switch, an Ethical Wall must be erected to isolate the paralegal from any involvement with the matter giving rise to the conflict, and the client must provide informed consent, in writing, to the continued representation of the firm.

then compared against a computer database of information about the firm's present and former clients. If a match or conflict is disclosed, members of the firm will then determine whether it is a disqualifying conflict. See Chapter Eleven for additional information on performing conflicts checks.

Paralegals who work in large cities are usually advised to maintain a list of clients whose files they have worked on so that if they desire to switch jobs, the new firm can run a conflicts check. In fact, NFPA's ethics rules require paralegals to create and maintain an effective recordkeeping system to identify conflicts. When a new client comes into the firm, check the new client's information against your list. If you have any doubt about whether you have a conflict, inform your supervisor so a determination can be made. Give only enough information so that a conflicts check can be performed: the client's name (and perhaps the names of related parties and attorneys). Do not disclose confidential information. Always keep an updated list of the matters on which you are working.

5. Communication with Adverse Parties

One of the most important ethical rules is the ABA's Model Rule 4.2, which provides that an attorney shall not communicate about a matter with a person the attorney knows is represented by another attorney unless the latter attorney consents to the contact. Thus, once you know that a party is represented by counsel, you may not contact that party for any reason connected with the case unless the party's attorney consents. All communications must be with the party's attorney. This rule ensures that legal professionals do not attempt to take advantage of adverse parties.

6. Duties with Regard to Financial Matters

A review of state bar journals and disciplinary records reveals that a significant number of attorneys are reprimanded, censured, or disbarred over issues relating to money. The following are the areas that cause the most trouble.

- **Setting fees.** Generally, state statutes do not mandate the fees that attorneys may charge for their services. These statutes typically require only that the fee be "reasonable" and that agreements between attorneys and their clients regarding fees be in writing. California's new legislation regulating paralegals (see Chapter Two) specifically states that paralegals may not establish the fees to be charged for services to a client; the attorney must set the fee. Similarly, many paralegal ethical codes state that paralegals may not set legal fees (see NALA's Guidelines). Generally, fees are dictated by the marketplace, and clients who believe one attorney's fees are excessive will usually retain other counsel. In some matters, such as the probating of estates, attorney fees may be set by statute.

- **Segregating client funds.** Attorneys and law firms generally maintain two types of bank accounts: one for general office operating expenses and one for client funds. When clients engage the services of an attorney or law firm, a written fee agreement will be provided to the client that fully explains how fees and expenses for legal services will be calculated. For example, a fee for preparing a trademark application may be a flat fee, a fee for preparing a merger agreement may be set on an hourly basis, and a fee for handling a medical malpractice case may be based on a **contingent fee agreement**, in which case the client will be

Contingent fee agreement
Agreement by client to pay legal fees only if attorney is successful in case; often used in personal injury cases

obligated to pay the firm a stated percentage of any recovery obtained in a lawsuit; if the firm is unsuccessful, the client will owe no fees (but is usually required to reimburse the firm for expenses incurred, such as court filing fees, fees for postage, copying, and travel expenses). Clients are often required to pay an advance fee or deposit funds with the firm, usually called a **retainer**, to retain the services of the firm. Attorneys also receive various fees on behalf of clients when they settle cases, receive funds relating to a business transaction, and so forth. Retainer fees, settlement proceeds, and the like must be maintained by the attorney in a special interest-bearing bank account, called a **trust account**. The attorney may not mix or **commingle** general operating funds with these client trust funds and may not borrow from the trust account for any reason. The funds in this account (and any interest thereon) belong to the clients, and the firm must maintain scrupulous records identifying which funds belong to which clients. See Figure 3-3 for a discussion of **IOLTA accounts**, which are special client accounts the interest on which is used to fund legal services for the needy.

■ **Fee splitting.** While attorneys from different firms may split or share fees that arise from their joint representation of a client, attorneys generally are not permitted to split fees with nonattorneys, including paralegals. If an attorney or firm has had a successful year, the attorney may well provide a discretionary bonus to a paralegal; however, a fee paid by a particular client may not be shared by the attorney with nonattorneys, primarily because only the licensed attorney may engage in the practice of law and those who share fees might try to influence a case and its strategy. Also, a paralegal cannot be paid for referring business to the attorney. Guideline 10

Retainer
Initial sum paid by a client to engage services of a law firm or an attorney

Trust account
Special, segregated interest-earning accounts for client funds

Commingling
Mixing of funds; specifically, mixing of attorney's own funds and those of clients

IOLTA account
Interest on Lawyers' Trust Account; special accounts funded with nominal or short-term funds of clients, the interest on which is used to fund legal services for the needy or other similar projects

---

FIGURE 3-3

IOLTA—USING INTEREST ON CLIENT FUNDS FOR THE PUBLIC GOOD

Attorneys and firms often receive small sums of money for clients or funds for a very short period, perhaps a few days before a settlement is paid to a client. By 1995, all 50 states had developed IOLTA (Interest on Lawyers' Trust Account) programs so that the interest earned on these funds can be used for charitable purposes, such as legal services for the poor, funding of law libraries, victim assistance programs, and legal scholarships.

An attorney must make an initial determination whether a particular client's funds are significant enough to generate income in the firm's interest-bearing trust account. If not, the attorney will deposit the nominal funds into an IOLTA account, which is a single, interest-bearing account into which attorneys in the state pool funds. Banks forward the interest earned on IOLTA accounts (less service charges) to the state IOLTA program, which then uses the money to fund charitable causes. An attorney may put into an IOLTA account only those funds that are not capable of generating any net interest to clients. Thus, none of the individual deposits placed in IOLTA accounts could generate interest on its own for an individual client because the program is expressly restricted to amounts that are too insignificant or deposits that are too short-term to yield any interest for the clients who own the funds. The IOLTA programs thus succeed in generating income where the individual deposits could not, and the IOLTA accounts then fund valuable legal services for the community.

of the ABA's Guidelines on utilizing paralegals provides that a paralegal may be compensated based on the quantity and quality of his or her work and the value of that work to a practice, but the paralegal's compensation may not be contingent, by advance agreement, upon the profitability of the practice.

- **Billing practices.** Attorneys generally charge clients for work performed by a firm's paralegals. Typically, the paralegal will keep track of his or her time spent on a client's case and then a bill will be prepared describing the nature of the work, the date it was performed, and the cost. Thus, if a paralegal's hourly billable rate is $90 and a letter to a client requires one and one-half hours to research and write, the client will be billed $135 for this task. Fees charged for paralegal time must be for the performance of paralegal duties. Thus, if a paralegal spends three hours performing a purely clerical task, such as routine photocopying, the client may not be billed for any of this time. Some tasks may appear somewhat clerical but might actually be billable. For example, assembling documents for the closing of a merger and ensuring that the appropriate exhibits are attached to the merger agreement call for the type of skill and knowledge typically possessed by paralegals. Thus, clients may be charged for the paralegal's time in performing this task. While timekeeping and billing will be discussed more thoroughly in Chapter Eleven, it is important at this point to understand the most important thing about timekeeping: Always be scrupulously honest in recording your time. Neither inflate nor discount the time spent on a task.

7. Duties with Regard to Solicitation and Advertising

Closely related to financial matters are the duties imposed on attorneys and paralegals not to solicit employment from a prospective client with whom there is no family, personal, or prior professional relationship when a significant motive for doing so is financial gain. Hunting for prospective clients in such an aggressive fashion is usually called "ambulance chasing" and direct one-on-one solicitation is prohibited because of the possibility of unduly influencing persons who may be vulnerable due to illness, grief, or injury. Direct, in-person, live telephone, and real-time electronic contact is generally prohibited. Furthermore, attorneys may not use paralegals to solicit clients for them or compensate paralegals for referring business to them. Most states have statutes that prohibit the use of individuals, usually called **runners** or **cappers**, who are paid to procure business for attorneys.

Runner
An individual paid to procure business for an attorney; also called a *capper*

Although attorneys and paralegals may not solicit clients directly, they may engage in limited forms of advertising. Advertising in various media (radio, television, print ads, or correspondence) is permissible so long as the advertisement is not false or misleading and does not constitute improper in-person solicitation.

Until 1977, all attorney advertising was prohibited, and nearly all attorneys believed that advertising was undignified and offensive. Advertising is now permissible because it does not involve the same pressures that in-person solicitation might. It is easy for a person to throw out a mailer or turn off the television; it is much more difficult to resist in-person or direct entreaties.

Most attorneys do advertise, even if those advertisements are only entries in telephone book yellow pages or law firm websites. While aggressive television advertising is still frowned upon by most in the profession, many proponents believe that competitive advertising makes legal services more accessible and affordable for those in need. See Figure 3-4 for information about advertising and cyber ethics.

> ## FIGURE 3-4
> ## CYBER ETHICS ISSUES
>
> Although various states are in the process of formulating ethics rules relating to communications in cyberspace, a few general principles have emerged:
>
> - Law firm websites are usually viewed as communications or "advertisements" rather than as unlawful solicitations; thus, so long as their content is neither false nor misleading, they are permissible. Many law firms include disclaimers on their websites that a person's visit to the site does not constitute an attorney-client relationship.
> - A law firm's domain name (its Internet address) may not be false or deceptive and it may not falsely imply any special expertise. Some states have concluded that a for-profit law firm should not use the "org" suffix because it implies the firm is a nonprofit entity.
> - Advertising past victories on an Internet site may be problematic if it indicates that other clients may expect similar results. Disclaimers that "results vary from case to case" may help ensure that discussions of past successes do not constitute an unlawful guarantee of results of the representation.
> - E-mail announcements and invitations to law firm seminars should be labeled as "advertisements."
> - Attorneys may not solicit clients through Internet chat rooms (namely, by real-time communications between the attorney and a would-be client).

NFPA's position is that freelance paralegals who work on a contract or case-by-case basis for attorneys may advertise so long as the advertisements indicate the nonlawyer status of the paralegal, are not misleading or false, are aimed at attorneys rather than members of the public, and comply with attorney advertising guidelines in the relevant jurisdiction. Similarly, independent paralegals (those who offer their services directly to the public) may advertise on the same basis as freelance paralegals.

8. Duty to Avoid the Unauthorized Practice of Law

a. Introduction

The ABA Guidelines state that it is the attorney's responsibility to take reasonable measures to ensure that clients, courts, and other attorneys are aware that a paralegal who is employed by the attorney is not licensed to practice law. Similarly, both NALA and NFPA flatly prohibit paralegals from engaging in the unauthorized practice of law, commonly referred to as "UPL." **Unauthorized practice of law** refers to engaging in the practice of law without a license to do so.

All states have statutes that prohibit any nonlawyers from practicing law so that members of the public are protected from incompetence. Unfortunately, few of the statutes define what it means to "practice law." Most legal professionals agree, however; and the ABA Guidelines provide that paralegals may not engage in the following activities:

- Establishing an attorney-client relationship;
- Establishing a fee to be charged for legal services; or
- Providing a legal opinion or legal advice to a client.

Unauthorized practice of law
Practicing of law by one without a license to do so; usually called *UPL*

Many other codes and guidelines add another activity that constitutes the practice of law: representing a party before a court or tribunal.

When called upon to determine whether a certain challenged activity is the "practice of law," courts often consider three factors: whether the activity is one traditionally performed by an attorney; whether the activity requires professional judgment and legal skills not commonly possessed by lay persons; and whether harm has been caused to the consumer of the service or activity.

Most UPL statutes are criminal statutes and their violation may result in a variety of sanctions, including fines and incarceration. Moreover, attorneys may be reprimanded, censured, suspended, or disbarred by their bar associations, and paralegals may have their memberships in their voluntary associations terminated. In addition, a client may sue both the attorney and paralegal for malpractice. Recall the statutory scheme in California for regulation of paralegals and its prohibition against UPL. A first violation of the law subjects the paralegal to a fine of up to $2,500 as to each consumer to whom a violation occurs; subsequent violations subject the paralegal to additional fines or imprisonment or both. Moreover, injured consumers are specifically authorized to sue paralegals.

b. Giving Legal Advice

Traditional paralegals and freelance paralegals who work with lawyers and law firms are more likely to violate the rule prohibiting them from giving legal advice than the rules prohibiting them from establishing an attorney-client relationship or setting legal fees. Because a paralegal is often a client's primary liaison with a firm and because paralegals often have such close and continuing contacts with clients, there is a great temptation for clients to ask paralegals for advice and for paralegals to respond to those requests. Similarly, highly competent paralegals are often asked for advice by friends and family members. Advice given by paralegals may be taken more seriously by members of the public than advice given by someone without legal training. Thus, casual advice given by a paralegal may be more strictly scrutinized than an offhand comment by a neighbor that "you ought to sue your boss." Moreover, the fact that a paralegal may not be compensated for the advice is irrelevant. One may engage in UPL whether one is paid or not.

Paralegals can clearly relay information to clients, provide status reports, and communicate general information about clients' cases. They may also relay an attorney's legal advice to a client. Consider the following statements made to clients:

UPL	**Permissible Statements**
You should file an application to register your trademark with the Patent and Trademark Office.	*Attorney Jones has asked me to tell you that he advises that we file an application to register your trademark with the Patent and Trademark Office.*
We think you should appeal the denial of the motion to change venue.	*Attorney Smith is reviewing the court order denying the motion to change venue and will contact you shortly to discuss this matter.*
These are the two options you may pursue to recover damages from the doctor who committed malpractice against you.	*Attorney Diaz will contact you to discuss your case.*

> *This isn't legal advice, but if I were*
> *you, I'd sue for breach of contract.*

> *You will need to check with an*
> *attorney to determine your rights.*

When in doubt, always err on the side of caution. When a client is pressing you for information or advice, tell the client that you will check with the attorney and have the attorney respond to the client's questions. Simply state that you are not an attorney and therefore are not licensed to give legal advice. Introducing legal advice with a disclaimer such as, "I'm not an attorney, but I think . . . " will not protect you from an allegation of UPL.

c. Representing Clients in Court and Before Agencies

As discussed in Chapter Two, although the general rule is that only attorneys may represent clients, there are some exceptions to this rule: When authorized by law, paralegals may represent clients at both federal and state administrative hearings. For example, the Social Security Administration and the Immigration and Naturalization Service allow nonlawyer representation. Recall that ten states allow nonlawyers to appear before their various state administrative agencies. To illustrate, California allows paralegals to represent clients in workers' compensation matters if the client consents and the paralegal is supervised by an attorney.

d. Permissible Activities

Although it is impossible to identify every activity in which paralegals may engage, there is some general agreement that the following tasks are permissible (with appropriate supervision):

- Communicating with clients, both orally and in writing, so long as legal advice is not being given and the paralegal's status as a nonlawyer is clear;
- Relaying an attorney's legal advice to a client so long as the client is informed that the opinion is that of the attorney, not of the paralegal;
- Preparing legal documents, including wills, business agreements, and other forms, so long as the paralegal either works under the supervision of an attorney or, if the paralegal is an independent paralegal, merely fills in forms as instructed by a consumer and does not modify any answers;
- Conducting research and preparing pleadings and briefs to be submitted to court and other litigation documents so long as the paralegal's work is supervised and the documents are signed by a licensed attorney;
- Meeting with clients;
- Representing clients at administrative hearings if allowed by law;
- Assisting at trial and sitting at counsel's table (in many courts); and
- Teaching about the law (for example, explaining probate principles or writing an article about patent infringement);
- Identifying oneself as a paralegal on a business card (or letterhead in most states) so long as one's nonlawyer status is clear; and
- Identifying oneself as a "Certified Legal Assistant," "Certified Paralegal," or "PACE-Registered Paralegal" if those designations are true.

Note that the ABA Guidelines specifically provide that an attorney may identify paralegals by name and title on the attorney's or firm's letterhead, and paralegals may be identified on firm business cards.

e. Prohibited Activities

The following are some tasks that are usually designated as acts of UPL by paralegals:

- Giving legal advice;
- Agreeing to represent a client;
- Establishing legal fees;
- Signing legal documents, such as settlement agreements or partnership agreements (although the paralegal may draft the documents with adequate supervision);
- Conducting depositions (although the paralegal may help prepare the person to be deposed, attend the deposition and take notes, and summarize the deposition transcript);
- Signing documents to be filed in court; and
- Negotiating settlements (although the paralegal may relay offers and responses to clients under the supervision of an attorney).

f. Avoiding UPL

Because the consequences of UPL can be so severe and because it can be easy to casually cross over the line between providing information and giving legal advice, there are a number of precautions you can take to avoid UPL, including the following:

- **Disclose your status.** Always clearly disclose your status as a paralegal. Use of either "paralegal" or "legal assistant" is acceptable. A statement such as "I'm with Fuller and Hanley" or "I work for Martin Anderson" is not sufficient to inform members of the public of your status.
- **Indicate your position on firm materials.** Make sure that any firm letterhead, stationery, business cards, or documents that include your name clearly identify your position, as in *Caroline Edwards, Paralegal*. Correspondence to clients should likewise indicate your position.
- **Identify the source of advice.** If you are relaying information that might be construed as a legal opinion or advice, clearly indicate that the source of the information is the attorney for whom you work and that you are not permitted to give legal advice.
- **Request supervision.** If you have any concerns that a letter you are writing or information you provide to a client may be viewed as UPL, ask your supervising attorney to review the materials, meet with the client, and sign the documents. The attorney must remain responsible for your final work product.
- **Avoid excessive client contact.** Be sure that your supervising attorney meets with his or her clients and has contact with them. If all law firm contact is with you, it may create the impression that you are an attorney or that you are qualified to provide legal advice.
- **Do not sign court documents.** Ask your supervising attorney to review all documents that you draft that may be submitted to a court, and ensure that the attorney's signature appears on any such document.

g. New Developments in UPL: Self-Help Materials

Some of the newer issues and cases in UPL examine do-it-yourself legal publications, legal software packages, and information provided on the Internet.

No doubt you have seen "Do It Yourself Divorce" kits and books offering information on preparing wills, negotiating a merger transaction, or evicting a tenant. Most of these publications include forms and tips for completing the forms. Generally, publications that merely attempt to describe the law in abstract terms for an individual's self-help rather than providing specific advice to a client do not constitute UPL. Some courts that have considered the issue have noted that there is no client relationship of trust and confidence arising from the mere purchase of a book; other courts have focused on the fact that every individual has a right to represent himself or herself and do-it-yourself publications are a natural extension of this right.

The same principles generally apply to software packages that consist of forms for various matters, such as wills, the formation of a partnership, and the sale of a business. Similarly, there are thousands of legal forms accessible on the Internet—some that are free and some that are fee-based. These generally do not constitute the practice of law for the reasons given above.

Most publications, software packages, and Internet sites include a standard disclaimer that the information is provided for general informational use only, that an attorney should be retained to respond to questions, that the information does not constitute legal advice, and that no attorney-client relationship is created by providing such information.

h. Freelance and Independent Paralegals

You will recall that a freelance paralegal is an individual who works on a case-by-case basis for an attorney or firm, and when a project is completed, the freelancer moves on to another firm. The discussion above relating to UPL as to traditional paralegals employed in firms applies to freelance paralegals as well. Thus, generally, so long as there is adequate supervision by the attorney, a freelance paralegal is not engaging in UPL.

Independent paralegals, on the other hand, are individuals who provide legal services directly to consumers. They are therefore more at risk for engaging in UPL. A number of courts have examined situations involving independent paralegals. The following general principles have emerged:

- Providing general published factual information that has been written or approved by an attorney and that pertains to legal procedures or rights to a person who is presenting himself or herself is not UPL.
- If an independent paralegal merely provides forms to an individual who then directs how the forms should be completed, there is no UPL.
- If an independent paralegal advises individuals which forms to use and provides assistance and advice in completing the documents, the independent paralegal is likely engaging in UPL.

California has codified these principles in Business and Professions Code §§ 6400-6415 by providing that a registered Legal Document Assistant may complete legal documents (in a ministerial manner) if the documents are selected by a person who is representing himself or herself by typing or otherwise completing the documents at the person's specific directions. Any advertisements by Legal Document Assistants are required to state, "I am not an attorney. I can only provide self-help services at your specific direction."

These approaches suggest that independent paralegals function almost exclusively in an administrative or secretarial capacity by merely completing or typing documents at someone else's direction. They may not suggest which form to use, and the requirement that they complete the form at another's direction often means that even if they observe or know of an error, they may not suggest that a correction be made.

As certain professions become more highly specialized, legislators have acknowledged that qualified individuals may engage in limited activities that might otherwise constitute the practice of law. Thus, for example, accountants often represent their clients in tax hearings, real estate agents and brokers prepare legally binding contracts and explain their terms to their clients, and so-called "jailhouse lawyers" assist other inmates in preparing court briefs and motions. As noted earlier, California now regulates Legal Document Assistants and paralegals.

As the need for affordable legal services increases, the role of paralegals is expected to expand as well. For example, a court appearance by a paralegal to request a continuance agreed upon by all parties may well become the norm rather than the exception.

9. Duty to Report Misconduct

a. Reporting by Attorneys

Model Rule 8.3 provides that an attorney who has knowledge of another attorney's serious violation of an ethical rule must report this attorney to the appropriate disciplinary body. Note the use of the word "serious," which has generally been interpreted to mean a violation that reflects on the attorney's honesty or fitness to practice law. Not every violation requires a report. In some instances, a violation may be minor, inadvertent, or unintentional, and informal office counseling can resolve the problem. Many firms have ethics committees to handle ethics issues. They engage in informal counseling, advise individuals to take ethics classes, and assign inexperienced attorneys and paralegals to more experienced individuals who mentor them in order to provide professional representation to the firm's clients. The duty imposed on attorneys to report serious violations by other attorneys extends to paralegals as well.

b. Reporting by Paralegals

Are paralegals required to report ethics violations or misconduct by paralegals? NFPA answers this question in the affirmative and requires the "whistleblower" to make a confidential written report to NFPA's Disciplinary Committee, which might then issue a letter of reprimand, require attendance at an ethics course, impose a fine, or refer the matter to the appropriate authority for criminal prosecution.

In addition, NFPA's Model Code requires its members to advise the appropriate authorities of dishonest or fraudulent acts by any person (including attorneys as well as paralegals) pertaining to the handling of funds, securities, or other client assets or any act by any legal professional that demonstrates fraud, dishonesty, or misrepresentation. The Model Code then goes a step further and provides that failure to report such knowledge is in itself misconduct. The report may be made to a law firm ethics committee or to the bar association or prosecutor, depending on the nature of the misconduct.

c. What to Do if You Observe Misconduct

Follow these guidelines if you become aware of misconduct or unethical behavior by a legal professional:

- Review your jurisdiction's ethics codes to be sure that the activity in question is a violation and not merely a case of aggressive advocacy for a client;
- Do not participate in any activity that you believe may be an ethics violation;
- Report your concerns to your paralegal coordinator, your supervising attorney, or the firm's ethics committee or ethics liaison (assuming this is not the person whom you suspect of misconduct);
- Contact your paralegal association, and, without providing confidential information or names, discuss the problem; and
- Consider retaining legal counsel to advise you on the proper course of conduct.

You may also contact your state bar association's ethics division (again, without disclosing confidential information or naming names). Almost all states have an "ethics hotline" that provides general information by telephone or e-mail. While the ethics division will not give you legal advice, it may refer you to an appropriate ethics code, rule, or opinion that may provide guidance.

If your employment is terminated or you are retaliated against for reporting misconduct, you may be protected under your state's whistleblower statutes or under common law for wrongful discharge from employment.

d. Consequences of Violations of Ethical Duties

As discussed earlier, voluntary organizations (such as the ABA, NALA, and NFPA) have the right to terminate the membership of a member who violates the organization's rules. Moreover, NFPA's Model Code provides that it may refer information about criminal activity of a paralegal to the appropriate authority.

Violations by an attorney of his or her state bar association rules of ethics may result in a public reprimand, censure, suspension, or disbarment of the attorney. In many instances, state bar associations require offending attorneys to make restitution to wronged parties and take ethics training. Because attorneys are required to supervise the acts of those who work for them, including paralegals, violations by paralegals may give rise to sanctions against attorneys.

Violations of state statutes (such as those prohibiting UPL by paralegals) generally result in fines or, in extreme cases, imprisonment. Criminal activity such as defrauding clients or obstructing justice may also result in a misdemeanor or felony conviction, which could lead to fines or imprisonment.

Clients who are harmed by an attorney's or paralegal's misconduct may initiate civil lawsuits against the attorney or paralegal for damages caused by the wrongful acts or negligence. Tort law requires that all individuals act with reasonable care. Missing a deadline, preparing a document improperly, or failing to represent a client competently are all negligent acts. While attorneys and paralegals are not expected to possess extraordinary legal skills, they are expected to possess the skills and knowledge normally possessed by members of their profession. Failure to act in accordance with those standards is actionable as negligence. Finally, as a practical matter, an attorney is required to disclose to his or her malpractice insurer any claims made against the attorney or arising from representation of clients. Thus, frequent complaints by clients (even if they do not result in a verdict) may result in increased malpractice premiums, causing a financial hardship to the attorney or firm.

NET RESULTS

www.abanet.org/cpr/ model_def_home.html	ABA home page for its Center for Professional Responsibility with links to a variety of ethics information, including the Model Rules of Professional Conduct
www.abanet.org/ legalservices/paralegals	Home page for ABA's Standing Committee on Paralegals with link to ABA Model Guidelines for Utilization of Legal Assistant Services
www.nala.org/98model.htm	NALA's Model Standards and Guidelines for Utilization of Legal Assistants
www.paralegals.org	Select "Professional Development" for NFPA's Model Code of Ethics and Professional Responsibility and Guidelines for Enforcement and related information on ethics issues.
www.law.cornell.edu/ethics	The American Legal Ethics Library offered by Cornell Law School provides excellent information on ethics issues.
www.megalaw.com	Select "Law Topic Pages" and then "Ethics & Law" for links to a variety of sites relating to ethics and professional responsibility.

CASE ILLUSTRATION

Paralegal Conflicts of Interest

Case: *Rubin v. Enns*, 23 S.W.3d 382 (Tex. Ct. App. 2000)

Facts: Inda Crawford, a paralegal, left her employment with her previous law firm and went to work for opposing counsel in a case. The previous law firm sought to have the new law firm disqualified from continuing to represent the client.

Holding: The new firm was not disqualified. Although there is a presumption that a paralegal shares confidential information with a new employer, the presumption can be overcome if the new firm instructs the paralegal not to disclose information learned during her prior employment, tells her not to work on any matter on which she worked while employed at the previous firm, and takes reasonable measures to erect an Ethical Wall to reduce any potential for misuse of client confidences. This reasonable approach also fosters the ABA's suggestion that restrictions on a paralegal's employment be kept to the minimum necessary to protect confidentiality of client information. The court reviewed various barriers the new firm implemented to safeguard client information and determined they were appropriate in this case.

KEY TERMS

Model Rules of Professional Conduct
Model Guidelines for the Utilization of Legal Assistant Services
Code of Ethics and Professional Responsibility
Model Standards and Guidelines for Utilization of Legal Assistants
Model Code of Ethics and Professional Responsibility
Informed consent
Attorney-client privilege
Work product

Conflict of interest
Imputed conflict
Ethical Wall
Conflict check
Contingent fee agreement
Retainer
Trust account
Commingling
IOLTA account
Runner
Unauthorized practice of law

CHAPTER SUMMARY

Rules Governing Legal Professionals	Most jurisdictions have adopted some form of the ABA's Model Rules of Professional Conduct; thus, there is significant uniformity in the nation as to the ethics rules for legal professionals. Violation of an ABA Model Rule will result only in termination of membership in the ABA; however, violation of a state rule may result in an attorney's reprimand, suspension, or disbarment.
Ethics Rules Governing Paralegals	Ethics rules for paralegals are imposed by the voluntary organizations to which paralegals belong. In addition, attorneys are required to ensure that paralegals comply with the ethical rules governing attorneys.

Duties of Competency and Confidentiality	Attorneys and paralegals are required to provide competent legal representation. Thus, they must possess a reasonable level of knowledge and skill and must be thorough and prompt. Attorneys and paralegals are required to maintain the confidential information of clients, former clients, and prospective clients.
Avoiding Conflicts of Interest	Attorneys and paralegals are required to avoid conflicts of interest and may not represent clients whose interests are directly adverse. The duty extends to former clients as well. If a paralegal changes jobs and a conflict arises between clients at the new firm and the old firm, the new firm should obtain the client's written informed consent and create an Ethical Wall to isolate the paralegal and thereby protect the client's confidences.
Segregation of Funds	Money belonging to clients may not be commingled with funds in an attorney's general operating account. Client funds must be segregated and retained in accounts separate from general operating funds.
Prohibition Against Solicitation	Attorneys and paralegals generally may not solicit clients directly. General advertising is acceptable if it is not false or misleading.
Prohibition Against Unauthorized Practice of Law	State statutes prohibit the unauthorized practice of law. Thus, paralegals may not establish an attorney-client relationship, set legal fees, give legal advice, or appear in court on behalf of a client. Violations of this duty may result in fines or even imprisonment.
Duty to Report Misconduct	Paralegals have a duty to report serious ethical misconduct of attorneys and paralegals that reflects on honesty or fitness to represent clients.

TRIVIA

- A 1995 ABA report on nonlawyer activity and UPL found that many paralegals operate without "meaningful supervision." The same report noted that many attorneys desire that court rules be changed to permit paralegals to appear in court for routine and previously agreed-to matters.
- Eighty percent of lawyers send confidential or privileged information by e-mail. The overwhelming majority does not encrypt these e-mail communications; they rely solely on a confidentiality statement that accompanies the transmission.
- The Montana Supreme Court recently publicly censured three members of a law firm who initiated a wrongful death action on behalf of one client against another of the firm's clients and then dropped the defendant client when he objected to the conflict.

DISCUSSION QUESTIONS

1. Discuss whether the following activities and statements by Mike, a paralegal working for a law firm, might constitute the unauthorized practice of law.
   - A statement by Mike to a client that "You should consider suing your landlord."
   - An article by Mike on avoiding probate.
   - Status reports written by Mike for the firm's clients reporting the progress of their cases.
2. Sue, a client of a law firm, has limited financial resources and cannot afford the firm's services. She has therefore offered to make the firm a partner in her real estate partnership in lieu of fees. Is this acceptable? Discuss.
3. The law firm Brown & Henry represents the plaintiff in a breach of contract case. May Harry, a paralegal at the firm, contact the defendant, who is represented by Moran & Moran, to obtain some very basic factual information from the defendant?
4. Harry, the paralegal at Brown & Henry, decides to leave the firm and is hired by Moran & Moran. Will Moran & Moran be required to withdraw from representing the defendant in the breach of contract case described above? Discuss.
5. One of Harry's first tasks at Moran & Moran is to visit the survivors of a factory explosion to see if they need legal representation. Moran & Moran has informed Harry that Harry will be paid $1,000 for every client he "signs up." Discuss the propriety of such actions.
6. Harry is impressed with the clients at his new firm and tells his roommates that he is lucky that he is employed by the firm that represents United Airlines and that United Airlines is considering buying a smaller airline. Has Harry breached any ethical duties? Discuss.
7. Harry's firm is handling a complicated divorce case for Mr. Davidson. One day, during a meeting discussing money to be paid to his spouse, Mr. Davidson yells, "That's it. I'll kill her!" Later in the day, Mr. Davidson's daughter calls Harry and asks how the case is progressing. Discuss the confidentiality issues involved.

CLOSING ARGUMENTS

1. Access the ABA website and locate the ABA Model Rules of Professional Conduct. When is a lawyer responsible for the conduct of a person that would be a violation of the Rules of Professional Conduct if engaged in by a nonlawyer? What Rule governs your answer?
2. Access NALA's website and select information relating to NALA's Certified Legal Assistant program, specifically, the "CLA Fact Sheet." What topics are covered in the ethics portion of NALA's examination?
3. Access NFPA's website and select "Professional Development." Review NFPA's Confidential Ethics and Disciplinary Opinion 95-1 and answer the following question: May an individual employed by a corporation use the title "paralegal" when the corporation does not employ in-house counsel to supervise or be accountable for the individual's work?
4. Access the website for the California Alliance of Paralegal Associations. What is the Association's first ethical guideline?

CHAPTER 4

THE AMERICAN LEGAL SYSTEM

I'M NO IDEALIST TO BELIEVE FIRMLY IN THE INTEGRITY OF OUR COURTS AND IN THE JURY SYSTEM—THAT IS NO IDEAL TO ME, IT IS A LIVING, WORKING REALITY. GENTLEMEN, A COURT IS NO BETTER THAN EACH MAN OF YOU SITTING BEFORE ME ON THIS JURY. A COURT IS ONLY AS SOUND AS ITS JURY, AND A JURY IS ONLY AS SOUND AS THE MEN WHO MAKE IT UP.

—ATTICUS FINCH IN *TO KILL A MOCKINGBIRD,* BY HARPER LEE

CHAPTER OVERVIEW

To be an effective paralegal, you need to understand how the American legal system is structured. Once you know the difference between criminal and civil law and procedural and substantive law and understand which cases may be brought in which courts, you will readily grasp the hierarchy within a given court's structure, which gives greater emphasis to cases from higher courts than to those from lower courts.

A. INTRODUCTION TO THE AMERICAN COMMON LAW TRADITION

The American legal system is part of what is referred to as the **common law** tradition. "Common law" is defined in part by *Black's Law Dictionary* 293 (8th ed. 2004) as that body of law that derives from judicial decisions rather than from statutes or constitutions. The common law system began in England several hundred years ago. Since at least 1300 A.D., people who may have been training to be lawyers began "taking notes" on what occurred during trials. When judges were called upon to decide cases, they then began referring to these written reports of

Common law
The body of law that develops and derives from judicial decisions as distinguished from statutes or constitutions

earlier cases and making decisions based on prior cases concerning similar situations where people were treated in the same manner. The English referred to this system as the "common law" because it was applied equally throughout England and replaced a less uniform system of law. The system of following similar previous cases was considered the most equitable way of resolving disputes.

B. SOURCES OF LAW

1. Judicial Opinions

Stare decisis
Latin for "let the decision stand"; concept of relying on judge-made case law in similar cases

Precedent
A case or legal authority that governs a later case

There are several sources of law in the United States. Because this is a common law country, the role of cases is paramount. The concept of following previous cases, or precedents, is called **stare decisis**, which is a Latin phrase meaning "to stand by things decided." In the broadest sense, the doctrine of stare decisis means that once courts have announced a principle of law, they will follow it in the future in cases that are substantially similar. It is this doctrine of stare decisis that serves to protect litigants from unfairness. If the judge is required to follow **precedent**, he or she may not rule against an individual based on race, sex, or religion. Similarly, those precedents will guide a judge who is unacquainted with a certain area of the law. In this way, stare decisis advances fairness and consistency in our legal system.

Moreover, stare decisis promotes stability in our judicial system. It would not only be chaotic but manifestly unfair if a judge treated each case that came before him or her as being severed from our great body of legal tradition and then rendered different and inconsistent rulings on a daily basis. You can imagine the frustration of a client who seeks advice of counsel on the division of assets in a dissolution of a marriage only to be informed that the division depends on which judge hears the case. A client's rights would be totally dependent upon an arbitrary assignment to a judge. Such a result is not only unjust but also unpredictable. Thus, stare decisis not only encourages stability in our legal system but also aids those in the legal profession in advising clients as to the likely disposition of their cases.

Civil law
A body of law depending more on legislative enactments than on case law, often seen in non-English-speaking countries

In contrast, many other countries are said to be part of the **civil law** tradition, which means that they follow a comprehensive set of codes, as was the case under Roman law. In general, civil law countries place much heavier reliance on their collections of statutes than on their much smaller collections of cases. Germany, France, Japan, Mexico, Korea, Spain, Italy, China, Austria, and many of the countries of Africa are all civil law countries. Typically, English-speaking countries or those that are prior British Commonwealth colonies are part of the common law system (and are greatly dependent on cases used as precedents), while non-English-speaking countries are usually part of the civil law system (which is greatly dependent on codes or statutes). Note that every state in the United States except Louisiana, and every Canadian province except Quebec, is part of the common law tradition. Because Louisiana and Quebec were settled by the French, their legal systems are largely patterned after the law of France, a civil law country.

Under the common law system the "law" is found in the written decisions of judges, and these decisions serve as precedents to be followed in later cases involving substantially similar issues. Thus, the first source of law in the United States is judge-made case law.

2. Constitutions

A second source of law in the United States is constitutions. A **constitution** sets forth the fundamental law for a nation or a state. It is the document that provides the principles relating to organization and regulation of a federal or state government. We have a United States Constitution, our supreme law of the land, and each state has its own constitution.

Constitution
A document setting forth the fundamental law for a nation or state

3. Statutes

A **statute**, or law, is defined by *Black's Law Dictionary* 1448 (8th ed. 2004) as "a law passed by a legislative body." In the United States, legislatures did not become particularly active in enacting statutes until the early to mid-1800s, when our economy began changing from a very rural one to a more urban one. This major change in American society was coupled with a tremendous population growth, due largely to immigration, and it became clear that rather than deciding disputes on a case-by-case basis, which was slow and cumbersome at best, broader laws needed to be enacted that would set forth rules to govern behavior of the public at large.

Statute
A law passed by a legislative body

4. Administrative Regulations

A fourth source of law in the United States is found in the vast number of administrative rules and regulations promulgated by federal agencies such as the Federal Communications Commission (FCC), the Food and Drug Administration (FDA), the National Labor Relations Board (NLRB), and numerous other agencies. Agencies exist in the individual states as well, and these also enact rules and regulations.

The agencies play a unique role in our legal system because they function quasi-legislatively and quasi-judicially. You may recall from basic history and civics classes that our government is divided into three branches: the legislative branch, which makes laws; the judicial branch, which interprets laws; and the executive branch, which enforces laws. Each exercises its own powers, and, by a system usually called "checks and balances," each functions separately from the others.

The agencies, on the other hand, perform two functions: They act like a legislature by promulgating rules and regulations that bind us; and they act like a judiciary by hearing disputes and rendering decisions.

While you may not have given a great deal of thought to the effect of the agencies in your daily life, their influence is significant and far-reaching. For example, the radio you listen to and the television you watch are regulated by the FCC, and the cosmetics you use and the food you eat are regulated by the FDA.

5. Executive Branch

While the primary function of the federal executive branch is to enforce the law, it serves as a source of law itself in three ways: First, treaties are entered into by the executive branch with the advice and consent of the U.S. Senate. These agreements between the United States and other nations affect your daily life and serve as a source of law because they may relate to trade and import matters, economic cooperation, or even international boundaries and fishing rights. Second, the President, our chief executive, can issue executive orders to regulate and direct federal agencies and officials. Third, the executive branch exerts influence on the law through policies on enforcing laws. For example, if federal laws relating to possession of small amounts of drugs are rarely enforced, the effect is as if the law does not exist despite the fact that a statute clearly prohibits such acts. Nevertheless, while such an approach by the executive branch influences the law as well as societal behavior, such influence on the law is indirect and remote. In the event the government prosecutes an individual for violation of a previously unenforced law, the individual usually may not raise the previous laxity as a defense.

The executive branches of the federal and state governments also serve as sources of law in that the chief executive (the President or a state governor) is required to sign a bill to make it legally effective and can veto a bill (although legislatures usually can override such vetoes, generally upon a two-thirds vote).

C. JURISDICTION AND VENUE

1. Introduction

Jurisdiction
The power of a court to hear a case

Before a lawsuit can be initiated in a court, certain requirements must be met. Not all courts are permitted to hear all cases. For example, in Kentucky, cases involving disputes in excess of $4,000 are heard in the state's circuit courts, while cases involving lesser amounts of money are heard in the state's district courts. In brief, a court must have jurisdiction to hear a case. **Jurisdiction** is usually defined as the power or authority to hear a case. Before a litigant may bring a lawsuit, he or she must ensure that the court has jurisdiction over the subject matter involved in the case as well as jurisdiction over the persons or property involved in the case. Once a determination is made that a court has jurisdiction, it must be determined which location, or venue, is proper for the case.

2. Subject Matter Jurisdiction

Subject matter jurisdiction
The power of a court to hear a certain kind of case

Subject matter jurisdiction refers to the authority of a court to hear a particular type of case, often depending on the type of matter being litigated, the amount of damages claimed, or the status of the parties involved. For example, in Virginia all divorces are heard in Virginia's circuit courts, while all mental commitment hearings must take place in Virginia's district courts. Thus, one would say that in Virginia the circuit courts have subject matter jurisdiction over divorce cases. Other state courts and the federal courts have similar organizations. In fact, the first decision a litigant usually makes is whether a case should be brought in federal court or in state court.

Federal question jurisdiction
The power of a federal court to hear a case based upon the fact the case arises under the U.S. Constitution or a U.S. law or treaty

The federal courts are empowered to hear two types of cases: those involving federal questions and those involving diversity. As to the first category, federal courts may decide cases that involve a **federal question**; that is, any case arising under the U.S. Constitution, a U.S. (or federal) law, or any treaty to which the United States is a party. Cases arising under the U.S. Constitution include cases alleging racial, sexual, or age discrimination; cases involving freedom of speech; and cases involving a defendant's right to a fair trial.

The other category of cases that is handled by federal courts, those based on **diversity jurisdiction**, is determined not by the issue itself (as are federal question cases) but by the status of the parties to the action. Imagine you are a New York resident on vacation in Montana, where you become involved in an automobile accident with a Montana resident. You may have some concern whether a court in Montana would treat you, an outsider, the same as it would treat its own citizens, particularly in a locality in which the residents elect their judges. To ensure that litigants are treated fairly and to eliminate any bias against an out-of-state litigant, the federal courts may resolve cases based on the diversity of the parties; that is, in general, federal courts may hear cases in civil actions between citizens of different states. Note, however, that diversity jurisdiction is conditioned on satisfying another key element: The amount in controversy must exceed $75,000, exclusive of interest and court costs. For example, if a resident of Oregon sues a resident of Idaho for breach of contract and alleges (in good faith) damages in the amount of $80,000, the matter may be instituted in federal court.

> **Diversity jurisdiction**
> A basis upon which federal courts take cases, due to the different or diverse citizenship of the parties in the case

State courts usually have broad jurisdiction to hear almost all cases affecting their citizens, including negligence cases, breach of contract cases, and wrongful death cases. As discussed above, however, some courts in the state may be empowered to hear certain kinds of cases (for example, probate cases or cases involving certain amounts of money) while others may be empowered to hear other kinds of cases (for example, misdemeanor traffic cases).

A party may allege that a court lacks subject matter jurisdiction at any time. In fact, lack of subject matter jurisdiction is such a fatal defect that any judgment rendered by a court that lacks such jurisdiction is void.

3. Types of Jurisdiction Exercised by Courts

Closely related to the issue of subject matter jurisdiction is the specific type of jurisdiction a court has. Courts are classified in a variety of ways with regard to the types of cases they have the authority to hear.

- **General jurisdiction.** A court of **general jurisdiction** may hear any type of civil or criminal case. For example, Alabama's trial courts are courts of general jurisdiction because they may hear both civil and criminal cases.
- **Limited jurisdiction.** A court with **limited jurisdiction** may hear only a certain type of case—for example, probate cases or juvenile cases.
- **Original jurisdiction.** A court is said to have **original jurisdiction** if it acts as a trial court and is the court in which an action is initiated.
- **Appellate jurisdiction.** Courts with **appellate jurisdiction** serve as reviewing courts and review decisions of other courts.
- **Exclusive jurisdiction.** A court with **exclusive jurisdiction** is the only court that may hear a certain type of case. Thus, the U.S. Bankruptcy Courts have exclusive jurisdiction over bankruptcy cases; bankruptcy cases may not be brought in any other courts.
- **Concurrent jurisdiction.** If a case may be brought in more than one court, jurisdiction is said to be **concurrent**. For example, in New York, if an alleged criminal offender is 16 years of age or older, the case may be brought either in Family Court or Criminal Court because both have jurisdiction.

> **General jurisdiction**
> The power of a court to hear almost any type of a case
>
> **Limited jurisdiction**
> Limitation on a court as to the types of cases it may hear
>
> **Original jurisdiction**
> The power of a court to hear a trial
>
> **Appellate jurisdiction**
> The power of a court to hear appeals from other courts
>
> **Exclusive jurisdiction**
> The sole power of a court to hear a case
>
> **Concurrent jurisdiction**
> The shared power of two or more courts to hear a case

4. Personal Jurisdiction

Personal jurisdiction
Authority of a court to
exercise jurisdiction over the
person of a defendant; also
called *in personam jurisdiction*

No court may require a party before it to pay damages or perform any activity
unless the court has **personal jurisdiction** over the party. The theory underlying
personal jurisdiction, also called **in personam jurisdiction**, considers whether it
is fair for the court to exercise jurisdiction over the person of the defendant. Courts
always have personal jurisdiction over residents of the state in which the courts are
located. Similarly, courts have personal jurisdiction over corporate "residents" of the
state so that a corporation incorporated in Florida may always be sued in Florida.
In addition to jurisdiction based on residency, states also have jurisdiction over
those physically present in the state. Thus, if a resident of Ohio is involved in an
automobile accident in Michigan, Michigan may exercise jurisdiction over the
Ohio resident.

Long-arm statute
Statute that allows a state to
exercise jurisdiction over
nonresidents

Moreover, most states have enacted **long-arm statutes**, which permit the
state to extend its jurisdiction to individuals or entities not residing in the state.
Typically, these statutes allow the states to reach into other states and "grab" defendants if those defendants commit a tortious act in the state, transact business in the
state, own real estate in the state, or engage in certain activities in the state. The general principle is that states may exercise jurisdiction over nonresidents if there are
sufficient minimum contacts or ties with the state such that it is reasonable under
traditional notions of fair play and substantial justice to permit the state to exercise
personal jurisdiction. For example, McDonald's Corporation is a Delaware corporation. Because it does business in every state in the nation, it may be sued in any
state. By doing business in a state, McDonald's accepts the benefits and privileges of
acting in the state; thus, it is fair and reasonable to subject McDonald's to the personal jurisdiction of any state court.

On the other hand, if a person or company does not have such sufficient minimum contacts with a state, it cannot be subject to personal jurisdiction in the state.
Thus, if a corporation does business solely in Georgia, it cannot be required to
defend itself in Iowa.

Finally, parties can always consent to jurisdiction. For example, many contracts
have clauses in them by which a party agrees that if there is any dispute regarding
the contract or its terms, litigation may be brought in a designated court in a designated state.

Thus, in sum, personal jurisdiction is based on citizenship, physical presence, a
long-arm statute coupled with minimum contacts, or consent. Under Federal Rule
of Civil Procedure 4(e)(1), a federal court may exercise personal jurisdiction whenever the state in which it is located would have personal jurisdiction.

5. In Rem Jurisdiction

In rem jurisdiction
Jurisdiction exercised by a
court over a "thing" located
in the court's jurisdiction

Courts also exercise a type of jurisdiction called **in rem jurisdiction** (Latin for
"against the thing") when an action relates to property located within a state. Thus,
if there is a dispute between two parties relating to land in California, the action
may be brought in California, whether or not the parties reside there. Actions relating to real property are brought in the state in which the property is located. In rem
actions involve not only real property but also personal property, such as automobiles, boats, and other property. In a modern application of in rem jurisdictional

principles, disputes over Internet domain names (for example, *www.ibm.com*) may be brought in the jurisdiction in which the domain name registrar is located. For example, in one recent case, a Chinese news company was sued in Virginia although nearly all of its users were located in China because the domain name registry, Verisign, was located in Virginia. Thus, in rem jurisdiction served as a substitute for personal jurisdiction. *Cable News Network, L.P. v. CNNews.com*, 162 F. Supp. 2d 484 (E.D. Va. 2001).

6. Venue

Somewhat related to the issue of jurisdiction is that of **venue**—namely, determining the specific county in which a civil or criminal action is to be brought. Generally, venue is proper in any county in which the defendant resides or where the acts giving rise to the action occurred. Thus, in a breach of contract case, venue may be appropriate in two places: where the defendant resides and where the contract was breached. In such cases, the plaintiff has the option to select the venue, often based on matters of convenience, trial tactics, and strategy. If an action involves real property, venue is proper in the county in which the property is located. While a defendant may request a change of venue, a change is usually ordered only when there is good cause; moreover, a trial may be moved only to a court that has proper jurisdiction. Generally, if a defendant does not object to venue, he or she will be held to have waived the right to object to any judgment rendered by the court. In sum, jurisdiction relates to the power or authority of a court to hear a case, and venue relates to the particular locality where a matter will be heard.

Venue
The appropriate locality for a trial

D. TYPES OF LAW

1. Introduction

Generally, there are two types or categories of cases: those involving criminal law and those involving civil law. In addition, issues that arise in criminal or civil cases are classified as matters of substantive or procedural law.

2. Criminal and Civil Law

A **crime** is an act committed in violation of a law. Society itself is considered to be the victim of a crime and thus the state (or federal government, if a federal crime such as bank robbery is involved) will prosecute the offender. The injured party may be a witness in the case, but the plaintiff is either the state or the federal government (which acts on behalf of the injured public), and the case name typically will read *State v. Peterson* or *People v. Smith* or *Commonwealth v. Jones* or *United States v. Allen*. In contrast, a **civil action** is a case brought by a private party to redress some wrong done that causes injury to the private party but that does not harm society as a whole. In these actions, the case name will read, for example, *Jones v. Smith* or *Nike Corp. v. Jackson*. In some instances, the same conduct may be a crime and also give rise to civil liability. For example, if you are injured in an automobile accident caused by a drunk driver, the driver will be subject to criminal liability for breaking applicable laws relating to driving while intoxicated and will also be subject to

Crime
An act against society committed in violation of a statute

Civil action
Action brought by a private party to redress injury to the party

a civil action by you to recover damages caused by the driver's wrongful conduct. In addition to the different plaintiffs who initiate the cases, there are some other key differences in the way criminal and civil cases are handled:

- **Burden of proof.** In a criminal case the state or federal government must prove its case "beyond a reasonable doubt" while in a civil case the plaintiff need only show it is entitled to relief by a "preponderance of the evidence." The severe punishments that can be imposed on a criminal defendant justify the higher burden of proof. In contrast, proving something by a preponderance of the evidence merely means that something is more likely than not.

- **Right to a jury trial.** The Sixth Amendment to the Constitution guarantees the right to a jury trial in criminal cases, and the state or federal government pays the costs associated with a jury trial. In civil cases, a party who desires a jury trial must pay for that privilege. In some instances, a party may forgo a jury. For example, in late 2003, in the famous case involving celebrity Rosie O'Donnell and the publisher Gruner + Jahr USA Publishing, there was no jury. The parties tried the case only before a judge, a process known as a **bench trial.** In criminal cases, the verdict rendered by the jury must usually be unanimous, but this is not the rule for civil cases in all states. In addition, the size of a jury may vary from state to state. For example, in some states, a jury of six may decide civil cases. If the required number of jurors is not able to reach a decision, the jury is said to be a **hung jury**, and either the prosecutor in a criminal case or the plaintiff in a civil case must decide whether to retry the case.

- **Right to an attorney.** In a criminal case, the defendant has a right to have an attorney. If the defendant cannot afford an attorney, one will be provided at the government's expense. In a civil case, however, there is no absolute right to an attorney. If a party cannot afford an attorney, the party may represent himself or herself or seek the services of a legal aid society or a law firm, many of which offer legal services **pro bono publico**, meaning at no cost.

- **Punishments and remedies.** The punishments or sanctions imposed in criminal and civil cases differ. In criminal cases, if a defendant is found guilty, courts may impose a fine, probation, imprisonment, or the death penalty. If a fine is imposed, it is paid to the state (or federal government), not to the injured party. In most civil cases, if a defendant is found liable, damages will be awarded and will be paid to the plaintiff to compensate him or her for losses sustained. If the defendant's conduct was particularly malicious, egregious, or reckless, **punitive damages** may be imposed to punish the wrongdoer. In other types of civil cases, courts may impose injunctions against the defendant to compel or forbid him or her to do a certain act. In a divorce case, the court may order dissolution, award custody of any children, and impose child and spousal support obligations.

- **Right to appeal.** In a civil case, either side may appeal the verdict. In a criminal case, the defendant may appeal a guilty verdict, but the government may not appeal if a defendant is found not guilty because of the prohibition against double jeopardy in the U.S. Constitution. Either side in a criminal case may appeal with respect to the sentence that is imposed after a guilty verdict.

3. Substantive and Procedural Law

Both criminal and civil law are governed by substantive principles and procedural rules. **Substantive law** defines and regulates rights while **procedural law** relates to

---

Bench trial
A case heard by a judge alone, with no jury

Hung jury
A jury that cannot reach a decision in a civil or criminal case

Pro bono publico
Latin for "for the public good"; representation of parties by attorneys or law firms at no cost to the party

Punitive damages
Damages imposed on a party to punish him or her for willful, reckless conduct

Substantive law
Law that defines and regulates rights and obligations, such as family law or torts

Procedural law
Law that relates to the methods of enforcing substantive rights

the methods of enforcing those rights. Thus, contracts, real property, trusts, corporations, and intellectual property are fields of substantive law. The rules that govern the format of documents that are filed in courts are matters of procedural law. Paralegals must be conversant both with substantive law (for example, by knowing the elements required to prove a breach of contract case) and with procedural law (for example, by knowing that the U.S. Supreme Court requires that briefs submitted to the Court be in Roman 11 point or larger type). Failure to follow procedural rules may be fatal to a case, and courts may refuse to accept pleadings and documents that do not comply with court rules.

All federal district courts follow the Federal Rules of Civil Procedure, which provide rules on pleadings, motions, discovery, and civil trials. While these rules are not binding on state courts, most states have modeled their own civil procedural rules after the Federal Rules of Civil Procedure. Similarly, there are Federal Rules of Criminal Procedure to which all federal district courts are subject. These rules govern matters such as indictments, arraignments, and venue of criminal trials.

In a civil diversity case brought in a federal district court, the court will follow the procedural rules found in the Federal Rules of Civil Procedure but will apply the substantive law of the state in which the court is located. For example, if an Ohio resident sues a Texas resident in a federal court in Texas for breach of contract, the trial court will follow the Federal Rules of Civil Procedure but will follow Texas law in interpreting the contract.

E. TRIAL AND APPELLATE COURTS

In all legal systems, whether state or federal, some courts act as trial courts and others act as appellate courts, which review decisions of other courts. In trial courts, evidence is introduced, witnesses testify, motions are made, and a judgment is entered in the case. The work of trial courts and litigation is discussed in Chapter Eight. After the trial court judgment, if the losing party (usually called the **appellant** but sometimes called the **petitioner)**, wishes to appeal the decision, he or she initiates an appeal by filing a notice of appeal with the appropriate court. Procedural rules require that the notice of appeal be timely filed. Trials are conducted by a single judge; appeals are considered by a bank or panel of judges, often acting in groups of three.

Appellant
The person who appeals an adverse decision; also called *petitioner*

Many litigants are opting to forgo trials in favor of **alternative dispute resolution** (ADR), a cost-effective and quick alternative to litigation by which the parties select a neutral party to help them resolve their dispute. ADR is discussed in depth in Chapter Eight.

Alternative dispute resolution
A quick and cost-effective alternative to trial whereby a neutral party attempts to resolve a dispute

In general, litigants are entitled to one appeal as a matter of right; further appeals are subject to the discretion of the appellate court. Moreover, the appellant is not entitled to a reversal of the trial court decision simply because he or she is unhappy with the outcome. The appellant must show that an error of law occurred at the trial. For purposes of appeal, the appellate court will assume that the facts found at the trial were true (unless those facts are totally unsupported by the record). Thus, if a jury determines a defendant was driving at a speed of 80 miles per hour and this caused an accident that injures a plaintiff, an appellate court may not substitute its judgment for that of the jury and determine the defendant's rate of speed was 45 miles per hour. The appellate court may, however, decide that a prejudicial error of law was committed at the trial and this affected the jury's verdict. Examples of such errors of law include admission of evidence, such as hearsay, that should have been excluded, errors given in the instructions to the jury, and exclusion of evidence that should have been admitted. A common description of the delineation of duties of trial and appellate courts is that trial courts determine questions of fact while appellate courts determine questions of law.

Even if an error of law occured at the trial, the appellate court will not reverse the lower court decision unless this error was clearly erroneous or prejudicial to the appellant. Many errors can occur in a trial. Harmless errors, however, are not reversible. A **prejudicial error** is one that likely affected the outcome of the case. If a prejudicial, reversible error occurred, the appellate court usually remands or sends the case back to the trial court for retrial.

Generally, appellate courts give great weight to the trial court's conduct of a trial because the trial court was in the best position to evaluate the credibility of witnesses and to make "on the spot" determinations. Only if the trial court clearly erred or abused its discretion will its decisions be reversed.

Because of the difficulty in meeting these strict requirements and because of the high costs involved, the vast majority of trial court decisions are not appealed.

Prejudicial error
An error that affects the outcome of a case; reversible error

F. FEDERAL COURTS

1. Introduction

Article III, Section 1 of the Constitution created the federal court system. This section provides in part that "the judicial power of the United States shall be vested in one Supreme Court and in such inferior courts as Congress may from time to time ordain and establish." Thus, only the existence of the Supreme Court was assured. It was left up to Congress to determine the Court's composition and to create any other federal courts. In fact, the first Congress created the federal court structure that still exists today. While the numbers of courts and judges have increased, the basic structure of our federal court system remains the same as it was in 1789: district courts, intermediate courts of appeal, and one U.S. Supreme Court. Judges appointed to these courts are often referred to as **Article III judges**.

Article III judge
Judge appointed to a federal court under Article III, Section 1 of the U.S. Constitution

2. Ground Rules for Cases

Even if a federal question or diversity exists and even if the requirements for personal jurisdiction are satisfied, there still remain some ground rules that must be satisfied before a federal court will hear a case. While the following discussion relates primarily to federal cases, these ground rules must usually be satisfied for cases brought in state courts. In large part, these rules are rooted in Article III of the Constitution, which establishes the jurisdiction of federal courts and restricts federal courts to resolving "cases" and "controversies." There are three ground rules. First, with very few exceptions, federal courts will not consider issues that are "moot" or already resolved. In fact, it is a fraud on a court to continue with a case that is moot. Parties before the court must be involved in an existing, current controversy. Second, a close corollary to this first rule is that federal courts will not render advisory opinions even if asked by the President. The federal courts are constitutionally bound to resolve actual ongoing disputes, not to give advice. Finally, a plaintiff must have personally suffered some actual or threatened legal injury; that is, the plaintiff must be adversely affected by some conduct or threatened conduct of the defendant. The plaintiff may not base a claim on the rights or interests of some other persons. This requirement is referred to as **standing.** Standing ensures that parties before the court have a personal stake in the outcome of the controversy.

There are three levels of courts in the federal system. Starting with the lowest courts, they are the district courts, the courts of appeal, and the United States Supreme Court. All judges in the federal court system are appointed by the President with the advice and consent of the United States Senate.

3. United States District Courts

The district courts are the trial courts in our federal system. At present, there are 94 district courts scattered throughout the 50 states, the District of Columbia, and the territories and possessions of the United States. There is at least one district court in each state, and the more populous states, such as California, New York, and Texas, have as many as four within their territorial borders. Other less populous states, such as Alaska and Utah, each have only one district court (although they may have divisions in other parts of the state to allow easy access for litigants). While Congress has the authority to create new district courts, it has not done so since 1971, when a new district was created by splitting an existing district in Louisiana. See Figure 4-1 for a list of the district courts.

These district courts have jurisdiction over a wide variety of cases. One day a district court judge may hear a case involving a bank robbery and the next day may resolve a civil rights question followed by a case involving a crime committed on a military base. Bankruptcy courts are considered units of our district courts with judges appointed by the courts of appeal for 14-year terms. Each district includes a U.S. Bankruptcy Court.

The number of judges assigned to a particular district court will vary depending on the number of cases the court is called on to adjudicate. Thus, there may be only one district court judge assigned to a district court or there may be nearly 50 judges, as is the case for the increasingly busy Southern District of New York.

The district court judges, who are paid more than $158,000 annually, usually sit individually; that is, they hear cases and render decisions by themselves rather than as a panel or group like the U.S. Supreme Court Justices.

The vast majority of all federal cases end at the district court level; only approximately 10 percent of these federal cases are appealed. In recent years, the number of civil filings in the district courts has remained relatively stable, perhaps as a result of litigants seeking various forms of alternative dispute resolution, such as mediation and arbitration, and reforms aimed at reducing the number of frivolous petitions filed by prisoners. In 2004, nearly 360,000 cases were commenced in the various district courts.

4. United States Courts of Appeals

The 13 U.S. courts of appeals, sometimes called the circuit courts, are the intermediate courts in our federal system. The theory of our judicial system is that a litigant should have a trial in one court before one judge and a right to an appeal in another court before a different judge. In fact, a federal statute directs that no judge may hear an appeal of a case originally tried before him or her.

FIGURE 4-1
UNITED STATES DISTRICT COURTS AND COURTS OF APPEALS

Alabama	11th Cir.	**Kansas**	10th Cir.
M.D. Ala.		D. Kan.	
N.D. Ala.		**Kentucky**	6th Cir.
S.D. Ala.		E.D. Ky.	
Alaska	9th Cir.	W.D. Ky.	
D. Alaska		**Louisiana**	5th Cir.
Arizona	9th Cir.	E.D. La.	
D. Ariz.		M.D. La.	
Arkansas	8th Cir.	W.D. La.	
E.D. Ark.		**Maine**	1st Cir.
W.D. Ark.		D. Me.	
California	9th Cir.	**Maryland**	4th Cir.
C.D. Cal.		D. Md.	
E.D. Cal.		**Massachusetts**	1st Cir.
N.D. Cal.		D. Mass.	
S.D. Cal.		**Michigan**	6th Cir.
Colorado	10th Cir.	E. D. Mich.	
D. Colo.		W.D. Mich.	
Connecticut	2d Cir.	**Minnesota**	8th Cir.
D. Conn.		D. Minn.	
Delaware	3d Cir.	**Mississippi**	5th Cir.
D. Del.		N.D. Miss.	
District of	D.C. Cir.	S.D. Miss.	
Columbia		**Missouri**	8th Cir.
D.D.C.		E.D. Mo.	
Florida	11th Cir.	W.D. Mo.	
M.D. Fla.		**Montana**	9th Cir.
N.D. Fla.		D. Mont.	
S.D. Fla.		**Nebraska**	8th Cir.
Georgia	11th Cir.	D. Neb.	
M.D. Ga.		**Nevada**	9th Cir.
N.D. Ga.		D. Nev.	
S.D. Ga.		**New Hampshire**	1st Cir.
Hawaii	9th Cir.	D.N.H.	
D. Haw.		**New Jersey**	3d Cir.
Idaho	9th Cir.	D.N.J.	
D. Idaho		**New Mexico**	10th Cir.
Illinois	7th Cir.	D.N.M.	
C.D. Ill.		**New York**	2d Cir.
N.D. Ill.		E.D.N.Y.	
S.D. Ill.		N.D.N.Y.	
Indiana	7th Cir.	S.D.N.Y.	
N.D. Ind.		W.D.N.Y.	
S.D. Ind.		**North Carolina**	4th Cir.
Iowa	8th Cir.	E.D.N.C.	
N.D. Iowa		M.D.N.C.	
S.D. Iowa		W.D.N.C.	

FIGURE 4-1 (CONTINUED)
UNITED STATES DISTRICT COURTS AND COURTS OF APPEALS

North Dakota	8th Cir.	**Vermont**	2d Cir.
D.N.D.		D.Vt.	
Ohio	6th Cir.	**Virginia**	4th Cir.
N.D. Ohio		E.D. Va.	
S.D. Ohio		W.D. Va.	
Oklahoma	10th Cir.	**Washington**	9th Cir.
E.D. Okla.		E.D. Wash.	
N.D. Okla.		W.D. Wash.	
W.D. Okla.		**West Virginia**	4th Cir.
Oregon	9th Cir.	N.D.W. Va.	
D. Or.		S.D.W. Va.	
Pennsylvania	3d Cir.	**Wisconsin**	7th Cir.
E.D. Pa.		E.D. Wis.	
M.D. Pa.		W.D. Wis.	
W.D. Pa.		**Wyoming**	10th Cir.
Rhode Island	1st Cir.	D. Wyo.	
D.R.I.		**Miscellaneous**	
South Carolina	4th Cir.	**Canal Zone**	5th Cir.
D.S.C.		D.C.Z.	
South Dakota	8th Cir.	**Guam**	9th Cir.
D.S.D.		D. Guam	
Tennessee	6th Cir.	**N. Mariana Islands**	9th Cir.
E.D. Tenn.		D.N. Mar. I.	
M.D. Tenn.		**Puerto Rico**	1st Cir.
W.D. Tenn.		D.P.R.	
Texas	5th Cir.	**Virgin Islands**	3d Cir.
E.D. Tex.		D.V.I.	
N.D. Tex.		**U.S. Court of**	Fed. Cir.
S.D. Tex.		**Appeals for the**	
W.D. Tex.		**Federal Circuit**	
Utah	10th Cir.	**U.S. Court of**	Fed. Cl.
D. Utah		**Federal Claims**	

It is critical to remember the difference between the district courts, which are trial courts that hear evidence, listen to witnesses testify, and render decisions, and the courts of appeal, whose primary function is to review cases from these district courts. The courts of appeal do not retry a case. They merely review the record and the briefs of counsel to determine if a prejudicial error of law was made in the district court below. A second important function of the U.S. courts of appeals is to review and enforce decisions from federal administrative agencies such as the FCC or NLRB.

The United States is divided into 11 geographical areas called "circuits," and there is a court of appeals in each of these circuits. In addition, there is a Court of Appeals for the District of Columbia and a Court of Appeals for the Federal Circuit, located in Washington, D.C., which hears primarily patent cases. Figure 4-2 shows the grouping of states that are included in each circuit. It is not critical to know which states or district courts fall within the boundaries of which circuits.

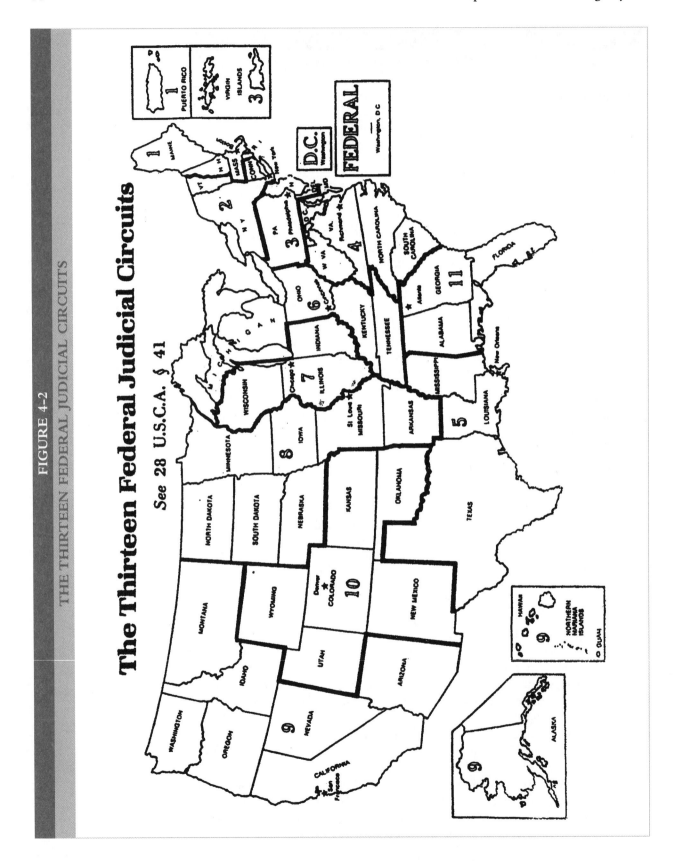

FIGURE 4–2

THE THIRTEEN FEDERAL JUDICIAL CIRCUITS

The Thirteen Federal Judicial Circuits

See 28 U.S.C.A. § 41

Maps of the circuit courts are readily available in the front of each volume of West's *Federal Reporter*, a set of books that reports decisions from the various courts of appeal. You should, however, know which circuit covers the state in which you will be working and that most of the circuits are assigned a number and will have several states (and their district courts) within it. For example, the Ninth Circuit covers California and most of the Western states. Thus, if a trial occurs in the Northern District of California, the appeal is filed in the Ninth Circuit Court of Appeals. Similarly, if a trial occurs in the Southern District of New York, the appeal is filed in the Second Circuit Court of Appeals.

Each of the intermediate circuit courts of appeals is free to make its own decisions independent of what the other circuits have held; in practice, however, the circuit courts are often guided by decisions from other courts. Decisions by the U.S. Supreme Court often resolve conflicts among the circuits.

Congress has the authority to create additional circuits, but it has not done so since 1981, when it created the Eleventh Circuit by dividing the Fifth Circuit, which had seen an increasingly heavy caseload as the population grew in the South.

Each of the courts of appeals has at least six judges and as many as 28 judges assigned to it, depending on the caseload for the circuit. The judges usually hear the appeals from the district courts as a panel of three judges, although they may sit **en banc**, with all judges present. These federal judges earn an annual salary of approximately $167,600. The U.S. courts of appeals typically issue more than 15,000 opinions each year (although not all of them are published).

> **En banc**
> The hearing of a case by a full court

For the vast majority of litigants, these intermediate courts of appeal represent the last opportunity to prevail. As you will see, the popular notion that everyone has access to the Supreme Court is unfounded. For most litigants, the court of appeals is the last chance to win, because one who wishes to appeal a case to the U.S. Supreme Court is largely dependent on the Court's discretion in accepting the case for review.

5. The United States Supreme Court

The U.S. Supreme Court consists of eight Associate Justices and one Chief Justice. While the Chief Justice is paid more than the Associate Justices (roughly $203,000 to their annual salaries of $194,300), and while he or she has prestige and certain authority by virtue of seniority, the Chief Justice's vote counts equally with that of any Associate Justice. Nevertheless, as the presiding officer of the Supreme Court, the Chief Justice is responsible for administration of the Court and the leadership of the federal judicial system. Upon the death or resignation of a Chief Justice, the President may either appoint one of the eight existing Associate Justices to the position of Chief Justice or may appoint an "outsider" as Chief Justice.

Like all of the approximately 1,700 judges in the federal system, the Supreme Court Justices are appointed by the President and hold office "during good behavior." This means they are not subject to mandatory retirement and may sit as federal judges until they voluntarily resign or retire. Many have served for extremely long periods—notably Chief Justice John Marshall, widely regarded as the finest jurist produced by the United States, who served for 34 years, and Associate Justice William O. Douglas, who served for 36 years. While federal judges may be impeached by Congress, this drastic remedy is seldom used. Only a handful of judges have been removed through impeachment.

The individuals who sit on the U.S. Supreme Court (or state supreme courts) are usually referred to as "justices," while the individuals who sit on lower courts are referred to as "judges." Occasionally, individuals who sit on intermediate appellate courts are also referred to as "justices," although typically the term "justice" is reserved for individuals on the U.S. Supreme Court or a state supreme court.

In addition to their primary activities of hearing cases and writing opinions, each Supreme Court Justice is assigned to one of the federal judicial circuits for the purpose of handling special and emergency matters such as stays of execution and injunctions. Because there are 13 federal circuits and only 9 Supreme Court Justices, some Justices are assigned to more than one circuit. Assignment to the circuits is made annually by the Chief Justice.

By federal law, the term of the Court commences on the first Monday in October, and the term typically ends at the end of June. In recent years, the Court has been reducing the number of cases on its docket. During the 1980s, the Court routinely decided roughly 150 cases each term. In its 2003-2004 term, the Court issued only 79 written opinions, although the average number of pages and footnotes per opinion has increased steadily over the years.

By the authority of the Constitution, the U.S. Supreme Court has the jurisdiction to act not only as an appellate or reviewing court but also in very limited instances (usually disputes between two states) may act as a court of original jurisdiction or trial court. The Court usually hears less than five original jurisdiction cases per term. See Figure 4-3 for a chart showing the jurisdiction of the Supreme Court.

The most important function of the U.S. Supreme Court is its appellate jurisdiction—namely, its authority to review decisions from lower courts. Cases may come to the Supreme Court from the lower federal courts or from the highest court in any state.

While a few cases, such as some cases under the Interstate Commerce Act, are directly appealable from the district courts to the U.S. Supreme Court, the vast majority of federal cases that the Supreme Court reviews proceed to the Court in

---

FIGURE 4-3

JURISDICTION OF UNITED STATES SUPREME COURT

I. Original Jurisdiction
   A. Controversies between two or more states (exclusive jurisdiction)
   B. Actions in which ambassadors or other public ministers of foreign states are parties (non-exclusive jurisdiction)
   C. Controversies between the United States and a state (exclusive jurisdiction)
   D. Actions by a state against the citizens of another state (non-exclusive jurisdiction)
II. Appellate Jurisdiction
   A. Cases from federal courts
      1. United States district courts (special statutes allow direct appeals as well as appeals from three-judge district courts granting or denying injunctive relief to be directly appealed to the United States Supreme Court)
      2. United States courts of appeals
         (a) Certiorari
         (b) Certification (granted only in exceptional cases)
   B. Cases from highest state courts

the expected "stair step" fashion: trial in the district court, an intermediate appeal to the appropriate circuit court, and a final appeal to the U.S. Supreme Court.

The most widely used means to gain access to the U.S. Supreme Court from the lower circuit courts of appeals is the writ of **certiorari.** *Certiorari* is a Latin word meaning "to be informed of." A litigant who has lost an appeal in the intermediate circuit court will file a document or petition with the Supreme Court called a Petition for Writ of Certiorari, which sets forth the basis for appeal.

The Supreme Court will either grant the petition and direct the lower court to send its records and files to the Supreme Court or will deny the petition, meaning that the lower court decision will stand. In the vast majority of cases, issuance of the writ, or "granting cert," is discretionary with the Supreme Court. Seldom does a litigant have an absolute right to have the Supreme Court review a case.

Approximately 8,000 petitions for certiorari are filed with the U.S. Supreme Court each year, and the justices typically grant certiorari in fewer than 100 of these cases. Full, signed opinions are issued in about 80 cases, and the remaining cases are disposed of without oral argument or formal written opinions.

There are no clearly articulated or published criteria followed by the Justices in determining which petitions will be deemed "cert worthy." The guideline most frequently given is that certiorari will be granted if there are "compelling" reasons for doing so. In general, however, a review of the cases accepted by the Supreme Court reveals some common elements: If the lower courts are in conflict on a certain issue and the circuit courts of appeals are issuing contradictory opinions, the Supreme Court often grants certiorari so that it can resolve such a conflict; or if a case is of general importance, the Court may grant certiorari.

Denial of the writ of certiorari is not to be viewed as an endorsement by the Court of a lower court's holding but rather its determination that for reasons of judicial economy not every case can be heard. Once a petition for certiorari has been granted, the attorneys or parties are notified and instructed to submit their written arguments, called briefs, which are then filed with the Court and made public. Oral arguments are then scheduled, after which the Justices meet in conference to decide the case. A preliminary vote is taken to determine the Court's disposition of the case. The Justice who is the most senior in the majority group then assigns the opinion to be drafted by another Justice or may decide to author the opinion himself or herself. Drafting the majority opinion may take weeks or even months. Justices who disagree with the result may write **dissenting opinions,** and Justices who agree with the result but disagree with the majority's reasoning may write **concurring opinions.** Finally, the opinion is circulated to the Justices for comment and then released to the public and authorized for printing in the *United States Reports*, the official publication of the Court's work.

While most cases arrive at the Court from the various U.S. courts of appeals by means of the writ of certiorari, there is one other means by which cases from lower federal courts may be reviewed by the Supreme Court: by certification. **Certification**, which is rarely used, is the process by which a court of appeals refers a question to the Supreme Court and asks for instructions.

Cases from the state courts may be appealed to the U.S. Supreme Court from the highest court in a state if and only if a federal question is involved. Even then, the Court may, in its discretion, refuse to grant certiorari, thus rendering the state court decision final. State court litigants seeking access to the U.S. Supreme Court have no absolute right to an appeal; they are entirely dependent on the Court granting certiorari, which it does in roughly 1 percent of cases. See Figure 4-4 for a diagram of our federal court structure.

Certiorari
Latin for "to be informed of"; method of gaining a discretionary appeal

Dissenting opinion
Opinion written by a judge in the minority

Concurring opinion
Opinion that agrees with result in a case but not its reasoning

Certification
Referral of a question to the U.S. Supreme Court by a federal court of appeals

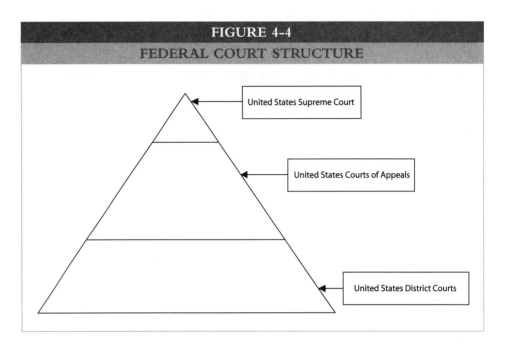

FIGURE 4-4

FEDERAL COURT STRUCTURE

United States Supreme Court

United States Courts of Appeals

United States District Courts

6. Specialized Courts

In addition to the district courts, the intermediate circuit courts of appeals, and the U.S. Supreme Court, certain specialized courts exist in the federal judicial system to determine particular issues, such as the U.S. Tax Court, which issues decisions in tax matters, and the U.S. Court of Federal Claims, which considers certain claims seeking monetary damages from the U.S. government. Other specialized courts include the U.S. Court of Appeals for Veterans Claims and the U.S. Court of International Trade. These specialized courts are referred to as "**legislative courts**," as distinguished from the district courts, intermediate courts of appeals, and Supreme Court, which are referred to as "**constitutional courts**" because they exist under Article III of the Constitution.

G. STATE COURTS

In addition to the federal court structure discussed above, each of the 50 states and the District of Columbia has its own arrangement for its court system. While the names of these courts vary from state to state, the general organization is the same: A trial is held in one court and the losing party will usually have the right to at least one appeal in an appellate court.

Illinois's court system, typical of many states, is shown in Figure 4-5.

Note that in some states, trials involving lesser amounts of money and misdemeanors are held in courts called municipal courts or district courts, while trials involving greater amounts of money and felonies are held in the superior courts or circuit courts. In Illinois, intermediate appeals are heard by the court of appeals, with the Illinois Supreme Court serving as the court of last resort.

While the majority of states have a two-tier appellate system, in ten states (Maine, Montana, Nevada, New Hampshire, North Dakota, Rhode Island, South

Legislative courts
Specialized federal courts not created by the U.S. Constitution

Constitutional courts
Federal courts created by Article III of the U.S. Constitution—namely, district courts, intermediate circuit courts of appeals, and the U.S. Supreme Court

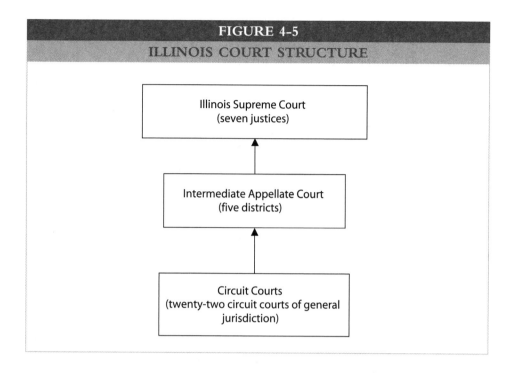

FIGURE 4-5

ILLINOIS COURT STRUCTURE

Illinois Supreme Court
(seven justices)

Intermediate Appellate Court
(five districts)

Circuit Courts
(twenty-two circuit courts of general jurisdiction)

Dakota, Vermont, West Virginia, and Wyoming), and in the District of Columbia there is no intermediate court of appeals. Dissatisfied litigants proceed directly from the state trial court to the court of last resort in the state, usually called the supreme court.

In almost all states, the highest state court is called the supreme court. Maryland, however, calls its highest court the court of appeals. New York also calls its highest court the court of appeals and calls one of the courts below it, which handles felonies and miscellaneous civil actions, the supreme court, which can cause some confusion.

Decisions by the highest courts in all states are rendered by odd-numbered panels of justices who function in a collective fashion. Seventeen of the 50 states are composed of a five-member supreme court; 28 of the states are composed of a seven-member supreme court; and five of the states are composed of a nine-member supreme court.

The average annual salary for justices on the highest state courts is approximately $125,292. The average annual salary for state trial court judges is approximately $112,724. Note that all of these salaries are significantly lower than the starting salaries paid to new attorneys in the nation's largest law firms, where annual salaries range from $125,000 to $140,000.

While all judges in the federal system are appointed by the President and are confirmed by the U.S. Senate, there is great variation among the states with regard to the selection of state court judges. The majority of states use a merit selection method (somewhat similar to the federal presidential appointment method) in which the governor appoints a judge from a list of nominees provided to him or her by a judicial nominating commission. Other states elect their judges either by vote of the state legislature or the general population for specific terms.

H. REMEDIES

1. Courts of Equity and Courts of Law

In England, the remedies available to an injured party were limited. Typically, only monetary compensation or items of value could be awarded, and the courts that awarded these items were referred to as **courts of law**. Because these courts were restricted as to the types of remedies they could award, litigants sometimes petitioned the king for additional relief. The creative remedies fashioned by the king and his chancellor were referred to as equitable remedies, and the courts that awarded them were called the **courts of equity**. Generally, litigants were required to select either an action at law (for which monetary damages could be obtained) or an action in equity (in which additional remedies could be sought).

In nearly all states, the courts of equity and law have merged so that any court may grant any type of remedy. Nevertheless, there are still some distinctions between legal and equitable remedies.

2. Legal Remedies

The following are the types of remedies that a plaintiff in a civil action may obtain.

- **Compensatory damages. Compensatory damages** are intended to compensate an injured party for the damages he or she has sustained. Thus, a party harmed by a breach of contract should be placed in the same position after the breach as he or she was in before the breach. Compensatory damages are further divided into general damages and special damages. **General damages** compensate an injured party for injuries that have no certain value, such as injuries for pain and suffering or loss of consortium. **Special damages** compensate an injured party for direct out-of-pocket expenses, such as medical expenses and lost wages.
- **Punitive damages. Punitive damages** are allowed in many cases to punish the defendant for particularly willful and reckless behavior and to ensure that the defendant and others are deterred from similar wanton behavior.
- **Nominal damages. Nominal damages** are awarded when a plaintiff has suffered no actual harm but a defendant has nevertheless acted wrongfully.
- **Liquidated damages.** In many contracts, parties to the contract specify in advance what the damages will be for a breach of the contract. Thus, a clause in a contract requiring a builder to pay a penalty of $1,000 for each day of delay in completing a construction project is a **liquidated damages clause**. Such clauses are generally enforceable so long as they are reasonable.

3. Equitable Remedies

Equitable remedies are generally granted only when legal remedies (usually meaning money) are inadequate. Following are the most common types of equitable remedies.

- **Injunctive relief.** In many instances, money does not compensate a plaintiff and the plaintiff desires that the court order that a party do some act (or cease doing some act). For example, a court may order a defendant to cease building a condominium project or to cease using an infringing trademark.

- **Declaratory relief.** In some instances a party is uncertain of its duties and obligations. The party may then initiate a declaratory action and ask a court to declare its rights and duties. No damages are awarded.
- **Specific performance.** A court may order a party to specifically perform its obligations under a contract. For example, a court may require a party to sell real property that it previously agreed to sell to a buyer.
- **Rescission.** A court may order a contract rescinded or annulled in certain instances, usually if the contract was procured by fraud or mistake.
- **Reformation.** A court may order that a contract be reformed to comply with the intent of the parties to the contract when the written document does not reflect their intentions.

Declaratory relief
A court order delineating the rights and duties of a party

Specific performance
A court order requiring a party to comply with contractual obligations or to perform an act

Rescission
The annulment of a contract, usually for fraud

Reformation
The revising of a contract to comply with the intentions of the parties

NET RESULTS

www.law.cornell.edu	Cornell Law School's site providing direct links to Federal Rules of Civil Procedure, Federal Rules of Criminal Procedure, and Federal Rules of Evidence
www.uscourts.gov	Official listing of all federal courts with direct links to district courts, circuit courts of appeals, and United States Supreme Court
www.fjc.gov	Federal Judicial Center, the education and research agency for the federal courts
www.supremecourtus.gov	Website of U.S. Supreme Court with general information about the Court and access to opinions
www.megalaw.com	Select "State Law" and then the desired state for access to each state's courts, statutes, and cases
www.ncsconline.org	National Center for State Courts offering diagrams for each state's court structure and statistics about state court caseloads

CASE ILLUSTRATION

Personal Jurisdiction

Case: *Zippo Mfg. Co. v. Zippo Dot Com, Inc.*, 952 F. Supp. 1119 (W.D. Pa. 1997)

Facts: The defendant operated an Internet website in California from which it sold subscriptions to an Internet service to residents in

Pennsylvania. The defendant had no offices or employees in Pennsylvania. The plaintiff sued the defendant for trademark infringement in Pennsylvania. The defendant alleged there was insufficient basis for personal jurisdiction.

Holding: The defendant was subject to personal jurisdiction in Pennsylvania. Its contacts with Pennsylvania residents were more than fortuitous. If a party merely posts information or advertises its products and services on a passive website, jurisdiction cannot be exercised over a nonresident defendant; however, if the defendant is actively conducting business or entering into contracts, as was the case here, jurisdiction can be exercised. The middle ground, in which a website owner engages only in some limited interaction with users, is closely scrutinized by courts to determine the specific nature of the interactions. If interaction is significant, jurisdiction may be imposed.

KEY TERMS

Common law

Stare decisis

Precedent

Civil law

Constitution

Statute

Jurisdiction

Subject matter jurisdiction

Federal question jurisdiction

Diversity jurisdiction

General jurisdiction

Limited jurisdiction

Original jurisdiction

Appellate jurisdiction

Exclusive jurisdiction

Concurrent jurisdiction

Personal jurisdiction, in personam jurisdiction

Long-arm statute

In rem jurisdiction

Venue

Crime

Civil action

Bench trial

Hung jury

Pro bono publico

Punitive damages

Substantive law

Procedural law

Appellant, petitioner

Alternative dispute resolution

Prejudicial error

Article III judge

Standing

En banc

Certiorari

Dissenting opinion

Concurring opinion

Certification

Legislative courts

Constitutional courts

Courts of law

Courts of equity

Compensatory damages

General damages

Special damages

Punitive damages

Nominal damages

Liquidated damages

Injunctive relief

Declaratory relief

Specific performance

Rescission

Reformation

CHAPTER SUMMARY

Sources of Law	America is a common law jurisdiction with the following sources of primary law: cases, constitutions, statutes, and administrative regulations. Additionally, the executive branch serves as a source of and an influence on law.
Jurisdiction	■ A court may not hear a matter unless it has both subject matter jurisdiction and personal jurisdiction. ■ Federal courts have jurisdiction to hear cases arising under federal laws and the U.S. Constitution and cases involving citizens with diverse citizenship (so long as the claim in question exceeds $75,000). ■ Courts have personal jurisdiction over their residents and can exercise long-arm jurisdiction over nonresidents if those nonresidents have minimum contacts with the state such that it would be reasonable for the state to exercise such jurisdiction. ■ Courts may exercise in rem jurisdiction over a thing, such as real estate, located in the state.
Venue	Venue is proper in any county in which a defendant resides or where the acts giving rise to an action occurred. Venue for actions involving real estate is proper in the county in which the real estate is located.
Criminal Actions	A crime is an act against society and criminal actions are brought by the state. The standard of proof is "beyond a reasonable doubt," and the defendant has a right to a jury trial and an attorney.
Civil Law	A civil action is one brought by a private party for harm done to him or her. The standard of proof is a "preponderance of the evidence," and there is no right to a jury trial or an attorney.
Substantive and Procedural Principles	All cases are governed by substantive principles, which define and regulate rights, and procedural principles, which relate to the methods of enforcing those rights.

Courts: Basic Principles	In all legal systems, some courts act as trial courts and hear cases and other courts act as appellate courts and review cases from other courts. Trial courts decide questions of fact and appellate courts decide questions of law. To bring an action, a party must have an actual controversy and must have standing, meaning a personal stake in the outcome of the case.
Federal Court Structure	The federal court structure is composed of the following: 94 district courts scattered throughout the country, which serve as trial courts; 13 intermediate courts of appeals, which review decisions from the district courts and administrative agencies; and the U.S. Supreme Court, which reviews cases from the intermediate federal courts of appeals and the highest state courts. Obtaining review by the U.S. Supreme Court is difficult because one who wishes to appeal a case to the Court is largely dependent on the Court's discretion in accepting the case for review.
State Court Structures	All states have trial and appellate courts. Most states have trial courts, intermediate courts of appeals, and a state supreme court. Cases from the state supreme courts may be appealed to the U.S. Supreme Court if a federal question is involved and if the Court, in its discretion, grants certiorari and takes the case.
Remedies Granted by Courts	Courts can grant a variety of remedies. Remedies at law usually involve money damages both to compensate the injured party and punish the wrongdoer, and equitable remedies often involve injunctions or other court orders.

TRIVIA

- The present composition of nine Justices on the Supreme Court has existed since 1869. At its beginning, the Court had only six Justices. At one time, it had ten Justices.
- A 1995 nationwide poll by the *Washington Post* revealed that while 50 percent of those polled could name the Three Stooges, only 17 percent of those polled could name three of the nine Supreme Court Justices.

■ Since the late 1800s, as the Justices take their seats on the bench and at the beginning of the case conferences at which they meet and review cases, each Justice formally shakes hands with each of the other Justices. This handshake serves as a visible reminder that while the Justices may offer differing views of the law, they are united in their purpose of interpreting the Constitution.

■ On rainy days, the early Justices would enliven case conferences with wine. On other days, even if the sun was shining, Chief Justice John Marshall would order wine anyway, saying, "Our jurisdiction is so vast that it must be raining somewhere."

DISCUSSION QUESTIONS

1. Sue, a resident of New Jersey, sues her employer for violation of the Federal Family and Medical Leave Act. In which court may Sue initiate her lawsuit? Why? Identify the type of jurisdiction involved.

2. Luis, a resident of Minnesota, was involved in an automobile accident in North Dakota with Dan, a resident of North Dakota. Luis is claiming that he has been damaged in the amount of $75,000. May Luis initiate an action in federal court? Why or why not?

3. Racial discrimination is a violation of the Fourteenth Amendment and a violation of California state law. In which court may Jack, a victim of such discrimination, bring a lawsuit alleging such discrimination? What is this specific type of jurisdiction called?

4. ABC Inc. was incorporated in Delaware but conducts business in Pennsylvania. Where may it be sued? Why?

5. Cal's Auto Inc. sells cars only in the state of Florida. One of its cars was recently driven into Georgia, where it was involved in an accident. The plaintiff is alleging that the car was defective when Cal's sold it. May Cal's be sued in Georgia? Why or why not?

6. Classify the following as matters of substantive or procedural law:
   a. A federal law prohibiting copyright infringement
   b. The right to a trial by jury in a criminal case
   c. A court's requirement that pleadings be prepared on white, opaque paper
   d. A state statute providing that corporations must hold annual shareholder meetings
   e. A policy by a state commissioner of corporations that two copies of incorporation papers must be submitted to it

7. Tim was recently convicted of armed robbery. He would like to appeal his conviction on the basis that the prosecution twice called him Jim. Gina was recently convicted of a drug violation and would like to appeal her conviction on the basis that she was not given her Miranda warnings (notifying her of her right to remain silent) when she was arrested and then confessed to the crime. Discuss whether the two convictions might be reversed.

8. Hal has breached a contract with Kyle by refusing to repair Kyle's roof. Kyle was required to obtain the services of another roofer. Hal also refused to transfer title to a car to Kyle that Kyle bought from Hal. Discuss the remedies that Kyle might seek from Hal.

CLOSING ARGUMENTS

1. Use Cornell Law School's site to access the Federal Rules of Civil Procedure. How is time computed by federal courts? For example, if the last day to answer a complaint falls on a Saturday, Sunday, or legal holiday, when must the answer be filed?

2. Access the website for the Ninth Circuit Court of Appeals. What is the physical or street address of the Office of the Clerk of the U.S. Court of Appeals for the Ninth Circuit?

3. Access the website for the U.S. District Court for the Eastern District of Texas (located in the Fifth Circuit). What size font must be used when one submits pleadings to the court?

4. Access the U.S. Supreme Court's website and answer the following questions:
   a. What type of pens are used in the courtroom of the U.S. Supreme Court?
   b. Locate the following case from the 2002 term and give its docket number and identify the Justice who delivered the opinion of the Court: *Hillside Dairy, Inc. v. Lyons.*
   c. Review the Rules of the Supreme Court. What color cover must be used when one submits a petition for certiorari to the Court?

PART

II

PARALEGAL SKILLS

CHAPTER

5

LEGAL RESEARCH AND ANALYSIS

RESEARCH IS NEVER COMPLETED. . . . AROUND THE COR-
NER LURKS ANOTHER POSSIBILITY OF INTERVIEW, ANOTHER BOOK
TO READ, A COURTHOUSE TO EXPLORE, A DOCUMENT TO VERIFY.
—CATHERINE DRINKER BOWEN (1959)

CHAPTER OVERVIEW

This chapter introduces you to the authorities used in legal research and to techniques used to analyze those authorities. Legal research is a "hands on" subject. The
best way to learn about legal research is to do it. Performing legal research can be
both frustrating and gratifying. It can be frustrating because there is often no one
perfect answer and because there are no established guidelines on how much research
to do and when to stop. On the other hand, legal research is gratifying because you
will be rewarded by finding the right case, statute, or other authority to help a client.

A. PRIMARY AND SECONDARY AUTHORITIES

1. Introduction

While the United States adheres to a uniform common law tradition, there is no one
single legal system in this country. Federal laws are enacted by the United States
Congress, and cases are decided by the federal courts. Moreover, unless an area of the
law has been preempted by the U.S. Constitution or the federal government, each
state is free to enact laws as well as to decide cases dealing with state or local concerns.

Thus, there is a tremendous body of legal literature on the shelves of law
libraries: federal cases and statutes; state cases and statutes; federal and state administrative regulations; and numerous other texts and journals that explain the law.

Primary authorities
Official pronouncements of
the law by any of the three
branches of federal or state
government

Secondary authorities
Any legal authority that is
not a primary authority

All of the great mass of legal authorities can be classified as primary authority or secondary authority. **Primary authorities** are official pronouncements of the law by the executive branch (namely, treaties and executive orders), legislative branch (namely, constitutions, statutes, and administrative regulations and decisions), and judicial branch (namely, cases).

If a legal authority does not fall within one of the previously mentioned categories, it is a secondary authority. **Secondary authorities** may consist of legal encyclopedias, law review articles written about various legal topics, books or other treatises dealing with legal issues, law dictionaries, and expert opinions on legal issues. In general, the secondary authorities provide comment, discussion, and explanation of the primary authorities, and, equally important, they help you locate the primary authorities.

It is critical to understand thoroughly the differences between primary and secondary authorities because only primary authorities are binding on a court, agency, or tribunal. That is, if your argument relies on or cites a case, constitution, statute, or administrative regulation that is relevant to the legal issue, it must be followed. The secondary authorities, on the other hand, are persuasive only. See Figure 5-1 for a chart showing primary and secondary authorities and other legal research tools.

FIGURE 5-1
LEGAL RESEARCH AUTHORITIES

Primary Authorities (binding)

Authorities	Source
Cases (state and federal)	Judiciary
Constitutions (state and federal)	Legislature
Statutes (state and federal)	Legislature
Administrative regulations (state and federal)	Administrative agencies
Executive orders and treaties (federal only)	Executive branch

Secondary Authorities (persuasive)

Encyclopedias
Legal periodicals
Texts and treatises
Restatements
A.L.R. annotations
Dictionaries

Finding Tools

Digests

Updating Tools

Shepard's Citations (in print and on LEXIS)
KeyCite (on Westlaw)

2. Using the Descriptive Word Approach to Conduct Legal Research

Although there is variation in the way that legal authorities are arranged, in most instances, the typical approach used to locate legal authorities is the same. Many sets of law books have indexes at the end of the set. These indexes are alphabetically arranged. To use a set of books, locate the index at the end of the set and try to think of key words or phrases that describe the problem you are researching. For example, if you are researching duties of landlords, look for descriptive words such as landlord, lessor, tenant, or lessee in the index and you will then be directed to the appropriate volume and section or page within the set of books you are using. This finding technique is usually called the **descriptive word approach,** and it is the most common means used by legal researchers to find the law.

Descriptive word approach
Method of conducting research using alphabetically arranged indexes

B. FINDING THE LAW USING PRIMARY AUTHORITIES

1. Federal Statutes

a. *United States Statutes at Large*

As each federal law is passed by Congress, it is published by the United States Government Printing Office as a looseleaf unbound pamphlet or sheet of paper, referred to as a **slip law.** At the end of each congressional session, these slips are taken together and are placed in chronological order in a hardback set of volumes called *United States Statutes at Large.* All of our federal laws since 1789 are contained in this set.

Slip law
Federal law initially published on looseleaf sheet(s) of paper

The laws in *United States Statutes at Large* appear in chronological order—namely, in the way in which they were passed by Congress—making the slip laws extremely difficult to research. Moreover, there is no one master index to this set. Thus, *United States Statutes at Large* serves more as a historical overview of Congress's work than as a viable research tool.

b. *United States Code*

Because the organization and lack of indexing of *United States Statutes at Large* makes research using the set so difficult, it became readily apparent to researchers that a set of books should be developed to eliminate these barriers to efficient research. The process of developing a set of books that compiles currently valid laws on the same subject together with any amendments to those laws is referred to as **codification.** The current codification of *United States Statutes at Large* that legal professionals use to find federal statutes is called the *United States Code* (U.S.C.). The set of U.S.C. arranges all federal laws by topic or subject matter into 50 different alphabetically arranged categories, called **titles** (see Figure 5-2).

Codification
Arrangement of statutes, bringing together all valid laws on the same subject with their amendments

Titles
Categories of statutes

For example, Title 11 includes all federal bankruptcy laws and Title 35 contains all patent laws. Within the titles, statutes are further divided into sections. Citations to federal statutes in U.S.C. are as follows:

42	U.S.C.	§	1390	(2000)
Title	*Set*	*Abbr. for section*	*Section no.*	*Year of code*

FIGURE 5-2

TITLES OF THE *UNITED STATES CODE*

1. General Provisions	28. Judiciary and Judicial Procedure
2. The Congress	29. Labor
3. The President	30. Mineral Lands and and the States
4. Flag and Seal, Seat of Government,	Mining
5. Government Organization and	31. Money and Finance
Employees	32. National Guard
6. Surety Bonds	33. Navigation and Navigable Waters
7. Agriculture	34. Navy (see Title 10, Armed Forces)
8. Aliens and Nationality	35. Patents
9. Arbitration	36. Patriotic Societies and
10. Armed Forces	Observances
11. Bankruptcy	37. Pay and Allowances of the
12. Banks and Banking	Uniformed Services
13. Census	38. Veterans' Benefits
14. Coast Guard	39. Postal Service
15. Commerce and Trade	40. Public Buildings, Property, and
16. Conservation	Works
17. Copyrights	41. Public Contracts
18. Crimes and Criminal Procedure	42. The Public Health and Welfare
19. Customs Duties	43. Public Lands
20. Education	44. Public Printing and Documents
21. Food and Drugs	45. Railroads
22. Foreign Relations and Intercourse	46. Shipping
23. Highways	47. Telegraphs, Telephones, and
24. Hospitals and Asylums	Radiotelegraphs
25. Indians	48. Territories and Insular Possessions
26. Internal Revenue Code	49. Transportation
27. Intoxicating Liquors	50. War and National Defense

It is not important to know what subject each of the 50 titles refers to. It is sufficient to understand that there are in fact, 50 groups or titles of federal statutes, that they are arranged alphabetically, and that these titles are permanently established, which means, for example, that any federal statute relating to patents will always be found in Title 35.

Official
Publication of law or case as mandated or directed by statute or court rule

The *United States Code* is **official,** a term meaning that its publication is approved by the government. A new edition of the *United States Code* is published every six years.

c. Annotated Versions of the United States Code

While the *United States Code* is an efficiently organized set of federal statutes, it has one glaring drawback from the perspective of legal researchers: While it includes the exact language of our federal statutes, it does not send researchers to cases that might interpret those statutes. Under the concept of stare decisis, discussed in Chapter Four, it is not the naked statutory language that controls a given situation but a court's interpretation of that statute. Thus, because the *United States Code* simply recites the exact text of a federal statute without providing any comment regarding the law or any reference to any cases that may have interpreted the law, two private publishers, West Group (West) and LEXIS Publishing (LEXIS) have separately assumed the task of providing this critical information to legal professionals. Because the publication of their sets is not government-approved, these publications are referred to as **unofficial**. Note that the terms "official" and "unofficial" relate to whether the publication of a set is government-approved or not. The terms do not relate to the accuracy or credibility of a set. The text of a statute will be the same whether it is published in the official set, U.S.C., or in one of the unofficial sets—namely, U.S.C.A. or U.S.C.S. Both U.S.C.A. and U.S.C.S. are referred to as **annotated** codes, meaning that they include "notes" referring readers to cases interpreting statutes.

You will see from the discussion below that the two sets are highly similar. Generally, researchers will use one set rather than another, primarily based on habit, convenience, and availability. In most respects the two sets are competitive, which means they are equivalent. For a typical research project you would ordinarily use one set—not both.

(1) United States Code Annotated *and* United States Code Service

West's set of federal statutes is called *United States Code Annotated* (U.S.C.A.) and LEXIS's set is *United States Code Service* (U.S.C.S.). Both are divided into the same 50 titles as the *United States Code* and both include a multivolume general index at the end of the set. These sets are not valuable because they provide the language of federal statutes—the *United States Code* provides that. These unofficial sets are valuable because of the extra features they provide, which are nearly identical (although they may have different names). These features are shown in Figure 5-3 and include the following: historical notes (showing the evolution and development of the statute you are researching); cross references (directing you to other helpful statutes); library references (sending you to other helpful sources); and the critical annotations. These annotations are the most valuable part of U.S.C.A. and U.S.C.S. because they will direct you to cases that have interpreted the statutes you read. You will be given a one-sentence description of the case and then its citation. You may then decide whether to read the case in full. Both U.S.C.A. and U.S.C.S. organize these annotations for you by topic, making it easy for you to select the right cases to read.

(2) Pocket Parts

Because federal statutes are amended so frequently, both U.S.C.A. and U.S.C.S. are kept current by the most typical method of updating legal research volumes: annual cumulative reports. A slit or "pocket" has been created in the back cover of each hardcover volume of U.S.C.A. and U.S.C.S. During each year, West and LEXIS mail small softcover pamphlets called **pocket parts** to law firms and law libraries. A pocket part slides into the slit in the back of each volume of U.S.C.A. and U.S.C.S. The pocket part provides current information about the statutes in that volume, including amendments to the statute and references or annotations to cases decided since the hardcover volumes were placed on the library shelves. Eventually, if a book becomes worn out, the publisher will replace that single volume. On occasion, a softcover book, called a **supplement**, is placed on the shelf next to a hardcover volume to update it.

Unofficial
Private publication of law or case; publication not mandated by statute

Annotated
Literally, "with notes"; manner of publishing statutes together with case summaries interpreting statutes

Pocket parts
Pamphlets inserted into back covers of legal books to provide current information

Supplement
A softcover book that updates a hardcover volume

FIGURE 5-3
STATUTE FROM U.S.C.A.

§ 1174. Liquidation

On request of a party in interest and after notice and a hearing, the court may, or, if a plan has not been confirmed under section 1173 of this title before five years after the date of the order for relief, the court shall, order the trustee to cease the debtor's operation and to collect and reduce to money all of the property of the estate in the same manner as if the case were a case under chapter 7 of this title.

Pub.L. 95–598, Nov. 6, 1978, 92 Stat. 2644.

Historical Notes

Historical and Revision Notes

Notes of Committee on the Judiciary, Senate Report No. 95-989. Section 1174 permits the court to convert the case to a liquidation under chapter 7 if the court finds that the debtor cannot be reorganized, or if various time limits specified in the subchapter are not met. Section 77 [former section 205 of this title] does not authorize a liquidation of a railroad under the Bankruptcy Act. If the railroad is not reorganizable, the only action open to the court is to dismiss the petition, which would in all likelihood be followed by a State court receivership, with all of its attendant disadvantages. If reorganization is impossible, the debtor should be liquidated under the Bankruptcy Act.

Legislative Statements. Section 1174 of the House amendment represents a compromise between the House bill and Senate amendment on the issue of liquidation of a railroad. The provision permits a party in interest at any time to request liquidation. In addition, if a plan has not been confirmed under section 1173 of the House amendment before 5 years after the date of order for relief, the court must order the trustee to cease the debtor's operation and to collect and reduce to money all of the property of the estate in the same manner as if the case were a case under chapter 7 of title 11. The approach differs from the conversion to chapter 7 under section 1174 of the Senate bill in order to make special provisions contained in subchapter IV of chapter 11 applicable to liquidation. However, maintaining liquidation in the context of chapter 11 is not intended to delay liquidation of the railroad to a different extent than if the case were converted to chapter 7.

Although the House amendment does not adopt provisions contained in sections 1170(1), (2), (3), or (5), of the Senate amendment such provisions are contained explicitly or implicitly in section 1123 of the House amendment.

Cross References

Cross References

Conversion of
    Chapter 7 cases, ssee section 706 of this title.
    Chapter 11 cases, see section 1112 of this title.
    Chapter 13 cases, see section 1307 of this title.
Dismissal of
    Chapter 7 cases, see section 707 of this title.
    Chapter 9 cases, see section 927 of this title.
    Chapter 11 cases, see section 1112 of this title.
    Chapter 13 cases, see section 1307 of this title.

Library References

Library References

Bankruptcy ☞851.   C.J.S. Bankruptcy § 1085.

Annotations

Notes of Decisions

Construction with other laws 1
Futility of reorganization 2
Limitations on court 3

FIGURE 5-3 (CONTINUED)

STATUTE FROM U.S.C.A.

1. Construction with other laws

Court was without jurisdiction to consider and approve equitable liquidation of estate of railroad in reorganization, since an adequate remedy at law was available through the Regional Rail Reorganization Act of 1973, section 701 et seq. of Title 45. In re Erie Lackawanna Railway Co., D.C.Ohio 1975, 393 F.Supp. 352.

Regional Rail Reorganization Act of 1973, section 701 et seq. of Title 45, does not provide a process of reorganization which is fair and equitable to the estate of a railroad undergoing reorganization pursuant to this title in that it precludes a form of liquidation under this title. In re Lehigh & H. R. Ry. Co., D.C.N.Y.1974, 377 F.Supp. 475.

2. Futility of reorganization

Liquidation of railroad undergoing reorganization should be considered only as last resort. In re Reading Co., D.C. Pa.1973, 361 F.Supp. 1351.

Liquidation of bankrupt railroad is not called for until futility of every reasonable effort to put railroad into sound financial condition becomes apparent. Id.

3. Limitations on court

In exercising its statutory power to convert capital assets of debtor to cash, railroad reorganization court must act within bounds of U.S.C.A.Const. Amend. 5 and may not by selling assets authorize unconstitutional taking of property of mortgage bondholders. In re Penn Central Transp. Co., C.A.Pa.1974, 494 F.2d 270, certiorari denied 95 S.Ct. 147, 419 U. S. 883, 42 L.Ed.2d 122.

There are few invariable or inflexible rules in legal research. One of them is that you must always consult a pocket part if the volume you are using is updated by a pocket part pamphlet.

d. Research Techniques

Researchers generally use one of the three following techniques to find federal statutes:

- **Descriptive word approach.** Both U.S.C.A. and U.S.C.S. have a multi-volume general index, which is arranged alphabetically and is usually located after Title 50, the last title in each set. When you are assigned a legal research problem, think of key words and phrases that describe the problem and then look up these words or phrases in the general index of either U.S.C.A. or U.S.C.S., which will then direct you to the appropriate title and section you need. This is the simplest and most reliable way to locate federal statutes.

- **Title/topic approach.** You may become so familiar with the organization of U.S.C.A. or U.S.C.S. that when given a research problem you can bypass the general index and go directly to the appropriate title. This is the title or topic approach. For example, if you know that a bankruptcy statute is in Title 11, you can retrieve the appropriate volume and look at the table of contents for Title 11 at the beginning of Title 11 or go directly to the index for all of the bankruptcy statutes found at the end of the title. You will then be able to review the statutes and annotations.

- **Popular name approach.** Because some statutes are known by their popular names (often the names of the sponsoring legislators, such as the Taft-Hartley Act), you can find statutes by examining the alphabetically arranged tables of statutes by popular name provided by both U.S.C.A. and U.S.C.S.

2. State Statutes

Session laws
Initial compilation of laws passed by state legislatures

The organization, publication, and process of finding state statutes is almost identical to that for federal statutes. State statutes are enacted by state legislative bodies and are then signed into law by the governor of the state. The state statutes initially appear in slip form and are then compiled in sets of books generally called **session laws**. The session laws are analogous to *United States Statutes at Large* in that they contain the laws of a particular state, but due to their chronological arrangement, they are not particularly helpful to researchers. Thus, the states have codified their session laws to bring together all the current laws on the same subject and eliminate repealed laws. Some states arrange their statutes by title and chapter, such as Va. Code Ann. § 8-102 (West 1998). Other states, usually the more populous ones, arrange their statutes in named titles—for example, Cal. Evid. Code § 52 (West 1998). Most states have annotated codes, which means that after you are given the wording of the pertinent statute, you will be directed to cases that interpret the statute.

While the publication of each state's statutes varies somewhat and while the publication may be unofficial or official, most state codes share the following features:

- The state's constitution is usually included in the state's code;
- The statutes will be organized by subject matter so that all of the corporate statutes are grouped together, all of the probate statutes are grouped together, and so forth;
- There will be a general index to the entire set and often each title (such as Probate) begins or ends with its own index;
- The statutes are kept current through annual cumulative pocket parts;
- Annotations will be provided to direct you to cases interpreting the statutes, typically through the use of a one-sentence summary of the case, similar to the organization of U.S.C.A. and U.S.C.S. annotations; and
- Extra features, such as historical notes and library references, will be provided to assist you in interpreting the statute.

The same techniques used to locate federal statutes are used to locate state statutes, namely, the descriptive word approach, the title/topic approach, and the popular name approach.

3. United States Constitution and State Constitutions

While the U.S. Constitution is not one of the 50 titles of the *United States Code,* nevertheless both U.S.C.A. and U.S.C.S. contain volumes for the Constitution. Similarly, as noted, most state constitutions are included with the state's codes. When conducting constitutional research in U.S.C.A., U.S.C.S., or in a state code, you will be provided with the text of the pertinent constitutional provision and its amendments, and then, by the use of annotations, you will be referred to cases that interpret them. The three primary research techniques described above should also be used when you research a constitutional law issue. Don't forget to review the pocket parts.

4. Administrative Regulations

Both the U.S. Congress and state legislatures delegate various powers to administrative agencies. Thus, a federal agency such as the Federal Aviation Administration regulates federal aviation matters, and a state agency such as the Texas Insurance Commission handles insurance matters in Texas. These agencies have the power to issue binding statements, called **rules** or **regulations**. Someone who violates an agency rule or regulation may be punished, just like someone who violates a federal or state statute. All of our federal regulations are initially published in a journal or pamphlet called the *Federal Register*, which is published every weekday. Because the *Federal Register* is difficult to use, it has been codified into a set of books published annually called the *Code of Federal Regulations* (C.F.R.). C.F.R. is divided into 50 titles and is organized similarly to the federal statutes contained in U.S.C. The C.F.R. set includes a one-volume index. To conduct research and locate federal rules and regulations, use the descriptive word approach and use words in the index that describe your research problem. You will be directed to the appropriate title and section or part of C.F.R.

> **Rules**
> Binding statements issued by agencies; also called *regulations*

To research state administrative rules and regulations, locate the state administrative code (usually located near the state statutes) and use the descriptive word approach to find rules and regulations.

5. Case Law

a. Official and Unofficial Publication of Cases

Not all cases are published. Generally, trial court decisions are not published. Moreover, not every appellate court case is published. Typically, because many cases involve similar issues, courts mark a case for publication only if it advances legal theory or represents a change in the law. The books in which cases are published are referred to as **reports** or **reporters,** and each one has a specific abbreviation. If cases are published pursuant to some statutory directive or court rule, the sets of books in which they are collected are referred to as **official reports**. Cases published without this type of governmental approval are collected in sets of books called **unofficial reporters**. The terms "official" and "unofficial" have nothing to do with accuracy or quality. The terms relate solely to the method of publication. The fact that many cases are published both officially and unofficially means that researchers have a choice as to which set of books to use to locate a case. As discussed previously, statutes are also published officially and unofficially. It is also important to understand the difference between official and unofficial sets because in many instances the rules of citation require one form of citation over another.

> **Reports, reporters**
> Books that compile cases
>
> **Official reports**
> Case books publishing cases as directed by statute or court rule
>
> **Unofficial reporters**
> Case books publishing cases without direction by statute or court rule

For example, consider the following citation: *Jones v. Smith*, 236 Va. 109, 402 S.E.2d 16 (1995). Citations to cases always include the same elements: the name of the case; a reference to the volume number, name of the set, and page number on which the case begins; the date of decision; and the deciding court, if not apparent from the name of the set. Thus, the citation given above informs the reader that the case named *Jones v. Smith* can be located in volume 236 of a set of books called the Virginia Reports at page 109, and the same case can also be located in volume 402 of a set of books called the South Eastern Reporter, Second Series, at page 16. The case was decided in 1995. The two citations are called **parallel citations.** The first citation, 236 Va. 109, is the official citation, and the second, 402 S.E.2d 16, is the unofficial citation. The opinion in the case itself will be exactly the same in both sets because what the judge has said in issuing the opinion is "etched in stone." What will vary will be type size, quality of paper, and some extra features provided by the respective publishers.

Cases are first published in **slip form** and are then published in **advance sheets**, which are temporary publications that appear a few weeks after release of the court's opinion. Eventually, after a few months, the cases will be published in hardcover volumes and the softcover advance sheets will then be discarded.

You may have noticed that some of the case reports on the shelves are titled on their spines, for example, Pacific Reporter, while others are titled Pacific Reporter 2d Series. The switch to a new series by a publisher merely indicates newer cases. Thus, any case in Federal Reporter 3d Series is newer than any case in Federal Reporter 2d Series, and so forth.

b. Elements of a Case

Cases that are published or reported typically include the following elements (See Figure 5-4).

- **Case name.** The name or title of a case identifies the parties involved in an action. A case name with a "v." in its title indicates an adversarial matter, and a case name such as *In re Stone* indicates a nonadversarial case, such as a probate or bankruptcy matter. A case name such as *State v. Smith* or *United States v. Henry* usually indicates a criminal proceeding brought by a state or the federal government, respectively.
- **Docket number and deciding court.** Immediately beneath the case name you will be given the docket number of the case, which is a number used by the court to identify the case as it progresses through the court system. Following the docket number, the deciding court is often identified.
- **Date of decision.** The date the case was decided by the court will be given. If two dates are given, one will be identified as the date the case was argued and the other will be the date the case was decided. For citation purposes, the critical date is the date of decision.
- **Case summary or synopsis.** Before you are given the actual opinion of the court, you will be provided with a brief paragraph summarizing the nature and background of the case, a description of the parties, a summary of what occurred in the court below, and an overview of this court's decision. This summary is typically prepared by the legal publishing companies (usually West), not by the court. This case summary serves as a quick introduction to the case, but it can never be quoted from or relied on as authority because it was not prepared by the court.
- **Headnotes.** Before the actual opinion of the court, you will be provided with short paragraphs, each of which is assigned a number and a name, such as "**4. Damages.**" These are called **headnotes.** Each point of law discussed in the case is assigned a

---

Parallel citations
Two or more references to a case

Slip form
Initial publication of cases and other materials on looseleaf paper

Advance sheets
Initial publication of cases in disposable softcover pamphlets

Headnotes
Brief, numbered paragraphs of points of law in a case

FIGURE 5-4

PUBLISHED CASE

(1st Cir.1989) (per curiam); *Carter v. Tisch,* 822 F.2d 465, 467–69 (4th Cir.1987); *Jasany v. United States Postal Serv.,* 755 F.2d 1244, 1251–52 (6th Cir.1985); *Daubert v. United States Postal Serv.,* 733 F.2d 1367, 1370 (10th Cir.1984).

Headnotes

Accordingly, we find that Mason has not established a claim under the Rehabilitation Act and therefore is not entitled to reinstatement or any other relief.[6]

The judgment is affirmed.

Case Name

Terry Lynn **ANDERSON,** Appellant,

v.

Carl **WHITE,** Superintendent, Algoa Correctional Center, Appellee.

Docket Number

No. 93–2915.

Deciding Court

United States Court of Appeals, Eighth Circuit.

Dates of Argument and Decision

Submitted June 14, 1994.

Decided Aug. 5, 1994.

Case Summary or Synopsis

Petitioner sought habeas corpus relief, claiming that he had been mentally incompetent at time of assaults and at time of guilty pleas. The United States District Court for the Western District of Missouri, Russell G. Clark, Senior District Judge, denied the petition. Petitioner appealed. The Court of Appeals, Wollman, Circuit Judge, held that: (1) the claims were procedurally defaulted where the petitioner did not file a timely state postconviction petition, and (2) no evidence indicated that the petitioner's posttraumatic stress disorder after he served in Vietnam prevented him from understanding his position or making a rational choice about whether to seek postconviction relief and, thus, his

6. We note that Mason does have another avenue for employment with the Postal Service. The Postal Service hires handicapped individuals

alleged incompetency was not cause for the procedural default.

Affirmed.

---

1. Habeas Corpus ⟲365

Petitioner's claims that he had been mentally incompetent at time of assaults and at time of guilty pleas were procedurally defaulted where petitioner did not file timely state postconviction petition. V.A.M.R. 24.-035; 28 U.S.C.A. § 2254.

2. Habeas Corpus ⟲364

State habeas corpus petitions did not resurrect procedurally defaulted claims, absent showing that state Supreme Court ruled on merits of federal habeas claims. V.A.M.R. 24.035, 91.01 et seq.; 28 U.S.C.A. § 2254.

3. Criminal Law ⟲998(1)

Defendant is competent to waive postconviction remedies if he is not suffering from mental disease, disorder, or defect that may substantially affect his capacity to appreciate his position and make rational choice with respect to continuing or abandoning further litigation.

4. Habeas Corpus ⟲405.1

No evidence indicated that petitioner's posttraumatic stress disorder after he served in Vietnam prevented him from understanding his position or making rational choice about whether to seek postconviction relief and, thus, alleged incompetency was not cause for procedural default of not filing timely state postconviction petition raising claims that petitioner had been mentally incompetent at time of assaults and at time of guilty pleas. V.A.M.R. 24.035; 28 U.S.C.A. § 2254.

5. Habeas Corpus ⟲401

Narrow exception to cause and prejudice standard applied to procedurally defaulted claims exists if petitioner demonstrates that federal habeas review of his claims is necessary to prevent fundamental miscarriage of justice. 28 U.S.C.A. § 2254.

who cannot meet the requirements of entry-level positions on a noncompetitive basis through the Missouri Division of Vocational Rehabilitation.

FIGURE 5-4 (CONTINUED)

PUBLISHED CASE

Names of Counsel

William J. Fleischaker, Joplin, MO, argued, for appellant.

Stacy Louise Anderson, Jefferson City, MO, argued, for appellee.

Before WOLLMAN, Circuit Judge, FLOYD R. GIBSON, Senior Circuit Judge, and WELLFORD,* Senior Circuit Judge.

Author of Opinion

WOLLMAN, Circuit Judge.

Terry Lynn Anderson appeals from the district court's [1] order denying on the merits his petition for a writ of habeas corpus filed pursuant to 28 U.S.C. § 2254. We affirm.

I.

On February 23, 1990, Anderson pled guilty to second-degree assault in Missouri state court. Execution of his two-year sentence was suspended and he was placed on probation. While on probation, Anderson again was charged with second-degree assault. On August 28, 1992, he pled guilty to the second charge and admitted that he had violated the conditions of his probation on the first charge. The state trial court revoked Anderson's probation and ordered that his two-year sentence for the first charge be executed concurrently with his four-year sentence for the second charge. In this habeas petition, Anderson alleges that he was mentally incompetent when he committed the assaults, as well as at the time of his pleas.

II.

[1, 2] Anderson did not file a timely motion for state post-conviction relief pursuant

* The HONORABLE HARRY W. WELLFORD, Senior United States Circuit Judge for the Sixth Circuit, sitting by designation.

1. The Honorable Russell G. Clark, Senior United States District Judge for the Western District of Missouri.

2. Pursuant to Missouri Supreme Court Rule 91, Anderson filed state habeas petitions in the circuit court of Cole County and the Missouri Supreme Court, which were denied. These petitions, however, do not resurrect Anderson's procedurally defaulted claims, for Anderson has not shown that the Missouri Supreme Court addressed the merits of his federal claims. *See State ex rel. Simmons v. White*, 866 S.W.2d 443,

to Missouri Supreme Court Rule 24.035. His incompetency claims therefore are procedurally defaulted.[2] *Jennings v. Purkett*, 7 F.3d 779, 781–82 (8th Cir.1993). "In all cases in which a state prisoner has defaulted his federal claims in state court pursuant to an independent and adequate state procedural rule, federal habeas review of the claims is barred unless the prisoner can demonstrate cause for the default and actual prejudice as a result of the alleged violation of federal law." *Coleman v. Thompson*, 501 U.S. 722, 750, 111 S.Ct. 2546, 2565, 115 L.Ed.2d 640 (1991); *Maynard v. Lockhart*, 981 F.2d 981, 984 (8th Cir.1992). Accordingly, we must determine whether Anderson has established cause for his procedural default.

[3, 4] Anderson argues that his alleged incompetency establishes cause for his failure to file a timely Rule 24.035 motion.[3] A defendant is competent to waive post-conviction remedies if he is not suffering from a mental disease, disorder, or defect that may substantially affect his capacity to appreciate his position and make a rational choice with respect to continuing or abandoning further litigation. *Rees v. Peyton*, 384 U.S. 312, 314, 86 S.Ct. 1505, 1506–07, 16 L.Ed.2d 583 (1966) (per curiam). The record demonstrates that Anderson suffers from post-traumatic stress disorder as a result of his service in Vietnam. The record, however, contains no evidence establishing that during the time for filing a motion for post-conviction relief, *see* Mo.Sup. Ct.R. 24.035(b), Anderson, as a result of his mental condition, could not understand his position or make a rational decision concern-

446 (Mo.1993) (en banc) (holding that state habeas corpus may be used to challenge a final judgment after an individual's failure to pursue post-conviction remedies only to raise jurisdictional issues or in circumstances so rare and exceptional that a manifest injustice results).

3. Because we conclude below that Anderson has not established that he was incompetent, we do not consider the state's argument that a petitioner's alleged incompetence is not an "objective factor external to the defense." *Murray v. Carrier*, 477 U.S. 478, 488, 106 S.Ct. 2639, 2645, 91 L.Ed.2d 397 (1986). Cf. *Cornman v. Armontrout*, 959 F.2d 727, 729 (8th Cir.1992) (petitioner's below-average intelligence and pro se status are not objective factors external to the defense).

FIGURE 5-4 (CONTINUED)

PUBLISHED CASE

ing the trial judge's directions regarding a Rule 24.035 motion. A showing that Anderson suffers from a mental disorder, "without more, is wholly insufficient to meet the legal standard that the Supreme Court has laid down" for determining a defendant's competence to pursue post-conviction relief. *Smith v. Armontrout,* 865 F.2d 1502, 1506 (8th Cir.1988) (en banc).

We note that soon after the time for filing a Rule 24.035 motion had expired, Anderson was competent enough to file a motion to file out of time a post-conviction relief motion. Moreover, he did not allege in that motion that his mental condition had prevented him from filing a timely motion, alleging instead that the inadequacy of the prison library was the cause. Accordingly, we conclude that Anderson's unsupported allegation that he was incompetent during the time period for seeking post-conviction relief does not establish cause for his procedural default. *See Williams v. Groose,* 979 F.2d 1335, 1338 (8th Cir.1992) (per curiam) (finding no cause where petitioner merely alleged but did not show that his mental problems had prevented him from presenting his claims in earlier habeas petitions); *Stanley v. Lockhart,* 941 F.2d 707, 709–10 (8th Cir.1991) (finding no cause for petitioner's procedural default when record did not establish that petitioner was incompetent). As Anderson has failed to establish cause for his procedural default, we need not consider the issue of prejudice.

[5] A narrow exception to the cause and prejudice standard exists where the petitioner demonstrates that federal review of his claims is necessary to prevent a fundamental miscarriage of justice. *See Coleman,* 501 U.S. at 750–51, 111 S.Ct. at 2565. Anderson, however, has made no such showing. He is therefore barred from seeking federal habeas relief.

Decision —

The district court's order denying Anderson's petition for a writ of habeas corpus is affirmed.

Ralph BUSSARD, Appellant,

v.

A.L. LOCKHART, Director, Arkansas Department of Corrections, Appellee.

No. 93–3231.

United States Court of Appeals, Eighth Circuit.

Submitted April 12, 1994.

Decided Aug. 5, 1994.

Defendant petitioned for habeas corpus relief after he was convicted of felony-murder and the Arkansas Supreme Court, 300 Ark. 174, 778 S.W.2d 213, affirmed. The United States District Court for the Eastern District of Arkansas, Garnett Thomas Eisele, Senior District Judge, denied relief. Defendant appealed. The Court of Appeals, John R. Gibson, Senior Circuit Judge, held that one remark by the prosecutor during closing argument was at most veiled reference to defendant's failure to testify, and a Biblical reference to Proverbs about whether flight would suggest consciousness of guilt was not an attempt to invoke wrath of God against defendant or a suggestion that jury could apply divine law as an alternative to state law, and, thus, defense counsel's decision not to object was reasonable and was not ineffective assistance of counsel.

Affirmed.

1. Criminal Law ⚖️641.13(2.1)

In reviewing claim of ineffective assistance of counsel premised on failure to object to prosecutor's closing argument, question is whether prosecutor's comments were so improper that counsel's only defensible choice was to interrupt them with objection; question is not whether comments were improper. U.S.C.A. Const.Amend. 6.

2. Criminal Law ⚖️641.13(2.1)

Prosecutor's remark during closing argument was at most veiled reference to de-

headnote. Thus, if the case discusses 12 points of law, there will be 12 headnotes. The headnotes provide a condensed overview or snapshot of the case and reduce the time you might spend reading a case that ultimately proves to be of no value to you. Because the headnotes are typically prepared by publishers, not judges, you cannot rely on them or quote from them, although they serve as excellent overviews of the issues in the case that follows. West reporters also include a pictorial diagram of a key, a topic name, and a number. This Key Number System is a method of finding numerous cases on the same topic. This system is discussed in detail below.

- **Names of counsel.** The names of the attorneys who represented the parties in the case are provided so that you can make contact with them.
- **Opinion.** The beginning of the opinion of the court is almost always marked by an identification of the author of the opinion. This is a signal that everything that follows is the court's opinion. Most opinions begin with a recital of the facts of the case. There are various types of opinions.

  - □ **Majority opinions** are those written by a member of the majority after the court has reached its decision. The holding of the majority is the law and serves as binding authority.
  - □ **Concurring opinions** are opinions written by justices who agree with the actual result reached in a case (for example, that the case should be affirmed) but who disagree with the reasoning of the majority opinion. Concurring opinions are persuasive only, not binding.
  - □ **Dissenting opinions** are those written by members of the minority. They are persuasive only.
  - □ **Per curiam opinions** are opinions of the whole court in which no specific author is identified.

- **Decision.** The final element in a case is the actual decision reached by the court. The final decision may be to affirm or uphold the determination of the lower court, to reverse or overturn the determination reached below, or to remand or return the case to the lower court for further action consistent with the court's findings.

c. Publication of State Cases

In 1879, West created and published the *North Western Reporter* to publish decisions from the Northwestern region of the United States. In many instances, these cases were already being published officially. For example, a Minnesota case would appear both officially in the *Minnesota Reports* and unofficially in the *North Western Reporter*. Practitioners became so enthusiastic about the various features offered by West's *North Western Reporter* and its groupings of cases from neighboring states that West followed it by creating reporters for other geographical regions of the United States. West's sets of books that collect state and federal cases are collectively referred to as the **National Reporter System.** Within the *National Reporter System* there are various units or sets of case books. The states that are included in each unit of the *National Reporter System* are shown in Figure 5-5.

Majority opinion
Case opinion written by a member of the majority, which is binding authority

Concurring opinion
Opinion written by justice who agrees with result reached in a case but not with the reasoning; persuasive only

Dissenting opinion
Opinion written by a member of the minority; persuasive only

Per curiam opinion
Opinion of the whole court in which no author is identified

National Reporter System
Sets of books published by West Group that report cases

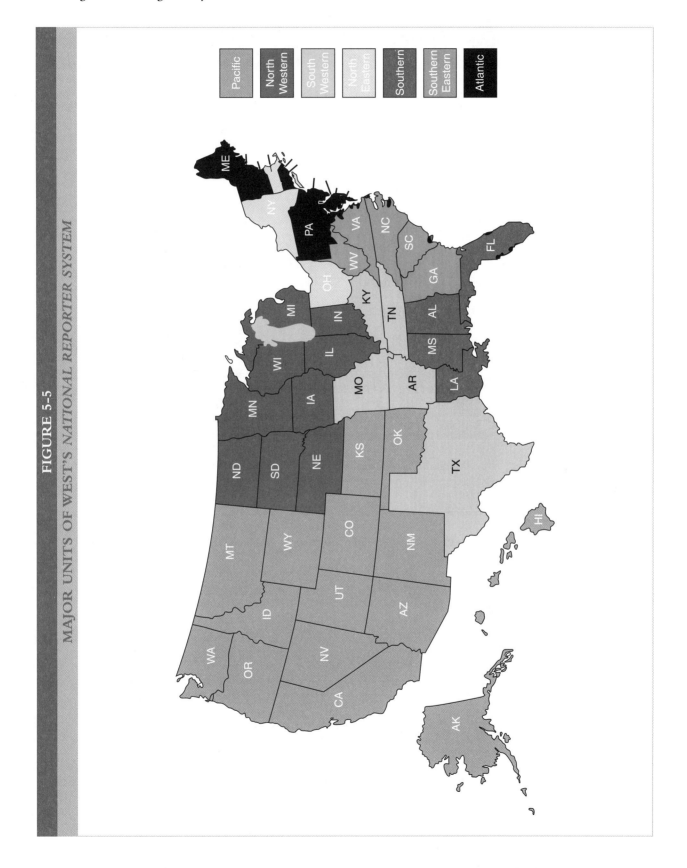

FIGURE 5-5

MAJOR UNITS OF WEST'S NATIONAL REPORTER SYSTEM

FIGURE 5-5 (CONTINUED)

MAJOR UNITS OF WEST'S *NATIONAL REPORTER SYSTEM*

Name of Case Reporter and Abbreviation	Courts Covered
North Western Reporter N.W., N.W.2d	State courts in Iowa*, Michigan, Minnesota*, Nebraska, North Dakota*, South Dakota*, Wisconsin
Pacific Reporter P., P.2d, P.3d	State courts in Alaska*, Arizona, California, Colorado*, Hawaii, Idaho, Kansas, Montana, Nevada, New Mexico, Oklahoma*, Oregon, Utah*, Washington, Wyoming*
North Eastern Reporter N.E., N.E.2d	State court cases in Illinois, Indiana*, Massachusetts, New York, Ohio
Atlantic Reporter A., A.2d	State court cases in Connecticut, Delaware*, Maine*, Maryland, New Hampshire, New Jersey, Rhode Island*, Vermont, Washington, D.C.*
South Western Reporter S.W., S.W.2d, S.W.3d	State court cases in Arkansas, Kentucky*, Missouri*, Tennessee*, Texas*
Southern Reporter So., So. 2d	State court cases in Alabama*, Florida*, Louisiana*, Mississippi*
South Eastern Reporter S.E., S.E.2d	State court cases in Georgia, North Carolina, South Carolina, Virginia, West Virginia
New York Supplement N.Y.S., N.Y.S.2d	Cases from various New York state courts
California Reporter Cal. Rptr., Cal. Rptr. 2d	Cases from the California Supreme Court and California Court of Appeals
Illinois Decisions Ill. Dec.	Cases from the Illinois Supreme Court and Illinois Appellate Court
Supreme Court Reporter S. Ct.	Cases from U.S. Supreme Court
Federal Reporter F., F.2d, F.3d	Cases from U.S. Courts of Appeal
Federal Supplement F. Supp., F. Supp. 2d	Cases from U.S. District Courts
Federal Rules Decisions F.R.D.	Cases interpreting federal rules of civil procedure and criminal procedure

* State does not publish official versions of its cases

After West created the regional units to report decisions from groups of neighboring states, the publishing company created specialized sets for three states because of the volume of litigation in those states: *California Reporter, Illinois Decisions,* and the *New York Supplement*. Thus, there may be three parallel citations to a California case, as follows:

Taylor v. Gregory, 34 Cal. 3d 119, 682 P.2d 190, 120 Cal. Rptr. 19 (1989). This citation shows that the *Taylor* case can be located in three separate sets of books. The opinion issued by the court in *Taylor* will be the same no matter which of the three sets you select to locate the case. What will differ, however, may be the color of the covers, the quality of the paper used, the typeface, and the editorial enhancements such as headnotes and the case summary or synopsis.

One of the advantages of the *National Reporter System* units lies in its groupings of states. A law firm in Ohio that purchases the official *Ohio Reports* will acquire a set of books that contains cases only from Ohio. If that firm purchases the *North Eastern Reporter*, however, it acquires a set of books that contains decisions not only from Ohio but also from Illinois, Indiana, Massachusetts, and New York. This allows legal professionals to review decisions from other neighboring states, which decisions might be helpful if a case of first impression arises in Ohio.

The sets of books in the *National Reporter System* offer a variety of useful features, including the following: an alphabetical table of the cases in that volume; a table of statutes directing you to cases in the volume that interpret statutes; and a table of words and phrases directing you to cases in the volume that interpret a word or phrase (for example, "assault"). Moreover, all books in the *National Reporter System* participate in West's Key Number System, a method of allowing researchers to locate cases. The system is discussed below.

Because of the popularity of West's *National Reporter System*, about 20 states have stopped publishing their cases officially. Generally, the states that have stopped official publication are smaller states (for example, North Dakota and Iowa). In those states, you will be able to locate cases only in West's respective regional reporter, and there will only be one citation for the case. Figure 5-5 indicates with asterisks those states that have ceased official publication.

d. Publication of Federal Cases

(1) United States Supreme Court Cases
United States Supreme Court cases are published in the following three sets of books: *United States Reports* (the official set), *Supreme Court Reporter* (West's unofficial set), and *United States Supreme Court Reports, Lawyers' Edition* (LEXIS's unofficial set, commonly called *Lawyers' Edition*). Thus, all U.S. Supreme Court cases can be found in three different sets of books. In addition, cases from the U.S. Supreme Court are published in the weekly journal *United States Law Week*. The Court also publishes its opinions on its website at *www.supremecourtus.gov*.

(2) Lower Federal Court Cases
Cases decided in the lower federal courts—namely, the intermediate courts of appeal and the district courts—are not published officially. West is the exclusive publisher of cases from these courts. West's set, the *Federal Reporter*, publishes decisions from the intermediate courts of appeal and West's set, the *Federal Supplement*, publishes some decisions from the district courts, which are the trial courts in our federal system.

e. Finding Cases Through the Use of Digests

(1) Introduction
While you know that you can locate cases by using a citation or annotated codes (which send you to cases interpreting statutes), some cases do not interpret statutes and

Digests
Books or indexes that arrange one-sentence summaries or "digests" of cases by subject

Key Number System
West's method of classifying the law to enable researchers to find cases on similar topics

Key Number
Number assigned by West to a topic of the law to enable researchers to find cases on similar topics

thus cannot be found through the use of annotated codes such as U.S.C.A. or U.S.C.S. One way to find cases is through the use of sets of books called **digests.** Digests serve as case finders. They arrange cases by subject matter so that, for example, all of the battery cases are brought together and all of the contracts cases are brought together. These digests, however, do not reprint in full all of the battery cases; rather, they print a brief one-sentence summary or "digest" of each battery case and then provide you with a citation so you can determine whether to retrieve and read the case. While there are several varieties of digests, all of them function in a similar manner. Most are published by West. The most comprehensive digest set published by West is called the *American Digest System*. Once you understand how to use this digest set, you will be able to use all other West digests because they are all organized in the same manner. Almost all West publications show pictures of keys that inform the reader that the set is a participant in the West digest system, sometimes called the **Key Number System**.

(2) Organization of West's **American Digest System**

West has categorized all of American case law into various topics. In fact, West has created more than 400 topic names for areas of law (for example, Corporations, Trespass, and Negligence) and has assigned various numbers, called **Key Numbers,** to specific areas of law. When an editor at West receives a case from a court, the editor reads the case; divides it into separate issues of law, each of which is represented by a headnote; and then assigns each of the headnotes one of West's more than 400 topic names and a number, the Key Number. For example, West might assign the topic name and Key Number "Landlord and Tenant 166" to a case dealing with injury to a tenant's property in leased premises. Every time thereafter that any portion of a case reported in the *National Reporter System* discusses injury to a tenant's property in leased premises, West will create a headnote for the case and assign it the topic name and Key Number "Landlord and Tenant 166."

West then gathers all of the headnotes into the *American Digest System*, which allows researchers to readily find numerous cases from all over the country that deal with the same issue. The *American Digest System* comprises sets of books with each set covering a ten-year period called a Decennial. Thus, the Tenth Decennial (Parts 1 and 2) covers the period 1986-1996; the Ninth Decennial (Parts 1 and 2) covers the period 1976-1986, and so forth, all the way back to the First Decennial, which covers 1897-1906.

(3) How to Find Cases Using Digests

Assume you are asked to research whether a tenant may recover damages from her landlord when the tenant's valuable rug is ruined by rain caused by a leak in the roof at the leased premises. Further assume that you need to find cases from all over the United States on this issue.

Locate the most recent Decennial, which is the Eleventh Decennial, Part 1. Locate the volume(s) called the Descriptive Word Index. Use the descriptive word research approach and look up words in this index that describe your research problem (for example, "landlord," "tenant," "leased premises," and so forth). You will be given your topic name (Landlord and Tenant) and your Key Number (166).

Once you have your topic name and Key Number, you merely look these up in the various decennial units of the *American Digest System*, which are arranged alphabetically on the library shelves. Thus, if you look up "Landlord and Tenant 166" in the Eleventh Decennial, Part 1, you will be presented with all of the headnotes from all of the cases reported in the various units of the *National Reporter System* that were decided between 1996-2001 (the five-year period covered by the Eleventh Decennial, Part 1) that relate to injuries to a tenant's property. The entries are carefully arranged, with federal cases given first and then state cases arranged alphabetically. If you do not find what you need in the Eleventh Decennial, Part 1, proceed back through each of the Decennial units, ending with the First Decennial, which covers 1897 to 1906.

As an alternate to the descriptive word approach, if you know the name of a case, you can research it in an alphabetically arranged Table of Cases (which accompanies most Decennial units). You will be given the citation(s) to the case and a list of the topics and Key Numbers under which it has been digested.

(4) Specialized Digests

The *American Digest System* is most useful when conducting comprehensive research, because it covers all federal and state cases from 1897 to the present time. If you do not need to conduct such thorough research, West has created several specialized digests that will assist you in locating cases from a specific jurisdiction, region, or state, all of which are organized identically to the *American Digest System*. The following specialized digests are kept up to date by annual cumulative pocket parts.

- **United States Supreme Court digest**. This digest provides headnotes and references only to U.S. Supreme Court cases.
- **Federal practice digests.** West has created several digests that serve as casefinders for cases from the federal courts.
- **Regional digests.** West has created the following regional digests, which allow researchers to locate cases from a given region: *Atlantic Digest, North Western Digest, Pacific Digest*, and *South Eastern Digest*.
- **State digests.** West publishes state-specific digests for 47 of the states (Delaware, Nevada, and Utah are excluded) and the District of Columbia, allowing researchers to readily locate cases from a given state when such is sufficient for their research purposes.
- **Other specialized digests.** West has created other digests as well, such as the *Bankruptcy Digest* and the *Military Justice Digest*.

C. FINDING THE LAW USING SECONDARY AUTHORITIES

Secondary sources lack the binding authority of relevant primary authorities; they are persuasive only. Nevertheless, they are often highly respected for summarizing, criticizing, and explaining the primary authorities. Moreover, the secondary authorities often help you locate relevant primary sources. Some of the better-known secondary sources include the following sets of books.

1. Encyclopedias

Legal encyclopedias function in the same way as any other encyclopedias in that they discuss various topics. Legal encyclopedias thus explain legal subjects, in alphabetical order, from abandonment to zoning. The multivolume sets are arranged alphabetically and provide articulate (but often basic) discussions of legal topics in a sentence-by-sentence format. You will be directed to cases and other authorities that support these narrative statements through the use of footnotes. The narrative sentences appear on the top half of each page, and the supporting footnotes are found on the bottom half. Encyclopedias are kept current through the use of annual cumulative pocket parts.

There are two competing general encyclopedias that attempt to explain all of American law: C.J.S. (short for *Corpus Juris Secundum*, meaning "body of law, second") and Am. Jur. 2d (short for *American Jurisprudence*, Second Series). Both sets are now published by West. In addition to these general sets, some states, usually the more populous ones, such as California, New York, and Texas, have their own local sets. Use the descriptive word approach or topic approach to access all encyclopedias.

Remember that encyclopedias are considered somewhat elementary in their approach. Thus, they are seldom cited in court documents. Rather, they are most useful for familiarizing you with an area of law and sending you to cases that will provide more thorough analysis.

2. Legal Periodicals

Just as you might subscribe to a periodical publication such as *Sports Illustrated*, law firms and legal professionals subscribe to a variety of publications that are produced on a regular or periodic basis. The two best-known types of periodicals are the publications by law schools and the specialized publications for those in the legal profession sharing similar interests.

Most law schools produce a periodical publication generally referred to as a "law review," such as the *Harvard Law Review*. These are typically published several times each year. Law reviews provide thorough and scholarly analysis of legal topics and are routinely cited with approval by the courts.

Just as individuals interested in fashion might subscribe to *Vogue*, legal practitioners who have an interest in a specialized area of law might subscribe to a specialized periodical. Thus, the *American Bankruptcy Law Journal* will be of interest to practitioners working in the area of bankruptcy law. There are hundreds of specialized periodicals that help keep practitioners current in their chosen fields.

The primary means used to conduct research and to find a relevant periodical article is to use a separately published index, generally either the *Index to Legal Periodicals & Books* or the *Current Law Index*. Both allow you to find articles using three approaches. You can look up the subject you are interested in (for example, aviation law), an author you are interested in (for example, Laurence H. Tribe), or the name of a case you are interested in (for example, *Bush v. Gore*). You will be referred to various articles about the topic of interest, or written by the relevant author, or about the case you selected. You will then retrieve the articles, read them, and locate other authorities discussed in the periodical article. Although periodical publications are not primary authorities, they are highly respected and are often cited in briefs and court documents.

3. Texts and Treatises

Treatises
Books or texts on various legal topics that are written by expert authors

Texts written by legal scholars that focus on one topic of the law are referred to as **treatises.** Treatises comment upon and analyze an area of law. They are usually multi-volume sets such as the six-volume set *McCarthy on Trademarks and Unfair Competition*, and they are usually written by academics or practicing attorneys. The discussion of the topics within the set is typically presented in a sentence-by-sentence narrative form, and footnotes at the bottom of each page send readers to supporting cases and other authorities.

Treatises are easy books to use because there is a comprehensive index in the last volume of the set. Use the descriptive word research approach, look up words in the index that describe your problem, and you will be sent to the appropriate volume and section in the set. Most treatises also provide a thorough table of contents in the first volume, making it easy to find the particular discussion in which you are interested. Treatises are kept current either by annual pocket parts or through individual replacement pages.

4. Restatements

The Restatements are multivolume sets of books on specific topics. They are the product of a group of legal scholars called the American Law Institute (ALI). The goal of ALI is to restate U.S. case law in a clear and concise manner. Each Restatement (for example, Restatement (Second) of Torts) typically consists of only three to five volumes. Each volume is arranged in chapters, and the chapters are arranged in sections. Each section relates to a principle of the law in clear straightforward language printed in bold typeface. These Restatement sections are followed by "Comments" and "Illustrations" that serve to explain the principle further.

The easiest way to locate a pertinent Restatement provision is to use the descriptive word approach. Consult the alphabetically arranged index to your Restatement, which is usually found in the last volume of the Restatement set. Look up words or phrases that describe your research problem and you will be directed to the appropriate section of the Restatement. Alternatively, you may be directed to a pertinent Restatement section in the course of your research; for example, a case you may be reading may refer to a Restatement section. The Restatements are kept current through appendix volumes, which contain pocket parts.

Because the Restatements are a secondary source, courts are not required to adopt or follow the Restatement positions. Nevertheless, the Restatements have been cited in cases more than 100,000 times. Many legal experts believe the Restatements are the most highly regarded of all of the secondary authorities. You should freely rely on them and cite to them in your research projects.

5. A.L.R. Annotations

American Law Reports (A.L.R.) is a West publication that publishes selected appellate court decisions as well as comprehensive and objective essays, called Annotations, relating to the legal issues raised in a case. The editors at West select cases they believe are interesting or present novel issues and publish them in A.L.R. The editors or various authors then prepare thorough and scholarly monographs or articles that examine the area of law discussed in the case.

The most current set is called A.L.R.5th. There is another set called A.L.R. Fed. that publishes selected federal cases and articles about these cases. To find an A.L.R. annotation, use the multivolume index called the A.L.R. Index and then use the descriptive word approach to look up words or phrases in this index that describe your research issue. You will then be directed to the appropriate annotation. Since 1965, A.L.R. has used annual cumulative pocket parts to update its annotations.

6. Miscellaneous Secondary Authorities

While the most frequently used secondary authorities are encyclopedias, legal periodicals, treatises, Restatements, and A.L.R. annotations, there are numerous other secondary authorities that researchers often use. The following are the most commonly used of these miscellaneous secondary authorities.

- **Legal dictionaries.** A legal dictionary will give you the spelling, pronunciation, and meaning of a legal word or phrase such as "en banc" or "abatement." The best known of the legal dictionaries is the thorough *Black's Law Dictionary* (8th ed. 2004).
- **Form books.** Much of a legal professional's time is spent drafting documents. Some documents are litigation-related, such as complaints or answers, while others are transaction-related, such as a partnership agreement. Form books help practitioners get a jump start on drafting these documents by providing sample forms. Most sets of form books are multivolume sets with an alphabetically arranged index that allows you to use the descriptive word research method to locate desired forms.
- **Looseleaf services.** Looseleaf services are sets of ringed binders with individual loose sheets of paper, which are easily removed and replaced. The looseleaf services are a variety of treatises. Many are devoted to rules and regulations promulgated by our federal agencies, such as the service titled *Labor Law Reporter.* The looseleaf services usually include both primary authorities (such as cases, statutes, and administrative regulations) as well as secondary authorities (such as commentary and discussion of the topic and recent developments). Generally, looseleaf services function as "finding" tools in that they provide general background information about a topic of the law and then direct you to relevant primary authorities. Use the descriptive word approach and look up words in the alphabetically arranged index to be directed to the appropriate volume and paragraph or section in the set.
- **Directories.** Directories are lists of lawyers. The best-known directory is the *Martindale-Hubbell Law Directory,* which includes biographical information for attorneys. The set, consisting of more than 20 volumes, is produced annually. It is arranged alphabetically by state and then alphabetically by city and law firm name. The set also includes two volumes, usually called the State Digests, which provide a brief overview of some of the laws of all 50 states. While *Martindale-Hubbell* will not include all of the laws of these jurisdictions, it will provide a summary of some of the more common laws of each state. Thus, for example, you will be able to determine the fees for creating a corporation in each state, residency requirements to obtain a divorce, and so forth. The State Digest volumes are arranged alphabetically, from Alabama to Wyoming, allowing easy access to information. See Figure 5-6 for a chart reviewing legal authorities.

	FIGURE 5-6				
	CHART OF LEGAL AUTHORITIES				
Authority	**Overview**	**Identification of Sets**	**Supplemen-tation**	**Research Techniques**	**Use Notes**
Statutes (Federal) and U.S. Constitution	Statutes are arranged by topic into "titles"; U.S. Constitution is arranged by articles and amendments	U.S.C. (official set); U.S.C.A. and U.S.C.S. (unofficial sets)	Annual cumulative pocket parts	Descriptive word approach; topic approach; or popular name approach	Unofficial sets contain highly useful annotations or references to cases inter-preting statutes
Statutes (State) and State Constitutions	Statutes are arranged by topic; state constitutions are arranged by articles and amendments	Various sets, both official and unofficial, depending on state	Annual cumulative pocket parts	Descriptive word approach; topic approach; or popular name approach	Nearly all sets contain highly useful annotations or references to cases interpreting statutes
Cases	Arranged in sets of books called "reports" or "reporters" in chronologi-cal order	Reporters may be official or unofficial	None; new cases appear in softcover, tem-porary "advance sheets"	Use annotations in statutes or digests to find cases	Digests are excellent case finders
Encyclo-pedias	Alphabetically arranged narrative statements of hundreds of legal topics, supported by cases in footnotes	General sets are C.J.S. and Am. Jur. 2d; about ten states have their own local sets	Annual cumulative pocket parts	Descriptive word approach or topic approach	Good introductory information but somewhat elementary in their approach
Legal Periodicals	Publications produced on a periodic basis on a variety of topics	Law school publications and special interest publications	No supple-mentation	*Index to Legal Periodicals & Books* or *Current Law Index*	Periodicals are often scholarly and well respected

FIGURE 5-6 (CONTINUED)
CHART OF LEGAL AUTHORITIES

Authority	Overview	Identification of Sets	Supplemen-tation	Research Techniques	Use Notes
Texts and Treatises	Texts written by scholars on one topic that analyze cases and statutes	Multivolume sets include thorough analysis	Annual cumulative pocket parts; new pages; or softcover supplements	Descriptive word approach; topic approach; table of cases approach	Many treatises are highly regarded
Restatements	Statements of the law in clear language	Multivolume sets on selected areas of the law, such as trusts	Annual cumulative pocket parts	Descriptive word approach; topic approach	Restatements are highly authoritative
A.L.R. Annotations	Thorough essays or "annotations" on various legal topics	Multivolume sets	Annual cumulative pocket parts	Descriptive word approach	A.L.R. annotations are very well respected
Dictionaries	Books providing definitions of legal words and phrases	One-volume alphabetical arrangements of words and phrases	No supple-mentation; each volume is complete	Alphabetical approach	Useful to determine meaning of a word or phrase
Form Books	Sets of books with standard forms to help in drafting documents	Multivolume sets of books	Pocket parts	Descriptive word approach; topic approach	Used primarily to assist in preparing documents
Looseleaf Services	Type of treatise devoted to one area of law	Multivolume sets of ringed binders	Replacement pages	Descriptive word approach	Services provide a thorough overview of an area of law
Directories	Lists of lawyers	Multivolume sets; *Martindale-Hubbell* includes useful "State Digest" volumes	New set issued annually	Alphabetical approach	Used to locate attorneys and law firms; State Digest volumes pro-vide brief summaries of some laws of all states

D. RESEARCH STRATEGIES

There are few inflexible rules in legal research: You are usually asked to provide an answer to a legal question. To reach that answer, there are a number of strategies available to you.

Before you begin grabbing books, spend a few minutes thinking about the issue you are researching. Develop a list of descriptive words and phrases. Because almost all legal authorities are accessed by alphabetically arranged indexes and the descriptive word research approach is usually the most efficient method of using an index, a list of descriptive words will help you begin your research. If you have trouble thinking of words, expand your list by thinking of related words, such as synonyms and antonyms. Consider using the "TAPP Rule" recommended by the former Lawyers Cooperative Publishing Company in determining which words to use to access an index:

T	Consider the <u>T</u>hing involved in the problem.
A	Consider the <u>A</u>ct committed or the cause of <u>A</u>ction (or defense) a party would assert.
P	Consider the <u>P</u>ersons involved in a problem.
P	Consider the <u>P</u>lace involved.

The following are some tips to ensure your research is sufficiently thorough:

- Always examine the statutes. Use an annotated code because it will refer you to cases.
- Use encyclopedias (C.J.S., Am. Jur. 2d, or a local set for your state) to obtain introductory information about the issue you are researching.
- If you cannot locate cases through an annotated code (because the issue is not dealt with by statutes), use digests. The Decennial digests may be used for a global approach, and federal- or state-specific digests may be used to locate cases from certain federal courts or states.
- If you are presented with numerous cases, consider the following strategy: read newer cases before you read older cases; read cases from higher courts before you read cases from lower courts; and always read cases from your own or forum jurisdiction before you read cases from a foreign jurisdiction.
- If there is a well-known treatise or text on your topic, examine it because it will provide excellent analysis as well as references to cases.
- For a thorough overview of a topic, consult A.L.R. (or A.L.R. Fed. for federal issues).
- For discussions of new or controversial issues or a comprehensive examination of an issue, find periodical articles through the *Index to Legal Periodicals & Books* or *Current Law Index*.
- Use *Shepard's Citations* or KeyCite (see Section F of this chapter) to locate other cases, legal periodicals, and sources. See Figure 5-7 for a blueprint for legal research.

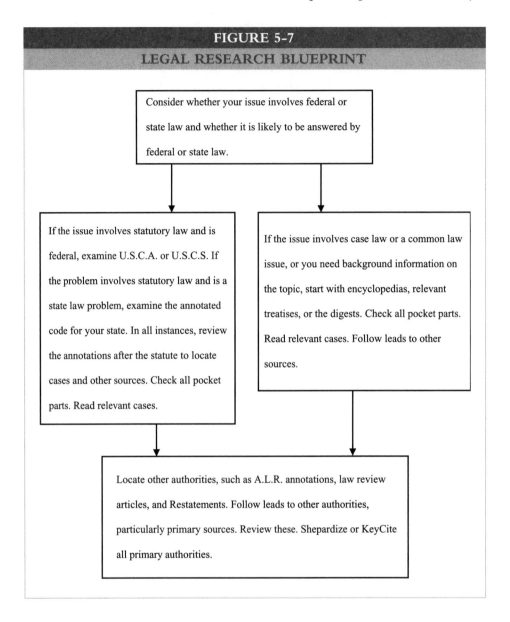

FIGURE 5-7

LEGAL RESEARCH BLUEPRINT

Consider whether your issue involves federal or state law and whether it is likely to be answered by federal or state law.

If the issue involves statutory law and is federal, examine U.S.C.A. or U.S.C.S. If the problem involves statutory law and is a state law problem, examine the annotated code for your state. In all instances, review the annotations after the statute to locate cases and other sources. Check all pocket parts. Read relevant cases.

If the issue involves case law or a common law issue, or you need background information on the topic, start with encyclopedias, relevant treatises, or the digests. Check all pocket parts. Read relevant cases. Follow leads to other sources.

Locate other authorities, such as A.L.R. annotations, law review articles, and Restatements. Follow leads to other authorities, particularly primary sources. Review these. Shepardize or KeyCite all primary authorities.

E. CITATION FORM

1. Introduction

A critical part of the writing process in many documents is citing to legal authorities. Every legal assertion made in a document must be supported by legal authority. These supporting authorities appear as **citations** in your document. Citations must appear in a standard and consistent format so that any reader will be able to retrieve the legal authority you cited and verify that you have accurately represented the status of the law. Thus, legal writers communicate using the same "language" or citation form.

Citation
A reference to a legal authority, such as a case

2. Citation Systems

There are two primary guides to citation form in the United States:

- The **Bluebook.** The oldest and best-known system of citation is found in *The Bluebook: A Uniform System of Citation* (Columbia Law Review Ass'n et al. eds., 18th ed. 2005) (the "*Bluebook*"). The *Bluebook* is complex and the rules are often poorly worded with few examples. Nevertheless, because most judges and practicing professionals were taught to use the *Bluebook* for citation format, at present it is the most commonly used citation manual.

- *ALWD.* In 2000, the Association of Legal Writing Directors and Professor Darby Dickerson produced an alternative to the *Bluebook*: ALWD & Darby Dickerson, *ALWD Citation Manual* (2d ed., Aspen Publishers 2003). Called *ALWD* (pronounced "all wood"), the citation system was intended to provide an easy to learn and user-friendly alternative to the *Bluebook*. In many instances, the *ALWD* format is identical to *Bluebook* format. There are, however, several differences, and the presentation and numerous examples in *ALWD* make it far easier to use than the *Bluebook*.

Bluebook
Citation manual providing rules for citing legal authorities

ALWD
Citation manual providing rules for citing legal authorities

While there are other guides to citation form, the most notable of which is the *Chicago Manual of Legal Citation*, usually referred to as the *Maroonbook* and used primarily in the Chicago metropolitan area, the *Bluebook* is probably the best-known system at this time, although *ALWD* continues to attract a great deal of interest because of its sensible rules and approach. Follow your school, firm, or office practice. Note, however, that if local citation rules exist for a court or jurisdiction, they must be followed and will supersede any citation system.

See Figure 5-8 and Appendix G for examples of citation form for both the *Bluebook* and *ALWD*.

FIGURE 5-8

QUICK REFERENCE: CITATION FORM

Citations provide information enabling readers to locate references to primary and secondary authorities relied upon by legal writers. While citation form is discussed more in depth in Appendix G, following are some basic rules and examples of citation form for statutes and cases.

Statutes: **Cite federal statutes to the title of the code, name of the set, section number, and year of code (and if you cite to U.S.C.A. or U.S.C.S., include the name of the publisher). Unless otherwise noted, the forms shown for federal statutes are acceptable for both the *Bluebook* and *ALWD*.**

- 35 U.S.C. § 602 (2000)
- 35 U.S.C.A. § 602 (West 1999)
- *ALWD:* 35 U.S.C.S. § 602 (LEXIS 2003)
- *Bluebook:* 35 U.S.C.S. § 602 (LexisNexis 2003)

Cite state statutes as shown in *Bluebook* Table 1 and *ALWD* Appendix 1.

- Wis. Stat. Ann. § 12-204 (West 1998)
- Cal. Prob. Code § 6450 (West 2002)

FIGURE 5-8 (CONTINUED)
QUICK REFERENCE: CITATION FORM

Cases: **Generally, cite cases to the name of the case, volume number of the set, name of the case reporter, page on which the case begins, and year of decision. There is some variation between the *Bluebook* and *ALWD*.**

- U.S. Supreme Court: *Allen v. Taylor*, 420 U.S. 166 (1999)
- Federal courts of appeal: *Kim v. Gray*, 909 F.2d 18 (4th Cir. 1987)
- Federal district courts: *In re Lee*, 899 F. Supp. 16 (S.D.N.Y. 1992)
- Iowa case: *In re Olson*, 681 N.W.2d 90 (Iowa 1995)
- Kansas case: *Peters v. Mills*, 452 Kan. 199, 18 P.3d 877 (1999)*

* Local rules may require parallel cites in some instances.

F. VALIDATING YOUR RESEARCH

1. Introduction

Before you cite any primary authority in any document you prepare, you must be sure it is still good law. This is an inflexible rule of legal research. Updating and validating your authorities can be conducted manually (using a set of books called *Shepard's Citations*) or electronically on LEXIS (using *Shepard's Citations*) or on Westlaw (using its system called **KeyCite**). In the "old days," when everyone used the conventional printed sources, the process was always called **Shepardizing.** This term is often used today to describe the process of ensuring your authorities are still valid. Few people validate their authorities manually any longer because validating electronically is quicker and provides more current information.

While the primary reason for validating your authorities is that it is an act of legal malpractice not to do so, another reason to validate is that when you Shepardize or KeyCite, not only will you be informed whether your authorities are still good law, you will also be referred to other sources in the law library that discuss or mention your case or other authority, allowing you to access additional authorities and expand your research efforts. For example, when you Shepardize a case, you are referred to every case that mentions your case thereafter, as well as other authorities, such as law review articles, A.L.R. annotations, and other authorities that mention or discuss your case.

2. Using *Shepard's Citations* in Print Form

There is a set of *Shepard's Citations* books for each set of case books in a law library. For example, *Shepard's Pacific Citations* is used to validate cases published in the *Pacific Reporter.* Follow these steps to Shepardize a case (assume the case is *Henry v. Jones,* 182 Cal. 3d 118):

- Locate the set of *Shepard's California Citations* (this four- or five-volume set is usually located after the last volume of California cases on the law library shelf).

KeyCite
West's online software program that validates primary authorities to ensure they are still valid

Sheperdizing
Process of validating primary authorities to ensure they are still valid

- Open the first volume of *Shepard's California Citations* and look in the upper left- and right-hand page corners for a boldface **Vol. 182** (because the *Henry* case is located in volume 182 of the *California Reports*).
- Scan down the page looking for a boldface number **118** (because the *Henry* case begins on page 118).
- Examine the entries given. You will be given the parallel citation for the *Henry* case in parentheses. You will be given other entries that do not appear in parentheses. These nonparenthetical references direct you to other sources that have mentioned *Henry* since the time of its decision. *Shepard's Citations* uses an elaborate system of abbreviations to tell you about the status of a case. Thus, if you were to see the entry "r192Cal4th104," this would tell you that the *Henry* case was reversed by a case located at 192 Cal. 4th 104. Similarly, the letter "f" is an abbreviation for "followed," and the letter "c" means criticized. Each volume of *Shepard's Citations* includes a full explanation of the abbreviations it uses. Review any references that indicate that *Henry* may no longer be good law.
- Continue this process in all relevant volumes of *Shepard's California Citations*.

3. Electronic Validation

Validating primary authorities electronically provides more up-to-date information than using conventional print volumes of *Shepard's Citations* and is easily accomplished. There is no need to learn quirky abbreviations such as "m" for modified. Negative history, such as reversal of a case, is spelled out in plain English. Moreover, there is no need to gather together numerous bulky volumes of *Shepard's Citations*.

The most common way citation updating is now performed is through the use of *Shepard's Citations* online (through the LEXIS computerized research system) or through the use of West's online product, KeyCite.

The process of validating your authorities is much the same for either *Shepard's Citations* online or KeyCite. An icon or screen indicator will appear on your computer screen indicating either "*Shepard's*" or "KeyCite." When you select the indicator, you then type in your citation and the case will be immediately validated.

You are now ready to interpret your results. You will be informed in plain English whether your case has been followed, distinguished, criticized, and so forth. You will also be given the full citation for your case and any parallel citations.

Because keying in a series of citations can be time-consuming, both LEXIS and Westlaw offer software programs that automatically extract citations from an entire document and check their validity at one time. A printed report is produced with the results of the check. LEXIS's software program is called "CheckCite" and Westlaw's product is called "WestCheck." Both are easy to use.

4. Validating Other Authorities

In addition to validating cases, you must also validate other primary authorities— namely, statutes, constitutions, and administrative regulations. Moreover, you are also able to update other authorities. For example, if you have read an interesting law review article, you can update it to see if any more recently published law review articles discuss it. The process of validating these other authorities is identical to the processes described above.

G. COMPUTER-ASSISTED LEGAL RESEARCH

1. Introduction

There are two major competing computer-assisted research services: LEXIS and Westlaw. These research systems provide access to a tremendous variety of cases, statutes, administrative regulations, and numerous other authorities that a law firm or other employer may not otherwise be able to afford. The more familiar you become with LEXIS or Westlaw, the more efficient you will be at locating the information you need. LEXIS and Westlaw operate in essentially the same manner; most users, however, eventually develop a preference for one or the other.

Each service consists of thousands of databases. The databases include cases, statutes, administrative regulations, and other materials for you to access. In general, research using LEXIS and Westlaw is very similar. Both allow easy retrieval of cases, statutes, and other materials when you already have a citation. You merely type the citation into an open field and click on "Go" or a similar button. When you do not have a citation, you will usually access the appropriate database (such as selecting federal cases or state cases) and then formulate a search question by using **Boolean searching** (a search method using symbols, word fragments, and numbers rather than plain English) or by using plain English.

Boolean searching
Method of searching for legal authorities on the computer using numbers, symbols, and connectors rather than plain English terms

Both LEXIS and Westlaw offer training courses and written materials describing their systems. Often a complete tutorial package is available consisting of written descriptions of the systems as well as floppy disks or CD-ROMs to demonstrate use of the system. Contact:

LEXIS-NEXIS	West Group
P.O. Box 083	610 Opperman Drive
Dayton, OH 45401	Eagan, MN 55123
24-hour toll-free customer service:	Toll-free customer service:
1 (800) 543-6862	1 (800) Westlaw
www.lexis.com	*www.westlaw.com*

While LEXIS and Westlaw are the acknowledged giants in the field of computer-assisted legal research, a number of other companies offer access on a fee basis to legal materials through the Internet. Most charge moderate fees and appeal to smaller firms and sole practitioners. One of the better known is Loislaw (*www. loislaw.com*) a system offering case law, statutes, administrative law, and court rules for all states and federal courts.

2. Getting Started Using LEXIS or Westlaw

Getting started usually requires you to sign on to either LEXIS or Westlaw and to type in an identification signal and password assigned to you by your school or employer. When performing research on the job, you will usually enter a client's name or number so that the client can be billed for the time spent conducting the research. In most firms, legal professionals have desktop computer access to LEXIS, Westlaw, or both.

The first screen presented to you after sign-on usually allows you to retrieve a document or case (if you know the citation), check a citation (either through *Shepard's Citations* or KeyCite), or to construct a search if you do not have a citation.

3. Boolean Searching

You will find that computers are extremely literal. They will not search for cases containing the word "collision" if you search for "collide." Thus, Boolean searching allows you to use symbols, numbers, and connectors to overcome the literalness of the computer. For example, both LEXIS and Westlaw use an exclamation point (!) to substitute for any number of additional letters at the end of a word. Thus, "colli!" will locate "collide," "collision," "colliding," and so forth. Of course, words such as "collie" will also appear, so use the symbols carefully. Using connectors such as "or" also helps locate additional documents. A search for "tenant or lessee" will locate documents containing either or both of these words. Both LEXIS and Westlaw offer publications that explain the use of search symbols, numbers, and connectors.

These symbols and connectors help you limit your search and make it more manageable. If you merely entered "First Amendment," LEXIS and Westlaw would retrieve thousands of documents containing these two words. A more effective search would be "first amendment /50 free! and press." This instructs LEXIS and Westlaw to locate only documents that contain the phrase "first amendment" within 50 words of the words "freedom" or "free" and "press."

4. Plain English Searching

Recognizing that many individuals find working with Boolean connectors awkward, LEXIS has introduced "Freestyle" and Westlaw has introduced "WIN" (an acronym for "Westlaw Is Natural") to allow you to enter your issue in plain English and eliminate the need for symbols, numbers, and connectors. Thus, you could enter a search question such as "When can unmarried or single individuals adopt children?"

Construct your searches before you sign on so that you work efficiently and do not incur excessive costs. Draft some sample queries and search terms. Although using natural language is easier when constructing queries, using Boolean searching usually produces more precise results.

5. Summary of Computer-Assisted Legal Research

Both LEXIS and Westlaw are extremely cooperative in training and assisting researchers. Both provide toll-free numbers, worksheets, tutorials, and interactive training. Contact LEXIS and Westlaw and ask for help and information at the addresses given above.

Keep in mind that some tasks are best performed by using conventional legal research tools such as books while others are best performed by using LEXIS or Westlaw. Still other tasks might call for you to blend both methods of research. Knowing which method to use requires an analysis of many factors, including the complexity of your task, the costs involved, and time constraints. Many teachers urge students to first become familiar with the conventional print tools before becoming too wedded to computer-assisted legal research. Strong skills in manual legal research provide a good foundation for using LEXIS and Westlaw more effectively.

Use conventional print sources when:

- You need to "get your feet wet" and get some background about an area of the law.
- You need a thorough and comprehensive analysis of an area of the law, such as that provided by a treatise.

- You are having difficulty formulating research queries for LEXIS or Westlaw because you are unfamiliar with the issue you are researching.
- It would be more cost-effective and easier to use traditional print sources to get a quick answer to a question than to incur costs by using LEXIS or Westlaw.

Use computer-assisted legal research when:

- You already have a citation to a known case or other authority.
- You are looking for cases involving a known party, attorney, or judge.
- The area of law is new or evolving.
- You are looking for the most current information available.
- You are validating your primary authorities (by Shepardizing or KeyCiting).

Computer-assisted legal research is a valuable tool. The services provide rapid access to a wide range of materials that no law firm could afford to purchase or shelve. Nevertheless, computer-assisted legal research may be expensive and will only produce useful results if you understand how to make the system work effectively for you. This takes practice and experience. Legal research is not as easy as merely typing some words into a query box. Effective researchers use a combination of computer-assisted legal research and conventional research techniques to obtain the best results for clients.

H. USING THE INTERNET FOR LEGAL RESEARCH

1. Introduction

Every year more and more cases, statutes, and other legal authorities are available on the Internet. While the Internet will likely never replace conventional research methods and while there are some significant drawbacks to Internet legal research, it is an extremely efficient and timesaving method to obtain some legal materials at no cost, 24 hours each day.

The advent of the Internet has dramatically changed legal research, allowing professionals immediate access to cases, statutes, forms, legislative materials, and much more. In some instances, cases are posted to the Internet within hours after their release by a court. Nevertheless, resist the temptation to over-rely on the Internet. Most legal research instructors believe that students who thoroughly master conventional research techniques before using electronic or Internet tools are better and more precise researchers.

The general duty imposed on legal professionals to have a sufficient level of competence to represent clients is broad enough to require competence in new and emerging technologies. Clients are increasingly technologically proficient and expect their legal team to be equally proficient.

Start page
A reliable website used to begin research using the Internet

2. Using a Good Start Page

There is probably no better strategy for conducting legal research on the Internet than to begin your project with one good "start page." Your **start page** should be reliable and easy to use. The advantage of always beginning at the same place or start page is that you will quickly become familiar with the page and it will serve as an excellent jumping-off point for your research tasks.

Some sites are considered more reliable than others. Generally, the "gov" (government) sites are probably the most authoritative, followed by the "edu" (educational) sites, followed by the "com" (commercial) and "org" (organization) sites.

To begin searching on the Internet, log onto your computer, double click on the icon that identifies your Internet service provider (for example, AOL), and type either an Internet address (such as *www.sec.gov*) into the address box at the top of your page or type a word or phrase into the search box that appears when you access AOL or other Internet service provider.

While there are many start pages from which you can begin your legal research, the following are some well-known legal favorites:

- *www.law.cornell.edu*. The Legal Information Institute of Cornell Law School is an excellent and reliable starting place for legal issues and offers direct links to cases, statutes, and numerous other materials.
- *www.washlaw.edu*. The site of Washburn University School of Law lists legal materials, courts, and states in alphabetical order, making it very easy to locate materials of interest.
- *www.findlaw.com*. FindLaw is one of the best-known commercial sites. It directs users to a vast array of legal materials, including cases, statutes, forms, reference materials, and legal periodicals. Links to hundreds of sources of interest to legal professionals are provided, including special links for students. Although FindLaw is a commercial site (rather than an educational one) it is highly reliable and easy to use. FindLaw is part of West Group.
- *www.megalaw.com*. MegaLaw is a portal to numerous other sites. It provides links to federal and state law, forms, court rules, and materials on legal topics. The site is user-friendly and comprehensive.

One excellent all-purpose site for finding nearly anything is the site called "Google" at *www.google.com*. Type in a citation, a question, or a phrase into the search box and you will be given a list of sites. The site is easy to use and highly reliable. The practice is so well known that it is called **Googling**. For example, to locate information on strategies to improve classroom learning, simply Google "study skills" or a similar term. You will be presented with a list of relevant sites that offer information on study skills and academic success.

Keep in mind that most government sites offer excellent information, publications, guides, and links to relevant statutes. In many instances you can "guess" at website addresses for government agencies. For example, the website of the Internal Revenue Service is *www.irs.gov*.

Googling
Method of Internet research in which user types key terms or words into the search box provided on Google's website at *www.google.com*

3. Internet Legal Research Strategies

It is far easier to get distracted when researching on the Internet than when researching using conventional print volumes. A site piques your interest so you click on it. Another site looks promising and you click on that one. Before you know it, you have drifted away from your topic. Following are some tips and strategies to help ensure that your Internet research is as efficient as possible:

- **Take notes.** Rather than jumping from site to site, jot down the sites that look promising and visit them later. Stay focused on the task at hand.
- **Use bookmarks.** When you determine that there are certain sites that you continually visit or that provide you with useful information, "bookmark" them or add them to your "favorites" list so that you can readily return to them.
- **Avoid reading the screen.** Do not spend too much time reading the screens. Reading material on a computer screen is often tiring and causes eyestrain. If an article or case appears promising, print it and read it in hard-copy form.
- **Never rely completely on the Internet.** While the Internet provides some excellent information and is often the easiest and cheapest way to find a case or statute, it is not a substitute for a law library. Relying solely on the Internet for legal research will result in a research project that lacks in-depth analysis. Many unpublished cases find their way onto the Internet. No one edits out the "dog" cases. Some courts prohibit citations to unpublished decisions. Thus, you should exercise care.
- **Be aware of gaps in information.** While a law library and LEXIS and Westlaw offer all federal court cases, some Internet sites offer only more recent lower federal court opinions. Thus, research on the Internet cannot be a complete substitute for other means of research.
- **Review materials.** Retrieving a case is not the same as analyzing it. Locating a case or statute is just the beginning of a research task. Cases that interpret the statute must be analyzed and other secondary authorities should be consulted.
- **Be cautious.** Much of the material that appears on the Internet is anonymous. Thus, you do not know the credibility or reputation of the author. Those who post articles and information on the Internet may be reliable experts. Then again, they may not be; there is no way to know for sure. Even the most reputable-seeming sites are subject to abuse.

So long as you remember these cautionary notes, the Internet remains a valuable and efficient tool for beginning a research project or obtaining some cases and statutes. Nevertheless, it can never substitute for a full, in-depth analysis of legal materials.

4. Using the Internet to Impress Clients

While you may be tempted to think that the Internet is primarily useful in performing legal research, it can also be used in a number of far more practical ways. First, you will need to understand how to navigate around the Internet to obtain basic information, such as confirming the correct spelling and punctuation of a corporate client's name (use *www.hoovers.com*) or obtaining directions to the client's place of business (use *www.mapquest.com*). Second, consider using the Internet to keep in touch with a client's activities. For example, you can obtain the following information with the click of a keystroke:

- Current price at which a client's stock is trading (use *www.nyse.com* or *www.nasdaq.com*);
- Information about the client's new office locations and expansion plans and descriptions of the company's product lines and competitors (use *www.hoovers.com*); and

■ Updated financial information for publicly traded companies and descriptions of their key officers and players (use *www.sec.gov* or *www.hoovers.com*).

Make a point of periodically visiting your client's website. Look for any information that is newly posted. One useful section offered by many companies is "Press Releases." This section provides any information the company has released to the press, often about important company developments, changes in executive positions, and increased profits. In addition, you should Google your client's name every week or two to see if any other information has been published about the client. Make a conscious effort to mention this information when you speak with the client. Nothing impresses a client more than the fact that the legal team cares about the client's business and takes the time to educate itself about the client's plans and future.

I. ANALYZING THE LAW

Merely finding relevant legal authorities is not sufficient. Legal professionals must analyze these authorities and then apply them to the client's particular fact situation. Following are some techniques and comments about analyzing the various authorities that have been discussed in this chapter.

1. Analyzing Statutes and Regulations

Many statutes and regulations are extremely long, with several phrases embedded within a single sentence and several unfamiliar words included. On many occasions, statutes include limiting language and exclusions. Consider 35 U.S.C. § 101 (2000), the federal statute that defines what material is patentable:

> Whoever invents or discovers any new and useful process, machine, manufacture, or composition of matter, or any new and useful improvement thereof, may obtain a patent therefor, subject to the conditions and requirements of this title.

Although the statute is not lengthy, it does include several words that are unfamiliar in this context, such as "manufacture" or "composition." Furthermore, you cannot assume that your ordinary interpretation of a word such as "improvement" applies in the statute. "Improvement" may mean something slightly different, as interpreted by the courts. Even the word "whoever" needs interpretation. Does it mean that only natural persons may obtain a patent? May a corporation or artificial entity be "whoever" such that it could obtain a patent?

In analyzing statutes (and regulations), consider the following approaches:

■ If the statute or regulation is lengthy or awkwardly written, "take notes" on it and summarize its major components.
■ Identify each component of the statute and determine its meaning. Thus, for the statute above, determine the meaning of "invent," "discover," "useful," "process," and so forth. See if definitions are provided in patent statutes. Many laws begin with a list of defined terms and elements. For example, 35 U.S.C. § 100, the statute section preceding the statute above, defines the terms "invention" and "process." Review these definitions.

- If terms are not defined by statutes, use the cases that follow an annotated statute to locate cases that will provide definitions or interpretations of terms in the statute.
- Read cases that have interpreted the statute to determine how courts have construed and applied the statute.
- Apply the statute to the client's factual problem or issue you are researching.
- Reach a conclusion based on the statute and its various interpretations.
- Shepardize or KeyCite the statute and any cases to ensure they are still valid.

2. Canons of Construction and Statutory Interpretation

Canons of construction
Rules followed by courts in interpreting statutes

Courts have developed some guidelines, usually called **canons of construction**, to assist them in interpreting law. Some of the more common canons are as follows:

Plain meaning rule
Rule followed by courts that words in a statute will be interpreted according to their ordinary meaning

- Under the **plain meaning rule**, courts assume that when terms are not specifically defined, the legislature intended that these words be given their ordinary everyday meaning.
- When an item or term is not mentioned in a statute, courts assume the legislature meant to exclude it.
- Statutes should be construed in such a way as to ensure that they are effective.

Legislative history
The background of a statute; may be examined by courts in interpreting statutes

If courts still cannot discern the meaning of a statute, they may, in their discretion, review the legislative history of a statute. The **legislative history** of a statute is the background underlying a statute. Thus, courts may consider various versions of the bill as it passed through the legislature and compare and contrast these. They may review legislative committee reports and analyze floor debates on the matter to determine the intent of the legislature when it enacted the statute.

3. Analyzing Cases

a. Introduction

Some cases are easier to read and understand than others. Judges often fail to explain or define Latin terms or legal terms of art, because they believe that their audience will readily understand the language in a case. Moreover, many of the issues cases deal with are complex. Thus, reading cases takes some practice. Don't be concerned if it takes you several readings of a case to understand it. You may need to take notes and prepare a diagram or flowchart showing the path the case followed in reaching a court and the relationship of the parties to each other.

b. Techniques for Legal Analysis: Analogizing, Distinguishing, and Synthesizing

On point
A case that will serve as a precedent because it is factually similar and legally relevant; also called a case *on all fours*

Stare decisis means more than simply following settled cases. It means following cases that are factually similar and legally relevant to the case or problem you are researching. Such a case from a court in your jurisdiction equivalent to or higher than the court that will hear your particular case is said to be **on point** or **on all fours** with your case. The goal of case research is to be able to locate cases on point with your particular case. Such cases are binding and must be followed by the court hearing your case. You will probably never find a published case that is exactly the same as the one you are researching. Some facts will be different; some additional issues may be raised in your case that were not dealt with in the published opinion. Thus, legal analysis requires you to read cases, reflect on their similarities and differences, compare and contrast them to your research problem, and then reach a conclusion.

One of the common techniques used in analyzing cases is **analogy**—namely, finding similarities in cases and comparing them to your research issue. If a case you locate is not identical to your case, don't discard it out of hand. Consider whether the differences are immaterial; if so, that case may still serve as a case on point and be binding.

How will you know whether differences are material or immaterial? A key issue or fact, usually called a **relevant issue** or **relevant fact,** is one that contributes to a court's decision. Had the fact or issue been different, the ultimate decision in the case would have been different as well. For example, assume you are researching whether a client committed a burglary when he used fraud or deception to enter a person's house and took money and jewelry. Cases consistently define "burglary" as the act of breaking and entering the house of another with intent to commit a felony therein. When you locate burglary cases, it will probably not be material *which* particular felony a defendant intended to commit or whether the defendant was a man or woman. On the other hand, it will be relevant to the client's particular situation for you to locate cases in which no physical act of "breaking" occurred but rather access to a house was gained by similar means of artifice and fraud.

A technique similar to using analogy to find cases on point is **distinguishing** cases. If you locate cases that are adverse to the client's position, you will attempt to show the court that those cases are inapplicable by distinguishing them from your client's case. You will point out as many differences as possible to show the reader that the case cannot govern the client's case. Try to show that the differences are more than merely superficial differences; that they are so significant that the case is not on point.

The final technique in case analysis is **synthesizing** cases, or bringing together several cases to show how, as a whole, they serve as precedent for the client's case.

Nearly anyone can read a case and then summarize it for a reader. Listing and summarizing cases is not legal analysis. True legal analysis requires you to see the interrelationships among cases, even those that initially appear dissimilar, and show the reader how and why they apply to your research issue.

c. The "IRAC" Method of Analyzing Authorities

In discussing and analyzing authorities, many writers follow what is referred to as the "**IRAC**" method. IRAC is an acronym for Issue, Rule, Analysis or Application, and Conclusion. First, the issue is presented: (*Does the Uniform Partnership Act govern a partnership that has no written agreement?*). Next, the rule or legal authority that governs the issue is discussed. Then the writer analyzes and applies the rule to the writer's particular case situation. After a thorough analysis in which authorities are compared and contrasted, a conclusion is presented.

Other writers use a variation of IRAC, usually called "**CRAC**" (for Conclusion, Rule, Application, and Conclusion). In this type of analysis, the conclusion is given first, followed by the rule of law that supports the conclusion. The rule is explained and illustrated through citation to legal authorities. The rule is then

Analogy
Method of analyzing cases by comparing similarities in cases

Relevant issue
An issue that contributes to a court's decision; if issue were different, court result would be different

Relevant fact
A fact that contributes to a court's decision; if fact were different, court's result would be different

Distinguishing
Method of analyzing cases by showing differences in cases

Synthesizing
Method of analyzing cases by bringing together cases to show how they serve as precedents

IRAC
Method of analyzing cases by setting forth case issue, rule, analysis, and conclusion

CRAC
Method of analyzing cases by setting forth conclusion, rule, analysis, and conclusion

applied to the writer's particular case, and then the conclusion is restated. The CRAC method is often used by authors of court briefs, which are persuasive documents, because stating the conclusion first is a more powerful way to begin an argument than to merely identify the issue the document will examine. While methods of analyzing cases vary, some techniques are common to all analysis:

- Analyze rather than merely summarize the legal authorities on which you rely. Describe the cases you rely on, giving sufficient facts from those cases so the reader may readily see how and why those cases apply to your case.
- Give the holding and the reasoning from the cases you rely on. Then compare and contrast the cases you rely on with your case.
- Convince the reader by applying the holding and reasoning from the cited authorities to your case. Complete the analysis by providing a conclusion. Don't force the reader to guess at a conclusion.

J. BRIEFING CASES

Case brief
Short, written summary of a published case

Trial brief
Written argument submitted to a trial court

Because case analysis can be difficult, many researchers routinely brief the cases they locate so they remain focused on the important parts of the case and obtain a thorough understanding of the case and its reasoning. A **case brief** is a short, written summary and analysis of a case. In some instances you will prepare case briefs for your own benefit. In other instances, attorneys will ask you to provide briefs of cases so that the attorneys can more efficiently analyze case law and prepare their written arguments (also called "briefs" or **trial briefs**) for a court. These trial briefs are discussed in Chapter Six.

While you may be tempted to view case briefing as busywork and may believe you can understand a case by simply reading it through, research has shown that people tend to read quickly and see words in groupings. Briefing a case will force you to slow down and concentrate on the critical aspects of the case. After you have mastered case briefing and thus trained yourself to analyze cases properly, you likely will be able to dispense with written briefs and will be able to brief cases by merely underlining or highlighting the key portions of cases.

There is no one perfect format for a case brief. Some large law firms provide suggested formats. If no form is provided, you should use a form that best suits you and helps you understand the case and its significance as a precedent for your research problem. Resist the temptation to read only the headnotes or to skim the case. A close scrutiny of the case may reveal critical analysis likely to be overlooked in a cursory reading.

No matter what their format, good case briefs share the following elements:

- They use complete sentences.
- They do not overquote from the opinion.
- They do not include unnecessary distracting citations.
- They do not include the writer's personal opinions.
- They are brief, ideally one page in length.

The most common elements to be included in a case brief are the following:

- **Citation.** The case name and full citation (including any parallel citations) should be given.
- **Procedural history.** Include a brief summary of the holdings of any previous courts and the disposition of the case by this court. A procedural history describes how the case got to this court and how this court resolves the case. Start by briefly identifying the parties and stating the relief they were seeking or the defenses they raised. Then proceed to discuss what the court(s) below held and the final disposition by this reviewing court.
- **Statement of facts.** A case brief should include a concise statement of the facts of the case. You need not include all facts but rather only the most significant facts relied on by the court in reaching its decision. Identify the parties by name and indicate whether a party is a plaintiff, defendant, and so forth. The facts are more readable if they are presented in a narrative or sentence-by-sentence format rather than in an outline or "bullet" format. Generally, discuss facts in chronological order and in the past tense.
- **Issue(s).** You must formulate the question(s) or issue(s) being decided by this court. Focus on what the parties asked the court to determine. In some instances, courts will specifically state the issues being addressed. In other instances, the issues are not expressly provided and you will have to formulate them. Phrase the issue so that it has some relevance to the case at hand. Thus, rather than stating the issue in a broad fashion ("What is an assault?") state the issue so that it incorporates some of the relevant facts of the case ("Does a conditional threat constitute an assault?"). Generally, issues should be phrased in a direct-question format. If there is more than one issue, number them and format them in a list.
- **Answer(s).** Provide an answer to each question being resolved by this court. Rather than merely stating "yes" or "no", phrase the answer in a complete sentence and incorporate some of the reasons for the answer. For example, if the issue is as stated above, rather than merely state "no", state "A conditional threat does not constitute an assault because a condition negates a threat so that the hearer is in no danger of immediate harm." If you have set forth three issues, you will need three separate, numbered answers. Strive for one-sentence answers. Do not include citations.
- **Reasoning.** The reasoning is the most important part of a case brief. This is the section in which you discuss *why* the court reached the conclusions it did. Were prior cases cited? Did the court adopt a new rule of law? Is the decision limited to the facts of this particular case, or is the decision broad enough to serve as binding precedent in similar but not identical cases? Fully discuss the reasons why the court reached its decision and its thought processes. Re-read your questions and then be sure that the reasoning is directly responsive to the questions you framed. Citations should be included only if they are critical. Use your own words in summarizing and explaining the court's reasoning rather than overquoting from the case. This will help ensure that you understand the rationale for the court's decision.
- **Holding.** Include the actual disposition of this case, such as "affirmed."

See Figure 5-9 for a sample case brief.

FIGURE 5-9

SAMPLE CASE BRIEF

Fonovisa, Inc., v. Cherry Auction, Inc., 76 F.3d 259 (9th Cir. 1996)

Facts

The plaintiff and appellant, Fonovisa, Inc., owned copyrights and trademarks in various music recordings. The defendant, Cherry Auction, Inc., owned and operated a swap meet in California where customers came to purchase various merchandise from individual vendors who paid a daily fee to Cherry Auction in return for booth space. Cherry Auction received an entrance fee from customers attending the swap meets. It also provided parking and advertising and retained the right to exclude vendors for any reason. Vendors at the swap meet sold counterfeit music recordings, a fact of which Cherry Auction was aware, and which infringed the copyrights and trademarks of Fonovisa.

Procedural Background

Fonovisa sued Cherry Auction in the U.S. District Court for the District of Oregon for contributory copyright and trademark infringement and vicarious trademark infringement. The district court dismissed all claims and Cherry Auction appealed. The Ninth Circuit Court of Appeals reversed.

Issue

Is the owner of a swap meet liable for acts of copyright and trademark infringement by its vendors?

Brief Answer

Yes. Liability for contributory and vicarious copyright infringement and contributory trademark infringement may be imposed on an owner who can control the premises and who obtains a financial benefit arising from the infringing activities.

Reasoning

Even in the absence of an employer-employee relationship one may be vicariously liable for the acts of others if it has the right and ability to supervise and control wrongful activity and also has a direct financial interest in such activities. In this case, Cherry Auction had the right to terminate vendors for any reason and through that right had the ability to control vendors on its premises. Moreover, Cherry Auction promoted the swap meet and controlled the access of customers to the swap meet area. Finally, Cherry Auction received financial benefits from the vendors, who paid daily rental fees; it also received financial benefits in the form of admission fees, concession stand sales, and parking fees, all of which flowed directly from customers who wanted to buy counterfeit recordings at reduced prices. Because Cherry Auction provided the site and facilities for the infringing activities, had the right to control the activities, and received direct financial benefit from the activities, a claim was stated for contributory and vicarious copyright infringement and contributory trademark infringement.

Holding

The Ninth Circuit Court of Appeals reversed the holding of the district court.

NET RESULTS

www.lawschool.cornell.edu/library/ guide/legresearch/4.html	Cornell Law School's site offers information on how to conduct legal research.
www.ll.georgetown.edu	Go to "Select" and then "Legal Research" for Georgetown University Law Center's site for a variety of "how to" research guides.
www.washlaw.edu	This site provided by Washburn University School of Law is easy to navigate and provides links to cases, statutes, legal forms, and numerous other legal materials and documents.
www.findlaw.com	FindLaw is arguably the best-known legal site on the Internet and provides direct links to both primary and secondary materials.
www.megalaw.com	MegaLaw is a general legal site, allowing you to find cases, statutes, administrative regulations, and a wide variety of other legal materials.
www.virtualchase.com	Provided by a law firm, the Virtual Chase provides tips and techniques for conducting legal research as well as general and factual research.

CASE ILLUSTRATION

Importance of Legal Research

Case: *Smith v. Lewis*, 530 P.2d 589 (Cal. 1975)

Facts: The plaintiff alleged that her attorney, the defendant, negligently failed in a divorce action to assert plaintiff's community property interest in certain retirement benefits of her husband. The defendant attorney contended that the law was unclear at the time he represented the plaintiff.

Holding: At the time the attorney represented the plaintiff, the law relevant to division of retirement benefits was clear. Information on this area of law had been reported in a number of California cases and was readily available to the defendant attorney. While an attorney is not liable for every mistake he may make, he is expected to possess knowledge of elementary principles of law and to discover those additional rules of law, which although not commonly known, may easily be found by standard legal research techniques. Even with respect to an unsettled area of the law, an attorney has an obligation to undertake reasonable research to ascertain relevant legal principles. In this case, the defendant failed to perform such adequate research, which justified the jury's award of $100,000 to the plaintiff.

KEY TERMS

Primary authorities
Secondary authorities
Descriptive word approach
Slip law
Codification
Titles
Official
Unofficial
Annotated
Pocket parts
Supplement
Session laws
Rules
Reports, reporters
Official reports
Unofficial reporters
Parallel citations
Slip form
Advance sheets
Headnotes
Majority opinion
Concurring opinion
Dissenting opinion
Per curiam opinion
National Reporter System

Digests
Key Number System
Key Number
Treatises
Citation
Bluebook
ALWD
KeyCite
Sheparinding
Boolean searching
Start page
Googling
Canons of construction
Plain meaning rule
Legislative history
On point
Analogy
Relevant issue
Relevant fact
Distinguishing
Synthesizing
IRAC
CRAC
Case brief
Trial brief

CHAPTER SUMMARY

Primary and Secondary Authorities	Legal authorities are divided into primary authorities (cases, constitutions, statutes, and regulations), which are binding law, and secondary authorities (anything that is not a primary authority), which are not binding.
Descriptive Word Approach	Most researchers use the "descriptive word approach" to locate legal authorities. This approach involves looking up words and phrases in alphabetically arranged indexes to be directed to the appropriate section, volume, or page in a set of books.
Publication of Statutes	■ Federal statutes are published officially in the *United States Code*. Two unofficial annotated versions of the *United States Code*, U.S.C.A. (West's publication) and U.S.C.S. (LEXIS's publication) are usually used by researchers to find federal statutes and cases interpreting those statutes. ■ Statutes are updated and kept current through the use of pocket parts. ■ State statutes are also published officially and unofficially. Most researchers use annotated state codes to find state statutes.
Publication of Cases	■ Federal and state cases are published officially (meaning their publication is government-approved) or unofficially (meaning there is no statute that directs their publication). ■ West's *National Reporter System* is a series of sets of case reporters that publish cases from state appellate courts and from federal trial and appellate courts.
Using Digests to Find Cases	Digests are used by researchers to find cases. West's digest system, often called the Decennial digest system, uses topic names and Key Numbers to direct researchers to relevant cases from all American jurisdictions.

Secondary Sources	Secondary sources comment upon and criticize primary sources. They also help researchers locate relevant primary sources. The better-known secondary sources are as follows: encyclopedias, legal periodicals, texts and treatises, Restatements, *American Law Reports*, and several miscellaneous sets of books, including dictionaries, form books, and looseleaf services.
Citation Form	Citation form is used to direct readers to legal authorities. The two best-known guides to citation are the *Bluebook* and *ALWD*.
Validating Primary Authorities	All primary authorities must be validated, either manually through the use of *Shepard's Citations* or electronically through the use of *Shepard's Citations* (when using LEXIS) or KeyCite (when using Westlaw).
Modern Research Tools	Both computer-assisted legal research and Internet legal research are valuable research tools. Skillful paralegals are familiar with all methods of conducting legal research.
Analyzing and Understanding Legal Authorities	Researchers must not only be able to locate legal authorities, they must also be able to analyze them. Some researchers use the IRAC or CRAC technique to analyze legal issues. Briefing cases can help readers understand the reasoning of a case.

TRIVIA

- West was founded by two brothers, John and Horatio West, in 1872 in Minnesota. Their first product, the *Syllabi*, a weekly record of excerpts from Minnesota courts later expanded into the *National Reporter System*.
- The first volume of the *National Reporter System* was published in 1877. By 1887, the set provided coverage of all state and federal court cases.
- The computer research system LEXIS was introduced in 1973 and Westlaw was introduced in 1975.
- In 2004, more than nearly 360,000 civil cases were initiated in the United States district courts. Lawsuits alleging personal injuries represented the largest number of suits filed.

DISCUSSION QUESTIONS

1. Assume you are researching a First Amendment issue and the annotated code provides references to nearly 100 cases. What research strategies should you adopt when you are confronted with masses of authorities?
2. What are primary and secondary authorities and what are the differences between them?
3. What is the difference between cases that are published officially and those that are published unofficially?
4. What is the purpose of citation systems such as the *Bluebook* and *ALWD?* Why do legal professionals follow citation rules?
5. Assume you are researching liability of directors of a corporation, an area of law that is new to you. Where might you begin your research efforts?
6. What are the two inflexible rules of legal research, of which the failure to follow constitutes legal malpractice?

CASE BRIEF ASSIGNMENT

Brief the case *Missouri v. Jenkins*, 491 U.S. 274 (1987). The case may be accessed through FindLaw, at *www.findlaw.com*.

RESEARCH QUESTIONS AND SHEPARDIZING

Use conventional print research tools to locate the answers to the following questions.

1. Use U.S.C.A. What federal statute relates to fines, penalties, and forfeitures for sales of bald eagle eggs?
2. Use the Popular Name Tables for U.S.C.A. Give the citation to the Drug Free Workplace Act of 1998.
3. Under 18 U.S.C.S. § 3603, does the fact that a defendant did not receive notice of the conditions of supervised release in writing and that the defendant might not have received information required under federal law preclude the district court from revoking supervised release when the defendant committed another crime and violated conditions of supervised release? Answer the question and cite the best case to support your answer.
4. Locate the case at 532 U.S. 661 (2001).
   a. What is the name of the case?
   b. What is the date of decision?
   c. What is the docket number?
   d. Who delivered the opinion of the Court?
   e. Who dissented?
   f. What statute or federal law does the case construe?

5. Locate the case published at 448 S.E.2d 785 (Ga. Ct. App. 1994).
   a. What is the name of the case?
   b. What does headnote 8 discuss?
6. Use the Descriptive Word Index to the Tenth Decennial Digest, Part 2.
   a. What topic and Key Number relate to the allowance of paralegal fees in divorce cases?
   b. Locate a 1996 South Carolina appellate court case relating to this issue.
7. Use the Descriptive Word Index to the Tenth Decennial Digest, Part 2. What topic and Key Number relate to the issue of a certificate for stock at less than par value?
8. Use the A.L.R. Quick Index to A.L.R. 3d, 4th, and 5th.
   a. What annotation deals with tort liability for personal injury or death directly resulting from operations of a termite exterminator?
   b. Review the annotation. What Indiana court of appeals case discusses this issue?
9. Use Am. Jur. 2d. What volume, title, and topic generally deal with raising the defense of intoxication in homicide cases?
10. Use the *Index to Legal Periodicals & Books*. Cite a summer 2003 article relating to the controversy over Indian mascots.
11. Locate *Collier on Bankruptcy* (15th ed. revised).
    a. What section generally discusses the privilege against self-incrimination?
    b. Review the section mentioned in question 11a. May an adverse inference be drawn in a bankruptcy case against a debtor who relies on the Fifth Amendment privilege even if the debtor does so properly?
    c. What statute supports this rule of law?
12. Locate Restatement (Second) of Torts § 577.
    a. What does this section relate to?
    b. Review the illustration for this section. Has slander been published when *A* and *B* are in the woods on a hunting trip and during a quarrel, *A* accuses *B* of murder but no one hears the accusation?
13. Which C.F.R. provision relates to the requirements for bunk beds?
14. Give the correct citations for the following (using either *Bluebook* or *ALWD*). You may need to make up some information.
    a. 17 USC Section 106.
    b. A U.S. Supreme Court case titled Bruce Davidson versus Helen Nelson, published at volume 532, page 109, with a quotation appearing on page 120.
    c. A case from the Eighth Circuit Court of Appeals, decided in 2003, titled Bailey Brothers versus Pat Taylor Association, published at volume 98 of the Federal Reporter, Third Series, at page 909.
    d. Section 141 of a book written by Timothy T. James called "Health Care Law," third edition, published in 1998.
15. Use *Shepard's Citations* for U.S. Reports, Supplement 2000-2002. Shepardize 532 U.S. 661. What was the first case in the ninth circuit to follow this case?

CLOSING ARGUMENTS

1. Access THOMAS, Congress's website. Locate information relating to the 108th Congress. What does Senate Bill No. 499 (S 499) commemorate?
2. Start with FindLaw (*www.findlaw.com*) and access the website for the United States Supreme Court.
    a. Give the citation to a case in which the defendant's name is Bakke.
    b. Who announced the judgment of the Court?
3. Use FindLaw to access the *United States Code*.
    a. Use the popular name approach to locate the citation to the "Bald Eagle Protection Act."
    b. What is the general subject matter of 18 U.S.C. § 706?
4. Use FindLaw to access the California statutes. Browse the list of codes and then browse the California Corporations Code. Which statute provides general discussion relating to amendment of a corporation's articles of incorporation?

CHAPTER 6

LEGAL WRITING AND COMMUNICATIONS

THERE ARE TWO THINGS WRONG WITH ALMOST ALL LEGAL WRITING. ONE IS ITS STYLE. THE OTHER IS ITS CONTENT.
—FRED RODELL, *GOODBYE TO LAW REVIEWS*,
23 VA. L. REV. 38, 38 (1936)

CHAPTER OVERVIEW

This chapter introduces you to legal writing and communications. Capable writing skills are a prerequisite for any successful paralegal. In fact, the American Association for Paralegal Education has identified general communications skills, in particular effective writing skills, as one of the core competencies for paralegal programs. Mastering the "mechanics" of good writing (namely, grammar, punctuation, and spelling) is critical so that your final product will accurately communicate to your intended audience. If you need a quick review of these mechanics, see Appendix H.

Once these mechanics have been mastered, you must focus on making your writing effective by achieving the key requirements of legal writing: accuracy, clarity, readability, and conciseness. This chapter reviews these key requirements and then introduces you to the five main types of legal writing: correspondence, memoranda, court briefs, pleadings, and transactional documents. Electronic communications are also discussed. The chapter then discusses the post-writing steps of proofreading and document design and concludes with an overview of common writing errors.

A. CHARACTERISTICS OF EFFECTIVE LEGAL WRITING

1. Introduction and the Plain English Movement

The cornerstone of the legal profession is communication—communication with an adverse party, a colleague, client, or judge. In most cases the communication will be in written form. Even in those instances in which you communicate orally, you will often follow up with a written letter or memo to a file. Thus, effective legal writing is critical to success as a paralegal.

One of the recurring criticisms of legal writing is that it is nearly incomprehensible to the average reader because of its heavy use of jargon, redundant expressions, and archaic phrases. Consequently, the current movement in legal writing is toward using "plain English," and many government agencies (including the Federal Trade Commission and Securities and Exchange Commission) require that certain documents be written in plain English.

Writing in plain English is not always an easy task. Many legal concepts are complex and translating them into a more simple style can be difficult. Similarly, some use of "legalese" may be unavoidable in certain documents such as wills, complaints, and deeds. See Figure 6-1 for some of the SEC's guidelines for writing in plain English.

FIGURE 6-1

SEC GUIDELINES FOR PLAIN ENGLISH

- Use short sentences.
- Use definite, concrete, everyday language.
- Use the active voice rather than the passive voice.
- Use tables and lists to present complex information.
- Avoid legal and financial jargon and highly technical terms.
- Avoid multiple negatives.
- Avoid weak verbs, abstract terms, and superfluous words.
- Enhance readability through attractive design and layout.

The four key features of effective legal writing, accuracy, clarity, readability, and conciseness, are discussed below.

2. Accuracy

The most important characteristic of legal writing is accuracy. Clients rely on the information given to them by legal professionals. Judges, adversaries, and others will assume the information provided to them is correct. Therefore, being right is fundamental to effective legal writing. Be accurate with regard not only to the "big" issues, such as the legal conclusions and arguments, but also to the "small" elements of a writing, such as names, dates, dollar amounts, and numbers. An error in the client's name will attract more attention than anything else in a project.

Following are three tips to achieve accuracy in your legal writing.

- **Use the right word.** The selection of an incorrect word causes imprecision in your writing. There is a world of difference between a contract that states *The Buyer may deposit the purchase price by May 15, 2005,* and one that states *The Buyer must deposit the purchase price by May 15, 2005.* Use a dictionary or thesaurus to select the right word and pay special attention to the following words, which are commonly misused and confused.

☐ **Affect, effect** used as a verb. *Affect* means *to influence,* as in *I was affected by her testimony. Effect* means *to cause or bring about,* as in *The effect of the increased rainfall was flooding.* If these verbs are confusing to you, don't use either one. Use their synonyms (*influence,* or *produce,* or *result*).

☐ **Among, between.** *Among* is used to refer to *more than two objects or persons,* as in *The agreement was entered into among Andrews, Baker, and Carr. Between* is used to refer to *two objects or persons,* as in *The settlement was reached between Daley and Espinosa.*

☐ **And/or.** Many experts dislike the use of *and/or,* which can be confusing. Use either *and* or *or,* as in *Either the plaintiff or the defendant, or both, will attend the hearing.*

☐ **Compose, comprise.** *Compose* means *to make up,* as in *The contract is composed of three sections. Comprise* means *to include,* as in *Lee's collection comprises modern art and sculptures.* Do not use *of* with *comprise* (just as you would not write *includes of*).

☐ **Guilty, liable.** The word *guilty* refers to criminal conduct. *Liable* refers to responsibility for a civil wrong. Thus, it is correct to say *Defendant Smith was found guilty of embezzlement while Defendant Jones is liable for damages of $45,000 for slander.*

☐ **Memoranda, memorandum.** *Memoranda* refers to several documents (plural) while a *memorandum* is a single document.

☐ **Oral, verbal.** *Oral* means *something spoken,* as in *The plaintiff's oral testimony at trial was inconsistent with her earlier deposition testimony.* The word *verbal* means *a communication in words* and may refer to either a written or a spoken communication.

☐ **Principal, principle.** *Principal* refers to *the supervisor at a school, a sum of money on which interest is paid,* or *a dominant item,* as in *Our principal office is in Akron, Ohio. Principle* refers to *a fundamental rule,* as in *The principles of physics are complex.*

Remember that if you have difficulty remembering which word to select, either use a dictionary or avoid using a confusing word. For example, rather than stating *The company's principal office is in Akron,* write, *The company's chief office is in Akron.*

■ **Use concrete words**. Use concrete and descriptive words. Avoid vague words such as *matter, issue, situation, development, process,* and *problem,* which carry little if any meaning. Thus, write *I am writing to you about your lease* rather than *I am writing to you about this matter.* The words *it* and *this* are often used in a vague manner. Pay special attention when you use *it* and *this* to make sure the reader will understand what is being discussed.

■ **Consider word connotations.** Many words have more than one meaning and some have subtle connotations. There is a great difference between referring to a person as *candid* and referring to the same person as *blunt.* Similarly, there is a world of difference between the words *determined* and *stubborn.* Use care when selecting words to ensure they have the connotations you intend and do not carry hostile undertones.

3. Clarity

The second feature of effective legal writing is clarity—namely, ensuring that your project is easily understood by the reader. Your writing style should be invisible. It is bad writing that is noticeable. Because legal writings are read not for pleasure but for function, readers expect you to make your point clearly and quickly.

Following are three tips to help you achieve clarity in your legal writing.

- **Avoid elegant variation.** "Elegant variation" refers to the practice of substituting one term for another in a writing to avoid repetition of a term. For example, a writer might refer to the *Buyer* of property. Later in the same document, the writer might use the word *Purchaser* to avoid repeating the term *Buyer*. In legal writing, however, such elegant variation is fatal because readers will assume that you have selected a different word for a reason and that you are drawing a distinction between the words or terms. Thus, once you select a label or term, such as *Plaintiff, Employer,* or *Landlord,* you must use the term consistently thereafter. Use the "find and replace" feature of your word processor to ensure terms are used consistently.
- **Avoid multiple negatives.** The overuse of negatives can be confusing to readers. Using more than two negative words in a sentence usually forces the reader to stop and convert the negative terms to positive ones. For example, when you use *not unlikely,* the reader must convert the phrase to *likely* or *probable.* Remember that there are many more negative terms than the obvious ones: *no, not,* and *never.* Words such as *deny, except, fail, preclude,* and *refuse* function in a negative fashion. While you cannot purge your writing of all negative terms, carefully review your projects to ensure that you have not used too many negative terms. They not only obscure meaning, they are also less forceful than affirmative expressions.
- **Use "standard" word order.** The most common sentence structure in English is the placement of the subject first, the verb second, and the object third. Most readers expect sentences to be phrased in this way. While you may not want to compose every sentence in a project in the same fashion, remember that excessive variation from this standard and expected word order may cause confusion. One of the other benefits of placing the subject first in a sentence is that such placement produces a sentence in the active voice.

4. Readability

Because the subject matter discussed in many legal writings is complex, and often rather dull, you need to make your project as readable as possible. Keep in mind that the more complicated a topic is, the more important the need for readability. To enhance readability, follow these five strategies:

- **Prefer the active voice.** The *active voice* focuses attention on the subject of the sentence that performs or causes action. The active voice is consistent with standard sentence structure of subject, verb, and object. The *passive voice* focuses attention on the object of the action by placing it first and relegating the subject (the actor) of the sentence to an inferior position.

Passive Voice	**Active Voice**
The decision was issued by the judge.	The judge issued the decision.
The brief was filed by the attorney.	The attorney filed the brief.

The active voice is stronger and more forceful than the passive voice. Readers do not have to search through the sentence looking for the actor or subject. An additional advantage of using the active voice is that it often results in shorter sentences.

- **Use lists.** Another way to enhance readability is to use lists when discussing complex matters. Lists not only enable readers to comprehend information quickly, they also create visual interest because they are usually set apart from the rest of the text. Lists can be structured in several ways, but to increase interest:
  - ☐ Ideally, set the list off from the rest of your narrative by adding spaces above and below the list;
  - ☐ Indent your list;
  - ☐ Identify the items in your list with numbers, letters, or "bullets" (■); and
  - ☐ Punctuate correctly by putting a semicolon after each item (except the last) and include *or* or *and* before the last item.

  The grammatical structure of all of the items in any list must be identical or parallel. Thus, if the first word in a list is a verb, all of the following items must begin with verbs.

Incorrect Parallel Structure	**Correct Parallel Structure**
In my last job, I was responsible for the following tasks:	In my last job, I was responsible for the following tasks:
- preparing trial exhibits;	- preparing trial exhibits;
- interviewing witnesses; and	- interviewing witnesses; and
- drafted pleadings.	- drafting pleadings.

- **Avoid nominalizations.** A *nominalization* occurs when you take an adjective, verb, or adverb and turn it into a noun. While a nominalization is grammatically correct, overuse of nominalizations drains your writing of interest and makes it read as if written by a bureaucrat.

Nominalizations	**Preferred**
The defendant made an argument.	The defendant argued.
Consideration was given to our options.	We considered our options.
Enforcement of the contract was effected.	The contract was enforced.

  As you can see, nominalizations not only take strong action words such as verbs and convert them into dull nouns, they also tend to make your writing overlong. Writing in the active voice will reduce nominalizations.

- **Avoid legal jargon.** The use of "legalese" frustrates readers and results in stodgy writing. Legalese or jargon includes not only archaic and stuffy words such as *aforesaid, opine,* and *whereas*, but also words and phrases that are unfamiliar to a reader such as Latin phrases or legal terms (*res judicata* or *laches*). Try to avoid using legal jargon. Often archaic or jargon-filled phrases can be omitted entirely or replaced with more familiar terms.

Legal Jargon	**Preferred**
Witnesseth, this Agreement is made and entered into this Fourth day of May, 2004, by and between . . .	This Agreement is entered into May 4, 2004, between . . .

You may not be able to omit all the legal jargon you would like, particularly when drafting wills, deeds, contracts, pleadings, and other legal documents that have more rigid structures. These documents are often drafted in accordance with standard forms and conventions of many years ago, and there has been no aggressive movement to modernize them. Nevertheless, try to eliminate as much legal jargon as you can. Similarly, avoid "made-up" words such as *dialogued, interfaced,* and *mentee.* While English is an evolving language, do not use a word before it has evolved into an entry in a standard dictionary.

- **Keep subjects and verbs in proximity.** The two most critical parts of a sentence are the subject and the verb; readers typically look for these first to make sense of a sentence. Legal writing is famous for creating large gaps between the subject of a sentence and its verb. When too many words intervene between the subject and the verb, readers no longer remember what the sentence is about by the time they locate the verb. Generally, when there is a large gap between the subject and the verb, you can revise the sentence by taking the intervening words and making them into their own sentence.

Disfavored	**Preferred**
The corporation, an entity organized under Ohio law and reincorporated in Delaware in 1995, is bankrupt.	The corporation is bankrupt. It was organized under Ohio law and reincorporated in Delaware in 1995.

5. Conciseness

The length of a document does not necessarily translate into quality. While almost all writers agree in principle that conciseness is an admirable goal in legal writing, it is not easily accomplished. Because courts routinely impose page limits and word count limits on documents, you must be merciless. Your reader's time is at a premium, and you cannot afford to frustrate the reader by redundancy and continuous rehashing of previous material. To achieve conciseness:

- **Omit needless words and phrases.** There are numerous phrases in English that we use simply by habit. Many of these can be eliminated or reduced to a concise word or phrase. Consider the following substitutions and ask yourself if you absolutely need a phrase and whether there is an effective replacement for it.

Long-Winded Phrases	**Substitutions**
Due to the fact that	Because
As a result of	Consequently
During the time that	While
With regard to	Regarding, concerning
It is interesting to note that	Note
In order to	To

- **Avoid redundant expressions.** The legal profession is wedded to redundancy. Writers cannot resist saying *null and void and of no legal effect whatsoever.* Are all of these words needed? The redundant doublings of words has persisted in legal writing. If you find yourself using these stock redundancies, stop and ask your-self whether one word in the pair or series is sufficient.

Common Redundancies
Alter or change or modify
Cease and desist
Due and owing
Each and every
Full and complete
Null and void and of no legal effect
Refuse and fail
True and correct

B. TYPES OF LEGAL WRITING

There are five main types of legal writing: correspondence, memoranda, court briefs, pleadings, and transactional documents. This section provides a brief overview of each type of document.

1. Correspondence

While there are different types of letters written by legal professionals, there are certain "basics" that are common to all correspondence. The elements of legal correspondence are similar to those of general business letters. Thus, all letters include a letterhead, a date, an inside address, a salutation, and the like. Follow your firm or office practice for the elements and format for letters. Generally, letters are single-spaced and then double-spaced between component parts (for example, between the salutation and the body of the letter) and between paragraphs.

There are three types of legal correspondence:

a. General Correspondence

General correspondence letters may include letters requesting information, responding to requests for information, cover letters that accompany documents, letters that confirm meetings, or letters providing a status report to a client. These letters are often brief: They may be only a paragraph or two in length. Watch the details: If you misspell the client's name, this will attract more attention than the substance of the letter. Always send a confirming letter to confirm dates, amounts, or any other matter, such as an extension of time to respond to a complaint. Send a copy to the client to keep the client informed.

b. Demand Letters

Demand letters set forth a client's demands. The most common type of demand letter is a collection letter, which outlines the basis for a debt due to a client and demands that the debt be paid. Make sure your tone is firm and business-like, not overly aggressive. Include the facts underlying the client's claim and then state the client's demand as clearly as possible. If money is due, specify the exact amount. Finally, give an exact date for compliance. Do not write, *You must pay the sum of $10,000 within two weeks.* Give a specific date, as in *You must pay the sum of $10,000 by June 15, 2005.* See Figure 6-2 for a sample demand letter.

Demand letter
A type of letter demanding some action, such as the payment of a debt

---

FIGURE 6-2

SAMPLE DEMAND LETTER

Ramirez & Powell, L.L.P.
1200 Coast Street
Los Angeles, CA 22103
(213) 766-0100

January 30, 2005

Mr. Anthony Lovell
Vice President
Lovell Finance, Inc.
3268 Wilshire Boulevard
Los Angeles, CA 22909

Re: J-Tech Associates. Inc.

Dear Mr. Lovell:

This law firm represents J-Tech Associates, Inc. (J-Tech) regarding its legal affairs. As you know, on August 12, 2004, Lovell Finance, Inc. (Lovell) entered into a written agreement with J-Tech, by the terms of which J-Tech was required to provide information technology consulting services to Lovell—specifically, the design of specialized accounting software for Lovell, and Lovell was to pay the sum of $38,500 therefor.

J-Tech has informed us that it has provided all of the services required by it to be performed under the terms of the contract, and Lovell is presently using the accounting software designed for it. Although Lovell made one payment to J-Tech in the amount of $14,000 in October 2004, it has made no payments since, despite numerous requests by J-Tech for such payments.

This letter is a formal demand that Lovell pay the sum of $24,500 to J-Tech on or before February 15, 2005. J-Tech has asked us to advise you that if this sum is not paid as directed, it will initiate litigation against Lovell for the money due it as well as attorneys' fees and interest, as provided in the written contract signed by Lovell.

Please contact us within the time provided to confirm your compliance with the terms of this letter and to avoid litigation being filed against Lovell.

Sincerely,

Maria M. Ramirez

MMR: jjp
cc: Alex Jackson,
J-Tech Associates, Inc.

---

c. Opinion Letters

Opinion letter
A letter that provides legal advice

An **opinion letter** provides advice to a client. While letters offering legal advice or opinions may be signed only by attorneys, paralegals often play a major role in researching the law and writing the first draft of these opinion letters. An opinion letter usually includes the following elements:

- **Introductory language.** The first part of an opinion letter often reminds the client why the opinion is being provided and states the issue that the letter will address.
- **Review of facts.** An opinion letter should always set forth the facts on which it is based. Even a minor factual error can result in an incorrect opinion. Thus, include the facts so the reader understands that the accuracy of the opinion depends on the specific facts recited.
- **The opinion.** The essence of an opinion letter is the advice given to the client. If the opinion is one that will be welcome to the client, give the opinion first and then explain the law supporting the opinion. If the news or opinion will be unwelcome to the client, consider explaining the law first and then give the opinion. This approach prepares the reader for the unfavorable outcome.
- **Explanation.** This portion of the letter explains the law on which the opinion is based. Because most opinion letters are for laypersons, avoid detailed discussion of or citation to statutes and cases. It is sufficient to summarize the legal authorities in a general fashion, as in *The legal authorities in this state provide that . . .*
- **Recommendation.** Many letters conclude with a recommendation to the client, such as recommending that the client initiate litigation or settle a case. Be clear without being unduly optimistic. Bad news must be unmistakably conveyed.

See Figure 6-3 for a listing of the elements of letters and Figure 6-4 for some ethical tips in letter writing.

FIGURE 6-3
QUICK REFERENCE: ELEMENTS OF LETTERS

- **Letterhead.** The sender's name, address, and other pertinent information, usually centered
- **Date.** Usually centered three lines below letterhead with no abbreviations
- **Inside address.** Recipient's name and address, at left margin, two lines below date
- **Special notations.** Indications of method of sending, privileges claimed, and so forth, at left margin, two lines below inside address
- **Reference notation.** Reference to case name, topic of letter, and so forth, at left margin, or indented five spaces, two lines below special notations (usually shown as "Re:")
- **Salutation.** Opening greeting, addressing all individuals as Mr. or Ms. unless directed otherwise and followed by a colon, placed two lines below reference notation
- **Body of letter.** Begins two lines below salutation, single spaced, with double-spacing between paragraphs, which may be indented five spaces or not indented
- **Complimentary closing.** A closing phrase or word such as "Sincerely," centered, appearing two lines below last line of body of letter
- **Signature block.** Writer's name and title, aligned with complimentary close, four lines below complimentary close
- **Final notations.** References to writer's and typist's initials, enclosures, and indications of those who will receive copies of letter, all appearing at left margin, beginning two lines below signature block, each appearing one line below the other

FIGURE 6-4

ETHICS TIPS IN LETTER WRITING

- Conduct research to ensure the letter is appropriate. For example, in some states, certain types of litigation may not be instituted unless a notice of the claim is first sent to the potential defendant.
- Only a properly licensed attorney may give legal advice.
- It is a violation of ethics codes to correspond with a person who is represented by counsel. Make sure the recipient is not represented by counsel before you send any letter.
- It is unethical to threaten criminal prosecution if the reader will not comply with a demand. Review your state's code of professional conduct.
- Most states have consumer protection laws regulating demands for payments of certain types of debts. Review your state's consumer debt laws and the federal Fair Debt Collection Practices Act at 15 U.S.C. § 1692 (2000).

d. Electronic Communications

New forms of communication—namely, electronic communications, have arisen in the past several years, and they have changed the way people communicate in the workplace. While many of them are great timesavers, others may be traps for the unwary writer.

(1) Communicating by E-Mail

E-mail is becoming an increasingly common method of communication, both within the workplace and with clients. E-mail creates an air of informality, and the ease with which a message can be composed and sent causes countless errors. Many firms and offices have formal policies as to the types of communications that may be sent by e-mail, and most include automatically inserted confidentiality notices at the conclusion of each e-mail message.

Because e-mail is almost instantaneous, and the time between sending a message and receiving a response is so reduced, e-mail is more conversational than traditional paper communication. Thus, the style for e-mail communications must be adjusted. Consider the following when using e-mail in a business setting:

- Because e-mail is often dashed off without a great deal of planning, it tends to be abrupt and brusque. Readers will not be able to hear voice intonation or see any body language. Thus, attempts at humor, irony, or sarcasm are often misperceived.
- Spell-check all e-mail and proofread it for accuracy. If necessary, print a hard copy of the message, proof it, correct it, and then send it.
- Follow the same rules of courtesy and tone as are used in traditional communications. When in doubt, leave it out.
- Be brief and to the point. Many people receive a great number of e-mails during the day and won't bother reading a long, rambling message. Make the "subject" or "re" line specific. Do not overuse "urgent."
- Understand that once you send a message, you have no control over its distribution. Your message may be sent to numerous others without your permission or even awareness.

■ E-mail is not an effective forum for handling sensitive matters or resolving disputes. Once an electronic conversation becomes even slightly confrontational, end it and agree to speak over the phone or meet in person.

(2) Communicating by Facsimile

Communicating by facsimile is so commonplace that many firms and offices use traditional mail only for more critical matters or for sending original documents. Most office facsimile cover sheets include a confidentiality notice. (See Chapter Eleven and Figure 11-3 for a sample confidentiality notice.)

Either preprogram frequently called numbers into the facsimile machine or always double-check the facsimile number before pressing "send." Call the recipient and tell him or her that a document will be sent, especially if the document is confidential or the facsimile machine is in an open location or shared with others. Remember that once the document is sent, it cannot be re-called.

(3) Communicating by Telephone and Voice Mail

Although conference calls and voice mails can both reduce the time you spend on communications and eliminate certain forms of written communications, there are some guidelines you should follow when communicating by telephone:

■ Treat conference calls as meetings and be prompt in dialing in to the conference number.

■ Make sure that introductions are made for all participants.

■ Always ask for permission before placing someone on a speakerphone, and always disclose that another is listening with you if you are using a speakerphone.

■ Do not leave overly long or rambling messages on voice mail.

■ Clearly state your name and phone number on voice mail messages. Repeat both at the end of your message for those unfamiliar with you so they do not have to replay the message to obtain your name and number.

■ Place a note in the file to confirm that you left or received a voice mail. For example, use the following format: "V/M 5/16/05 re: preparation of employment K" (meaning that you left a message by voice mail on May 16, 2005, regarding the preparation of an employment contract).

■ Do not disclose confidential information over a car phone, cell phone, or on voice mail. Messages may be easily intercepted, and you do not know who may be listening.

2. Legal Memoranda

A **legal memorandum** or research memorandum is a document designed to provide information about a case or matter. Usually, you will be asked to research a question, and your answer will be provided in the form of a written memorandum or "memo." The **memo** is an internal document, which means it is prepared for use within a law firm or company. It is generally protected by the work product privilege and thus is not discoverable by an adverse party. Because it is not discoverable, its primary characteristic is its objectivity. The most difficult part of writing a memo is remaining neutral and objective. You must point out any weaknesses and flaws in the client's case. Your goal is to explain the law, good and bad, not to argue it.

Legal memorandum
A research document that analyzes a legal problem in an objective manner; for interoffice use only; also called a *memo*

In addition to research memoranda, many firms use memoranda to report the results of client interviews or investigations. Some law firms use specific formats for their memos. Most memos, however, share the following common features:

- **Introductory information.** This section identifies the document, the person for whom the memo is prepared, the author's name and position, the subject matter of the memo, and the date it is prepared.
- **Question(s) presented.** This section sets forth the legal questions or issues the memo addresses. If the memo discusses more than one issue, number each one. Most writers use a true question form, such as *In Florida, are punitive damages recoverable in fraud actions?*
- **Brief answer(s).** This section of the memo briefly answers the questions you set forth in the order you presented them. Each answer should be no more than one or two sentences. Do not include formal citations.
- **Statement of facts.** The statement of facts will be based on what you know about the case, what the client has said, and your review of the file. Remember to be objective and include all the facts, even if they are unfavorable to the client's position. The most common approach in stating the facts is to present them in the past tense and in chronological order.
- **Analysis or discussion.** The heart of the memorandum is the analysis or discussion section. This portion of the memo provides an in-depth analysis of the issues presented. Cases, statutes, and other legal authorities will be discussed. Citations usually appear in the body of the memo rather than as footnotes. Consider using the IRAC approach (discussed in Chapter Five) to analyze the issues. Use headings and subheadings throughout this section to alert the reader to new topics. Write in the third person in your discussion.
- **Conclusion.** The conclusion should be brief (probably no more than one paragraph) and should not include formal citations. The conclusion should summarize your analysis section.

See Figure 6-5 for elements of a typical memorandum.

3. Legal Briefs

When a party requests action from a court (for example, a request for change of venue), it makes a motion requesting the action. The document filed in support of the motion and attached to the motion is usually called a **brief,** although it may be called a Memorandum of Law or Memorandum of Points and Authorities. Remember that the word "brief" may also refer to a short, written summary of a case, as discussed in Chapter Five.

Brief
A document submitted to a court that includes legal argument

Briefs differ from letters and memoranda in their purpose and audience. While letters and memoranda are intended primarily to inform and explain, briefs are intended to persuade judges. Trial briefs are submitted in pending cases, and appellate briefs are used to appeal an adverse decision (or are submitted in support of a decision) made by a trial court.

There are three primary guidelines for preparing court briefs:

- **Be persuasive.** Aim at being persuasive throughout every portion of the brief. Use the table of contents and headings to persuade. For example, rather than

FIGURE 6-5
ELEMENTS OF A TYPICAL MEMORANDUM

MEMORANDUM

To:

From:

Re:

Date:

ISSUES

1.

2.

BRIEF ANSWERS

1.

2.

STATEMENT OF FACTS

ANALYSIS

1.

2.

CONCLUSION

using a neutral heading such as *Punitive Damages*, use a more persuasive one, such as *Defendant's Willful and Reckless Conduct Entitles Plaintiff to Punitive Damages*.

■ **Be honest.** While you need not present the adversary's argument, you have an ethical duty to be honest and to bring to the court's attention anything that would assist the court in reaching a decision. If you discover cases that do not support the client's position, address them in a straightforward fashion, and then show the reader why they do not apply.

■ **Know the rules.** Most courts issue rules relating to documents submitted to them. Some of these rules relate to the paper used, citation form, length of the document, and the elements required in a brief. Many courts now establish maximum page limits. Failure to comply with the rules can be fatal. Many courts, including the U.S. Supreme Court, have posted their rules on their websites. Table T.1 of the *Bluebook* provides each state's judicial website, Table BT.2 of *Bluebook* Bluepages refers to local citation rules, and Appendix 2 of *ALWD* provides local court citation rules for each state.

For information on the elements and format of court briefs, use a form book, such as *American Jurisprudence Pleading and Practice Forms, Revised*, which consists of more than 30 volumes of forms relating to litigation and appeals.

4. Pleadings

Typically, the word **pleading** encompasses almost anything filed with a court in the course of a pending action. All jurisdictions have rules relating to the content and format of pleadings. Some courts have preprinted and fillable forms available on the Internet. For example, the Judicial Council of California provides a variety of pleading forms at its website at *www.courtsinfo.ca.gov/forms.*

Form books provide suggested forms and models for preparing pleadings. Most states have state-specific form books, and law firms that engage in litigation have numerous sample forms that may be used as guides. Make sure that you do not view forms as mere fill-in-the-blank documents. Use the form books as helpful guides, but modify forms when needed. Some form books are identified below. A sample complaint is shown in Chapter 8 in Figure 8-1.

5. Transactional Documents

The term **transactional documents** usually refers to documents used in various legal transactions, such as contracts, leases, employment agreements, and corporate minutes. Legal professionals seldom draft these documents from "scratch." Generally, they rely on forms or models that have proven useful in other instances. In many cases, there is not a great deal of creativity in transactional documents, nor should there be. Moreover, because the document must protect the client in the future against interpretations that were unforeseen at the time the document was created, transactional documents tend to be overlong as they attempt to foresee and forestall every possible future problem raised by a hostile reader.

There are numerous well-known form books that provide suggested forms, language, and checklists for transactional documents. Most law firms and offices have numerous standard forms that have served clients well. These are excellent starting places. Create your own form files of documents so you have samples on hand. Following are some well-known form books used in drafting transactional documents.

- *American Jurisprudence Legal Forms 2d.* This set consists of more than 25 alphabetically arranged volumes of forms and provides forms for contracts, wills, leases, and hundreds of other topics.
- *West's Legal Forms 2d.* This 30-volume set contains a variety of forms used in general law practice.

A sample transactional document (namely, a joint venture agreement) is provided in Chapter 9 in Figure 9-1.

C. PREWRITING STEPS AND GETTING STARTED

One of the best investments of your time can be the time spent before you begin the actual writing process. Consider using an outline to organize the structure of your writing. A formal, numbered outline is not always needed. Index cards or looseleaf sheets that you can shuffle around are excellent organizational tools. Similarly, jotting down in list form all the words and phrases that you can think of that relate to your project may give you some ideas on how to structure your project. Plan your topic sentences, which announce the theme or subject matter of the paragraph to follow.

For many writers, the most difficult task in writing is getting started. The best cure for this common problem is to write something. Write anything. Just get started. If the idea of beginning an argument paralyzes you, don't begin there. Start with the section of the document you are most comfortable with, even if it is not in the correct order. If you are familiar with the facts, begin with a statement of facts. If you know how you want to conclude your project, begin there. The mere act of writing any section of a document will relieve some anxiety about writing.

Consider "telling the story" of your project to a friend or colleague. This may help you organize your thoughts and give you ideas on how to begin the project. Set small goals for yourself. Challenge yourself to complete a task by a certain time. Consider making a list of all items that need to be done for the project. Do the easiest tasks first, even if these are purely clerical, such as copying exhibits. These techniques may help you get started.

TIPS

Strategies for Successful Writing

One of the best strategies for successful writing is to invest time in the prewriting phase of a project. Two threshold questions are of particular importance in helping you shape your writing. Always ask yourself "What is the purpose of this writing?" and "Who will be reading this writing?" Once you have focused on these questions, you will automatically adopt the correct style and tone.

D. FINISHING ON TIME AND POSTWRITING STEPS

1. Finishing on Time

If you have been given a deadline date, you may find it helpful to work backward from this date and establish a writing schedule. Set a date by which all of the research is to be done, another for completing the first draft, and so forth. If you are a habitual last-minute worker, it may be helpful to "go public" and announce a deadline to your supervisor. Telling someone he or she will have a finished project by Monday will commit you to meeting this deadline. Once a deadline is established, allow some room for emergencies, such as illness, equipment breakdowns, and the like. Set small and reasonable goals for yourself. Tell yourself "I will have the statement of facts done by 3:00 P.M. today." These self-imposed deadlines will help you tackle the project bit by bit and meet your deadline.

2. Proofreading and Reviewing

One of the most difficult writing tasks begins only when most writers think they have finished a project. Steps taken in the postwriting stage provide a final opportunity to ensure a document is correct in all respects.

The best technique for successful proofreading and reviewing is to get some distance from the project. Try to allow at least a few hours (and, if possible, overnight or longer) to pass between the completion of your first draft and your initial review. It is extremely difficult to review effectively a project with which you are too familiar. If you can come to the review cold, you will be better able to detect flaws.

You cannot review (literally, "re-see") for all errors at the same time. Thus, divide your review into two parts. During phase one, review for content and meaning. Ask yourself if the reader will understand the writing. Focus on the purpose of the writing. If the project is a court brief, its purpose is to persuade. Check to see if the writing meets this goal. Review to ensure the writing flows smoothly and that its organization assists the reader's comprehension. Read the project aloud to help you locate awkward phrasing, repetitive sections, and missing transitions.

During phase two, review for technical errors—namely, errors in grammar, punctuation, and spelling. While a spell-checker is a wonderful tool, it has its limitations because it cannot distinguish the correct usage of a word so long as it is spelled correctly. Because readers naturally read groups of words and phrases rather than isolated words, force yourself to slow down and focus on each word. Try these techniques:

- Slide a ruler or piece of paper under each line as you read down the pages of the document. This will prevent you from jumping ahead.
- Read sections out of order to ensure you stay focused on the mechanics of grammar, punctuation, and spelling, and do not begin yet to concentrate on content.
- Read the document aloud to yourself or read it with a colleague who has a copy of the document. You will not only hear what is being read but also see it.
- Check the "details" one last time. Make sure the page numbering is correct. Check to see that the numbering of headings and subheadings is correct. Do one final review to ensure dates, names, and money amounts are accurate.

Use the standard proofreaders' marks used in editing to show changes. See Figure 6-6 for the most commonly used proofreaders' marks.

3. Document Design

Even if your project is well written, clear, and readable, it should be presented in such a manner that it creates a favorable impression on the reader. Thus, use document design to enhance your writing. Follow the guidelines below to make your project more visually appealing:

- Use the highest-quality paper possible.
- Use 12-point type and use a conventional typeface such as Times New Roman.
- Allow adequate white space on each page to give the reader's eye a rest from blocks of text.
- Use headings and subheadings to alert the reader to topic changes and to create visual drama on the page.

FIGURE 6-6
COMMONLY USED PROOFREADERS' MARKS

Mark	Explanation	Example
≡	Capital letters	senator Kennedy
/	Lowercase letters	the next Witness
~	Boldface	January 30, 2004
⌒	Close up space	can not
¶	Begin new paragraph	¶ The motion
⟍	Delete	The order was was
Stet	Let original text stand	The judgment awarded
∧	Insert	The witness and his attorney
#	Add space	to the court.The deponent then
∼	Transpose	compliant
[	Move left	[any juror
]	Move right	] any juror
⌃	Insert comma	the witness Kyle Ryan stated
⌄	Insert apostrophe	the shareholders lawsuit
⊙	Insert period	to the judge The motion also
○	Spell out	San Diego, CA

E. COMMON ERRORS IN LEGAL WRITING

There are several blunders commonly committed by beginning legal writers. Some are oddly phrased constructions; others are defects in reasoning and analysis. Pay careful attention to these common errors in legal writing.

■ **Labels and numbering.** Never label an item *A* or *I* unless a *B* or *II* follows.
■ **Defined terms.** Once you define a term or use a label, it must be used consistently. Thus, once you tell a reader that the plaintiff Lynn Ryan will be referred to as *Ryan*, you must continue this reference and not later refer to her as *Ms. Ryan* or *the Plaintiff*.

Plagiarism
Taking another's ideas, thoughts, or expressions and representing them as one's own

Paraphrasing
Putting the words or ideas of another into one's own words

■ **Supporting authorities.** Do not conclude that a test or element of an argument is satisfied without supporting authority. Every assertion you make or conclusion you provide must be supported by some legal authority. See Figure 6-7 for information about **plagiarism, paraphrasing,** and citing to authorities.
■ **Use of headnotes.** Never quote from headnotes in a case. Headnotes are summaries of what the court said that are prepared by book publishers. Rely on the

---

FIGURE 6-7
PLAGIARISM

Plagiarism is taking another's ideas, thoughts, or expressions and representing them as your own. The word *plagiarism* is derived from the Latin for *literary thief* or *kidnaper*. Plagiarism is a serious ethics violation. It is perfectly acceptable, however, to paraphrase another's material. *Paraphrasing* is taking the ideas or expressions of another and putting them in your own words. Nevertheless, even paraphrased material must be attributed to the original author. Follow these guidelines in legal writing, as in all writing:

■ When you quote from any authority, use quotation marks and give the full citation and the pinpoint, namely, the page on which the specific material appears.
■ When you paraphrase an authority, give the full citation and the pinpoint.
■ When an entire paragraph includes paraphrased material and the sentences in the paragraph are closely connected, it is acceptable to give the citation at the end of the paragraph, rather than giving citations at the end of each sentence. Similarly, it is permissible to give a citation to a legal authority, such as a case, and give the facts from that case in several sentences without repeating the citation at the end of each sentence.
■ Do not assume that material in the public domain (for example, statutes and cases) can be used without attribution. When you rely upon such materials, give the full citation and the pinpoint.
■ Using material from the Internet is not only an ethics violation, it may also be a copyright violation. Just as it is easy for a writer to find material on the Internet and "cut and paste" the material into a writing, it is easy for the reader to locate the original source on the Internet and realize that you have plagiarized.
■ Understand that in law firms and office settings, professionals routinely share their writings, memos, and briefs with each other. This sharing of materials is considered practical and cost-effective for clients. Such use with the permission of another is not plagiarism.
■ When in doubt, err on the side of caution and give a citation.

majority opinion itself. When you read a case, find the author of the opinion. The author's name is a signal that every word thereafter was written by the court.

■ **Addressing readers.** Do not address the reader of a document by name. Thus, in a letter, do not write, *Ms. Ryan, you should therefore . . .* It is sufficient to write *You should therefore . . .*

■ **Use of third person.** Do not use the first person (*I, my, our, us, we,* and so forth) in any document other than correspondence. In memos and court briefs, do not write *We will show;* rather, write *the Plaintiff will show.* In most instances you are writing on behalf of the client; thus, third person is appropriate.

■ **Including facts.** Be sure to include facts from the cases you rely on so the reader can easily see why the authorities you cite apply to your case.

■ **Over-quoting.** Don't include so many quotations from legal authorities that it appears your project was assembled from a hodgepodge of authorities rather than being the result of your own analysis. Don't just drop quotations into a project without explaining their relevance to your analysis.

■ **Headings.** Always provide sufficient headings that the reader can readily determine the topic that will next be addressed. Review each heading to make sure each is parallel and that each advances your argument.

■ **New topics.** Do not introduce any new issues or topics in a conclusion that have not been previously analyzed in the document. A conclusion summarizes material previously presented; it does not introduce new topics.

■ **Shifts in tense.** Use the correct tense. Use the past tense when describing events that occurred previously or the facts, procedural background, and holding of a case. Use the present tense when discussing what the law is, whether you discuss a statute, case, or regulation. Thus, for example, write *the Lanham Act provides that . . .* Do not shift tenses unless there is an actual change in time.

■ **Citation form.** Always follow local, *Bluebook,* or *ALWD* rules of citation. Improper citation form casts doubt on your professionalism and attention to detail.

NET RESULTS

www.gpoaccess.gov/ stylemanual/index.html	The Government Printing Office Style Manual is the most widely accepted manual on English usage. The entire Style Manual is available at this site.
www.plainlanguage.gov	This website, offered by a group of government volunteers, provides excellent information on plain writing as well as its major guidance document, Writing User-Friendly Documents.
www.lclark.edu/~legalwrt	Lewis & Clark Law School's Legal Writing Department offers links to several excellent legal writing sites.

CASE ILLUSTRATION

The Meaning of the Word *Between*

The following case illustrates the importance of selecting the precise word in legal documents.

Case:	*LeFeavre v. Pennington*, 230 S.W.2d 46 (Ark. 1950)
Facts:	The Arkansas Supreme Court was called upon to interpret a will that read "The Bal. to be divided equally between all of our nephews and nieces on my wife's side and my niece, Nathalee Pennington." There were 22 nieces and nephews on the wife's side and they contended that the property should be distributed equally among all of the beneficiaries so that each would receive one twenty-third.
Holding:	The court divided the property into two equal shares, stating that the use of the word "between" showed that the testator intended to divide the property in two equal shares; had the testator intended otherwise, the word *among* would have been used.

KEY TERMS

Demand letter	Pleading
Opinion letter	Transactional document
Legal memorandum	Plagiarism
Brief	Paraphrasing

CHAPTER SUMMARY

Goal of Legal Writing	The goal of legal writing is to communicate. No matter what style or form the legal writing takes, its mechanics (grammar, punctuation, and spelling) must be correct.
Plain English	Legal writers should write in "plain English" and reduce the wordiness and jargon seen in many legal documents.
Characteristics of Effective Legal Writing	The characteristics of effective legal writing are accuracy, clarity, readability, and conciseness.

Legal Correspondence	There are various types of legal correspondence. Letters may be general correspondence, demand letters (which set forth a client's demands, usually for payment of money), or opinion letters (which provide advice to a client).
Electronic Communications	Be especially careful when using electronic methods of communication such as e-mail or facsimile communications. Once a message is sent, it cannot be recalled. E-mail is often highly conversational and may result in a brusque tone or frequent errors in spelling and grammar.
Legal Memoranda	A legal memorandum provides an overview of the issues in a particular case. Its primary characteristic is its objectivity. The memo is intended to inform the reader about the law rather than to argue or persuade.
Court Briefs	Briefs are legal arguments submitted to trial or appellate courts. These briefs are persuasive in their tone.
Pleadings	Pleadings are documents submitted to court in pending cases. Their format is usually dictated by court rules, and some legalese is common.
Transactional Documents	Transactional documents are writings used in legal transactions, such as contracts, leases, and other agreements.
Reviewing and Proofreading	Reviewing and proofreading of writings is critical to ensure the project is correct in all respects.
Document Design	Consider the design of a document to enhance its readability.

TRIVIA

- The Gettysburg Address has only 286 words; one federal statute relating to Medicare has more than 700 words.
- In mid-2000, the Kentucky Supreme Court suspended a lawyer for 60 days for a "virtually incomprehensible" brief and dismissed his client's case.
- Supreme Court rules recognize legal writers' tendency to try to squeeze additional wording into a brief by using a small typeface. The rules provide that

"increasing the amount of text by using condensed or thinner typefaces, or by reducing the space between letters is strictly prohibited." Sup. Ct. R. 33.

DISCUSSION QUESTIONS

Note that Questions 1 and 2 may require you to review Appendix H, which covers writing basics (grammar, punctuation, and spelling).

1. Select the correct word.

   ■ Either Ronald or Raymond was/were involved.
   ■ The corporation had their/its annual meeting last week.
   ■ The photograph, together with the video display, was/were powerful.
   ■ The principal/principle office location of the corporation is in New York City.

2. Select the correct pronoun.

   ■ Frank and her/she attended the trial.
   ■ It was the witness who/whom I saw.
   ■ The evidence which/that was introduced had a strong effect on the jury.

3. Correct the following negative expressions.

   ■ We are not unaware of the effect of the witness's testimony.
   ■ It is not unreasonable to assume that the meeting was not held.

4. Rewrite the following sentences to omit legalese and redundant expressions.

   ■ We are pleased to request that you forthwith execute the enclosed will in the space placed contiguously to your typed name.
   ■ It is at this point in time that the opinion of this law firm is that you have a cause of action for fraud. We would appreciate it if you could contact this office at your earliest convenience so we may dialogue about this matter.
   ■ We have definitized the lease and are enclosing it herewith for your execution.

5. What is the primary difference in style between an internal office memorandum and a brief submitted to a court?

6. Give some of the reasons why the legal profession has been resistant to adopting "plain English" principles for drafting documents.

7. Write a letter to your firm's client, Janet Young of Los Angeles, California, providing her with the amended corporate bylaws that she requested the firm prepare.

8. Write a letter to Jonathan Petersen of Cleveland, Ohio, your firm's client, confirming a meeting next week at your office to discuss his answers to interrogatories propounded to him.

CLOSING ARGUMENTS

1. Access the GPO Style Manual.
   a. What does the Latin abbreviation "in lim" stand for and what does it mean?
   b. Review the section on punctuation. What is the plural possessive form of the word "Congress"?
2. Access the site *www.plainlanguage.gov* and select "Plain English at a Glance." What advice is given regarding the use of justified right margins?
3. Access the SEC's Plain English Handbook. In the chapter titled "Writing in Plain English," what are the most common problems identified by the SEC in documents?

CHAPTER

7

INTERVIEWING AND INVESTIGATING

W E NEVER STOP INVESTIGATING. WE ARE NEVER SATIS-
FIED THAT WE KNOW ENOUGH TO GET BY. EVERY QUESTION WE
ANSWER LEADS TO ANOTHER QUESTION.

—DESMOND MORRIS

CHAPTER OVERVIEW

Paralegals often interview potential clients, clients, and a variety of nonclients, such as witnesses and experts. Effective interviewers spend almost as much time preparing for an interview and reporting the results of an interview as conducting the interview itself. Similarly, paralegals often conduct a variety of investigative tasks—from locating witnesses, to obtaining police reports, to determining information about companies and entities. This chapter examines the two related tasks of interviewing and investigating and the skills needed to ensure that you obtain the best results in the least amount of time and that you obtain evidence that will be admissible at trial.

A. INTERVIEWING

1. Introduction

Interviewing is such a critical skill that the American Association for Paralegal Education (AAfPE) identifies interviewing as a core competency for paralegals. Specifically, AAfPE has concluded that graduates of paralegal programs should be able to do the following:

- Develop a list of questions for an interview;
- Conduct an effective interview; and
- Record the results of the interview in an accurate manner.

While "interviewing" sounds like a formal process, keep in mind that nearly every conversation you have is a form of interview, with questions asked and information exchanged. Thus, even paralegals who will not conduct many legal interviews can likely learn some techniques to help improve their communications skills.

2. Initial Client Interviews

a. Prospective Clients

A firm's prospective client or new client will likely be very apprehensive about the nature of the relationship to follow. If the client has been sued, the level of anxiety is greatly increased. Thus, the initial meeting with a client is key because it sets the tone for the legal relationship, which may continue for several years. The initial interview should thus serve two purposes: for the parties to get acquainted so that each becomes comfortable with the other and begins to have trust and confidence in the other, and for the legal team to obtain sufficient information so that it can begin representing the client.

If the client has not yet engaged the firm, he or she may be in the position of "interviewer" and the firm the "interviewee" as the client attempts to gain enough information to determine whether the firm can capably handle the client's case. Similarly, the attorney will obtain information to determine the nature of the client's legal needs. In some instances, the prospective client's telephone call to schedule a meeting may not have revealed the particular type of case for which representation is needed. The initial meeting may then disclose that the firm either has a disqualifying conflict of interest (see Chapter Three) or that the firm is not well suited to handle the particular legal issue the case might present. To avoid confusion, most attorneys provide written confirmation clarifying that they will not be representing the individual.

Engagement letter
Letter prepared by attorney or paralegal and signed by attorney and client that retains the attorney to represent the client and sets forth fee arrangements

If the client has had no previous relationship with the attorney, the attorney need not sell himself or herself but should be prepared to describe his or her background and why the client should engage the firm. Thus, at the initial meeting the supervising attorney should describe his or her educational background and experience and expertise and describe how the firm "works"—namely, how communications and billing are handled, who will be assigned to the case, whom the client may contact for information, and so forth. If the parties agree, the client will likely sign an **engagement letter** that formally engages the firm and sets forth the fee arrangements. The attorney will complete a formal conflicts check to ensure that representation of the new client does not violate any ethical duties to any current or former clients, the client will pay a retainer, and a follow-up meeting will be scheduled. See Chapter Three for additional information about conflicts checks and retainers. While some firms have paralegals initially meet with prospective clients, most firms use either an attorney-paralegal team or have an attorney conduct the initial meeting alone, primarily because only licensed attorneys may establish an attorney-client relationship and establish the legal fees. In any event, there are a variety of steps you can take to facilitate the initial meeting:

- Reserve a conference room or ensure that there will be a quiet place to meet so that the meeting will be confidential, and arrange for calls and pages to be held;

- Call or write the potential client to confirm the meeting and to make sure the individual has directions to the office and has all information relating to parking, transportation, and the like;
- Arrange to have coffee or other beverages available;
- Have sufficient copies of the firm's brochure, marketing materials, or the attorney's resume so the potential client may review these;
- Make sure you have your own business cards as well as those of any attorneys who attend the meeting;
- Have paper and pens available for the prospective client if he or she wants to take notes;
- Dress appropriately—when in doubt, dress up rather than down;
- Meet the prospective client promptly in the reception area, exchange a polite and friendly greeting, clearly indicate your position, and escort him or her to the conference meeting room or office;
- Take your cues from the attorney and take notes if requested, and keep an eye on whether the prospective client needs additional beverages or note paper;
- Escort the individual back to the reception area; and
- Ask your supervising attorney what follow-up is necessary—for example, whether you should begin the first draft of an engagement or nonengagement letter, work on the conflicts check, or open the file.

Keep in mind that while it is probably far easier to take notes on a laptop computer (and the resulting notes are more legible than handwritten notes), many clients find the use of a laptop computer at an initial meeting a bit mechanical and off putting.

b. Post-Engagement Client Interviews

It is possible that a client has already engaged the attorney before you meet the client. If this is the case, you will likely have been assigned to the case by your paralegal manager or supervising attorney and are now being asked to obtain additional information from the client so the work of representing the client may begin in earnest.

While a telephone interview will produce a great deal of information, you should take the opportunity to meet the client in person and establish a relationship. If the client is elderly or infirm, offer to meet the client at his or her residence or at a mutually convenient location. Calling the appointment a "meeting" rather than an "interview" may reduce some anxiety.

Because the initial meeting will have disclosed the type of matter for which the client needs representation, you will be able to plan for this subsequent meeting. For example, once you know the client intends to sue another for breach of contract, review form books and complaints for breach of contract, and determine the type of information you will need. Similarly, for a medical malpractice action, you will need to conduct some research to determine whether your state requires that the potential defendant doctor be notified before an action is filed. Thus, use your basic research skills to help establish a game plan. Make a list of the information and documents you need. Plan ahead so that you can make just one telephone call to the client to request that this information be brought to the meeting. Approaching this problem in a haphazard manner and making numerous telephone calls to say "and bring the addendum too" will make the client think you are disorganized. Ideally, you should confirm the meeting by letter and identify in writing the particular information and documents you need. See Chapter Six for information about general correspondence letters.

See Chapter Six for information about general correspondence letters.

Intake sheet
A form or checklist used by legal professionals to obtain information from clients

Intake memo
A memo that describes a client meeting and the client's case

If you routinely work on the same types of cases—for example, divorce or bankruptcy cases, develop your own forms or checklists to help you ask the right questions. These forms are usually called **intake sheets** that remind you to obtain information. See Figure 7-1 for a portion of a sample new-client intake sheet used in bankruptcy cases. After a client meeting, many paralegals prepare an **intake memo** to describe the meeting and the client's particular case.

3. Conducting Interviews

We all know that there is a great deal more to communication than merely speaking. Body language, facial expression, posture, and numerous other cues give information to listeners. While there are several books to consult about effective communication techniques, in many instances you can improve your interviewing skills by following some common-sense approaches. Effective interviewers of clients and nonclients share four characteristics: they are prepared, they are thorough, they are flexible, and they are good listeners.

a. Preparing for Interviews

Just as students always know when a teacher is unprepared, so clients can readily determine whether you have prepared to meet with them. Following are some suggestions for getting ready for an interview or client meeting.

- **Review the file.** Before the interview, review the client's file and refresh your memory about the client's name, case, and any other pertinent issues. Make copies of documents you will need to review at the meeting, and have extra copies made for the client.
- **Conduct legal research.** Conduct some preliminary legal research to familiarize yourself with the area of law the client's case involves. Your research will likely suggest additional topics to explore during the interview. Conversely, your research may disclose that certain topics need not be covered. For example, if you know that your state is a no-fault divorce state, there may be no need to ask about adultery of the other spouse. Asking the wrong questions wastes time and displays a lack of professionalism.
- **Prepare some questions.** After you have reviewed the file and conducted some basic research, you will be able to prepare a checklist of some questions for the client. Ask the attorneys working on the case if they have any specific information they need from the client. Give some thought to the purpose of the meeting because this will also help you frame some questions.
- **Prepare the setting.** Consider the physical setting for the interview. Reserve a conference room. If you will be using your own office, make sure it is uncluttered and that no other client files are visible. Make sure you have supplies (paper, pens, and sticky notes) for both you and the client. Have your business cards ready.
- **Analyze the seating arrangements.** If you conduct the interview in a conference room, give some thought to the seating arrangements. If you sit at the

---

FIGURE 7-1

CLIENT INTAKE FORM (PARTIAL)

GENERAL INFORMATION

Please fill out ALL the information requested in these forms. If a question or section does NOT apply to you, write "N/A" in the space. (N/A means "not applicable.") The more information you provide in these forms, the faster your bankruptcy petition can be prepared. There will be a delay if we need to verify or obtain more information concerning a specific asset, debt or creditor; so please provide as much detail as you can and fill in ALL the information requested on these forms. Thank you for taking the time to be thorough and complete, resulting in faster turnaround.

Name, First	Middle (spell out)	Last
Social Security Number		Date of Birth
Street Address		
City	State	Zip
County of Residence	Length of Time at This Address	
Home Phone	Other Phone	
Email address		
SPOUSE, First Name	**Middle (spell out)**	**Last**
Social Security Number		**Date of Birth**
Address (if living separately)		
City	**State**	**Zip**

DEPENDENTS

Name	Age	Relationship to You	Is this person/child living with you?
1. _____	____	_____	☐ YES ☐ NO
2. _____	____	_____	☐ YES ☐ NO
3. _____	____	_____	☐ YES ☐ NO
4. _____	____	_____	☐ YES ☐ NO

Have you ever filed bankruptcy before? ☐ Yes   ☐ No   If yes, what year? _____

Are both you and your spouse filing this bankruptcy together?   ☐ Yes   ☐ No

Has either you or your spouse been known by any other name during the past 6 years? (Example: maiden name, last name from previous marriage, legal name change, etc.)
☐ Yes ☐ No   If yes, write the **NAME** and **DATE(S) USED** below:

Name Used _____ Dates Used _____ thru _____
Name Used _____ Dates Used _____ thru _____

Client Intake Forms developed by The Lawyer Assistant, http://www.lawyerassistant.com

head of the table, you may unwittingly project a superior attitude. Sitting next to a client conveys an impression of collegiality, but it also allows a client to observe your notes. If you wish to ensure that the client cannot read your notes, you may want to sit on the opposite side of the table.

b. Conducting a Thorough Interview

Always be sure that you are on time for the initial interview. Clients will be impressed if you greet them promptly, remind them of your name and position, provide them with your business card, and then escort them into an office or conference room that has obviously been readied for them. Remind them of the purpose of the meeting. For example, you might say "Our goal today is to obtain some background information about your heart surgery last year." Tell the interviewee that you will be taking notes so that the file will be complete and so that you can later share the information with the attorney working on the case. Remind the client that anything disclosed is confidential (see Chapter Three). Avoid jargon such as "Tell me about your subdural hematoma." Instead say "Tell me about your injuries." Consider asking if the client or interviewee has any questions before you begin. If so, make sure that you do not respond by giving legal advice.

You are now ready to begin. There are a number of ways to obtain needed information from clients or other interviewees. Following are some typical approaches.

■ **The story approach.** Many clients are upset and emotional about their cases. They may be ready to burst with information. In such cases, allow the client to vent with minimal interruption. Ask the interviewee to give you a general overview of the event or to tell the story in chronological order. If you think of questions you'd like to ask or information that needs clarification, jot down these questions so you can ask them later.

■ **Remaining silent.** Don't forget that silence can be used to obtain information. Many people are uncomfortable with silence and will rush to fill the awkward moment by speaking. Thus, consider remaining silent on occasion to elicit information.

■ **The question approach.** Some clients may be more comfortable responding to questions than initiating discussion. There are several types of questions interviewers use to obtain information.

□ **Open questions. Open questions** (also called **open-ended questions**) are those that require an explanation rather than a yes–no response. Thus, questions such as "How can we help you?" or "Can you tell me about the accident?" are open questions because they do not restrict the interviewee to providing a short response but rather allow full dialog and explanation. The advantage of open questions is that they allow the responding party to control the response; the disadvantage of open questions is that they may encourage rambling and long responses. Open questions also allow you to observe the interviewee and determine his or her credibility and possible effectiveness as a witness.

□ **Closed questions. Closed questions** (also called **closed-ended questions**) require a yes–no answer or a very short answer. Examples of closed questions are "Did you sign the lease?" and "When did the surgery occur?" Such closed

Open question
A question that requires an explanation as a response; also called an *open-ended question*

Closed question
A question that requires a yes–no or brief answer; also called a *closed-ended question*

questions are helpful in clarifying information previously given and in directing individuals who tend to ramble. Such questions, however, generally produce only a very direct response and may encourage the speaker to omit other important information because it wasn't specifically asked.

☐ **Leading questions. Leading questions** are those that suggest an answer, as in "You weren't speeding, were you?" or "You signed the contract, didn't you?" Leading questions can be dangerous because a hesitant interviewee will be tempted to provide the answer your question suggests. Leading questions are most often used at trial with hostile witnesses who are reluctant to communicate information to the "other side."

☐ **Hypothetical questions. Hypothetical questions** are those based on speculation, such as, "If a person suffers a broken hip, what type of physical therapy is generally recommended?" or "If a car is traveling at a speed of 85 miles per hour and is involved in a head-on collision, what injuries are its occupants likely to sustain?" Hypothetical questions ask the interviewee to assume certain facts and are frequently used when interviewing or examining expert witnesses.

☐ **Prompting questions. Prompting questions** are those used to obtain information when the client or interviewee is hesitant to provide information. Ask, "What happened next?" or "Then what occurred?" to help the interview progress.

Leading question
A question that suggests the desired response

Hypothetical question
A question that is based on speculation and asks the respondent to assume certain facts

Prompting question
A question that motivates an interviewee to provide information

After you have obtained an overview of the event or responses to your questions, ask any additional questions you may have to clarify confusing statements the interviewee has given and that fill in the details you need.

c. Being Flexible

A serious obstacle to an effective interview is the interviewer's inflexibility. Beginning interviewers are usually somewhat nervous and want to make sure that they receive an answer to every question on their interview checklist. Thus, they often fail to listen to what is being said and become overly focused on completing their question checklist.

For example, you may be interviewing a client about injuries she sustained in an automobile accident. In the course of describing the accident, the client may casually mention that at the time of the accident she was on her way to the doctor for treatment for a back condition. An effective interviewer will catch this seemingly incidental remark and ask additional questions (either at the time or later) to make sure that the injuries she sustained in the accident were unrelated to her previous back problems. An interviewer who is focused on obtaining answers to the checklist questions will likely miss this opportunity and resume with a planned question such as "How fast were you driving at the time?"

Thus, be flexible. Allow the speaker to ramble a bit and feel free to leave your checklist to explore a new avenue that opens during the course of the interview. Follow up with logical questions that arise from comments the interviewee makes.

d. Cultivating Listening Skills

You will not be an effective interviewer unless you cultivate an ability to listen to the interviewee. If you are so busy thinking of the next question you intend to ask or are focused on the other cases you are handling, you will not be able to absorb the information the interviewee is providing and later relay it to your supervising attorney. More important, if you have to ask the interviewee to repeat information already given to you, it will be obvious that you weren't paying attention and the client will rightly feel that the case isn't important to you.

Active listening
Communication technique that lets speaker know that the listener is attentive

A technique commonly taught in communications seminars is that of **active listening,** a style of communication that lets the speaker know that you have heard what has been said. Active listening includes the following strategies:

- Using nonverbal cues, such as making eye contact, nodding your head, or taking notes, all of which let the speaker know that you are paying attention;
- Using verbal cues, such as "yes," "go on," "that's interesting," "I understand," "um-hmm," or "and then?" or other similar short verbal expressions that let the speaker know you are being attentive;
- Repeating or restating what the speaker has said by using expressions such as "Let me see if I understand this" or "Let me make sure I have all of the facts" and then paraphrasing what the speaker has said; and
- Sympathizing with the speaker by using expressions such as "I know this is difficult for you" or "I understand that was a tense confrontation for you."

Fidgeting, reviewing phone messages, taking other calls, interrupting, and looking at your watch give strong cues to the interviewee that you are impatient and lack interest in the speaker. If you find that your attention wanders during a long interview, force yourself to take careful notes because this will make you focus on what is being said. Similarly, be attentive to the speaker and offer to take a break if you think he or she is becoming distracted. You can then refocus the interview when it resumes. Remain silent for a few moments to encourage the interviewee to speak.

e. Ending the Interview

As the interview is nearing completion, take a minute and review your notes to make sure you have covered all topics. Review your checklist of questions. Consider providing a very brief summary to the client of the important points discussed in the interview. Confirm critical dates, names, and money amounts. Ask the interviewee if there is anything else he or she would like to add.

Conclude the interview by reviewing the next steps to be taken (such as obtaining documents and addresses). If you need the client's signature or authorization to obtain documents, such as a form authorizing doctors or hospitals to release the client's medical records to your office for review, explain the form and make sure the client has a copy. Tell the interviewee you appreciate his or her time and ask if there are any questions. Remind interviewees that you are available, and be sure they know how to reach you.

Prepare a letter thanking the interviewee and confirming any tasks that need completion. Prepare a memo to the file or to your supervising attorney as soon as you can, while the interview is fresh in your mind. Don't wait till you obtain outstanding facts or dates. These can be inserted later. Attach any pertinent documents to the memo or report so that if a new paralegal or attorney is assigned to the file, the file will be complete. See Chapter Six for information on preparing memoranda and Figure 7-2 for some tips for interviewing.

FIGURE 7-2
STRATEGIES FOR EFFECTIVE INTERVIEWS

Following are ten tips for conducting effective interviews.

1. Plan ahead by reviewing the file, conducting your legal research, and drafting some preliminary questions.
2. Start on time.
3. Make sure the interviewee understands you are not an attorney. Provide your business card.
4. Take copious notes, although be careful that you are not so focused on your note taking that you fail to listen attentively to what is being said.
5. Start any tape or video recording by introducing yourself, give the date and time, and ask the interviewee to confirm that he or she has consented to the tape recording. Many individuals find a recorded or videographed conversation intimidating, and it may well inhibit the flow of conversation.
6. Provide adequate supplies and useful documents.
7. Be observant to nonverbal cues, such as fidgeting, poor eye contact, and fatigue. Take frequent breaks when needed.
8. Be open, flexible, and nonjudgmental. Just because you had a bad experience with a landlord does not mean that all landlords are bad. Resist prejudging the client or the case.
9. Use a different colored pen for questions and topics that occur to you as the interview progresses. At the conclusion of the interview, it will be easy for you to return to these areas and obtain needed information.
10. Follow up after the interview. Call the interviewee a few days after the interview and ask if there is anything else he or she would like to add. In many cases, the interview jogs the memory, and a new idea or thought may have occurred to the interviewee.

---

f. Conducting Witness Interviews

(1) Introduction

In many respects, interviewing witnesses is similar to interviewing clients in that you will need to be prepared, thorough, flexible, and attentive. Nevertheless, there are some differences in style in interviewing clients and nonclients, such as witnesses.

Generally, there are two types of witnesses in a case: **lay witnesses**, or ordinary individuals who may have observed or experienced the events in question—for example, a person who saw an accident occur; and **expert witnesses**, or individuals who are specially qualified by education or experience to provide an opinion about the case—for example, an engineer who testifies about the speed and direction of cars in an accident. Interviews with clients may yield the names of additional witnesses, such as those who observed the accident or were present when certain events occurred.

In some instances, experts will be hired by the firm as consultants to help the firm prepare its case. These consultants may not be deposed (questioned under oath) by the adverse side unless they will testify. Witnesses who will testify for the client may be deposed by the other side so that the adverse party can fully prepare its case

Lay witness
Non-expert witness who has observed or experienced events that are testified about

Expert witness
Witness qualified by training or education to provide an opinion about a case or event

and perhaps hire its own expert to refute the opponent's expert's opinion, the so-called "battle of the experts."

In some cases, experts are retained even before the firm accepts a case. For example, if a prospective client asks the firm to represent her in a malpractice action against a doctor, the firm will want to first determine that malpractice has likely occurred. To take a patient's word that her doctor was incompetent without first consulting other doctors to determine whether the individual's doctor breached the applicable standard of care may be legal malpractice.

Friendly witness
Witness who is supportive of a client's position

Expert witnesses retained by the firm or lay witnesses who are friends and family of the client are often called **friendly witnesses** because they are supportive of the client's position. Other witnesses, such as eyewitnesses to an accident may have a neutral position and may not care which party succeeds; they are interested only in relaying the information they possess. Still other witnesses, usually those experts who have been retained by the adverse party or who have some personal relationship with the adverse party, are called **hostile witnesses**, because their stance is unsympathetic to the client.

Hostile witness
Witness who is hostile to client's position

(2) Witness Interview Techniques

As stated earlier, many of the skills required for conducting any interview apply equally to witness interviews. Thus, it is always critical to provide your name and position, start on time, avoid giving legal advice, and refrain from speaking with anyone represented by counsel. There are, however, some techniques that are specific to witness interviews, including the following:

- The conventional wisdom is that hostile or unfriendly witnesses should be interviewed as soon as possible so that your firm can develop a plan to minimize the effect of their anticipated testimony.
- Recognize that hostile witnesses are unlikely to share a great deal of information. Thus, asking a closed question ("Did you see skid marks at the accident scene?") will likely lead only to a curt "Yes" response. An open question ("What did you see when you visited the accident scene"?) will likely produce more information.
- Be especially careful not to lead friendly witnesses. These witnesses want to help the client. Thus, a question such as "Dan had his seat belt on, didn't he?" will likely produce the response the witness believes you want. Try and uncover the actual facts rather than this witness's perhaps favorably colored perception of the event.
- Be professional and courteous to hostile witnesses to ensure that they don't become even unfriendlier to the client. You will likely have only one opportunity to interview a hostile witness and therefore you want to make the most of this occasion.
- Pay special attention to the witness's demeanor. Form an opinion whether the witness will be effective or whether the witness is confused, defensive, inarticulate, or rambling. The firm needs to know how to prepare for trial, and judging how the witness will perform on the stand is important.
- Determine whether the expert witness is qualified. The witness likely has a résumé that describes his or her experience, articles written, and professional associations. Review this and other details relating to the witness's qualifications to ensure the witness is in fact competent to testify about the subject matter in question.

■ For witnesses who are reluctant or unfriendly, try to determine the basis for this attitude. Do they have something to gain if the other side is successful? Are they related to the adverse party? If so, their bias may be disclosed in court.

(3) Witness Statements

While preparing a careful memo or report of every interview is important, it is even more important for interviews of potential witnesses. Why? In many cases, a **witness statement**, a written and signed record of the witness's interview, may be discoverable by the adverse party. You will need to consult with your attorney to determine whether you should prepare a simple memo to the file that summarizes what was said and includes your impressions of the witness's demeanor (and that would not be discoverable because it is the firm's work product) or whether you should prepare a formal witness statement that the witness will review and sign and that may then be used at trial to refresh the witness's recollection or to impeach the witness by showing inconsistencies in testimony.

Witness statement
Written record of a witness's interview, signed by witness

B. INVESTIGATING

1. Introduction

Closely related to interviewing is **investigating** or locating information. While a great deal of information can be obtained through interviews of clients, nonclients, and witnesses, some factual information can be obtained only through investigation, such as reviewing motor vehicle records, visiting the scene of an accident, or locating assets. While some investigations, usually called **field investigations**, are done outside of the law office, the advent of comprehensive databases and powerful search engines has made investigating at once easier (because so much can be done on the Internet at your own office) and more difficult (because there is so much more information to check). In some instances attorneys ask paralegals to investigate while in other cases a commercial or professional investigator may be engaged.

Investigating
Locating information

Field investigation
Investigation done outside of a law office

2. The Rules of Evidence

No matter what type of investigation is being conducted, some understanding of the rules of evidence is important because only certain types of evidence may be introduced at trial. The term **evidence** refers to any information that may prove or disprove a fact. Generally, each state has its own rules of evidence and nearly all of these are based on the **Federal Rules of Evidence**, which were adopted in 1975, and govern federal trials. You will always need to research your own state's rules of evidence to determine what evidence may be introduced at trial. Such evidence is referred to as **admissible evidence.** The fact that evidence is allowed at trial does not necessarily mean it is true; it is the jury's function to make that determination.

While trial lawyers are fully knowledgeable about the rules of evidence, paralegals generally need to understand only fundamental principles relating to evidence so that they understand whether the fruits of their investigations (both statements and documents) will be admissible. The discussion that follows will provide you with a brief overview of the most fundamental evidentiary principles.

Evidence
Information that may prove or disprove a fact

Federal Rules of Evidence
Rules of evidence used in all federal courts and on which state rules of evidence are based

Admissible evidence
Evidence that may be introduced at a trial

a. Types of Evidence

Generally, there are two broad categories of evidence: direct and circumstantial. **Direct evidence** refers to information that proves (or disproves) the existence of a fact without relying on other facts or any inferences. **Circumstantial evidence** (sometimes called **indirect evidence**) is evidence that creates an inference or presumption that a fact exists. For example, if you saw Hal rob a bank, this is direct evidence. If Hal is found near the bank with a great deal of money for which he has no explanation, this fact is circumstantial evidence because it doesn't directly prove Hal robbed the bank but suggests that fact. There is nothing wrong with circumstantial evidence. Because of the difficulty of obtaining eyewitness accounts of criminal acts, many criminal convictions are based entirely on an accumulation of circumstantial evidence.

b. Forms of Evidence

Evidence can take several forms:

- **Real or physical evidence. Real** or **physical evidence** consists of any tangible item, such as a bullet, a glove, or a drop of blood.
- **Documentary evidence. Documentary evidence** consists of written records or documents, such as wills, employment agreements, photographs, or computer records.
- **Testimonial evidence. Testimonial evidence** consists of the testimony of a witness under oath.

To be admissible, both real and documentary evidence must be **authenticated,** or proven to be genuine or what is claimed. To authenticate documents, witnesses usually testify and identify the document and who prepared it or signed it. For example, to authenticate an employment agreement, the employer can authenticate that it is what it purports to be and that he or she signed it. The requirement of authentication for real and documentary evidence arises from the fact that such objects cannot be cross-examined. To ensure the jury does not place too great an emphasis on such items, they must thus be authenticated. Some evidence is **self-authenticating**, which means that it is presumed that it is genuine with no further proof. Thus, a certified copy of a death certificate is automatically deemed authentic.

Courts can dispense with the introduction of formal evidence in some cases and take judicial notice of certain facts. **Judicial notice** refers to the process of admitting evidence without formal proof. Thus, courts will take judicial notice that January 30, 2004, fell on a Friday and that the moon was full last Sunday evening. These are matters that are not subject to reasonable dispute and that could so easily be proven that courts won't require formal proof.

c. The Requirements of Relevancy and Competency

Evidence may not be introduced at trial unless it is relevant. **Relevant evidence** is evidence that tends to make the existence of any fact that is of consequence to the determination of the action more probable or less probable than it would be without the evidence. Fed. R. Evid. 401. In our example, evidence that Hal was in debt would be relevant because it tends to prove he had a motive for the bank robbery. Although

---

Direct evidence
Information that proves or disproves a fact without relying on any other evidence

Circumstantial evidence
Evidence that creates an inference that a fact exists; also called *indirect evidence*

Real evidence
Evidence consisting of a tangible item; also called *physical evidence*

Documentary evidence
Evidence consisting of written records or documents

Testimonial evidence
Evidence consisting of a witness's testimony under oath

Authenticated
Evidence that must be proven to be genuine or what is claimed

Self-authenticated
Evidence that is presumed to be genuine, with no further proof

Judicial notice
Concept that courts will admit some evidence without formal proof (generally, because it could be easily proven)

Relevant evidence
Evidence that tends to prove that a fact is more or less probable

relevant, some evidence may be excluded. Thus, evidence that would unfairly prejudice the jury, confuse the issues, or waste time may be excluded even though it is relevant. For example, evidence that a party has liability insurance is generally not admissible in a negligence action because it might well cause the jury to rule against a defendant on the basis that a verdict won't cost the defendant anything because his insurer will pay.

Another fundamental rule of evidence is that evidence must be **competent,** which means that a witness must understand the obligation to tell the truth, must have personal knowledge of the matter testified about (if the person is a lay witness), and must be able to communicate. Thus, a person with a limited I.Q. or a young child might be incompetent to testify. The trial judge will make the determination as to competency. Although a witness may be competent or legally fit to testify, he or she might not be credible or believable. The terms "competency" and "credibility" are not synonyms.

Generally, lay witnesses are competent to testify only as to matters about which they have personal knowledge or matters about which any person is likely able to testify, such as the speed of vehicles, size, distance, and the like. Lay witnesses may testify as to what they observed ("I watched Hal leave the bank with a bag" or "I signed the contract"), and may tell what they have perceived, but generally they may not offer an opinion or give a legal conclusion ("Hal is the bank robber" or "The contract is valid"). Expert witnesses need not have such personal knowledge to form an opinion and testify about it. An attorney who wishes to offer expert testimony must first establish a **foundation** or background information to show the witness's expertise, such as testimony or evidence as to the expert's credentials, education, experience, and particular skill.

d. Hearsay

Closely related to the requirement that lay witnesses may testify only as to matters within their personal knowledge is the evidentiary rule excluding hearsay evidence. **Hearsay** is any statement made by a declarant or speaker outside of a hearing or trial that is presented at the hearing or trial to prove the truth of the contents of the statement. Often called **secondhand information,** hearsay is excluded because it is viewed as unreliable because the person who made the original statement is not available for cross-examination.

> Example: Jill tells Rashida, "I saw Hal leave the bank the day it was robbed." At trial, Rashida cannot testify, "Jill said that she saw Hal leave the bank the day of the robbery." Rashida has no firsthand knowledge of the event. Jill, who does have firsthand knowledge of the event, should testify as to what she saw and then be subject to cross-examination so that witnesses can observe Jill's demeanor and assess her credibility.

Not all statements made out of court are hearsay; only those offered to prove the truth of the matter stated are hearsay. Thus, if Rashida testifies, "Jill told me she saw Hal leave the bank the day of the robbery" to show that Jill speaks English or that Jill is biased against Hal, such is not hearsay because the statement is not offered to prove that Hal actually left the bank on the day of the robbery; it is offered for some other purpose.

Moreover, hearsay consists of more than mere oral statements. Statements in the form of letters, memos, diaries, and computer files all constitute hearsay when

---

Competent evidence
Evidence that is legally sufficient (generally meaning that witness must understand the obligation to tell the truth, must have personal knowledge of the event, and must be able to communicate)

Foundation
Requirement of proving background before evidence is introduced

Hearsay
Out-of-court statement offered at trial to prove the truth of the matter asserted; also called *secondhand information*

they are offered to prove the truth of their contents. Thus, Jill's diary entry, "I saw Hal enter the bank today" is inadmissible hearsay. Similarly, hearsay may consist of conduct, such as pointing.

There are numerous exceptions to the hearsay rule, and much hearsay is admitted at trial under exceptions (most of which show that the statement was made under conditions that show a significant degree of reliability). Following are some of the common hearsay exceptions:

- **Excited utterances.** Statements made at the time of a startling event are admissible hearsay. Thus, a statement such as "Oh no! That car just hit the pedestrian!" is admissible because such an outburst is likely to be true.
- **Statements against interest.** A statement that is contrary to the declarant's interest is usually admissible if the declarant is unavailable as a witness. Thus, a statement such as, "Hal told me he robbed the bank" would be admissible hearsay (assuming Hal is unavailable to testify) because it is unlikely Hal would make a statement against his own interest unless it were true.
- **Dying declarations.** A statement made by an unavailable declarant who believes his or her death is imminent concerning the cause of death is admissible because a person who is facing death is unlikely to lie about the cause of death. For example, the statement, "Frank just shot me!" made just before a person dies is admissible.
- **Then-existing mental, emotional, or physical condition.** A statement made to show a declarant's then-existing state of mind, emotion, or physical condition is admissible. For example, if Alex testifies, "Hal told me he was desperate about his financial condition and would do anything to fix it" is admissible to show Hal's then-existing emotional state.
- **Business records.** Business records kept in the ordinary course of business activity are admissible. Thus, bank records showing Hal made an inquiry about his account on the day of the robbery are admissible.

e. Other Evidence Rules

There are two other evidence rules that are important. The **best evidence rule** requires that to prove the content of a writing, recording, or photograph, the original is usually required (although the adverse party can agree that a copy may be submitted). The **parol evidence rule** generally provides that oral evidence may not be introduced to contradict the terms of a written document.

f. Excluded Material and Privileged Material

Some evidence is inadmissible, even though it may be relevant and genuine. Generally, the evidence is excluded because there is a **public policy,** or societal advantage, to excluding the evidence. Some common types of such evidence that are inadmissible are the following:

- **Settlement offers.** Almost all civil cases engender settlement discussions and offers. These are inadmissible because otherwise parties would not freely engage in settlement negotiations, and courts always favor out-of-court settlements.
- **Remedial measures.** Measures taken after an incident to remedy a defect are inadmissible. Thus, if a defendant repairs her steps after the plaintiff has tripped

Best evidence rule
Evidentiary rule that original is usually required to prove the content of a writing

Parol evidence rule
Evidentiary rule that oral evidence may not be introduced to vary the terms of a written document

Public policy
Societal reason for a rule or regulation

on the steps and has been injured, information relating to the subsequent repair of the steps is inadmissible. This policy encourages defendants to repair and remedy dangerous conditions.

■ **Insurance coverage.** Information relating to a party's insurance coverage is inadmissible to prove liability. If jurors know a defendant is insured, they may be likely to rule against him or her, believing that the defendant won't be harmed by a judgment that the insurer will pay. Insurance coverage is discoverable before a trial because knowing policy limits may encourage settlement; however, evidence of insurance coverage may not be admitted at trial to prove liability.

Closely related to excluded material is **privileged material,** matter that is inadmissible because of the relationship between parties who engage in confidential discussions. One who holds a privilege cannot be forced to testify about the privileged matter. Thus, be alert to the status of certain parties in a case because it may not be possible to obtain information from them during your investigation. Generally, in these cases, public policy dictates that preserving the confidentiality of discussions between certain parties is more important than requiring disclosure of the confidential matter. The following are the most common privileges:

Privileged material
Matter that is inadmissible because of the relationship between parties in confidential discussions

■ **Attorney-client privilege.** Under the **attorney-client privilege,** attorneys and clients may not be compelled to disclose communications between them relating to the representation of the client. The attorney may, however, disclose the information with the consent of the client. (See Chapter Three.)

Attorney-client privilege
Evidentiary rule preventing legal professionals from testifying about confidential client information

■ **Doctor-patient privilege.** Under the **doctor-patient privilege**, doctors and patients may not be compelled to disclose communications between them relating to the treatment of the patient. If the patient consents, however, the doctor may testify.

Doctor-patient privilege
Evidentiary rule preventing doctors from testifying about confidential patient information

■ **Priest-penitent privilege.** Under the **priest-penitent privilege**, members of the clergy and penitents may not be compelled to disclose any confidential matters relating to the spiritual guidance of the penitent. The clergy member may disclose the communications if the penitent consents.

Priest-penitent privilege
Evidentiary rule preventing clergy members from testifying about confidential communications by their penitents

■ **The marital privilege.** Under the **marital privilege**, spouses may not be compelled to testify about their confidential discussions or communications. Thus, one spouse may not be compelled to testify against the other. If both spouses consent, a spouse may testify. The privilege usually survives divorce: Even after a marriage is dissolved, a former spouse may not be forced to testify against the other. The privilege does not apply if the spouses are engaged in litigation against each other.

Marital privilege
Evidentiary rule preventing spouses from being compelled to testify about their confidential communications

■ **Privilege against self-incrimination.** Under the **privilege against self-incrimination**, provided by the Fifth Amendment to the Constitution, in a criminal case a person may not be compelled to testify or provide information that could incriminate him or her. Thus, a criminal defendant may not be forced to answer questions about the alleged crime or to testify at the trial of the matter. This privilege is often referred to as the "right to remain silent."

Privilege against self-incrimination
Constitutional provision preventing an individual from being compelled to testify against himself or herself

3. Conducting the Investigation

The type and scope of an investigation is entirely dependent on the nature of the case. For example, in automobile accident cases, you will need to review police reports and motor vehicle records. In medical malpractice cases, you will need to obtain hospital and other medical records, locate expert witnesses, and calculate expenses and lost wages. In patent infringement cases, you will need to obtain copies of files from the Patent and Trademark Office. Thus, there is no one perfect approach that works for all investigations. There are, however, some strategies that can be used for most investigations.

a. Planning the Investigation

In most cases, the supervising attorney will give you instructions as to what items need to be investigated. Perhaps witnesses need to be located, title records need to be reviewed, or medical reports need to be obtained. Once you have your assignment, carefully review the file to determine if there are any preliminary leads in the file. For example, the file may identify the names and addresses of some witnesses or the dates of transfer of a parcel of real estate. Similarly, you may need to contact the client to see if he or she has any additional information.

If you haven't already done so, conduct some legal research to determine what the client needs to prove to prevail. This research will give you some guidance in planning your investigation. For example, if your client is sued for causing a car accident, an appropriate defense may be that the plaintiff caused the accident or contributed to her own injuries. A logical, common-sense starting point for the defendant is to review the police report to see if the reporting officer commented whether the plaintiff was at fault or was wearing her seat belt. Similarly, reports of insurance companies relating to the accident will be helpful.

Once you know your assignment and have obtained as much helpful information as you can from the file and the client, it is time to prepare a plan for your investigation—namely, a list of the steps you will follow to obtain the needed information. Use a logical approach and break down the investigation into chunks or units. For example, consider the following broad categories:

- **People**
- **Documents**
- **Physical evidence**
- **The scene**

For each category, identify what you need and how you plan to go about obtaining it. To illustrate, for "People," identify the various people you need to contact (by name if you know them, by description if you do not), indicate how you intend to locate them, and then note whether you will schedule a personal interview. Consider the following plan:

- **People**
  - ☐ Sandra Jones, witness (identified in police report; address provided in police report; call to schedule a personal interview to discuss her recollection of accident.)
  - ☐ Bystander who witnessed accident (talk to client and Sandra Jones to see if either remembers the bystander's name; talk to reporting police officer and insurance representative to see if either knows the bystander's name; consider placing notice in newspaper to locate bystander; once located, call to schedule a personal interview).

■ **Documents**

☐ Police report (obtain report and any accompanying photographs and diagrams).

☐ Insurance report (obtain report and any accompanying photographs and diagrams).

☐ Hospital and doctors' records (obtain all information about plaintiff's injuries, treatment, and costs of treatment).

☐ Employment records (obtain records to determine days of work missed due to injuries, and obtain salary information in order to establish damages).

☐ Vehicle information (obtain records of Department of Motor Vehicles relating to registration and records relating to repair of vehicle post-accident).

For litigation matters, another approach for preparing an investigation plan is to review the complaint filed by the plaintiff and the answer filed by the defendant. Identify each item or source needed for the plaintiff to prevail in each cause of action of the complaint or each item needed to support each defense asserted by the defendant. You can then make a list of the witnesses, documents, and physical evidence needed for each cause of action or defense and proceed with your investigation.

You should be aware that confidential records or records subject to privileges, such as medical records, are generally not accessible without a written authorization from the person affected by the records. If you are obtaining records related to the client, it will be easy to obtain the appropriate written release or authorization from the client. If an adverse party will not voluntarily provide authorization for you to review records, you may need to ask the court to issue a subpoena for them. A **subpoena** is a court order directing a person to appear at a trial or deposition (or to produce certain documents, in which case it is called a **subpoena duces tecum**). The subpoena will be directed to the hospital, doctor, records custodian, or the like, ordering the release and copying of the pertinent records. (See Chapter Eight, Civil Litigation, for additional information.) Similar rules apply for obtaining employment records and educational records.

Subpoena
A court order directing a person to appear at trial or deposition

Subpoena duces tecum
A court order directing a person to bring documents or other items to a proceeding

Once you have prepared your plan, review it with the supervising attorney to ensure that the plan is complete and that there are no ethical concerns relating to your plan. Finally, identify the tasks that you can complete at the office (such as using computer databases, the telephone, or the Internet) and those tasks that will require you to work in the field. Arrange the tasks in a logical order so that you work efficiently and do not end up retracing your steps.

b. Ensuring a Successful Investigation

As you investigate, keep a checklist or log identifying your progress, identifying your task, the date you interviewed witnesses or obtained evidence, the location of interviews, and the current status of the task or the date it was completed. Use electronic tools and reminders to help you track interviews and investigations. Consider adding some notes reflecting your personal observations, such as "witness seems reluctant to provide information" or "witness is cooperative and articulate." Make sure the log is complete and legible. If you cannot read the witness's address or you neglect to include the name of the investigating police officer, you will have to repeat these tasks.

Remember that the value of the case and the client's resources will dictate the scope of the investigation. It would be impractical in the extreme to conduct a

$10,000 investigation in a breach of contract case that alleges damages in the amount of $15,000. Discuss the scope of the proposed investigation with your supervising attorney before you begin. Ask if there is a budget for the investigation. Agree that you will report back to the attorney after a certain number of hours to provide an oral progress report. In some instances, a client may have significant resources and much of the investigation will be conducted by professional or commercial investigators. Your role may then be limited to coordinating the investigation, compiling or summarizing the results, and presenting them to the attorney and the client.

Be creative and flexible. If one source or approach isn't productive, don't give up; instead consider alternative ways of obtaining the information. Be thorough and persistent and follow each lead to its logical conclusion. If you hit a dead end, regroup by consulting with your supervising attorney, colleagues, and the client to determine if you would be able to find the results by some other method. Brainstorm by preparing a list of all the tasks you need to complete and the information you need to obtain. If your law firm employs a law librarian, work with him or her. Law librarians are specially trained to track down information and are invaluable sources with creative ideas for locating information.

Do not allow an unproductive investigation to consume all your time and efforts. If you believe that your investigation is proceeding too slowly or is not producing useful information, meet with your supervising attorney and report your results thus far, indicating how much time has been spent. You can then jointly agree on the next steps to be taken to ensure the client obtains the best results for the least amount of money.

Most of the resources that follow are free Internet services that allow access to various records.

c. Locating People

In some cases, clients or records such as police reports will provide the correct names and addresses of individuals that you need to track down. In other instances, you may only have someone's educated guess as to a name. Start with the easiest approach: Use a conventional telephone directory or call directory assistance. Old telephone directories are often maintained at your local library. Visit the last known address. If the person has moved from the address, talk to neighbors and landlords who may have information about the individual's whereabouts. Remember that finding a relative of the person may provide you with a lead.

While professional investigators are excellent at locating individuals (for example, experts and witnesses), you may be able to locate individuals yourself using the following sources:

■ **The Internet.** Popular search engines, such as Yahoo! (*www.yahoo.com*) or Google (*www.google.com*) provide or can link you to online telephone and address directories. When using Yahoo!, use the "People Search" tabs. When using Google, simply type in as much information as you know about the person into the search box (for example, you could type in "John Larkin, Philadelphia, teacher"). Alternatively, try the Internet search services Switchboard (*www.switchboard.com*) or Bigfoot (*www.bigfoot.com*). Both provide free access to some of their databases to allow you to locate persons and determine their addresses. More detailed information (such as background checks or information on judgments entered against a person) is offered for a fee. Once you locate an individual, you can use Mapquest (*www.mapquest.com*) to obtain directions to the address. Many sites also offer reverse directories, so that if you know only an address or a telephone number, you can then obtain the name of the individual. Such a "reverse look-up" is offered by The Virtual Chase, an excellent website maintained by a private law firm, which has numerous articles, tips, and strategies on conducting legal research and investigations. The site also offers "People Finder" and other links. Access *www.virtualchase.com.*

- **Electronic legal research services.** The two computer-assisted legal research services, LEXIS and Westlaw, both maintain databases for locating individuals. Your law firm will likely have access to one or both of these services. LEXIS's service, LexisNexis, allows searching of multiple records to find an individual even if you do not have complete information or the correct spelling of the individual's name. Westlaw's database is called "People Locator." It will provide addresses, phone numbers, information on professional or commercial licenses held by the person, and other information.

- **Court records.** If an individual has been the plaintiff or defendant in a civil action or a defendant in a criminal action, the court record will provide significant information, including the attorney who represented the person, perhaps facilitating contact with the individual through the attorney. If you know the county where the individual resides, check the records at the clerk's office at the courthouse. Records are usually maintained by the names of the plaintiff and defendant. If you know either name, you can usually obtain any court records for actions in which the person was a party.

- **Vital records.** To obtain vital records (birth, death, marriage, and divorce records), contact the county or state where the event occurred. Alternatively, use the site Vital Records at *www.vitalrec.com*, which provides information about how to obtain vital records from each state. Most states or counties charge nominal fees for providing copies of these records.

- **Property records.** If you know the person's address, you may be able to identify the person's name by reviewing property records for the county or city in which the property is located (assuming the individual owns the real estate rather than rents it). Many jurisdictions have placed these records online, making access convenient and free.

- **Post office records.** If the person has moved from his or her prior address, the post office will usually forward mail to the new address (if the individual has requested such) for one year. Mark the envelope "Change Service Requested" and you will be provided with a notice of the new address or reason for non-delivery. See the U.S. Postal Service website at *www.usps.gov* for additional information on obtaining addresses and forwarding information.

- **Motor vehicle records.** Most local jurisdictions require that automobiles used in the jurisdiction be registered on an annual basis. Title and registration information is usually maintained by the state department of motor vehicles. Information availability varies from state to state. You may need to submit a written request for information together with a fee. Direct links to each state's department of motor vehicles can be found at *www.usatrace.com/ssmv.html.* Review the pertinent state's policies on releasing driving records. Alternatively, you may call or visit your local department of motor vehicles to determine its policies.

■ **Social Security records.** Generally, individuals and businesses are able to obtain the Social Security numbers of other individuals. Information is available at the website of the Social Security Administration at *www.ssa.gov.* A person's Social Security number reflects the location of the office that issued the number. For example, New York issues Social Security numbers beginning with the digits 050-134, and all Social Security numbers issued in Alaska begin with the digits 574. The Social Security Administration website provides tables showing how numbers are assigned. Thus, if you know a person's Social Security number, you will be able to determine the state the individual resided in at the time the number was applied for, and you may then begin your search in that state.

■ **Other sources.** Consider visiting some Internet genealogy sites. Many of these offer excellent search tips and free searching. Some of the better-known sites are *www.ancestry.com* and *www.genhomepage.com.* The U.S. Census Bureau maintains many records at its site, *www.census.gov/genealogy.com.* Consider also whether the person may belong to a trade association. For example, if the person is a doctor, review the websites of the American Medical Association and other medical associations to determine if the person is a member of the association and whether location information is provided.

d. Locating Experts

Many cases depend on expert testimony from doctors, engineers, accountants, and the like. One of the best-known services is Technical Advisory Service for Attorneys (TASA), which provides experts in hundreds of areas for litigation and nonlitigation matters. TASA has been in existence for more than 40 years and is highly regarded. If your client needs to locate a witness who can testify about technical matters, such as the speed of vehicles, construction techniques, or an arson investigation, contact TASA at *www.tasanet.com.*

e. Locating Businesses

Obtaining general information about businesses is relatively easy and efficient because most companies have a presence on the Internet. In addition, if the company's stock is publicly traded, there will be a wealth of information available about the company and its principals.

For business information, consider starting with information that may be maintained by your state's secretary of state, which is the agency responsible in most states for corporate records and filings. Links to each state's secretary of state may be found at *www.premiercorp.com/statelinks.htm.* Many state sites allow basic searching, enabling you to determine the address of a corporation, its agent for service of process, and whether it is in good standing in the state.

Use the following free Internet sources to obtain information about businesses:

www.yahoo.com	Use Yahoo! "Yellow Pages" to find basic information about a company.
www.switchboard.com	Switchboard provides business and company information.
www.hoovers.com	Hoover's Online is an excellent source of information about companies. You may search by company name, stock ticker number, or a variety

	of other elements. You will then be provided with the company's address, telephone number, a brief factual description of the company's business and competitors, and an identification of its key people.
www.sec.gov	The website of the Securities and Exchange Commission permits searching of filings made by publicly traded companies. These public filings, including annual reports, offer a treasure trove of information about a company, including its assets, liabilities, key people, business activities, and subsidiaries.
Company websites	Don't forget that most companies now have websites that offer significant information about the company. If you do not know a company's website, consider guessing. For example, the website for IBM is *www.ibm.com* and the website for the Ford Motor Company is *www.ford.com*. Alternatively, try a general search engine, such as Google, to locate a company's website.

LEXIS and Westlaw also offer information about businesses and companies, although you will be charged a fee for accessing their databases. Many law firms, however, have subscription agreements with LEXIS and Westlaw that allow unlimited searching. In such a case, these services provide excellent, thorough, and reliable information. For example, Westlaw's "Business & Corporate Information" database provides information on corporate records, business registration filings, bankruptcy records, company profiles, lawsuit filings, and securities filings. Westlaw's "Asset Locator" database offers information about real property records, tax assessments, and motor vehicle records.

f. Locating Government and Public Records

Locating federal and state government records is relatively easy. Much information is available to the public, and a great deal is accessible on the Internet. The first step for any search of federal, state, or local records is to access the site FirstGov at *www.FirstGov.gov,* the official gateway to all government information. FirstGov offers direct links to the U.S. Congress, all courts, all federal agencies, state governments, and local governments. FirstGov provides access to the most comprehensive collection of government resources anywhere on the Internet. In addition to FirstGov, a variety of other Internet sources offer information.

(1) Obtaining Federal Government Records

There are numerous sources where you can find federal records, including the following:

- **United States Government Manual.** Unless you are certain which agency or department maintains the records you desire, consult the *United States Government Manual*, the official handbook of the federal government, which has comprehensive information on the agencies of the legislative, judicial, and executive branches.

The *Manual* is now available online, at *www.gpoaccess.gov/gmanual/index.html*. The *Manual* provides extensive information for the three branches of government (judicial, legislative, and executive), for agencies such as the Department of Commerce, and for independent establishments, such as the Environmental Protection Agency. Each section includes an organization chart, a list of key officials, a description of the role of the agency or department in the federal government, and a description of its programs and activities. Names, addresses, and phone numbers are provided to allow contact with the agency or department.

■ **Agency and department websites.** While it is fairly easy to guess at the websites for most federal agencies (for example, the website of the Department of Labor is *www.dol.gov*), a complete listing of all federal government agencies, boards and commissions, from the Accounting and Auditing Policy Committee to the Yucca Mountain Site Characterization Project, is available at *www.lib.lsu.edu/gov/fedgov.html*. The websites of most agencies and departments offer a wealth of information, including contact information, free publications, and e-mail access.

■ **Court records.** The website of the courts of the United States, *www.uscourts.gov*, provides links to the websites of all federal courts in the nation, including the U.S. Supreme Court, the courts of appeal, and all district courts. Available information varies from site to site, and all information is free. One fee-based service, PACER (Public Access to Court Electronic Records), a service of the U.S. Judiciary, allows users to obtain case and docket information from federal appellate, district, and bankruptcy courts. The PACER system offers electronic access to a listing of all parties and participants in cases, documents filed for certain cases, a chronology of dates of case events entered in the case record, and other useful information. Access the site at *http://pacer.psc.uscourts.gov* and register to use the system. The fee is presently $0.07 per page, whether or not pages are printed, viewed, or downloaded (although no fee is owed until a user accrues more than $10 worth of charges in a calendar year). Note that if your firm provides LEXIS or Westlaw access, these services may be more affordable than PACER.

(2) Obtaining Records and Information from Federal Agencies

The chief method by which one obtains records and information from government agencies is through the **Freedom of Information Act** (FOIA, pronounced "foy-ya") located at 5 U.S.C. § 552 (2000). FOIA allows any person to request records from various federal government agencies. A great deal of information is available, including information about how the agencies operate and any information an agency has about you. Any individual may make a FOIA request. These requests are often used to obtain records relating to public health, the environment, consumer product safety issues, and federal spending. Moreover, each agency must make certain records available to the public electronically and maintain an "electronic reading room" with final opinions and orders and other materials. Some information may not be obtained, such as information relating to national security, trade secrets, or information that would impede law enforcement activities. Additionally, FOIA does not apply to records held by Congress, federal courts, state and local governments, private businesses and organizations, or private individuals.

Each federal government agency website maintains a "FOIA page" with information on how to obtain records from the agency. Usually, a sample request form is provided. See Figure 7-3.

Freedom of Information Act
Federal law allowing individuals to obtain records and information from government agencies (known as *FOIA*)

FIGURE 7-3
SAMPLE FOIA REQUEST LETTER

[Letterhead]
[Date]

Freedom of Information Act Request
Agency Head or FOIA Officer
Name of agency or agency component
Address

Dear _____:

Under the Freedom of Information Act, 5 U.S.C. § 552 (2000), I am requesting copies of [identify the records as clearly and specifically as possible].

If there are any fees for searching or copying the records, please let me know before you fill my request. [Or, please supply the records without informing me of the cost if the fees do not exceed $_____, which I agree to pay.]

If you deny all or any part of this request, please cite each specific exemption that you believe justifies your withholding of information. Notify me of appeal procedures available under the law. [Optional: If you have any questions about handling this request, you may telephone me at _____ (home phone) or at _____ (office phone).]

                                                   Sincerely,
                                                   [Name]
                                                   [Address]

To obtain information, submit a FOIA request to the pertinent agency that reasonably describes the information and records you desire. The agency must respond within ten days and inform you whether your request will be fulfilled. You may be charged for the agency's costs of searching for documents, reviewing them to see if they should be provided, and costs of duplicating the documents.

The American Civil Liberties Union website (*http://archive.aclu.org/library/foia.html*) provides an excellent article about FOIA, *Using the Freedom of Information Act*, with information and tips on making requests and appealing refusals by agencies to release information.

(3) Obtaining State and Local Records

If you know the name of the state or local agency that maintains the records you need, contact that entity. If you are unsure which agency will have the desired records or documents, start with your state or local government website. To locate the pertinent state or local website, use these sources:

www.FirstGov.gov	The official portal to all government information, FirstGov offers direct links to each state's home page, state agencies, state legislatures, state governors, and a variety of state and local resources.

www.statelocalgov.net	State and Local Government on the Net is a directory of links to government-sponsored resources on the Internet. The site provides access to websites of thousands of state agencies and city and county governments.
www.searchsystems.net	This commercial site provides links to public records databases, including civil and criminal court filings, property records, professional licenses, and numerous other records. Most records are free but some require the payment of a fee.

Many states have acts similar to FOIA that allow individuals to obtain public records. Review your state's statutes for additional information.

g. Conducting a Physical Investigation

In many instances, you will need to leave the office to investigate a physical location, such as an accident scene, employment location, or parcel of property. Try to visit the scene as soon as possible after the event because the scene will change over time. Replicate the conditions of the event to the best extent possible—for example, visit an accident scene at the same time of day and during the same weather conditions as the time of the accident. Make diagrams and sketches and take numerous photographs. Use a digital camera if you have one. Have the photographs developed or downloaded as soon as you can and carefully label them with the date taken, your name, and a description of what the photograph shows. Alternatively, consider videotaping the scene or physical evidence or hiring a professional photographer or videographer to do so.

h. Using LEXIS and Westlaw for Investigations

The computer-assisted legal research services, LEXIS and Westlaw, contain numerous libraries and databases of information. Moreover, the information has been reviewed and scrutinized by professionals at LEXIS and Westlaw, thus enhancing its reliability and credibility. If your firm provides LEXIS or Westlaw access (almost all firms do), consider researching some very basic information yourself through the Internet and then log on to LEXIS or Westlaw, access the appropriate database, and refine your results. Both LEXIS and Westlaw offer research assistance seven days a week, 24 hours a day. Contact LEXIS at (800) 543-6862 and Westlaw at (800) 733-2884. Alternatively, review their websites at *www.lexis.com* or *www.westlaw.com* for additional information about support services.

i. Using Professional Investigators and Attorneys' Services

Some firms make a practice of using professional investigators for all investigations. The firm will have an established relationship with an investigator it trusts and may refer all but the most routine investigation requests to this professional. Alternatively, if your investigation hits a dead end, the firm may refer the matter to a professional investigation service. If the firm does not have an established relationship with an investigator, enter the term "Professional Investigator" into the Google site at *www.google.com* and you will be provided with information on numerous professional investigators. If the firm engages the services of a professional investigator, your role will likely be limited to providing instructions and information to the investigator, reviewing the results of the investigation, and summarizing and then reporting those results to the attorney and the client.

In some instances, your assignment may be straightforward, such as "get me a copy of the client's name change document." If you can readily and easily obtain the document, do so. Alternatively, consider using your local Yellow Pages and contact an **attorneys' service.** These are companies that specialize in helping attorneys by photocopying medical records, filing and serving papers at courthouses, and retrieving public documents. Most law firms have established relationships with attorneys' service companies and routinely rely on these services to obtain copies of public records. If the records are not located in your locality, the attorneys' service will contact an affiliate or other company in the other possible locations and arrange for the documents to be obtained and provided to you. Fees are generally reasonable.

> **Attorneys' service**
> Professional company that assists attorneys and paralegals in filing and serving court documents, retrieving public documents, and performing related tasks

j. Evaluating Results of Investigations

Once records and information are obtained, they must be evaluated. Remember that while the Internet is a wonderful tool, in many cases you do not know who posted the information or how current it is. Because many sites link to others, an error at one site is easily carried over to others. Thus, if a person's date of death was erroneously reported as January 31, 2004, rather than January 30, 2004, it may appear incorrect in a number of databases. Generally, government Internet sites (those that end with the suffix .gov) are highly reliable. Similarly, those sites maintained by educational institutions (those that end with the suffix .edu) are credible. Commercial sites (those that end with .com, .net., or .org) vary in their reliability.

Similarly, be skeptical when interviewing witnesses and clients. Observe their demeanor and body language. Be attentive to inconsistent statements.

k. Reporting Results of Investigations

After you complete your investigation, you will need to report your results to the supervising attorney (and usually to the client). In many instances, results are reported in the format of a standard legal memorandum, discussed in Chapter Six. Many investigation reports or memos begin with an **executive summary,** a short and concise overall review of the report. The executive summary gives a preview of the longer report to follow and includes your results, conclusions, and any recommendations you may have. The more detailed report follows. The full report summarizes the purpose and scope of your investigation, describes the approaches you followed to obtain information, identifies each person or source you contacted with a description of the information obtained from the person or source, identifies the dates you conducted any interviews or investigations, gives your overall impressions of witnesses, provides conclusions you have reached, and gives any suggestions you have for obtaining additional information.

> **Executive summary**
> Short, concise written review provided before a full report

If there are photographs or diagrams, these should appear as appendices to the report. Similarly, include a separate source appendix that specifically identifies each source you contacted. For individuals, include full names, addresses, and telephone numbers. Indicate the dates you contacted the individuals and any direct statements or quotations you obtained. For Internet sources, provide the full Internet site (some sites are transient) and the dates you reviewed the sites. For physical evidence and inspections, identify the dates you viewed the scene or physical evidence and identify where the negatives of the film are stored or where computer files of digital photos can be located. Attach copies of any public records or other related documents. Such information is better placed in a separate appendix following the report so that it does not interrupt the flow of your narrative discussion.

After you provide the report to the supervising attorney, schedule a meeting to discuss the results and any additional investigation that may be needed and to determine whether the results should be provided to the client.

Consider preparing a "lessons learned" memorandum for yourself to identify which sources were helpful and which were time-wasters. Your next investigation will then benefit from what you learned.

NET RESULTS

Although this chapter has identified numerous useful Internet websites, following are five that are "the best of the best."

www.khake.com/page66.htm	This site offers numerous articles and tips on interviewing and general communications skills.
www.FirstGov.gov	FirstGov is a gateway or portal to a vast array of federal, state, and local sites, allowing easy access to important information.
www.google.com	Google is a popular, all-purpose search engine. When the site appears, simply type words that describe your task or question into the search box. Google provides excellent results, usually ranked in their order of usefulness or importance.
www.law.cornell.edu/rules/ fre/overview.html	The Federal Rules of Evidence are offered by Cornell Law School.
www.virtualchase.com	This excellent website is offered by a private law firm and provides links to other sites and strategies for finding the law and conducting investigations. It offers useful "People Finder," "Court Records," and "Public Records," features, among other useful links. Articles and tips on conducting research and investigations are offered.

CASE ILLUSTRATION

Exclusion of Evidence of Insurance

Case: *Citti v. Bava*, 266 P.2d 954 (Cal. 1928)

Facts: The plaintiff was a passenger in the defendant's car when an accident occurred. The plaintiff was injured and sued the defendant. At trial, the plaintiff introduced evidence that was intended to inform the jury that the defendant was insured. The jury ruled for the plaintiff and the defendant appealed.

Holding: The court reversed the judgment because evidence of insurance is highly prejudicial. Evidence of insurance is inadmissible to prove negligence or wrongdoing. The purpose of the rule excluding evidence of insurance is to prevent the prejudicial use of evidence of liability insurance in an action against the insured.

KEY TERMS

Engagement letter
Intake sheet
Intake memo
Open question
Closed question
Leading question
Hypothetical question
Prompting question
Active listening
Lay witness
Expert witness
Friendly witness
Hostile witness
Witness statement
Investigating
Field investigation
Evidence
Federal Rules of Evidence
Admissible evidence
Direct evidence
Circumstantial evidence
Real evidence
Documentary evidence

Testimonial evidence
Authenticated
Self-authenticated
Judicial notice
Relevant evidence
Competent evidence
Foundation
Hearsay
Best evidence rule
Parol evidence rule
Public policy
Privileged material
Attorney-client privilege
Doctor-patient privilege
Priest-penitent privilege
Marital privilege
Privilege against self-incrimination
Subpoena
Subpoena duces tecum
Freedom of Information Act
Attorneys' service
Executive summary

CHAPTER SUMMARY

Interviews	Paralegals are often involved in interviewing clients and nonclients, such as witnesses and experts.
Effective Interviewers	Effective interviewers are prepared, thorough, flexible, and are good listeners. While a list of questions or an intake sheet may be useful starting points, good interviewers go beyond printed questions and follow up on unexpected avenues of information.
Different Types of Questions Used in Interviews	Different types of questions are useful in eliciting information. For example, an open question such as "Tell me what happened," encourages the speaker to tell the story at his or her own pace. A closed question such as "How fast was the car going?" can serve to direct and focus a rambling speaker.
Active Listening Skills	Use active listening skills (letting interviewers know you are paying attention) to encourage interviewees to share information.
Communicating Results of Interviews	Always prepare a memo reflecting the results of any interview.
Evidentiary Rules	■ Paralegals need to understand some evidentiary rules to ensure that their investigations focus on material that will be admissible at trial. ■ Generally, evidence must be authentic, relevant, and competent. ■ Some evidence is excluded from trials. Thus, hearsay (unless it falls within one of the numerous hearsay exceptions), settlement offers, evidence of insurance or repairs, and privileged material are generally inadmissible at trial.
Investigation Plans	Develop an investigation plan before you conduct any investigation. Use a logical approach and keep accurate notes and a log of all your activities.

Useful Investigation Tools	The Internet is an extremely useful source of information and, in many cases, a great deal of investigatory work can be done in the office by using helpful websites. In other instances, an investigation will move into the "field," so that physical evidence and scenes can be examined.
Communicating Results of Investigations	Provide a report of your investigation results to your supervising attorney. Use a standard memorandum format and provide an executive summary.

TRIVIA

- FOIA has been used to obtain information from both the FBI and CIA about the assassination of President Kennedy.
- The total number of FOIA requests received by all federal departments and agencies in fiscal year 2002 was 2,402,938.
- The cost of all FOIA-related activities for all federal departments and agencies in fiscal year 2002 was more than $300 million.
- TASA, the group that refers experts for litigation and nonlitigation matters, receives more than 13,000 requests for experts each year.

DISCUSSION QUESTIONS

1. Assume your office represents the plaintiff in a case involving an automobile accident. Why would it be important to find out from an interviewee that he was employed by the defendant in the case?
2. In the above question, may you obtain your client's medical records from the client's doctor? May you obtain a witness's medical records? Discuss.
3. What is the best way to obtain records from the Department of the Army?
4. What are the advantages and disadvantages of the following forms of questions:
   - "Why don't you go ahead and tell me about the accident?"
   - "He didn't repair the roof, did he?"
5. Francie testifies at trial, "Jim told me, 'I sure wish I hadn't had so much to drink before I drove on the night of the accident.' " Is the statement admissible? Why?
6. What purpose would an executive summary serve in a 30-page investigation report?
7. What cautions should you exercise in evaluating investigation results from the Internet?

CLOSING ARGUMENTS

1. Access the FirstGov website.
   a. What is the address of the Secretary of the Navy?
   b. What is the phone number for the FOIA contact for the Alcohol, Tobacco, Firearms, and Explosives Bureau (Justice)?
   c. Link to "State Government." What is the fee for ordering a birth certificate by mail in Texas?
2. Access the Google website.
   a. Who were the founders of Procter & Gamble and in what year was the company founded?
   b. What is the stock ticker symbol for Target Corp. and on what exchange is the company's stock traded?
   c. What are the visiting hours for the United States Senate and the Capitol?
3. Locate the Federal Rules of Evidence. Is evidence of subsequent remedial measures admissible to prove negligence or a defect in a product? Give the answer and cite the rule that governs your answer.

PART

III

PARALEGALS IN THE WORKPLACE

CHAPTER

8

CIVIL LITIGATION

D

ISCOURAGE LITIGATION. PERSUADE YOUR NEIGHBORS TO
COMPROMISE WHENEVER YOU CAN. POINT OUT TO THEM HOW
THE NOMINAL WINNER IS OFTEN A REAL LOSER—IN FEES,
EXPENSES, AND WASTE OF TIME. AS A PEACEMAKER THE LAWYER
HAS A SUPERIOR OPPORTUNITY OF BEING A GOOD MAN. THERE
WILL STILL BE BUSINESS ENOUGH.

—ABRAHAM LINCOLN (CIRCA 1850)

CHAPTER OVERVIEW

Because more paralegals are involved in litigation than in any other practice area
and because litigation crosses over to nearly every other practice field in which
paralegals work, this chapter explores the role of paralegals in litigation in more
detail than in other practice fields, which are discussed in the following chapter. The
chapter follows the litigation "life cycle" from the filing of the complaint to trial.
The handling of complex and large-scale litigation (such as the massive cases involving tobacco and asbestos claims) are addressed, and the specific tasks likely to be performed by paralegals engaged in litigation work are examined. The chapter then
reviews alternative dispute resolution and other alternatives to litigation.

A. THE CIVIL LITIGATION LIFE CYCLE

1. Introduction

The National Association of Legal Assistants (NALA) reports that nearly half of all
paralegals employed by law firms work in the litigation field. As a result, nearly all

Civil litigation
A lawsuit between private parties

Criminal litigation
A lawsuit brought against a person by a governmental entity for an alleged criminal violation

paralegal programs offer courses in litigation or trial procedures. This chapter will focus on **civil litigation**, actions between two parties, rather than **criminal litigation**, which involves actions brought against defendants by either a state or the federal government for alleged violations of law. Civil litigation overlaps with many other practice areas because a lawsuit may allege breach of an employment agreement, medical malpractice, patent infringement, or failure to comply with an order entered in a divorce action. There are, however, matters common to all lawsuits. Before reading the following discussion of litigation, you may wish to review Chapter Four's discussion of jurisdiction, venue, the distinction between trial and appellate courts, and the remedies available to litigants.

2. Before the Lawsuit Is Filed

Generally, before a lawsuit is filed, most parties try to resolve the matter amicably. Recall from Chapter Six that an aggrieved party will usually send a demand letter to the other party, setting forth his or her demands and requesting that some action be taken. If informal attempts to resolve a matter are not successful, the injured party may begin the litigation process. As discussed, the process will be governed by either the Federal Rules of Civil Procedure (if the action is brought in federal court) or the pertinent state's rules of civil procedure (which are modeled on the Federal Rules of Civil Procedure). These rules govern the format of documents submitted to court, the number of copies required to be submitted, filing fees, the method of filing and serving court papers, the discovery process, jury selection, and trial and appellate procedures. Courts require strict compliance with their rules, and paralegals involved in litigation thus need to be intimately familiar with these rules. Many courts now post their rules on their websites, making compliance fairly straightforward. Always double-check court rules before filing any documents with a court.

3. Initiating the Lawsuit

a. The Plaintiff's Complaint

Complaint
The document setting forth a plaintiff's claims and which initiates litigation

Caption
The heading in a court pleading that identifies the court, parties, title of action, and so forth

Docket number
The number assigned to a file by a court

Parties
In litigation, plaintiffs and defendants

Once a firm determines that a party has a claim and that jurisdiction and venue are proper (see Chapter Four), the first step in the litigation process begins: the drafting of the **complaint**, which is the document that initiates litigation and sets forth the plaintiff's demands. The complaint must comply with the appropriate rules as to its form and content. Generally, the complaint "tells the story" of the plaintiff's claims. Some courts provide sample forms for straightforward civil actions; the plaintiff then completes the appropriate form.

The first page of the complaint displays the **caption**, a heading that sets forth the name of the court, the title of the action, the court's **docket number** (an identifying number assigned to the case by the court clerk, that remains the same during the lawsuit throughout the trial), and the names of all **parties** (the plaintiffs and defendants).

In addition to the caption, the complaint includes the following three elements:

■ **Jurisdictional statement.** The complaint will indicate the grounds on which the court's jurisdiction depends and a reference to the pertinent statute, if any.

The statement is usually very concise, such as, "This Court has jurisdiction pursuant to 28 U.S.C. § 1253 (2000)."

- **Plaintiff's claim.** The body of the complaint will set forth the claim showing that the plaintiff is entitled to relief. Courts generally require only that this be a "short and plain statement." Each part of the claim appears in its own paragraph, each of which is numbered. If the plaintiff has more than one claim or **cause of action** against the defendant, these will be stated as separate **counts.**
- **Request for relief.** The plaintiff concludes the complaint by asking the court to enter judgment for the plaintiff and to grant certain relief, which is usually money damages but could be a request for an injunction or other remedy. This section is usually called the **prayer.**

Cause of action
A claim against a defendant

Count
A plaintiff's statement of his or her cause of action

Prayer
Request for relief made in plaintiff's complaint

The complaint will then be signed by the plaintiff's attorney (although it will be signed by the plaintiff if he or she is acting pro se—that is, in his or her own behalf). The signature constitutes a representation that the person who signed has read the complaint and reasonably believes everything stated to be true. Fed. R. Civ. P. 11. Some jurisdictions require that complaints and other pleadings be **verified**, which means that the person on whose behalf they are submitted must declare under penalty of perjury that what is stated is true. See Figure 8-1 for a sample complaint.

Verified
Process of swearing under penalty of perjury that a pleading is true

b. Filing and Serving the Complaint

After the complaint is prepared, it is filed with the clerk of the court. Either the paralegal files the complaint or the firm's attorneys' service (see Chapter Seven) will do so. Because court rules vary, you will need to call the clerk and determine how many copies are required and the amount of the filing fee. Many courts require a **cover sheet** to identify certain basic information about the case, which will aid the clerk in assigning the case to an appropriate judge. Some jurisdictions allow filing of complaints by facsimile or electronically, using the Internet, but most courts require hand delivery to the clerk's office.

Cover sheet
In litigation, document that accompanies plaintiff's complaint

The clerk then assigns a docket number to the case and issues a **summons**, which is a document informing the defendant that he or she is being sued and ordering the defendant to appear and respond to the complaint within a certain time period. The summons also tells the defendant that a failure to respond may result in a default judgment being entered against him or her.

Summons
A document by which a court orders a party to appear before the court

The next step in the lawsuit is that the plaintiff must effect **service of process** on the defendant, which means that the summons and the complaint must be delivered to the defendant. While the general rule is that anyone over 18 who is not a party may serve the summons and complaint, most law firms either use professional process servers or pay a court official to effect service. The best method of service is **personal service**, which means hand delivering the summons and complaint to the defendant. In many instances this is impracticable, and most court rules allow service by leaving a copy of the documents at the defendant's residence or place of business with a person of suitable age and discretion. If these methods are not successful, most courts allow a defendant to be served by mail. Some courts require an official notice to be published in a newspaper if service is effected by mail. The rules relating to service of process are quite strict because courts want to ensure that defendants have the opportunity to defend themselves if they have been sued.

Service of process
Delivery of court documents

Personal service
Hand-delivery of court documents

Once service is effected by some means, the individual who served the documents completes and files with the court the **proof of service**, a document that

Proof of service
Verification that documents have been served

FIGURE 8-1

SAMPLE COMPLAINT FOR BREACH OF CONTRACT

Anna T. Carr
Carr & Nelson, LLP
1010 Second Avenue
Suite 1700
San Diego, CA 92110
State Bar No: 12898
(619) 276-1090
Attorney for Plaintiff

SUPERIOR COURT OF THE STATE OF CALIFORNIA
COUNTY OF SAN DIEGO

Liberty Associates, LLC	) CASE NO: 03-1088
	)
Plaintiff,	) COMPLAINT FOR
	) BREACH OF CONTRACT
	)
	)
v.	)
	)
Jackson Enterprises, Inc., and	)
	)
Does 1 through 10	)

Defendants

Plaintiff complains and for causes of action alleges as follows:

FIRST CAUSE OF ACTION

(For Breach of Contract Against Jackson Enterprises, Inc.)

1. Plaintiff Liberty Associates, LLC ("Plaintiff") is a Limited Liability Company organized and existing under the laws of the State of California with its principal offices in the City of San Diego, County of San Diego.
2. Defendant Jackson Enterprises, Inc. ("Defendant") is a corporation organized and existing under the laws of the State of California with its principal offices located at 1800 Pomerado Road, in the City of San Diego, County of San Diego.
3. Plaintiff is ignorant of the true names and capacities of Defendants sued as DOES I through X, inclusive, and therefore sues these Defendants by such fictitious names. Plaintiff will amend this Complaint to allege their true names and capacities when ascertained.
4. Plaintiff is informed and believes and thereon alleges that each of the Defendants was the agent and employee of each of the remaining Defendants and was at all times acting within the purpose and scope of such agency and employment.
5. On or about February 15, 2003, in the City of San Diego, County of San Diego, State of California, Plaintiff and Defendant entered into a written agreement, a copy of which is attached hereto as Exhibit "A" and made a part hereof. By the

FIGURE 8-1 (CONTINUED)
SAMPLE COMPLAINT FOR BREACH OF CONTRACT

terms of the written agreement Defendant agreed to pay Plaintiff for certain construction services performed by Plaintiff for Defendant.

6. The consideration set forth in the agreement was fair and reasonable.
7. Plaintiff has performed all conditions, covenants, and promises required by it on its part to be performed in accord with the terms and conditions of the written agreement.
8. On or about September 1, 2003, the Defendant breached the agreement by failing and refusing to pay Plaintiff for the services provided by Plaintiff to Defendant.
9. By reason of Defendant's breach of the contract as alleged in this Complaint, the Plaintiff has suffered damages in the sum of Seventy Five Thousand Dollars ($75,000).
10. By the terms of the written agreement, the Plaintiff is entitled to recover reasonable attorney fees incurred in the enforcement of the provisions of the agreement. By reason of the aforementioned breach of the Defendant, the Plaintiff has been forced to secure the services of the law firm Carr & Nelson LLP to prosecute this lawsuit.

WHEREFORE, Plaintiff requests judgment against Defendants, and each of them, as follows:

1. For compensatory damages in the sum of $75,000;
2. For interest on the sum of $75,000 from and after September 1, 2003 to date of judgment;
3. For reasonable attorney fees according to proof;
4. For costs of suit incurred; and
5. For such other and further relief as the court may deem proper.

VERIFICATION

I, Timothy F. Delgado, am a member of Liberty Associates, LLC, Plaintiff in the above-entitled action. I am authorized to act on behalf of Liberty Associates, LLC. I have read the foregoing Complaint for Breach of Contract and know the contents thereof. The same is true of my own knowledge, except as to those matters that are alleged on information and belief, and as to those matters, I believe them to be true.

I declare under penalty of perjury that the foregoing is true and correct and that this declaration was executed at San Diego, California.

Date:_____   _____

                                          Timothy F. Delgado
                                          Member, Liberty Associates, LLC

verifies to the court that the defendant was in fact served, and describes when and how he or she was served.

A corporation doing business in a state is required to appoint an agent to receive service of process for the corporation. The name of the agent may be obtained from the state's secretary of state. Alternatively, most statutes provide that service on any corporate officer is effective service. In addition, a defendant may waive formal service by agreeing to accept the summons and complaint. To encourage defendants to waive service (which saves time and money), many courts give defendants who waive service an additional period of time to respond to the complaint.

c. The Defendant's Response to the Complaint

Generally, the defendant in a civil action has a choice of three responses to the complaint:

Default judgment
Judgment entered against a defendant who fails to respond to a complaint

Answer
A defendant's response to a plaintiff's complaint

Affirmative defense
Allegation by a defendant that negates a plaintiff's right to relief

- **Default judgment.** A failure to respond by the defendant will result in the entry of a **default judgment** against the defendant. The defendant will be liable for the full amount the plaintiff requested in the complaint.
- **Answer.** The defendant may respond to the complaint by filing an **answer**, a pleading that responds to each and every allegation of the complaint and sets forth **affirmative defenses**, defenses that negate a plaintiff's right to relief. Examples of affirmative defenses include pleading that the statute of limitations bars the plaintiff's claim, that the claim has been discharged in a bankruptcy action, and that fraud precludes the plaintiff from recovering. If a defendant does not deny an allegation by the plaintiff, it is deemed admitted. The defendant's responses must be set forth in numbered paragraphs that respond to the allegations in the plaintiff's complaint. The answer must be filed within specified time limits; in federal courts, the answer must be filed within 20 days after service of process.

Motion to dismiss
A request that a court dismiss litigation (sometimes called a *demurrer*)

- **Motion to dismiss.** The defendant may file a **motion to dismiss** the complaint and ask the court to dismiss the action for a variety of reasons, including the following: the court lacks jurisdiction; the defendant was not properly served; or the complaint did not state a basis for which relief could be sought. In some jurisdictions, including California, a motion to dismiss is called a **demurrer.**

Counterclaim
A claim by a defendant against a plaintiff

Cross-claim
A claim by one defendant against another

Third-party practice
A claim by a defendant against one not a party to pending litigation

Third-party plaintiff
A defendant who makes a claim against one not a party to pending litigation

d. Counterclaims, Cross-Claims, and Third-Party Practice

If a defendant has a claim against the plaintiff arising out of the same event or occurrence complained of by the plaintiff, the defendant must assert it in the ongoing action by filing a **counterclaim.** The plaintiff must then respond to the allegations asserted by the defendant. If the action involves several defendants and one of them wishes to sue another or others, the defendant files a **cross-claim,** a claim asserted by one defendant against another. A defendant may also file an action against a party not named in the original action, in a procedure known as **third-party practice**. The defendant is now called the **third-party plaintiff** because he or she is in the position of making a claim against someone else. As you can see, litigation can be quite complex, with a variety of actions being filed by parties against each other and the joining of new parties.

e. Amendments to Pleadings

During the litigation process, the parties may wish to amend their pleadings as new issues arise and new facts are uncovered. Parties may agree or **stipulate** to allow each other to amend a pleading. If the other party does not agree, one may ask leave of court to amend. Leave is usually freely given when justice requires.

f. The Scheduling Conference

After the complaint and answer have been filed with the court, the court usually schedules a conference with the parties, called either the **scheduling conference** or the **pre-trial conference**, to discuss possible settlement and efficient disposition of the case. The court will issue a **scheduling order** limiting the time to file motions and complete discovery.

4. Discovery

a. Introduction and Scope of Discovery

After the initial pleadings have been filed, the next phase in a lawsuit is **discovery,** the investigation conducted by parties before trial to obtain information from each other and from witnesses so they can prepare for trial. There are five discovery devices: interrogatories, depositions, requests for production of documents, requests for admissions, and requests for physical or mental examinations.

All the discovery devices are intended to give the parties to a lawsuit information about the other party's claims, defenses, witnesses, insurance coverage, financial status, and other matters. Courts highly favor discovery because information gained before a case may facilitate settlement, which courts always encourage. Moreover, discovery will eliminate surprise and reduce delay at trial, leading to a more efficient trial. Discovery also helps narrow the issues, because it may reveal that an issue is not contended by the other side, thus eliminating the need for proof of that issue at trial. Finally, discovery may help preserve testimony from witnesses who may not be available at trial.

The discovery devices share some common features:

- Except for orders for physical and mental examinations, each method is **extrajudicial**, which means that the court is not involved;
- The scope of discovery is the same for all methods: the materials sought must be relevant to the subject matter of the lawsuit (or reasonably calculated to lead to relevant information) and may not be privileged;
- Each request for discovery must be signed by the attorney requesting it; and
- The court can fashion a variety of protective orders to ensure discovery has not been used to harass a party, cause delay, and so forth.

Paralegals probably play a more significant role in discovery than in any other litigation phase and are intimately involved in preparing interrogatories, summarizing depositions, assisting in document production, and numerous other discovery-related tasks.

Stipulation
A voluntary agreement to take action or refrain from taking action

Scheduling conference
Conference held by court to determine disposition of a case; also called *pre-trial conference*

Scheduling order
Order issued by court indicating dates related to trial

Discovery
Investigation conducted by parties before trial to obtain information from each other

Extrajudicial
A proceeding that does not involve a court

b. Interrogatories

Interrogatories
Written questions propounded by one party to another

Interrogatories are sets of written questions propounded by one party to another. Interrogatories may be sent only to plaintiffs and defendants; they may not be used to obtain information from nonparties. They must be answered under oath and returned within 30 days after service (unless the parties stipulate to an extension of time). Interrogatories can be used, for example, to locate documents, determine a person's medical condition, or inquire about the existence of expert witnesses. Some states impose limits on the number of interrogatories a party may send to ensure one side doesn't outspend the other.

Paralegals often play a major role in drafting interrogatories. Most offices have files of sample interrogatories that can serve as models. Form books are also helpful in drafting interrogatories. Paralegals also help clients formulate and refine their responses to interrogatories. As soon as your office receives a set of interrogatories, calendar the response date so that you do not miss this critical deadline.

c. Depositions

Deposition
Out-of-court examination of party or witness under oath

Depositions are oral examinations of witnesses under oath. Depositions are the one discovery device that can be used to obtain information from witnesses. All other discovery devices are directed exclusively to parties in the lawsuit. The deposition usually takes place in an attorney's conference room. A court reporter will attend, administer the oath to the witness, and transcribe the witness's answers to the questions asked. Depositions may also be audiotaped or videotaped. Many attorneys consider depositions the most useful discovery device because the witness (and not his or her attorney) will be providing the responses. If a corporation is a party, it must appoint the appropriate person to attend the deposition.

The deposition of a party to the litigation may be taken by simply providing a notice to the party setting forth the time, date, and place where the deposition will be taken. Paralegals frequently assist in scheduling depositions. A notice of deposition directed to a party may be coupled with a request that the proposed deponent bring various documents to the deposition. If a nonparty witness will not appear at a deposition voluntarily, a subpoena (a court order directing a person to appear and give testimony) will need to be prepared by the desiring party and signed by a judge. If the attorney wants the nonparty witness to bring documents or other things to the deposition, a subpoena duces tecum is presented to the judge for signature. The subpoena duces tecum orders the individual to bring various documents and items at the time of the deposition.

Transcript
Booklet providing testimony of witnesses at depositions or trial

After the deposition is completed, the reporter will prepare a booklet or **transcript** of the witness's testimony. Paralegals often play a major role in reviewing and summarizing these deposition transcripts. See Figure 8-2 for information on summarizing depositions.

Paralegals may prepare a preliminary checklist of questions and attend a deposition with the attorney who will conduct the questioning. In a newer trend, many litigation support companies provide interactive realtime depositions (allowing attendees to "see" the testimony on their laptop screens as it is spoken and affording easy note taking and marking of key passages of the testimony). Transcripts are later prepared in both traditional booklet form and on disks, often called e-transcripts. See Chapters Eleven and Twelve for additional information about litigation support software.

FIGURE 8-2
SUMMARIZING DEPOSITIONS

Paralegals frequently summarize or digest depositions, generally to condense a voluminous transcript into a shorter and more readable format and to help the attorney prepare for trial by locating critical or inconsistent testimony. Some commercial firms specialize in preparing deposition summaries, and some sophisticated litigation software packages now generate deposition summaries and allow "real time" interaction, which means that as the court reporter transcribes the witness's testimony, it appears nearly immediately on the attorney's or paralegal's laptop screen, allowing the team to mark key parts of the testimony during the deposition itself (see Chapter Eleven for additional information). Although there are different formats, there are some general rules common to all forms of deposition summaries:

- **Get instructions from the attorney.** Determine whether the summary is being prepared for use in the firm or will be sent outside the firm, perhaps to an insurance company. Find out what format the attorney prefers and whether there are any key topics in which he or she is particularly interested.
- **Review the file before you begin.** Review the client's file to determine the causes of action alleged, defenses asserted, and so forth, so that you understand the critical issues in the case.
- **Skim the deposition before beginning your digest.** Because witnesses often ramble and repeat information, skim the deposition so you can flag critical topics and topics that are repeated several pages apart.
- **Keep it short.** The summary must be short enough to be useful. If the format is a narrative, three to five pages should be sufficient. If the format is in a topic format, try to keep to a ratio of 10:1, so that for every ten pages of testimony, there is a one-page summary.
- **Use the witness's words when needed.** In many instances, the witness's own words are critical. For example, if the witness says, "I believe Mary was wearing her seat belt," don't change this to "Mary was wearing her seat belt."
- **Include page numbers.** No matter what form of deposition summary you prepare, include the page numbers (and line numbers, which are usually included down the left margin of each page) so a reader can readily locate the pertinent testimony.
- **Omit extraneous information.** Omit any discussion between attorneys, attorneys' objections, introductory remarks made by attorneys or by witnesses, questions asked by the attorneys, and repetitive information (although you must flag inconsistent testimony).

There are three well-known formats for deposition summaries. A narrative summary simply summarizes the testimony in sentence-by-sentence, paragraph-by-paragraph form. Narrative summaries are usually used when providing status reports to insurance companies. Use topic headings throughout the summary. For example, if the witness is an expert, topic headings might be "Education," "Professional Experience," and "Accident Reconstruction."

A topic format is probably the most common type of deposition summary. This format is often called a deposition index. Each page indicates the topics discussed and the nature of the testimony given about the topic. Ideally, all of the testimony relating to medical care is then brought together, all of the testimony relating to damages is brought together, and so forth, allowing the reader to locate quickly topics of interest. One variety of a topic format is to present the information in chronological order, a technique that is especially helpful when the timing or the

FIGURE 8-2 (CONTINUED)
SUMMARIZING DEPOSITIONS

sequence of events in a case is critical. Because many deponents skip around when testifying, you may need to prepare a cover sheet or table of contents for the deposition index, indicating where, for example, the reader can locate information on various topics such as injuries, lost wages, and medical care.

Depositions are also sometimes cross-indexed. For example, you may be asked to review six different transcripts to determine what each witness recalled about the weather at the time of a car accident.

Examples

Narrative Form

Deposition of Patricia Allen, M.D.

(January 30, 2004)

<u>Background</u>

Patricia Allen is a practicing physician whose office is located in Chicago, Illinois (2:6-16). She has been the pediatrician for the plaintiff's child since 1995 (3:6-14). Dr. Allen obtained her undergraduate degree at the University of Chicago and her medical degree at the University of Minnesota (7:18-28).

<u>Description of Medical Care</u>

Dr. Allen first saw the minor child on July 10, 2003, when the child was brought in for examination for a fever of 103 degrees. Dr. Allen prescribed bed rest and Tylenol and ordered a throat culture to determine if the child had strep throat. The culture was negative. Five days later the child began having convulsions. After a phone call with the child's mother, Dr. Allen instructed the mother to take the child to Northwestern Memorial Hospital in Chicago (8-11).

Index Form

Deposition of Patricia Allen, M.D.

(January 30, 2004)

<u>Topic</u>	<u>Page</u>	<u>Testimony</u>
Practice	2: 6-16	Allen's pediatrics practice is in Chicago.
Education	7: 18-28	Allen has an undergraduate degree from Univ. of Chicago and medical degree from Univ. of Minn.
Office visit and medications	8: 2-9	Allen saw child on 7/10/03 when child brought in to office with fever of 103. Allen prescribed bed rest and Tylenol and performed a throat culture for strep throat, which was negative.

FIGURE 8-2 (CONTINUED)
SUMMARIZING DEPOSITIONS

Convulsions and hospitalization	9: 10-26 10, 11: 1-19	The child began having convulsions on 7/15/03 and Allen instructed mother to take child to Northwestern Memorial Hospital in Chicago.

Cross-Index Format

Topic: **Medications ordered by physician Patricia Allen, M.D.**

Deponent	Page	Testimony
Patricia Allen, M.D.	8:2-9	Allen ordered that the child receive Tylenol for the fever.
Jayne Nelson	16:4-10	Dr. Allen did not recommend that the child take any medicine.
Paula Rainey	8: 12-26	The child's mother asked Rainey, the school nurse, to make sure the child received Tylenol during the week of July 10, 2003.

d. Requests for Production of Documents

A party may request that another party produce documents that are relevant to the litigation. Copies of contracts, invoices, medical records, insurance agreements, and the like can be obtained. In addition, items of physical evidence, such as an allegedly defective fuel pump or a parcel of real property may be examined. A party cannot avoid the duty to disclose by placing documents or items with another person. A party must produce any documents in his or her custody, possession, or control.

e. Requests for Admission

A **request for admission** is a written document served by one party on another asking the other to admit the truth of some matter or the genuineness of some document. For example, a party might ask another, "Do you admit that Exhibit A attached to the Complaint in this matter is a true and correct copy of the contract signed on July 10, 2005?" and "Do you admit you signed the contract?" Requests for admission help narrow and frame the issues for trial. If a party admits that a copy of the contract is valid and that he or she signed it, there is no need to prove this at trial, thus ensuring a more efficient and speedy trial.

Request for admission
A written request that a party admit the truth of some matter or the genuineness of some document

f. Requests for Physical and Mental Examinations

A party may ask a court to order that another party undergo a physical or mental examination if the party's physical or mental health is at issue in the case. These discovery devices tend to be used in personal injury lawsuits when the plaintiff has alleged physical injury or mental trauma caused by the defendant.

g. Discovery of Electronic Evidence

Discovery allows a party to obtain not only conventional paper evidence but also electronic evidence in the form of voice mail, e-mail, electronic calendars, information stored on computers, spreadsheets, and other such information. This process is often referred to as *electronic discovery.* Because e-mail is so common in the workplace, a number of experts have called it a "smoking gun," and some lawsuits alleging sexual harassment in the workplace have relied on e-mail at the employer's workplace to show a persistent pattern of harassment or hostile work environment.

h. Exclusions from Discovery

Recall that parties may obtain discovery of any matter that is not privileged that is relevant to the subject matter of the pending lawsuit. It does not matter that the information will not be admissible at trial; it may still be discoverable. For example, evidence that a party has insurance coverage is inadmissible to show fault; nevertheless, it is discoverable because it might lead to a settlement.

Work product
Written mental impressions, conclusions, and opinions of attorneys and paralegals

In addition to privileged material (see Chapter Seven), an attorney's or paralegal's work product is not discoverable. **Work product** refers to the written mental impressions, conclusions, opinions, or legal theories of counsel prepared for use in a case.

i. Sanctions and Protective Orders

Except for requests for physical or mental examinations, discovery proceeds without court intervention. Usually, a court has no idea who is being deposed, whether interrogatories have been sent, and so forth. If a dispute arises, however, the court will become involved. For example, if a party simply refuses to respond to interrogatories, you may seek an order compelling discovery. If the party continues to refuse to comply, the court can impose a variety of **sanctions** or punishments: The court may order that certain facts are deemed established; it may forbid the disobedient party from asserting certain claims or defenses; and, in particularly egregious cases, it may dismiss the plaintiff's case or enter a judgment against the defendant.

Sanction
Punishment imposed by a court

The potential for abuse in discovery is clear. For example, one party might attempt to bury another under an avalanche of interrogatories. Such practices cause delay and subvert the legitimate purposes of discovery. Thus, courts may fashion **protective orders** to protect parties from discovery requests that are unduly burdensome or are intended to delay or harass. A court may eliminate some items of discovery altogether. For example, in one case, interrogatories were over 2,000 pages. The court struck the entire set. A court may control the time and place of discovery to ensure a party is not inconvenienced. Moreover, a court may seal a deposition to protect trade secrets or order that discovery not be had at all.

Protective order
Order issued by a court to protect a party from harassment or harm

5. Pre-Trial Activities

Dismissal with prejudice
Dismissal of a case such that it cannot be reinstituted at a later date

Not all cases go to trial; in fact, the vast majority are settled out of court. Discovery may disclose the weakness of a case and thus spur settlement discussions. A plaintiff may dismiss his or her case **with prejudice**, which means the plaintiff may not later reinstitute the case; or **without prejudice,** which means the plaintiff may later reinstitute the case.

Dismissal without prejudice
Dismissal of a case that may later be reinstituted by the plaintiff

In addition, either the plaintiff or the defendant may move for **summary judgment**, asking the court to grant a judgment in its favor without a trial. A court will grant a motion for summary judgment if there are no material facts in dispute and the only questions are those of law, which a judge is competent to decide.

Before the trial, parties may also make **motions in limine,** which are motions to exclude evidence or certain issues; for example, to exclude privileged information, hearsay, or work product.

Most courts require the parties to hold a pre-trial conference, at which time the parties' stipulations, list of witnesses to be called, and issues to be litigated will be reviewed. Some courts combine this with settlement conferences, which represent another opportunity for the court to urge the parties to settle the case themselves.

6. Trial

Not all civil cases are heard by juries; some occur at bench trials, which are conducted solely by judges. For example, some trials may involve highly scientific information, and the attorneys may decide a jury would be overwhelmed with the technical nature of the testimony and evidence. A party who desires a jury trial must file a demand for it and serve the demand on the other party. If a jury is requested, each attorney will question the prospective jurors in a process known as **voir dire.** Attorneys may challenge jurors to exclude them. Attorneys have an unlimited number of **challenges for cause**, a challenge based on the juror's bias, personal involvement in the case, and the like. Attorneys have a limited number of **peremptory challenges**, challenges for which no reason need be given. A limit of three peremptory challenges is common.

One task commonly performed by paralegals is maintaining the **trial notebook,** a binder with all pertinent information the attorney may need at trial, including information about witnesses, summaries of deposition transcripts, copies of needed documents, and lists of exhibits to be presented.

The trial begins with **opening statements** by the attorneys, if desired. The plaintiff makes his or her opening statement first, followed by the defendant. Following the opening statements, the plaintiff's attorney will present the plaintiff's case. The attorney engages in **direct examination**, which is questioning of a witness by the party who called him or her. During direct examination, the attorney may not ask leading questions (those that suggest the desired answer). Hostile witnesses may be asked leading questions.

After direct examination of a witness by the plaintiff, the defendant may cross-examine each of the plaintiff's witnesses. The scope of the cross-examination is limited to what was testified about during the direct examination. After cross-examination, the plaintiff may engage in **redirect examination,** perhaps to clarify a confusing point or to rehabilitate a witness who faltered under cross-examination.

After the plaintiff has presented all of his or her evidence, the defendant may move for **judgment as a matter of law,** which, like the motion for summary judgment, alleges that there are no material facts in dispute and that defendant is entitled to judgment in his or her favor at this time. If this motion is not successful (very few are), the defendant will present his or her case (although, because the plaintiff has the burden of proof in a civil suit, there is no requirement that the defendant prove anything). Once again, the process is direct examination by the defendant, cross-examination of the defendant's witnesses by the plaintiff, and

Summary judgment
Pre-trial motion asking court to enter judgment for a party

Motion in limine
Request that a court exclude evidence or issues at trial

Voir dire
The process of questioning prospective jurors

Challenge for cause
Request to eliminate a prospective juror for a valid reason, such as bias; unlimited in number

Peremptory challenge
Request to eliminate a prospective juror with no reason given; limited in number

Trial notebook
Binder prepared for trial with all information and documents needed at trial

Opening statement
First statement made at a trial by an attorney

Direct examination
Questioning of a witness by the party who called him or her

Redirect examination
Examination of a witness by plaintiff after defendant has cross-examined the witness

Motion for judgment as a matter of law
Request that a court enter judgment for a party

possible redirect examination by the defendant. After the defendant's case is completed, the plaintiff may rebut new evidence the defendant introduced or make a motion for judgment as a matter of law.

Closing statements will be made and the judge will then instruct the jury about the rules of law that apply to the case. At the beginning of a case, each party usually provides a set of requested jury instructions to the judge, who will decide (outside the presence of the jury) which ones will be read. The jury is then given its instructions, often in an "if-then" format, as in, "If you find the defendant breached the contract, then you must award monetary damages to the plaintiff to compensate her for damages caused by the defendant's breach." Once the jury reaches its verdict, the court will enter the judgment in the formal court records. Entry of judgment starts the clock running for an appeal. In most states, an appeal must be filed within 30 days after entry of a final judgment. Additional information about appeals is provided in Chapter Four, Section E. See Figure 8-3 for a diagram showing the litigation lifecycle.

7. The Paralegal's Role in Litigation

Paralegals are involved at every stage of the litigation process. Before a case is initiated, paralegals may engage in client interviews and investigations (see Chapter Seven) and may draft demand letters. They also engage in the following activities:

- Conducting legal research in preparation for drafting complaints, answers, and briefs;
- Preparing pleadings, notices of motion, and proposed orders;
- Reviewing court rules to ensure pleadings comply with court requirements;
- Maintaining the litigation calendar, docketing dates for responsive pleadings, discovery deadlines, court hearings, and so forth;
- Locating and tracking case and docket information with courts;
- Arranging for filing and service of the complaint and other litigation pleadings and documents;
- Participating in all phases of discovery, including the following:
  - Drafting discovery requests, including interrogatories, notices of depositions and preliminary deposition questions, requests for production of documents, requests for admissions, and requests for physical and mental examinations;
  - Coordinating deposition schedule and reserving conference room and engaging court reporter;
  - Meeting with clients before depositions, attending depositions and taking notes at depositions;
  - Meeting with clients to obtain information so answers to interrogatories may be prepared;
  - Drafting responses to various discovery requests;
  - Summarizing and digesting transcripts of deposition testimony;
  - Assisting in document production and attending document production;
  - Coding, indexing, and reviewing documents produced by other parties; and
  - Assisting in preparing motions for protective orders or to compel discovery.
- Assisting with preparation of pre-trial briefs and related research; conducting legal research; cite-checking; validating citations through *Shepard's* or KeyCite;

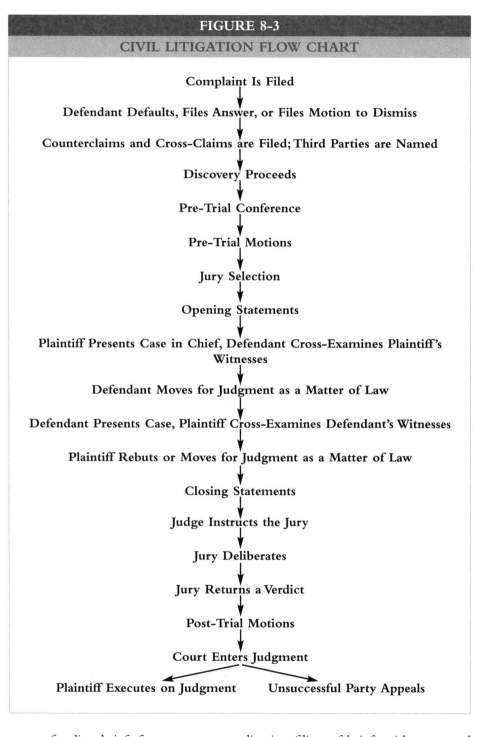

FIGURE 8-3

CIVIL LITIGATION FLOW CHART

Complaint Is Filed

Defendant Defaults, Files Answer, or Files Motion to Dismiss

Counterclaims and Cross-Claims are Filed; Third Parties are Named

Discovery Proceeds

Pre-Trial Conference

Pre-Trial Motions

Jury Selection

Opening Statements

Plaintiff Presents Case in Chief, Defendant Cross-Examines Plaintiff's Witnesses

Defendant Moves for Judgment as a Matter of Law

Defendant Presents Case, Plaintiff Cross-Examines Defendant's Witnesses

Plaintiff Rebuts or Moves for Judgment as a Matter of Law

Closing Statements

Judge Instructs the Jury

Jury Deliberates

Jury Returns a Verdict

Post-Trial Motions

Court Enters Judgment

Plaintiff Executes on Judgment   **Unsuccessful Party Appeals**

proofreading briefs for accuracy; coordinating filing of briefs with court and service on parties;

■ Attending settlement conferences and meetings, preparing and proofreading settlement agreements, monitoring compliance with obligations of settlement, preparing and filing dismissals of action (if representing plaintiff);

■ Assisting in pre-trial conferences and meetings;

- Preparing a trial notebook with all key documents and witness information;
- Helping prepare clients and witnesses for court appearances;
- Drafting jury instructions;
- Organizing trial exhibits;
- Attending trial and taking notes;
- Coordinating scheduling for witnesses;
- Ordering transcripts;
- Assisting in collecting damages, if awarded; and
- Drafting and filing notice of appeal, if desired.

See Figure 8-4 for information on utilization of paralegals in litigation.

8. Complex Case Management

While paralegals are highly involved in all litigation matters, class actions and other complex cases such as those involving asbestos claims or breast implant litigation rely on paralegals even more extensively. For example, the March/April 2004 issue of *Legal Assistant Today* reported that a paralegal in New York was responsible for organizing 15 million pages of documents for a high-profile securities class action. The paralegal stated that the key to success in these cases is the effective use of technology and following a firm-initiated protocol for organizing and tracking documents. Generally, one paralegal will be assigned to the case as the **project manager,** who will supervise other paralegals and assume the lead role in the case. See Chapter Eleven for additional discussion of complex case management and the use of technology tools that allow the storing of all transcripts and pleadings on a laptop computer, allowing easy searching for inconsistent testimony and eliminating the need to carry boxes of documents to court.

Among the tasks paralegals perform in these mega-cases are the following:

- Determining the particular type of software programs needed to manage the case;
- Developing databases to facilitate the accessibility of documents;

Project manager
Lead paralegal in a complex case, often a litigation case

FIGURE 8-4

USE OF PARALEGALS IN LITIGATION

According to the ABA Survey on the utilization of paralegals, among firms that engage in litigation and that use paralegals:

- 71% use paralegals to maintain litigation calendars;
- 88% use paralegals to review, organize, and index documents produced by parties;
- 65% use paralegals to summarize deposition transcripts;
- 54% have paralegals attend document productions;
- 31% use paralegals to obtain lists of prospective jurors and biographical information on jurors;
- 82% use paralegals to organize and mark trial exhibits;
- 67% use paralegals to prepare trial notebooks; and
- 55% have paralegals attend trials to take notes and handle exhibits.

- Working with vendors or other legal team members to code documents through the use of Bates numbering (see Chapter Eleven) or other systems;
- Working with vendors or other legal team members to scan documents and effect optical character recognition so that full-text searching of documents is facilitated;
- Using case management software packages to construct chronologies and witness lists, respond to discovery requests, prepare a "paperless" case, and collaborate with others on the team;
- Conducting searches of documents to prepare chronologies and to prepare for discovery and trial;
- Assisting in production of documents; and
- Assisting in training of other team members on effective use of technology.

B. ALTERNATIVE DISPUTE RESOLUTION

Alternative dispute resolution (ADR) is the term given to an umbrella of activities that are designed to resolve disputes without trial. Because going to trial is expensive, time-consuming, and stressful, a number of disputing parties elect ADR. In many instances, clauses in contracts between parties will require ADR. In other instances, courts order some form of ADR. It has proven especially useful in commercial cases.

ADR usually takes the form of **mediation**, in which a neutral third party acts as a facilitator to help parties resolve their differences. The mediator has no power to render a decision. The ADR may also take the form of **arbitration,** in which a neutral third party renders an actual decision, much like a judge at trial. ADR not only saves time and money; it preserves the confidentiality of the parties because the discussions, hearing, and related matters are not a matter of public record, as is a trial.

A new method of dispute resolution, called **med-arb**, is a combination of mediation and arbitration: If preliminary and informal mediation does not produce a result, the parties immediately proceed to arbitration, often using the same neutral third party. Another form of ADR is the **mini-trial**, in which the parties make presentations of their cases and either a judge selected by them renders a binding decision or the parties themselves (or their decision makers) meet to resolve the dispute based on the presentations of evidence. Another form of ADR is called **rent-a-judge**, in which case the parties engage the services of a retired judge to hear their dispute and either render a decision or coach them into a settlement. Finally, a new form of ADR is **online dispute resolution**. For example, parties involved in disputes relating to Internet domain names must resolve their disputes online. All papers and arguments are submitted electronically, and a decision is rendered by the Internet Corporation for Assigned Names and Numbers.

Commercial companies such as JAMS (Judicial Arbitration and Mediation Services, Inc.) provide ADR services, as does the nonprofit American Arbitration Association. Generally, the parties agree on a neutral third party (often a retired judge) and then pay the costs associated with the process. The results are confidential and the process is less formal than a trial. Discovery is usually streamlined. If the procedure is an arbitration, it may be binding, in which case the arbitrator's decision is treated like that of a trial judge, or it may be nonbinding, in which case an unhappy party may proceed to trial after the arbitrator's decision. One law firm,

Alternative dispute resolution
Method of resolving disputes without trial

Mediation
Process by which a neutral party attempts to help parties resolve their differences

Arbitration
Process by which a neutral party renders a decision affecting disputing parties

Med-arb
Combination of mediation and arbitration in which arbitration is commenced after an unsuccessful mediation

Mini-trial
Form of alternative dispute resolution in which parties present evidence to either a judge selected by them or a panel of their decision makers

Rent-a-judge
Form of alternative dispute resolution in which parties engage the services of a retired judge to hear their dispute and render a decision or facilitate settlement

Online dispute resolution
New form of alternative dispute resolution in which all documents and evidence are submitted electronically and a decision is rendered electronically as well

Morse, Barnes-Brown & Pendleton, P.C., has estimated that the average cost of a hotly disputed employment discrimination case is approximately $150,000, while the average cost of an employment discrimination arbitration is about $20,000. The firm believes that ADR is usually cheaper because the proceedings are simpler and typically there is no appeal.

Paralegals are usually involved in the following ADR-related activities:

- Reviewing documents to determine if ADR is required under the terms of an agreement;
- Inserting ADR clauses into contracts drafted by the office, if desired by clients;
- Reviewing rules relating to ADR procedures;
- Drafting a demand for arbitration;
- Reviewing the background of proposed neutral parties;
- Coordinating arrangements for arbitration or mediation, including scheduling witnesses;
- Preparing discovery requests and responses;
- Preparing documents and exhibits to be produced at the ADR hearing;
- Drafting settlement agreements;
- Monitoring settlement agreements for compliance; and
- Enforcing the arbitrator's award, if any.

NET RESULTS

www.law.cornell.edu/rules/frcp	Cornell Law School provides the text of the Federal Rules of Civil Procedure at this site.
www.findlaw.com/01topics/ 29litigation/	FindLaw offers links to a variety of journals, articles, message boards, and other useful sites relating to litigation and ADR.
www.megalaw.com	MegaLaw offers direct linking to numerous sites relating to civil procedure and litigation, including articles on preparing for depositions and links to "wacky court cases."

CASE ILLUSTRATION

Policies Underlying Discovery

Case:	*Pacific Telephone and Telegraph Co. v. Superior Court*, 465 P.2d 854 (Cal. 1970)
Facts:	After being ordered by the San Diego Superior Court to answer 97 questions propounded in interrogatories, the plaintiffs sought

to restrain the court from enforcing its order on the basis that the questions were not relevant.

Holding: Discovery was allowed. The discovery statutes allow wide discretion to trial courts in granting or denying discovery, and a party seeking to show that a trial court abused its discretion bears an extremely heavy burden. Any doubts about the relevancy of information sought to be discovered should generally be resolved in favor of permitting discovery. The discovery of information does not depend on its admissibility at trial. So long as the information will reasonably lead to the discovery of admissible evidence or be helpful in preparation for trial, it should be discoverable.

KEY TERMS

Civil litigation
Criminal litigation
Complaint
Caption
Docket number
Parties
Cause of action
Count
Prayer
Verified
Cover sheet
Summons
Service of process
Personal service
Proof of service
Default judgment
Answer
Affirmative defense
Motion to dismiss
Counterclaim
Cross-claim
Third-party practice
Third-party plaintiff
Stipulation
Scheduling conference
Scheduling order
Discovery
Extrajudicial

Interrogatories
Deposition
Transcript
Request for admission
Work product
Sanction
Protective order
Dismissal with prejudice
Dismissal without prejudice
Summary judgment
Motion in limine
Voir dire
Challenge for cause
Peremptory challenge
Trial notebook
Opening statement
Direct examination
Redirect examination
Motion for judgment as a
    matter of law
Project manager
Alternative dispute resolution
Mediation
Arbitration
Med-arb
Mini-trial
Rent-a-judge
Online dispute resolution

CHAPTER SUMMARY

Litigation Paralegals	More paralegals are engaged in litigation than in any other practice area. Paralegals are involved in every step of the litigation process, from the filing of the complaint, through discovery and trial, to an appeal, if necessary. Paralegals are utilized extensively in the discovery process to prepare and respond to discovery requests.
Initiating and Responding to the Lawsuit	A lawsuit is initiated by the filing of a complaint by the plaintiff. The defendant may answer, move to dismiss the complaint, or fail to respond. Other parties may be brought in by either the plaintiff or defendant.
Purpose of Discovery	The parties to litigation may engage in discovery, a process intended to allow the parties to discover information about the other's case and possibly facilitate settlement or eliminate surprise at trial.
Scope of Discovery	A party may discover any relevant information or information that may lead to relevant information that is not privileged.
Discovery Devices	The discovery devices are interrogatories, depositions, requests for production of documents, requests for admissions, and requests for physical or mental examinations. All but the last device proceed without court intervention.
Trial	If a case is not resolved, it will proceed to trial with the plaintiff proceeding first. A jury may or may not be involved in a civil case.
Complex Cases	Some large-scale cases involve reams of documents, requiring paralegals to use sophisticated software packages to manage the case.
Alternative Dispute Resolution	As an alternative to trial, a party may elect (or a contract may require) mediation (in which case a neutral party helps the parties resolve their dispute) or arbitration (in which case a neutral party renders a decision). ADR reduces costs and is an efficient alternative to trial.

T R I V I A

- Over the past ten years, civil and criminal caseloads for our nation's federal and state courts have increased by 30 percent.
- A 1998 ABA survey on the use of paralegals in private practice reported that smaller law firms (those with four to ten attorneys) make the most use of paralegals in the litigation field, with nearly 70 percent of those firms using paralegals to prepare pleadings, discovery responses, and deposition summaries and outlines. Only 23 percent of law firms with more than 100 attorneys used paralegals to perform these litigation tasks.
- According to the ABA Survey, 88 percent of firms that use paralegals in litigation have them engaged in discovery-related tasks, such as reviewing, organizing, and indexing documents produced.
- The ABA Survey also reported that nearly 70 percent of those firms that spend some time on litigation have paralegals attend trial to take notes and handle exhibits.

D I S C U S S I O N   Q U E S T I O N S

1. Tim is a paralegal employed by a law firm that is representing the defendant in a litigation matter. The firm has been overwhelmed with numerous sets of interrogatories served on the defendant. What might the firm consider doing to protect its client, and what role would Tim play?
2. Anna has sued Jeff for breach of a contract to repave her driveway. Jeff thinks Anna must be mentally disturbed to make such a ridiculous claim. May Jeff obtain a court order to compel Anna to submit to a mental examination? Discuss.
3. Kevin has sued George for injuries Kevin sustained when the two were involved in a car accident. George is convinced that Kevin is either faking it or has dramatized the extent of his injuries. May George obtain a court order to compel Kevin to submit to a physical examination? Discuss.
4. During a trial, an attorney asks the expert she has hired: "You didn't find any injuries when you examined the plaintiff, did you?" Is this a proper question? Discuss.
5. Describe the difference between mediation and arbitration.

C L O S I N G   A R G U M E N T S

Unless directed otherwise, use a general search engine, such as Google, to locate the answers to these questions.

1. Review the Civil Cover Sheet (Form JS 44) used for complaints filed in all U.S. district courts. In Section II, titled "Basis of Jurisdiction," what four options may a plaintiff select?

2. Review the Manual for Complex Litigation, Third, issued by the Federal Judicial Center in 1995. Review § 20.153, relating to considerations in imposing sanctions. May monetary sanctions imposed on an attorney be passed along to the client?
3. Access the website for JAMS. Locate a "Neutral" for the Boston, Massachusetts, area whose area of expertise is real property disputes. Identify this individual and the sports-related matter he settled.

CHAPTER
9

PARALEGAL PRACTICE SPECIALTIES: WHAT PARALEGALS DO

CHOOSE A JOB YOU LOVE, AND YOU WILL NEVER HAVE TO
WORK A DAY IN YOUR LIFE.

—ATTRIBUTED TO CONFUCIUS

CHAPTER OVERVIEW

In some firms, a paralegal may be the proverbial jack of all trades who works on
contracts, civil litigation cases, criminal matters, real property cases, wills and estates,
and a variety of other types of work. In other firms, a paralegal may be assigned to
a certain practice group, which will handle only a specialized type of case—for
example, intellectual property cases or securities matters. Perhaps reflecting the continuing trend of attorney specialization, a November 2002 survey conducted by the
International Paralegal Management Association reported that 77 percent of the
respondents assigned paralegals to a specific practice area and only 15 percent
assigned paralegals to a general assignment pool.

There is no agreed-upon number of legal specialties. As a guideline, the website of the National Federation of Paralegal Associations identifies 27 paralegal specialty areas, from alternative dispute resolution to workers' compensation.

Because a great number of legal issues arise from either contract law or tort
law, these areas of the law are introduced at the outset. In all likelihood, you will be
taking separate classes on contracts, torts, and some of the other practice fields discussed in this chapter. Thus, the information provided on those areas is meant to be
a quick review. Because it is impossible to discuss with specificity each practice area
in which paralegals might be involved, this chapter then focuses in depth on the
four most significant practice areas (exclusive of litigation, discussed in the previous
chapter) identified by the ABA's 1998 survey, "Utilization of Legal Assistants Among

TIPS

Paralegals who are employed in the practice areas discussed in this chapter often spend a great deal of time drafting forms and documents. While you should never blindly rely on canned legal forms, many offer drafting ideas and tips on structuring agreements, documents, and pleadings. Many Internet sites offer legal forms.

See MegaLaw's site at *www.megalaw.com* for forms for use in many areas of legal practice, including corporate and business law, real estate, estate planning, and family law. Other sites offering or linking to forms are *www.washlaw.edu* and *www.ilrg.com*.

Private Practitioners" (ABA Survey) in their order of utilization: business and corporate law (including contract issues); real estate; estate planning and probate; and family law.

Each section in this chapter includes a brief substantive discussion of the pertinent area of law followed by a discussion of the tasks specifically performed by paralegals employed in that area.

The chapter concludes with an overview of some of the other specialty fields in which paralegals are employed and a discussion of the roles and responsibilities of paralegals who are employed "in house"—namely, in company legal departments.

A. CONTRACTS

1. Introduction

Contract
Promise enforceable in court

A **contract** is a promise that is enforceable in court. The word *agreement* is often used interchangeably with *contract*. Attorneys and paralegals are frequently involved in preparing contracts, amending them, and then enforcing them through litigation. A contract may be a complicated agreement of merger between two industry giants, a simple partnership agreement, an employment agreement, or a one-page agreement not to disclose confidential information.

Uniform Commercial Code
Uniform law adopted by all states, except Louisiana, governing contracts and the sale of goods

Contracts are governed primarily by state statutes and case law. In addition, contracts are governed by the **Uniform Commercial Code** (UCC), a comprehensive set of rules governing contracts. The UCC has been adopted in some form by all states (but only partially in Louisiana). Article 2 of the UCC, which governs contracts for the sale of goods, includes a variety of important rules, such as rules governing warranties that goods sold are fit for their purpose.

Statute of frauds
Law in all states requiring some contracts, such as those for the sale of land, to be in writing

Generally, agreements may be written or oral, although under state statutes called **statutes of fraud**, some contracts (primarily, those involving the sale of land, those that by their terms cannot be performed within one year, and those for the sale of goods valued at $500 or more) must be in writing to be enforceable. All states have statutes delineating which contracts must be in writing to be enforceable. In addition, under the parol evidence rule (discussed in Chapter Seven), oral evidence may not be introduced to vary the terms of a written agreement. Also, there may be special state or federal laws governing certain types of contracts. For example, most states give consumers three days to cancel certain types of consumer contracts.

2. Elements of a Valid Contract

To be valid, a contract must include the following four elements:

- **Competent parties.** The parties to a contract may be individuals or entities, such as corporations. However, all parties must have **capacity,** the legal ability to enter into a contract. Thus, contracts involving minors or incompetents are void-able at the option of the minor or incompetent.

- **Agreement.** A contract must include a mutual agreement, or an offer by one party and an acceptance by another. The terms must be sufficiently definite that a court would be able enforce the agreement. Once an offer is made by the **offeror**, the other party, called the **offeree**, may accept it, reject it, or make a counteroffer. If an offer is accepted according to its terms, a contract is formed (assuming all other requirements are satisfied). An offer will remain open until its stated termination time. If no time is set for termination of the offer, it will remain open for a reasonable time. An open-ended offer may be revoked at any time before it is accepted.

- **Consideration.** Adequate consideration must support the agreement. **Consideration** is usually defined as something of value given in exchange for a promise. For example, if you agree to paint a bedroom for your friend Bill for $500, your consideration is your obligation to perform the labor and Bill's consideration is his agreement to pay you $500. Each party has received some benefit and each has parted with something of value. Consideration is usually money, but it may consist of an act, a forbearance (refraining from taking action), or some other benefit or detriment. Courts will usually not second-guess parties to a contract and inquire whether the consideration is adequate, so long as there is some consideration—namely, so long as what has been promised has been bar-gained for and can be distinguished from a mere gift or a one-sided promise.

- **Legality.** The subject matter of the contract must be legal. Thus, a contract to import cocaine is not enforceable.

3. Performance and Remedies for Breach

Generally, contracts are completed or discharged by performance, which means each party has performed what he or she agreed to do. Failure to perform one's agreed-upon promise is a **breach of contract**, for which the law provides various remedies, including the following:

- **Monetary damages.** Courts may award compensatory damages to compensate a party for the losses caused by the breaching party. The parties may agree in advance what damages will be awarded in the event of a breach and courts will enforce this **liquidated damage clause** so long as the agreement is reasonable.

Capacity
Legal ability to take action, such as entering into contract

Offeror
Party making an offer

Offeree
Party receiving an offer

Consideration
Bargained-for item of value, usually money, that induces another to enter into contract; all contracts must be supported by consideration

Breach of contract
Failure to perform duties required by terms of contract

Liquidated damage clause
Clause in contract imposing damages (intended as a penalty) in a specified amount in the event of breach

Specific performance
Remedy compelling
performance of an act

- ■ **Specific performance.** If monetary damages are not adequate to compensate a party, a court may order **specific performance** and compel a party to perform its obligations. Thus, for example, if a party breaches an agreement to sell land or a rare painting, a court could order the party to perform his or her obligations.

Rescission
A remedy canceling a
contract, usually due to fraud,
and restoring parties to the
positions they occupied prior
to contract

Reformation
Modifying a contract to
reflect parties' true intentions

- ■ **Rescission and reformation.** A court may order **rescission** or cancellation of the contract (and return the parties to the positions they occupied before the contract was entered) if the contract was procured by fraud, duress, or mistake. Courts can also order **reformation** or correction of a contract to reflect the true intention of the parties.

4. Defenses to Breach of Contract

Unconscionable contract
Contract that is oppressive
and unreasonable

A party accused of breach of contract may assert a variety of defenses, some of which have already been addressed. Thus, a party may allege that he or she lacked capacity to enter into the contract; that there was no mutual assent to the agreement due to mistake, fraud, or duress; or that according to the statute of frauds, the contract was required to be in writing. In addition, courts will not enforce **unconscionable** contracts: those that are commercially unreasonable and oppressive. Finally, if the contract is not capable of being performed (perhaps because of a party's death or incapacity), it is unenforceable.

5. Rights of Third Parties

Assignment
Transfer of all or part of one's
rights

Third parties often acquire rights under contracts. For example, one party to a contract may **assign** or transfer all or some contract rights to another. Using the above example, you could assign your right to receive the $500 payment from Bill to your landlord. While parties may usually freely assign their rights under a contract, assigning duties or obligations is more problematic. Generally, parties may not assign duties that call for their personal services.

Third-party beneficiary
Party who receives some
benefit from a contract or
transaction although he or
she is not a party to the
contract or transaction

An individual may have a right under a contract as a **third-party beneficiary:** Although the person is not a party to the contract, the contract was made for his or her benefit. Thus, if you name your child Francie as a beneficiary under the terms of your life insurance policy, Francie is a third-party beneficiary of the contract and may enforce its terms upon your death.

6. The Paralegal's Role in Contracts

Paralegals involved in every phase of law practice need to understand basic contract principles because they routinely draft, review, and proofread various agreements. There are numerous form books used by paralegals when preparing agreements (see Chapter Six, Section B.5, relating to transactional documents). Paralegals conduct legal research to determine whether various terms may be included in agreements. Paralegals also perform many tasks relating to litigation involving contract disputes, as discussed in the previous chapter. See Figure 9-1 for a form of contract, a joint venture agreement.

FIGURE 9-1
JOINT VENTURE AGREEMENT

This Joint Venture Agreement ("Agreement") is entered into on _____, _____, by and among _____, an individual residing at _____, an individual residing at _____, and _____, and _____, an individual residing at _____ (collectively referred to as the "Joint Venturers").

WHEREAS, the Joint Venturers desire to form a joint venture (the "Venture") pursuant to the laws of the State of _____ and the terms and conditions of this Agreement;

NOW, THEREFORE, for good and valuable consideration, the receipt and sufficiency of which are hereby acknowledged, the Joint Venturers agree as follows.

1. <u>Formation and Business Purpose</u>. The parties do hereby form the Venture for the purpose of _____ and any purpose reasonably related thereto.

2. <u>Principal Place of Business</u>. The principal place of business of the Venture shall be located at _____.

3. <u>Contributions</u>. Each Joint Venturer has made the contribution set forth after his or her respective name:

Name	Contribution
_____	$_____
_____	$_____
_____	$_____

In the event additional contributions are necessary or reasonable for the operation of the Venture, the Joint Venturers shall make such additional contributions in the same proportion as their original contributions bear to the total contributions originally made to the Venture as provided herein.

4. <u>Term</u>. The Venture shall commence on the date provided hereinabove and shall continue until terminated as provided in Section 11 hereof.

5. <u>Profits and Losses</u>. The Joint Venturers agree that their interest in any gross profits and interest in any losses or liabilities that may result from the operation of the Venture shall be borne in the same proportion as their original individual contributions (together with any later contributions) bear to the total contributions made to the Venture (the "percentage of participation"). Profits made during the term of the Venture shall be distributed to each Joint Venturer in accordance with his respective percentage of participation in the Venture within ninety (90) days after the Venture's receipt of such profits, except that the Joint Venturers may decide to retain reasonable sums in bank accounts established for the Venture for operation of the business of the Venture.

6. <u>Management</u>. The Venturers shall jointly manage, control, and operate the business and affairs of the Venture and shall each have as many votes on each issue to be decided by the Venture as is equal to his percentage of participation. All issues relating to the management and operation of the Venture shall be decided by majority vote. No Joint Venturer shall have the authority to incur any debt, obligation, expense, or liability on behalf of the Venture in excess of the amount of $5,000 without the prior written consent of all other Venturers. If a Venturer breaches the foregoing provision, that Venturer shall bear full responsibility and any liability arising therefrom, and the remaining Joint Venturers shall have no

FIGURE 9-1 (CONTINUED)

JOINT VENTURE AGREEMENT

responsibility or obligation to indemnify or reimburse the breaching Venturer for such breach.

7. <u>Admission of New Joint Venturers</u>. No new joint venturer may be admitted to the Venture without prior written approval of all Joint Venturers.

8. <u>Expenses.</u> Joint Venturers shall be entitled to be reimbursed for expenses reasonably incurred in connection with the business of the Venture.

9. <u>Return of Contributions</u>. No Joint Venturer shall have the right to withdraw his contribution or demand a return of such contribution except as provided herein.

10. <u>Liability</u>. The Joint Venturers shall have no liability to each other for any loss or damage suffered that arises out of a Joint Venturer's act or omission so long as such act or omission was in the best interests of the Venture and did not constitute gross negligence, misconduct, or a breach of this Agreement.

11. <u>Termination</u>. This Venture shall terminate and be dissolved upon the occurrence of the first of the following to occur:

    a. The withdrawal, removal, or death of any Joint Venturer or the filing of a petition under the U.S. Bankruptcy Act by or for a Joint Venturer, except that in the event of any of such occurrences, the remaining Joint Venturers may agree to continue the business of the Venture.

    b. The sale of all or substantially all of the assets of the Venture;

    c. Completion of the purpose of the Venture; or

    d. Mutual written agreement of the Joint Venturers.

12. <u>Liquidation and Distributions</u>. Upon dissolution of the Venture, the Joint Venturers shall liquidate the assets and liabilities of the Venture and shall distribute any assets as follows: After payment of all expenses, obligations, and liabilities, of whatever nature and kind of the Venture, each Joint Venturer shall receive his percentage of participation of any assets remaining.

13. <u>General Provisions</u>.

    a. The books and records of the Venture shall be located at its principal place of business and shall be available for inspection by any Joint Venturer upon reasonable advance notice.

    b. The bank accounts of the Venture shall be maintained at _____.

    c. In the event that any provision of this Agreement is held to be invalid, such invalidity shall not affect the remainder of this Agreement.

    d. In the event of a dispute between or among the Joint Venturers that cannot be amicably resolved, the Joint Venturers shall submit the dispute for binding arbitration by the American Arbitration Association.

    e. This Agreement constitutes the entire agreement of the Joint Venturers with respect to the Venture and supersedes any prior oral or written agreement and can be modified only by a written agreement signed by all parties hereto.

    f. No Joint Venturer may assign any interest in the Venture to any other party without the prior written consent of all other parties except that a Venturer may assign his right to receive profits or distribution to another upon written notice to the Venture.

    g. Notices required or permitted to be given hereunder shall be addressed to the Venture and to each Joint Venturer at the addresses provided hereinabove. Notice shall be deemed received three (3) days after notice is deposited in the U.S. Mail, postage prepaid.

> h. This Agreement shall be governed by the laws of the State of _____.
>
> IN WITNESS WHEREOF, this Agreement is executed as of the date provided herein.

B. TORTS

1. Introduction

A **tort** is a civil wrong for which the injured party may bring a civil action for damages. There are three general categories of torts: intentional torts, negligent torts, and strict liability torts.

2. Intentional Torts

An **intentional tort** is a deliberate commission of a wrongful act. Intentional torts thus require that the actor intend the consequences of his or her act. Some intentional torts (for example, assault and battery) may also constitute crimes for which punishment may be imposed. The following are the most common intentional torts:

- **Assault.** An **assault** is an attempt that places a person in fear of an immediate offensive touching.
- **Battery. Battery** is a harmful and offensive touching of another (without consent or justification). Thus, slapping someone in the face is both an assault and battery because the victim would fear the slap and would be harmed by it, while a punch to a victim's back would be battery only, because the victim would not see or apprehend the harm to come.
- **Conversion. Conversion** is the unauthorized taking of another's property and treating it as one's own.
- **Defamation.** An action for **defamation** lies if a person makes untrue statements to another about a victim that harm the victim's reputation. **Libel** is written defamation and **slander** is oral defamation. Statements that are true cannot be defamatory. Moreover, statements made about public figures (such as politicians and celebrities) are wrongful only if they are made with *actual malice,* meaning with knowledge of falsity or a reckless disregard for the truth of the statement.
- **False imprisonment. False imprisonment** is the confinement or restraint of another without justification. Some of the most common actions for false imprisonment are brought against stores that confine suspected shoplifters for an unreasonable amount of time or in an unreasonable manner.
- **Fraud.** An action for **fraud** may be brought if one knowingly or recklessly makes a material misrepresentation to another person of a factual matter (or omits a material fact), intending the other person to take action in reliance on the statement,

Tort
Civil wrong; may be intentional or based on negligence or strict liability

Intentional tort
Tort in which actor intended consequences of his or her action

Assault
Attempt or threat to cause immediate harm to another

Battery
Harmful and offensive intentional touching of another

Conversion
Taking and using of another's property as one's own

Defamation
Publication of false information about another that harms the other's reputation

Libel
Written defamation

Slander
Spoken defamation

False imprisonment
Wrongful confinement or restraint of another

Fraud
Material misrepresentation or omission upon which another justifiably relies to his or her detriment, causing damage

which the other justifiably does and is injured thereby. Thus, selling your house to another without disclosing that the house rests on a toxic waste site is fraud.

- **Intentional infliction of emotional distress.** Extreme and outrageous conduct may support an action for the tort of **intentional infliction of emotional distress.** There is no requirement of physical harm, but the conduct must be extreme and must cause severe emotional distress to the victim.

- **Interference with contract.** An action for **interference with contract** may be brought when a person induces another to breach a contract. Actions for interference with a business relationship or a prospective economic advantage are also actionable.

- **Invasion of privacy. Invasion of privacy** occurs when one party appropriates or uses another's image or likeness for commercial purposes without consent or when one intrudes on another's right to seclusion.

- **Trespass.** Unauthorized entry on the land of another will support an action for **trespass.**

Various defenses may be asserted to claims of intentional torts. The defenses most often asserted are consent, self-defense, or privilege. Thus, giving permission to another to enter land would constitute consent to a claim of trespass; defending oneself in a fight would constitute self-defense to a claim of battery; and testimony given in court is privileged although it may invade another's privacy.

3. Negligence

Negligence is generally defined as a failure to exercise due care toward another. The duty owed is one to act as a reasonably prudent person would in like circumstances. If an individual such as a doctor has special skill and expertise, his or her conduct must be consistent with that of similar professionals. Moreover, the defendant's actions must be the proximate cause of the plaintiff's injuries. Some courts use a "but for" test. Thus, if the plaintiff would not have been injured but for the defendant's acts, the defendant's acts proximately caused the plaintiff's injuries and the defendant is liable. Moreover, the plaintiff must show that injury to him or her was reasonably foreseeable.

The most common instances that give rise to actions for negligence include the following: automobile accidents, premises liability (liability imposed on landowners for injuries sustained on their property, such as occurs when a customer slips and falls in a store), and professional negligence (for example, actions asserted against doctors, lawyers, and accountants). Negligence actions may allege either personal injury or wrongful death. Damages may include general damages for losses that have no precise value (such as pain and suffering), special damages to cover out-of-pocket expenses (such as lost wages and medical bills), and punitive damages—damages intended to punish the wrongdoer when malice, intent, or reckless and gross conduct is shown.

The most common defenses asserted in negligence actions are the following:

- **Contributory negligence. Contributory negligence** is an act by the plaintiff that contributed to the plaintiff's damages. An example of contributory negligence is the failure of a plaintiff to wear a seat belt in an accident caused by a defendant. In a few jurisdictions, if the plaintiff has contributed in any way to his or her injuries, he or she may not recover any damages from the defendant. Even

Intentional infliction of emotional distress
Intentional, outrageous, and extreme conduct that causes injury to another

Interference with contract
Wrongful act of interfering with another's contract so as to cause breach of the contract

Invasion of privacy
Wrongful act that interferes with another's right of seclusion or privacy

Trespass
Wrongful entry on another's land

Negligence
Failure to exercise the duty of due care that a reasonable person would exercise in like circumstances

Contributory negligence
Act by plaintiff that contributed to his or her injury and which may preclude award to plaintiff

if the plaintiff is contributorily negligent, if the defendant had the *last clear chance* to avoid harm, then the plaintiff may recover.

- **Comparative negligence.** To ameliorate the harsh effects of contributory negligence, more than 40 states have adopted the doctrine of **comparative negligence,** in which each party's fault is calculated. Thus, if the plaintiff's failure to wear a seat belt caused 25 percent of his or her injuries, any recovery awarded to him or her will be reduced by 25 percent. In some states, however, the plaintiff must be no more than 50 percent at fault. In these states, for example, if the plaintiff is determined to be 52 percent at fault, then the plaintiff is precluded from any recovery. Other states follow a "pure" comparative negligence approach and allow the plaintiff to recover even if he or she is more at fault than the defendant.

- **Assumption of risk.** Those who knowingly place themselves in harm's way are said to have **assumed the risk** of injury and may not later recover for any damages sustained. For example, it has generally been held that spectators at sporting events assume the risk of being hit by balls or other objects.

4. Strict Liability, Product Liability, and Toxic Torts

Under the doctrine of **strict liability,** liability is imposed on a defendant for his or her actions or product regardless of fault. Thus, defendants are strictly liable when they engage in inherently dangerous activities, such as keeping wild animals or using dynamite, no matter how much care they may exercise to prevent harm to others. In addition, under the doctrine of **product liability** (a form of strict liability), the maker and seller of a defective product (from tires to hair dryers) is strictly liable for injury to a consumer that is caused by the product, regardless of negligence. The product's defects may arise from its design, manufacturing, or marketing (as is the case when warnings or instructions are inappropriate). Any of those in the stream of commerce (sellers, assemblers, distributors, retailers, and so forth) may be liable for defective products, whether or not they have exercised due care.

A newer trend in tort law is allegations involving **toxic torts,** cases brought alleging personal injury or wrongful death caused by chemicals, pollutants, or other toxic substances. Toxic tort cases are often brought as class action suits involving huge numbers of claims because the toxic substance affects significant numbers of people. Examples of toxic tort cases involve claims relating to latex allergies, lead-based paint, and asbestos claims. The asbestos litigation cases are the longest-running mass tort litigation in U.S. history and involve more than 500,000 claimants. Toxic tort cases may be brought under either negligence theory or strict liability theory.

Defenses asserted in strict liability and product liability actions include assumption of risk, comparative negligence, and product misuse (although sellers are required to foresee that some people will misuse the product and must guard against such). Some products, such as guns and knives, are viewed as well-known dangerous products, and thus manufacturers are generally not required to warn of the dangers associated with such products.

5. The Paralegal's Role in Torts

Paralegals involved in tort law primarily perform litigation-oriented tasks, as discussed in the previous chapter. Paralegals also conduct interviews and investigations, locate witnesses, and obtain medical reports and other documents.

Comparative negligence
Doctrine that determines fault of each party in a negligence action

Assumption of risk
Defense to negligence in which a plaintiff is precluded from recovery because he or she knew of danger and proceeded willingly

Strict liability
Imposition of liability on a party even when no fault is shown and party exercised reasonable care; usually imposed for inherently dangerous conditions and activities

Product liability
Responsibility of those in the stream of commerce to ensure that products are free from defects

Toxic tort
Wrongful act in which injury arises from harmful chemicals, pollutants, or the like

C. BUSINESS AND CORPORATE LAW

1. Introduction

According to the ABA Survey, more than two-thirds of attorneys who practice in the areas of business and corporate law use paralegals. Similarly, according to NALA's 2004 National Utilization and Compensation Survey Report (the NALA Survey), except for litigation, corporate work represents the largest specialty practice area for paralegals, with 29 percent of paralegals engaged in some corporate work. While business and corporate clients may be involved in lawsuits, such suits are handled by the firm's litigation group; the business and corporate group handles the formation, management, and dissolution of business enterprises, ongoing business and corporate counseling, mergers and acquisitions, and so forth.

While each state has its own statutes relating to business entities, these statutes are often based on model legislation, and thus there is significant uniformity in state law relating to business organizations. State regulation is usually effected through each state's secretary of state.

2. Types of Business Entities

The following are brief descriptions of the six main types of business entities in the United States. These business organizations are briefly discussed in Chapter Eleven because a law firm may operate as one of these business structures (except that it may not operate as a limited partnership and if it elects to operate as a corporation, it must be as a professional corporation).

- **Sole proprietorships.** A sole proprietorship is a business owned and operated by one person who makes all business decisions and retains all profits. Sole proprietorships are formed and operate with very little government regulation. A business license may need to be obtained, and the sole proprietor may need to file a fictitious business name statement in the county or state in which he or she does business if the business name does not include his or her surname. A sole proprietor has unlimited personal liability, meaning that the liability for business debt extends beyond what the sole proprietor has invested in the business to personal assets, such as savings accounts and art collections. Sole proprietorships have pass-through taxation; all of the income earned in the business is passed through to the sole proprietor who then pays tax at whatever rate is applicable.
- **General partnerships.** A general partnership is a voluntary agreement by two or more persons who agree to do business together. Like sole proprietorships, general partnerships may be formed and operated with little, if any, government involvement. As with sole proprietorships, a business license may be needed and the partnership may need to file a fictitious business name statement if the business name does not include all of the partners' surnames. The partnership agreement need not be written, although a written agreement lends certainty in the event of disputes. The partners may choose to manage and operate the partnership business any way they desire, although if they fail to agree on how profits, losses, management, and control will be shared, state statutes provide that these matters will be shared equally, regardless of a partner's contribution to the partnership. General partners owe fiduciary duties to act in the utmost good faith with regard to each other. Like

sole proprietorships, general partnerships offer pass-through taxation. The partnership files an information tax return with the government, but the tax return's purpose is solely to verify that the individual partners declared their appropriate share of partnership profits (or losses).

- **Limited partnership.** A limited partnership is a partnership having one or more general partners and one or more limited partners. It may only be formed by strict compliance with state statutes, by filing a certificate or application form with the secretary of state in the state where its principal office is located and formally applying to do business in any other states in which it will do business. The general partners have the same status and rights as general partners in a general partnership (they have the right to manage and control the partnership, they have fiduciary duties to all partners, and they have unlimited personal liability for business obligations). The liability of the limited partners, however, is limited to their agreed-upon investment, and they may not manage or control the affairs of the partnership. The limited partnership has pass-through taxation.

- **Limited liability partnership.** A limited liability partnership (LLP) is a new form of business entity that modifies one principle of partnership law: The liability of all partners is limited so that they are not subject to unlimited personal liability for the negligence of their co-partners (and in most states, for the contractual obligations of the partnership). Partners in this business enterprise retain liability for their own wrongful acts and those by persons they direct or supervise. LLPs are formed only by complying with state statutes that require the filing of an application with the appropriate state agency. The LLP agreement may be written or oral. LLPs have the pass-through taxation of general partnerships. This form of business structure is very attractive to law firms and other professional associations because it allows partners to manage the firm's business as they desire without imposing personal liability on partners for each other's wrongful acts.

- **Limited liability companies.** A limited liability company (LLC) is an entirely new form of business enterprise that offers its members full protection from personal liability whether it arises in tort or contract. LLCs must be formed by filing articles of organization with the appropriate state agency. The LLC will be governed by its operating agreement, which is usually written. LLCs provide the pass-through taxation of a general partnership.

- **Business corporation.** Corporations are "persons" that are created under state statute. They exist separate and apart from their owners, the shareholders. Corporations offer limited liability for their shareholders, directors, and officers, because the corporation itself is liable for its own debts and obligations. Corporations are formed by the filing of **articles of incorporation** with the applicable state agency and are permitted to do business in other jurisdictions if they apply to do so. The internal affairs of a corporation are governed by the corporation's **bylaws.** Ownership in a corporation is evidenced by a **stock certificate** and is easily transferred to others. Corporations are managed not by their owner-shareholders but by their directors, who are elected by the shareholders. The directors appoint officers to carry out the day-to-day operations of the corporation. Corporations are subject to double taxation: The income of the corporation is taxed, and when profits are distributed to shareholders in the form of dividends, the shareholders also pay tax on the money received. While shareholders generally do not have liability for corporate obligations, if the shareholders fail to observe corporate formalities (for example, they fail to hold meetings or elect directors) or

Articles of incorporation
The document that creates a corporation

Bylaws
Rules governing a corporation's internal affairs

Stock certificate
Piece of paper that evidences one's ownership interest in a corporation

Piercing the corporate veil
Process of imposing liability on corporate shareholders for corporate obligations, usually due to commingling of funds or lack of corporate formalities

Securities laws
Federal laws that regulate corporations whose stock is publicly offered

Blue sky laws
State laws that regulate corporations whose stock is publicly offered

commingle the funds of the corporation with their personal funds, courts will **pierce the corporate veil** and impose liability on the shareholders. If a corporation wishes to sell its stock publicly, it must comply with various federal laws, generally called **securities laws**, and with state laws, generally called **blue sky laws**. Federal securities laws require that corporations that sell their stock to the public publish and file various reports with the Securities and Exchange Commission and post these reports with the SEC's electronic system called "EDGAR" (Electronic Data Gathering, Analysis, and Retrieval).

3. Business and Corporate Transactions

In addition to forming various business entities, legal professionals maintain the entities by providing ongoing assistance, such as ensuring that annual filings and reports are timely made to the appropriate state agencies, meetings are held and minutes of those meetings are prepared, and various records are kept in good order. Because the business entities described may conduct business in other jurisdictions, research may need to be conducted to ensure compliance with various other states' requirements. Moreover, business entities engage in transactions with each other. One may merge with another, one may buy another's assets, or one may buy another's stock. Transactions such as these involve a great deal of planning. Agreements must be prepared, assets and property must be transferred to the surviving entity, and various filings must be made with government agencies. There are many tasks for paralegals engaged in such changes to business structures. The work is fast-paced, challenging, and document-intensive, and requires keen organizational skills.

4. The Paralegal's Role in Business and Corporate Law

Paralegals play a major role in business and corporate law practice. They may engage in the following activities:

- Meeting with clients and obtaining information so various agreements and filings can be prepared;
- Conducting research regarding state regulation of business entities;
- Preparing form files of required forms and lists of filing fees imposed by the state's secretary of state;
- Preparing fictitious business name statements and assisting clients in obtaining business licenses;
- Drafting documents to form business entities (such as drafting partnership agreements and articles of incorporation);
- Filing documents with the secretary of state to create business entities;
- Drafting operating agreements for LLCs and bylaws for corporations;
- Filing documents to ensure business entities may transact business in other states (and obtaining certificates of good standing from state agencies so the entity may conduct business elsewhere);
- Amending documents when required;
- Maintaining business records such as lists of partners;
- Preparing stock certificates and maintaining stock ledger books;
- Calendaring dates for annual meetings and annual reports to be filed with secretaries of state;

- Preparing notices and agendas for meetings;
- Preparing annual reports and proxy statements for annual shareholder meetings;
- Attending meetings and preparing minutes of meetings;
- Drafting corporate resolutions;
- Drafting various agreements to be used in business entities (for example, drafting a noncompetition agreement to be signed by a corporation's officers);
- Drafting federal registration statements for companies wishing to sell their stock publicly;
- Managing the EDGAR filings for companies that sell their stock publicly;
- Conducting state-by-state blue sky research for registration of stock in individual states;
- Participating in **due diligence**, or review of documents for business-related transactions;
- Preparing documents relating to mergers and acquisitions and preparing **closing binders** containing all documents related to a business transaction such as a merger;
- Preparing press releases announcing corporate activities such as mergers; and
- Preparing documents relating to dissolution of business entities.

Due diligence
Careful review of documents and transactions

Closing binder
Binder containing all documents relating to a transaction

D. REAL PROPERTY

1. Introduction

The term **real property** (or real estate) refers to land and is distinguishable from **personal property,** an area of the law dealing with tangible items such as jewelry, cars, and rare coins, and **intellectual property**, an area of the law dealing with the fruits of creative endeavors, such as trademarks, copyrights, and patents.

Real property
Land

Personal property
Tangible items of property

Intellectual property
The fruits of creative endeavors, such as trademarks, copyrights, and patents

Most real estate cases deal with one of the following issues: acquisition or sale of real property (whether for residential or commercial purposes); matters relating to financing of real property; cases relating to landlord-tenant relations; litigation in which real property is involved; and corporate transactions involving real property. Thus, there is some overlap with other areas of law. For example, a corporation that buys real estate needs to have a board of directors meeting to discuss and authorize the purchase, and minutes of the meeting need to be prepared.

The NALA Survey reported that nearly 25 percent of paralegals are involved in real estate work (although this may not be the only specialty area in which they are involved). Transactions are often pressure-filled and document-intensive. The "deal" may need to close on a specific date, and the legal team may work all night preparing and reviewing documents for the transaction. The work can be intense and challenging.

2. Real Property Ownership

Following are the ways in which most interests in real property are owned:

- **Ownership in fee simple.** The broadest type of real property ownership is ownership in **fee simple**, which means absolute ownership rights over the property. It is presumed that property is owned in fee simple unless stated otherwise. A fee simple owner may sell the property, lease it, or treat it in any way he or she desires. Upon the owner's death, the property passes to the owner's heirs.

Fee simple
Type of land ownership in which owners exercise absolute ownership rights over property

Life estate
Use of land during one's lifetime

Joint tenancy
Type of land ownership in which multiple parties own land; upon death of one, property belongs to the other(s)

Tenancy in common
Type of land ownership in which multiple parties own land; upon death of one owner, his or her interest passes to heirs, not to other tenant(s) in common

Eminent domain
Power of governmental entity to seize real property for the public good

Easement
Right to use the property of another

Community property
Type of property ownership of married couples in which all property acquired during marriage is owned equally by husband and wife; recognized in nine states

■ **Life estate.** A **life estate** is an interest in real property granted to another to use during his or her lifetime. Upon the life tenant's death, the property reverts to its fee simple owner. The life tenant may not dispose of the property because he or she is not the absolute owner of it but rather merely a holder during lifetime.

■ **Joint tenancy. Joint tenancy** is a form of real property ownership by multiple parties; upon the death of one joint tenant, the other(s) automatically succeeds to the decedent's share. Most husbands and wives hold real property by joint tenancy; upon the death of the husband, for example, the wife then owns the property by right of survivorship.

■ **Tenancy in common. Tenancy in common** is another form of real property ownership by multiple parties, each of whom has an undivided interest in the property. Upon the death of one tenant in common, his or her interest passes to the heirs (rather than to the survivor, as is the case with joint tenants).

Real property may be subject to certain restrictions or encumbrances. For example, local ordinances may preclude a party from operating a business in an area zoned for residential use. Similarly, through the exercise of the power of **eminent domain**, a government entity may seize real property for the public good (often for needed roads), although the owner must be fairly compensated for the taking of the property. Real property may also be subject to **easements,** the right of another to use the property for a specified purpose. For example, most property is subject to various easements for sewers, telephone and cable lines, and so forth. One party may have an easement over a neighbor's property to gain access to a road.

In addition, nine states (Arizona, California, Idaho, Louisiana, Nevada, New Mexico, Texas, Washington, and Wisconsin) are **community property** states, which means that they view that all property acquired during a marriage (except gifts and inheritances) and all income earned during the marriage as owned equally by the husband and wife.

3. Transfers of Real Property

Real property may be acquired in a number of ways. A party may inherit a parcel of real estate or may purchase it from another. Inheritance rights will be discussed in the next section of this chapter.

Purchase transactions involving real property are governed by standard contract principles. Thus, one party makes an offer, another party accepts the offer, and the offer must be supported by adequate consideration. The usual consideration supporting a contract or agreement is money. Thus, if real property is sold for $100,000, the sum of $100,000 is the consideration. The parties must have the legal capacity to contract, which means that they must have attained the age of majority and must not be incompetent.

Offers for the sale of real property must be in writing and must include sufficient terms such that it can be determined that the parties have entered into a valid agreement. Thus, the offer must describe the property, the consideration, and any other conditions. Many times property is sold upon certain conditions, called **contingencies,** such as a requirement that the buyer be able to obtain financing or that the property pass various inspections.

The parties may negotiate through a series of offers and counteroffers. Ultimately, an agreement is signed and is as binding as any other contract. The buyer

Contingencies
In real property law, a condition that must be satisfied before title is transferred

usually provides a deposit, typically called earnest money, to demonstrate commitment to the transaction. In the event of a default or breach by the buyer, the seller retains this deposit.

Generally, once an agreement has been reached, the parties engage the services of an **escrow agent**, a person or company that holds documents or funds for both parties. The escrow agent represents both parties and acts only on instructions of both parties. Thus, the escrow agent will not release the deed to the property to the buyer until the seller has received the full purchase price and agrees to the release of the deed.

The buyer usually requires a **title examination** to ensure that the seller actually has title to the property, has the right to sell it, and to determine if the property is subject to any liens or encumbrances, often called **clouds on the title.** Thus, if the seller owes outstanding real property taxes on the parcel, the seller must satisfy this obligation before the transfer of the property. The buyer purchases title insurance, a type of insurance policy that guarantees that the title is clear and that the seller has the right to convey the property.

Unless the buyer has enough cash to purchase the property outright, the buyer needs to borrow money to finance the purchase. The buyer signs a **promissory note,** which is a document promising to repay the money borrowed. The buyer also signs a *mortgage,* a document whereby the buyer agrees that if he or she does not make the payments required by the promissory note, the lender may take back or **foreclose** on the real property. The real property is the **security** for the loan, because the lender feels "secure" in the knowledge that it can recapture the property in the event of a default.

The time and place at which the property is actually transferred is called the **closing** or the **settlement.** At the closing, the parties sign various documents, the seller receives the agreed-upon consideration, and the escrow agent delivers the **deed,** the document transferring title to the property. Various closing costs are incurred, such as fees to be paid to the lender, the escrow agent, and the title company.

4. Leases of Real Property

The owner of real property (the premises) may choose to allow another person to occupy the premises. The owner is called the **landlord** or **lessor** and the party who uses the real property and pays rent therefor is called the **tenant** or **lessee.** The agreement whereby the tenant agrees to occupy the premises may be oral or written and may be for a specified term or may be **at will,** which means that either party has the right to terminate the lease on notice to the other. Whether the lease is oral or written, each party must abide by its terms, as is the case with any contract. Moreover, the law may impose additional obligations on the landlord. For example, if a state statute requires that landlords must provide 30 days' notice to a tenant before evicting the tenant, the landlord may not circumvent that law by requiring otherwise.

The landlord-tenant relationship is subject to a number of rights, duties, and responsibilities. For example, the landlord must deliver physical possession of the premises to the tenant. The landlord may not allow a former tenant to occupy the space and inform the incoming tenant that it is the new tenant's responsibility to take possession.

Escrow agent
Neutral party or company that acts for both buyer and seller of real property

Title examination
Review of records pertaining to parcel of real property

Cloud on title
Defect that affects title to parcel of real property

Promissory note
A written promise to repay money borrowed

Foreclose
Reacquisition of real property, usually by bank that loaned funds for purchase of property and usually because of buyer's default

Security
An item that may be seized in the event of default in a promise by the promisor

Closing
Consummation of transaction (sometimes called *settlement*)

Deed
Document transferring title to real estate

Landlord
One who owns real property but rents it to another (sometimes called *lessor*)

Tenant
One who rents real property from landlord (sometimes called *lessee*)

Tenancy at will
Rental of property for no specific term or duration

Right of quiet enjoyment
Right of tenant to use and enjoy property leased from landlord

Constructive eviction
Impairment of basic rights of tenant, such as rights to water or heat, such that tenant is virtually evicted from leased premises

Retaliatory eviction
Eviction of tenant by landlord in retaliation for exercise of lawful rights by tenant

Assignment
Transfer of all or part of one's rights

Sublease
Transfer of rented premises to another for less than the term of the original lease

Unlawful detainer
Name of action by which landlord evicts tenant from leased premises

All tenants have a **right of quiet enjoyment,** which means they have a right to use and enjoy the premises for the purpose for which the premises are intended without interference. If the landlord permits raucous parties or allows other tenants to destroy the premises, a tenant may have the right to terminate the lease on the basis that the landlord has breached the covenant of quiet enjoyment.

Landlords may not evict tenants without notice. Even in the event the tenant fails to pay rent, the landlord must provide the tenant with notice and an opportunity to cure the default. Similarly, the landlord is generally prohibited from **constructive eviction** of the tenant by impairing the tenant's rights such that the tenant might as well have been physically evicted. Thus, the landlord may not shut off heat, water, or other essential services. Landlords are also prohibited from **retaliatory eviction,** or evicting tenants who have exercised certain statutory rights, such as complaining to local authorities about the condition of the premises.

The tenant may be restricted as to use of the premises, however. In some commercial leases, for example, business tenants often negotiate for a written covenant by the landlord that a similar business will not be allowed to lease premises in the building or space.

Generally, tenants have a duty to maintain the leased premises in good condition; however, tenants are not required to repair defective plumbing, wiring, and so forth. Moreover, a tenant may not typically be charged for ordinary wear and tear of the premises. Tenants may not alter the premises without the landlord's approval. Landlords must maintain common areas, such as parking lots and hallways, and must maintain the major systems in good condition, such as by repairing leaks and roofs, but landlords have no duty to improve the premises.

The amount charged for rent of the premises is subject to agreement of the parties. Rent need not always be paid in cash. The parties are free to work out other arrangements. For example, the landlord may provide one year's free rent in exchange for an advantageously long rental term. The parties may agree that the rent will increase periodically. The increase may be established in advance or may be based on increases in the consumer price index or some other relevant statistical index. If there is no written lease agreement and the tenant rents at will, the landlord may increase the rent on reasonable notice, usually one month.

Generally, the landlord may assign or transfer his or her interest in the leased premises. A tenant, however, seldom has the right to transfer his or her rights without prior approval of the landlord, because the landlord has the right to interview and screen potential tenants to ensure they will be reliable. An **assignment** of a lease is a transfer of all of the renter's interest in the space to someone else. A **sublease,** however, is a transfer of the premises for a period less than the term of the lease agreement. The tenant remains responsible for the lease obligations.

In the event of a breach by the landlord, a court may allow the tenant to cease or abate its rent for some period of time or may terminate the tenant's obligations under the lease. In the event of a breach by the tenant, the landlord must usually initiate an eviction action (called an **unlawful detainer** action) in court. Evidence is presented and the court renders a decision. If eviction is ordered, the tenant is usually given a certain period of time to vacate the premises. If the tenant fails to do so, a sheriff will forcibly evict the tenant. If the tenant vacates the premises before the agreed-upon term, the tenant remains liable for the rent owed under the lease, although the landlord has an affirmative duty to mitigate damages by making a good faith effort to lease the premises to a third party.

5. The Paralegal's Role in Real Property

Paralegals play significant roles in real estate matters. They may be engaged in the following tasks:

- Preparing drafts of offers, counteroffers, and real estate purchase agreements;
- Monitoring purchase agreements to ensure contingencies have been met and deadlines observed;
- Assisting in or arranging for a title search and title insurance and various inspections of property;
- Preparing documents for corporate parties, such as resolutions authorizing purchase or sale of property and authorizations of corporate officers to sign documents,
- Conducting searches of public records to verify the chain of title and to ensure property is not subject to liens and encumbrances;
- Drafting and reviewing loan documents, including promissory notes;
- Coordinating closings, preparing a checklist for a closing, attending the closing, and preparing a closing binder with all relevant documents;
- Drafting and reviewing leases, subleases, and assignments of leases;
- Preparing notices for landlords and tenants—for example, a notice of default in rent or notice of eviction for a landlord or notice of breach for a tenant;
- Assisting in all phases of litigation, including drafting complaints for unlawful detainer or breach of lease and answers thereto, drafting discovery requests and responses, assisting with trial preparation, and arranging for a tenant's eviction by a sheriff.

E. ESTATE PLANNING, WILLS, AND TRUSTS

1. Introduction

Estate planning is the general term used to describe the way by which a person will dispose of his or her property (whether the property is real property, personal property, or intellectual property). A **will** declares how a person's property should be disposed of on the person's death, while a **trust** provides for the handling and disposition of property either during a person's lifetime or after death. **Probate** refers to the court-supervised process of ensuring that a decedent's will is valid and that the decedent's estate is properly administered. Because they are interrelated, the fields of estate planning, wills, and trusts are usually grouped together as one specialty field. NALA's Survey reported that approximately 18 percent of its respondents engaged in probate, trusts, and estate-related work.

2. Estate Planning

While a person may plan for distribution of his or her property by a will, there is more to estate planning than merely drafting a will and putting it in a safety deposit box. Individuals may use trusts and outright gifts as a means of distributing their assets to others. Individuals may need **advance medical directives** (sometimes called **living wills** or **health care proxies**) to indicate their intentions as to medical care if they become incapacitated and to appoint others to carry out their

Estate planning
Method by which a person disposes of his or her property

Will
Document that declares how a person's property should be distributed upon death

Trust
Document that provides for handling of property during person's lifetime or after death

Probate
Court-supervised process of ensuring a decedent's will is valid and administering decedent's estate

Advance medical directive
Directions given to indicate a person's desires as to medical treatment if incapacitated (sometimes called *living will* or *health care proxy*)

intentions. An advantage of using a trust or a gift to dispose of property is that these estate planning devices are not subject to probate, a court-supervised process that can be expensive and time-consuming. Paralegals who assist in estate planning often assist clients in gathering financial information, work with accountants, prepare tax calculations, and draft wills and trusts.

3. Wills and Intestate Succession

a. Introduction

A will is a written document that provides a person's directions for distribution of his or her property upon his or her death. The will may also include provisions naming guardians for minor children or adults who may be legally incompetent. The will usually names a person, called an **executor**, to carry out or execute these directions. If no executor is identified in the will, the court will appoint a **personal representative** or **administrator** to carry out these functions. The person who makes a will is called a **testator** (if a male) or **testratrix** (if a female) and upon death, this person is said to have died testate, which means having a will. A person who dies without a will is said to die **intestate**, and the state in which the decedent resided dictates how the decedent's property will be distributed, a process called **intestate succession.**

b. Requirements for a Valid Will

Each state has strict requirements for the contents and execution of a will, in part to ensure that there is no fraud. Consequently, failure to comply with state requirements usually invalidates a will. Nevertheless, there is no requirement that an attorney prepare a will. Following are the requirements in most states for a valid will.

■ **Requirement of a writing.** In almost all states, wills must be in writing. Few states accept oral wills. While a videotaped will may be useful to demonstrate that the testator was competent at the time the will was made, a videotaped will by itself is usually not valid. Although the will must be in writing, it need not be typed. Many states allow a **holographic will**, a will that is written entirely in the testator's own handwriting and is dated and signed by the testator but is not witnessed. The document must state that it is a will; thus, a letter leaving your jewelry to a niece is not a valid will.
■ **Requirement of capacity.** The testator must be legally competent to make a will. Generally, this means that the person must be of sound mind at the time the will is made and must have attained the age of majority, eighteen years.
■ **Requirement of a signature.** The testator must sign the will (although if the testator is incapacitated, he or she may direct another to sign on his or her behalf so long as the will is signed in the testator's presence). The will must be signed in the presence of witnesses.
■ **Requirement of witnesses.** Witnesses must sign the will, generally to demonstrate that the testator was competent and voluntarily signed the will. Most states require two witnesses, but some states require three. Generally, those who will receive assets under the will, the **beneficiaries,** should avoid serving as witnesses to ensure there are no later disputes over whether someone exercised undue

Executor
Person named in will to carry out instructions in will

Personal representative
Person appointed by court to carry out functions of executor if no executor is named in will; also called *administrator*

Testator
A male who makes a will

Testatrix
A female who makes a will

Intestate
A person who dies without having made a will

Intestate succession
Process of distributing property of a decedent who dies without making a will

Holographic will
A handwritten will

Beneficiary
Person who will receive assets or property under a will or trust

influence over the testator. In some states beneficiaries may not be witnesses. In many cases, paralegals, doctors, or neighbors serve as witnesses.

c. Additional Elements of Wills

Wills often contain a variety of other elements. They may name personal guardians for minor children (which directions are generally followed if a court believes the guardian will act in the best interests of the children); they may expressly disinherit certain individuals (although a surviving spouse is entitled to some portion of the estate by law). In community property states, the surviving spouse is entitled to his or her one-half of the community property.

A will may include information as to desired funeral and burial arrangements and may place conditions on gifts—for example, by leaving money to a child only to be used for college expenses. It is unlawful, however, to leave money to a beneficiary that is conditioned on the beneficiary obtaining a divorce, getting married, changing religion, or any such condition that is against public policy.

d. Revisions to Wills

Wills are often revised. The testator may divorce and remarry and wish to change beneficiaries. A death of another family member may cause the testator to change a will. The testator may either make a change or addition to the existing will, called a **codicil**, or may execute an entirely new will that expressly revokes the prior will. A codicil is a separate document that must be prepared, signed, and witnessed with the same formalities as the original will.

Codicil
A change to an existing will

e. Intestate Succession

If a person dies without a will, state statutes dictate how the estate is to be distributed. Generally, if there is a surviving spouse, the surviving spouse takes the entire estate. If there is no surviving spouse, the children of the decedent share the estate equally. If there are no surviving children, the parents of the decedent share the estate in equal portions, and so forth.

Similarly, in community property states, on the intestate death of one spouse, his or her half of the community property goes to the surviving spouse.

4. Probate

After the decedent's death, if there is a will, it is admitted to probate for court-supervised administration. The executor named in the will files various documents with the court, including the original will. The executor is charged with gathering the testator's assets, paying debts and taxes, and distributing the remaining assets to the designated beneficiaries or heirs. The executor often engages attorneys and accountants to help with the administration of the estate. The executor is not required to serve; he or she may decline to do so, in which case the court will appoint an administrator. The court will also appoint an administrator in the case of intestate succession. Certain assets are not handled by the probate court. For example, a small estate may pass "outside of probate," which means there is no court involvement.

Probate is often a fairly complicated process, and courts usually require written inventories of assets, various interim reports, formal accountings, and so forth.

The executor or administrator sets up a formal bank account to pay expenses of the estate. If a party contests the will, a hearing is held. During probate, formal notices are sent to creditors, and claims against the estate, including taxes, are paid. Eventually the estate is distributed to the named beneficiaries. The executor is entitled to a fee according to state statute. For example, in California, the executor is entitled to receive a maximum fee in the amount of 4 percent of the first $100,000 of the estate, 3 percent of the next $100,000 of the estate, and so forth. These statutorily set fees may be increased for exceptionally difficult cases.

5. Trusts

Trust
A written document by which one party conveys legal title to property to another property to manage on behalf of a third party

Trustor
The person who establishes a trust (sometimes called *grantor* or *settlor*)

Trustee
The person to whom legal title to trust assets is conveyed

Corpus
Money or items placed in trust (sometimes called the trust *principal*)

Living trust
A trust established during the grantor's lifetime; also called an *inter vivos trust*

Declaration of trust
The formal name of a document that establishes a trust

Testamentary trust
A trust created by will

Charitable trust
A trust established for the benefit of some public, charitable, or like purpose

Spendthrift trust
A trust established for a beneficiary who the grantor believes is incapable of handling the entire trust

A **trust** is a written document by which one party (called the **trustor, settlor,** or **grantor**) conveys legal title to property to another party (called the **trustee**) to manage on behalf of a third party, the beneficiary. For example, if your Uncle Ed transfers $100,000 to the Bank of America to be managed for you, Uncle Ed is the trustor, the bank is the trustee, and you are the beneficiary. The item or money placed in trust is called the **corpus** or **principal**. Trustees have fiduciary duties to manage the trust principal for the best interests of the beneficiary and as directed by the trustor. There are several types of trusts:

- **Living trust.** A **living trust,** also called an **inter vivos** (literally, "between the living") **trust** is one established by a grantor during his or her lifetime. The grantor transfers legal title to certain assets to the trustee to be managed for the beneficiary. A living trust may be revoked by the grantor at any time (although the trust document may provide that it is irrevocable, in which case the grantor may not change or terminate the trust). A person can name himself or herself as trustee and thus manage the property during his or her lifetime. Upon the death of the grantor, a successor trustee distributes property as directed by the trust instrument, usually called a **declaration of trust**. Living trusts are attractive estate planning vehicles because the property in the trust is not subject to probate.
- **Testamentary trust.** A **testamentary trust** is one created by will. It becomes effective only on the death of the trustor, and the will that establishes the trust must be probated.
- **Charitable trust.** A **charitable trust** is one established for the benefit of some public, educational, charitable, or scientific purpose. Usually, the trustor places his or her assets into an irrevocable trust, and the trustor receives profits or income from the trust during the trustor's lifetime. On the trustor's death, all of the assets in the trust are given to the designated charitable beneficiary.
- **Spendthrift trust.** A **spendthrift trust** is established by a grantor for a beneficiary who the grantor believes is incapable of handling the entire trust estate. The beneficiary usually receives only a certain portion of the trust assets as directed by the trustor. The assets in the trust cannot be reached by creditors.

6. The Paralegal's Role in Estate Planning, Wills, and Trusts

With the exception of providing legal advice, paralegals may and do perform almost every task involved in wills, trusts, and estate planning, including the following:

- Drafting wills and codicils to wills;
- Filing a will with a court on the death of a decedent;
- Obtaining certified copies of death certificates;
- Filing documents for probate of wills;
- Preparing inventory and appraisal of a decedent's assets and estate;
- Preparing claims to receive proceeds of a decedent's insurance policies and death benefits;
- Reviewing claims of creditors;
- Supervising probate;
- Locating beneficiaries;
- Preparing documents to ensure title to assets is transferred to beneficiaries;
- Transferring assets to beneficiaries;
- Reviewing trustee's fees;
- Drafting declarations of trust;
- Coordinating transfer of assets into trust;
- Reviewing and monitoring trustee's actions and administration of trust to ensure that the trust estate is not wasted;
- Preparing and filing various tax returns;
- Assisting in periodic distributions of income and principal to trust beneficiaries; and
- Distributing trust assets to trust beneficiaries.

F. FAMILY LAW

1. Introduction

The practice of family law includes activities related to marriage, divorce, custody, spousal and child support, adoption, and juvenile law. In some cases, the activities are similar to those in litigation because a divorce or **dissolution** of a marriage is begun by filing a petition in court, and a trial may be held (although there is no jury trial in such actions). Similarly, court matters involving juveniles share some issues in common with criminal proceedings. Thus, there is overlap between family law and other practice specialties. NALA's Survey reported that 13 percent of its respondents were involved in family law. Family law is an interesting and challenging field, with a number of emerging issues, such as those relating to same-sex couples and grandparent visitation rights. Paralegals often report significant job satisfaction in this specialty field because they are directly involved in helping clients during a time of great need. On the other hand, there is significant stress as well because clients are often highly emotional over the dissolution of their marriage, juvenile delinquency actions involving their children, and the difficulties inherent in the adoption process.

Dissolution
Termination of a relationship; in marital law, a term used interchangeably with *divorce*

2. Marriage, Separation, Annulment, and Divorce

a. Prenuptial Agreements

Before a couple marries, they may desire a **prenuptial** or **antenuptial agreement** that sets forth the parties' agreement as to how their assets will be divided in the event

Prenuptial agreement
Agreement entered into by couple before marriage, specifying how assets will be divided in event of death or divorce; also called *antenuptial agreement*

of death or divorce. Although statistics vary, about one-third of all marriages end in divorce. These divorced individuals often remarry and wish to ensure by agreement that assets brought with them into a later marriage will be preserved for the benefit of their children. In addition, individuals who marry later in life often have significant assets and wish to ensure those assets will be protected in the event of a divorce.

Prenuptial contracts are governed by the general principles relating to all contracts. Thus, they can be invalidated on the basis of fraud, unfairness, or duress. For example, if one party does not fully disclose assets or one party is not represented by counsel and does not understand the nature of the agreement, the agreement may be invalidated. Moreover, a court always has the power to determine what is in the best interests of minor children, no matter what the parents have agreed.

b. Marriage

State laws regulate marriage by specifying who may marry, what age they must be, whether they may be related in any way, and whether the individuals must satisfy any health requirements, such as verifying they are not subject to certain diseases. Generally, couples desiring to get married must obtain a marriage license from their local government (usually a county) and must wait for a period of time before becoming married. A ceremony must be performed by an individual licensed by the state (usually a member of the clergy or judicial officer). After the marriage ceremony, the marriage license is recorded with the local governmental entity, often a county.

Common law marriage
Marriage formed by mutual consent and for which no marriage license is issued

Despite public perception to the contrary, few states (fewer than 20) recognize **common law marriages,** marriages formed by mutual consent and for which no marriage license is issued. If a common law marriage has been formed (generally by the couple holding themselves out as husband and wife), it is as valid as a ceremonial marriage in every way, and it may only be dissolved by annulment, death, or divorce.

c. Separation, Annulment, and Divorce

A couple may prefer to obtain a legal separation rather than a divorce. For example, they may wish to remain legally married for insurance, tax, or religious reasons. In a legal separation, the parties remain married, but a court may divide their assets and make orders relating to support, custody, and visitation.

Annulment
Invalidation of a marriage

Divorce
Court decree terminating a marriage

An **annulment** is a court decree that invalidates a marriage, usually because the marriage was procured by fraud, one of the parties was not of legal age, or one of the parties was already married. An annulled marriage is viewed as if it never existed, although children born during the marriage are deemed legitimate.

No-fault divorce
A proceeding that does not require that one party prove the other committed an unsavory act to obtain a divorce

A **divorce** is a court decree that terminates or dissolves a marriage. All states allow **no-fault divorce,** which means that one party need not demonstrate that the other party committed some unsavory act, such as adultery or domestic cruelty, and no consent from the other spouse is required to end the marriage. Generally, most states require only a showing that the marriage has irretrievably broken down (many states use the term **irreconcilable differences**). Many states impose a waiting period or require that the couple be separated for some period of time before a divorce will be granted. For example, the Commonwealth of Virginia requires that a couple be separated for one year before a divorce will be granted. Almost all states require that a spouse be a resident of the state for some period of time before initiating a divorce.

Irreconcilable differences
A common ground for divorce in which a party proves only that the marriage has irretrievably broken down

A divorce begins much like other types of litigation. A complaint (called a **petition** in many states) is filed and a summons is issued by the court. The complaint and summons must be served on the other party. The other party (called either the defendant or the respondent) will file a response with the court. Discovery commences, and a hearing is held in front of a judge, who resolves any disputes between the parties. During the process of the litigation, the court may enter a variety of temporary orders, including orders relating to payment of bills or to custody and visitation of minor children. A judge may also issue a **temporary restraining order** to prevent one spouse from harassing or abusing the other or from disposing of marital property or removing a child from the jurisdiction. A hearing is held to determine whether the temporary order should be made permanent. Ultimately, a divorce is final when a judge signs a judgment of dissolution or divorce.

If the parties agree on all issues relating to division of property, payment of debts, spousal support, and child support and visitation, it is usually not necessary for the parties to appear in court; however, their agreement on these issues must be set forth in writing and filed with the court.

Some states, including California, have new procedures for a **summary dissolution** if the couple has been married fewer than five years, has no children, has few assets and few debts, and agrees on how property is to be divided. A filing fee is paid and there are no hearings before the court. After six months, a decree of dissolution is entered.

Many states require mediation in an effort to induce the parties to reach a voluntary agreement. In fact, few divorce cases proceed to trial. The costs of the mediator are usually paid by the court if the mediator is engaged to resolve issues relating to custody and visitation. If an agreement is reached, it is filed with the court. Courts usually approve voluntary agreements reached by parties. Once the court is satisfied that all property, custody, and visitation issues have been resolved, the court enters various orders confirming these arrangements and issues a decree of divorce. The parties may later modify their agreement voluntarily. If a voluntary agreement cannot be reached, either party may return to court after the decree of divorce is entered if there have been substantial changes in their circumstances that require a court to modify any previous order.

d. Custody, Visitation, and Child and Spousal Support

Courts prefer that parties reach voluntary agreements on parenting issues. If the parties agree on a parenting plan, it becomes part of the court's final order. If the parties cannot agree on custody and visitation, the court may appoint a **guardian ad litem** (literally, a guardian "for the suit") to represent the interests of any minor children. Courts consider a variety of factors in determining custody and visitation; as a general rule, however, courts are guided by the best interests of the child and can fashion creative arrangements. **Legal custody** refers to rights to make decisions about the child's health, education, and welfare; **physical custody** refers to the place the child resides. Many courts order **joint custody**, which means that the parents share decision making and the child spends time living with each parent on a routine basis. Generally, the noncustodial parent is awarded **visitation rights,** the right to see the child on some specified schedule. Visitation is denied to a parent only in extreme cases, such as when the child would be endangered by

Petition
A document that initiates a court proceeding, as in a divorce petition

Temporary restraining order
Temporary order issued by court to prevent a person from taking certain action

Summary dissolution
A form of divorce recognized by many states that expeditiously ends a marriage, usually one of short duration and with few assets

Guardian ad litem
A person appointed to represent the interests of another, often a minor or incompetent, in court

Legal custody
Court order that allows a party to make decisions about all matters affecting a child

Physical custody
Court order that determines where a child will reside

Joint custody
Court order that allows parents to share decision making about child, and child spends time residing with both parents

Visitation rights
Court order allowing a parent to see a child on a specified schedule

Child support
Court order determining
financial support for a child

spending time with the parent. A court may order supervised visitation so that a third party is present when the parent has contact with the child.

Parents are always responsible for their children's financial support, called **child support**, usually until the child reaches the age of 18. The amount of support to be paid by a parent is determined by the court after considering a variety of factors, chief among them how much time each parent spends caring for the child and the income each parent earns. Many states have formal guidelines they follow in determining awards of child support and use pre-established formulas to calculate child support. Generally, child support may not be withheld by the paying spouse merely because the receiving spouse fails to abide by orders relating to visitation.

Spousal support
Court order determining
financial support for a spouse
after a divorce; also called
alimony or *maintenance*

Spousal support (sometimes called **alimony** or **maintenance**) refers to payments made by one spouse to the other after dissolution of the marriage. Courts take several factors into account when determining spousal support, including the amount needed by the receiving spouse to maintain his or her standard of living; the financial needs of each; the obligations, assets, and earnings of each spouse; the length of the marriage; and the ages and health of the spouses. Spousal support may be temporary (for some period of time or perhaps until the receiving spouse obtains education or training that would enable him or her to be self-supporting) or permanent, as is often the case with lengthy marriages. Permanent spousal support obligations usually terminate only on the death or remarriage of the supported spouse. Spousal support payments are tax deductible for the paying spouse and are taxable income for the receiving spouse.

After dissolution of a marriage, parties may voluntarily agree to modify custody, visitation, and child and spousal support decisions. The modified agreement should be submitted to the court and entered as an order. Many agreements provide for automatic increases; thus, if one spouse is awarded a bonus or raise, the support payments to the other spouse automatically increase.

If the parties cannot voluntarily agree on modifications, one party may request a change or modification, which will usually be granted only on a showing of significant changes in circumstances (for example, significant health changes or changes in income). Any court order may be enforced, and courts may hold a defaulting party in contempt of court. States also now assist each other by statute in enforcing various support orders so that a party cannot escape support obligations by relocating to a different state.

Child support and spousal support obligations may not be discharged in bankruptcy, and wages may be garnished or attached (up to certain amounts) so that payments go directly to the receiving spouse or parent rather than to the employee who is obligated to pay support.

Civil union
A legal relationship between
same-sex partners that affords
some benefits of marriage;
presently recognized only in
Vermont

Gay marriage
A legal relationship between
same-sex partners that would
create a marriage relationship
for all purposes; presently
recognized only in
Massachusetts

e. Civil Unions, Gay Marriage, and Domestic Partnerships

At the time of writing of this text, only Vermont recognizes **civil unions,** a legal relationship that grants gays and lesbians the same rights as married individuals. A civil union performed in Vermont is not recognized in other states, and a dissolution of the union may be accomplished only in Vermont. A true **gay marriage,** however, results in the creation of a marriage relationship for all purposes, so that the marriage is recognized in all states, the couple may file their income taxes jointly, each spouse is entitled to various federal benefits (for example, Social Security survivor benefits), and a divorce or dissolution can take place in any state.

At the time of writing of this text, Massachusetts has recognized gay or same-sex marriages, but neither the federal government nor any other state recognizes such marriages performed in Massachusetts as valid, primarily because of the Defense of Marriage Act, a federal law passed in 1996 that provides that states have the right to refuse to recognize laws of other states relating to same-sex marriages.

Some states and localities have enacted **domestic partner laws**, which grant same-sex partners some of the rights of married heterosexual couples—for example, allowing hospital visitation during medical emergencies and extending health, retirement, and life insurance benefits and other benefits such as bereavement leave to the same-sex partner. In addition to recognition of same-sex benefits by state and local governments, a number of private employers voluntarily grant same-sex benefits. In some states, such as California, to be entitled to such benefits, the domestic partners must register with the secretary of state by completing a certain form, which must then be canceled in the event of termination of the relationship.

Domestic partner law
State law granting same-sex partners some of the rights of married heterosexuals

3. Adoption

Generally, any adult may adopt a child, although some states prefer married couples rather than single parents. Florida currently bars gays and lesbians from adopting. It is often harder for single individuals to adopt than married couples because courts may determine it is in the best interests of the child to have two parents. There are three main types of adoption:

- **Agency adoptions. Agency adoptions** involve placement of a child with adoptive parents by either a public or a private agency. Public agencies generally place children who have become wards of the state because the state has terminated parental rights (often because of neglect or abuse) or the child has been abandoned. In many cases, the children are older or have special needs. Private agencies are licensed by the state and usually place children when the mother or both parents plan in advance of the child's birth to place the child for adoption. Agencies are highly experienced in adoptions and provide counseling and help with the extensive paperwork involved in adoptions.

Agency adoption
Adoption in which child is placed with adopting parents by a public agency or a private agency

- **Private or independent adoptions. A private** or **independent adoption** is an adoption arranged between the birth parent(s) and the adoptive parents without any agency involvement. Prospective parents often seek expectant mothers through doctors, clergy members, attorneys, or advertisements. These adoptions are often quicker than agency adoptions but can be very costly. Some adoptions are **open**, which means that the adopting parents and birth parent(s) have contact with each other throughout the birth mother's pregnancy and may agree to continue some contact after the birth of the child. Some states regulate private adoptions carefully to ensure babies are not "sold." Generally, the adoptive parents may pay the birth mother's medical expenses during pregnancy but are not permitted to pay someone for the express purpose of giving up a child. In some instances, once the adopting parents and the birth mother locate each other, they engage the services of a private agency to assist with the legal process of the adoption.

Private adoption
Adoption arranged between birth parent(s) and adopting parents without agency involvement; also called *independent adoption*

Open adoption
Adoption in which adopting parents and birth parent(s) have contact with each other

- **International adoptions.** In an **international adoption**, the adopting parents adopt a child from a foreign country. The process can be complicated and involves numerous immigration issues. The child is granted U.S. citizenship upon

International adoption
Adoption of a child from a foreign country

entering the United States. Many gays and lesbians have pursued international adoptions due to extensive agency waiting lists and because most birth mothers prefer to place their children with a traditional married couple.

In addition to the adoptions described above, there may be stepparent adoptions (in which case an adult adopts the children of his or her spouse with a former partner) or a relative or kinship adoption (in which case a relative adopts children, often because of the death of the children's parent or parents).

Home study
Evaluation of environment of home into which an adopted child will be placed

All adoptions must be approved by a court, and because the process can be complicated, almost all adoptions involve attorneys. The adopting parents must file a petition for adoption and a hearing is held. Most states require a **home study,** which evaluates the environment into which the child will be placed to ensure it is beneficial for the child. Notice must be given to anyone who is required to consent to the adoption (generally, the biological parents). If the judge finds that the adoption is in the best interests of the child, the judge will enter an order approving and finalizing the adoption. Adoption creates a parent-child relationship in every way, and the child will now be known by the name the adopting parents have selected.

4. Juvenile Law

Juvenile
A minor; generally, a person under 18 years of age

Delinquency matter
Proceeding alleging criminal conduct by a juvenile

Dependency matter
Proceeding alleging abuse or neglect of a juvenile

Matters relating to **juveniles,** meaning minors, generally fall into two categories: delinquency matters and dependency matters. A **delinquency matter** relates to criminal violations of the law; a **dependency matter** involves cases alleging the abuse or neglect of a juvenile by a parent or guardian. Both matters are heard in juvenile court, a special court designated to resolve issues relating to juveniles.

Most cases handled by juvenile courts are delinquency matters. Some involve offenses that are violations of the law only because they are committed by minors, such as truancy matters and curfew violations. The goal of delinquency proceedings is rehabilitation of the juvenile rather than punishment.

House arrest
Order by a court that an individual be confined to his or her home pending court determination of guilt

Once a juvenile is arrested, he or she will be taken to a special detention facility for juveniles, usually called juvenile hall. A probation officer is assigned to the juvenile and a court hearing is held within a few days to determine whether the juvenile should continue to be detained or whether he or she may be released to the care of parents, on **house arrest**, pending the next court date or hearing. There is no bail in juvenile proceedings.

The juvenile is arraigned or formally charged with a criminal offense, and a hearing is held in juvenile court to determine whether the juvenile should be tried as an adult or as a minor. Juveniles may be tried as adults for serious crimes, such as murder or rape. Juvenile trials, often called hearings or adjudications, have a great deal in common with other criminal trials. The juvenile has a right to an attorney (and a public defender will be provided if the juvenile cannot afford counsel). The juvenile has a right to confront and cross-examine witnesses, must be proved guilty beyond a reasonable doubt, and retains the right against self-incrimination provided by the Fifth Amendment to the U.S. Constitution. There is no jury trial, however; the matter is conducted exclusively by the juvenile law judge. While the juvenile's parents and attorney may attend the trial, the public is generally excluded.

If the juvenile is found guilty, he or she may be placed on probation, may be required to perform public service, or may be incarcerated at a juvenile detention facility. If the juvenile has been tried as an adult, incarceration may be at an adult facility. Recommendations made by probation officers carry great weight. The juvenile's parents may be required to pay a victim's medical expenses or make the victim whole if the court orders restitution. Not all juvenile records are sealed.

In dependency actions, if a court finds that a juvenile has been abused or neglected, the court may cancel a parent's rights or place the juvenile in foster care or send the juvenile to live with a relative. The parent has a right to counsel in dependency matters, and courts usually appoint a lawyer for the juvenile as well.

5. The Paralegal's Role in Family Law

Paralegals play a vital role in family law matters. The paralegal generally has a great deal of client contact to obtain information so that various documents can be drafted and filed. Some of the activities paralegals engage in are as follows:

- Preparing prenuptial agreements;
- Obtaining background information from clients relating to income, assets, support, employment, and so forth to prepare for hearings relating to custody and support issues;
- Drafting legal separation agreements and petitions for dissolution of marriage;
- Assisting in discovery in marriage dissolution proceedings;
- Preparing requests for temporary restraining orders;
- Drafting parenting agreements and property division agreements;
- Reviewing and investigating assets of a client and a client's spouse to determine support payments;
- Calculating support payments;
- Modifying custody, visitation, and support agreements and orders;
- Assisting in enforcement of court orders relating to custody, visitation, and child and spousal support;
- Drafting petitions for adoption and preparing for various hearings relating to adoption; and
- Assisting in preparing for juvenile delinquency and dependency hearings.

G. OTHER PARALEGAL PRACTICE SPECIALTIES

While more paralegals are involved in the civil litigation, corporate and securities, real property, wills and trusts, and family law fields than any other specialty practice areas, the following is a brief overview of some other practice areas in which paralegals play a significant role (arranged in order of paralegal involvement in these fields, according to NALA's Survey):

- **Personal injury litigation.** Many law firms specialize in personal injury and medical malpractice actions. They may represent the injured party as the plaintiff or they may represent the defendant. In many cases, the defendant has insurance that covers the alleged loss; law firms that represent the insurance company are said to be engaged in insurance defense work. Paralegals involved in this practice field (which is a variety of tort law) conduct field investigations, perform research, and engage in all of the tasks discussed earlier that paralegals engaged in litigation perform. (See Chapter Eight and Section B of this chapter, covering litigation and torts, respectively.)

■ **Administrative law.** Administrative law is the field of law relating to administrative agencies, such as the SEC, the Occupational Safety and Health Administration, or the Internal Revenue Service. State agencies exist as well. Federal agencies implement their policies by promulgating rules and regulations, which are published in the *Code of Federal Regulations* (see Chapter Five). Paralegals may help clients obtain benefits from agencies (such as the Social Security Administration), file claims with certain agencies (such as claims filed with the National Labor Relations Board), and ensure clients comply with agency rules and regulations (such as the Federal Trade Commission's regulations governing franchises). Corporations that sell stock publicly are closely regulated by the SEC and must file periodic reports with the SEC. Paralegals are intimately involved with both preparing and filing these reports (see discussion of corporate and securities law earlier in this chapter).

■ **Labor and employment law.** The field of labor and employment law covers an array of employer-employee relations, including employee benefits (such as grants of stock options and employee retirement and pension plans), formation and termination of the employment relationship, claims by employees of discrimination or retaliation by employers, sexual harassment, health care, and workers' compensation matters. Generally, law firms engaged in employment law represent either employees or employers but not both. Paralegals may also interact with various federal agencies, such as the Equal Employment Opportunity Commission or the Department of Labor, and with state agencies as well.

■ **Bankruptcy.** Bankruptcies are governed exclusively by federal law and are intended to help a debtor obtain a fresh start and to protect the rights of the debtor's creditors. All bankruptcy matters are heard in bankruptcy courts, which are units of the U.S. district courts. Bankruptcies are initiated by the filing of a **voluntary petition** (in which case the bankruptcy is initiated by the debtor) or an **involuntary petition** (in which case the bankruptcy is initiated by creditors). The three most common types of bankruptcies are those filed under Chapters 7, 11, and 13 of the Bankruptcy Act (11 U.S.C. §§ 101 et seq. (2000)). In a Chapter 7 proceeding, the debtor has no hope of financial recovery, so the debtor's property and most of the debtor's assets are liquidated for the benefit of creditors. A Chapter 11 proceeding is usually referred to as a **reorganization** because the debtor hopes to reorganize its debts and emerge from bankruptcy. A Chapter 13 proceeding allows individuals to adjust and repay their consumer debts. New legislation enacted in spring 2005 will likely result in fewer people being able to file under Chapter 7; more will be forced to file under Chapter 13 and repay their debts. In addition, debtors must seek credit counseling before they file for bankruptcy. Once a bankruptcy is initiated, the court appoints a trustee to collect the bankrupt's assets and pay the creditors' claims. Paralegals involved in the bankruptcy field interview debtors, review lists of assets, file petitions to initiate bankruptcy proceedings, file notices of claims on behalf of creditors, and prepare various documents related to bankruptcy matters.

■ **Intellectual property.** The field of intellectual property (IP) comprises the following four related fields: trademarks (protecting designs, logos, and slogans); copyrights (protecting original works of authorship such as books and music); patents (protecting new and useful inventions); and trade secrets (protecting confidential

Voluntary petition
In bankruptcy, a proceeding initiated by a debtor

Involuntary petition
In bankruptcy, a proceeding initiated against a debtor by creditors

Reorganization
In bankruptcy, a restructuring of debtor's obligations rather than a liquidation of assets

business information). Paralegals play a significant role in the IP practice areas and conduct trademark and patent searches. They file applications for trademark, copyright, and patent registrations; monitor those applications; assist in litigation involving infringement of IP rights; work with foreign clients and attorneys to obtain U.S. protection of their IP rights; and prepare ancillary documents, such as IP license and assignment agreements. According to the NALA Survey, paralegals who spent more than 40 percent of their time working in the IP field earned approximately 16 percent more than the average annual compensation for a paralegal. Working on IP projects is interesting and challenging work and often provides an opportunity for close client contact while learning about a client's business goals and strategies.

- **Criminal law.** NALA's Survey reported that approximately 7 percent of the respondents indicated they devoted more than 40 percent of their time to criminal law matters. Paralegals may work for public prosecutors and assist in the prosecution of criminal defendants or may assist in criminal defense work, either by working for a public defender's office or a private law firm devoted to criminal defense work. A growing area is white-collar criminal defense. Paralegals conduct investigations, perform legal research, draft documents, assist at trial, and help with the appeal process, if necessary.

In addition to the fields previously discussed, paralegals are involved in appellate practice, aviation law, communications law, construction law, energy and environmental law, government contracts, immigration, international trade, and tax law, among other specialty practice areas. Thus, there is a practice field for nearly every interest.

H. IN-HOUSE PARALEGAL DUTIES

You will learn in Chapter Eleven that paralegals who work "in house" work directly for a company in its legal department, which may have one or several attorneys. The "client" is the company itself, and it may be involved in numerous activities that require assistance from the legal team.

Paralegals who work in-house assist the in-house counsel with a variety of tasks, including the following:

- Drafting and reviewing employee and vendor contracts;
- Preparing shareholder agreements, stock option plans, and employee benefit plans;
- Administering employee benefit plans;
- Calendaring deadline dates for corporate matters such as filing of various reports, payment of annual taxes, filing of periodic reports with the SEC, and so forth;
- Maintaining corporate records, including the corporate minutes book, and recording resolutions and taking minutes at corporate meetings;
- Filing required corporate forms, such as annual corporate reports, with the secretary of state;
- Developing various in-house compliance policies, such as policies relating to Internet use, display of company trademarks, and sexual harassment;
- Working closely with the company's human resources department and assisting in hiring, firing, and ongoing employee-related issues and disputes;

■ Assisting in employee training to ensure compliance with various government regulations and laws, such as training on avoiding sexual harassment, compliance with the Family Medical Leave Act, and so forth; and

■ Serving as a liaison with outside counsel to monitor matters being handled by outside counsel, including litigation involving the company.

NET RESULTS

www.bls.gov/oco/ocos114.htm	The Department of Labor's Bureau of Statistics provides information about the paralegal profession and the nature of the tasks performed by paralegals.
www.nala.org/Survey_Table.htm	NALA's 2004 National Utilization and Compensation Survey is produced in full, showing the duties and responsibilities of paralegals, specialty areas, billing rates, and salary and compensation levels.
www.paralegals.org	The National Federation of Paralegal Associations provides an excellent review of the roles and responsibilities of paralegals in more than 20 different specialty practice fields. Select "Consumer Education" and then "Paralegals' Roles and Responsibilities."
www.paralegalmanagement.org	The International Paralegal Management Association provides survey information relating to the specialty practice fields in which paralegals are involved. Select "Utilization Survey."
www.abanet.org	The ABA provides (for a fee) its booklet titled "Utilization of Legal Assistants Among Private Practitioners," showing the specialty areas in which paralegals are involved and the types of tasks commonly performed by paralegals in those fields.
www.megalaw.com	MegaLaw offers free legal forms on a variety of topics, including real estate, estate planning, and family law.

CASE ILLUSTRATION

Grandparent Visitation Rights

Case: *Troxel v. Granville*, 530 U.S. 57 (2000)

Facts: After their son died, the plaintiffs sought broad visitation rights so they could visit their two granddaughters under a Washington statute that provided that any person could petition for visitation rights of a child at any time and that visitation would be granted if it was in the best interests of the child. The children's mother wished to curtail visitation.

Holding: The Washington statute was held unconstitutional. It was "breathtakingly broad" because it allowed any third person at any time to petition for and receive visitation rights subject only to the standard that such visitation would be in the best interests of the child. Thus, the statute interfered with the fundamental right of parents to rear their children. So long as a parent adequately cares for his or her children, there is no need for the state to inject itself into the private realm of the family. Although in an ideal world, parents might always seek to cultivate the bonds between grandparents and their grandchildren (and although all 50 states have statutes that provide for grandparent visitation in some form), the statute in question unconstitutionally infringed the mother's fundamental right to make decisions relating to the care, custody, and control of her children.

KEY TERMS

Contract
Uniform Commercial Code
Statute of frauds
Capacity
Offeror
Offeree
Consideration
Breach of contract
Liquidated damage clause
Specific performance
Rescission
Reformation
Unconscionable contract
Assignment
Third-party beneficiary
Tort
Intentional tort
Assault
Battery
Conversion
Defamation
Libel
Slander
False imprisonment
Fraud

Intentional infliction of emotional distress
Interference with contract
Invasion of privacy
Trespass
Negligence
Contributory negligence
Comparative negligence
Assumption of risk
Strict liability
Product liability
Toxic tort
Articles of incorporation
Bylaws
Stock certificate
Piercing the corporate veil
Securities laws
Blue sky laws
Due diligence
Closing binder
Real property
Personal property
Intellectual property
Fee simple
Life estate

Joint tenancy
Tenancy in common
Eminent domain
Easement
Community property
Contingencies
Escrow agent
Title examination
Cloud on title
Promissory note
Foreclose
Security
Closing
Deed
Landlord
Tenant
Tenancy at will
Right of quiet enjoyment
Constructive eviction
Retaliatory eviction
Assignment
Sublease
Unlawful detainer
Estate planning
Will
Trust
Probate
Advance medical directive
Executor
Personal representative
Testator
Testatrix
Intestate
Intestate succession
Holographic will
Beneficiary
Codicil
Trust
Trustor

Trustee
Corpus
Living trust
Declaration of trust
Testamentary trust
Charitable trust
Spendthrift trust
Dissolution
Prenuptial agreement
Common law marriage
Annulment
Divorce
No-fault divorce
Irreconcilable differences
Petition
Temporary restraining order
Summary dissolution
Guardian ad litem
Legal custody
Physical custody
Joint custody
Visitation rights
Child support
Spousal support
Civil union
Gay marriage
Domestic partner law
Agency adoption
Private adoption
Open adoption
International adoption
Home study
Juvenile
Delinquency matter
Dependency matter
House arrest
Voluntary petition
Involuntary petition
Reorganization

CHAPTER SUMMARY

Paralegal Specialization	In smaller firms, paralegals may be "generalists" working on many types of cases. Most paralegals, however, tend to specialize in a certain practice field. The practice areas in which most paralegals are employed are litigation (often arising from contract or tort matters), business and corporate law, real estate, estate planning (including wills and trusts), and family law.
Contracts Paralegals	Contracts are promises enforceable in courts. They may be written or oral. Paralegals are actively involved in drafting and reviewing contracts.
Torts Paralegals	Torts are civil wrongs and may be based on intentional conduct, negligent conduct, or strict liability. Paralegals involved in tort law are generally involved in the entire litigation life cycle.
Real Estate Paralegals	Paralegals in the real estate field draft leases, handle landlord-tenant cases, prepare for the closing or settlement of real property transactions, and attend the closing of the transaction by which real property is transferred to another.
Estate Planning Paralegals	The practice area of estate planning, wills, and trusts affords significant opportunities for paralegals, who draft wills and trusts, prepare appraisals and inventories of estates, and shepherd cases through the probate process.
Family Law Paralegals	Paralegals involved in family law have significant client contact as they assist clients in divorce actions, particularly with regard to custody and visitation issues as well as those involving child support and spousal support. The fields of adoption and juvenile law also provide unique opportunities to help clients in need. Family law practice is challenging but may be stressful as well because clients may be going through a difficult divorce or adoption or dealing with a delinquency matter.
Other Specialty Practice Areas	Paralegals are also involved in a variety of other specialty areas of law, including personal injury

	cases (which are almost always litigation cases), administrative law (the area of law dealing with the powers and procedures of federal and state agencies), bankruptcy (dealing with debtor and creditor relations), labor and employment law (handling a wide range of issues for employees and employers), intellectual property (the law of trademarks, copyrights, patents, and trade secrets), and criminal law (involving actions brought by a state or federal government for criminal conduct).
In-House Paralegals	Paralegals who are employed "in house" perform tasks nearly identical to those performed by paralegals employed in private practice, including drafting documents, assisting in litigation, and working on a variety of employment-related issues.

TRIVIA

- The ABA Utilization Survey reported that about 40 percent of the lawyers who work with paralegals indicated that knowledge of a particular area of law practice is very important.
- The ABA Survey also reported about half of the attorneys who worked with paralegals had expanded the role of their paralegals during the three years before the survey (primarily to achieve skill development and economic efficiencies).
- A 2000 report by the General Counsel Roundtable, a group of in-house counsel, strongly urged general counsel to delegate more tasks to paralegals and concluded that some legal departments of corporations have been able to save millions of dollars by shifting work to paralegals.
- In addition to the field of intellectual property, other high-paying paralegal practice specialties include the securities, corporate, and banking fields.

DISCUSSION QUESTIONS

1. Georgia has discovered that her written contract with Ann does not include a provision requiring liquidated damages, as the parties agreed. Ann will not voluntarily amend the contract. What remedy may Georgia seek from a court in this case?
2. In a hotly contested political campaign, one candidate charges (knowing it is false) in written advertisements that Pam Tyler, another candidate, failed to pay her income taxes last year. What type of action should Ms. Tyler bring, if any?

3. Why have most large law firms begun operating as limited liability partnerships rather than as general partnerships?

4. Your law firm's client, a landlord, is furious that one of his tenants complained to the local health and safety department that many of the smoke detector systems at the premises are not working. The landlord would like to evict the tenant, who does not have a written lease. Discuss whether the landlord may commence an eviction action.

5. One of your law firm's clients has died without a will. The client is survived by two daughters (one of whom is adopted) and four grandchildren. Discuss how the property will be divided.

6. What advantages does a living trust afford over a will?

7. One of your law firm's clients, Jessica, did not receive her spousal support payment last month. She is now refusing to allow her former spouse to visit the children of the marriage, although there is a visitation order in effect. Discuss whether this approach is appropriate and what the firm might do to protect Jessica's interests. Because Jessica's former husband recently received a cost of living increase, Jessica would like to modify the spousal support and child support orders in effect. Discuss whether such a modification is likely to be granted.

CLOSING ARGUMENTS

Unless directed otherwise, use a general search engine, such as Google, to locate the answers to these questions.

1. What is the filing fee in Colorado to file articles of incorporation for a for-profit corporation?

2. Use FindLaw to find the pertinent state statutes to answer these questions.
   a. In Washington, how would a landlord terminate a month-to-month tenancy?
   b. In Florida, what does the term "probate of will" mean?
   c. In Minnesota (review Domestic Relations statutes), does a 16-year-old have the legal capacity to be married?
   d. Using the Illinois Code of Civil Procedure, determine the statute of limitations for personal injury actions, generally.
   e. Review the Virginia statute of frauds for lease contracts. Is an oral lease for a term of one year enforceable if the monthly rent is $400?

10

CAREER STRATEGIES: GETTING A JOB, KEEPING A JOB, AND QUITTING A JOB

NEVER CONTINUE IN A JOB YOU DON'T ENJOY. IF YOU'RE HAPPY IN WHAT YOU'RE DOING, YOU'LL LIKE YOURSELF, YOU'LL HAVE INNER PEACE. AND IF YOU HAVE THAT, ALONG WITH PHYSICAL HEALTH, YOU WILL HAVE HAD MORE SUCCESS THAN YOU COULD POSSIBLY HAVE IMAGINED.

—JOHNNY CARSON

CHAPTER OVERVIEW

This chapter provides an overview of some of the most important and delicate tasks you will ever undertake: getting a job, keeping the job, quitting the job, and looking for another one. All of these career issues require a great deal of planning and work. This chapter begins by focusing on strategies to help you find your first job, including résumé preparation and interview techniques. There are many places to look for a job, but probably the most important source of a job is your network of personal contacts. After you obtain your first job, you need to devote time to career advancement, to ensuring that you continue learning and take the initiative so your job remains rewarding and challenging. The chapter then addresses ways for you to leave a job professionally and with dignity. The chapter concludes with some strategies on obtaining a second job and some law-related jobs you may wish to consider.

A. GETTING YOUR FIRST JOB

1. Introduction

You have probably heard the saying that "getting a job is a job." The expression is certainly true in the sense that you need to put time and effort into obtaining a job;

seldom if ever does the perfect job (or any job) present itself to you. Many of the same qualities that will make you successful in keeping a job will help you get one: preparedness, persistence, creativity, and hard work.

Although your paralegal school or local paralegal association may have placement and career services, the ultimate responsibility for finding a job rests with you. Do not wait until after graduation. Begin now. Even if you do not intend to work until after you graduate or sometime thereafter, prepare yourself by reading want ads to keep tabs on the job market in your locality, drafting your résumé so it is ready to go at any time, and joining your local paralegal association and attending its events and meetings. Take classes if you need to brush up on any computer skills. Assemble copies of your transcripts, diplomas, awards, and writing samples so you will be ready to provide them on request. Ask permission from the individuals whom you intend to ask to serve as references and prepare this list of references.

2. Setting Objectives

Just as you would never start a long road trip without a map, you need direction and planning in searching for a job. Investing time on the front end of your job search will pay off when you find the job that is right for you.

Because you are likely new to the paralegal profession, you may be wondering, "How will I know where I want to work and what type of work I want to do?" While it is certainly true that it is impossible to know with certainty what a particular employment situation will be like until you have worked there for some time, it is equally true that careful planning and thoughtful analysis will reduce the chances that you will make a mistake in job selection.

Job-hunting notebook
A binder containing all notes and materials relating to a job search

Take this phase of the job search seriously. Many experts recommend a **job-hunting notebook,** which is usually a looseleaf binder that contains all notes and information relating to your job search. Create separate sections for your initial planning stage, notes and articles on the job market in your locality, salary surveys, résumés, writing samples, networking contacts, list of references, and notes on the activities you have undertaken. The most important section is an alphabetical list of each potential employer to whom you send a résumé. It should indicate the dates you sent the résumés and cover letters, dates of interviews, and dates of follow-up activities, including your thank-you notes. Be sure to include notes on the individuals you meet, contact names and addresses, notes on salary negotiations, and brief overviews of your impressions of the firm and the interview. If you go on several interviews at different firms, this section will help remind you of topics discussed at each firm.

Your first step in your career planning should be to identify your career goals and objectives. Rather than merely run through some goals mentally, take the time to write these down in the planning section of your notebook. Ask yourself what types of jobs you had in the past that gave you the most satisfaction. Once you have listed a few of those jobs, try to identify why they provided you with satisfaction: Was it the salary you earned? The people you worked with? The type of work you were doing? The opportunity to learn new skills? The ability to work independently?

Similarly, ask yourself what types of jobs you have had in the past that gave you the least satisfaction. Once again, identify in writing why those jobs made you unhappy: Was it a low salary? Lack of benefits? Were you engaged in routine tasks with no variety? Were you isolated from other workers? Were you "micromanaged," with no opportunity for independence?

Don't skip this stage merely because you have been a student for most of your life and have not had the opportunity to have significant job experience. Go ahead and answer the questions *as if* you have had prior work experience. Do you think salary is more important than doing meaningful work? Do you generally prefer to interact with people in a small setting, or are you comfortable in large groups or classes? In school, did you prefer classes when a published syllabus was carefully followed and the class had structured goals, or did you enjoy classes in which there was little structure and a great deal of open and wide-ranging discussion?

Give careful thought to your answers to these questions because they should provide insight into your career objectives. Consider whether you would be willing to make some trade-offs. For example, would you be willing to work for a lower salary in return for a job situation that was close to home?

Many companies draft mission statements, concise descriptions of the company's purpose and values. Draft your own mission statement for getting a job. Start with the phrase, "I want a job that . . . " and complete the sentence as quickly as you can with as little self-censoring as possible. Your mission statement may provide you with insight as to what you really want in a job.

Don't forget that you are not the only one affected by your job. Your family and friends will also be affected by the decisions you make. If you take a job in which overtime or travel is the norm, your personal relationships may be strained. On the other hand, if you have student loans or financial or family commitments, salary may be the most important factor in any job, and you may be willing to trade a long commute for a higher salary.

Finally, it is possible that you will be attempting to find a job in a very tight market and may not have the luxury of deciding whether you want to work for a small firm or a large one, in litigation or in real estate, and so forth. You may have decided that you need to find a job as soon as possible and that you will accept the first respectable offer, no matter what type of work is involved. There is absolutely nothing wrong with this approach, and indeed, it is not only very common in certain job markets but also a realistic approach in a difficult economy. Nevertheless, ask yourself the questions outlined in this section and attempt to clarify your long-term career goals so that if you make a job change in the future you will have already done some of the planning work.

3. Self-Assessment

Your next step in getting a job should be to assess your abilities and candidly evaluate what skills you will bring to an employer. Be honest and don't let your ego get in the way. Consider your values, interests, and skills.

For example, in assessing your core values, consider questions like the following:

- Is a high salary important to you at this time?
- Is achieving a proper work-and-life balance more important than salary?
- Is having a prestigious job at a "name" law firm important to you?
- Is working near your home more important than salary?

- Is making a contribution to your community more important to you than salary and other perks of a job?

In assessing your interests, consider the following questions:

- Would you prefer to work in a small firm or a large one?
- Is there an area of the law that particularly appeals to you, such as family law or corporate law?
- Would you rather work independently or in a group or team setting?

Finally, in assessing your skills, remember that while the skills you have learned in a paralegal program are invaluable, you undoubtedly have other skills as well. Ask yourself the following:

- Are you organized?
- Do you pay attention to detail?
- Are you a good team player?
- Do you have computer skills?
- Do you speak a language other than English?
- Have you had experience in managing other people?
- Do you have a business or financial background?
- Do you have good oral and written communications skills?

Even if you have been out of the job market for a while and are "retooling," you likely have some hidden skills and talents that will be valuable to an employer. Consider the following true stories:

- Against all conventional wisdom, a paralegal included on her job résumé that she was a marathon runner. The paralegal included this information because she needed any prospective employer to understand that there would be certain times during any year when she would be participating in training and marathons and would need time off from her job. Every employment agency told her that including this information would be the "kiss of death" and that employers should not be told in advance about personal needs and commitments. The paralegal got an excellent job offer from the largest law firm in Washington, D.C., where she has now worked for several years. The hiring attorney told her that anyone who could run a marathon was obviously a disciplined and conscientious individual and that was unquestionably what the firm was looking for in its employees.
- Once again, flying in the face of conventional wisdom, a law firm job applicant who was changing jobs included "married, four children" on her professional résumé. Most experts counseled that such information might convey a message that the worker would be distracted by her considerable family commitments. Nevertheless, she got the job for which she applied. The hiring attorney commented that anyone who could work while managing a marriage and a large family was clearly organized and efficient, and those qualities were exactly what were needed.

Thus, consider not only work activities in which you have learned skills, but also school activities, volunteer work, and so forth. Perhaps you have published a school or neighborhood newsletter. Perhaps you have organized fundraisers or planned events for a charity or have served as treasurer for your church or some other group. The planning and organizational skills needed in such activities translate well into any job setting.

Consider your school experience. For example, if you have a background in finance or business, your experience matches well with tax and with corporate and securities work. If you were a criminal justice major, either criminal law or juvenile law may be ideal areas for you to pursue. If you have an engineering or science background, consider whether being a patent paralegal would be a good fit for your skills. If you have done informal counseling through your church or synagogue, consider pursuing family law jobs.

After you have given some thought to your skills, be equally honest in analyzing your weaknesses. If your computer skills are weak, take a class to brush up. Sign up for the free classes offered by LEXIS and Westlaw (or log on and take tutorials online). If your organizational skills could be improved, read books and articles on time management. If your writing skills could be sharpened, ask your writing instructor for additional assignments and exercises. Seek out feedback on ways to improve. Rewrite a paper or project, incorporating your instructor's suggestions, and ask for an additional critique.

4. Evaluating the Marketplace

The best source of information about the market for paralegal jobs in your community is your local paralegal association. It will not only maintain a **job bank**—a listing of available jobs in the community—but also provide inside information about trends in your locality. You need to know what's hot and what's not in your community. In some instances, a downturn in one practice field results in an upturn in another. For example, in a poor economy, merger and acquisition work often dries up, but bankruptcy work abounds.

Job bank
A listing of available jobs maintained by an entity or school

The paralegals in your local association are probably the most knowledgeable individuals about the job market for paralegals in your community. They know which firms are hiring, which ones are having trouble, which firms have been selected as counsel for new companies, and the like. These paralegals are an invaluable source of information about market trends and salary information. They know not only where the good jobs are but also which firms have unusually high turnover, which signals a general level of employee unhappiness. Attend association meetings, go to luncheons and dinners, sign up for the job bank services, and, most important, ask for help! Tell the paralegals you meet that you are looking for a job. Ask their advice. Give them your business card with a handwritten "interested in family law" note. This will remind them of your career desires.

To determine market trends in your area, you can also read the business section of your local newspaper. Pay attention to the section detailing the formation of new businesses and bankruptcy filings. Review the legal newspaper or journal in your area. There is a publisher of a daily or weekly newspaper for the legal community in most large cities. The publication will include news about law firm mergers and announcements relating to court rules, court dockets, and job advertisements.

For example, legal professionals in Los Angeles usually subscribe to the *Los Angeles Daily Journal*, a daily newspaper with information about the legal community and advertisements for law-related jobs.

Your paralegal program may subscribe to several of these journals. Alternatively, your law library will undoubtedly subscribe to these journals, and they will be maintained in the reference section or reading room. Make a point of reading these periodicals to find out general trends and information in your area. For example, if the newspaper reports that the Baker firm was just selected as lead counsel in a huge class action case, you can usually bet that the firm will "staff up" for the new case and will be looking to hire paralegals. Be smart: Know what's happening in your legal community.

If you do not have easy access to a legal journal or other periodical, see if any journals are offered online. Similarly, review legal websites (such as *www.findlaw.com* and *www.law.com*) to determine trends in the nation and in your market.

Be realistic about downward trends in the market. For example, if you have your heart set on doing intellectual property work but that practice sector is stagnant in your locality, rather than sending your résumé exclusively to IP firms, focus on larger firms that have an IP department. You may be able to start working in the firm's litigation department and then move over to the IP department when the market is stronger.

Be sure to think "outside the box" by considering nontraditional paralegal jobs. Remember that not all paralegals work in law firms. Some work in corporations, banks, trust companies, human resource departments, law libraries, employee benefit planning groups, and other similar non-law firm jobs.

5. Where to Look for a Job

There are a variety of places to look for jobs. The following are the most common sources for finding a job:

Networking
Using personal contacts and relationships to further one's career

- **Personal contacts.** Usually called **networking**, the use of personal contacts is especially helpful in finding a job. Some surveys have revealed that more people find jobs through networking than through any other means. Moreover, employers are thrilled to hire someone who comes with a personal recommendation (and no agency fee). Tell everyone you know that you are looking for a job. Most people will be more than willing to pass along your name and résumé to a potential employer. In addition to telling your family and friends that you are looking for a job, tell your teachers. Many of them have extensive contacts within the legal community and are happy to recommend good students.

- **Professional associations.** Remember that your local paralegal association will not only give you a host of networking opportunities; it may well have a job bank available for its members. Go to lunches and meetings. Attend the educational seminars. Volunteer to work on a committee. You will then be able to meet working paralegals. These paralegals who are currently employed will often share the news that their firm or company has hiring needs. Moreover, practicing paralegals are excellent sources for insider information, such as which firms pay overtime, which ones have high billable-hour requirements, and the like. Your paralegal association may publish a periodic newsletter that has job announcements. Some paralegal associations publish job postings on their websites (usually accessible to association members only).

- **School placement offices.** If your paralegal program has placement services of any kind, use them. You may be able to get assistance in preparing your résumé, and there may be workshops to help you prepare for job interviews. The placement office may provide you with postings of job vacancies in your area. At a minimum, the placement office will have information about salaries and hiring trends in your area.
- **Newspaper advertisements.** The most common print source for job searching is the classified advertisement section of your daily newspaper. Look for ads grouped under the heading "Paralegals" or "Legal Assistants." Look for other law-related positions, such as postings for law librarians, legal editors, research assistants, and so forth. Remember that if your community has a daily or weekly legal newspaper, this is probably the best source for job listings. Most legal newspapers publish numerous ads for paralegal positions in each issue. See Figure 10-1 for two sample paralegal job advertisements.
- **Legal placement agencies.** Most communities have placement agencies, also called recruiting firms or **headhunters**, devoted exclusively to placement of lawyers, paralegals, and legal secretaries. Check your yellow pages directory to locate these placement services. Alternatively, your school program office should know of several legal placement services in your locality. Law firms and companies looking for legal professionals contact the agency and describe their needs. The agency will fill the vacancy by sending several candidates to the prospective employer for interviews. If a candidate is hired, the employer will pay the agency a placement fee. In large cities, there may be agencies devoted solely to the placement of paralegals. These agencies are extremely knowledgeable about skills required, salary levels, and career opportunities for paralegals. Agency fees are typically paid by the employer, not the employee; be especially wary of any agency

Headhunter
A recruiter who places candidates for employment

FIGURE 10-1
PARALEGAL JOB ADVERTISEMENTS

PARALEGAL

The Kennedy Center seeks a legal assistant/paralegal. Must have Bachelor's degree with two years of legal and/or office management experience. Strong interpersonal, computer, and organizational skills required. Send cover letter indicating Job Title 35/Legal Assistant and current résumé by June 22, 2004 to _____. EOE.

From *Legal Times*, June 14, 2004

PARALEGAL

Busy business bankruptcy boutique in Century City seeks full-time paralegal/legal assistant. Bankruptcy experience preferred. Strong computer skills and knowledge of Windows W-9, Word, and Excel required. Competitive salary and benefits. Please fax résumé and salary requirements to _____.

From *Los Angeles Daily Journal* June 4, 2004

that asks you for a fee to place you with an employer. There is one significant barrier to obtaining employment through a legal placement agency: Most will place only professionals who have experience. Thus, many of them will not work with paralegals attempting to get their first job. Most placement agencies will carefully screen candidates before sending them on interviews. Thus, be prepared to take quizzes on proofreading, cite-checking, and computer skills. In addition, these agencies will check your references before sending you to any interview. Working with an agency can be helpful because the agency knows the firm needs a paralegal and will be able to help you prepare for the interview and may help you polish your résumé as well to target the firm's specific needs. It is acceptable to work with more than one agency, although you should disclose this fact.

- **General employment agencies.** If your community does not have a legal placement agency, use the services of a general employment agency. Employment agencies function similarly to legal placement agencies, but are likely not as knowledgeable about placing paralegals in law firms and in companies.

- **Online searching.** The number of paralegal positions posted online is growing. NFPA's website (*www.paralegals.org*) allows job searching through its Career Center. You may not only search for jobs in the region you desire: you may post your résumé as well so that potential employers can view it. The site also provides information about employers and recruiting firms in your area. Similarly, IPMA posts job notices for both paralegal managers and paralegals on its site (*www. paralegalmanagement.org*), and Paralegal Gateway (*www.paralegalgateway.com*) provides free searching for job seekers. You may search for jobs, post your résumé, find out who is hiring in your market area, and request automatic e-mail notification when new jobs are posted. In addition to the sites devoted exclusively to paralegals and paralegal managers, general legal websites may be useful. For example, recent searches of American Lawyer's site LawCom (*www.law.com*) for paralegal jobs usually disclose about 100 job openings. You can refine your search by requesting jobs only in certain states. Finally, don't forget about general commercial websites such as *www.monster.com* and *www.careerbuilder.com*. These sites offer numerous listings for paralegals. For example, a recent search for paralegal openings in Florida yielded more than 150 matches. In many instances, however, the job openings are posted by legal placement agencies. Both the "monster" and "career builder" sites also allow job seekers to post their résumés online, and neither website charges any fee to the job seeker. Fees are paid by employers who post their job openings.

- *Martindale-Hubbell* **and mass mailing.** *Martindale-Hubbell Law Directory* is the best-known law directory in the United States. It identifies lawyers and law firms in the United States and gives brief biographical information about attorneys and an overview of the type of practice engaged in by the firm. The set has several volumes and is published annually. Listings are alphabetical by state, city, and law firm name, making it easy to find all law firms in Seattle, for example. *Martindale-Hubbell* is available in all law libraries, and you can find a great deal of information online as well at *www.martindale.com*. Use *Martindale-Hubbell* to locate law firms in your area. You can then target your résumé to firms that focus on the area of law in which you are interested. *Martindale-Hubbell* is generally used when job seekers send their résumés in a **mass mailing** directed to numerous firms whether or not they may be looking for paralegals. Generally, a mass mailing is not a particularly effective method of finding a job because you waste a great deal of

Mass mailing
Mailing to numerous individuals or firms who have not requested the communication

time sending your résumé to firms that have no present hiring needs. Review the biographical information listed for attorneys and consider directing your résumé to an attorney from your alma mater, fraternity, and so forth. This individual may be more inclined to schedule an interview with you than someone who has no connection with you. Because *Martindale-Hubbell* lists a law firm's website, go to the site and determine if the firm has posted any information about vacancies and job openings. You can then send your résumé in response to the posting. This is a better strategy than the shotgun approach of sending your résumé to every firm in your city. Other online sources for locating lawyers and law firms include West Legal Directory, available through FindLaw at *http://lawyers.findlaw.com*, and MegaLaw (*www.megalaw.com*), which includes links to numerous law firms and other legal directories such as "Immigration Lawyers on the Web."

■ **Temporary employment agencies.** One avenue to explore when looking for a job is to register with a temporary employment agency (usually called "temp" agencies). These agencies place employees with employers on a temporary basis. For example, if a law firm is selected as lead counsel in a mass torts case, it may need an immediate infusion of legal talent to handle the responsibilities of the new case. On the other hand, the firm may not want to hire individuals on a permanent basis because the case may settle or because it will only last a short time. The solution is to hire workers on a temp basis. Once the case or project is finished, the firm has no responsibility to retain the workers. Moreover, the temp workers usually receive no benefits from their employers. Working as a temp paralegal allows you the opportunity to see what different law firms are like before you commit to a permanent job. Many law firms are so impressed with their temp workers that they hire them on a permanent basis; however, there is no guarantee of permanent employment.

■ **Government jobs.** Paralegals are employed in numerous federal agencies, not only in Washington, D.C., but also in those agencies' branch offices throughout the United States. If you are interested in obtaining a job with the federal government, a good place to start is at the Office of Personnel Management website at *www.opm.gov*. The OPM's website allows you to search for job vacancies and create and store your résumé so you can apply for one of the nearly 18,000 jobs posted. To locate paralegal openings, go to *www.usajobs.gov.opm* and select "search jobs." Enter "paralegal" in the search box and you will be provided with all the paralegal openings. You may refine your search by state or locality. The federal government no longer requires the cumbersome job application form 171 that it previously used. Applicants may now apply for jobs using a résumé, the government's form OF-612 (the "Optional Application for Federal Employment," available on the OPM website), or any other written format. For state and local government jobs, either visit your local employment office or view its website. Most state and local agencies post job vacancies on their websites, making locating and applying for these jobs relatively easy.

6. Writing an Effective Résumé

a. Introduction

You must have a résumé to obtain a job. While the primary purpose of a résumé is to provide information as to your background and qualifications, its secondary purpose is to create such a strong first impression that it will win an interview for you. Because studies show that most hiring managers spend only about half a minute reviewing a résumé, your résumé is a marketing document that should sell you. A hiring manager may receive hundreds of résumés in response to a single job notice. Other batches of résumés may show up unsolicited. Thus, your résumé should advocate for you. If there is one single misspelling or typographical error in your résumé, it will provide an opportunity for the reviewer to reject you. To survive the first review the résumé must be polished in its appearance and relatively short (ideally, one page in length).

Many individuals prepare several versions of their résumés, each of which emphasizes different aspects of their backgrounds and experience. Because of the ease of preparing different versions of a résumé on your word processor, consider whether you need individualized résumés that emphasize your education, your experience, your volunteer work, and so forth. Similarly, don't be afraid to revise your résumé to fit the requirements of a particular job posting. Your résumé should be directly responsive to the job you are seeking. Review the firm's website and gather ideas on how to target your résumé to this specific firm. For example, if you notice that the firm has several offices overseas, you could emphasize your foreign language skills or your travel or education experience abroad.

In every instance, your résumé must be accurate and honest. While you may use certain terms and phrases to showcase your abilities and present yourself in the best light possible, make sure that every date, title, degree, and award can be verified.

b. Résumé Content

There is no one perfect résumé format. Good résumés, however, have the following elements in common:

- **Heading.** Your résumé should prominently indicate your personal information (name, address, phone number, e-mail address, and fax number). Most individuals center this information at the top of the page.
- **Education.** Identify every educational institution you have attended, in reverse chronological order, giving your most recent educational experience first. Give the full name of the institution and the city and state where it is located. Omit information related to high school unless your high school is extremely well known or you have not attended college. Give the dates you attended college and list the degrees awarded (and any special awards or honors, such as graduating *cum laude*). Following are some other tips about education-related entries on your résumé:
  - ☐ Give your grade point average or class standing only if they are distinctive (generally, if you have above a 3.0 grade point average or are in the top 25 percent of your class).
  - ☐ If you are currently in a paralegal program, give the date you anticipate completion (for example, "Certificate anticipated 2006"), and if it is an ABA-approved institution, indicate such.
  - ☐ Consider listing the major courses you have studied, such as legal research and writing, litigation, corporate law, contracts, and so forth. If the section on your experience and prior employment is brief because you are new to the job market, enhance the legal education section and list additional courses. Target

this section to the job you seek. For example, if you are responding to an ad for a litigation paralegal, strengthen this section so it includes any civil procedure or litigation classes you took, identifies litigation documents you drafted, and details any litigation projects your class performed. Note, however, that some experts advise omitting this section because it takes a great deal of room and the information is duplicated on your transcript.

☐ For undergraduate work, identify your major and minor.

☐ Spotlight information relating to any awards or unique paralegal school projects, such as internships, mock trials, or pro bono activities.

■ **Experience.** In this section, you should identify the jobs you have held. Develop this section so it is responsive to the position for which you are applying. As is the case with education, list your work experience in reverse chronological order. Give the full name of each employer and its city and state. Generally, give only years (2001-2003) rather than full dates (July 1, 2001-May 18, 2003) of your employment. For your current job, for example, indicate "2002 to present." Provide any job titles you have held. Following are some strategies to enhance this section of your résumé:

☐ Use parallel structure. Thus, write "organized exhibits, prepared for trial, and scheduled pre-trial discovery" rather than "organiz<u>ed</u> exhibits, prepar<u>ed</u> for trial, and schedul<u>ing</u> of pre-trial discovery."

☐ You may describe your current responsibilities in the present tense (for example, "drafting discovery requests and assisting in all phases of trial preparation" or perhaps "prepare real estate purchase contracts and attend real estate settlements") and your previous job responsibilities in the past tense (for example, "improved conflicts checking systems"). Do not shift between past and present tense within any one section of your résumé. Thus, do not write "drafted responses to interrogatories and prepare summaries of deposition transcripts."

☐ Emphasize writing and communication skills whenever you can. Indicate that you drafted agreements, formulated policies, authored memoranda, participated in daily meetings, and so forth (if accurate).

☐ Use strong verbs. For example, rather than stating that you "read deposition transcripts," write that you "analyzed" or "summarized" the transcripts. Do not write that you "did research" but rather that you "performed" or "conducted" research. Other strong action verbs include *coordinated, created, developed, designed, directed, formulated, generated, implemented, improved, managed, operated, organized, resolved,* and *supervised.*

☐ Be prepared to explain. If there are gaps in your work experience, perhaps because you have been a homemaker for several years, there is no need to mention this in your résumé, but you should be prepared to discuss the gap in an interview. Similarly, if you have had numerous jobs all of short duration, be prepared to explain what might appear to be a lack of commitment. If possible, anticipate this issue and label the jobs "summer position," if accurate.

☐ If this section of your résumé is brief because your primary job has been that of a student or you have interrupted work to raise a family, emphasize other parts of your résumé, such as the education section or the "other experience" section. In addition, while it is unethical to claim you did a job you did not, there is nothing wrong with using strong, descriptive words to characterize your work experience. Rather than merely stating "sales clerk," consider other responsibilities you may have had in the position, such as training new employees, supervising others, reconciling daily accounting and financial records, performing inventory analysis, processing sales records, designing market displays, engaging in customer relations, and serving as liaison to management.

☐ This section may also include any volunteer work or fundraising activities in which you have been involved. Use this section to emphasize your organizational and leadership skills, ability to supervise others, and attention to detail. If significant, give the monetary amount raised by any charity fundraiser in which you played a part.

■ **Other experience.** You may wish to include a catch-all section that describes other distinctive skills and experiences you may have. For example, if you volunteer at your library, have served as treasurer of your homeowners' association, or participated in other community activities, describe these. Indicate military service and any school activities such as working on the school newspaper or organizing social events. Give the budget for any group for which you have performed secretarial or treasurer services. You may identify activities in which you participate (playing with a jazz group, coaching Little League, and the like if they show special talents), especially if they show discipline, leadership, or resourcefulness. Do not use the word "hobby" in describing these activities, and do not include common activities such as "reading" or "enjoy travel."

■ **Other skills.** Think about special skills you may have. Perhaps you have designed a website, speak other languages, were awarded a scholarship, or possess a real estate license. Identify these special talents. Indicate your level of proficiency in other languages by stating whether you are "fluent" or "familiar with" or some similar phrase.

■ **Computer skills.** Identify the computer programs with which you are familiar (for example, Microsoft Word, PowerPoint, or Excel). Indicate if you have received training on the computer-assisted legal research systems, LEXIS and Westlaw. Almost all paralegals are expected to have excellent computer skills. If your skills are rusty, take classes.

■ **Memberships.** Identify any memberships in any paralegal associations or groups and indicate whether you serve on any committees in your organization.

■ **References.** Generally, most résumés conclude with a brief statement that "references are available upon request." If you are fortunate enough to have a well-known person serve as a reference for you (perhaps a local judge or the president of the local bar association), you may wish to identify these individuals by name in this section. You should prepare a separate sheet with your list of references (full names, titles, job addresses, and telephone numbers), and be prepared to provide this during interviews. Never identify an individual as a reference for you unless you have first asked for permission and given the person a "heads up" to alert him or her to the fact that he or she will likely be called for a reference. A list that includes three or four references is probably sufficient. Use references that can verify your work habits and diligence. Thus, teachers and former employers are excellent sources for references. The reference sheet should include your heading information from your résumé (your name, address, etc.).

c. Sensitive Areas in Résumés

The following are some tips on how to deal with sensitive issues or problem areas in résumés:

- **Employment gaps and too many jobs.** To handle gaps in your employment history or too many jobs, consider one of the following approaches:
  - ☐ Omit months from any listing. Thus, if you were employed only three months in 2004, rather than indicating "July 2004-October 2004," indicate "2004." During an interview you can explain why the job was of such short duration.
  - ☐ Omit dates altogether. Rather than indicating a five-year gap in employment, simply list all of your employment history under the general heading of "Experience" or "Employment Background." You may include a broad date reference, such as "1995-present" and list all of your jobs under this one entry.
  - ☐ Focus on your skills and experience rather than on dates and job titles. Those individuals who are changing careers often use this type of résumé, often called a **functional résumé**, to deflect attention from gaps in employment. This type of résumé generally does not include a chronological listing of jobs; rather, it identifies and focuses on the applicant's skills and experience in certain areas. Headings in a functional résumé may be "Supervisory Experience" and "Document Management Experience."

  Functional résumé
  A résumé that focuses on skills and experience rather than individual listings of prior employers

- **Confidentiality.** If you are concerned that a current employer will find out that you are looking for a job, indicate "Confidential" across the top of your résumé and then confirm this in the **cover letter** that accompanies your résumé.

- **Personal information.** Following are some suggestions on including personal information in your résumé.

  Cover letter
  A letter that accompanies a document such as a résumé and explains it

  - ☐ Do not include a photograph.
  - ☐ Some résumés begin with an employment objective statement, such as "A position in a firm engaged in family law where I can use my skills." Such statements are probably unnecessary verbiage, but you may include one if you wish.
  - ☐ Your first name will usually indicate whether you are male or female. If your name is unusual or doesn't clearly convey information (such as "Pat Ryan"), include "Mr." or "Ms." on your résumé.
  - ☐ If you are changing careers or are concerned that your age may be an initial barrier to getting an interview, omit the dates that you graduated from school and the dates of your earliest jobs.
  - ☐ Consider omitting references to political and religious groups of which you are a member (unless you have held a high-level or significant political position). Most employers are not interested in this information, and it is impossible to predict what the readers of your résumé will think if you include such affiliations.
  - ☐ The conventional wisdom is to omit any reference to marital status or children; however, as noted above, in some instances this may be helpful. The safest course may be that "when in doubt, leave it out."
  - ☐ Do not include any salary requirements in your résumé. This topic will be discussed in an interview.
  - ☐ Ideally, keep your résumé to one page in length.

d. Polishing Your Résumé

The appearance of your résumé is critical. If there are spelling or typographical errors, you will not be given an interview. Because attention to detail and careful review are critical in any legal job, such errors will immediately disqualify you.

You will need to proofread, proofread, and proofread again. Then ask someone else to proofread for you to catch any errors you missed.

The following are some strategies to improve your chances of being called in for an interview:

- Use high-quality paper. Purchase 8 1/2 × 11 inch bond paper that is at least 20-pound weight. Use white, ivory, or light gray. Buy plenty of paper because you must use a matching paper for your cover letter. Buy legal size envelopes to match. These stationery items are available at your local office supply store.
- You may print your résumé on your own printer if your printer produces a professional result. Otherwise, put your résumé on a disk and take it to a copy shop and do your printing there.
- Use 12-point type in a conventional typeface, such as Times New Roman. Courier, or Century Schoolbook. Use the bold form of your typeface for your headings. Don't get fancy and use unusual typefaces and different fonts. Keep it clean.
- Leave sufficient margins and white space so that your résumé is readable. It's better to go to a second page than to have a one-page résumé that looks cluttered.
- Be consistent. If you decide to underscore your job title for one job, do so for all.
- Discuss education and experience before you discuss any other areas.
- Proofread one more time.

See Figure 10-2 for a sample paralegal résumé.

7. The Cover Letter

No matter what job you apply for, your résumé must be accompanied by a *cover letter,* a short letter that introduces you to the potential employer. The cover letter should be typed in the same font and typeface as your résumé and should be printed on paper that matches your résumé. The letter should be short: no more than three brief paragraphs.

If you are responding to a job announcement or advertisement for a job, address your cover letter to the individual identified in the ad. If no individual is identified, try calling the firm or office to determine the name of the individual in charge of hiring. If this method is not successful, address the letter to the Paralegal Manager or Human Resources Manager and use the salutation "Dear Sir or Madam." Respond to an advertisement as directed. For example, if the ad states "no telephone calls," do not call. If the ad requests that you respond by e-mail, do so. Generally, if you respond by e-mail, you should send a hard copy by regular mail as well.

When responding to an advertisement, your first paragraph should refer to the advertisement, as in "I am responding to your recent advertisement in the *New York Law Journal* for a litigation paralegal." If you are not responding to an advertisement, indicate that you are sending your résumé in the hope that a position is available, and, if not, that the firm will keep your résumé on file for future reference.

Proceed to discuss briefly why you are qualified for the particular position (such as indicating your litigation experience, education, and so forth). Stress something positive about yourself such as superior academic performance or relevant experience. Indicate that your résumé is enclosed and that you hope to hear from the prospective employer soon or that you are available for questions and comments.

FIGURE 10-2

SAMPLE RÉSUMÉ FOR PARALEGAL

Humphrey Nowell
674 U Street, N.W.
Washington, DC 20001
(202) 538-6324
hnowell@vtu.edu

EDUCATION

Paralegal Certificate expected December 2006
Georgetown University, Washington, DC; ABA Approved
Courses

Introduction to Legal Research & Writing	Advanced Legal Research & Writing
Commercial & Contractual Relations	Advanced Legal Writing Seminar
Introduction to Litigation	Corporate Law Practice
Legal Ethics/Legal Technology	Legal Specialty I
Advanced Litigation & Trial Practice	Legal Specialty II
Torts	Paralegal Series I, II, III

Bachelor of Science in Economics, December 2001
Virginia Polytechnic Institute & State University (Virginia Tech), Blacksburg, VA

EXPERIENCE

Data Entry Associate, April 2003–Present
Stone Street Capital (Financial Firm), Bethesda, MD
- Maintain and update multiple inventories in database and spreadsheet format
- Review documents and correct any errors upon inspection
- Retrieve company records
- Track and review billing

Server/Cook/Host, August 2000–April 2003
Damon's (Restaurant), Bristol, VA
Gobblertown Tavern (Restaurant), Blacksburg, VA

Computer Support, May 2000–August 2000
WXLZ 107.3 FM, Lebanon, VA
- Provided support at the hardware and software level and general user support
- Assisted in computer assembly
- Performed computer repair

COMPUTER SKILLS AND MEMBERSHIPS

Word, WordPerfect, Access, Excel, Explorer, Netscape, Westlaw, LEXIS

Member of the National Capital Area Paralegal Association

REFERENCES

References provided upon request.

If confidentiality is important, add that you prefer that you be contacted at your home telephone number rather than at your present place of employment.

Because the employer will likely receive numerous responses, try to sell yourself in your cover letter by showing that you are the best fit for the particular job. For example, if the job announcement is for a litigation paralegal, mention any relevant coursework, and identify any litigation documents you have prepared.

Proofread your letter carefully, and then mail it after typing or printing rather than handwriting the address on the envelope. Enter all pertinent information in your job notebook such as where the advertisement was placed, the nature of the position advertised, the date of the advertisement, the individual and firm you responded to, and the date you mailed your résumé.

8. Preparing for Interviews

Don't wait until you are contacted for an interview to prepare for it. Be sure you have several folders or portfolios ready for any interview. Each folder should include additional copies of your résumé, your transcripts, a copy of your certificate from your paralegal program, your list of references, and writing samples.

Writing samples may consist of projects prepared for your research and writing class, such as letters, memoranda, and court documents. Copies of litigation documents (sample complaints or sample answers) and transactional documents (copies of agreements you drafted) should also be included. Make sure that all writing samples are "clean" copies, not the ones marked by your instructors. If your folder is voluminous, consider preparing an index for it and having the materials placed in a spiral binder. In every part of the job-seeking process, be professional. A professional portfolio creates a good first impression and showcases your organization skills.

Before going to any interview, do some homework. Find out about the firm or company. Read the firm's entry in *Martindale-Hubbell* so you will know what type of law the firm practices, its representative clients, the firm's size, and other pertinent information. Review the firm's website. Most larger firms post pictures and bios of their attorneys; if you know who will be interviewing you, you will be able to find out some information about the interviewer. Make a point of mentioning during the interview that you reviewed *Martindale-Hubbell*, even if you comment on something general such as, "I noted that the firm opened an office in Atlanta last year." This will demonstrate not only your familiarity with an important research tool but also your initiative. Take note of the fact that it could be embarrassing if you ask a question that you should have known the answer to by reviewing *Martindale-Hubbell* or the firm's website.

If you are nervous about interviewing, ask friends or colleagues to participate in mock interviews with you. Ask them to ask you difficult questions about your grades, career expectations, and salary demands. Do not go on an interview just for practice. This is disingenuous and wastes the time of employers.

If the position is for a certain practice group, such as litigation or corporate law, review your books and notes and brush up on this area of the law so that you can demonstrate your familiarity with the relevant concepts. If possible, bring writing samples relevant to the position.

At the interview, you will be asked if you have questions about the firm or the position. Be prepared to ask a few questions, such as whether there is a defined career track for paralegals, the nature of the work, or how the firm utilizes its paralegals.

Consider preparing a short written list of questions and bringing it with you to the interview. See Section 9(d) below for some ideas on questions to ask

Similarly, be prepared to explain any problem areas in your résumé, such as a poor academic record or employment gaps, and to explain why you left a job (or are looking for a new position). Rehearse your answers to these questions. Be ready to discuss salary by reviewing salary survey information from your local paralegal association or NALA, NFPA, or IPMA, so you will be prepared and realistic when you are asked about your salary requirements.

9. The Interview

a. The Formalities

Before you go for your interview use the potential employer's website (or Mapquest, at *www.mapquest.com*) to obtain directions. Allow plenty of time. If you arrive more than ten minutes early, wait in the lobby or go get a cup of coffee nearby. Plan on being at the office ten minutes early. If you are late, you will in all likelihood not get the job (and you may not even get the interview). Bring at least ten extra copies of your résumé. Allow some time in your schedule so that you do not need to rush out or so that if you are asked to lunch, you can attend.

Do not attend the interview with a chip on your shoulder or make demands on the receptionist. In many instances, law firms rely greatly on the impressions of the clerical staff and an observation by the receptionist that you were rude to her or him will result in your disqualification. Be courteous to everyone you meet.

Unless you have been specifically directed to wear business casual attire, wear conservative business attire, meaning a suit and tie for a man and a skirted suit or dress for a woman. It is considered somewhat risky for women to wear pants suits to an initial interview. When in doubt, dress up, not down. Do not call in advance to ask if you may wear business casual clothing.

You will likely be met in the reception area. Stand and greet the person with a firm handshake. Make eye contact. You may be interviewed by any number of people, including the paralegal manager, human resources director, and the paralegals and attorneys with whom you might work. Address the individuals you meet as "Mr." or "Ms." unless directed otherwise. In some instances, the interview may be a preliminary or screening interview, and you will meet only with the paralegal manager. If the paralegal manager believes you may be a good candidate, another interview will be scheduled, at which time you will meet the attorneys with whom you would work. You may be interviewed by a panel or group of individuals. Some firms (usually the larger ones) will greet you with a brochure about the firm and your interview schedule, indicating whom you will meet with and when.

b. The Actual Interview

There are as many interview styles as there are individuals. Some individuals have experience conducting interviews and others may be inexperienced, in which case the first question asked of you may be "What can we tell you about us?" or "Tell me about yourself," forcing you to take the lead during the meeting. You may be asked very pointed questions, testing your knowledge. For example, you may be asked, "How would you go about obtaining medical records from a doctor in a personal injury case?"

In all likelihood, you will be asked to discuss your strengths and weaknesses. Give some thought to how you plan to answer this question. For strengths, consider your organization and communication skills and your ability to work as an effective team member. Try to turn any weaknesses into positive attributes. For example, indicate that you may have a tendency to be so interested in your work that you lose track of time or that you sometimes continually review a project until you are sure it's right. Do not say that you have no weaknesses. Consider indicating that you are currently working on improving your proofreading or computer or other skills. See Figure 10-3 for NFPA's guide to answering difficult interview questions.

FIGURE 10-3
NFPA'S GUIDE TO ANSWERING DIFFICULT INTERVIEW QUESTIONS

Q: How much money do you want?
A: Only indicate what you are presently earning and that salary is one of several factors you are considering. Emphasize that the opportunity is the most important consideration.

Q: Tell me about yourself.
A: Emphasis on your recent experience is most important; however, brief coverage of previous experiences and education can also be useful.

Q: What are some situations in which your work was criticized?
A: Give only one or two examples and emphasize how you addressed the criticism and how it is now not a problem. Ensure that you show you are open to constructive criticism.

Q: What do you think of your boss?
A: Create a positive image, even if this is not the case.

Q: How long would it take you to make a meaningful contribution to our company?
A: Realistically speaking, experience and requirements of the job will influence your making a meaningful contribution.

Q: Why haven't you found a new position before now?
A: Explain that finding the right job is more important than just finding a job. This can be a difficult task as the current economy may be a factor.

Q: Why were you laid off?
A: Be as positive as possible. Do not discuss interpersonal conflicts, regardless of how sympathetic the interviewer may seem. Discuss economic conditions. Do not go into much detail unless asked.

Q: Why should we hire you? or Are you interested in this job?
A: Explain why this is a logical position for you, sum up your work history and re-emphasize your strongest qualities and achievements. Above all, let the interviewer know that you will be an asset to the company.

From *www.paralegals.org* (website of NFPA)

Listen carefully to the questions you are asked, and do not interrupt the interviewer. If you do not understand a question, say so, or ask if the interviewer can give you an example.

Be honest. If you are asked if you can travel, but family commitments preclude this, say so. You may wish to leave the door open a bit and say, "at present, I am not able to travel, but I would like to do so in the future." Similarly, if the firm asks your availability to work overtime in the evenings and you are taking classes two nights each week, disclose this. Do not indicate you can travel or work overtime when you cannot. If you try to fudge these issues, they will come back to haunt you—usually during the first week on the job. If the fit between the employer and you is not right, it's better to determine this now rather than later.

One difficult issue that may arise for women is to have an interview while pregnant, especially in the early stages when the pregnancy is not obvious. The dilemma is whether the applicant should disclose the pregnancy (and risk losing a job offer) or wait to reveal it until after an offer is made or the job has commenced (and risk having the employer think the employee hid something during the interview process). While it is illegal to discriminate against a woman on the basis of pregnancy, it can and does happen. The applicant may never know if she was not hired because of the pregnancy or for some other reason. Under the Family and Medical Leave Act, an employee who has been with an employer that has 50 or more employees for at least one year may have 12 weeks of unpaid leave. Some states and employers have more generous policies. Thus, the employer will not be required to extend leave to the pregnant applicant. Some pregnant job applicants wait until an offer is extended, accept, and then disclose the pregnancy and indicate their maternity leave needs. There is no perfect way to handle this delicate situation, but job applicants should keep in mind that an organization that will punish an applicant for being pregnant is probably not a good organization to work for anyway.

If you are asked if you are able to draft a complaint or summarize a deposition, but you have never done so, respond by saying, "I have not had the opportunity to do that as yet, but I am eager to learn and would be willing to study this or take a class on my own time. I am a quick learner and think I would be able to get up to speed on this very quickly." Do not indicate that you can do a task when you cannot. Simply state the truth, and indicate your willingness to learn.

In many instances, what you say is not as important as how you say it and how you react to questions. Most firms believe they can readily train paralegals to do the specific tasks required. What they are interested in is someone who has core values of diligence and persistence and who can fit in with the team and work in a collaborative environment.

c. Illegal Questions

Some questions are illegal—namely, those relating to your national origin, religion, race, age, affiliations, marital and family status, disabilities or health conditions, and arrest records. Sometimes, handling such questions calls for tact and diplomacy. The interviewer may be inexperienced and may have no intent to discriminate against you but is instead trying to be friendly. Thus, questions such as, "Are you married?" or "How does your spouse feel about your commuting into the city to work?" may be asked in all innocence.

There are really only two ways to handle such questions. If you point out that the question is a violation of federal law or offends you, you will probably not get the job. Even a tactful reminder that the question is objectionable may embarrass the interviewer and doom your chances of getting the job. Thus, consider trying to finesse your answer. Perhaps you could say, "Everyone I know is excited that I might work in the city. I have many friends who work here and they really enjoy it." If the question relates to whether you plan to have a family, consider responding, "Right now I'm really focused on my career and that is where my priorities lie at present." On the other hand, if the questions reveal blatant discrimination, you may wish to end the interview; you would not want to work for such an employer.

d. Your Role in an Interview

As mentioned, during the course of an interview, you will undoubtedly be asked what questions you have about the job or the firm. You need only ask two or three questions. Asking a long list of questions conveys the impression that you are doing the interviewing. Consider the following questions:

- Are paralegals assigned to individual attorneys or to practice groups?
- What specific types of responsibilities do paralegals have in this organization?
- What attributes or skills are required to be successful in this position?
- What is the most pressing case or project that I would be working on?
- Does the firm focus on any particular specialties or practice areas?
- How are paralegals in the firm evaluated and reviewed?
- Is there growth in the paralegal ranks?
- What reference sources does the firm have? A law librarian? LEXIS? Westlaw?
- What computer technology and software programs does the firm use?
- Do paralegals have client contact?
- Is there opportunity for continuing legal education? Is there in-house training for paralegals?
- Is there a minimum number of hours paralegals are required to bill?
- Is there opportunity to do pro bono work?
- What support assistance is available to paralegals? Is there a secretarial pool or are secretaries assigned to attorneys, paralegals, and practice groups?

Be cautious when asking questions about billable hours and overtime. You want to ensure your questions convey your honest attempt to understand the firm and its policies rather than send the subtle message that you are not interested in working hard. Similarly, avoid questions about vacation policies and benefits that might imply you are more interested in what the firm can do for you than what you can do for the firm.

Do not discuss salary unless the interviewer raises the issue. If you are asked about your salary requirements, give a range (based on your research of the market and the average salary paid to paralegals in your field). Additional information on salary negotiations is provided below.

If you meet with several people, you may ask the same questions of different individuals. In fact, this may well help you obtain an accurate view of the employment environment.

Don't forget that you are interviewing the firm as well. You not only need to find a job, you need to find the right job. Try to learn as much as you can about the firm. Notice the interaction between people. Observe the layout of the office. Are people working in teams and group settings or is everyone sequestered in offices behind closed doors? Are workers permitted to display personal items on their desks? All of these visual cues offer information about the work environment.

e. Concluding the Interview

At the end of the interview, indicate that you are strongly interested in the job. Show some enthusiasm. For example, say, "I'm impressed with the firm and everyone I met. I would really appreciate the opportunity to work here." If you want the job, go ahead and say so. Mention something positive—for example, that you enjoyed meeting the other paralegals. If you misstated something earlier, use this opportunity to correct or clarify a previous answer. Be sure you have the business card of everyone you interview with so you can write the appropriate follow-up thank-you notes. If you have not been asked for them, offer your transcript, writing samples, and list of references. Ask if any additional copies of your résumé are needed.

You will probably be escorted back to the reception area by the paralegal manager, who will then tell you what the next step will be (usually, either another round of interviews or a telephone contact after the firm has completed its interviews). If you do not receive this information, ask the firm's expected time frame for making a decision. Thank the individual for allowing you to interview with the firm; express your interest in the position once again; and firmly shake hands.

10. Post-Interview Activities

After the interview, enter in your job notebook the name of the firm, the date of the interview, and the identities of the interviewers. Indicate what salary discussions took place (if any) and note any critical information you gained (for example, that the job requires overtime or that employment will begin on the first of the next month). When you attend several interviews, these facts will tend to run together, so unless you take good notes you may forget which firm is which. Write down your overall impressions of the firm and the people, whether they seemed friendly, stressed, and so forth.

On the same day as the interview, write and mail your thank-you notes. If you have met several people, you may either write separate thank-you notes to each of them (this is the better approach) or you may direct your letter to the paralegal manager and indicate that you enjoyed meeting the other individuals and then list their names. A combination approach is to write thank-you notes to the paralegal manager and the attorney with whom you may be working. This puts your name in front of the people who make the hiring decision. Make sure the spelling of each name is correct. Check the business cards or the website to ensure correct names and titles. Some individuals have e-mailed their thank-you notes, but this is a minority approach; the traditional approach is to send a formal note by regular mail.

Thank-you notes may be either handwritten or typed (using stationery and envelopes that match those you used for your résumé and cover letter). If you type your thank-you note, type the address on the envelope as well.

The note should include three components: Thank the individual for meeting with you, reiterate your interest in the job, and indicate where you can be contacted. Try to mention something that was discussed in the interview. See Figure 10-4 for a sample thank-you note.

FIGURE 10-4

SAMPLE THANK-YOU NOTE

[Your letterhead or personal information]

April 14, 2005

Ms. Teresa McCoy
Paralegal Manager
Bates & Anderson, L.L.P.
3490 Easton Avenue
Philadelphia, PA 45066

Dear Ms. McCoy:

Thank you for taking the time to meet with me last Tuesday to discuss the opening at Bates & Anderson L.L.P. for a litigation paralegal. I enjoyed meeting you and Ms. Anderson and learning more about the firm. I was particularly impressed with the law library and the firm's commitment to technology.

I am very interested in the litigation paralegal position. Please let me know if you have any questions or comments or if you need any additional information. I look forward to hearing from you.

Sincerely,

James K. Hays

If you do not hear from the firm right away, do not assume that you have been rejected. Law firms, especially large ones, have several levels of management. The hiring partner may be on vacation. A crisis may have arisen in a case. Wait seven to ten days and then telephone the paralegal manager or the person who interviewed you to determine the status of your application. Ask if the firm has made a decision and whether there is anything you can provide that will help the firm make its decision. Enter the dates of your thank-you notes and your follow-up call in your job notebook.

If you are informed that the firm has hired another candidate, thank the individual and move on to the next opportunity. If you believed the interview went well and that you were qualified for the job, consider asking whether there was anything you could have done or said that would have made a difference. Try to learn from the experience. Consider the following true story:

> Cheryl, a legal professional, went on a job interview. She felt she was perfect for the job and loved everything about the potential employer. Both of her interviews were very successful, and Cheryl was certain she would be hired. She was crestfallen when the interviewer called to say that another candidate had been hired. After worrying over the matter for two weeks, she telephoned the hiring manager and simply stated how disappointed she was that she didn't get the job, and, to help her learn from the experience, asked how she could have handled things better or differently. The manager indicated that the candidate who had been offered the job had just rejected it, and the firm offered the job to Cheryl on the spot. Cheryl was a little disappointed to be "second

choice," but she still believed her instincts were right about the firm. She took the job and worked there happily for several years.

If you have gone on several interviews and are in the enviable position of having an offer on the table from Firm A but prefer to work for Firm B, consider the following strategy: Ask Firm A for a few days (three to five) to respond to its offer. Call Firm B and, without being dramatic, indicate that you have an offer from another firm and ask when Firm B might be ready to make a decision. Do not give up a sure thing for a speculative opportunity.

11. Evaluating an Offer

Generally, when an offer is made to a job applicant, it will include all of the terms of employment. Smaller firms will make the offer to you telephonically (and perhaps follow it up with a written letter), but larger firms will usually provide you with a written offer. At a minimum, an offer should indicate the following: title of position, starting date, salary, and benefits. If an offer does not include these elements, don't be afraid to ask. You need not accept an offer on the spot. It is customary and reasonable to ask for a few days to evaluate the offer.

You may need a job right away and think that almost any job will do so long as the salary and benefits are adequate. On the other hand, if you are in an employee market or you have some time before you must make a decision, remember that salary is only one part of a job (although it is usually the most important factor for most workers), and consider the following when you are evaluating any offer:

- **Compensation issues.** Are wages paid every two weeks or once per month? How frequently are raises given? Are salary decisions made by the firm as a whole or by your particular supervisor? Are bonuses awarded? Are bonuses based on hours billed?
- **Benefits.** What benefits are provided? What is the nature of the health insurance offered? What portion of the premiums do employees bear? Are life and disability insurance provided? Maternity and parenting coverage? Dental and vision insurance? Are there "flex" or "cafeteria" plans? Are there any employee retirement, pension, or 401(k) plans? If so, what contributions, if any, does the employer make to these plans? What is the vacation policy? Is parking provided? Tuition assistance? Continuing education? Will paralegal association dues be paid? How and when are expenses reimbursed?
- **Career advancement.** Is the work in a field you will enjoy? Will your work be interesting and challenging? Will there be opportunities for advancement? Will you have client contact? Will you learn important skills so that if you need to find another job, this job will prepare you?
- **Work environment.** Will you be happy working in this environment? Is the employer located in a nice area? How will you commute to work? Is the location convenient for you? What have you heard about turnover at this firm? Is the firm stable? Does the job offer some flexibility so that if you have a doctor's appointment one day you can simply work a bit longer the next day rather than having to take a vacation day? Do any professionals work part-time? Do any professionals telecommute on occasion? Is there training? Will you be required to travel? Will you be required to work overtime? Is the firm nationally known?

If so, it may be easier for you to obtain another job if you relocate because the firm has branch offices in other cities or is prominent in legal circles.

■ **Legal market.** If the competition for jobs in your area is intense, you may not have the luxury of considering the above factors. If you don't take the job, there may be many other individuals ready to do so. Thus, temper your desire for the "perfect" job with the realities of the market in your locality. If you reject a job because the salary is $500 less than you had hoped and you then spend two months looking for another job, have you gained anything?

12. Salary Negotiations

In many cases, the stated salary will be listed in the job advertisement. If so, there may be very little room for negotiation. If no salary is stated, the issue may arise during the interview or during the offer stage. Be prepared by carefully studying all of the national and local survey information that is available. In addition to being prepared, you must also be realistic. If the average annual salary for starting paralegals in your community is $34,000 and you demand $40,000, you will price yourself out of the job. On the other hand, if you have unique talents that the firm needs, such as language skills, you should ask for more than the average.

If you are asked for your salary demands, consider avoiding undervaluing yourself by indicating that you will consider any reasonable offer. If you are already employed, you can merely provide current salary information. It is implicit that you want a salary higher than your current one. If pressed, respond with a range (for example, $32,000 to $36,000). Understand that you may well be offered a job at the low end of the range, so the amount you set at the low end should be one you are prepared to accept.

If the salary is a bit lower than you would like, but everything else about the job is right, consider saying so and then ask whether your salary could be reviewed after three or six months. If your work is acceptable, you may then be awarded a raise within a short period of time. Such an approach displays confidence in your skills because it conveys the message to the employer that you know you will be such a good worker that you will undoubtedly get a raise.

One of the advantages of working with a recruiter is that he or she will often participate in salary discussions and serve as both a liaison and advocate for you. The recruiter will have experience in evaluating your skills, the market, and the firm's needs and will be able to advise you on setting and accepting a reasonable salary.

If you know you will reject the offer, do so right away, so the employer can proceed to the next candidate.

13. Offer Contingencies

It is becoming increasingly common for law firms to ask paralegal candidates to commit to stay in the firm for at least two years, primarily because it is expensive for an employer to go through the hiring process and train a paralegal only to have the paralegal leave for another job opportunity. Such a request is unfair, however, because the firm will probably not make a corresponding two-year commitment to you.

Responding to such a request calls for a great deal of tact and diplomacy. You may be considering a move, starting a family, continuing your education, or some other goals that would preclude you from working for two full years. Consider the following response to such requests: "At present, I have no definite plans that would interfere with my ability to work for the firm for two years." This statement is true unless you have already been accepted to school or have made some similar commitment. In truth, none of us ever knows with certainty what we will be doing next year or in two years. Thus, if you can make such a statement in good faith, do so. Just as the firm's position is likely to be that you will be employed so long as you are a productive worker and the firm has adequate business, it is only fair that your position is that you will remain in the job so long as you are treated fairly and professionally and unforeseen circumstances do not arise.

14. Offer Reneges

Carefully consider any job offer, because once you accept it, you may not renege on it (unless unforeseen circumstances arise, such as a family crisis or geographic relocation). Reneging on an acceptance is considered highly unprofessional, and the decision may come back to haunt you. Even in a large city, the legal community is insular, and word of your conduct will spread and impair your ability to get a job later. Moreover, because you represent yourself and your paralegal program, your reneging will hurt other students who are in your program and the program itself.

In some rare instances, employers have reneged after making offers to legal professionals. Sometimes called blow-up offers, these reneges happen far more often to newly hired attorneys than paralegals. If an offer extended to you is revoked, you will simply have to move forward. You may, however, ask if the firm or employer has any leads for other jobs or any outplacement services that it can provide you.

15. What to Do if Nothing Works

If your search efforts produce no results, start all over again. Redouble your efforts. Start with your personal contacts and let them know you are still looking. Review your job notebook and contact anyone with whom you interviewed to see if there are other job openings. Contact your school placement office or program director and ask for suggestions. Rewrite your résumé so it has a fresh appearance. Finally, there are three approaches that may yield results:

- Ask your school to place you in a short internship with a firm or ask someone who has a job if you can "shadow" him or her for a few days. Although an internship is usually unpaid, it will widen your circle of contacts, it may lead to a job offer, and it may give you sufficient experience such that a placement agency will now work with you. If your school does not provide such services, contact a placement agency or send résumés to large law firms in your locality asking to do a two- or three-week unpaid internship.
- Do volunteer legal work. Work in a legal clinic. Contact your local bar association to find out what pro bono activities are available. You will learn a great deal, and you may well meet individuals who can help you find a permanent job or serve as references for you. You will be able to describe this work experience in your résumé. Also, once you have some experience, a placement agency may be willing to work with you.
- Use the services of a temp agency and find a temporary legal job. You will have the opportunity to learn about various law firm environments and different practice

fields. More important, in many cases, if you prove to be a diligent and competent worker, the employer may try to find a position for you as a permanent employee.

If none of these approaches yields the desired results, consider jobs outside of law firms, such as in a corporation or working for a government agency or trade association. Apply to work in a courthouse as a court clerk or research assistant. Apply to legal aid societies, the public defender's office, and the public prosecutor's office. Consider writing an article and submitting it to a paralegal publication to enhance your résumé. Look for jobs in law-related fields. Apply for jobs in law libraries.

16. Two Post-Acceptance Tasks

After you receive and accept a job offer, take the time to do two things:

- **Contact your network.** Be sure you call or send e-mails to all your personal contacts, letting them know that you got a job, where you'll be working, and when you start. The people you asked for help will want to know the results of your job search. Thank anyone who helped give you advice or any lead. Send a formal thank-you note expressing your appreciation for his or her help. This is not only the courteous thing to do; it will also serve you well if you need help in the future.
- **Contact your paralegal program.** Let your school know of your new position. If your program is ABA-approved, it must conduct periodic surveys of former students. It will thus need to know how to contact you to obtain basic information about your tasks, salary, and other work-related information. Moreover, if your school has current information about your job situation, it can be passed on to new students to help them in their job-hunting activities. Finally, your program director and instructors want to know about you and share in your success.

17. Applying for a Job Using the Internet

More and more job announcements are being posted on Internet sites, such as those posted on NFPA's site at *www.paralegals.org*. Similarly, you may wish to post your résumé and announce your availability. The process of applying for a job using the Internet is highly similar to that used to find other jobs in that you will submit a cover letter and résumé, but keep in mind the following cautions:

- There may be less confidentiality than that in a conventional job-hunting situation. Once you post your résumé, you have gone public and announced to the world that you are in the market for a new job. Similarly, once you send your résumé electronically over the Internet, you have no control over any subsequent use or distribution of it. Mark your documents "Confidential."
- When you reply to a posting, treat your e-mail response as a mini-cover letter and try to sell yourself. Don't let the informality of e-mail fool you into thinking the process is casual. Double-check the e-mail address and your e-mail message for accuracy. Make sure the appropriate documents are attached so you don't have to later send an "oops" message.

B. KEEPING A JOB

1. Introduction

Getting a job is not the end of your career story. You must work even harder at keeping your job than you did to get it. Each day you will need to demonstrate that the employer made the right decision in hiring you. Moreover, you will be happier if you know you are doing the best job you can.

2. Strategies for On-the-Job Success

All employers understand that while your paralegal program will have provided an excellent foundation and important skill sets, you will need a training period to learn the employer's policies and preferences. In addition, it will take a bit of time for you to apply the principles you learned in school to the real-life cases on which you will work. Although employers are prepared to train you in a practice field and allow you some time to learn more about a substantive area of law, there are six characteristics you will be expected to have on the first day of your job.

- **Punctuality.** You will quickly discover that lawyers work very hard. If the work-day begins at 9:00 A.M., slipping behind your desk as the clock strikes 9:00 every day will brand you as an apathetic worker. Always give a little bit extra to your employer. Lawyers expect to hit the ground running each day. If every morning begins with your supervising attorney wondering where you are, you will quickly be shown the door. Be willing to come in a little early and work a little late, at least during the first few weeks or months of your job and until your employer gets to know you and your work habits. Similarly, show up a few minutes early for office meetings. Making others wait for you is unprofessional and disrespectful. If you know you will be late arriving at the office or returning from a break, call and let someone know.
- **Diligence.** Work hard. Accept assignments willingly. There are no successful lawyers who are clock-watchers. If you always dash out at noon for lunch and immediately leave the office at 5:00 P.M., your professionalism and work ethic will be questioned. While no one expects you to understand everything about the law or your practice field, you will be expected to give your best efforts to every assignment.
- **Excellence.** The standard in the legal environment is one of excellence. Do not turn in a project that is "good enough." Give every assignment your full attention. Keep working on a project until you are satisfied that it is of the highest quality possible.
- **Collegiality.** It is highly unlikely that you will work alone or in an isolated environment. You will be expected to be a team player. Your entire team works for one person: the client. Thus, you need to get along with others, share information, and lend a helping hand. It is not enough to simply do your share of the work. Offer to help others. Establish rapport with others. You will need help from others in the course of your employment. Thus, you need to build up a reservoir of goodwill so that others are willing to help you. There may well be individuals at your office who are difficult to get along with or who are unproductive. Recognize that the work environment is not a social situation. You should not

expect to be best friends with everyone at work. Maintain your focus on the client's needs and work on establishing professional relationships. If social friendships develop at work, that's an added bonus, but the primary reason you are at work is to help your employer assist the clients.

■ **Respect.** Treat everyone in your work environment with respect. While your immediate supervisor may be the one who determines whether you receive a raise, every individual in the office deserves respect. Be courteous to the receptionist, the office supply team, and the clerical staff. Respect the opinions of your colleagues even if you disagree with their approach. Show respect to the client by working diligently and being honest with regard to your timekeeping on the client's case. Finally, respect your work environment as well by keeping your work area neat and organized. Do not take supplies or equipment. Do not use your employer's time to conduct your personal business. Remember to give an honest day's work for your wages.

■ **Professionalism.** The way you dress and present yourself communicates information about you. Treat your employer with respect by dressing and acting appropriately in the workplace. More and more law firms are moving from business attire (suits and ties for men, skirted suits or dresses and skirts for women) to business casual attire. Business casual attire varies from office to office, but generally it means that men may wear long or short sleeve shirts without jackets or ties or may wear collared "polo" type shirts with dressy pants (often khaki-colored). Women may wear skirts without hose, casual tops, and dressy slacks. Many offices forbid jeans, t-shirts, open-toed shoes for women, and any type of athletic shoes (except perhaps on a casual Friday). Follow your office policy. While your office may well permit casual attire, consider the image you want to project. One paralegal reported that she discovered she was treated with more respect by the attorneys at her office when she dressed a bit more formally and conservatively than was required. In any event, keep some extra and more formal clothes at the office so that if you are unexpectedly called into a meeting with a client or need to go to court, you will be prepared.

3. Performance Evaluations and Salary Negotiations

a. Planning for Your Performance Evaluation

During the course of your employment you will be evaluated on a continuing basis. Every project you work on provides an opportunity for a review of your work. At some time, however, you will receive a more formal evaluation of your performance, usually in connection with a salary increase or career development. Some employers conduct performance evaluations annually while others conduct them more sporadically. Similarly, in large firms the review process is more formal, while in a small firm, the process may consist of a casual chat over coffee. Whatever the nature of your work environment, you should be ready for your performance review.

During the course of the year, ask for feedback from your supervisors. When a case is completed, ask what you could have done better. Don't wait until the end of the year to find out that your supervisor is unhappy with something you do or don't do. Ask for a quick review of your performance so you can adjust your work habits accordingly.

The best way to prepare for a formal performance review is to keep accurate records of your accomplishments. The person who makes the final determination as to whether you receive a salary increase or a promotion may not be familiar with your work. Thus, you will need to be your own advocate. Keep notes on the projects you worked on, indicating the type of work you performed and the results reached for the client. Perhaps a client's transaction was completed in record time. Perhaps an appeal was filed on a tight deadline. Keep track of your billable hours. If your hours are lower than average, be prepared to explain why. Indicate any tasks or projects that were extraordinary. Perhaps you were required to travel a good while during the year. Tell your supervisor about the efforts you have made to continue your legal education by taking classes, writing articles, or mastering new software programs. Have you had any ideas that saved money or time for the firm or its clients? Did you receive any special recognition during the year for work on any one case? Have you served as a mentor to new paralegals?

You will be well-prepared for your review if you maintain a working or personal portfolio, with copies of the documents, briefs, and other matters you worked on during the year. Just as paralegal students should keep a job portfolio or notebook so they are prepared to showcase their talents when they are looking for a job, be prepared to showcase your accomplishments during the year. If you complete continuing education courses, keep copies of the syllabi and certificates of completion.

b. Learning from Your Performance Evaluation

While it is possible that a determination of your salary and performance will simply be announced to you, it is far more likely that you will have a face-to-face review with your paralegal manager or your supervising attorney. Listen carefully and don't be defensive. Try to learn as much as possible from your review. Remember that the employer is not trying to hurt you. It is in everyone's best interest that you are as productive and skillful as possible. The employer wants this for you just as much as you do. Accept any criticism graciously. If a particular problem area or weakness of yours is pointed out to you, ask for specific suggestions on how to improve. Ask to be directed to a mentor who possesses the desired skill so you can improve the area of weakness. For example, if it is noted that your files are disorganized, offer to take a class on organization skills and ask whose files in the office are a model of organization. You can then speak with this person and learn how to improve. Showing a positive outlook and taking the initiative to improve will impress your employer.

If your performance evaluation reveals a number of weaknesses, ask to meet more frequently with your supervisor—perhaps every six or eight weeks—so you can mutually determine whether you are achieving the goals established during your performance review. If a problem is noted during your performance evaluation and there is no later showing that you are attempting to work on it, you will likely lose your job.

During the performance review, you will probably have an opportunity to comment on your work environment. If there is a particular problem that needs solving, don't merely present the problem; suggest possible solutions. If you would like more challenging work or greater responsibility, say so. Volunteer to work on other projects. Offer to assist another practice group to sharpen your skills.

c. Salary Negotiations During Your Performance Evaluation

Expect to address the issue of a salary increase during your review. Just as you did during your job search, be prepared. Review the national surveys released by NALA, NFPA, and IPMA. Check with your local paralegal association to determine the average salaries in your market for paralegals with your level of experience and in your practice area.

Check with colleagues as to what the average increase has been in your locality during the preceding year. While sharing specifics of salary information is generally awkward or even taboo, most colleagues will volunteer that the average salary increase was 3 percent, for example.

The firm may have already released information as to an expected range of salary increases. Therefore, if the firm announces that raises will be between 2 and 6 percent, based on performance, you then have some guidelines. When such an announcement is made, generally only extraordinary achievement will result in any raise at or above the stated maximum.

Review your billable hours and compare them against the average in the firm. Consider the nature of your work. Perhaps your team has participated in a complex transaction or your job has required travel—factors that would justify an increase greater than the average. Don't just say that you need a raise. Show that you deserve one. Consider whether your firm offers other benefits (flexible work hours, extra vacation days, telecommuting, and so forth) that offset a slightly lower than average raise.

Be realistic about the firm's financial position. If the economy is weak, your firm lost a major client or downsized during the year, or you have heard through the office grapevine that times are tough, be prepared to forgo a raise this year. Read the legal journals and newspapers for your locality. They will indicate whether the market is strong or weak and which firms are enjoying successes. Be knowledgeable about the external factors that will influence your compensation.

Be realistic about your work performance. If your learning curve was longer than anticipated and your billable hours were low, understand that your raise will likely be average or slightly lower than average.

If you work in a setting in which there are few, if any, formal evaluations, be sensitive about your timing. If you have just completed work on a successful project or you have been assigned additional duties, this may be an excellent occasion to request a raise. On the other hand, if your firm just lost its biggest client to a competitor, this is not the time to make demands.

If you are disappointed with your raise or weren't given one, ask what you can do to ensure that you will receive one at the next review. Confirm the duties expected of you in your job. Verify the number of hours you are expected to bill. Set a date for another review so you can make sure you are on the right track. Don't threaten to leave unless you are prepared to carry through. Generally, employees who threaten to leave are responded to with an invitation to do so.

End the review by thanking the reviewer for his or her time and comments, and indicate that you will immediately set about correcting any weaknesses. Impress the reviewer with your professionalism.

4. Career Advancement

There is more to your job than your salary. You need stimulating and challenging work. If your firm has an established career track and your work is exemplary, you will advance to a senior paralegal position in accordance with this track. If you wish to advance in your career, you need to take an active role. Consider the following strategies:

- **Ask for more work.** A common complaint among paralegals is that they are underutilized by their employers. It is possible that your employer simply does not know your skills or talents. Volunteer to summarize a deposition, cite-check a court brief, draft an agreement, or some other task. Indicate that you will do this "on your own" as a learning experience (without billing the client or asking for overtime) and ask for feedback. Once your employer sees the work you are capable of, you may be given more challenging responsibilities.
- **Continue learning.** Continue your education. Take classes or attend lectures offered by your local paralegal association. Attend any firm seminars. Let others know about the classes you take. Share the knowledge you gain in seminars by preparing memos summarizing the information and providing copies of any pertinent handouts. Read the same publications that your supervisor does so you stay current in your field and can discuss cutting-edge issues. Subscribe to some of the online legal journals to stay informed of new developments. Many websites, such as FindLaw (*www.findlaw.com*) will send you a daily bulletin with important developments in the legal field. If you are in a specialty practice area, subscribe to an online newsletter devoted to your field. For example, professionals working on intellectual property matters often subscribe to GigaLaw's daily newsletter (*www.gigalaw.com*), which reports on new IP developments.
- **Take the initiative.** Write an article for publication in a paralegal journal. Run for office in your paralegal association. Volunteer to be a mentor to newly hired paralegals. Tell your paralegal manager that you are available for special projects. Serve on the firm's committees. Perform pro bono work. Organize an event in the firm. Volunteer to help out when you see that a practice group or colleague needs assistance. This type of initiative demonstrates leadership.

C. QUITTING A JOB

1. Planning to Quit

The days when people stayed in a job for a lifetime are history. Most people change their jobs and even their careers several times during their working years. You may want to leave your job for any number of reasons: desire for change, lack of opportunity and advancement, low salary, general dissatisfaction with your work or colleagues, geographic relocation, family issues, or a host of other reasons.

Before you take the leap and quit, spend as much time analyzing why you would like to leave as you did in getting the job in the first place. Perform another assessment. Write down the pros and cons of your current situation. In many instances, there is only one negative factor about a job, but it colors a worker's feelings about the entire work environment. Carefully review your list. Can you fix the problem? Don't forget that there will be difficult colleagues, unreasonable supervisors, and boring tasks at any job. If your immediate boss is the only problem, consider whether you can improve your work environment by changing to a different practice field within your firm. Perhaps your firm has another office location where you can work.

Think about other job changes you have made. If every time you have left a job, it has been because your co-workers are difficult to get along with, it may be possible that your expectations are unreasonable or that you are part of the problem.

Meet with your paralegal manager or supervising attorney. Express your concerns about your job but be sure to raise some possible solutions as well. Be specific. A general complaint that "there's too much work," is not as effective as showing that your team is tasked with working overtime far more than any other team in the office. If you're planning on leaving anyway, a candid discussion won't hurt your chances for advancement. Make sure that you have evaluated the job market before you burn any bridges. If the market is weak, you may have to be patient and continue trying to resolve the problems from within.

Many experts note that the most critical issues for most workers, advancement and compensation, are the most difficult to discuss. Thus, many employers have no idea that employees are unhappy until the employee presents a resignation letter. Consider whether you will stay with your employer if your employer tries to keep you by giving you a raise. In some instances, an employee who resigns and then retracts the resignation goes on to have a healthy working relationship at the firm. In many instances, however, the employee is viewed as having been disloyal and having bullied his or her way into an out-of-sequence raise. Of course, staying with your employer is not an option if you have already accepted another offer.

It is unusual, but possible, that you will be asked to leave immediately on giving notice, and you will not be able to work the usual final two weeks. Unless you have an employment agreement, your employer is free to terminate you at any time. Plan for this contingency, and make sure you have sufficient accrued vacation time or savings to meet your financial obligations until you receive your next paycheck.

2. The Resignation Process and Your Resignation Letter

While the conventional wisdom is that you should stay in a job for at least one year, if you are miserably unhappy and there is no workable solution, you should probably go ahead and leave your position, but be prepared to explain to prospective employers why your tenure was so short. You must do this without making negative comments about your former employer.

Resign with professionalism. Meet with your paralegal manager or supervising attorney and indicate that you are leaving. Do not give advice on how the firm could be better managed. Resist the temptation to settle scores. The fact that you are leaving speaks for itself. Moreover, the legal community is small and you never know when you may encounter your colleagues in the future. Plan on giving two weeks' advance notice, which is the generally accepted standard. Never walk off a job with no notice to the employer (unless you are the victim of a legitimate case of sexual harassment or some similar situation, in which case you must still meet with a supervisor to explain why you cannot stay in the work environment).

Work out a reasonable transition plan, promise to complete critical projects, and mutually agree on your final date. Prepare a formal resignation letter, and then tell your colleagues rather than letting them find out through the office grapevine. The resignation letter should be gracious and dignified. It will be the top item in your personnel file, so you want it to provide continuing evidence of your professionalism. There is no need to explain in your letter why you are leaving, although if you are leaving to continue your education or because of a relocation, you may wish to include that information. Prepare a memorandum on the status of each matter on which you have been working. Indicate what tasks need action and when. Place a separate copy of the memo in each file and give another copy to your supervisor. Create a good last impression. See Figure 10-5 for a sample resignation letter.

While you may ask for a letter of reference, most legal employers will not issue a blanket reference. If a prospective employer calls a former employer to ask for a reference, most employers merely verify dates of employment, job title, and salary. You will probably need to rely on other sources for written references.

FIGURE 10-5

SAMPLE LETTER OF RESIGNATION

Joanna T. Lindsey
1238 Fairfax Street
Cleveland, OH 19099

October 10, 2005

Ms. Sandra Cruz
Paralegal Manager
Adam & Baker, L.L.P.
1703 Eighteenth Street
Cleveland, OH 18998

Dear Ms. Cruz:

This letter is my formal letter of resignation from Adam & Baker, L.L.P. As we discussed, my last day will be October 24, 2005.

I will do everything possible to ensure a smooth transition during my remaining time here. I have enjoyed working for Adam & Baker and appreciate the opportunities I have had to learn about corporate and securities law.

I wish both you and Adam & Baker continued success and I thank you for allowing me to be part of the Adam & Baker team. Please let me know if there is anything I can do to assist you in making sure that my remaining time here is productive.

Sincerely,

Joanna T. Lindsey

D. GETTING THE NEXT JOB

1. Introduction

Getting a second or later job is usually easier than getting your first job because you already have the one asset required by many employers: experience. In some instances, a job may fall into your lap through your network of personal contacts. Alternatively, legal recruiters or headhunters are known for calling currently employed paralegals and inquiring if they are interested in making a job change.

You may be ready for a new experience or a different field of practice, or you may have reached the top of the salary range or career path at your present job. These are all valid reasons for changing jobs.

Your résumé should always be ready to go. Each time you receive an award or recognition, update your résumé. Each time you work on a new or complicated project, include this in your résumé. If you are then called by a friend who tells you that his or her firm has an immediate opening, you can respond right away.

2. Looking for the Next Job

The process of obtaining your next job duplicates that of getting your first job. Establish your objectives. In most cases, this will be easier for you than when you did this for your first job. With the experience you have gained from your first job, you may have definite ideas on the size of the firm you wish to work for, the type of work you'd like to do, and the benefits that are important to you. In addition, as a working member of the legal community, you now have a better grasp of how strong the market is in your locality, which fields of practice are strong, and which firms are known for certain specialties.

After you set your objectives, review your job-hunting notebook and consider the strategies that worked well for you the first time. Review section A.5 of this chapter ("Where to Look for a Job"). Step one of any job search is to let your friends, family, and colleagues know that you are looking for a new job. You need to let your contacts know that your search is confidential if you do not want your present employer to know you are searching for another position. Networking alone may land you a job. Review advertisements placed in legal newspapers and general newspapers, look at the job bank postings of your local paralegal association, and see if your school placement office offers job support services for second jobs. Because you now have experience, you will be able to use the services of a legal placement agency. A general employment agency will also help place you. Consider looking at online job postings. Review the legal directories (such as *Martindale-Hubbell*) and the websites of law firms. Consider whether you wish to explore something entirely different, such as working in-house, teaching, being a law firm administrator, managing paralegals, working in a placement company, and so forth.

3. Some Special Concerns When Looking for Another Job

There are five key items that are relevant only to second and subsequent jobs.

Blind ad
Advertisement that does not identify the person or firm that placed it

- **Blind ads.** Many ads placed by law firms and legal employers are **blind ads,** which means they do not identify the employer by name. For example, the ad may simply say, "large, nationally known firm is seeking experienced litigation paralegal," and you will be directed to respond to a newspaper post office box. Imagine your embarrassment if you find out you are responding to your own law firm's ad. Imagine what your supervisor will say when she finds out that you are looking for another job. This has happened. Most job sections of newspapers tell you how to handle this, generally by marking your envelope with a notation similar to the following: "Do not give to the law firm of Adam & Baker."

■ **Confidentiality.** When you send your résumé to a potential employer, write "Confidential" on both the cover letter and your résumé. In the cover letter include the statement, "Please do not contact present employer without prior notice." This will help to ensure that the hiring manager who receives your résumé doesn't immediately contact your present employer and ask why you are leaving. Interestingly, a confidentiality notice is a signal that you are employable and that your present employer values you.

■ **Writing samples.** You will likely have a number of real-world (rather than purely academic) writing samples to provide to prospective employers. You may have, for example, drafted corporate resolutions, prepared employment agreements and wills, summarized deposition transcripts, and so forth. While these documents make excellent writing samples and showcase your experience, in most cases they are confidential client documents. Thus, you will need to **redact**, or black out or white out, any information that identifies the client. Include the notation "Redacted for Confidentiality" at the top of any such document. Documents filed with courts, such as complaints and briefs, are public records and may usually be freely provided to others.

Redact
Striking out of material on a document, usually for confidentiality reasons

■ **Client conflict list.** As discussed in Chapter Three, you need to maintain a current conflicts list so that a prospective employer can determine whether hiring you would pose an ethical problem or disqualify the firm from representing a client. Always keep your conflict list up to date. Be realistic: Although a firm may want to hire you, it will probably not if doing so causes a conflict, even if the conflict is one a client may waive.

■ **Use of current employer's e-mail.** Do not use your present employer's e-mail or other systems to send your résumé, confirm an interview, or engage in any other activities related to your search for a new job. Such practices are disloyal and unprofessional. Use your cell phone and lunch breaks to conduct your job search. It is acceptable to maintain your résumé and conflicts list on your office computer because these may be needed in your present employment.

4. The Interview and Offer

In all likelihood you will be far more comfortable in the interview process for your second job than in your first. You have experience to relate, and you know what questions to ask. Be prepared to explain why you are leaving your present job, but never badmouth your current employer. Not only is such a practice unprofessional; it will make prospective employers wonder if you will badmouth them next time around. It is acceptable to state that you are looking for new opportunities, wish to work in a new practice field, want additional responsibilities, and so forth. As you did for your first job, send a thank-you note after any interview and keep your job notebook updated.

You probably will feel more adept in salary negotiations because you have a baseline (your current salary) from which to judge an offer. Once again, give careful consideration to the nonsalary aspects of a job. Are you willing to trade a lower salary for lower stress? Is the location or reputation of a firm important to you? Again, once you accept an offer, you may not renege on it.

5. Law-Related Jobs

After working in a law firm, you may be ready to work in a different setting. Consider the following jobs that may be easier for you to get now that you have some experience:

- Law librarian or research specialist
- Bank, insurance, or trust department paralegal
- Title searcher or other real estate-related position
- Legal recruiter
- Freelance paralegal
- Law office administrator
- Court clerk
- In-house paralegal
- Legal editor
- Legislative aide
- Paralegal teacher
- Nonprofit or lobbying work

Once you have proven yourself in one law job, a host of other opportunities are available to you, in both traditional roles and nontraditional positions.

NET RESULTS

www.paralegals.org	Select "Career Center" to be directed to NFPA's job center where you can post and edit your résumé, look for jobs, and review articles and tips on preparing résumés and cover letters and going on interviews.
www.paralegalmanagement.org	Select "Job Bank" for IPMA's job bank, which includes postings for paralegal jobs and paralegal manager jobs.
www.opm.gov	The Office of Personnel Management's website posts paralegal job vacancies for federal government positions.
www.job-interview.net	This site provides résumé and interview guides, practice interviews, sample questions to ask on interviews, and related job-searching information.

www.jobweb.com   Select "Résumés & Interviews" for articles
                                    and tips on preparing résumés and cover
                                    letters and on interview strategies.

www.greedyassociates.com   This website offers the "inside story" on
                                    law firms from associates' points of view.

CASE ILLUSTRATION

Résumé Falsification

Case: *Mathis v. Boeing Military Airplane Co.*, 719 F. Supp. 991 (D. Kan.
             1989)

Facts: The plaintiff, Mathis, alleged that the defendant, her former
             employer, had discriminated against her on the basis of race and
             sex, in violation of Title VII of the Civil Rights Act. The defen-
             dant denied any unlawful discrimination and stated it terminated
             the plaintiff's employment because the plaintiff had not disclosed
             a prior felony conviction on her employment application and
             had not revealed that she had been terminated for cause by three
             federal agencies.

Holding: The defendant employer was entitled to summary judgment. The
             omissions on the résumé/employment application were material
             and related directly to the plaintiff's employment by defendant.
             Under these circumstances, the plaintiff could not recover under
             Title VII.

KEY TERMS

Job-hunting notebook   Functional résumé
Job bank   Cover letter
Networking   Blind ad
Headhunter   Redact
Mass mailing

CHAPTER SUMMARY

Planning to Get a Job	Getting a job requires a great deal of planning. You must set your objectives, assess your strengths and weaknesses, evaluate the marketplace, and then begin the search process.
Places to Search for Jobs	There are numerous places to search for a job, including through personal contacts, paralegal associations, school placement offices, newspaper ads, legal and general employment placement agencies, online searching, law directories, and temporary employment agencies. Of all methods, using your network of personal contacts is likely to be the most effective.
Job-Hunting Notebook	Maintain a job-hunting notebook with all the information relating to your search activities, including the dates you sent résumés, results obtained, dates of interviews, and your impressions of potential employers.
Résumé	Your résumé must be a persuasive marketing document that "sells" you to an employer. Its content should be accurate and it should present you in the best light possible. It should be professional and polished in its appearance, and it should be accompanied by a brief cover letter introducing you to the prospective employer.
Interview Process	The interview process can be stressful, but if you plan ahead, you can reduce a great deal of anxiety. Participate in mock interviews, conduct research to obtain information about the prospective employer, and plan your answers to anticipated questions. After your interview, follow up with a thank-you letter.
The Offer	When you receive an offer, you should take a few days to think it over because once you accept an offer, you cannot renege on it.
Keeping a Job	To keep a job, you must be punctual, diligent, highly competent, a team player, and respectful.
Performance Evaluations	During the course of your job, your performance will be evaluated. Prepare for your evaluations by

	maintaining a list of your projects. Conduct research about salaries so you are prepared to engage in salary negotiations.
Advancing Your Career	During your job, to advance your career, continue learning, take the initiative to work on new projects, and ask for work.
Quitting a Job	If you decide to leave your place of employment, do so professionally and with class. Giving two weeks' notice is the accepted standard. Provide a formal resignation letter.
Getting Your Second Job	Getting your second job may well be easier than getting your first job because you will have the experience desired by so many employers. In addition, a variety of law-related jobs will be available to you.

TRIVIA

- Studies show that more than 20 percent of employment data about previous jobs on résumés or employment applications is falsified.
- In 2004, the Bureau of Labor Statistics reported that the median number of years that wage and salary workers had been with their current employer was 4 years. The median years of tenure tend to increase with the age of the worker.
- NFPA's website reports that some of the common errors individuals make in their cover letters are the following:
  - ☐ Spelling and grammar errors;
  - ☐ Addressing the recipient as "Dear Sir" (rather than by name or by "Dear Sir or Madam");
  - ☐ Failing to include contact information; and
  - ☐ Forgetting to put the letter in the envelope with the résumé.

DISCUSSION QUESTIONS

1. Draft a letter responding to the following job announcement posted in your local newspaper:

   Needed: Entry level litigation paralegal. The paralegal will need to oversee file maintenance and document production, perform cite-checking and Shepardize or KeyCite briefs and other pleadings, conduct factual and legal research, organize pleadings and discovery documents, draft basic memos and letters, summarize depositions, and interact with clients. Respond to Announcement 12345, L. Hendersen, Bell & Gray, 1134 Avenue of the Americas, New York, NY 10036.

2. During an interview, the comment is made to you, "Your name is interesting. What type of name is that? It sounds foreign." How should you respond?

3. After an interview, you are offered a salary that is $4,000 less than what you were expecting. What should you do?

4. You are considering leaving the firm you are with and looking for another job. You see an ad in the paper that asks you to respond to Box 505. What is the risk if you send your résumé in response to this ad? Can you do anything to minimize the risk?

5. During a job interview, when asked for writing samples, you give an employment agreement you drafted for one client and a complaint you drafted for another. Discuss whether there are any ethics issues related to providing these documents.

6. During an interview, you are asked if you have any questions about the prospective employer. What is the disadvantage of responding, "What is the salary for this job and what benefits will I get if I am hired?"

7. You have gotten a new job that requires you to start in five days. What should you do with respect to your current employer?

CLOSING ARGUMENTS

1. Access the NFPA website and select "Career Center."
   a. Review the information relating to effective résumés and cover letters. What is the recommended maximum length for a résumé?
   b. Select "Career Tools." Identify the different types of interviews.
   c. Select "Career Tools." What is NFPA's advice regarding the use of personal or professional references?
   d. Select "Career Tools" and review the article relating to setting goals for success. What are the four topics that job candidates need to consider and determine whether they are essential, desired, or optional?

2. Access the Executive Summary for NFPA's 2003 Paralegal Compensation and Benefits Report.
   a. What is the average salary reported?
   b. What is the average bonus reported?
   c. What percentage of paralegals reported receiving a bonus?

3. Access IPMA's Job Bank online and review the FAQ section relating to finding a job as a paralegal. What is IPMA's response to the question "Must I have a four-year degree?"

CHAPTER

11

THE LAW OFFICE ENVIRONMENT

N O ONE IS UNDER PRESSURE. THERE WASN'T A LIGHT ON WHEN I LEFT AT 2 O'CLOCK THIS MORNING.

—HOYT A. MOORE (1964) (QUOTED BY A PARTNER IN THE MANHATTAN LAW FIRM OF CRAVATH, SWAINE & MOORE)

CHAPTER OVERVIEW

As you learned in Chapter Two, most paralegals work in law firms. In fact, NFPA's 2003 annual survey reported that approximately 70 percent of the nation's paralegals work in law firms. NALA's 2004 survey results are the same. Thus, this chapter focuses primarily on law firms and secondarily on other work settings in which paralegals are employed. The business structures of law firms are examined; for example, whether the firm operates as a partnership or a professional corporation. The characteristics of both small firms and large firms are described, and law firm personnel are identified. Because time is money in private law practice, fee arrangements and timekeeping and billing practices are explained. This chapter examines various law office procedures in which paralegals are routinely involved, including conflicts checks, file maintenance, and docket and calendar control. The chapter then reviews the way technology has changed law firm practice and has allowed small firms to compete with larger ones. The chapter concludes with a brief look at nontraditional work settings for paralegals, such as working "in house" for a company or working in the public sector.

A. LAW FIRM STRUCTURES AND ORGANIZATION

1. Introduction

When the American Bar Association was formed in 1878 by 75 attorneys, most individuals entered the profession by apprenticing with attorneys. Most lawyers practiced by themselves or in partnerships of two or three individuals. Today, the Bureau of Labor Statistics estimates the total number of lawyers in the United States at 1,508,000 and the total number of paralegals at 211,000. Law firms range in size from solo offices to the giant Baker & McKenzie firm, which has more than 3,000 attorneys in 66 offices in 36 countries and an annual revenue in excess of $1 billion.

Thus, the variety and size of the settings in which the nation's paralegals are employed are diverse. Generally, attorneys and law firms operate as sole practitioners, partnerships, limited liability partnerships, limited liability companies, and professional corporations. Attorneys who work for themselves or who are employed by other attorneys are said to be in **private practice**, as opposed to being employed by a government entity or a corporation that is not engaged in the practice of law, such as a high-tech company.

2. Sole Practitioners

A **sole practitioner** is an attorney who practices by himself or herself. The sole practitioner makes all business decisions, retains all profits (and must bear all losses), and owns all of the business assets of the practice. Usually, the sole practitioner is a "jack of all trades" and handles a variety of matters, including family law matters (wills, divorces, and so forth), general business matters (such as forming partnerships or corporations for clients), and some criminal matters. The sole practitioner usually employs a secretary and may employ a paralegal.

3. General Partnerships

For hundreds of years, law firms of two or more attorneys operated as traditional **general partnerships** in which all partners shared decision-making responsibility, retained all of the profits of the firm, and were personally liable for all debts and obligations of the firm and for malpractice claims made against any attorney. **Personal liability** is liability for debts that may exceed that which one has invested in a business, and it may extend to one's personal assets. For example, under general partnership law, a partner in a law firm in Dallas will be personally liable for an error made by one of the attorneys in the firm's Atlanta office; the Dallas attorney's personal assets (checking account, savings account, art collection, and the like) are available to satisfy the malpractice claim. Under a concept known as **joint and several liability,** each partner is entirely responsible for all debts. Thus, a creditor can attack the assets of all or any combination of partners in order to satisfy a debt or obligation. Although this discussion focuses on liability, keep in mind that most law firms have significant malpractice insurance to cover potential losses, and thus, while a malpractice claim may well arise, the insurance may be sufficient to pay the claim, and the issue of a partner's personal liability may never arise.

In a traditional partnership, the **partners** are the owners of the firm and its assets. Newly licensed attorneys usually begin working for the firm as **associates** and after a period of time (often between seven to ten years) are elected to partnership status. Associates are employees of the firm and are paid a stated salary; partners, the owners of the firm, share in the profits of the firm. These owner-partners are oftentimes referred to as **equity partners**. Not every partner is equal. Some may own a 5 percent interest in the firm while another may own a 9 percent interest in the firm, and so forth. Ownership interests and profit calculations may be

Private practice
In law, attorneys who work for themselves or other attorneys rather than for a government entity or company

Sole practitioner
In law, an attorney who practices by himself or herself

General partnership
A business structure with shared decision-making and unlimited personal liability for its partners

Personal liability
Liability extending beyond what is invested in a business to one's personal assets

Joint and several liability
Liability for an entire debt

Partner
The owner of a firm or business operating as a partnership

Associate
A junior attorney

Equity partner
A partner who owns business assets

based on complicated formulas that factor in such elements as seniority, investment in the firm, and business generated. Management of the firm is often based on ownership interest, so that a partner with a 10 percent interest will have 10 percent of the voting power and will receive 10 percent of the profits distributed that year; however, partnerships are free to make other arrangements relating to management and profit distribution. Because partners share in profits of the firm, if profits drop off in a certain year, the associates, paralegals, and support staff will still receive their agreed-on salaries, but the partners' incomes may be decreased that year. To ensure that partners' profits remain high, the firm may downsize. The partners may elect one **managing partner** or may establish various committees, such as a compensation committee, a recruitment committee, and an ethics committee.

Until a few years ago, if an associate was not offered a partnership, he or she was expected to leave the firm. Now, in recognition of the varied career paths of attorneys, many firms recognize that there may be **permanent associates,** individuals who are employed by the firm who will never achieve equity partnership status (having ownership rights in the firm), but they are valued members of the firm and will continue to keep their jobs with the firm so long as the firm is profitable. A variety of names are assigned to these individuals, such as **senior attorney, of counsel,** and **nonequity partner.** The term **of counsel** is often reserved for older, semi-retired partners or possibly experienced attorneys who are hired by the firm after they have been employed for a number of years at another firm. These **lateral hires** are then given one or two years to prove themselves; if they do, they will be offered a partnership at the new firm.

Managing partner
A partner who directs or manages a partnership

Permanent associate
An attorney who will remain an employee of a firm rather than an owner; also called *senior attorney, of counsel,* or *nonequity partner*

Of counsel
Term usually assigned to older, semi-retired attorneys although it might refer to senior attorneys

Lateral hire
Attorney hired by one firm from another

4. Limited Liability Partnerships

The **limited liability partnership** (LLP) was first recognized in 1991 and was created to alter a fundamental principle of partnership law, that of unlimited personal liability, which is a significant risk in any law firm operating as a traditional general partnership. In an LLP (now recognized in all jurisdictions), the liability of partners is limited so that partners have no personal liability for the negligent acts and misconduct of their partners (unless they participated in the wrongful act or supervised the partner who committed the wrongful act). Recall that in our example, partners in the Dallas office were personally liable for the malpractice of the attorney in the firm's Atlanta office. If the firm is organized as an LLP, the Atlanta attorney and the firm itself are liable for the act of malpractice, but the personal assets of the Dallas attorneys cannot be reached to satisfy the obligation.

To form as an LLP or to convert from the traditional partnership form to the LLP form, the law firm needs to file an application with the state in which it maintains its principal office. You always know that a firm is an LLP because its name, letterhead, business cards, and so forth must include the designation "LLP" or some similar designation.

The LLP is managed much like a traditional partnership, and its professionals continue to be called partners and associates. Because of the tremendous advantage of doing business as an LLP, most of the nation's large firms have converted from operating as general partnerships to LLPs. Electing to operate as an LLP allows a law firm to manage its affairs like a traditional partnership but limits liability to those partners directly involved in a wrongful act. Thus, an LLP structure is an extremely attractive form in which law firms operate.

Limited liability partnership
Method of doing business that is governed by partnership law and protects partners from unlimited personal liability

5. Limited Liability Companies

Limited liability company
Method of doing business in which the business entity (which is neither a corporation nor a partnership) protects its members from unlimited personal liability

Member
A participant in a limited liability company

Like LLPs, **limited liability companies** (LLCs) are new business entities that are recognized in all American jurisdictions. LLCs, however, are not based on a partnership model (like LLPs are); they are a new form of business structure that combines features of partnership law and corporate law. Like the LLP, the LLC also provides protection for its participants (who are called **members** rather than partners) from personal liability for the wrongful acts of others in the LLC (unless, of course, the member participated in the wrongful act or supervised it).

Because the LLC is an entirely new type of business structure, law firms have been slow to adopt this form. Most prefer to operate as LLPs rather than LLCs because LLPs are based on partnership law, a comfortable and familiar way of doing business for law firms. In fact, in some states (including California and Rhode Island) professionals such as attorneys are precluded from operating as LLCs.

LLCs are formed much like LLPs: A document is filed with the state in which the firm maintains its principal office. Various annual filings may be required thereafter. A law firm operating as an LLC must include the designation "LLC" (or some similar designation) in its name and on all written material. The attorneys in an LLC who own the firm will be called members and the newer attorneys are usually called associates.

6. Professional Corporations

Professional corporation
Corporation formed to provide professional services, such as a law firm

Shareholder
The owner of a corporation

Director
The manager of a corporation

Law firms and attorneys may also conduct business as **professional corporations,** in which case they will be governed by corporate law rather than partnership law. The corporation is formed by filing state-required documents with the state in which it maintains its principal office. Like any corporation, it is owned by its **shareholders,** who will elect the managers, usually called **directors,** to govern the affairs of the corporation. Share ownership and management are usually restricted to the licensed attorneys. Both law firms and individual attorneys may practice as professional corporations. The professionals will have personal liability for their own acts of malpractice and the acts of others they supervise. A law firm or attorney operating as a professional corporation must use the designations "PC" (or a similar designation).

7. Office Sharing

Some sole practitioners may share office arrangements with each other. In outward appearance, the arrangement may appear to be a single law firm, but it is really a collection of sole practitioners gathered under one roof who share the reception area, conference rooms, law library, and personnel, such as a receptionist and secretarial pool. Such an arrangement allows sole practitioners low-cost access to nicer offices and amenities without sacrificing their ability to make all decisions (and retain all profits) for themselves.

B. LAW FIRM ENVIRONMENTS

1. Introduction

The ways in which law firms operate are as varied as the number of firms. There are, however, some generalizations that can be made about working in smaller firms and in larger firms. First, however, the designations "small" and "large" may be misleading. For example, in New York City, a small firm may be 40 attorneys while in Cedar Rapids, Iowa, such a firm would be considered quite large. While there is no absolute agreement then as to what constitutes a small, medium, or large firm, there are some general guidelines. For example, Altman, Weil, Inc., a prominent legal consulting firm, classifies a small law firm as one having fewer than 15 attorneys. Florida State University College of Law classifies medium firms as those having between 26 and 50 attorneys and large law firms as those firms with more than 50 attorneys. The following discussion highlights some of the broader differences in law firm environments.

2. Working for a Sole Practitioner or Small Firm

If a paralegal is employed by a sole practitioner or a small firm, the paralegal will likely be a jack-of-all-trades, much as the attorney is. Many paralegals report great job satisfaction working with a sole practitioner or in a small firm; the paralegal is a valued colleague and usually is able to assume as much responsibility as he or she likes. The work is varied and there is often a great deal of client contact and little, if any, of the bureaucracy and hierarchies seen in larger law firms, in which paralegals may be relegated to the role of supporting players. Working in a small law firm allows paralegals the opportunity to work on an array of both civil and criminal cases and provides an effective way for paralegals to find out what kinds of work they enjoy.

Paralegals usually report directly to attorneys, without any layers of management in between, which makes strong, personal relationships the norm. According to the 2004 National Utilization and Compensation Survey Report prepared by the National Association of Legal Assistants (NALA Survey), approximately 15 percent of the responding paralegals were employed by sole practitioners and 31 percent (the largest percentage reported) were employed by firms with two to five attorneys. In fact, 63 percent of the responding paralegals were employed by firms with ten or fewer attorneys.

There are some disadvantages to working with a sole practitioner or in a small firm. In many cases, the pay is less than that offered to paralegals by large firms. The office may lack some of the technological advancements often seen in larger firms, supplies may run low, and the law library may be small or nonexistent. However, most sole practitioners and small firms now take advantage of computerized legal research services designed especially for them, such as Loislaw (*www.loislaw.com*), thus eliminating the need for conventional print sources. In a small firm, everyone needs to pitch in and provide support services, such as buying supplies, word processing, and photocopying. Moreover, usually there is no other paralegal to share the workload; if an emergency arises, the paralegal will need to stay until the task is complete. Thus, paralegals who work for sole practitioners and small firms should always join their local paralegal association to meet other paralegals with whom they can share information and ideas. Similarly, in recognition of the special challenges for sole practitioners and small firms, the ABA has established the Standing Committee on Solo and Small Firm Practitioners to serve as a resource and support center for these firms. Although there are a number of demands in working in such a firm, the work environment may provide an exciting and challenging career opportunity because the paralegal is a true team member whose work is appreciated by both the attorney and the client.

3. Working in Medium-Sized Law Firms

Medium-sized law firms are generally those with between 10 and 25 attorneys. At the low end of the range, these firms strongly resemble small law firms while at the higher end of the range, these firms are similar to large law firms. Medium-sized law firms often employ a paralegal manager or coordinator who supervises and hires paralegals and controls the workflow. Because there will likely be other paralegals at the firm, sharing ideas, getting help, and working collaboratively is common. The NALA Survey reported that 27 percent of all paralegals are employed by firms with 11 to 50 attorneys.

4. Working in Large Law Firms

The nation's large, elite firms dominate the legal landscape and media reports relating to law practice management, mergers, salaries, and revenues. The NALA Survey reports that only 4 percent of all paralegals work for law firms with 100 or more attorneys. These large law firms usually offer generous starting salaries, a variety of employment benefits, guaranteed bonuses, and a number of interesting practice areas. Paralegals employed by a large firm may be assigned to just one practice group, such as bankruptcy, litigation, or intellectual property.

Everything is the best: The supply room is well-stocked with every possible type of pen and sticky note; the reception and conference rooms are beautifully appointed; all legal professionals will have desktop access to LEXIS and Westlaw; messengers and photocopy assistants await instructions; employees who work late will be driven home by a limousine; holiday parties are lavish; office kitchens are stocked with fruit juices, sodas, and cappuccino makers; health club memberships may be provided; and the clients represent a "Who's Who" of American businesses and individuals. Large firms routinely have offices throughout the United States and in a variety of foreign countries, making travel exciting and often allowing attorneys and paralegals the opportunity to work at one of the firm's overseas offices.

So why shouldn't everyone want to work at a large law firm? Paralegals who work for the nation's largest law firms often complain about their lack of job satisfaction. Beginning paralegals may be assigned mind-numbing tasks of labeling or indexing boxes of documents for months on end; they may be assigned to or pigeon-holed in one practice group with no hope of transferring to another more interesting field; they often have little client contact; and the pressure and work hours can be difficult in the extreme. Travel and overtime are frequently required. Moreover, paralegals often feel they are anonymous laborers whose work is not appreciated or rewarded. With numerous committees, branch offices, and layers of management, opportunities for career advancement may be frustrated. For example, in some large law firms, a paralegal is not eligible for a promotion until after serving at least a year with the firm. In a small firm, the attorneys have the discretion to reward a particularly skilled and hard-working paralegal, and the paralegal is not burdened by policies and rules imposed firmwide or even globally. In large firms, paralegals usually report directly to a paralegal manager or coordinator rather than to an attorney.

There is, of course, a certain amount of prestige and status in working for one of the nationally known megafirms. Moreover, because of the name recognition of such firms, there is often greater job mobility for paralegals who work at these firms; other firms readily recognize the firm name and are eager to hire paralegals who have been trained at these large firms. Similarly, paralegals employed by large firms often transfer to one of the firm's other offices.

5. Organization Within Law Firms

While the sole practitioner and his or her paralegal will handle a variety of different matters (often called a **general practice**), many other firms specialize in or establish certain niche practice groups. For example, while most small firms handle a wide array of cases, both civil and criminal, other small firms are known as **boutique firms**—small firms devoted to one type of practice such as intellectual property law or appellate work. Firms that engage in personal injury practice usually devote themselves either to representing plaintiffs, defendants, or insurers.

Many law firms are divided into two broad categories of work: litigation and **transactional work** (nearly any work that is nonlitigation, such as corporate, tax, and any work related to a legal transaction). Review the website of any large law firm and you can see the various practice groups within the firm. For example, a firm may be divided into the following practice areas: banking and finance, energy, international law, labor and employment, land use, mergers and acquisitions, real estate, securities, telecommunications, and international law. Both attorneys and paralegals may be assigned to a practice group depending on the firm's needs rather than on their own interests and desires, and they often find it difficult to move to another group within the firm.

General practice
Law firm practice that handles a wide variety of cases

Boutique firm
Law firm that handles only one type of case

Transactional work
Legal work related to business transactions rather than litigation

C. LAW FIRM PERSONNEL

While we have briefly discussed some of the personnel in law firms, following is a more detailed description of law firm employees and owners.

- **Support staff. Support staff** is the term broadly used to describe the nonprofessional staff in a law firm—namely, any individual who is not a paralegal or an attorney. Support staff in a larger firm can include a receptionist, file clerks, copy and mail personnel and messengers, accounting and billing clerks, and secretaries. In a small firm, one secretary performs all of these functions. Support staff usually report to and are managed by an office manager. Until about ten years ago, many firms hired one secretary for each attorney or paralegal. The ratio then changed to 2:1 (two attorneys or paralegals or a combination) for each secretary. As more and more attorneys and paralegals become proficient at preparing their own documents on word processors, the ratio in larger firms has changed to 3:1. In fact, the NALA Survey reported that 28 percent of all paralegals share a secretary with one or more attorneys. In smaller firms, experienced secretaries may perform paralegal duties such as drafting correspondence and preparing the first drafts of some documents.

  Support staff
  Personnel in a law firm other than attorneys and paralegals

- **Paralegals.** As described in Chapter Two, a paralegal is usually defined as a person who by training, experience, or both, performs substantive legal work under the supervision of an attorney. While paralegals may be required to perform some clerical functions in small firms (such as ordering supplies or doing photocopying), attorneys in small firms share these tasks as well. Some firms have various tiers of paralegals who have different titles and duties. For example, a firm may designate the new employees as "project assistants," more experienced paralegals as "legal assistants," and the most experienced individuals as "senior legal assistants." Such hierarchies are far more common in large firms than in small ones.

- **Paralegal managers.** Paralegal managers are generally found in larger firms with a number of paralegals. These managers hire, supervise, train, mentor, evaluate, and discharge the paralegals. In some firms, paralegal managers have nearly complete responsibility for the recruiting and hiring of paralegals. They develop programs for training, coordinate workflow, ensure that projects are staffed appropriately, and supervise all of the firm's paralegals. Recall that IPMA is the international organization for paralegal managers.

Law clerk
Law student hired by firms to perform research and other tasks

- **Law clerks.** Many law firms hire **law clerks**, who are often second- or third-year law students or recent law school graduates. In many cases, large firms have "summer associate" programs in which they hire law students to work for the firm during the summer between the students' second and third years of law school. If the arrangement is satisfactory, the firm may extend an offer to the summer associate to join the firm as a permanent associate upon graduation. Law clerks perform much of the same work that paralegals do, although they frequently perform more legal research than paralegals.

Law librarian
Individual specially trained in the law and in library science

- **Law librarians.** Large law firms hire professional **law librarians** to ensure the firm's law library is adequate and to assist with research problems. Many of these law librarians are not only law school graduates but also possess advanced degrees in library science. In today's information technology world, and as more and more law firms eliminate traditional print volumes of books in favor of computerized legal research and investigation, these law librarians have become increasingly skilled and proficient in locating information and conducting investigations with paralegals and attorneys.

- **Associates.** Associates are the new attorneys in a firm who often do the "grunt" work. In large firms, associates are compensated extraordinarily well (often being paid more than $120,000 per year) and as a result are expected to devote extraordinary time to the firm. As discussed earlier, after seven to ten years, the firm will usually extend a partnership offer (or shareholder offer, if the firm functions as a professional corporation) to the associate. Associates who elect to work part-time or have taken leaves of absence often depart from the **partnership track,** the firm's established course for becoming a partner, and may remain permanent associates, with titles of senior attorney, senior associate, of counsel, nonequity partner, and the like. In small firms, associates are expected to jump in on the first day of employment and immediately assume responsibility for cases, business development, and client relations. In contrast, in large law firms, new associates are often not given a great deal of responsibility and may compete with paralegals for interesting work. Just as some law firms hire contract paralegals or freelance paralegals to work on specific projects, some law firms hire **contract attorneys** to work on a case-by-case basis. When a case or transaction is complete, the contract attorney's relationship with the firm ends.

Partnership track
A firm's established course to become partner

Contract attorney
Attorney who is not an employee of a firm but who works for the firm on a project basis

- **Partners and shareholders.** As discussed, partners and shareholders are the senior attorneys in a firm who own the assets of the firm. They are usually paid from the profits of the firm rather than receiving a stated fixed salary. These attorneys manage the firm, implement all firm policies, and determine the firm's future. The partners or shareholders usually elect a managing partner or managing shareholder from their ranks and are expected to serve on various firm committees to ensure the firm operates smoothly. Generally, raising revenue by attracting new clients, called *rainmaking*, is required for continued success.

D. MONEY MATTERS

1. Introduction and Types of Fee Arrangements

As discussed in Chapter Three, only attorneys may establish fee arrangements with clients. Remember that in many instances the client will pay a retainer or advance fee to the firm, against which future fees are charged. Also, recall that attorneys have ethical obligations to segregate client funds from firm operating accounts. There are three common types of fee arrangements that firms and attorneys enter into with clients:

- **Contingency fees.** In a **contingency fee** arrangement, the attorney does not receive any fee unless he or she is successful in recovering money for the client. Contingency fee arrangements are most common in personal injury, medical malpractice, and collection cases. For example, it may be nearly impossible for a poor plaintiff to assume the burden of paying an attorney for several years of work in a complex medical malpractice action. Thus, the firm will agree that it will receive a stated percentage of any money recovered in the action. The fee is thus contingent on the firm's success in the case. If there is no recovery, the firm receives no fees for its services. Generally, clients are expected to pay for the costs and out-of-pocket expenses of the case as they are incurred, such as court filing fees, witness fees, photocopying and mailing fees, and the like. The percentage of the fee to be retained by the attorney must be set forth in a written agreement and varies depending on the nature of the case, the experience of the attorney, and so forth. Most contingent fee arrangements provide for a sliding scale. For example, a common approach is an agreement that if the case is settled out of court, the firm receives one-third of the recovery. If the case proceeds to trial, the firm will receive 40 percent of any recovery awarded at trial. Attorneys who work on a contingency basis must conduct careful analysis of the case prior to accepting it because the firm cannot be profitable if it works for free for several years on a case that is unlikely to be successful. Law firms that accept cases on a contingency basis will delegate as much of the work as possible to junior associates and paralegals so as to maximize the firm's recovery. Contingent fee arrangements are usually prohibited in criminal actions or domestic relations matters.

  > **Contingency fee**
  > Fee paid to law firm by client only if firm is successful in representing client; usually seen in personal injury practices

- **Flat or fixed fees.** A **flat** or **fixed fee** is a specific sum agreed on in advance by the firm and the client for the work to be performed. For example, a firm may charge a flat fee of $750 for preparing a trademark application or a flat fee for preparing a simple will or handling an uncontested divorce case. Flat fees are common in cases in which the attorney is so experienced in a field that he or she can easily predict how much time the matter will require. Flat fees are advantageous for clients because they know in advance how much money their matter will cost. As with contingent fee arrangements, the client is required to pay all costs and expenses incurred by the firm in connection with the representation. Many clients wonder why law firms cannot offer more services on a fixed-fee basis, much like the way the fee for an office visit to a physician is established

  > **Flat fee**
  > An agreed-upon sum that will be paid by a client to a law firm for performance of certain legal tasks, regardless of outcome of case; also called *fixed fee*

in advance. In law firms, however, many factors are outside of the firm's control, including court dockets and the responsiveness of other parties. As is the case with contingency fees, it is more advantageous to the firm to allow junior attorneys and paralegals to perform as much of the work as possible in cases being billed on a fixed-fee basis, to maximize profits. In a variation on flat fees, some firms agree to **transaction fees,** in which an entire transaction, such as a merger or acquisition, is completed for a fixed sum. Some clients offer their attorneys **success fees**, which are essentially bonuses for completing a transaction early. For example, a firm may receive a bonus of $50,000 if it can close a deal by a certain date or ensure that the client acquires title to real estate by a certain date. The law firm is then provided the incentive to work harder on the client's case to earn the success fee.

■ **Hourly fee.** Since the late 1960s, most law firms have charged **hourly fees**, or a certain amount for each hour of time spent on the client's case. Hourly fees are the norm because it is nearly impossible for a law firm to predict how much work a case will involve, especially when many factors are not within the firm's ability to control, such as crowded court calendars. Hourly rates vary based on market conditions, the reputation of the firm, the nature of the case, and, most important, the level of experience of the legal professional. The hourly rate may also vary according to activity so that conducting a deposition or appearing in court may require a higher fee. According to 2004 surveys by Altman, Weil, Inc., the following are standard average hourly billing rates in the United States for various legal professionals:

  ☐ Experienced equity partner $294
  ☐ Associate(five years' experience) $203
  ☐ Paralegal specialist $166
  ☐ Paralegal $127

Note that these are average rates. Large firms routinely charge in excess of $350 per hour for senior attorneys and more than $150 per hour for paralegals. Many law firms follow "the rule of thirds," which means that one-third of the revenue generated by hourly fees is allocated to law firm salaries, one-third to overhead (insurance, rent, computer services, and the like), and one-third to profit for the firm's partners or shareholders.

A newer form of fee arrangement is a **blended billing rate**, which allows law firms to bill a set hourly rate (for example, $175 per hour), regardless of which individual legal professional works on the case. Blended billing rates are more frequently charged in litigation matters than in transactional matters.

2. Concerns About Billable Hours

The obvious advantages of billing on an hourly basis are that it allows a firm to determine easily the productivity of attorneys and paralegals and allows clients to pay for the actual services rendered to them on a matter. The great disadvantage of **billable hours** (the time that can be charged to a client) is that it places tremendous pressure on legal professionals to bill more and more time in order to generate profit for the firm.

The problem is compounded by the fact that many firms require attorneys and paralegals to bill a stated number of hours each year. For example, a new associate

---

Transaction fee
Fee paid to law firm by client for an entire transaction

Success fee
Excess fees paid to law firm by client for achieving certain preestablished goals

Hourly fee
Fee paid by client for each hour of work performed on a matter

Blended billing rate
An hourly rate set by a law firm no matter which individual works on a particular client matter

Billable hours
Time that can be charged to a client for work performed

might be required to bill 1,900 hours, and a paralegal might be required to bill 1,400 hours each year. In fact, the NALA Survey reported that nearly one-third of all paralegals are expected to bill between 31 and 35 hours per week. A 2003 Altman, Weil survey disclosed that associates in the largest law firms (those with more than 150 attorneys) recorded a median of 1,969 hours.

Because legal professionals meet friends for lunch, attend firm business meetings, visit with colleagues, attend seminars, and so forth, not every minute during a workday is billable. Thus, there is tremendous pressure to meet the stated quotas to remain employed, receive a bonus, or be viewed as a productive and efficient team member.

When mandatory billable hours are set by a firm, attorneys and paralegals must work many hours more than those that are billed. At least one legal consulting firm has estimated that typically three hours are worked for every two hours that are billed. If that is the case, to bill 1,400 hours per year, a paralegal has to work 2,100 hours, which comes to 40 hours each week throughout the year. If the paralegal wishes to take a vacation or is sick, the time must be made up in some way, thus leading to a grueling pace and a temptation to pad time by recording hours in excess of those actually spent on client work.

In recognition of the corrosive effect of hourly billing, in 2002 the ABA formally acknowledged the "treadmill—the continuous push to increase billable hours" as a significant problem in the legal profession that "has caused the pace of law practice to become frenetic and has had a negative effect on mentoring, associate training, and collegiality." The ABA established a Commission on Billable Hours to study the problem and issued its findings in 2002. Among the findings of the ABA Commission were that over-reliance on billable hours:

- Results in a decline of the collegiality of law firm culture, an increase in the departures of associates, and a reduction in pro bono work;
- Encourages skipping steps;
- Provides no predictability of costs for the client because the client does not know the ultimate cost until the project concludes; and
- Puts the client's interests in conflict with the attorney's interests.

The Commission also determined that approximately 80 percent of the firms it surveyed used billable hours to determine associates' salaries and bonuses. The Commission recommended the use of alternative billing methods (such as billing based on the value of the work, partial contingency fees, task-based billing, and fixed rates) and elimination of strict, mandatory billable hours requirements.

Criticism of hourly billing continues. Because most firms do not give credit for time spent on nonbillable activities (such as community service, mentoring, pro bono work, and bar activities), few attorneys participate in such activities, and most perceive the law firm's message to be that the only thing valued by the firm is billable hours. Keep in mind that the emphasis on billable hours is not as great in public interest law firms, legal clinics, and government legal departments because these entities do not bill time to a paying client. To encourage pro bono work, some firms allow attorneys and paralegals to devote a certain number of hours to pro bono activities (for example, 50 hours per year) and count that time toward any minimum billable hour requirements.

3. Timekeeping Practices

a. Introduction

Timekeeping
Practice of tracking and entering time spent on client and other work

Because most firms use hourly billing as the method by which clients are charged for legal services, **timekeeping,** which is the detailed and accurate recording of the time spent and tasks performed on client matters, is critical. Even firms that take cases on a contingency basis or that use flat fees require timekeeping to measure productivity and assess whether the fees recovered are adequate to cover the firm's costs. Moreover, in cases in which the court may order the payment of attorneys' fees, the firm will need to be able to document the time it spent on the case to receive a fee award. In any event, the fee must be reasonable and must have been fully explained to the client. Ethical standards for timekeeping can be found in the ethical rules and opinions of the ABA, state bar associations, and paralegal associations.

b. How Time Is Calculated

Generally, law firms that engage in hourly billing divide the hour into either quarters or tenths as units of measurement. For example, assume your firm charges your time to the client at the rate of $100 per hour and the firm bills based on quarter hours—segments of 15 minutes. If you spent 30 minutes drafting a letter, the client would be billed $50, and if you spent 45 minutes preparing a document, the client would be billed $75. Generally, time is rounded up to the next nearest fraction of an hour. Some firms charge a minimum amount of time for certain tasks. For example, a firm may always bill a minimum of 30 minutes for every letter prepared. Generally, so long as such practices are disclosed to the client and they are reasonable, they are acceptable.

Many firms bill based on tenths of an hour, in which case every six minutes represents a billable entry. Consider the following example (again assuming the rate is $100 per hour):

Task	Time Spent	Entry on Bill	Charge to Client
Note to file	4 minutes	.1	$10
Phone call	10 minutes	.2	$20
Letter	45 minutes	.7	$70
Draft will	2 hours, 10 mins.	2.2	$220

Although it may seem unusual to divide an hour into six-minute segments, consider that this method allows easy calculation of fees based on the decimal system. Thus, it is a very common timekeeping approach.

When firms divide the hour into quarters, no task can be billed for less than one-quarter of an hour. Thus, if a phone call takes you ten minutes, you will record .25 for the time spent on the task. Similarly, when firms divide the hour into tenths, no task can be billed for less than one-tenth of an hour. Thus, if a quick telephone call takes four minutes, you should record .1 for the time spent on the task.

The NALA Survey reported that nearly 40 percent of paralegals bill more than $90 per hour.

c. How Time Is Recorded

If it is true, as Abraham Lincoln has been quoted, that "a lawyer's time and advice are his stock in trade," then it is critical to record the time you spend on client and other law firm work so that the client can be billed, and the firm can assess your productivity and efficiency.

In the early days of the legal profession, time was recorded on sheets of paper that legal professionals completed on a daily basis and then gave to the firm's office manager or billing clerk, who would then take the information and prepare a formal bill for the client. The entry reflected the client's name (or a client number assigned by the firm to the client), a description of the work performed, and the amount of time spent on the task. Entries on the time sheets were also made for various firm-related nonbillable activities, such as training, recruiting, interviewing potential employees, updating materials in the law library, and so forth. For ease of recording, most firms developed abbreviations, such as "t/c" for "telephone call" and "re" for "regarding." See Figure 11-1.

As time progressed, many firms migrated to tear-off or perforated slips of paper with carbon copies. Each slip was then sorted into appropriate files and bills were prepared based on these slips.

Almost all firms now use computerized systems for keeping time and preparing bills. These software systems merge both the timekeeping and billing systems so that after time is entered, a bill is automatically prepared and added to in further time increments. These systems allow immediate entry of time expended into a computerized database. Many systems include a stopwatch function to allow you to accurately track your time. Spelling checkers and custom abbreviations make entry of time efficient and accurate. See Figure 11-2 for a sample page from Timeslips®, a well-known software package for tracking time.

Attorneys also track expenses incurred on behalf of clients so these can be billed to the clients. Most law firms use highly sophisticated computerized systems so that making even one copy of a one-page document for a client requires entry of the user's employee number and the client billing number. Similarly, telephone calls, mailing, court or other filing fees, LEXIS or Westlaw research fees, and travel expenses are tracked. At the end of the month, these expenses are shown on the client's bill.

Most firms assign a **client number** to each client and then a **matter number** for each individual matter handled by the firm for the client. If a law firm represents Sanders Corporation, for example, it may assign the client number 79192 to the corporation. If the firm works on the corporation's purchase of another corporation's assets, that specific matter may be assigned the matter number 1023; if the firm works on amending the corporation's bylaws, that specific matter may be assigned the matter number 1024. The client receives separate bills for each of its matters so that it can readily understand the fees and expenses for each of its particular legal matters.

After the initial bills are prepared, they are usually reviewed by supervising attorneys to ensure they are accurate and in accord with any fee agreements. In many instances, a firm reduces the amount of bills or "write off" time. For example, if it takes a new paralegal four hours to draft a noncompetition agreement and it would have taken a more experienced paralegal only two hours to do the same task, the firm may write off the additional two hours because the firm understands that it takes some time for newly hired paralegals to become efficient. The lower starting salaries for new paralegals reflect this economic reality.

Client number
Number assigned to a client by a law firm

Matter number
Number assigned to each individual matter handled by a firm for a client

FIGURE 11-1
HAND-PREPARED TIME RECORD

Timekeeper: Susan Gregory   **Date: September 8, 2005**

Client Name	Client and Matter Number	Description of Work Performed	Time Spent
ABC Inc.	09981.0004	Draft Employment Agreement for Mr. Thomas; telephone call with Mr. Thomas re: same	1.8
Henry Reynolds	54421.0025	Summarize Deposition of Timothy Stevens	2.3
Allison Nelson	19981.0001	Telephone call to Ms. Nelson regarding motion for change of venue	.4
Admin.	00004	Attend training session on conflicts checks	1.5
Tri-Tech Inc.	65688.0001	Review records of USPTO for availability of TRITECH mark	1.4

FIGURE 11-2

TIMESLIPS® SLIP ENTRY

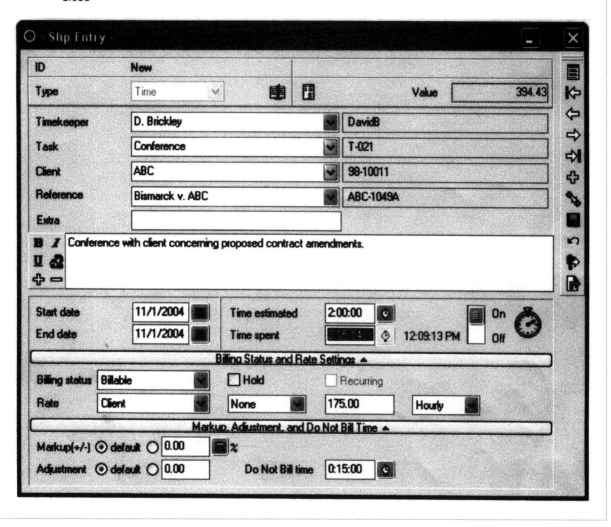

FIGURE 11-2

TIMESLIPS® SLIP ENTRY

d. Best Timekeeping Practices

No matter which method of timekeeping is used, there are several fundamental rules that must be followed by all paralegals and attorneys in timekeeping:

■ **Enter the time spent contemporaneously.** As you perform a task, immediately enter the appropriate client name or number, matter number, and a clear description of the work you performed. You may think that at the end of the day it will be easy for you to remember the work you did that day, but you will be surprised how difficult it can be to capture time that you didn't record contemporaneously with the task, primarily because you will work on several different matters during any given day and will be interrupted by telephone calls, meetings, and so forth.

- **Enter your time accurately.** According to ABA Formal Opinion 93-379, "it goes without saying that a lawyer who has undertaken to bill on an hourly basis is never justified in charging a client for hours not actually expended." Charging a client for work not performed or padding time is unethical. The ABA gives the following other examples of unethical billing practices:
  - ☐ Billing more than once for documents prepared once but sent to several parties;
  - ☐ Billing for "form" or standard law firm documents as if they were originally created rather than merely recycled;
  - ☐ Double billing by charging each client the full amount for time shared by more than one case. For example, if a paralegal must take a three-hour plane trip to visit a client and rather than watching a movie, he or she works on another client's file while on the plane, each client may not be billed for that three hours; generally, the time must be split between matters.

  The ABA position is that clients, not law firms, should benefit from economies of scale and other cost efficiencies that arise on the practice of law

- **Describe the tasks in detail.** Clients do not appreciate receiving a bill for $200 for such vague tasks as "reviewing file," "research," or "telephone call." Thoroughly describe the work you performed, such as "review Ms. Morton's answers to interrogatories propounded by plaintiff," "perform legal research regarding statute of limitations for medical malpractice action," or "telephone call with Mr. Diaz regarding motion for summary judgment."

4. Client Accounts

Although the issue of client funds and accounts is discussed in Chapter Three, a brief review of these important issues is useful when discussing billing practices and similar money-related issues.

Remember that law firms generally maintain two types of bank accounts: one for general law office operating expenses (mailing, supplies, rental of offices, salaries, coffee, and the like) and one for client funds. Retainer fees (fees initially paid to the attorney or firm by a client to retain the attorney's or firm's services), settlement proceeds, escrow proceeds, and similar funds must be placed in a special bank account—the client trust account—and the funds in this account may not be commingled with those in the general operating account. Some firms ensure that commingling cannot occur by maintaining the accounts at separate banks. The funds in the client trust account (and any interest on the funds) belong to the clients, and careful records must be kept to identify which funds are allocated to which client.

Also remember IOLTA accounts, special client accounts that are established for small sums or for short-term purposes, the interest on which is used for the public good—for example, to fund legal services for the poor and victim assistance programs.

E. LAW OFFICE PROCEDURES

1. Introduction

Because the expression "time is money" is a guiding principle at law firms, law firms consistently strive to streamline office procedures and eliminate waste so that as much productive time as possible can be spent on client-related work, thus increasing the firm's revenue. The efficient administration of law offices is a frequent topic of seminars, courses, books, an ABA practice section, and a critical focus of IPMA, the International Paralegal Management Association (see Chapter Two). In fact, the PACE Examination offered by the National Federation of Paralegal Associations specifically tests paralegals on the following procedures: conflicts checks, file maintenance, calendar systems, database systems, timekeeping and billing, coordinating vendor services, law office technology, and other related topics.

2. Policy Manuals

Many firms (and almost all large firms) have office procedure manuals that describe general employment-related issues (such as the firm's policies on vacation time, paid holidays, benefits, and so forth) and procedures for various office practices, such as instructions on how conflicts checks (see Chapter Three) are to be performed, how new files are opened, how documents should be prepared, how time is entered, and similar matters. Some firms distribute a looseleaf binder to new employees delineating these policies; others maintain their policies online. Typically, the larger the firm, the more policies and procedures it will have. For example, a large firm will want all of its correspondence to be uniform and will thus provide detailed instructions on preparing letters, including information on spacing, margins, and so forth. You will be expected to follow all of the law firm's policies, so review any manuals carefully.

3. Conflicts Checks

As you will recall from Chapter Three, before an attorney or firm agrees to represent a client, a conflicts check will be performed to ensure that representing the client will not create a conflict of interest. Paralegals are frequently engaged in conflicts checking.

In small firms, conflicts checks are conducted manually, while larger firms use sophisticated software to perform the check. Generally, attorneys complete a conflict of interest document after meeting with a prospective client. The form includes all information relating to the client. If the client is an individual, basic information such as the client's name, address, and the like is sufficient. If the client is a business entity, however, such as a corporation, far more detailed information is needed, including related companies, names of directors and officers, business relationships with other companies, and so forth. The same process is followed when an existing client asks for representation on a new matter, such as a new lawsuit against a new defendant.

The information gathered on the conflicts form will then be entered into the firm's database to see if a match is found with any existing or former clients. If a preliminary match is found by the paralegal, an attorney will usually review the matter to determine if an actual conflict exists. Most firms circulate a memo to everyone in the firm identifying the new client or matter and generally describing the nature of the case and identifying those attorneys and paralegals who will be working on it.

Because large firms routinely conduct thousands of conflicts checks each year (for example, the international law firm White & Case, which employs nearly 2,000 attorneys has 15 employees working full-time to screen for conflicts of interest), many have employed computer consulting companies to create customized software packages based on their specific requirements. Some systems are highly sophisticated: They provide full case management for firms, integrating conflicts checks, calendaring, client information, file tracking, and timekeeping and billing into one seamless package.

4. File Maintenance

Most firms have procedures relating to the organization of client files so that any attorney or paralegal in the firm can readily locate pleadings, correspondence, and other important documents. Poor file maintenance causes lost productivity while legal professionals aimlessly search through piles of paper. Similarly, time is lost when those in the office cannot locate critical information that should be readily available in the file. The 1998 ABA survey titled "Utilization of Legal Assistants Among Private Practitioners" reported that nearly 75 percent of the responding firms assigned file maintenance duties to paralegals. Avoid the temptation to think of law firm file maintenance as merely placing papers in files. Maintaining orderly files so information is readily available ensures that clients are satisfied and deadlines are met.

While some firms use an alphabetical filing system (so that the Allen files are located before the Baker files, for example), such a system is impractical for all but the smallest firms. Most firms now use numerical systems, at least partly to provide confidentiality concerning the clients' affairs. As discussed earlier, clients are usually assigned a client number and then each specific matter the firm handles for the client has its own assigned number. As each new matter is brought to the firm, the supervising attorney will prepare a **new matter memo** so that a new matter number will be assigned. In some instances, the client and matter numbers describe something about the case. For example, a firm might designate the initial number "4" to indicate litigation while the number "5" might indicate a corporate transaction. Similarly, the first two numbers in the sequence might indicate the year the file was opened, such as 04-5-0125.

Some firms use color-coded tabs on files or colored folders to provide visual cues about the matter or file contents. While smaller cases might be contained within one file folder, larger cases or transactions may require several folders or subfiles. Legal supply companies offer a variety of customized files. For example, there are special tri-fold files for trademark applications.

Most law offices maintain separate manila subfiles for correspondence, pleadings, notes, and so forth. Each subfile is usually kept in chronological order with the most recent item on top. Thus, the most current piece of correspondence is easily accessible. Documents (other than special documents such as wills and deeds, which should never be mutilated) are usually two-hole punched at the top and secured to the file folder by prong fasteners. For pleadings, the file usually includes "tabbed" documents (for easy retrieval of the document), and the top document is usually an

New matter memo
Memo prepared by attorney so a matter number will be assigned to a client's new transaction or case

index to the pleadings file, indicating some basic information about the document, as follows:

Document/Tab	Description	Filed by	Date Filed
1.	Complaint	Plaintiff Ellis	4/14/04
2.	Answer	Defendant Chu	5/10/04
3.	Motion to Compel Answers to Interrogs.	Plaintiff Ellis	8/30/04

Files may be kept in a central file room or kept in cabinets near the supervising attorney's office. When files are removed from cabinets or shelves, some law firms use a "check-out card" system that requires anyone who removes a file to sign for the file and indicate the date it was removed. The card is then placed in the slot where the file would be located. Anyone looking for the file will readily be able to determine its location. Because large law firms have thousands of matters they are handling, a new trend in facilitating the location of files is bar coding. Each file has a label with a bar code. At the end of each day, a firm employee will use an implement to scan all of the files on each attorney's and paralegal's desk (much the way checkers in grocery stores scan items for prices). When someone needs to know the location of the file, the bar coding system easily identifies the file's location.

When a lawsuit or a matter is concluded or settled, the file will be reviewed so that pleadings and documents that may serve as forms in the future can be copied and maintained in form files. The file will then be closed and the **inactive file** will usually be sent to a commercial storage site. Indexes are maintained of the closed and archived files so that if a document is later needed, it will be easy to locate the file. State statutes or codes of ethics usually require that attorneys maintain client files for some minimum period of time, often several years. If the firm offers to return the file to the client, it will usually retain another complete copy for itself. Most larger firms have policies on file retention and storage. Large firms often convert paper files to microfilm, computer zip drives, or use other similar methods, so that the files are more easily and inexpensively stored. Eventually, after several years the file will be destroyed, usually by shredding, so as to preserve confidentiality. There are many companies nationwide that specialize in the destruction of confidential files.

Inactive file
A client file for which work is completed

5. Form Banks

Many paralegals and attorneys keep their own form files of useful documents that may serve as guides or models in the future. For example, it is far more efficient to draft a settlement agreement based on a previous model than to start from scratch. Some law firms have policies on form files and request that all research memoranda be maintained in a central form bank, which will have an index, so that other professionals may take advantage of research previously conducted. The current trend is to maintain such files electronically in the firm's computer system rather than in hard-copy form. It is also common for legal professionals to e-mail their colleagues and simply inquire whether someone else has a form or document that has proven useful in the past. Collect and maintain your own form files so you can efficiently prepare needed documents.

6. Copying, Mailing, and Faxing

Every law office, no matter what its size, produces masses of paperwork. Multiple copies are often made of nearly every document. In large firms, employees are hired solely to staff the copy room. Attorneys and paralegals in these firms do not copy documents themselves; rather, they provide instructions to the employees as to how many copies are needed, desired binding, collating, and so forth. These firms use automated copy systems so that before any copying can be done, the client number, matter number, and employee number must be entered into the system using a keypad. The system then tracks the number of copies and the client's bill is automatically generated at the end of the month. Smaller firms use paper logs placed on the copy machine. Each user manually records the client name or number and the number of copies made so that the billing clerks in the office can charge the clients for these expenses at the end of the month. Outgoing mail is handled in the same way as copying.

Facsimile cover sheet
Top sheet that accompanies communications sent by facsimile with identifying information about the sender, recipient, and confidentiality

Procedures for sending communications by facsimile are identical to those used for copying, except that a **facsimile cover sheet** is used to identify the nature of the document that is being transmitted, how many pages are included, and other similar information. A confidentiality notice is placed on the fax cover sheet so that if the communication is inadvertently sent to an incorrect number, the recipient is instructed to return the document. See Figure 11-3 for a sample fax confidentiality notice.

The ABA's position is that attorneys who receive faxes sent to them in error must refrain from reading them, must notify the sender, and must abide by the sender's instructions as to disposition of the communication. Not all jurisdictions agree; for example, in the District of Columbia the reviewing attorney may use inadvertently produced documents if they have been read before the reader determines that he or she was not the intended recipient. Depending on the particular facts of the case, it is possible that the person who sent the fax in error may have violated ethics rules requiring attorneys and paralegals to use care and diligence in representing clients.

Thus, because confidential communications may lose their privileged status if they are sent to the wrong person, you should use extreme caution when sending faxes. Double-check the fax number, and use automated dialing features if your office has them.

See the additional discussion in Chapter Six regarding e-mail and fax communications.

FIGURE 11-3
SAMPLE CONFIDENTIALITY NOTICE FOR FACSIMILE COVER SHEET

This communication is privileged and confidential and is intended only for the use of the individual or entity identified above. If you are not the intended recipient, do not read, distribute, or make a copy of this communication. If you have received this communication in error, please notify sender immediately at the telephone number provided above.

7. Calendaring and Docket Control

Every paralegal and attorney lives with the pressure of deadlines. Statutes of limitations require that lawsuits be filed within a certain time. Litigation professionals know that answers to interrogatories must be served on the party who propounded them within 30 days. Transactional professionals understand that the closing of a merger must occur on a scheduled date. Failure to observe these deadlines constitutes legal malpractice. Thus, all firms use some form of calendar to track important dates and deadlines. This calendar is often referred to as the **docket.** The ABA survey mentioned earlier reported that approximately 70 percent of the responding firms and attorneys used paralegals to monitor deadlines and calendars.

> **Docket**
> Law firm's calendar of its pending matters and related deadlines (also refers to court's schedule of cases)

As with nearly all systems, the type of calendar or docket the firm maintains will vary based on the size of the firm and the nature of the practice. The most common manual systems are a large whiteboard calendar posted in the office in a central location with critical dates and tasks entered in the appropriate calendar square or an index card system. A separate 3×5 index card is prepared for each deadline date (with information relating to the client name, the client and matter number, the task to be completed, and so forth) and then each card is placed behind tabbed dividers for the appropriate month and date. The cards are reviewed on a routine basis, and reminders are sent to the responsible paralegal and attorney. These index card reminder systems are often called **tickler systems.**

> **Tickler system**
> A method of providing reminders to individuals of tasks that need completion or have pending deadlines

While these manual systems worked well for many years, today's megafirms with their significant caseloads require more sophisticated systems, usually electronic docket systems maintained by a professional docket clerk. After the appropriate data are entered, the system generates daily or weekly written reports and electronic reminders of the task. Some programs are customized to the firm's areas of practice so that once a certain task or date is entered, other related dates are automatically calendared. These calendar or docketing systems can also send reminders of recurring events such as weekly office meetings or paralegal association meetings. Because missed deadlines are a frequent cause of malpractice claims, some malpractice insurers require certain types of docketing systems with manual or other backup systems as well.

A number of electronic methods exist to track cases and monitor dockets. In addition to services offered by LEXIS and Westlaw, PACER (Public Access to Court Electronic Records), a fee-based service of the United States Judiciary, offers electronic access to most federal court case dockets so users can retrieve a listing of all parties in a case, a chronology of case events entered in the case record, judgments or case status, and a variety of other useful information. Many law firms subscribe to PACER, which allows paralegals easily to access information about pending cases.

To review some of the many valuable features provided by today's sophisticated software systems, see the product descriptions of CompuLaw, a calendar and docketing software package used by many of the nation's largest law firms (*www.compulaw.com*).

8. Complex Case Management and Technology

In recent years, the number of large-scale litigation cases has increased significantly. Many are class actions against drug companies, tobacco companies, or companies making dangerous products. The cases involving asbestos claims involve more than

500,000 claimants who have sued more than 6,000 defendants. Cases such as these involve millions of pages of documents that must be organized and accessible to the legal professionals involved in the case. Even smaller cases generate reams of paper.

As documents are received by lawyers, they must be organized. Many law firms continue to use a *Bates*® stamp, a device that places sequential numbers on documents. The documents are then **indexed**, a process by which the numbered document is described in a separate document. Thus, document number 12,264 might be described by its author, its recipient, date, subject matter, key terms, and so forth. Later, if someone wishes to see all documents written by a certain author or all documents relating to asbestos, the index can identify which numbered documents should be reviewed. Paralegals frequently **Bates stamp** and index documents. While Bates stamping was previously done manually by using an actual stamping machine, it is now commonly done by using peel-and-stick labels or various electronic methods of assigning sequential numbers to each page in each document in a case. Alternatively, bar codes may be assigned to each document and then a portable scanner is used to track and locate the documents.

The documents are then scanned into an electronic dababase. Electronic Bates stamping can be applied during the scanning process. An optical character recognition package converts the images into machine-readable text documents, which allows easy computerized searching of key terms, party names, dates, and so forth. The maintenance of paper documents in electronic format on disk or CD-ROM makes document review, storage, and production far easier than in the past, when documents were housed in boxes in room after room at a law firm. Most law firms engaged in complex cases still maintain a **war room** however, for tracking exhibits, trial preparation, and document productions. See Chapter Twelve for additional information on litigation support software packages such as "Summation" that gather all documents (pleadings, transcripts, and notes) into one paperless file to enhance trial preparation.

Sophisticated software packages are capable of managing all aspects of a case, including the following:

- Performing conflicts checks (once a party's name is entered into the system, it need never be entered again, and all later conflicts checks will locate that party's name);
- Allowing conflict voting so that each attorney or department head can review each conflict check;
- Preparing a fee agreement and client acceptance letter as soon as a new client meeting is scheduled;
- Maintaining calendars and automatically generating reminders of meetings and dates;
- Providing a full status history of cases from the date the file was opened to the date it was closed and moved off-site;
- Allowing relevant research from legal authorities to be "cut and pasted" into briefs and other documents;
- Allowing collaborative drafting of documents by several legal professionals;
- Locking a document so that others cannot modify it while it is being drafted;
- Affording access to documents by clients and co-counsel on a secure and confidential basis;
- Tracking of time, timekeeping, and bill generation; and
- Accounting of client trust accounts.

In addition, some systems include all federal and state rules of court to ensure that all dates for every motion, trial, discovery proceeding, and so forth are scheduled accurately. Many systems allow access from the Internet so that legal professionals can review and work on documents from remote locations at any time of the day. Others ensure confidential electronic chat rooms so that legal professionals from all over the country can discuss a case without incurring long-distance telephone charges.

While some of these systems are expensive in the extreme, they do level the legal playing field so that small firms are not "papered over" by larger firms. Attorneys and paralegals can go to meetings, conferences, and trials with laptops rather than boxes of documents. The searching capabilities of these systems allow the paralegal to locate easily a document or prior statement. For example, if an expert witness makes a statement at trial about the plaintiff's soft tissue injuries, the legal team can immediately enter the witness's name or the term "soft tissue injury" into the database and perhaps find a prior inconsistent statement or discrepancy.

These automated case management tools provide a streamlined way to find and review documents quickly, search testimony, collaborate with colleagues, and manage every aspect of a case.

F. OTHER WORK ENVIRONMENTS

1. Introduction

The vast majority of paralegals are employed by private law firms. In fact, the Bureau of Labor and Statistics (BLS) reports that 70 percent of paralegals are employed in private practices. NALA's Survey reports identical results. Most of the remaining 30 percent are employed by corporate legal departments and various government agencies. This section of the chapter discusses employment of paralegals outside the environment of private law firms.

2. Corporate Employment

A number of companies have legal departments, usually called **in-house legal departments.** These may range in size from one attorney to a staff of more than 300 legal professionals in some of the nation's "blue chip" corporations. In some instances, the attorney, called the **in-house counsel** (or **general counsel,** if he or she is the most senior attorney in the corporation), performs most of the company's legal work. In other instances, the in-house counsel performs only some of the work and delegates significant work to either one law firm or to several, who represent the company in a variety of matters.

Paralegals are employed at some of the nation's giants, such as E.I. DuPont de Nemours and Company, FedEx Corporation, and Exxon-Mobil Corporation. They are also employed by high-tech companies such as America Online, Inc. and by smaller companies. In fact, the NALA Survey reported that 14 percent of its responding paralegals were employed by corporations. Moreover, while the conventional wisdom is that pay is usually higher for paralegals employed in law firms, a 2002 salary survey by *Legal Assistant Today* shows otherwise, reporting that the average salary for paralegals in law firms was $42,582, compared with $49,467 for paralegals in the corporate environment.

In-house legal department
Group within a company that performs legal work for the company

In-house counsel
Attorney employed directly by a company to perform its legal work

General counsel
The most senior in-house attorney

While the work performed by paralegals in in-house company law departments may be similar to that performed by paralegals in law firms, there are some notable differences. Perhaps the most significant is that paralegals working for private companies do not generally track their time. There are no minimum billable hours, and legal professionals usually devote as much time as they believe is warranted on a task, with no artificial budget constraints. Most paralegals find that being "free from the clock" is liberating. Perhaps the downside to not billing their time is that paralegals who work in corporate law departments seldom receive overtime compensation. Altman Weil's 2003 survey on paralegal compensation reported that more than two-thirds of paralegals in law firms received overtime compensation, while only approximately 10 percent of paralegals in law departments received compensation for overtime work.

A hidden benefit of working as part of an in-house team is that while there may be many different tasks, there is only one client, the company, affording the opportunity to get to know everything about a company, including its finances, its vision for the future, and its culture. Paralegals who work in-house frequently attend various corporate meetings and are encouraged to offer ideas and suggestions for the overall benefit of the business. The ability to witness company action first-hand and learn about finance, business, and marketing is attractive and can lead to interesting employment opportunities in other fields. Also, many companies offer educational benefits, such as tuition reimbursement. Thus, paralegals who wish to take additional courses may do so at the company's expense.

Various tasks performed by in-house paralegals are discussed in Chapter Nine.

3. Public Sector Employment

The NALA Survey reported that only about 8 percent of all of its respondents were employed in the public sector or for any government branch or agency. Within the federal government the Department of Justice is the largest employer, followed by the Social Security Administration and the Department of Treasury. Other federal agencies employ paralegals as well, including the Patent and Trademark Office, the Equal Employment Opportunity Commission, and the Central Intelligence Agency. A 2002 Altman, Weil survey reported that there are approximately three paralegals for every ten attorneys in government agencies.

According to the Bureau of Labor Statistics, while the duties of paralegals who work in the public sector vary within each agency, in general, they "analyze legal material for internal use, maintain reference files, conduct research for attorneys, and collect and analyze evidence for agency hearings. They may then prepare informative or explanatory material on laws, agency regulations, and agency policy for general use by the agency and the public."

Because the "client" is the government entity, paralegals usually do not track their time. Generally, paralegals who work in the public sector work closely with attorneys. In many instances, their work is a mirror image of the work performed by paralegals in private law firms. For example, in a lawsuit brought by the Securities and Exchange Commission against a corporation for insider trading or some other violation of securities laws, paralegals on both sides perform much of the same type of work, including conducting legal research, indexing documents, coordinating pretrial discovery, reviewing documents produced, and assisting at trial. In one case the paralegal will be employed by the plaintiff agency, the SEC, while in the other the paralegal will be employed by the defendant's private law firm.

Because paralegals may appear before administrative agencies and because most government agencies are always looking for ways to save money, paralegals in the public sector often perform a wide array of interesting and challenging tasks. *Legal Assistant Today's* 2002 salary survey reflects an average annual salary of $37,681 for paralegals in the public sector, which is lower than that for paralegals working both in law firms and in corporate environments. Nevertheless, BLS has reported that paralegals in the public sector usually work a standard 40-hour week, which is often far less than the hours required of paralegals in the private sector. In addition, as discussed in Chapter Two, BLS has estimated that job opportunities for paralegals will expand in the public sector to provide assistance to the poor, aged, minorities, and middle-income families.

4. Other Employment Opportunities

Although the vast number of paralegals are employed by private law firms, in-house legal departments, and various government agencies, other employment opportunities also exist. For example, paralegals are employed by insurance companies, title companies, court systems, public defenders' offices, nonprofit organizations, banks, health care organizations, and consumer groups. Note, however, that the number of paralegals employed by such nontraditional employers is small: The NALA Survey reported that combined employment of paralegals by insurance companies, banks, court systems, and nonprofit organizations totaled only 5 percent.

NET RESULTS

www.nala.org; www.paralegals.org; www.paralegalmanagement.org	The websites of the National Association of Legal Assistants, the National Federation of Paralegal Associations, and the International Paralegal Management Association offer excellent information on issues of interest to paralegals, including law firm billing practices and practice management strategies.
www.abanet.org/lpm	The ABA has established a "Law Practice Management" section with information on law practice management.
www.abanet.org/genpractice/ home.html	The ABA's section on general practice offers excellent information for general practitioners, sole practitioners, and small firms.
www.abanet.org/govpub/ home.html	The ABA's section for government and public sector practitioners offers information for professionals in the public sector.

www.law.com   LawCom offers annual lists of the
                                 nation's largest law firms with informa-
                                 tion about their sizes and revenues.

www.greedyassociates.com   Greedy Associates is a site designed to
                                 let associates share inside information
                                 about their law firm employers, billing
                                 requirements, salary structures, and
                                 other related information.

CASE ILLUSTRATION

Billing Practices

Case: *Hensley v. Eckerhart*, 461 U.S. 424 (1983)

Facts: Attorneys who successfully litigated certain civil rights claims
             requested attorneys' fees under a statute that provided that in fed-
             eral civil rights actions, the court may allow reasonable attorneys'
             fees to the prevailing party.

Holding: A party who seeks an award of fees should submit evidence sup-
             porting the hours worked and the rates claimed. If documenta-
             tion of hours is inadequate, a request for fees may be reduced.
             Attorneys must also exclude from a fee request any hours that
             are excessive, redundant, or unnecessary. In this case, the hours
             spent on any claim that was unsuccessful should have been
             excluded from the fee request.

KEY TERMS

Private practice	Member
Sole practitioner	Professional corporation
General partnership	Shareholder
Personal liability	Director
Joint and several liability	General practice
Partner	Boutique firm
Associate	Transactional work
Equity partner	Support staff
Managing partner	Law clerk
Permanent associate	Law librarian
Of counsel	Partnership track
Lateral hire	Contract attorney
Limited liability partnership	Contingency fee
Limited liability company	Flat fee

Transaction fee
Success fee
Hourly fee
Blended billing rate
Billable hours
Timekeeping
Client number
Matter number
New matter memo
Inactive file

Facsimile cover sheet
Docket
Tickler system
Index
Bates stamp
War room
In-house legal department
In-house counsel
General counsel

CHAPTER SUMMARY

Law Firm Sizes and Organization	Law firms vary widely in their sizes and structures. Lawyers may practice by themselves as sole practitioners or with others. A newer trend for law firms is to organize as limited liability partnerships, a business structure that is governed by traditional partnership law but that limits liability so that attorneys are liable only for their own acts of malpractice and the acts of those they direct or supervise.
Smaller Law Firms	Working in a smaller firm generally provides paralegals with varied and challenging work with the opportunity for significant client contact. Salaries are often lower, however, and the amenities in small firms are not as luxurious as those found in larger law firms.
Larger Law Firms	Larger law firms often offer higher pay and opulent surroundings, but the work may be routine and may afford little opportunity for client contact.
Law Firm Personnel	The personnel in a law firm include support staff, paralegals, paralegal managers, associates, and partners or shareholders.
Fee Arrangements	Law firms enter into a variety of fee arrangements with their clients, including contingency arrangements (in which the firm is paid only if the client is successful), flat fees (in which a set fee is charged for certain tasks), and hourly billing arrangements.

Timekeeping	Nearly all paralegals are required to keep track of the time they spend on client matters so that clients may be billed for the work performed for them. Paralegals must be scrupulously honest in keeping and entering time.
Law Office Procedures	Paralegals are involved in a variety of law office procedures, including conflict checking, file maintenance, copying, calendaring and docket control, and case management.
Large-Scale Cases	Complex cases and large-scale litigation have given rise to elaborate software systems used by law firms for nearly every aspect of a case, from the opening of the file, to tracking documents, to keeping time and generating bills, to the ultimate closing of the file.
Employment Outside of Law Firms	Approximately 30 percent of the nation's paralegals are employed by private companies, government agencies, and employers other than private law firms. The duties of these paralegals vary widely depending on the employer. Generally, paralegals who work "in house" or for government agencies do not track their time because they have only one client: the company or the agency, respectively.

TRIVIA

- The ABA Commission on Billable Hours reported that of 570 firms that responded to its survey, only 22 did not have a minimum hour requirement for their legal professionals.
- The 1998 ABA survey on utilization of paralegals reported that nearly 90 percent of the firms bill clients for paralegal time.
- All states (except Idaho, Maine, and Michigan) now allow the award of fees for paralegal time at market rates.
- According to one legal consulting firm, in 1965 associates typically billed between 1,200-1,600 hours each year; by 1980 the minimum had increased to 1,600-1,800 hours per year; and by 2004 the number required for associates at large firms was from 2,000 to more than 2,400 hours in order to earn bonuses.
- The 1998 ABA survey reported that the general tasks most often assigned to paralegals were maintaining client files, drafting correspondence, conducting factual research, and monitoring dockets and deadlines.
- A 2002 Altman, Weil survey reported that there are three paralegals for every ten attorneys working in corporate legal departments.

DISCUSSION QUESTIONS

1. Ken is a partner in the Boston office of the law firm Smith & Stern LLP. Jack, an attorney in the firm's Denver office, forgot to file an appeal brief and the firm has been sued for malpractice. Describe the liability of the firm, of Ken, and of Jack. Would the situation be different if the firm operated as a general partnership? Discuss.
2. What concerns might clients have about a firm's policy of billing in increments of 15 minutes rather than in increments of 6 minutes?
3. Caitlin, a paralegal in the large law firm Miller & Powell PC, has been informed that she will receive a bonus at the end of this year if she bills 1,800 hours. In December, Caitlin realizes she has billed 1,600 hours for the year. Describe some ethical problems this situation might cause.
4. May a law firm pay a paralegal's salary from the client trust account? Discuss.
5. How often should you review your firm's calendar or docket? Daily? Weekly? Monthly?
6. How does technology put large firms and small firms on an equal footing?

CLOSING ARGUMENTS

Unless otherwise directed, use a general search engine such as Google to locate the answers to the following questions.

1. Locate the website of the law firm Morgan Lewis. What is the address of the firm's Los Angeles, California office?
2. Locate the website of the law firm Hogan & Hartson. Examine the firm's name. Under what organizational structure has the firm elected to operate?
3. Access the Law.Com Dictionary online. What does the term "of counsel" mean?
4. Review NALA's 2004 National Utilization and Compensation Survey Report. What percentage of paralegals was expected to bill between 31 and 35 hours per week?
5. Review the ABA's Model Rules of Professional Conduct. Must a lawyer's fee agreement be in writing? What rule governs your answer?
6. Access the website of the North Carolina State Bar. What is IOLTA?
7. When was the Bates Automatic Numbering Machine patented?

CHAPTER

12

PUTTING IT TOGETHER: STRATEGIES FOR SUCCESS IN THE WORKPLACE

THERE IS NO FUTURE IN ANY JOB. THE FUTURE LIES IN THE MAN WHO HOLDS THE JOB.

—GEORGE CRANE

CHAPTER OVERVIEW

Because learning does not stop once you leave the classroom, this chapter discusses skills and attributes you need to be successful on the job. Successful practicing paralegals share several characteristics: reliability, competency, and flexibility. They have mastered communications skills and have learned how to navigate the often difficult task of working in groups. The chapter provides some approaches to consider when you receive an assignment at work and concludes with strategies for time management.

A. SUCCESS IN THE WORKPLACE

1. Introduction

Not surprisingly, most of the skills and techniques that students use to achieve success in the classroom work equally well in workplace settings. Moreover, because paralegals perform a great deal of the work that was formerly performed by attorneys, paralegals need to possess the professionalism and attributes of their attorney colleagues. This section of the chapter discusses some of the common skills and attributes of successful practicing paralegals.

2. The Team Approach

In most instances, students are responsible solely for their own work product. While group projects may be assigned, generally students work on their own in learning and mastering the subjects in a paralegal program. The legal work environment is quite different: You will generally be working very closely with other paralegals and with attorneys and support staff. Moreover, you will interact on a daily basis with clients, witnesses, vendors, court personnel, and other members of your legal team. Your ability to do your job well will be critically compromised if your interpersonal skills are lacking.

The people you work with may be under a great deal of stress. Some clients may be going through a difficult divorce or may be engaged in a sensitive business transaction. They may be anxious and therefore abrupt. Other clients rightly believe that they are paying a great deal of money for legal services and may be highly demanding. Lawyers are notorious perfectionists. The clerical staff is generally overwhelmed with work and underappreciated. All of these individuals will be making demands on you.

Be sensitive to others' working styles. Other workers may have cluttered desks or odd working hours. Just because their method of approaching tasks is not one that you would use does not mean it is not effective.

You will be a productive team player with strong working relationships if you do three things:

- **Treat others with courtesy.** Treat every individual with whom you interact with respect and courtesy. Be polite when asking for something. Be appreciative when you get it.
- **Pull your weight and more.** It's not enough to do what you have been assigned to do. Do even more and do it in a timely manner. Don't make your team members wait to complete their tasks because you haven't yet completed yours. Work collaboratively, and be sure you do at least your share. Be the person everyone wants on a team.
- **Volunteer.** Volunteer to help when you see a need. You will quickly make yourself invaluable. Take the initiative and work on a task that needs completion. Don't ever say, "It's not my job."

3. Attributes of Successful Paralegals

Successful paralegals share the following characteristics:

a. Reliability

Successful workers can be relied on to get the job done. They do not need to be micromanaged and reminded to do their work. They arrive early to work and to meetings and can be counted on to stay until the work is completed. They understand the need to keep client confidences. They are self-starters who continually demonstrate their commitment to their profession, colleagues, and clients. When a task is assigned to them, they can be depended on to keep working until the work is completed, accurately, and on time.

b. Competency

Paralegals who are respected in the workplace have earned that respect by showing that they are knowledgeable about the core competencies required of all paralegals: research and writing skills, communication skills, analytical skills, interviewing skills, and general understanding of the basic legal principles and fields they studied in their paralegal programs. If they are assigned a new or unfamiliar task, they diligently learn how to do the task and remember the next time around. They pay attention to the details, knowing that an error in a decimal point may be fatal and that the misspelling of a client's name will attract more attention than anything else in a document.

c. Flexibility

Successful paralegals know to expect the unexpected. A crisis in a case will arise, a client will forget to respond to interrogatories, a needed book will be missing from the library. Flexible paralegals understand that there are numerous ways a task can be handled. They aren't afraid to abandon a method that isn't working in favor of a creative solution. They are resourceful in tackling problems and in finding needed information. They know how to move seamlessly to a new task when their work is interrupted by a phone call or when a crisis erupts that requires their attention to a new matter. They understand that their workday will be filled with interruptions and distractions, and they plan some "wiggle room" into their daily schedules to accommodate the unexpected.

B. THREE CRITICAL WORKPLACE SKILLS

While there are numerous skills that effective paralegals possess, there are three that deserve special attention: organization skills, communications skills, and computer skills.

1. Organization Skills

Being organized requires more than merely being neat. It means that you complete all your assigned tasks in the most efficient manner and in the least amount of time possible. Law firms and law offices are busy places. You will work on several different tasks and files during the course of each day. Thus, staying organized is a must. Moreover, if you are organized, you can achieve more during your workday, thus freeing up time for leisure. Finally, if you are organized, you will be able to manage stress more effectively because you won't spend time worrying that you won't be able to find an important document or that you'll miss a deadline.

There are two components to being organized: having the right tools and having the right system.

a. Organization Tools

You will need some basic tools to be well organized. You will need a calendar (either a traditional paper or desktop calendar or a handheld, computerized version, such as a Palm Pilot). Consider investing in a large, wall-mounted dry-erase calendar so you can see upcoming deadlines at a glance. Your desktop computer will likely have a calendar you can use with electronic messages and prompts to remind you of meetings and due dates. Your calendar will help you track assignments and will ensure critical commitments are met. Get different colored file folders to serve as instant visual cues. For example, use a red folder for "hot" projects, a yellow folder for projects on hold or projects for which you are awaiting a response from others, a blue folder for critical phone numbers, and so forth. Make sure that when you need something quickly, the answer is at your fingertips. Use colored sticky flags to serve as visual cues. Use any tools or supplies that help you to work efficiently and productively.

b. Organization Systems

Develop a few methods or systems to keep yourself and your work organized. The best approach is to maintain a "to do" list that identifies tasks that need completion. Mark the tasks high, medium, or low, depending on their priority. Work on the most important tasks that have critical deadlines before you work on a task with a lower level of priority. Your "to do" list will also serve as an excellent reminder of the projects you have worked on so that when it is time for your performance review, you'll be ready to discuss the cases and projects you were involved with during the year. Think about the things you need to know on a daily basis. For example, if you find that you routinely need to look up a client's Federal Express number, keep it on your desktop in a folder marked "Contacts." Use the "Favorites" or "Bookmarks" tool on your word processor for websites that you frequently visit. Keep your list of client and matter numbers handy so that you can enter your time swiftly. Don't procrastinate. Keep your files in order. Eliminate needless searches for documents. Realize that eventually you will have to file papers away. File them as soon as you can, so you do not waste time thinking about the filing you need to do. Moreover, if anyone else in the office needs the file, it will be complete. Even a bin marked "to be filed" is an improvement over stacks of paper on your desk.

Try to handle your mail or other papers just once. Remember an easy acronym to help keep your paperwork and mail organized: OHIO. Only Handle It Once. Otherwise, you'll waste time by picking up the same piece of paper over and over. As soon as any deadline or due date is set, mark it in your calendar or docketing system. If you let a due date slide, even for a day or two, the project may fall through the cracks. Know how your office operates so you can tap all available resources.

Keep your own form files of the documents you have drafted so you can prepare the next similar agreement or other document more efficiently without having to reinvent the wheel. At the end of a project or transaction, prepare checklists of the tasks you completed, the critical phone numbers and contacts you relied on, and a "lessons learned" memo. You can use your checklist or lessons on the next similar project you have so that it proceeds even more efficiently and smoothly. Be the person recognized in your office as the "go to" worker—the person with the best form files, the best samples of documents, and the best practices. There is no one perfect method of organization. Find a style that works for you and stick with it.

2. Communications Skills

a. Introduction

As mentioned in Chapter Six, the foundation of the legal profession is communication—communication with a colleague, client, adverse party, or judge. Some of the communications skills discussed in this section have been mentioned in earlier chapters. For example, written and e-mail communications are discussed in Chapter Six, and active listening skills are discussed in Chapter Seven. There are at least two parties in every communication; thus, there is the possibility for misunderstanding on both sides. It is probably true that in a law office setting, there is no such thing as too much communication. Each of the following four methods of communication requires attention to detail and commitment, but each method also has its own special characteristics.

b. Writing Skills

Written communications must be accurate in every aspect. Not only must information and conclusions be accurate; the details must also be accurate: names, dollar amounts, numbers, and so forth. Use a style manual and a dictionary to ensure that the mechanics (grammar, punctuation, and spelling) are correct and follow your office's desired format for letters, memos, and the like. Remember that a written document will remain in a file and continue to reflect on you and your abilities. Even handwritten notes placed in a file should be accurate, complete, and legible. Every writing conveys not only information; it also reveals information about you. Be sure that even informal methods of communication, such as e-mails, are accurate and professional. If an e-mail is going to a very senior team member, consider printing it out and reviewing a hard copy to make sure all the *i*'s are dotted and the *t*'s are crossed. Remember that providing status reports is an excellent way of communicating not only the nature of the projects you are working on but also serves to keep your name in front of your supervisor and reminds him or her that you are diligently working on a variety of matters. Once you prepare a standard format or template for status reports, you can continually add information or modify the form as you see fit. Most attorneys greatly appreciate receiving status reports because they serve as reminders of tasks they need to complete as well and provide an easy reference if a client calls asking about the status of a case.

c. Speaking Skills

Speaking well requires not only that you use proper grammar and that you accurately convey information but also that you are attentive to the listener. Watch for body language and nonverbal cues that suggest that the listener does not understand your message. Be attentive to the subtle signs that a listener is bored, needs a break, or lacks comprehension. If you have any concerns that a listener has not fully understood your message, follow up with a written memo or e-mail. Tailor your remarks to your audience. If you are explaining a concept to a client, you must use plain English and avoid legalese. On the other hand, if you are speaking with your supervising attorney, expressions such as "The TRO was served yesterday" will be readily understood. Exercise tact and diplomacy. If a conflict arises, avoid negativity. Explain your point of view calmly and suggest alternative approaches. Try to find a solution that works for everyone.

d. Listening Skills

Communication is a two-way street. Be attentive not only to the words of a speaker but also to subtle messages given by a speaker's body language and other nonverbal cues. Take notes. Ask for clarification when needed. Practice the active listening skills discussed in Chapter Seven. Focus on the message being conveyed to you, not on the messenger or his or her particular mannerisms.

e. Reading Skills

Review the information given in Chapter One about methods of reading material that enhance comprehension, such as the SQ3R method of reading. Attention to detail is critical when you review and proofread documents prepared by your office. You may spend a great deal of time proofing documents, checking figures, and locating differences between documents. Learn to sharpen your focus by giving your full attention to tasks. Reduce or eliminate distractions.

3. Computer Skills

Paralegals must be computer savvy to be successful in today's law firms and legal offices. You will be expected to possess some of the following computer skills.

a. Word Processing and Related Skills

At a minimum, you will be expected to be familiar with preparing and revising documents using a word processor. Some law firms prefer the WordPerfect® word-processing program but most use Microsoft Word. In fact, according to a recent survey commissioned by IPMA, approximately 90 percent of the respondents indicated that they used Microsoft Word. You will be more efficient if you know not only the basic features of each program, but also some of the tricks, shortcuts, and other features that help to improve your ability to produce documents quickly and effortlessly. You must understand how to access the firm's wide array of files, forms, and documents so you can easily prepare similar documents. You will undoubtedly be expected to understand the firm's "redlining" software—the package that allows users of documents to show and track changes they make to documents. If you need to improve your word-processing skills, take classes at your local community college. You can also check with computer stores near you because they almost always offer low-cost introductory word-processing classes. In addition, many free tutorials are offered online. Try Googling terms such as "Microsoft Excel tutorial" and the like. Remember that while word processing makes producing a new document easy (because you can often use one of the firm's earlier documents as a model), there is also a high likelihood of error. You may import another client's name or information. Thus, use your proofreading skills (and computer aids, such as the "Find and Replace" feature of your word-processing system) to ensure correctness.

b. Skills in Other Technology Applications

The more software applications you are able use, the more valuable you will be to your employer. Law firms use the PowerPoint® software package to make presentations both to clients and in courtrooms, Microsoft Excel™ to create spreadsheets and graphs, and a host of other applications to streamline law office practice. You will be expected to be able to use your firm's time and billing software so you can track your time. Some of the time and billing software and litigation software support tools have been discussed in Chapter Eleven. Law firms share documents and allow real-time collaboration, use conferencing software for virtual meetings, and perform conflicts checks using software tools. Many legal professionals make extensive use of automated calendaring, docketing, and reminder systems, and use various technology tools to set up meetings and conferences, confirm attendance, and send reminders before the meetings begin. Many discovery requests require production of electronically stored evidence. Complex litigation cases rely on paralegals' familiarity with automated case management tools. For example, many attorneys use sophisticated litigation software packages to manage documents. Four of the most commonly used litigation support software packages are Concordance®, Summation®, CaseMap®, and LiveNotes® (product descriptions and demos are available at *www.dataflight.com, www.summation.com, www.casesoft.com,* and *www.lexsolutio.com,* respectively), which are packages that streamline electronic and paper discovery, generate deposition summaries, and allow annotation or marking of electronically stored documents. Lex Solutio Corp., the provider of LiveNote®, has been awarded contracts to automate documents for the plaintiffs in the Enron civil litigation and expects to organize, store, and disseminate more than 20 million documents. See Figure 12-1 for additional information on Summation®, a powerful litigation support software package.

FIGURE 12-1
LITIGATION SOFTWARE TOOLS

Summation®, a software product designed by litigators to allow global searching, organizing, analyzing, and building of cases, is offered by Summation Legal Technologies, Inc. and was used in the antitrust action against Microsoft. Summation allows the litigation team to perform numerous useful tasks, including the following:

- Constructing chronologies and witness lists;
- Storing all case documents on a laptop computer, eliminating the need for boxes of paper documents;
- Responding to discovery requests;
- Managing and presenting deposition and trial exhibits, including placing all transcripts, documents, records, and images on the computer, together with one's own notes and comments;
- Performing optical character recognition (converting an image to text so that it can be easily searched);
- Offering real-time deposition transcription (which means that as a witness testifies at a deposition, the court reporter's transcription appears on the attorney's or paralegal's laptop computer screen almost instantaneously, thus allowing legal professionals to mark key testimony and making the testimony instantly available);
- Searching of databases and transcripts (allowing the search for a key term—for example, "fraud"—in pleadings, deposition transcripts, and images);
- Collaborating on a real time basis with others on the legal team; and
- Enhancing trial presentation, including the attaching of video files and video synchronization tools.

Source: *www.summation.com*

c. E-Mail Skills

You will be expected to use the firm's e-mail system to communicate with your colleagues and with the firm's clients. Moreover, you will need to know how to attach documents to your e-mail communications. E-mail is an excellent method of communicating information in the office and giving your supervising attorney a quick overview of your pending cases. Review the information in Chapter Six about communicating by e-mail, facsimile communications, and communicating using telephones and voice mail.

d. Internet Skills

The ABA has reported that nearly all legal professionals have access to the Internet at their offices. Paralegals use the Internet to obtain phone numbers, addresses, and directions, conduct investigations (see Chapter Seven), perform legal research (see Chapter Five), and provide information to clients. Legal professionals routinely take continuing legal education classes through the Internet and keep current on legal news through law-related websites and e-journals and newsletters. Additionally, more and more courts and agencies are accepting documents submitted electronically. For example, more than one-half of all trademark applications filed with the U.S. Patent and Trademark Office are now submitted electronically. Trademark paralegals are expected to be familiar with the PTO website, understand how to retrieve the form template for a trademark application, complete it, attach an electronic signature to it, arrange for electronic payment of the trademark filing fee, submit the application to the PTO, and monitor the application electronically throughout the entire trademark registration process. While employers will be willing to provide some training, the more familiarity with technology you have, the more likely you are to get the interview, the job, and the promotion you want. Most law firms have an **intranet**, an internal network within the firm that allows everyone in the firm access to certain shared documents and information but does not provide access to anyone outside the firm. Many law firms also use an **extranet**, a private network in which the firm's information and files are shared with those outside the firm (such as clients and adverse counsel) on a select, confidential basis. Clients may then use a password to access documents relating to their cases.

Intranet
Internal computer network within an office that allows workers to share documents

Extranet
Computer network within an office that allows some limited access by those outside the office

While you may not need to know all of these technology applications, the more you know, the more valuable you will be to an employer. Make a point of learning as much about the firm's technology systems as you can. Ask the firm's technology committee how to obtain training on some of the applications and software packages. Alternatively, as mentioned earlier, take classes at your community college. Hire a tutor. Go online to see if free tutorials are available. Your résumé will be enhanced with the addition of the technology tools you have mastered. Moreover, your ability to communicate with your firm from remote locations may enable you to telecommute if your office permits it.

C. WHAT TO DO WHEN YOU GET A WORK ASSIGNMENT

During the course of your paralegal career, you will routinely be asked to perform certain tasks and assignments. In some cases, the assignment will be clear or highly familiar to you. In other instances, the assignment may require you to perform a new task. If this is the case, follow these seven tips to ensure you satisfy the requirements of the assignment.

- ■ **Take notes.** If the assignment is given to you in person or at a meeting, take notes. Consider using the Cornell Note-Taking System discussed in Chapter One and shown in the chapter summaries in this text, and place your questions or concerns in the left-hand column on the page. Include the date of the assignment and the name of the assigning individual.

- ■ **Find out the due date.** In some cases, your supervisor will tell you when an assignment is due. If not, ask for a due date. Otherwise, the project will languish in your in-basket until it is specifically requested. If your supervisor persists in giving you vague comments, such as "within the next several days," take the initiative: Go public, and announce that you will have the task completed by next Monday, for example.

- ■ **Ask for clarification.** If there is any part of the assignment that is unclear to you, ask for additional clarification. If you get bogged down during the course of the task, either ask for a meeting with your supervisor or send a quick e-mail with your questions. Don't be afraid to ask questions. No one expects you to know everything. Consider the following approaches:
  - ☐ Is there any particular part of this task you'd like me to work on first?"
  - ☐ "Do you have any preliminary thoughts as to the best place to begin [my research] or [drafting the complaint]"?
  - ☐ "Is there any file that I should check first that might serve as a model for the agreement I will be drafting?"

  Similarly, consider sending an e-mail or short memo to your supervisor confirming your understanding of the task, especially for an extensive project. Your supervisor will then have the chance to redirect you if there's some confusion about what you have been asked to do. Attorneys often assume everyone is as familiar with a case as they are. A confirming memo will ensure you don't waste your time and the client's money.

- ■ **Provide status reports.** Give a quick status report when you are about one-fourth of the way finished with the project. This accomplishes two goals: It lets your supervisor know that you are working on the project, and it allows the supervisor to correct you if you have drifted off track. Similarly, if you have reached a stumbling block, say, "I'd like to give you a brief overview of what I've done so far and ask for a few suggestions." Your supervisor would prefer to know as soon as possible that you are encountering some difficulties with the task, not after you have billed 40 hours to the client without making any progress.

- ■ **Anticipate what is needed.** If, during the course of the assignment, you come across other avenues of interest, take the initiative and prepare a list of related tasks. Ask your supervisor if you should follow up on these items as well.

- ■ **Communicate your results.** Prepare a memo or other document with the results of your research or investigation. Handing your supervisor a sheaf of photocopied cases with a sticky note saying, "Here's what you wanted" is neither helpful nor professional. Prepare a formal memo or summary explaining what you have done, providing your results, and attaching any relevant documents. Be sure that the client and matter numbers appear on all documents, and identify

Chron file
A file of all documents prepared by an employee in a law office, kept in chronological order

any particular file name or path so your supervisor is able to retrieve the pertinent documents from the computer.

■ **Keep a "chron" file.** Most legal professionals maintain a separate file containing a copy of every document they prepare. This file is called the **chron file** because it provides a chronological record of their work. The most recent document is placed on top. Keeping a chron file allows ready access to all documents you have worked on in the event a question arises about a client matter. If you have a secretary, ask the secretary to maintain this file for you.

D. TIME-MANAGEMENT STRATEGIES

1. Introduction

We are each given 24 hours a day, yet some of us accomplish far more than others. Why? Some workers are simply more efficient and productive with their time. Managing time in the work world is often more difficult than managing time in the academic world. In school, your class time is scheduled, your syllabus tells you what to expect when, your exams occur on a specific day, and then you graduate. In the work environment, however, projects and assignments are far more fluid. No one can predict the course of a case, whether it will go to trial or whether it will settle, or what obstacles will occur during a transaction. You will probably not meet with a supervisor on the regular basis the way you have met with your instructors, and in some instances you may have little or no supervision. Missing a deadline in class may result in a grade point deduction; missing a deadline in a law firm may result in a malpractice suit. Thus, learning to be productive on the job may require a different approach to managing your time than that used in your school endeavors.

2. Setting Priorities

One of the common complaints of paralegals is that all of the tasks given to them are denoted as critical. Every attorney who gives you a project will likely think that his or her assignment is the most important task you have. There are a few techniques you can adopt to establish priorities among competing projects:

■ **Ask the assigning attorney or individual.** Always ask the individual who gives you the assignment what its priority is or whether there are any deadline dates associated with the project.
■ **Review the files.** Review the various files to determine if any correspondence or pleadings indicate a due date. Any statutory deadline or court due date will take priority over other matters. Review the correspondence files to see if commitments have been made to clients or opposing counsel as to when they will receive the document. A careful review of the files will likely disclose the proper ordering of the tasks you must perform.
■ **Ask your paralegal manager.** If you find that your projects still have conflicting priorities, ask your paralegal manager to help you establish the priorities for the work. Paralegal managers are expert in this area and will work with the attorneys involved to separate tasks and sort out conflicting priorities.
■ **Prepare a status report.** If your office does not have a paralegal manager, prepare a status report of the tasks you have been assigned and circulate it to each

attorney who has given you work. Indicate the case name, the assigning attorney, a brief description of task, and the due date. It is highly likely that attorneys in the firm are unaware that you are being overwhelmed with conflicting tasks. Your status report will serve as a wake-up call, so they will redistribute your workload or reestablish the priorities of the tasks you are to perform. Add a quick cover memo to the report asking for input on setting the priorities of the various conflicting matters.

3. Time-Management Techniques

The following are some of the most common suggestions to use your time more efficiently.

- **Use a "to do" list.** Almost all productivity experts recommend that workers prepare a list of the tasks that must be completed. Once all of the tasks are listed, identify each task as a "high," "medium," or "low" priority. If three categories are not sufficient, use a grading scale of A to F. If too many tasks are marked "high," you need to review the list and demote some tasks to a lower priority.
- **Formalize your to do list.** Once each task has been assigned a priority, prepare a log or calendar with tasks assigned to different days and times. Be realistic. Don't think you can cite-check an appellate brief in one hour. Identify the amount of time you think it will take to complete each task and schedule this time on your calendar. Use whatever method or calendar that works for you, whether it is a conventional desktop calendar or diary, an electronic calendar such as that offered by Microsoft Outlook, or a personal digital assistant. Allow some time for unexpected interruptions or delays. Revise your calendar or schedule as needed. Some workers maintain two separate lists, one for weekly goals and one for long-term goals.
- **Chunk your projects into smaller parts.** If certain projects seem overwhelming, break them down or chunk them into more manageable tasks. View each small task as important and reward yourself for completion. Avoid negative thoughts such as, "I'll never get this done." Challenge yourself to complete one of the small tasks in one hour. Remind yourself of how much you have done, and do not focus on how much there is left to do.
- **Use your to do list.** Your to do list will only work if you use it. Preparing the list is not your goal. Once the list is prepared, keep it handy, revise it as needed, and check off completed tasks. Keep the list handy so that if your supervisor asks how the project is coming along, you will be ready to provide an overview of the tasks that have been completed.
- **Adopt strategies for success.** Consider the following techniques to improve your efficiency as a worker.
  - □ **Find the right time to do your work.** Try to figure out when you are most productive. If you have more energy in the morning, do your most difficult tasks then. You will not only get the hard work out of the way, you will have a sense of accomplishment. Do routine tasks such as filing in the afternoon when your energy levels are lower.
  - □ **Set realistic goals.** You may want to complete ten tasks each day, but this may be unrealistic. Don't set yourself up for failure and stress by scheduling too many tasks for the day. Decide what can reasonably be accomplished

during the day, bearing in mind that unexpected tasks will arise and that you
need some time for work breaks and lunch.

☐ **Don't procrastinate.** The most effective workers are the "do it now and do
it once" types. These workers read an e-mail message and immediately decide
whether to respond to it or to delete it. They don't continually revisit old
e-mails while they decide when might be a good time to respond. They touch
their paper mail once rather than continually reshuffling it. They respond to
their phone messages promptly rather than accumulating a stack of messages
that take up room on their desks. Much procrastination occurs because workers view a task as overwhelming. They know the task will take a full day to
complete, and they cannot then allocate a full day to work on that one project. Again, break the project into smaller units. Work 30 minutes if that's all
the time you have. Don't allow yourself to become paralyzed by the thought
of a big project. Do some part of the project—any part, even if it is merely
photocopying the exhibits or preparing the FedEx envelopes. At least you will
have made some forward movement toward your goal of completion. Recall
that if you announce to your supervisor that you will have the project completed by a given date, this will force you to honor your spoken commitment.
If you find that procrastination is a continuing problem for you, see if you can
figure out what you are trying to avoid.

☐ **Move on if you're blocked.** If you find that you encounter an obstacle or
are completely blocked, move on to another task. Perhaps a quick break will
refresh you so you can return to your task energized. Brainstorm with colleagues for ideas on how to approach your task. Move to another project that
is completely different. You may suddenly get a great idea about how to
approach the first task.

☐ **Reduce interruptions.** Efficient workers know they cannot eliminate all interruptions, but they also know they can structure their environment in such a way
as to reduce them. While you need to be accessible to your colleagues, there is
nothing wrong with closing your door on occasion or asking that your calls be
held while you work on a critical part of your project. You may need to be
aggressive in carving out time for yourself and your work. One attorney who is
much admired by his colleagues for being efficient refuses to take any phone calls
(other than for emergencies) during the first hour or so of his workday. He closes
his office door, plans his day, and begins work on his most important tasks. Clients
and colleagues know that the attorney is simply not available until 10:00 a.m.
each morning. Try to finish one task or segment of a project before moving on
to the next. There will be plenty of interruptions you cannot control so try not
to interrupt yourself. Otherwise, you will need to reorient yourself to start again
by retrieving the first file, figuring out where you left off, and so forth. If you are
interrupted, jot down a few notes (either on your paper or on sticky notes placed
on your computer screen) as to what you planned to do or write next. These will
jog your memory when you return to the first task.

☐ **Make your environment work for you.** Reduce any distractions that
might impair your ability to work efficiently. Move your desk so that you cannot see the flow of traffic in the hallway near your office. Move to a quieter
place if your office is near the break room. Make sure you have the necessary
supplies to do your work. Know what makes you most productive, whether it
is frequent breaks, small rewards, background music, or adequate lighting.

☐ **Multitask.** There are many occasions when you can save some time by doing two tasks. While you are on hold on the telephone, review your e-mail. Bring a file with you to every meeting, so if the meeting starts late or a break is taken, you will be able to do some work. Keep professional journals with you so that if you are waiting for an appointment, you can catch up on your reading.

☐ **Manage stress.** Stress is part of every work environment. Stress in law firms is thought to be higher than in many other workplaces because the standards in the legal profession are so high, deadlines are so critical, and there are at least two sets of people making demands (attorneys and clients). Some workers are stress addicts and create tension even if none exists. Law firms may even encourage stress due to the emphasis on billable hours and productivity. To keep stress manageable, eat right, get sufficient sleep and exercise, and remember to take breaks and reward yourself. Don't obsess over mistakes. Learn from your mistakes, resolve not to repeat them, and move on. Studies show that 75 percent of all worries never occur, but the stress over these speculative events wastes a significant amount of time. Don't forget to enlist the support of your colleagues. Ask for help. Work with a mentor who can coach you through difficult moments. Realize that you will probably never remove tension entirely from your job, but you can manage stress so that you can be an efficient and productive team member.

E. SOME CLOSING THOUGHTS

The previous section of the chapter has focused on skills and techniques to ensure success in the workplace. There are four final items to learn if you want to be admired and respected by your colleagues.

- **All work has value.** Understand that there are boring and mindless tasks in any job. There may well be times when you feel you are being underutilized. Remember that all of the client's work has value. If documents need to be copied or envelopes need to be prepared, do it. The most senior partner in any law firm is willing to do the most mundane task to make sure the client is satisfied. You should be too.

- **Acknowledge mistakes.** You will undoubtedly make a mistake at some time. Own up to it as soon as possible, take responsibility for your part, and do not deflect blame onto someone else. Avoid making excuses. Simply acknowledge that you made a mistake, commit that it will not happen again, learn from it, and don't agonize over it. Similarly, learn to accept constructive criticism. Try to be objective and commit to making improvements suggested to you.

- **Commit to excellence.** Decide that your professional standard is excellence. Make sure every project you submit is one in which you have pride. Pay attention to detail. Take charge of your career. Take classes. Subscribe to online newsletters to keep current in your field. Write articles. Be a mentor.

- **Give back.** Give back to your community by volunteering or engaging in pro bono work. Participate in your employer's pro bono program if it has one; if it doesn't, start one. Call your local paralegal association or bar association to find out what opportunities exist for volunteering in your locality. You will achieve great personal satisfaction, expand your horizons, and help others in need. Check the ABA's website for its Standing Committee for Pro Bono & Public Service at *www.abanet.org/legalservices/probono/home.html* to find out what opportunities are available for you to help those in need of legal services.

The paralegal field is filled with both challenges and opportunities. Be excited by your profession and your role in it. Remember that you play a vital and indispensable part in helping clients. You will be rewarded not only monetarily, but also, and just as important, by having a career that brings you emotional satisfaction. Welcome!

NET RESULTS

www.paralegals.org	NFPA's site offers excellent career tips. Select "Career Center" from the top of the screen.
www.aafpe.org/core.html	The American Association for Paralegal Education identifies the core competencies required of successful paralegals.
www.abanet.org/ careercounsel/home.html	The ABA offers tips on finding jobs and maximizing a legal career. Articles related to career planning and success in the workplace are also provided.
www.mindtools.com	This site offers information on important life and career skills, including time management, stress reduction, and communications skills.
http://print.jobfind.com/	This site provides articles and information on career planning and job success strategies.
www.couns.uiuc.edu/ Brochures/time.htm	The University of Illinois offers excellent advice about time and stress management.

CASE ILLUSTRATION

Standards for Legal Professionalism

Case:	*5-H Corp. v. Padovino*, 708 So. 2d 244 (Fla. 1997)
Facts:	An attorney sought a writ to prohibit all judges of the Florida First District Court of Appeals from presiding over a case in which he represented certain parties. In an earlier case, the attorney made derogatory comments about his opposing counsel's arguments and used several expletives in a motion submitted to the court. The district court judge forwarded the motion to the Florida Bar to review the attorney for his lack of professionalism.

Holding: The petition to disqualify the judges was denied. The lower court
            had the right and the duty to maintain the integrity of the bar.
            Judges should participate in establishing and enforcing high
            standards of conduct and should require that attorneys be patient,
            dignified, and courteous. Courts should actively encourage
            reporting of improper conduct to maintain and promote attorney
            professionalism, high standards of conduct and decorum in the
            courtroom and in pleadings, and the general integrity of the legal
            profession.

KEY TERMS

Intranet   Chron file
Extranet

CHAPTER SUMMARY

Paralegal Attributes for the Workplace	Successful paralegals are those who are reliable, competent, and flexible. They work well in teams by respecting other team members, pulling their own weight, and volunteering to help when needed. They possess excellent organization skills, communications skills, and computer skills, so they can be efficient and productive workers.
Work Assignments	When receiving a work assignment, take notes, determine the due date, ask for clarification when needed, provide status reports to the assigning supervisor, anticipate what is needed, and communicate your results in a professional manner.
Time Management	To manage time effectively, set priorities, prepare a "to do" list, formalize the list, break projects into manageable chunks, set realistic goals, avoid procrastination, reduce interruptions, establish a good working environment, multitask when possible, and manage stress.
Closing Thoughts	Successful paralegals realize that all the work they perform has value, acknowledge their mistakes quickly, commit to maintaining the highest standards of excellence for themselves and their work product, and give back to their community.

TRIVIA

- IPMA's recent Legal Assistant Utilization Survey reported the following percentages of paralegals frequently used these technology applications:

Microsoft Word	95%
Corel WordPerfect	10%
Spreadsheets	55%
Litigation Support Software	
(such as Concordance)	55%
Presentation Software	39%
LEXIS	53%
Westlaw	54%

- The average person loses one hour each day due to disorganization.
- In a survey of recruiters from companies with more than 50,000 employees, communications skills were cited as the most significant factor in selecting managers.
- A recent ABA survey disclosed that 79 percent of all law firms are networked, 43 percent have an intranet, and 27 percent have an extranet to which clients and others outside the firm have access.

DISCUSSION QUESTIONS

1. As your first job, you have been assigned to draft a complaint to foreclose a mechanic's lien. You have no familiarity with this topic. What should you do?
2. All six of the attorneys in your firm have given you projects that they have stated are "absolutely critical." How do you handle these conflicting priorities?
3. You seem to be procrastinating in preparing a letter to a client. What might you do to stop delaying and begin working on the letter?

CLOSING ARGUMENTS

1. Access the Executive Summary for NFPA's 2001 Paralegal Compensation and Benefits Report.
   a. In what areas did paralegals report the greatest satisfaction with their jobs?
   b. In what areas did paralegals report the least satisfaction with their jobs?
2. Access IPMA's website.
   a. Access "Job Bank." What qualities do prospective employers say they deem most important in a legal assistant or paralegal candidate?
   b. Access "Resources" and review the article relating to the value of a legal assistant manager. What are the responsibilities of a legal assistant manager?
   c. Access the 2002 Utilization Survey.
      (1) Review the section relating to technology. What percentage of respondents frequently used the following technologies: document

management programs, databases, online document programs, and billing applications?

(2) Review the section on attorney utilization. What percentage of respondents stated that paralegals were proactive with their attorneys? What percentage of respondents reported that the paralegal program in their organization was a strong one?

A P P E N D I X

A

PARALEGAL ASSOCIATIONS

There are many paralegal associations throughout the country. Some are national in scope (such as NALA and NFPA); others are regional (for example, the Rocky Mountain Paralegal Association covers Colorado, Nebraska, South Dakota, Utah, and Wyoming); some are statewide (such as the Delaware Paralegal Association); and still others are local (for example, the San Diego Paralegal Association). Many of the smaller associations have no physical address: They maintain only post office boxes or websites to communicate with their members. The contact person identified is often an active member of the association, whose telephone number or address may frequently change. The following is a list of many paralegal associations together with an identification of their affiliation with NALA or NFPA (remember that not all paralegal associations elect to affiliate with NALA or NFPA). If the address or telephone number for an association is invalid, try linking directly to its website through the web addresses given below.

WEB LINKS

A number of websites provide direct links to national, state, and local paralegal associations, including the following:

www.nala.org/links.htm#afflinks
NALA provides direct links to its affiliated associations.

www.paralegals.org/displaycommon.
cfm?an=1&subarticlenbr=488
NFPA provides direct links to its member associations.

www.legalassistanttoday.com/assoc_links.htm
Legal Assistant Today offers links to national, state, and local paralegal associations.

www.paralegalgateway.com/associations.html
ParalegalGateway.com, a general website for paralegals, provides direct links to paralegal associations.

NATIONAL ORGANIZATIONS

American Alliance of Paralegals, Inc.
16815 East Shea Boulevard
Suite 110
PBM #101
Fountain Hills, AZ 85268
www.aapipara.org

American Association for Paralegal Education
19 Mantua Road
Mt. Royal, NJ 08061
(856) 423-2829
www.aafpe.org

American Association of Legal Nurse Consultants
401 N. Michigan Avenue
Chicago, IL 60611
(877) 402-2562
www.aalnc.org

American Corporate Legal Assistants Association, Houston Chapter
P.O. Box 941535
Houston, TX 77094
www.aclaa.net

Association of Legal Administrators
75 Tri-State International, Suite 222
Lincolnshire, IL 60069-4435
(847) 267-1252
www.alanet.org/home.html

International Paralegal Management Association
P.O. Box 659
Avondale Estates, GA 30002-0659
(404) 292-IPMA
www.paralegalmanagement.org

NALS
314 E. Third Street
Suite 210
Tulsa, OK 74120
(918) 582-5188
www.nals.org

National Association of Legal Assistants
1516 S. Boston
Suite 200
Tulsa, OK 74119
(918) 587-6828
www.nala.org

National Federation of Paralegal Associations
2517 Eastlake Avenue East, Suite 200
Seattle, WA 98102
www.paralegals.org

National Paralegal Association
Box 406
Solebury, PA 18963
(215) 297-8333
www.nationalparalegal.org

STATE AND LOCAL ASSOCIATIONS

Alabama

Alabama Association of Paralegals, Inc. (formerly known as Alabama Association of Legal Assistants) (NALA)
P.O. Box 55921

Birmingham, AL 35255-5921
www.aala.net

Gulf Coast Paralegal Association (NFPA)
P.O. Box 66706
Mobile, AL 36660
http://groups.msn.com/gcpa/_homepage.msnw?pgmarket=en-us

Alaska

Alaska Association of Paralegals (NFPA)
P.O. Box 101956
Anchorage, AK 99510-1956
(907) 646-8018
www.alaskaparalegals.org/main.htm

Arizona

Arizona Paralegal Association (NALA)
P.O. Box 392
Phoenix, AZ 85001
www.azparalegal.org

Legal Assistants of Metropolitan Phoenix (NALA)
P.O. Box 13005
Phoenix, AZ 85002
www.geocities.com/azlamp

Tucson Association of Legal Assistants (NALA)
P.O. Box 257
Tucson, AZ 85702
www.azstarnet.com/nonprofit/tala/index.html

Maricopa County Bar Association, Paralegal Division
(662) 262-0888
www.maricopaparalegals.org

Arkansas

Arkansas Association of Legal Assistants (NALA)
400 W. Capitol Avenue
Suite 2700
Little Rock, AR 72201
(501) 372-6175

California

California Alliance of Paralegal Associations
P.O. Box 1089
San Leandro, CA 94577-0126
www.caparalegal.org

California Association of Legal Document Assistants
www.calda.org

Inland Counties Association of Paralegals (NALA)
P.O. Box 143
Riverside, CA 92502-0143
www.icaparalegal.org

Los Angeles Paralegal Association (NALA)
P.O. Box 71708
Los Angeles, CA 90071
(310) 921-3097
www.lapa.org

Orange County Paralegal Association (NALA)
P.O. Box 8512
Newport Beach, CA 92658
(714) 744-7747
www.ocparalegal.org

Paralegal Association of Santa Clara County (NALA)
P.O. Box 26736
San Jose, CA 95159-6736
(408) 235-0301
www.sccparalegal.org

Sacramento Valley Paralegal Association (NFPA)
P.O. Box 453
Sacramento, CA 95812-8317
(916) 286-8317
www.svpa.org

San Diego Paralegal Association (NFPA)
P.O. Box 87449
San Diego, CA 92138-3488
www.sdparalegals.org

San Francisco Paralegal Association (NFPA)
P.O. Box 2110
San Francisco, CA 91426-2110
(415) 777-2390
www.sfpa.org

San Joaquin Association of Legal Assistants (NALA)
P.O. Box 28515
Fresno, CA 93729-8515
www.fresnoparalegal.org

Santa Barbara Paralegal Association (NALA)
1224 Coast Village Circle
Suite 32
Santa Barbara, CA 93108
www.sbparalegals.org

Sequoia Paralegal Association
P.O. Box 3884
Visalia, CA 93278-3884
(559) 737-4422
www.sequoiaparalegals.org

Ventura County Association of Legal Assistants (NALA)
P.O. Box 24229
Ventura, CA 93002
www.vcparalegal.org

Colorado

Colorado Association of Professional Paralegals and Legal Assistants (NALA)
www.cappla.org

Rocky Mountain Paralegal Association (NFPA)
P.O. Box 481864
Denver, CO 80248-1864
(303) 370-9444
www.rockymtnparalegal.org

Connecticut

Central Connecticut Paralegal Association, Inc. (NFPA)
P.O. Box 230594
Hartford, CT 06123-0594
www.paralegals.org/associations/2270/files/home154.html

Connecticut Association of Paralegals, Inc. (NFPA)
P.O. Box 134
Bridgeport, CT 06601-0134
(203) 382-8471
www.paralegals.org/associations/2270/files/home159.html

New Haven County Association of Paralegals, Inc. (NFPA)
P.O. Box 862
New Haven, CT 06504-0862
www.paralegals.org/associations/2270/files/home167.html

Delaware

Delaware Paralegal Association
P.O. Box 1362
Wilmington, DE 19899-1362
(302) 426-1362
www.deparalegals.org

District of Columbia

National Capital Area Paralegal Association (NFPA)
P.O. Box 27607
Washington, DC 20038-7607
www.ncapa.com

Florida

Central Florida Paralegal Association, Inc. (NALA)
P.O. Box 1107
Orlando, FL 32802
(407) 672-6372
www.cfpainc.com/pages/718816/index.htm

Gainesville Association of Paralegals, Inc.
P.O. Box 2519
Gainesville, FL 32602
(904) 462-2249
www.afn.org/~gala

Northeast Florida Paralegal Association, Inc. (NALA)
221 North Hogan Street
Box 164
Jacksonville, FL 32202
www.nefpa.org

Northwest Florida Paralegal Association (NALA)
P.O. Box 1333
Pensacola, FL 32502
www.nwfpa.com

Paralegal Association of Florida, Inc. (NALA)
P.O. Box 7073
West Palm Beach, FL 33403
(800) 433-4352
www.pafinc.org

South Florida Paralegal Association (NALA)
P.O. Box 31-0745
Miami, FL 33231-0745
(305) 944-0204
www.sfpa.info

Southwest Florida Paralegal Association, Inc. (NALA)
P.O. Box 2094
Sarasota, FL 34230-2094
www.swfloridaparalegals.com

Tampa Bay Paralegal Association, Inc. (NFPA)
P.O. Box 2840
Tampa, FL 33601
www.tbpa.org

Volusia Association of Paralegals (NALA)
P.O. Box 15075
Daytona Beach, FL 32115-5075
www.volusiaparalegals.com

Georgia

Georgia Association of Paralegals, Inc. (NFPA)
1199 Euclid Avenue, N.E.
Atlanta, GA 30307
(404) 522-1457
www.gaparalegal.org

Southeastern Association of Legal Assistants (NALA)
www.seala.org/index2.html

Hawaii

Hawaii Paralegal Association (NFPA)
P.O. Box 674
Honolulu, HI 96809
www.hawaiiparalegal.org

Idaho

Idaho Association of Paralegals
P.O. Box 1254
Boise, ID 83701
www.idahoparalegals.org

Illinois

Central Illinois Paralegal Association (NALA)
P.O. Box 1948
Bloomington, IL 61702
www.hometown.aol.com/cipainfo/myhomepage/club.html

Illinois Paralegal Association (NFPA)
P.O. Box 452
New Lenox, IL 60451-0452

(815) 462-4620
www.ipaonline.org

Indiana

Indiana Paralegal Association, Inc. (NFPA)
P.O. Box 44518
Indianapolis, IN 46204
www.indianaparalegals.org

Michiana Paralegal Association, Inc. (NFPA)
P.O. Box 11458
South Bend, IN 46634
www.paralegals.org/associations/2270/files/home165.html

Northeast Indiana Paralegal Association, Inc. (NFPA)
P.O. Box 13646
Fort Wayne, IN 46865
www.paralegals.org/associations/2270/files/home169.html

Iowa

Iowa Association of Legal Assistants (NALA)
P.O. Box 93153
Des Moines, IA 50393
www.ialanet.org

Kansas

Heartland Association of Legal Assistants (NALA)
P.O. Box 12413
Overland Park, KS 66282-2413
(913) 477-7625
www.accesskansas.org/hala

Kansas Association of Legal Assistants (NALA)
P.O. Box 47031
Wichita, KS 67201
www.accesskansas.org/kala

Kansas Paralegal Association (NFPA)
P.O. Box 1675
Topeka, KS 66601
www.accesskansas.org/ksparalegals

Kentucky

Kentucky Paralegal Association
P.O. Box 2675
Louisville, KY 40201-2675
www.kypa.org

Greater Lexington Paralegal Association, Inc. (NFPA)
P.O. Box 574
Lexington, KY 40589
www.paralegals.org/associations/2270/files/contactus.htm

Louisville Association of Paralegals
www.loupara.org

Louisiana

New Orleans Paralegal Association (NFPA)
P.O. Box 30604
New Orleans, LA 70190
(504) 467-3136
www.paralegals.org/associations/2270/files/home206.html

Louisiana State Paralegal Association, Inc. (NALA)
www.la-paralegals.org

Maryland

Maryland Association of Paralegals, Inc. (NFPA)
550 M. Ritchie Highway PMB #203
Severna Park, MD 21146
(410) 576-2252
www.paralegals.org/associations/2270/files/home202.htm

Massachusetts

Massachusetts Paralegal Association, Inc. (NFPA)
P.O. Box 1381
Marblehead, MA 01945
(800) 637-4311
www.passparalegal.org

Central Massachusetts Paralegal Association (NFPA)
Centralmassachusetts@paralegals.org

Western Massachusetts Paralegal Association, Inc. (NFPA)
P.O. Box 30005
Springfield, MA 01103
www.paralegals.org/associations/2270/files/home200.html

Michigan

Grand Rapids Bar Association—Legal Assistant Section
535 Fountain Street, N.E.
Grand Rapids, MI 49503
(616) 458-9400
www.firms.findlaw.com/grbala

Legal Assistants Association of Michigan (NALA)
P.O. Box 80125
Lansing, MI 48908-0125
www.laamnet.org

State Bar of Michigan Legal Assistants Section
www.michbar.org/legalassist

Minnesota

Minnesota Paralegal Association (NFPA)
1711 W. County Road B, #300N
Roseville, MN 55113
(651) 633-2778
www.mnparalegals.org

Mississippi

Mississippi Association of Legal Assistants, Inc.
(NALA)
P.O. Box 966
Jackson, MS 39205
www.mslawyer.com/mala

Missouri

Kansas City Paralegal Association (NFPA)
1912 Clay Street
N. Kansas City, MO 64116
(816) 421-0302
*www.paralegals.org/associations/2270/files/
home207.html*

Missouri Paralegal Association
P.O. Box 1016
Jefferson City, MO 65102-1016
www.missouriparalegalassoc.org

St. Louis Association of Legal Assistants (NALA)
P.O. Box 69218
St. Louis, MO 63169-0218
www.slala.org

Montana

Montana Association of Legal Assistants (NALA)
P.O. Box 9016
Missoula, MT 59807-9016
www.malanet.org

Nebraska

Nebraska Association of Legal Assistants (NALA)
P.O. Box 24943
Omaha, NE 68124
www.neala.org

Rocky Mountain Paralegal Association (NFPA)
P.O. Box 481864
Denver, CO 80248-1864
(303) 370-9444
www.rockymtnparalegal.org

Nevada

Paralegal Association of Southern Nevada (NFPA)
P.O. Box 1752
Las Vegas, NV 89125
www.nvparalegal.net

New Hampshire

Paralegal Association of New Hampshire (NALA)
P.O. Box 728
Manchester, NH 03105-0728
www.panh.org

New Jersey

Legal Assistants Association of New Jersey (NALA)
P.O. Box 142
Caldwell, NJ 07006
www.laanj.org/pages/1/index.htm

South Jersey Paralegal Association (NFPA)
P.O. Box 355
Haddonfield, NJ 08033
www.paralegals.org/associations/2270/files/home203.html

New Mexico

State Bar of New Mexico Paralegal Division
*www.nmbar.org/Template.cfm?Section =
Paralegals_Legal_Assistants*

New York

Capital District Paralegal Association, Inc. (NFPA)
P.O. Box 12562
Albany, NY 12212-2562
www.cdpa.info

Empire State Alliance of Paralegal Associations
www.timesunion.com/communities/cdpa

Long Island Paralegal Association (NFPA)
LongIsland@paralegals.org

Manhattan Paralegal Association, Inc. (NFPA)
P.O. Box 4006
Grand Central Station
New York, NY 10163
(212) 330-8213
www.paralegals.org/associations/2270/files/home162.html

Paralegal Association of Rochester, Inc. (NFPA)
Attn: Membership Committee
P.O. Box 40567
Rochester, NY 14604
(585) 234-5923
http://par.itgo.com/index.html

Western New York Paralegal Association (NFPA)
P.O. Box 207
Niagara Square Station
Buffalo, NY 14201
(716) 635-8250
www.wnyparalegals.org

North Carolina

Metrolina Paralegal Association (NALA)
P.O. Box 26260
Charlotte, NC 28236
www.charlotteareaparalegals.com

North Carolina Paralegal Association (NALA)
P.O. Box 36264
Charlotte, NC 28236-6264
(800) 479-1905
www.ncparalegal.org

North Dakota

Red River Valley Paralegal Association (NALA)
P.O. Box 1954
Fargo, ND 58107
www.rrvpa.org

Western Dakota Association of Legal Assistants (NALA)
www.wdala.org

Ohio

Cincinnati Paralegal Association (NFPA)
P.O. Box 1515
Cincinnati, OH 45201
(513) 244-4122
www.cincinnatiparalegals.org/index.htm

Cleveland Association of Paralegals, Inc. (NFPA)
P.O. Box 14517
Cleveland, OH 44114-0517
(216) 556-5437
www.capohio.org

Greater Dayton Paralegal Association, Inc. (NFPA)
P.O. Box 515
Mid-City Station
Dayton, OH 45402
www.paralegals.org/associations/2270/files/home188.html

Paralegal Association of Central Ohio (NFPA)
P.O. Box 15182
Columbus, OH 43125-0182
(614) 224-9700
www.pacoparalegals.org

Toledo Association of Legal Assistants (NALA)
P.O. Box 1322
Toledo, OH 43603-1322
www.tala.org

Oklahoma

Oklahoma Paralegal Association (NALA)
714 Maple Drive
Weatherford, OK 73096
www.okparalegal.org

Tulsa Association of Legal Assistants (NALA)
P.O. Box 1484
Tulsa, OK 74101-1484
www.tulsatala.org

Oregon

Oregon Paralegal Association (NFPA)
P.O. Box 8523
Portland, OR 97207
(503) 796-1671
www.oregonparalegals.org

Pennsylvania

Central Pennsylvania Paralegal Association (NFPA)
P.O. Box 11814
Harrisburg, PA 17108
www.paralegals.org/associations/2270/files/home158.html

Lycoming County Paralegal Association (NFPA)
Lycoming@paralegals.org

Montgomery County Paralegal Association (NFPA)
P.O. Box 1765
Blue Bell, PA 19422
www.paralegals.org/associations/2270/files/home215.html

Philadelphia Association of Paralegals (NFPA)
P.O. Box 59179
Philadelphia, PA 19102-9179
(215) 255-8405
www.philaparalegals.com

Pittsburgh Paralegal Association (NFPA)
P.O. Box 2845
Pittsburgh, PA 15230
(412) 344-3904
www.pghparalegals.org

Chester County Paralegal Association
P.O. Box 295
West Chester, PA 19831-0295
www.chescoparalegal.org

Rhode Island

Rhode Island Paralegals Association (NFPA)
P.O. Box 1003
Providence, RI 02901
www.paralegals.org/associations/2270/files/home149.html

South Carolina

Charleston Association of Legal Assistants, Inc. (NALA)
215 East Bay Street
Suite 404
Charleston, SC 29401
(843) 534-2628
www.nala.org/aff-roster-LINKS.htm

Grand Strand Paralegal Association, Inc.
743 Hemlock Avenue
Myrtle Beach, SC 29577

Palmetto Paralegal Association (NFPA)
P.O. Box 11634
Columbia, SC 29211-1634
(803) 252-0460
www.paralegals.org/associations/2270/files/home210.html

South Carolina Upstate Paralegal Association (NALA)
(formerly Greenville Association of Legal Assistants, Inc.)
www.scupa.org./default.asp

Tri County Paralegal Association, Inc. (NALA)
P.O. Box 449
Charleston, SC 29402
(843) 722-6319

South Dakota

Rocky Mountain Paralegal Association (NFPA)
P.O. Box 481864
Denver, CO 80248-1864
(303) 370-9444
www.rockymtnparalegal.org

South Dakota Paralegal Association, Inc. (NALA)
27328 Adrianna's Place
Tea, SD 57064
www.sdparalegals.com

Tennessee

Greater Memphis Paralegal Alliance, Inc. (NALA)
P.O. Box 3846
Memphis, TN 38173
(901) 527-6254
www.memphisparalegals.org

Memphis Paralegal Association (NFPA)
P.O. Box 3646
Memphis, TN 38173-0646
www.paralegals.org/associations/2270/files/home189.html

Middle Tennessee Paralegal Association (NFPA)
P.O. Box 198006
Nashville, TN 37219
www.mtpaonline.com

Tennessee Paralegal Association (NALA)
3295 Highway 45 South
Jackson, TN 30301
(800) 727-0622
http://firms.findlaw.com/TPA

Texas

Alamo Area Professional Legal Assistants, Inc.
P.O. Box 524
San Antonio, TX 78292
(210) 231-5791
www.aapla.org

Capital Area Paralegal Association (NALA)
P.O. Box 773
Austin, TX 78767
www.capatx.org

Dallas Area Paralegal Association (NFPA)
P.O. Box 12533
Dallas, TX 75225
(214) 991-0853
www.dallasparalegals.org

El Paso Paralegal Association (NALA)
P.O. Box 6
El Paso, TX 79940
www.elppa.org

Ft. Worth Paralegal Association
P.O. Box 17021
Ft. Worth, TX 76102
www.fwpa.org/default.asp

Houston Legal Assistants Association
Lyric Centre
440 Louisiana Street
Houston, TX 77002
(713) 236-7724
www.hlaa.net/index.html

Houston Paralegal Association
P.O. Box 6183
Houston, TX 77208-1863
www.houstonparalegalassociation.org

Metroplex Association of Corporate Paralegals
P.O. Box 201592
Arlington, TX 76006
www.macp.net/default.asp

South Texas Organization of Paralegals, Inc. (NALA)
P.O. Box 2486
San Antonio, TX 78299-2486
(210) 554-9135
www.southtexasparalegals.org/index.html

Southeast Texas Association of Legal Assistants (NALA)
P.O. Box 813
Beaumont, TX 77704
www.setala.org

State Bar of Texas—Legal Assistants Division
Texas State Bar
P.O. Box 12487
Austin, TX 78711
(800) 204-2222
www.lad.org

Utah

Legal Assistants Association of Utah (NALA)
P.O. Box 112001
Salt Lake City, UT 84147-2001
www.laau.info

Rocky Mountain Paralegal Association (NFPA)
P.O. Box 481864
Denver, CO 80248-1864
(303) 370-9444
www.rockymtnparalegal.org

Vermont

Vermont Paralegal Organization (NFPA)
P.O. Box 5755
Burlington, VT 05402
www.paralegals.org/associations/2270/files/home204.html

Virginia

Richmond Paralegal Association (NALA)
P.O. Box 384
Richmond, VA 23218-0384
www.ralanet.org

Roanoke Valley Paralegal Association (NALA)
P.O. Box 1505
Roanoke, VA 24007
www.rvpa.org

Washington

Washington State Paralegal Association (NFPA)
P.O. Box 58530
Seattle, WA 98138-1530
(866) 257-9772
www.wspaonline.com

West Virginia

Association of West Virginia Paralegals, Inc. (NALA)
www.lawv.org

Wisconsin

Madison Area Paralegal Association (NALA)
P.O. Box 2242
Madison, WI 53701-2242
www.madisonparalegal.org

Paralegal Association of Wisconsin, Inc.
P.O. Box 510892
Milwaukee, WI 53203-0151

(414) 272-7168
www.wisconsinparalegal.org

Wyoming

Legal Assistants of Wyoming (NALA)
P.O. Box 155
Caspar, WY 82602-0155
www.lawyo.com

Rocky Mountain Paralegal Association (NFPA)
P.O. Box 481864
Denver, CO 80248-1864
(303) 370-9444
www.rockymtnparalegal.org

APPENDIX B

STATE AND NATIONAL BAR ASSOCIATIONS

A number of websites provide direct linking to state, national, and local bar associations, including the following:

www.abanet.org/barserv/stlobar.html
The ABA website provides links to state and local bar associations.

www.palidan.com/statebar.htm
The Palidan Legal Resources website provides links to state and local bar associations.

www.hg.org/northam-bar.htm
Hieros Gamos, a general legal site, provides links to national, state, and local bar associations.

www.FindLaw.com/06associations/state.html
FindLaw, a general legal site, provides links to state and local bar associations.

SELECTED NATIONAL BAR ASSOCIATIONS

American Association of Corporate Counsel
1025 Connecticut Avenue, N.W.
Suite 200
Washington, DC 20036-5425
(202) 293-4103
www.acca.com

American Bar Association
321 N. Clark Street

Chicago, IL 60610
(312) 988-5000
www.abanet.org

Association of Trial Lawyers of America
1050 31st Street, N.W.
Washington, DC 20007
(800) 424-2725
www.atla.org

Federal Bar Association
2215 M Street, N.W.
Washington, DC 20037
(202) 785-1614
www.fedbar.org

National Bar Association
1225 11th Street, N.W.
Washington, DC 10001
(202) 842-3900
www.nationalbar.org

National Association for Public Interest Law
Equal Justice Works
2120 L Street, N.W., Suite 450
Washington, DC 20037-1541
(202) 466-3686
www.napil.org

National Association of Criminal Defense Lawyers
1150 18th Street, N.W.
Washington, DC 20036

(202) 872-8600
www.nacdl.org

National Lawyers Association
17201 E. 40 Highway
Suite 207
Independence, MO 64055
(800) 471-2994
www.nla.org

STATE BAR ASSOCIATIONS

Alabama State Bar Association
415 Dexter Avenue
P.O. Box 671
Montgomery, AL 36101
(334) 269-1515
www.alaba.org

Alaska Bar Association
P.O. Box 100279
Anchorage, AK 99501
(907) 272-7469
www.alaskabar.org

Arizona State Bar Association
4201 N. 24th Street
Suite 200
Phoenix, AZ 85016-6288
(866) 48- AZBAR
www.azbar.org

Arkansas Bar Association
400 West Markham
Little Rock, AR 78201
(800) 609-5668
www.arkbar.com

State Bar of California
180 Howard Street
San Francisco, CA 94105
(415) 538-2000
www.calbar.org

Colorado Bar Association
1900 Grant Street
Suite 900
Denver, CO 80203
(303) 860-1115
www.cobar.org

Connecticut Bar Association
30 Bank Street
P.O. Box 350
New Britain, CT 06050-0350
(860) 223-4400
www.ctbar.org

Delaware State Bar Association
301 N. Market Street
Wilmington, DE 19801
(302) 658-5279
www.dsba.org

District of Columbia Bar Association
1250 H Street, N.W.
Sixth Floor
Washington, DC 20005-5937
(2020 737-4700
www.dcbar.org

The Florida Bar
651 E. Jefferson Street
Tallahassee, FL 32399-2300
(85) 561-5600
www.flabar.org

State Bar of Georgia
104 Marietta Street, N.W.
Suite 100
Atlanta, GA 30303
(404) 527-8700
www.gabar.org

Hawaii State Bar Association
1132 Bishop Street
Suite 906
Honolulu, HI 96813
(808) 537-1868
www.hsba.org

Idaho State Bar and Idaho Law Foundation, Inc.
P.O. Box 895
Boise, ID 83701
(208) 334-4500
www2.state.id.us/isb/index.htm

Illinois State Bar Association
424 S. Second Street
Springfield, IL 62701
(800) 252-8908
www.illinoisbar.org

Indiana State Bar Association
230 East Ohio Street
Fourth Floor
Indianapolis, IN 46204-2199
(317) 639-5465
www.inbar.org

Iowa State Bar Association
521 East Locust
Des Moines, IA 50309-1939
(515) 243-3170
www.iowabar.org

Kansas Bar Association
1200 S.W. Harrison Street
Topeka, KS 66612-1806
(785) 234-5696
www.ksbar.org

Kentucky State Bar
514 W. Main Street
Frankfort, KY 40601-1883
(502) 564-3795
www.kybar.org

Louisiana State Bar
601 St. Charles Avenue
New Orleans, LA 70130-3404
(800) 421-5722
www.lsba.org

Maine State Bar Association
P.O. Box 788
Augusta, ME 04332-0788
(207) 622-7523
www.mainebar.org

Maryland State Bar Association
520 W. Fayette Street
Baltimore, MD 21201
(800) 492-1964
www.msba.org

Massachusetts Bar Association
20 West Street
Boston, MA 02111-1204
(617) 338-0500
www.massbar.org

State Bar of Michigan
306 Townsend Street

Lansing, MI 48933-2083
(800) 968-1442
www.michbar.org

Minnesota State Bar Association
600 Nicollet Mall, # 380
Minneapolis, MN 55402
(612) 333-1183
www.mnbar.org

The Mississippi Bar
P.O. Box 2168
Jackson, MS 39225-2168
(601) 948-4471
www.msbar.org

The Missouri Bar
P.O. Box 119
Jefferson City, MO 65102-0119
(573) 635-4128
www.mobar.org

State Bar of Montana
The Power Block
7 West 6th Avenue
Suite 2B
Helena, MT 59624
(406) 442-7660
www.montanabar.org

Nebraska State Bar Association
635 S. 14th Street
P.O. Box 81809
Lincoln, NE 68501
(800) 927-0117
www.nebar.org

Nevada State Bar
600 E. Charleston Boulevard
Las Vegas, NV 98104
(702) 382-2200
www.nvbar.org

New Hampshire Bar Association
112 Pleasant Street
Concord, NH 03301
(603) 224-6942
www.nhbar.org

New Jersey Bar Association
One Constitution Square

New Brunswick, NJ 08901-1520
(732) 249-5000
www.njsba.org

State Bar of New Mexico
P.O. Box 92860
Albuquerque, NM 87199-2860
(505) 797-6000
www.nmbar.org

New York Bar Association
1 Elk Street
Albany, NY 12207
(518) 463-3200
www.nysba.org

North Carolina Bar Association
P.O. Box 3688
Cary, NC 27519
(919) 677-0561
www.ncbar.org

State Bar Association of North Dakota
515 1/2 East Broadway
Suite 101
Bismarck, ND 58501
(701) 235-1404
www.sband.org

Ohio State Bar Association
1700 Lake Shore Drive
Columbus, OH 43204
(800) 282-6556
www.ohiobar.org

Oklahoma Bar Association
P.O. Box 53036
1901 N. Lincoln Avenue
Oklahoma City, OK 73152-3036
(405) 416-7000
www.okbar.org

Oregon State Bar
5200 S.W. Meadows Road
Lake Oswego, OR 97035-0889
(503) 620-0222
www.osbar.org

Pennsylvania Bar Association
100 South Street
P.O. Box 186

Harrisburg, PA 17105-0186
(717) 238-6715
www.pabar.org

Rhode Island State Bar
115 Cedar Street
Providence, RI 02903
(401) 421-5740
www.ribar.com

State Bar of South Carolina
950 Taylor Street
Columbia, SC 29202
(803) 799-6653
www.scbar.org

State Bar of South Dakota
222 East Capitol Avenue
Pierre, SD 57501
(800) 952-2333
www.sdbar.org

Tennessee Bar Association
221 Fourth Avenue North
Suite 400
Nashville, TN 37219
(615) 383-7421
www.tba.org

Texas State Bar Association
P.O. Box 12487
Austin, TX 78711
(800) 204-2222
www.texasbar.com

Utah State Bar
645 South
200 East
Salt Lake City, UT 84111
(801) 531-9077
www.utahbar.org

Vermont Bar Association
35-37 Court Street
P.O. Box 100
Montpelier, VT 05601-0100
(802) 223-2020
www.vtbar.org

Virginia State Bar
707 E. Main Street

Suite 1500
Richmond, VA 23219-2800
(804) 775-0500
www.vsb.org

Washington State Bar Association
2101 Fourth Avenue
Suite 400
Seattle, WA 98121-2330
(800) 945-9722
www.wsba.org

West Virginia State Bar
2006 Kanawha Boulevard East
Charleston, WV 25311-2204

(304) 558-2456
www.wvbar.org

State Bar of Wisconsin
5302 Eastpark Avenue
Madison, WI 53718-2101
(800) 728-7788
www.wisbar.org

Wyoming State Bar
500 Randall Avenue
P.O. Box 109
Cheyenne, WY 82003-0109
(307) 632-9061
www.wyomingbar.org

APPENDIX

C

ABA MODEL GUIDELINES FOR THE UTILIZATION OF LEGAL ASSISTANT SERVICES

The following Guidelines were adopted by the ABA's policymaking body, the House of Delegates, in 1991. Lawyers are the intended audience of these Guidelines. The Guidelines, therefore, are addressed to lawyer conduct and not directly to the conduct of legal assistants and paralegals. Both the National Association of Legal Assistants (NALA) and the National Federation of Paralegal Associations (NFPA) have adopted guidelines of conduct that are directed to legal assistants and paralegals.

The Guidelines were developed to conform with the ABA's Model Rules of Professional Conduct, decided authority, and contemporary practice. Lawyers are to be directed to Model Rule 5.3 of the Model Rules of Professional Conduct and nothing in these Guidelines is intended to be inconsistent with Rule 5.3. For more information, see the ABA Center for Professional Responsibility.

Note: The terms "legal assistant" and "paralegal" are used interchangeably. Annotations and commentary to the Guidelines (which were not adopted as official policy in 1991 by the House of Delegates) are not included below. They are currently being reviewed by the Standing Committee on Legal Assistants to see if they should be revised in light of current case law. A copy of the Guidelines with annotations and commentary is available through the ABA Legal Assistants Department staff office. (Phone: (312) 988-5616; Fax: (312) 988-5677; E-mail: *legalassts@abanet.org*).

GUIDELINE 1

A lawyer is responsible for all of the professional actions of a legal assistant performing legal assistant services at the lawyer's direction and should take reasonable measures to ensure that the legal assistant's conduct is consistent with the lawyer's obligations under the ABA Model Rules of Professional Conduct.

GUIDELINE 2

Provided the lawyer maintains responsibility for the work product, a lawyer may delegate to a legal assistant any task normally performed by the lawyer except those tasks proscribed to one not licensed as a lawyer by statute, court rule, administrative rule or regulation, controlling authority, the ABA Model Rules of Professional Conduct, or these Guidelines.

GUIDELINE 3

A lawyer may not delegate to a legal assistant:
(a) Responsibility for establishing an attorney-client relationship.
(b) Responsibility for establishing the amount of a fee to be charged for a legal service.
(c) Responsibility for a legal opinion rendered to a client.

GUIDELINE 4

It is the lawyer's responsibility to take reasonable measures to ensure that clients, courts, and other lawyers are aware that a legal assistant, whose services are utilized by the lawyer in performing legal services, is not licensed to practice law.

GUIDELINE 5

A lawyer may identify legal assistants by name and title on the lawyer's letterhead and on business cards identifying the lawyer's firm.

GUIDELINE 6

It is the responsibility of a lawyer to take reasonable measures to ensure that all client confidences are preserved by a legal assistant.

GUIDELINE 7

A lawyer should take reasonable measures to prevent conflicts of interest resulting from a legal assistant's other employment or interests insofar as such other employment or interests would present a conflict of interest if it were that of the lawyer.

GUIDELINE 8

A lawyer may include a charge for the work performed by a legal assistant in setting a charge for legal services.

GUIDELINE 9

A lawyer may not split legal fees with a legal assistant nor pay a legal assistant for the referral of legal business. A lawyer may compensate a legal assistant based on the quantity and quality of the legal assistant's work and the value of that work to a law practice, but the legal assistant's compensation may not be contingent, by advance agreement, upon the profitability of the lawyer's practice.

GUIDELINE 10

A lawyer who employs a legal assistant should facilitate the legal assistant's participation in appropriate continuing education and pro bono publico activities.

CHAPTER

D

NALA CODE OF ETHICS AND PROFESSIONAL RESPONSIBILITY

A legal assistant must adhere strictly to the accepted standards of legal ethics and to the general principles of proper conduct. The performance of the duties of the legal assistant shall be governed by specific canons as defined herein so that justice will be served and goals of the profession attained. (See Model Standards and Guidelines for Utilization of Legal Assistants, Section II.)

The canons of ethics set forth hereafter are adopted by the National Association of Legal Assistants, Inc., as a general guide intended to aid legal assistants and attorneys. The enumeration of these rules does not mean there are not others of equal importance although not specifically mentioned. Court rules, agency rules and statutes must be taken into consideration when interpreting the canons.

Definition: Legal assistants, also known as paralegals, are a distinguishable group of persons who assist attorneys in the delivery of legal services. Through formal education, training and experience, legal assistants have knowledge and expertise regarding the legal system and substantive and procedural law which qualify them to do work of a legal nature under the supervision of an attorney.

Canon 1.

A legal assistant must not perform any of the duties that attorneys only may perform nor take any actions that attorneys may not take.

Canon 2.

A legal assistant may perform any task which is properly delegated and supervised by an attorney, as long as the attorney is ultimately responsible to the client, maintains a direct relationship with the client, and assumes professional responsibility for the work product.

Canon 3.

A legal assistant must not: (a) engage in, encourage, or contribute to any act which could constitute the unauthorized practice of law; and (b) establish attorney-client relationships, set fees, give legal opinions or advice or represent a client before a court or agency unless so authorized by that court or agency; and (c) engage in conduct or take any action which would assist or involve the attorney in a violation of professional ethics or give the appearance of professional impropriety.

Canon 4.

A legal assistant must use discretion and professional judgment commensurate with knowledge and experience but must not render independent legal judgment in place of an attorney. The services of an attorney are essential in the public interest whenever such legal judgment is required.

Canon 5.

A legal assistant must disclose his or her status as a legal assistant at the outset of any professional relationship with a client, attorney, a court or administrative agency or personnel thereof, or a member of the general public. A legal assistant must act prudently in determining the extent to which a client may be assisted without the presence of an attorney.

Canon 6.

A legal assistant must strive to maintain integrity and a high degree of competency through education and training with respect to professional responsibility, local rules and practice, and through continuing education in substantive areas of law to better assist the legal profession in fulfilling its duty to provide legal service.

Canon 7.

A legal assistant must protect the confidences of a client and must not violate any rule or statute now in effect or hereafter enacted controlling the doctrine of privileged communications between a client and an attorney.

Canon 8.

A legal assistant must do all other things incidental, necessary, or expedient for the attainment of the ethics and responsibilities as defined by statute or rule of court.

Canon 9.

A legal assistant's conduct is guided by bar associations' codes of professional responsibility and rules of professional conduct.

NALA MODEL STANDARDS AND GUIDELINES FOR UTILIZATION OF LEGAL ASSISTANTS

NALA's study of the professional responsibility and ethical considerations of legal assistants is ongoing. This research led to the development of the NALA Model Standards and Guidelines for Utilization of Legal Assistants. This guide summarizes case law, guidelines, and ethical opinions of the various states affecting legal assistants. It provides an outline of minimum qualifications and standards necessary for legal assistant professionals to assure the public and the legal profession that they are, indeed, qualified. The following is a listing of the standards and guidelines.

Introduction

Proper utilization of the services of legal assistants affects the efficient delivery of legal services. Legal assistants and the legal profession should be assured that measures exist for identifying legal assistants and their role in assisting attorneys in the delivery of legal services. Therefore, the National Association of Legal Assistants, Inc., hereby adopts these Model Standards and Guidelines as an educational document for the benefit of legal assistants and the legal profession.

Standards

A legal assistant should meet certain minimum qualifications. The following standards may be used to determine an individual's qualifications as a legal assistant:

1. Successful completion of the Certified Legal Assistant certifying (CLA) examination of the National Association of Legal Assistants;

2. Graduation from an ABA-approved program of study for legal assistants;

3. Graduation from a course of study for legal assistants which is institutionally accredited but not ABA-approved, and which requires not less than the equivalent of 60 semester hours of classroom study;

4. Graduation from a course of study for legal assistants, other than those set forth in (2) and (3) above, plus not less than six months of in-house training as a legal assistant.

5. A baccalaureate degree in any field, plus not less than six months' in-house training as a legal assistant;

6. A minimum of three years of law-related experience under the supervision of an attorney, including at least six months of in-house training as a legal assistant; or

7. Two years of in-house training as a legal assistant.

For purposes of these Standards, "in-house training as a legal assistant" means attorney education of the employee concerning legal assistant duties and these Guidelines. In addition to review and analysis of assignments the legal assistant should receive a reasonable amount of instruction directly related to the duties and obligations of the legal assistant.

Guidelines

These guidelines relating to standards of performance and professional responsibility are intended to aid legal assistants and attorneys. The responsibility rests with an attorney who employs legal assistants to educate them with respect to the duties they are assigned and to supervise the manner in which such duties are accomplished.

Guideline 1

Legal assistants should:

1. Disclose their status as legal assistants at the outset of any professional relationship with a client, other attorneys, a court or administrative agency or personnel thereof, or members of the general public;
2. Preserve the confidences and secrets of all clients; and
3. Understand the attorney's Code of Professional Responsibility and these guidelines in order to avoid any action which would involve the attorney in a violation of that Code, or give the appearance of professional impropriety.

Guideline 2

Legal assistants should not:

1. Establish attorney-client relationships; set legal fees, give legal opinions or advice; or represent a client before a court; nor
2. Engage in, encourage, or contribute to any act which could constitute the unauthorized practice of law.

Guideline 3

Legal assistants may perform services for an attorney in the representation of a client, provided:

1. The services performed by the legal assistant do not require the exercise of independent professional legal judgment;
2. The attorney maintains a direct relationship with the client and maintains control of all client matters;
3. The attorney supervises the legal assistant;
4. The attorney remains professionally responsible for all work on behalf of the client, including any actions taken or not taken by the legal assistant in connection therewith; and
5. The services performed supplement, merge with, and become the attorney's work product.

Guideline 4

In the supervision of a legal assistant, consideration should be given to:

1. Designating work assignments that correspond to the legal assistant's abilities, knowledge, training, and experience.
2. Educating and training the legal assistant with respect to professional responsibility, local rules and practices, and firm policies;
3. Monitoring the work and professional conduct of the legal assistant to ensure that the work is substantively correct and timely performed;
4. Providing continuing education for the legal assistant in substantive matters through courses, institutes, workshops, seminars, and in-house training, and
5. Encouraging and supporting membership and active participation in professional organizations.

Guideline 5

Except as otherwise provided by statute, court rule or decision, administrative rule or regulation, or the attorney's Code of Professional Responsibility; and within the preceding parameters and proscriptions, a legal assistant may perform any function delegated by an attorney, including but not limited to the following:

1. Conduct client interviews and maintain general contact with the client after the establishment of the attorney-client relationship, so long as the client is aware of the status and function of the legal assistant, and the client contact is under the supervision of the attorney.
2. Locate and interview witnesses, so long as the witnesses are aware of the status and function of the legal assistant.
3. Conduct investigations and statistical and documentary research for review by the attorney.
4. Conduct legal research for review by the attorney.
5. Draft legal documents for review by the attorney.
6. Draft correspondence and pleadings for review by and signature of the attorney.
7. Summarize depositions, interrogatories, and testimony for review by the attorney.
8. Attend executions of wills, real estate closings, depositions, court or administrative hearings, and trials with the attorney.
9. Author and sign letters provided the legal assistant's status is clearly indicated and the correspondence does not contain independent legal opinions or legal advice.

NFPA MODEL CODE OF ETHICS AND PROFESSIONAL RESPONSIBILITY AND GUIDELINES FOR ENFORCEMENT

PREAMBLE

The National Federation of Paralegal Associations, Inc. ("NFPA") is a professional organization comprised [sic] of paralegal associations and individual paralegals throughout the United States and Canada. Members of NFPA have varying backgrounds, experiences, education and job responsibilities that reflect the diversity of the paralegal profession. NFPA promotes the growth, development and recognition of the paralegal profession as an integral partner in the delivery of legal services.

In May 1993 NFPA adopted its Model Code of Ethics and Professional Responsibility ("Model Code") to delineate the principles for ethics and conduct to which every paralegal should aspire.

Many paralegal associations throughout the United States have endorsed the concept and content of NFPA's Model Code through the adoption of their own ethical codes. In doing so, paralegals have confirmed the profession's commitment to increase the quality and efficiency of legal services, as well as recognized its responsibilities to the public, the legal community, and colleagues.

Paralegals have recognized, and will continue to recognize, that the profession must continue to evolve to enhance their roles in the delivery of legal services. With increased levels of responsibility comes the need to define and enforce mandatory rules of professional conduct. Enforcement of codes of paralegal conduct is a logical and necessary step to enhance and ensure the confidence of the legal community and the public in the integrity and professional responsibility of paralegals.

In April 1997 NFPA adopted the Model Disciplinary Rules ("Model Rules") to make possible the enforcement of the Canons and Ethical Considerations contained in the NFPA Model Code. A concurrent determination was made that the Model Code of Ethics and Professional Responsibility, formerly aspirational in nature, should be recognized as setting forth the enforceable obligations of all paralegals.

The Model Code and Model Rules offer a framework for professional discipline, either voluntarily or through formal regulatory programs.

§1. NFPA MODEL DISCIPLINARY RULES AND ETHICAL CONSIDERATIONS

1.1 A Paralegal Shall Achieve and Maintain a High Level of Competence

Ethical Considerations

EC-1.1(a)   A paralegal shall achieve competency through education, training, and work experience.

EC-1.1(b)   A paralegal shall aspire to participate in a minimum of twelve (12) hours of continuing legal education, to include at least one (1) hour of ethics education, every two (2) years in order to remain current on developments in the law.

EC-1.1(c)   A paralegal shall perform all assignments promptly and efficiently.

1.2 A Paralegal Shall Maintain a High Level of Personal and Professional Integrity

Ethical Considerations

EC-1.2(a)   A paralegal shall not engage in any ex parte communications involving the courts or any other adjudicatory body in an attempt to exert undue influence or to obtain advantage or the benefit of only one party.

EC-1.2(b)   A paralegal shall not communicate, or cause another to communicate, with a party the paralegal knows to be represented by a lawyer in a pending matter without the prior consent of the lawyer representing such other party.

EC-1.2(c)   A paralegal shall ensure that all timekeeping and billing records prepared by the paralegal are thorough, accurate, honest, and complete.

EC-1.2(d)   A paralegal shall not knowingly engage in fraudulent billing practices. Such practices may include, but are not limited to: inflation of hours billed to a client or employer; misrepresentation of the nature of tasks performed; and/or submission of fraudulent expense and disbursement documentation.

EC-1.2(e)   A paralegal shall be scrupulous, thorough and honest in the identification and maintenance of all funds, securities, and other assets of a client and shall provide accurate accounting as appropriate.

EC-1.2(f)   A paralegal shall advise the proper authority of non-confidential knowledge of any dishonest or fraudulent acts by any person pertaining to the handling of the funds, securities or other assets of a client. The authority to whom the report is made shall depend on the nature and circumstances of the possible misconduct, (e.g., ethics committees of law firms, corporations and/or paralegal associations, local or state bar associations, local prosecutors, administrative agencies, etc.). Failure to report such knowledge is in itself misconduct and shall be treated as such under these rules.

1.3 A Paralegal Shall Maintain a High Standard of Professional Conduct

Ethical Considerations

EC-1.3(a)   A paralegal shall refrain from engaging in any conduct that offends the dignity and decorum of proceedings before a court or other adjudicatory body and shall be respectful of all rules and procedures.

EC-1.3(b)   A paralegal shall avoid impropriety and the appearance of impropriety and shall not engage in any conduct that would adversely affect his/her fitness to practice. Such conduct may include, but is not limited to: violence, dishonesty, interference with the administration of justice, and/or abuse of a professional position or public office.

EC-1.3(c)   Should a paralegal's fitness to practice be compromised by physical or mental illness, causing that paralegal to commit an act that is in direct violation of the Model Code/Model Rules and/or the rules and/or laws governing the jurisdiction in which the paralegal practices, that paralegal may be protected from sanction upon review of the nature and circumstances of that illness.

EC-1.3(d)   A paralegal shall advise the proper authority of non-confidential knowledge of any action of another legal professional that clearly demonstrates fraud, deceit, dishonesty, or misrepresentation. The authority to whom the report is made shall depend on the nature and circumstances of the possible misconduct, (e.g., ethics committees of law firms, corporations and/or paralegal associations, local or state bar associations, local prosecutors, administrative agencies, etc.). Failure to report such knowledge is in itself misconduct and shall be treated as such under these rules.

EC-1.3(e)   A paralegal shall not knowingly assist any individual with the commission of an act that is in direct violation of the Model Code/Model Rules and/or the rules and/or laws governing the jurisdiction in which the paralegal practices.

EC-1.3(f)   If a paralegal possesses knowledge of future criminal activity, that knowledge must be reported to the appropriate authority immediately.

1.4 A Paralegal Shall Serve the Public Interest by Contributing to the Improvement of the Legal System and Delivery of Quality Legal Services, Including Pro Bono Publico Services

Ethical Considerations

EC-1.4(a) A paralegal shall be sensitive to the legal needs of the public and shall promote the development and implementation of programs that address those needs.

EC-1.4(b) A paralegal shall support efforts to improve the legal system and access thereto and shall assist in making changes.

EC-1.4(c) A paralegal shall support and participate in the delivery of Pro Bono Publico services directed toward implementing and improving access to justice, the law, the legal system or the paralegal and legal professions.

EC-1.4(d) A paralegal should aspire annually to contribute twenty-four (24) hours of Pro Bono Publico services under the supervision of an attorney or as authorized by administrative, statutory or court authority to:

    1) persons of limited means; or

    2) charitable, religious, civic, community, governmental and educational organizations in matters that are designed primarily to address the legal needs of persons with limited means; or

    3) individuals, groups or organizations seeking to secure or protect civil rights, civil liberties or public rights.

The twenty-four (24) hours of Pro Bono Publico services contributed annually by a paralegal may consist of such services as detailed in this EC-1.4(d), and/or administrative matters designed to develop and implement the attainment of this aspiration as detailed above in EC-1.4(a) B (c), or any combination of the two.

1.5 A Paralegal Shall Preserve All Confidential Information Provided by the Client or Acquired from Other Sources Before, During, and After the Course of the Professional Relationship

Ethical Considerations

EC-1.5(a) A paralegal shall be aware of and abide by all legal authority governing confidential information in the jurisdiction in which the paralegal practices.

EC-1.5(b) A paralegal shall not use confidential information to the disadvantage of the client.

EC-1.5(c) A paralegal shall not use confidential information to the advantage of the paralegal or of a third person.

EC-1.5(d) A paralegal may reveal confidential information only after full disclosure and with the client's written consent; or, when required by law or court order; or, when necessary to prevent the client from committing an act that could result in death or serious bodily harm.

EC-1.5(e) A paralegal shall keep those individuals responsible for the legal representation of a client fully informed of any confidential information the paralegal may have pertaining to that client.

EC-1.5(f) A paralegal shall not engage in any indiscreet communications concerning clients.

1.6 A Paralegal Shall Avoid Conflicts of Interest and Shall Disclose Any Possible Conflict to the Employer or Client, as Well as to the Prospective Employers or Clients

Ethical Considerations

EC-1.6(a) A paralegal shall act within the bounds of the law, solely for the benefit of the client, and shall be free of compromising influences and loyalties. Neither the paralegal's personal or business interest, nor those of other clients or third persons, should compromise the paralegal's professional judgment and loyalty to the client.

EC-1.6(b) A paralegal shall avoid conflicts of interest that may arise from previous assignments, whether for a present or past employer or client.

EC-1.6(c) A paralegal shall avoid conflicts of interest that may arise from family relationships and from personal and business interests.

EC-1.6(d) In order to be able to determine whether an actual or potential conflict of interest exists a paralegal shall create and maintain an effective recordkeeping system that identifies clients, matters, and parties with which the paralegal has worked.

EC-1.6(e)   A paralegal shall reveal sufficient non-confidential information about a client or former client to reasonably ascertain if an actual or potential conflict of interest exists.

EC-1.6(f)   A paralegal shall not participate in or conduct work on any matter where a conflict of interest has been identified.

EC-1.6(g)   In matters where a conflict of interest has been identified and the client consents to continued representation, a paralegal shall comply fully with the implementation and maintenance of an Ethical Wall.

1.7 A Paralegal's Title Shall be Fully Disclosed

Ethical Considerations

EC-1.7(a)   A paralegal's title shall clearly indicate the individual's status and shall be disclosed in all business and professional communications to avoid misunderstandings and misconceptions about the paralegal's role and responsibilities.

EC-1.7(b)   A paralegal's title shall be included if the paralegal's name appears on business cards, letterhead, brochures, directories, and advertisements.

EC-1.7(c)   A paralegal shall not use letterhead, business cards or other promotional materials to create a fraudulent impression of his/her status or ability to practice in the jurisdiction in which the paralegal practices.

EC-1.7(d)   A paralegal shall not practice under color of any record, diploma, or certificate that has been illegally or fraudulently obtained or issued or which is misrepresentative in any way.

EC-1.7(e)   A paralegal shall not participate in the creation, issuance, or dissemination of fraudulent records, diplomas, or certificates.

1.8 A Paralegal Shall Not Engage in the Unauthorized Practice of Law

Ethical Considerations

EC-1.8(a)   A paralegal shall comply with the applicable legal authority governing the unauthorized practice of law in the jurisdiction in which the paralegal practices.

§2. NFPA GUIDELINES FOR THE ENFORCEMENT OF THE MODEL CODE OF ETHICS AND PROFESSIONAL RESPONSIBILITY

2.1 Basis for Discipline

2.1(a)   Disciplinary investigations and proceedings brought under authority of the Rules shall be conducted in accord with obligations imposed on the paralegal professional by the Model Code of Ethics and Professional Responsibility.

2.2 Structure of Disciplinary Committee

2.2(a)   The Disciplinary Committee ("Committee") shall be made up of nine (9) members including the Chair.

2.2(b)   Each member of the Committee, including any temporary replacement members, shall have demonstrated working knowledge of ethics/professional responsibility-related issues and activities.

2.2(c)   The Committee shall represent a cross-section of practice areas and work experience. The following recommendations are made regarding the members of the Committee.

     1) At least one paralegal with one to three years of law-related work experience.

     2) At least one paralegal with five to seven years of law-related work experience.

     3) At least one paralegal with over ten years of law-related work experience.

     4) One paralegal educator with five to seven years of work experience; preferably in the area of ethics/professional responsibility.

     5) One paralegal manager.

     6) One lawyer with five to seven years of law-related work experience.

     7) One lay member.

2.2(d)   The Chair of the Committee shall be appointed within thirty (30) days of its members' induction. The Chair shall have no fewer than ten (10) years of law-related work experience.

2.2(e)   The terms of all members of the Committee shall be staggered. Of those members initially appointed, a simple majority plus one shall be appointed to a term of one year, and the remaining members shall be appointed to a term of two years. Thereafter, all members of the Committee shall be appointed to terms of two years.

2.2(f)   If for any reason the terms of a majority of the Committee will expire at the same time, members may be appointed to terms of one year to maintain continuity of the Committee.

2.2(g)   The Committee shall organize from its members a three-tiered structure to investigate, prosecute and/or adjudicate charges of misconduct. The members shall be rotated among the tiers.

2.3 Operation of Committee

2.3(a)   The Committee shall meet on an as-needed basis to discuss, investigate, and/or adjudicate alleged violations of the Model Code/Model Rules.

2.3(b)   A majority of the members of the Committee present at a meeting shall constitute a quorum.

2.3(c)   A Recording Secretary shall be designated to maintain complete and accurate minutes of all Committee meetings. All such minutes shall be kept confidential until a decision has been made that the matter will be set for hearing as set forth in Section 6.1 below.

2.3(d)   If any member of the Committee has a conflict of interest with the Charging Party, the Responding Party, or the allegations of misconduct, that member shall not take part in any hearing or deliberations concerning those allegations. If the absence of that member creates a lack of a quorum for the Committee, then a temporary replacement for the member shall be appointed.

2.3(e)   Either the Charging Party or the Responding Party may request that, for good cause shown, any member of the Committee not participate in a hearing or deliberation. All such requests shall be honored. If the absence of a Committee member under those circumstances creates a lack of a quorum for the Committee, then a temporary replacement for that member shall be appointed.

2.3(f)   All discussions and correspondence of the Committee shall be kept confidential until

a decision has been made that the matter will be set for hearing as set forth in Section 6.1 below.

2.3(g)   All correspondence from the Committee to the Responding Party regarding any charge of misconduct and any decisions made regarding the charge shall be mailed certified mail, return receipt requested, to the Responding Party's last known address and shall be clearly marked with a "Confidential" designation.

2.4 Procedure for the Reporting of Alleged Violations of the Model Code/Disciplinary Rules

2.4(a)   An individual or entity in possession of non-confidential knowledge or information concerning possible instances of misconduct shall make a confidential written report to the Committee within thirty (30) days of obtaining same. This report shall include all details of the alleged misconduct.

2.4(b)   The Committee so notified shall inform the Responding Party of the allegation(s) of misconduct no later than ten (10) business days after receiving the confidential written report from the Charging Party.

2.4(c)   Notification to the Responding Party shall include the identity of the Charging Party, unless, for good cause shown, the Charging Party requests anonymity.

2.4(d)   The Responding Party shall reply to the allegations within ten (10) business days of notification.

2.5 Procedure for the Investigation of a Charge of Misconduct

2.5(a)   Upon receipt of a Charge of Misconduct ("Charge"), or on its own initiative, the Committee shall initiate an investigation.

2.5(b)   If, upon initial or preliminary review, the Committee makes a determination that the charges are either without basis in fact or, if proven, would not constitute professional misconduct, the Committee shall dismiss the allegations of misconduct. If such determination of dismissal cannot be made, a formal investigation shall be initiated.

2.5(c)   Upon the decision to conduct a formal investigation, the Committee shall:

1) mail to the Charging and Responding Parties within three (3) business days of that decision notice of the commencement of a formal investigation. That notification shall be in writing and shall contain a complete explanation of all Charge(s), as well as the reasons for a formal investigation and shall cite the applicable codes and rules;

2) allow the Responding Party thirty (30) days to prepare and submit a confidential response to the Committee, which response shall address each charge specifically and shall be in writing; and

3) upon receipt of the response to the notification, have thirty (30) days to investigate the Charge(s). If an extension of time is deemed necessary, that extension shall not exceed ninety (90) days.

2.5(d)   Upon conclusion of the investigation, the Committee may:

1) dismiss the Charge upon the finding that it has no basis in fact;

2) dismiss the Charge upon the finding that, if proven, the Charge would not constitute Misconduct;

3) refer the matter for hearing by the Tribunal; or

4) in the case of criminal activity, refer the Charge(s) and all investigation results to the appropriate authority.

2.6 Procedure for a Misconduct Hearing Before a Tribunal

2.6(a)   Upon the decision by the Committee that a matter should be heard, all parties shall be notified and a hearing date shall be set. The hearing shall take place no more than thirty (30) days from the conclusion of the formal investigation.

2.6(b)   The Responding Party shall have the right to counsel. The parties and the Tribunal shall have the right to call any witnesses and introduce any documentation that they believe will lead to the fair and reasonable resolution of the matter.

2.6(c)   Upon completion of the hearing, the Tribunal shall deliberate and present a written decision to the parties in accordance with procedures as set forth by the Tribunal.

2.6(d)   Notice of the decision of the Tribunal shall be appropriately published.

2.7 Sanctions

2.7(a)   Upon a finding of the Tribunal that misconduct has occurred, any of the following sanctions, or others as may be deemed appropriate, may be imposed upon the Responding Party, either singularly or in combination:

1) letter of reprimand to the Responding Party; counseling;

2) attendance at an ethics course approved by the Tribunal; probation;

3) suspension of license/authority to practice; revocation of license/ authority to practice;

4) imposition of a fine; assessment of costs; or

5) in the instance of criminal activity, referral to the appropriate authority.

2.7(b)   Upon the expiration of any period of probation, suspension, or revocation, the Responding Party may make application for reinstatement. With the application for reinstatement, the Responding Party must show proof of having complied with all aspects of the sanctions imposed by the Tribunal.

2.8 Appellate Procedures

2.8(a)   The parties shall have the right to appeal the decision of the Tribunal in accordance with the procedure as set forth by the Tribunal.

DEFINITIONS

"Appellate Body" means a body established to adjudicate an appeal to any decision made by a Tribunal or other decision-making body with respect to formally-heard Charges of Misconduct.

"Charge of Misconduct" means a written submission by any individual or entity to an ethics committee, paralegal association, bar association, law enforcement agency, judicial body, government agency, or other appropriate body or entity, that sets forth non-confidential information regarding any instance of alleged misconduct by an individual paralegal or paralegal entity.

"Charging Party" means any individual or entity who submits a Charge of Misconduct against an individual paralegal or paralegal entity.

"Competency" means the demonstration of: diligence, education, skill, and mental, emotional, and physical fitness reasonably necessary for the performance of paralegal services.

"Confidential Information" means information relating to a client, whatever its source, that is not public knowledge nor available to the public. ("Non-Confidential Information" would generally include the name of the client and the identity of the matter for which the paralegal provided services.)

"Disciplinary Hearing" means the confidential proceeding conducted by a committee or other designated body or entity concerning any instance of alleged misconduct by an individual paralegal or paralegal entity.

"Disciplinary Committee" means any committee that has been established by an entity such as a paralegal association, bar association, judicial body, or government agency to: (a) identify, define and investigate general ethical considerations and concerns with respect to paralegal practice; (b) administer and enforce the Model Code and Model Rules and; (c) discipline any individual paralegal or paralegal entity found to be in violation of same.

"Disclose" means communication of information reasonably sufficient to permit identification of the significance of the matter in question.

"Ethical Wall" means the screening method implemented in order to protect a client from a conflict of interest. An Ethical Wall generally includes, but is not limited to, the following elements: (1) prohibit the paralegal from having any connection with the matter; (2) ban discussions with or the transfer of documents to or from the paralegal; (3) restrict access to files; and (4) educate all members of the firm, corporation, or entity as to the separation of the paralegal (both organizationally and physically) from the pending matter. For more information regarding the Ethical Wall, see the NFPA publication entitled "The Ethical Wall - Its Application to Paralegals."

"Ex parte" means actions or communications conducted at the instance and for the benefit of one party only, and without notice to, or contestation by, any person adversely interested.

"Investigation" means the investigation of any charge(s) of misconduct filed against an individual paralegal or paralegal entity by a Committee.

"Letter of Reprimand" means a written notice of formal censure or severe reproof administered to an individual paralegal or paralegal entity for unethical or improper conduct.

"Misconduct" means the knowing or unknowing commission of an act that is in direct violation of those Canons and Ethical Considerations of any and all applicable codes and/or rules of conduct.

"Paralegal" is synonymous with "Legal Assistant" and is defined as a person qualified through education, training, or work experience to perform substantive legal work that requires knowledge of legal concepts and is customarily, but not exclusively performed by a lawyer. This person may be retained or employed by a lawyer, law office, governmental agency, or other entity or may be authorized by administrative, statutory, or court authority to perform this work.

"Pro Bono Publico" means providing or assisting to provide quality legal services in order to enhance access to justice for persons of limited means; charitable, religious, civic, community, governmental and educational organizations in matters that are designed primarily to address the legal needs of persons with limited means; or individuals, groups or organizations seeking to secure or protect civil rights, civil liberties or public rights.

"Proper Authority" means the local paralegal association, the local or state bar association, Committee(s) of the local paralegal or bar association(s), local prosecutor, administrative agency, or other tribunal empowered to investigate or act upon an instance of alleged misconduct.

"Responding Party" means an individual paralegal or paralegal entity against whom a Charge of Misconduct has been submitted.

"Revocation" means the rescission of the license, certificate or other authority to practice of an individual paralegal or paralegal entity found in violation of those Canons and Ethical Considerations of any and all applicable codes and/or rules of conduct.

"Suspension" means the suspension of the license, certificate or other authority to practice of an individual paralegal or paralegal entity found in violation of those Canons and Ethical Considerations of any and all applicable codes and/or rules of conduct.

"Tribunal" means the body designated to adjudicate allegations of misconduct.

APPENDIX G

CITATION FORM

A. Introduction

A critical part of the writing process in many documents is citing to legal authorities. Every legal assertion made in a document must be supported by legal authority. These supporting authorities appear as citations in your document. Citations must appear in a standard and consistent format so that any reader will be able to retrieve the legal authority you cited and verify that you have accurately represented the status of the law. Thus, legal writers communicate using the same "language" or citation form. Errors in citation form will cause the reader to lose respect for the author of a document and conclude that if an author cannot be depended on to cite correctly, the author likely cannot be depended on to conduct a thorough analysis.

B. Citation Systems

There are two primary guides to citation form in the United States.

- **Bluebook.** The oldest and best-known system of citation is found in *The Bluebook: A Uniform System of Citation* (Columbia Law Review Ass'n et al. eds., 18th ed. 2005) (the *Bluebook*). The *Bluebook* is complex, and the rules are often poorly worded with few examples. Nevertheless, because most judges and practicing professionals were taught to use the *Bluebook* for citation form, it is the most commonly used citation manual.
- **ALWD.** ALWD & Darby Dickerson, *ALWD Citation Manual* (2d ed., Aspen Publishers 2003). In 2000, the Association of Legal Writing Directors and Professor Darby Dickerson produced an alternative to the *Bluebook*. Called

ALWD (pronounced "all wood"), the citation system is intended to provide an easy to learn and user-friendly alternative to the *Bluebook*. In many instances, the *ALWD* format is identical to *Bluebook* format. For example, the format for lower court cases, most statutes, constitutions, journals and periodicals, and encyclopedias is identical. Rules for spacing are identical, and most short forms are identical. There are, however, differences in many abbreviations for periodicals, and the presentation and numerous examples in *ALWD* make it far easier to use than the *Bluebook*.

While there are other guides to citation form, the most notable of which is the *University of Chicago Manual of Legal Citation*, usually referred to as the *Maroonbook* and used primarily in the Chicago metropolitan area, the *Bluebook* is probably the best-known system in use at this time, although *ALWD* continues to attract a great deal of interest because of its sensible rules and approach. Follow your school, firm, or office practice. Note, however, that if local citation rules exist for a court or jurisdiction, they must be followed and will supercede any citation system.

C. Law Reviews

According to *Bluebook* Rule 2.2, the main text of law review pieces contains no citations; instead, citations appear in footnotes. The presentation of citations in law review footnotes differs greatly from the style of citations used by practitioners. Thus, the *Bluebook* is primarily directed to showing how to cite in law review footnotes and presents information for practitioners in a separate section called the "Bluepages." While there are many differences between the two methods, the most noticeable are the following:

- Law review footnotes use "large and small capital letters" (as shown in the word "PATENT") for many citation forms, while practitioners never use large and small capital letters. Practitioners always use ordinary roman typeface (as shown in the word "Patent").
- Full case names are not italicized in law review footnotes unless they are grammatically part of the sentence. They are always underscored or italicized by practitioners.

ALWD does not differentiate between citation form for the footnotes in law review articles and for practitioners'

writings; *ALWD* endorses ordinary roman type and does not use any LARGE AND SMALL CAPITAL letters.

D. Using This Appendix

This Appendix is intended to provide a quick reference only to citation form; thus, the focus is on the most commonly encountered types of citations and their examples rather than explanations of the underlying rules for citation form because both the *Bluebook* and *ALWD* explain the rules. The examples in this section are fictitious.

E. Quick Reference for Citations (*Bluebook* and *ALWD* Forms)

Type of Citation and *Bluebook* and *ALWD* Rule	*Bluebook* Law Review Footnote Form	*Bluebook* Practitioner Form (Note that underscoring may be substituted for italics in any example.)	*ALWD* Form (Note that underscoring may be substituted for italics in any example.)
State Cases (in most instances) (*Bluebook* Rule 10 and Table T.1; *ALWD* Rule 12.4(c))	Allen v. Carr, 429 S.E.2d 118 (N.C. 1984) Harris v. Lee, 409 S.E.2d 90 (N.C. Ct. App. 1982)	*Allen v. Carr*, 429 S.E.2d 16 (N.C. 1984) *Harris v. Lee*, 409 S.E.2d 90 (N.C. Ct. App. 1982)	*Allen v. Carr*, 429 S.E.2d 16 (N.C. 1984) *Harris v. Lee*, 409 S.E.2d 90 (N.C. App. 1982)
U.S. Supreme Court Case (*Bluebook* Rule 10 and Table T.1; *ALWD* Rule 12.4)	Daley v. Fisk, 520 U.S. 103 (1998)	*Daley v. Fisk*, 520 U.S. 103 (1998)	*Daley v. Fisk*, 520 U.S. 103 (1998) (Note: *ALWD* permits parallel citations.)
U.S. Courts of Appeals (*Bluebook* Rule 10 and Table T.1; *ALWD* Rule 12.6)	Lawrence v. Mather, 103 F.3d 114 (8th Cir. 1999)	*Lawrence v. Mather*, 103 F.3d 114 (8th Cir. 1999)	*Lawrence v. Mather*, 103 F.3d 114 (8th Cir. 1999)
U.S. District Courts (*Bluebook* Rule 10 and Table T.1; *ALWD* Rule 12.6)	Blakely v. Yost, 742 F. Supp. 2d 942 (C.D. Cal. 2000)	*Blakely v. Yost*, 742 F. Supp. 2d 942 (C.D. Cal. 2000)	*Blakely v. Yost*, 742 F. Supp. 2d 942 (C.D. Cal. 2000)
U.S. Constitution (*Bluebook* Rule 11; *ALWD* Rule 13)	U.S. CONST. amend. IV	U.S. Const. amend. IV	U.S. Const. amend. IV
State Constitution (*Bluebook* Rule 11; *ALWD* Rule 13)	CAL. CONST. art. XX, § 4	Cal. Const. art. XX, § 4	Cal. Const. art. XX, § 4
Federal Statutes (*Bluebook* Rule 12 and Table T.1; *ALWD* Rule 14)	17 U.S.C. § 101 (2000); 17 U.S.C.A. § 101 (West 1998); 17 U.S.C.S. § 101 (LexisNexis 1998)	17 U.S.C. § 101 (2000); 17 U.S.C.A. § 101 (West 1998); 17 U.S.C.S. § 101 (LexisNexis 1998)	17 U.S.C. § 101 (2000); 17 U.S.C.A. § 101 (West 1998); 17 U.S.C.S. § 101 (LEXIS 1998)

Type of Citation and *Bluebook* and *ALWD* Rule	*Bluebook* Law Review Footnote Form	*Bluebook* Practitioner Form (Note that underscoring may be substituted for italics in any example.)	*ALWD* Form (Note that underscoring may be substituted for italics in any example.)
State Statutes (*Bluebook* Rule 12 and Table T.1; *ALWD* Rule 14)	ARIZ. REV. STAT. ANN. § 104 (1992); CAL. EVID. CODE § 52 (West 1998)	Ariz. Rev. Stat. Ann. § 104 (1992); Cal. Evid. Code § 52 (West 1998)	Ariz. Rev. Stat. Ann. § 104 (West 1992); Cal. Evid. Code Ann. § 52 (West 1998)
Federal Rules (*Bluebook* Rule 12.8.3; *ALWD* Rule 17.1)	FED. R. CIV. P. 12(b)(6)	Fed. R. Civ. P. 12(b)(6)	Fed. R. Civ. P. 12(b)(6)
Federal Regulations (*Bluebook* Rule 14.2; *ALWD* Rule 19.1)	Cheese Import Regulations, 42 C.F.R. § 131 (2003); or 29 C.F.R. § 605.89 (2004)	Cheese Import Regulations, 42 C.F.R. § 131 (2003); or 29 C.F.R. § 605.89 (2004)	42 C.F.R. § 131 (2003); or 29 C.F.R. § 605.89 (2004)
Federal Register (*Bluebook* Rule 14.2; *ALWD* Rule 19.3)	Standard Industrial Codes, 64 Fed. Reg. 278 (Dec. 6, 1997)	Standard Industrial Codes, 64 Fed. Reg. 278 (Dec. 6, 1997)	64 Fed. Reg. 278 (Dec. 6, 1997)
Administrative Decisions (*Bluebook* Rule 14.3; *ALWD* Rule 19.5)	Network Solutions, Inc., 18 F.C.C.2d 909 (2000); Stevens Textile Co., 403 N.L.R.B. 120 (1995)	*Network Solutions, Inc.*, 18 F.C.C.2d 909 (2000); *Stevens Textile Co.*, 403 N.L.R.B. 120 (1985)	*Network Solutions, Inc.*, 18 F.C.C.2d 909 (F. Commun. Commn. 2000); *Stevens Textile Co.*, 403 N.L.R.B. 120 (Natl. Lab. Rel. Bd. 1985)
Looseleaf Services (*Bluebook* Rule 19 and Table T.15; *ALWD* Rule 28.1)	*In re* Walmart Stores, Inc., 5 Bus. Franchise Guide (CCH) ¶ 42,201 (D.N.J. Aug. 12, 1995)	*In re Walmart Stores, Inc.*, 5 Bus. Franchise Guide (CCH) ¶ 42,201 (D.N.J. Aug. 12, 1995)	*In re Walmart Stores, Inc.*, 5 Bus. Fran. Guide (CCH) ¶ 42,201 (D.N.J. Aug. 12, 1995)
Attorneys General Opinions (*Bluebook* Rule 14.4; *ALWD* Rules 19.7, 20.7)	65 Op. Cal. Att'y Gen. 104 (1994); 49 Op. Att'y Gen. 918 (1988)	65 Op. Cal. Att'y Gen. 104 (1994); 49 Op. Att'y Gen. 918 (1988)	65 Cal. Atty. Gen. Op. 104 (1994); 49 Op. Atty. Gen. 918 (1988)
Books (*Bluebook* Rule 15; *ALWD* Rule 22.1)	2 J. Thomas McCarthy, MCCARTHY ON TRADEMARKS AND UNFAIR CMPETITION § 4:13 (4th ed. 1998); 7 Samuel Williston, TREATISE ON THE LAW OF CONTRACTS § 901 (Walter H. Jaeger ed., 3d ed. 1964)	2 J. Thomas McCarthy, *McCarthy on Trademarks and Unfair Competition* § 4:13 (4th ed. 1998); 7 Samuel Williston, *Treatise on the Law of Contracts* § 901 (Walter H. Jaeger ed., 3d ed. 1964)	J. Thomas McCarthy, *McCarthy on Trademarks and Unfair Competition* vol. 2, § 4:13 (4th ed., West 1998); Samuel Williston, *Treatise on the Law of Contracts* vol. 7, § 901 (Walter H. Jaeger ed., 3d ed., West 1964)

Type of Citation and *Bluebook* and *ALWD* Rule	*Bluebook* Law Review Footnote Form	*Bluebook* **Practitioner Form** (Note that underscoring may be substituted for italics in any example.)	*ALWD* **Form** (Note that underscoring may be substituted for italics in any example.)
Periodical Materials and Law Reviews (*Bluebook* Rule 16 and Table T.13; *ALWD* Rule 23.1)	David J. Hayes, Jr., *Due Process,* 41 EMORY L.J. 106 (1997); Janet R. Sanders, *Corporate Takeovers,* 12 J. BUS. L. 18 (2001)	David B. Hayes, Jr., *Due Process,* 41 Emory L.J. 164 (1997); Janet R. Sanders, *Corporate Takeovers,* 12 J. Bus. L. 18 (2001)	David B. Hayes, Jr., *Due Process,* 41 Emory L.J. 164 (1997); Janet R. Sanders, *Corporate Takeovers,* 12 J. Bus. L. 18 (2001)
Dictionaries (*Bluebook* Rule 15.8; *ALWD* Rule 25.1)	BLACK'S LAW DICTIONARY 791 (8th ed. 2004)	*Black's Law Dictionary* 791 (8th ed. 2004)	*Black's Law Dictionary* 791 (Bryan A. Garner ed., 8th ed., West 2004)
Legal Encyclopedias (*Bluebook* Rule 15.8; *ALWD* Rule 26.1)	76 AM. JUR. 2d *Trademarks* § 13 (1986); 95 C.J.S. *Trial* § 32 (1988); 14 CAL. JUR. 2d *Contracts* §§ 14-18 (1994)	76 Am. Jur. 2d *Trademarks* § 13 (1986); 95 C.J.S. *Trial* § 32 (1988); 14 Cal. Jur. 2d *Contracts* §§ 14-18 (1994)	76 Am. Jur. 2d *Trademarks* § 13 (1986); 95 C.J.S. *Trial* § 32 (1988); 14 Cal. Jur. 2d *Contracts* §§ 14-18 (1994)
Restatements (*Bluebook* Rule 12.8.5; *ALWD* Rule 27.1)	RESTATEMENT (SECOND) OF TORTS § 13 (1986)	Restatement (Second) of Torts § 13 (1986)	*Restatement (Second) of Torts* § 13 (1986)
A.L.R. Annotations (*Bluebook* Rule 16.6.6; *ALWD* Rule 24.1)	James W. Gray, Annotation, *Nuisance Theory,* 56 A.L.R.4th 145 (1990)	James W. Gray, Annotation, *Nuisance Theory,* 56 A.L.R.4th 145 (1990)	James W. Gray, *Nuisance Theory,* 56 A.L.R.4th 145 (1990)
Electronic Databases (*Bluebook* Rule 18; *ALWD* Rule 12.12)	Bowes v. Capital Group, No. 03-1765, 2004 U.S. App. LEXIS 1202, at *2 (4th Cir. Oct. 8, 2004); Green v. Taylor, No. 04-CAS-120, 2005 WL 44102, at *1 (D.N.J. Feb. 10, 2005)	*Bowes v. Capital Group,* No. 03-1765, 2004 U.S. App. LEXIS 1202, at *2 (4th Cir. Oct. 8, 2004); *Green v. Taylor,* No. 04-CAS-120, 2005 WL 44102, at *1 (D.N.J. Feb. 10, 2005)	*Bowes v. Capital Group,* 2004 U.S. App. LEXIS 1202 at *2 (4th Cir. Oct. 8, 2004); *Green v. Taylor,* 2005 WL 44102 at *1 (D.N.J. Feb. 10, 2005)
Internet Source (article available solely on Internet) (*Bluebook* Rule 18; *ALWD* Rule 40.1)	Brenda Sandburg, *PTO's Destination: Silicon Valley* (1999), *www.lawnewsnet.com/stories*	Brenda Sandburg, *PTO's Destination: Silicon Valley* (1999), *www.lawnewsnet.com/stories*	Brenda Sandburg, *PTO's Destination: Silicon Valley,* at *www.lawnewsnet.com/stories* (accessed June 28, 1999)

F. Special *Bluebook* and *ALWD* Citation Issues

1. General Comments

- Practitioners never use LARGE AND SMALL CAPITAL letters in citations. They always use ordinary roman type. LARGE AND SMALL CAPITAL letters are used for law review footnotes only in the *Bluebook* system. *ALWD* does not recognize LARGE AND SMALL CAPITAL letters as appropriate for any citation.
- Practitioners may underscore or italicize case names, book titles, names of articles in journals, and so forth. Select one method and be consistent. Use this same method for signals (such as *see* and *id.*)
- In citations, use the abbreviations "2d," "3d," and "102d Cong." rather than "2nd," "3rd," and "102nd Cong." All other ordinals (4th, 5th, and so forth) are the same as in general use. Do not use a superscript. Thus, use "8th" rather than "8th."

2. Abbreviations in Case Names: Bluebook and ALWD

- Under *Bluebook* Rule 10.2.1(c), when a citation appears in a textual sentence (meaning that the citation is needed to make sense of the sentence), you may abbreviate only well-known acronyms (such as FBI and CIA) and the following abbreviations in case names: "&," "Ass'n," "Bros.," "Co.," "Corp.," "Inc.," "Ltd.," and "No." (Rule 10.2). *ALWD* Rule 12.2(e) follows the same approach but uses the abbreviation "Assn."
- When a citation appears as a stand-alone citation—for example, after a declaratory sentence, you must abbreviate any of the nearly 170 words identified in Table T.6 of the *Bluebook* or Appendix 3 of *ALWD* such as "Hosp." or "Cas." even if the word is the first word in a party's name. Many of the *Bluebook* and *ALWD* abbreviations differ from each other.

Correct Example for Law Review Footnotes:

Trademarks may be abandoned by nonuse. Bates Constr. & Div. Auth. v. S. Maint. Comm., 499 U.S. 16 (1999)

Correct Example for Practitioners (for *Bluebook* and *ALWD*):

Trademarks may be abandoned by nonuse. *Bates Constr. & Div. Auth. v. S. Maint. Comm.*, 499 U.S. 16 (1999)

3. Spacing (*Bluebook* Rule 6.1(a), *ALWD* Rule 2.2)

- Close up adjacent single capital letters. Treat an ordinal (2d, 3d, 4th, and so forth) as a single capital letter.

Correct Examples: U.S.
F.3d
N.W.2d

- Place spaces before and after multiple letter abbreviations.

Correct Examples: F. Supp. 2d
Fed. R. Crim. P.
Cal. 4th

- Be careful with the abbreviations for the names of periodicals. Their spacing is odd. Mimic the spacing shown in *Bluebook* Table T.13 and *ALWD* Appendix 5.

Bluebook Correct Example for Law Review Footnotes:
46 B.C. L. REV. 190

Bluebook Correct Example for Practitioners:
46 B.C. L. Rev. 190

ALWD Correct Example for any purpose:
46 B.C. L. Rev. 190

- Always place a space after a section or paragraph symbol, as in 35 U.S.C. § 102 (2000). To pluralize sections, use two symbols, as in §§ 102-104.

4. Punctuation

- If the citation supports or contradicts a previous declaratory sentence, follow it with a period.
- If the citation is used as a clause within a sentence, follow it with a comma.
- If the citation is used in a "string" of other citations, separate the citations from each other with semicolons and follow the order required in *Bluebook* Rule 1.4 and *ALWD* Rule 45.

5. Pinpoints

Give a pinpoint citation (a reference to the page on which specific material appears) for all citations. (*Bluebook* Rule

3.2; *ALWD* Rule 5.2). See the examples below and the *Bluebook* and *ALWD* for rules relating to multiple pages.

Bluebook Correct Example for Law Review Footnotes:

☐ Hardy v. Bailey, 520 U.S. 118, 124 (1992)
☐ Jackson v. Emerson Inc., 691 N.W.2d 145, 150-51 (Wis. 1994)
☐ Steven Mills, *Bankruptcy Law*, 31 STAN. L. REV. 308, 314-15 (1998)

Bluebook and *ALWD* Correct Examples for Practitioners:

☐ *Hardy v. Bailey*, 520 U.S. 118, 124 (1992)
☐ *Jackson v. Emerson Inc.*, 691 N.W.2d 145, 150-51 (Wis. 1994)
☐ Steven Mills, *Bankruptcy Law*, 31 Stan. L. Rev. 308, 314-15 (1998)

Note that while the *Bluebook* requires one to drop repetitious digits for page spans, the *ALWD* approach is optional so that all digits may be retained if desired.

6. Quotations

The approach to presenting quotations is nearly identical in the *Bluebook* and in *ALWD*.

■ Quotations of 49 words or fewer are enclosed in double quotation marks (" ") and placed in the narrative portion of your text. Always put periods and commas inside your quotation marks. Quotations within quotations are shown by single quotation marks (' ').
■ Quotations of 50 words or more are indented left and right and appear without quotation marks (quotation marks within this block should appear as they do in the original). Place the citation at the left margin on the line immediately following the quotation, not within the block.
■ Use an ellipsis (. . .) to show an omission in the middle of a quoted sentence. Do not start a sentence with an ellipsis (*Bluebook* Rule 5.3; *ALWD* Rule 49.3(b)). Instead, use brackets, as in "[N]oncompetition agreements must be reasonable." If the omitted matter includes the end of a sentence, add another period to the ellipsis (. . . .).
■ Use brackets ([ ]) to show a minor alteration in a quotation, such as a change from upper case to lower case. Use the signal "[sic]" to show a misteak [sic] in the original material.

7. Short Forms

Short forms may be used for most citations once the citation has been given in full. The treatment of short forms is much the same in the *Bluebook* and in *ALWD*.

■ Use *id.* to send the reader to the most immediately preceding authority, no matter what the preceding authority is. *Id.* may be capitalized or not, depending on its location in a sentence.
■ Use the form "*id.* at 23" to send the reader to a different page from that in the preceding citation.

Bluebook Correct Example for Law Review Footnotes:

First reference: Thomas v. Murphy Bros., 520 U.S. 118, 124 (1995)
Second reference: *Id.* at 128-29.

■ Do not use the word "at" before a section symbol or paragraph symbol (*Bluebook* Rule 3.3). *ALWD* permits the use of "at" before the symbols (*ALWD* Rule 14.6).

Correct Example (*Bluebook*):

First reference: 42 U.S.C. § 101 (2000)
Second reference: *Id.* § 114

Bluebook and *ALWD*. Use one of the following forms to send a reader to a preceding case that is not immediately preceding:

Correct Examples for Practitioners:

First reference: *Geary Bros. v. Levy Ass'n*, 521 U.S. 16, 19 (2001)
Later references:
☐ *Geary*, 521 U.S. at 23
☐ 521 U.S. at 23
☐ In *Geary*, the Court also held . . . (See *Bluebook* Rule 10.9(c) and *ALWD* Rule 12.21(c), which allow a reference to a case by one of the parties' names without any further citation if the case has been cited in full in the same general discussion.)

■ Use the signal *supra* (meaning *above*) to send a reader to a previous secondary authority that is not the immediately preceding authority. The signal *supra* may not be used to send a reader to a case, statute, constitutional provision, or regulation. *Supra* always appears with the name of an author or the title of a work. (*Bluebook* Rule 4.2 and Bluepages Rule B8.2, *ALWD* Rule 11.4, requiring a note number with the *supra* reference). Thus, *supra* is used primarily to send readers to a previously cited book or law review article.

Bluebook Correct Example for Law Review Footnotes:

First reference: Susan Gray, DUE PROCESS § 12 (1999)

Later reference: Gray, *supra*, § 14.

- The first reference to a statute must give the full citation. Later references may use any short form that is understandable to the reader.
- While the *Bluebook* and *ALWD* clearly require a year and a reference to the publisher (unless the set is official) for citations for statutes, almost all practitioners omit the parenthetical.

Correct *Bluebook* and *ALWD* Example: 15 U.S.C. § 1051 (2000)

Example in Common Use: 15 U.S.C. § 1051

G. Differences Between the *Bluebook* and *ALWD*

Although the basic methods of citation are much the same in the *Bluebook* and *ALWD,* there are some notable differences, including the following:

- **Parallel citations for U.S. Supreme Court cases**. The *Bluebook* does not permit parallel citations for U.S. Supreme court cases. *ALWD* does.
- **Case names.** The abbreviations used in case names are different in the two citation systems. See *Bluebook* Table T.6 and *ALWD Appendix* 3. Additionally, if the United States is a party, the *Bluebook* requires reference to *United States*. *ALWD* cites as *U.S.*
- **Treatises and dictionaries.** The publisher of a treatise or dictionary is not included in the parenthetical with the date under the *Bluebook* approach but it is under the *ALWD* approach.
- **A.L.R. annotation.** The word *Annotation* is part of the citation under the *Bluebook* approach but is omitted when citing using *ALWD*.
- **Miscellaneous**. There are many differences in abbreviations between the *Bluebook* and *ALWD*. For example, the *Bluebook* abbreviates the word *Publishing* as *Publ'g* while *ALWD* abbreviates it as *Publg*.

APPENDIX
H

WRITING BASICS: GRAMMAR, PUNCTUATION, AND SPELLING

The following is a concise "Table of Contents" to the information in this Appendix so you may quickly find the information you need.

1. INTRODUCTION

Even if your research is flawless and you have found primary authorities "on point," these will do you no good unless you can communicate your results to a reader. Flaws in the communication process, such as improper spelling, awkward word usage and sentence construction, and errors in punctuation distract your reader from the message of your project, making the reader doubt your abilities and reflect on your carelessness.

Don't let the rules of grammar and its incomprehensible terms (such as *pluperfect* or *subjunctive*) intimidate you. You do not need to know all of the parts of speech to be a good writer, just as you do not need to know all of the parts of an oven to be a good cook.

2. GRAMMAR

Rules of grammar are used so that we can communicate clearly. The following are some of the most common grammatical errors made by beginning and even experienced writers.

a. Sentence Fragments

The sentence is the foundation of all writing. A well-written sentence conveys information to a reader while a poorly written sentence causes confusion and ambiguity. Legal writing is more formal than many other kinds of writing, and an incomplete sentence in a legal document will be noticed immediately.

Sentence fragments (also called *incomplete sentences*) are usually caused by a failure to include a subject and a verb in a sentence. Fragments also occur when writers assume that a *dependent clause* (one that cannot stand on its own) is a sentence by itself. To remedy sentence fragments, either attach the fragment to an adjacent complete sentence (usually by correcting punctuation) or make the dependent clause into a complete sentence.

Sentence Fragments	*Correct*
Janice viewed the exhibit. The one introduced by her attorney.	Janice viewed the exhibit, which was the one introduced by her attorney.
I proposed a change. Omitting section two of the agreement.	I proposed a change: omitting section two of the agreement. *or* I proposed a change. I proposed omitting section two of the agreement.

b. Run-On Sentences

In many ways, a run-on sentence is the opposite of a sentence fragment. A *run-on sentence* combines two sentences into one. Run-on sentences can usually be corrected by inserting the proper punctuation (usually a semicolon if the two clauses are closely related) or by dividing the run-on sentence into two separate sentences.

Incorrect	*Correct*
The corporate directors had voted, they agreed to hire a new president.	The corporate directors had voted; they agreed to hire a new president. *or* The corporate directors had voted. They agreed to hire a new president.

c. Subject-Verb Agreement

A subject must agree with its verb. Singular subjects correspond with singular verbs (as in *The <u>witness</u> <u>is</u> late*) and plural subjects must correspond with plural verbs (as in *The <u>witnesses</u> <u>are</u> late*). Most problems in subject-verb agreement occur when:

- A subject has more than one word;
- The subject is an indefinite pronoun (such as *everyone*) or a collective noun (such as *committee*); or
- Words or phrases intervene between the subject and the verb.

(1) Multiple Word Subjects

- **Rule One: Subjects joined by *and* usually take plural verbs.**

Incorrect	*Correct*
The jewelry and the stock was inventoried.	The jewelry *and* the stock *were* inventoried.

- **Rule Two: Subjects joined by *or* or *nor* usually take a singular verb.**

Incorrect	*Correct*
Neither the witness nor his attorney were present.	Neither the witness *nor* his attorney *was* present.

- **Rule Three: When the subject is composed of a singular word and a plural word joined by *or* or *nor*, the verb should agree with the nearer word.**

Incorrect	*Correct*
The landlords or the tenant have left.	The *landlords* and the *tenant has* left.

Note, however, that sentences such as these seem to sound better with plural verbs. Try to place the plural subject nearer to the verb.

Better

The *tenant* and the *landlords have* left.

- **Rule Four: When a compound subject is preceded by the words *each* or *every*, the verb is usually singular.**

Incorrect	*Correct*
Each exhibit, document, and model were given to the jury for review.	*Each* exhibit, document, and model *was* given to the jury for review.

(2) Indefinite Pronouns

Indefinite pronouns are pronouns that do not refer to a specific person or thing. Most of them end in *-one* or *-body.*

Indefinite pronouns can be singular (in which case they take singular verbs) or plural (in which case they take plural verbs). Following are some common indefinite pronouns:

Singular Indefinite Pronouns		*Plural Indefinite Pronouns*
anybody	everybody	both
anyone	everyone	few
each	neither	many
either	no one	several
every	somebody	
something		

Correct

- *Each* contract *includes* a liquidated damage clause.
- *Both* contracts *include* arbitration clauses.
- *No one was* present at the hearing.
- *Many* of the allegations *were* false.

Caution: A few indefinite pronouns (*all, none, any, some, more,* and *most*) can be singular or plural depending on the word to which they refer.

Correct

- *All* of the *directors were* at the meeting.
- *All* of the *complaint was* reviewed.

(3) Collective Nouns

Collective nouns (nouns that stand for a group of people or items) such as *committee, corporation, court, evidence,* and *jury* are usually singular. Watch for the word "the" before a noun because it is often a signal that the word to follow is singular.

Incorrect	*Correct*
The court have ruled on the issue.	The *court has* ruled on the issue.
The jury have adjourned for the day.	The *jury has* adjourned for the day.

If you wish to discuss the individuals composing the unit, for the sake of clarity use the following form.

Correct

- The *members* of the court *have* ruled on the issue.
- The *jurors have* adjourned for the day.

(4) Intervening Words

Subject-verb agreement problems often occur when several words or a phrase intervenes between a subject and a verb. To be correct, identify the subject of the sentence, ignore intervening words, and select the verb that agrees with the subject.

Incorrect	*Correct*
The remainder of the goods to be distributed have been identified.	The *remainder* of the goods to be distributed *has* been identified.

Caution: Intervening phrases or words such as *together with, including,* or *in addition to* do not change the form of the verb. If the subject is singular, select a singular verb; if the subject is plural, select a plural verb.

Correct

The *witness*, together with his attorneys, *has* reviewed the transcript.

d. Modifiers

Modifiers are words that limit, describe, or qualify another word or word group. Modifiers are said to be "misplaced" when they are located in a sentence in such a way as to cause ambiguity (and often humor). To avoid trouble with modifiers, move phrases and words close to the words they modify.

Misplaced Modifier	*Correct*
The defendant was described as a tall man wearing a hat weighing 180 pounds.	The defendant was described as a 180-pound tall man wearing a hat.

One type of common misplaced modifier is a prepositional phrase that is located in the wrong place in a sentence.

Misplaced Modifier	*Correct*
These guidelines provide tips for protecting your safety from our staff.	These guidelines from our staff provide tips for protecting your safety.

The following words, all of which are *limiting words* because they restrict the meaning of other words, are notorious causes of ambiguity and should be placed immediately before the word or words you intend to omit or restrict: *almost, even, hardly, merely, nearly, only, simply,* and *solely.* Review the following sentence: *The witness said Pete was the robber.* Now place the word *only* before each word in the sentence. Note that varying the placement of the word *only* in the sentence produces seven different meanings. For clarity, place these limiting words immediately before the word or words they are intended to limit or describe.

A modifier is said to "dangle" when it does not logically modify anything in its sentence. Most *dangling modifiers* occur in phrases introducing sentences, and while the phrases include a verb form, they do not include a subject. To remedy a dangling modifier, either identify the actor immediately after the introductory modifier, or reword the modifying phrase so that it identifies the actor.

Dangling	*Revised*
Waiting in the courtroom, his eyes became tired. (This sentence suggests that the eyes were waiting in the courtroom.)	As he waited in the courtroom, his eyes became tired.

e. Split Infinitives

An *infinitive* is the word *to* together with a basic verb, as in *to run* or *to plead.* An infinitive is said to be "split" when a word (usually an adverb) is inserted between the word *to* and the verb, as in *to quickly run* or *to convincingly plead.*

Most writing experts now recognize that there is no formal rule against splitting an infinitive, and split infinitives are commonly seen in nonlegal writing; however, legal readers tend to be conservative and may be annoyed or distracted by a split infinitive. Because most split infinitives are easily corrected (by simply moving the adverb that causes the "split" after the infinitive), correct them when you can and avoid splitting an infinitive unless you want to place emphasis on the adverb. See the "Tips" box for other "old" rules.

Split Infinitive	*Corrected Infinitive*
She asked me *to thoroughly review* pleadings.	She asked me *to review* the the pleadings *thoroughly.*

f. Pronouns

Pronouns are words that replace nouns. Thus, consider the sentences *Hal filed the brief* and *He filed the brief.* In the second sentence, the word *he* is a pronoun because it replaces the proper noun *Hal.* There are many different kinds of pronouns, including personal pronouns, indefinite pronouns, and reflexive pronouns, but all pronouns must agree with their *antecedents* (the word or phrase to which the pronoun refers).

(1) Personal Pronouns

Personal pronouns (*I/me, you, he/him, she/her, we/us, they/them*) change forms depending on whether they function as the subject of a sentence or the object of the sentence.

TIPS

The Old Rules

Because legal writing is more formal than other styles of writing and because legal readers are notorious perfectionists, err on the side of caution so readers will not be jarred by your usage. Thus, whenever possible, comply with the "old" rules of writing in legal documents:

■ Don't split an infinitive;
■ Don't start a sentence with a conjunction such as *and* or *but*; and
■ Don't end a sentence with a preposition.

Ending a sentence with a preposition is something up with which I will not put.
                                                        —Sir Winston Churchill

TIPS

For Pronoun Use

As an aid to determining which form of pronoun to use, omit or cover up the name and the word "and" and this will provide a clue as to which pronoun to use.

Example: You must give Ted and me the police report.

Cover up the words "Ted and" so that the sentence reads, *You must give me the police report.*

This reading makes it clear that the correct pronoun is *me.*

■ **Rule One: When the pronoun functions or replaces the subject of a sentence, use *I, he, she, we,* or *they.***

Incorrect	Correct
It was me who prepared the will.	It was *I* who prepared the will.
Jill and her drafted the brief.	Jill and *she* drafted the brief.
Either him or me will go.	Either *he* or *I* will go.

■ **Rule Two: When the pronoun functions as or replaces the object of a sentence, use *me, him, her, us,* or *them.***

Incorrect	Correct
The will was prepared by I.	The will was prepared by *me.*
The brief was drafted by Jill and she.	The brief was drafted by Jill and *her.*
Give John and I the directions.	Give John and *me* the directions.

(2) Pronoun Agreement

A pronoun must agree in number with its antecedent (the word the pronoun stands for or refers to). Singular antecedents take singular pronouns and plural antecedents take plural pronouns.

(a) Indefinite Pronouns

Some antecedents are indefinite, meaning that they do not refer to any specific person or thing. The most common indefinite pronouns that take a singular form are as follows (note that many end with *-body, -one,* or *-thing*): *anybody, anyone, anything, each, either, every, everybody, everyone, everything, much, neither, no one, one, somebody, someone, something.* When these indefinite words serve as antecedents of pronouns, select a singular pronoun.

Incorrect	Correct
Somebody forgot to file their papers.	*Somebody* forgot to file *his or her papers.*
Does everyone have their contract?	Does *everyone* have *his or her* contract?

Although the correct examples above show proper usage, you may wish to avoid the expression *his or her* if it strikes you as stuffy. As discussed below, there are several ways to remedy such constructions. For instance, the first example could be written as follows: *Somebody forgot to file the papers.*

(b) Collective and Generic Nouns

As discussed above, collective nouns (nouns that stand for a group of people or items) such as committee, corporation, court, and jury are usually singular and take a singular pronoun. Similarly, *generic nouns* (nouns that could refer to either men or women, such as athlete, defendant, or juror) usually take a singular pronoun.

Incorrect	Correct
The corporation is holding their annual meeting next week.	The *corporation* is holding *its* annual meeting next week.
A juror will be compensated for their time on the jury.	A *juror* will be compensated for *his or her* time on the jury.

g. Use of *Who* and *Whom*

Use *who* and *whoever* for all subjects, and use *whom* and *whomever* for all objects. Thus, use *who/whoever* whenever *I, he, she, we,* or *they* could be substituted for *who/whoever* and use *whom/whomever* whenever *me, him, her, us,* or *them* could be substituted for *whom/whomever.*

Correct

- *Who* will be going to the trial?
- *Whom* does the indictment name?
- This is the man *whom* I called.
- *Whom* do you trust?

h. Use of *That* and *Which*

That is used to introduce a *restrictive clause* (one that is necessary to the meaning of the sentence) and is not preceded by a comma. *Which* is used to introduce a *nonrestrictive clause* (a clause that is not necessary to the meaning of the sentence and that can be omitted without changing the meaning of the sentence). A *which* clause is almost always preceded by a comma.

The use of *that* or *which* depends on the writer's intent. If the writer wishes to convey essential information, *that* should be used to introduce the information; if the writer intends to define, add to, or limit information, *which* should be used to introduce the information.

Example: *The corporation that was formed in Ohio announced its profits.*

Explanation: The word *that* tells us which particular corporation announced its profits. There may be several corporations that announced their profits, but the writer is describing which particular corporation—namely, the one formed in Ohio (rather than others formed elsewhere) announced its profits. Use *that.*

Example: *My car, which is old, is underinsured.*

Explanation: The *which* clause adds information, but it can be dropped and the sentence still makes sense. Use *which.*

i. Reflexive Pronouns

The *reflexive pronouns* are the *self* pronouns, namely *myself, yourself, himself, herself, ourselves, yourselves,* and *themselves.* Reflexive pronouns usually reflect back on a subject, such

---

TIPS

Who vs. *Whom:* Remember "m" for *Whom*

In every use of *who* or *whom,* rephrase the question or clause to determine whether you would use *he* or *him* in its place. If *he* would be used, use *who.* If *him* would be used, use *whom.* Remember that the "m" in *him* matches up with the "m" in *whom.*

Example:	*Who is calling?*
Test:	Rewrite as <u>*He*</u> *is calling.* Replace *he* with *who.*
Example:	*This is the juror whom I mentioned earlier.*
Test:	Rewrite as *I mentioned* <u>*him*</u> *earlier.* Replace *him* with *whom.*
Example:	*Who do you trust?*
Test:	Rewrite as *I trust* <u>*him*</u>. Replace *him* with *whom.*

TIPS

That or *Which*

To determine whether to start a clause with *that* or *which*, consider these tips:

- If you can drop the clause and still retain the meaning of the sentence, use *which*. If you can't, use *that*.
- A clause beginning with *which* is almost always surrounded by commas.
- A clause beginning with *that* is not surrounded by commas.
- *That* introduces essential information; *which* does not.

as *He injured himself*. Do not substitute a *self* pronoun for a personal pronoun (*I, me, he, him,* and so forth).

Incorrect	Correct
Joe and myself witnessed the accident.	Joe and *I* witnessed the accident.
The trial was attended by Ted and himself.	The trial was attended by Ted and *him*.

j. Gender-Linked Pronouns

Avoid the use of gender-linked pronouns. For example, the sentence *A judge must give his instructions to the jury* is objectionable because it implies that all judges are male. There are several techniques you can use to avoid offending readers:

- **Change singular nouns to plural nouns.**

  Correct

  Judges must give *their* instructions to the jury.

- **Rewrite the sentence to avoid using any pronouns.**

  Correct

  A judge must *give instructions* to the jury.

- **Use *he/him* or *she/her*.**

  Correct

  A judge must give *his or her* instructions to the jury.

  (Note that continued use of *his or her* throughout a document is often clumsy.)

k. Coordinating Conjunctions: *And, But, For, Nor, Or, So, Yet*

Coordinating conjunctions join elements of equal grammatical status, such as in the statement *The witness and the attorney were on time,* in which the conjunction *and* joins two nouns. The coordinating conjunctions are *and, but, for, nor, or, so,* and *yet*. Many traditional writers dislike the use of a coordinating conjunction at the beginning of a sentence, although it is becoming increasingly common. When possible, avoid starting a sentence with a coordinating conjunction because it is likely to annoy some readers.

Disfavored	Revised
The jury awarded damages. But the award was later reduced.	The jury awarded damages, but the award was later reduced.

3. PUNCTUATION

Punctuation marks signal meaning to readers and allow them to know that a sentence has ended, a question has been asked, and so forth. There is some variation in punctuation. Given the same paragraph, two writers may punctuate slightly differently. When in doubt, err on the side of caution, and use the more conventional approach to punctuation rather than some unusual approach because legal writing is traditional.

a. Commas

A comma indicates a brief pause and is considered the most troublesome of punctuation marks due to its numerous uses. Use a comma:

(i) after the salutation of an informal letter and after the closing of any letter:

Dear Aunt Mary,   *Sincerely,*

(ii) to set off digits in numbers, dates, and addresses:

There are 5,012 pages in the transcript.

(Note, however, that *Bluebook* Rule 6.2 states to use a comma only where numbers contain five or more digits and would therefore write this number as "5012.")

The defendant began employment on July 3, 2003, and remained employed until March 14, 2004.

(iii) to set off an introductory word, phrase, or clause:

According to the plaintiff's witness, the contract was breached in June 2003. Consequently, the plaintiff suffered damages.

(iv) to set off interruptive or nonessential words or phrases:

While reviewing the exhibits, however, I noticed an error.

(v) to set off appositives (a word or words that explain previous words):

Susan James, the well-known doctor, testified for the plaintiff.

(vi) before a coordinating conjunction (*and, but, for, nor, or, so,* and *yet*) if it introduces an *independent clause;* namely, one that can function as a complete sentence. You may omit the comma if the clause is short (five words or less) or when the last part of the sentence is a subordinate or dependent clause (meaning that it does not make sense by itself):

Correct

- I intended to amend the complaint, but the statute of limitations had expired.
- The directors vetoed the resolution and refused to discuss it.
- The trial ended and we left.

(vii) to set off items in a series of three or more items. Although the final comma in a series (often called a *serial comma*) is optional in most writing, in legal writing it is required. For example, consider the following two sentences:

I give all my money to Abe, Betty, Clay, and Donna.

I give all my money to Abe, Betty, Clay and Donna.

In the first example, it is clear that each of the individuals will receive one-fourth of the money. In the second example, it is arguable that the money will be divided into thirds, with Abe and Betty each receiving one-third and the group composed of Clay and Donna sharing one-third. Because the omission of the last comma in a series can cause ambiguity, always include it to show readers that each item is separate.

(viii) before and after most quotations:

"Give me the will," Jim said. Lee replied, "Frank has it."

b. Apostrophes

Use an apostrophe:

(i) to show possession or ownership. If a word is singular, always add *'s* to show possession (even if the word ends in *s, k, x,* or *z*). When a plural word ends in *s*, add only an apostrophe (') to show possession.

Correct Singular Examples	**Correct Plural Examples**
The defendant's first witness	All workers' paychecks
Xerox's annual report	The ten shareholders' agenda
The clerk's docket	The four judges' chambers

Some plural nouns (such as *men, women, children,* and *mice*) do not end in *s*. Form the possessive just as you would for singular nouns (as in the *men's* shoes and the *women's* voices)

To form the possessive of a proper noun that ends in a sibilant (*s, x,* or *z*), add an apostrophe and an *s* (*'s*). To pluralize names that end in *s, sh, ch, s,* or *z*, merely add *es* (as in *The Lynches and the Joneses will vacation together this year*).

Correct

Texas's legislature
Congress's resolve
Mr. Jones's son and Mr. Smith's daughter will attend.
Lucas's car

Note that many grammar books permit the use of an apostrophe alone with a singular word ending in *s* when adding another *s* would make the word difficult to pronounce or look odd. Thus, you may see *Jefferson Davis' house* or *Marcus' book.* Nevertheless, the U.S. Government Style Manual, *The Elements of Style* by William Strunk, Jr. and E.B. White (4th ed. 2000), and most conventional grammar books suggest the *'s*, as in *Jefferson Davis's house* and *Marcus's book.* This form is always correct.

(ii) to indicate omissions of letters, as in contractions (although contractions are disfavored in legal and business writing because they are so informal):

can't	(for can<u>no</u>t)
hadn't	(for had n<u>o</u>t)
don't	(for do n<u>o</u>t)
it's	(for it <u>i</u>s)

One of the most common errors beginning writers make is confusing *it's* with *its*. The word *it's* is a contraction for *it is* (or *it has*). The apostrophe is used to indicate that the letter *i* (or *ha*) has been omitted. To form the possessive of it, use *its*. Only use *it's* when you intend to write *it is* or *it has*, not when you intend to indicate possession.

Correct

It's the duty of the hospital to care for *its* patients.

c. Colons

Use a colon:

(i) after the salutation of a formal letter.

Dear Mr. Howell: Dear Sir or Madam:

(ii) to introduce a list. Use a colon especially after expressions such as *as follows* or *the following*:

The plaintiff asserted the following causes of action: breach of contract, fraud, and negligence.

(iii) to indicate that something will follow.

We have implemented a new policy: Late forms will not be accepted.

(iv) to introduce a formal or long quotation.

The court stated in unequivocal terms: "Punitive damages are warranted because of the defendant's fraudulent conduct."

(Note that this quotation could also be introduced by a comma.)

Most writers capitalize the first word after a colon if the material following the colon can stand on its own as a sentence. Conversely, most writers do not capitalize the first word after a colon if the material cannot stand on its own as a sentence.

d. Semicolons

Use a semicolon:

(i) to connect two independent but related clauses.

This was my first trial; I was excited and nervous.

(Note that these two ideas could also be expressed as complete sentences separated by periods.)

(ii) to connect two independent clauses joined by a transitional word or conjunction such as *therefore*, *however*, or *nevertheless*.

The witness was convincing; however, the jury rendered a guilty verdict.

(iii) to separate items in a list containing commas or introduced by a colon.

The elements to be proved in an action for fraud are as follows: a material misrepresentation; reasonable reliance by the injured party; and resulting damage caused to the injured party.

(Note that these items could also be separated by commas.)

e. Quotation Marks

Use quotation marks:

(i) to indicate the exact words of a speaker.

Judge Powell stated, "The motion to dismiss is granted."

(ii) to explain or draw emphasis to a word.

The writer misspelled the word "rescission" in the brief.

Use quotation marks only for quotations of 49 words or fewer. For quotations of 50 words or more, block indent the quotation and use single spacing. Do not use quotations marks for these indented quotations; the indentation itself signals that the material is a direct quotation.

Always place commas and periods inside quotation marks. Place colons and semicolons outside quotation marks. When a quotation includes another quotation, single quotation marks (' ') are used.

"It was Defendant Jones," said the witness, "who said, 'I admit I sold the house to the plaintiff.'"

f. Parentheses

Use parentheses:

(i) to set off interruptions or explanations.

His first affirmative defense was laches (an unreasonable delay that causes prejudice to the other party).

(ii) to direct a reader to other information.

The plaintiff adequately alleged reasonable reliance (Compl. ¶ 4).

(iii)   to introduce abbreviations.

The plaintiff, Jackson Engineering Company ("JEC"), filed the complaint on January 30, 2004.

If what is included in the parenthetical is a complete sentence, place a period inside the parenthetical. Otherwise, the period is placed outside the ending parentheses.

g. Hyphens

Use a hyphen:

(i)   to divide words between syllables at the end of a line of text. Use a dictionary to ensure the word is hyphenated at the correct place. Modern word processors "wrap" words to the next line, eliminating the need to manually insert a hyphen at the end of a line.

(ii)   between parts of a compound adjective when it modifies the next word.

Correct

- Susan is a well-respected judge.
- Susan is well respected.

(iii)   after prefixes preceding proper nouns and after prefixes ending with a vowel (to avoid confusion).

anti-American	pro-English
co-op	anti-intellectual

(iv)   to form compounds, as in *two-year lease.*

h. Dashes, Exclamation Marks, and Slashes

Dashes, exclamation marks, and slashes are seldom seen in legal or formal writing because they are considered informal punctuation marks.

(i)   Use a dash to indicate a break or interruption or to substitute for the word *to* in dates or numbers.

Judith—not her sister—practiced law from 1995-1998.

(ii)   Use exclamation marks to emphasize an idea. In legal writing, they are generally used only as part of a direct quotation.

(iii)   A slash mark causes ambiguity and should be avoided. Avoid the construction *and/or.* Write *Either Don or Mike, or both, will be here.*

4. SPELLING

Because English is such a confusing language, many people have difficulty spelling. One of the most distressing results of misspelling is the effect produced in a reader's mind. If the aim of writing is to inform or persuade a reader and the reader is confronted with spelling errors, any value a project may have may well be overshadowed by the misspellings. Legal document readers, such as clients, attorneys, and judges, tend to be highly critical and perfectionistic. When confronted with spelling errors, they may react by assuming that if you cannot be trusted to spell correctly, you cannot be trusted to analyze properly. At best, spelling errors make readers believe the writer is careless. At worst, they make readers question the writer's intelligence.

The following are some tips and strategies to improve spelling:

- **Use a dictionary.** The only certain way to ensure that a word is spelled correctly is to use a dictionary. A legal dictionary, such as *Black's Law Dictionary*, includes words used in legal settings as well as Latin terms and phrases commonly used in the profession. Dictionaries with no definitions (those that list only spelled words) are more portable. Don't be afraid to write in your dictionary. Circle or highlight troublesome words. If you are given two spellings for a word, such as *canceled* and *cancelled*, use the first spelling because it is the preferred spelling. Use the "American" spelling of a word (for example, *labor, judgment*) rather than the "British" spelling (for example, *labour, judgement*).

- **Develop a "hit list" of commonly misspelled words.** Many writers routinely misspell the same words. On an index card, write the ten or twelve words you commonly misspell and keep the card near your computer or writing area. Write the correct spelling only. Refer to the list often and note the words that you misspell the most often so you can spend additional time on them. Once you learn the words on your list, make another one.

- **Learn some rules.** Many spelling rules are easy to remember (although most have exceptions). Remember "*i* before *e* except after *c*, and except when it sounds like *a* as in *neighbor* and *weigh*." Similarly, use mnemonic devices, such as "the princi*pal* of your school is your *pal*."

- **Pronounce your words carefully.** If you make a concerted effort to pronounce *than* differently from *then* and *affect* differently from *effect*, your spelling will improve.

■ **Don't overrely on your spell-checker.** Use a spell-checker to help you catch some spelling errors but recognize its limitations; namely, that it will not signal incorrect usage. Thus, if you write *form* rather than *from*, the spell-checker will not flag the incorrect word because it is spelled correctly.

■ **Proofread carefully.** In many instances, a misspelled word will not look "right" to you and you can readily locate your errors. If you find it difficult to catch your own errors, ask a colleague to proofread your project for spelling errors.

GLOSSARY

ABA Standing Committee on Paralegals An ABA committee that approves paralegal education programs and supports utilization of paralegals

Active listening Communication technique that lets speaker know that the listener is attentive

Administrator See *Personal representative*

Admissible evidence Evidence that may be introduced at trial

Advance medical directive Directions given to indicate a person's desires as to medical treatment if incapacitated (often called *living will* or *health care proxy*)

Advance sheets Initial publication of cases in disposable softcover pamphlets

Affirmative defense Allegation by a defendant that negates a plaintiff's right to relief

Agency adoption Adoption in which child is placed with adopting parents by a public agency or a private agency

Alimony See *Spousal support*

Alternative dispute resolution Method of resolving disputes without trial

ALWD Citation manual providing rules for citing legal authorities

American Bar Association A voluntary professional association for attorneys

Analogy Method of analyzing cases by comparing similarities in cases

Annotated Literally, "with notes"; manner of publishing statutes together with case summaries interpreting statutes

Annulment Invalidation of a marriage

Answer Defendant's response to a plaintiff's complaint

Antecedent The noun to which a pronoun refers

Antenuptial agreement See *Prenuptial agreement*

Appellant The person who appeals an adverse decision (also called *petitioner*)

Appellate jurisdiction The power of a court to hear appeals from another court

Approval The designation by the ABA that a paralegal education program meets ABA guidelines; approval is not accreditation

Arbitration Process by which a neutral party renders a decision affecting disputing parties

Article III judge Judge appointed to a federal court under Article III, Section 1 of the U.S. Constitution

Articles of incorporation The document that creates a corporation

Assault Attempt or threat to cause immediate harm to another

Assignment Transfer of all or part of one's rights

Associate Junior attorney

Assumption of risk Defense to negligence in which a plaintiff is precluded from recovery because he or she knew of danger or risk and proceeded willingly

Attorney-client privilege Rule of evidence that prevents an attorney or a paralegal from being forced to testify about confidential client information

Attorneys' service Professional company that assists attorneys and paralegals in filing and serving court documents, retrieving public documents, and performing related tasks

Authenticated Evidence that must be proven to be genuine or what is claimed

Bates stamp Implement that assigns sequential numbers to pages and documents; may be performed manually or electronically

Battery Harmful and offensive intentional touching of another

Bench trial A case heard by a judge alone, with no jury

Beneficiary Person who will receive assets or property under a will or trust

Best evidence rule Evidentiary rule that original is usually required to prove the content of a writing

Billable   Time that can be charged to a client for work performed

Blended billing rate   Hourly rate set by a firm no matter which individual works on a particular client matter

Blind ad   Advertisement that does not identify the person or firm that placed it

Blue sky laws   State laws that regulate corporations whose stock is publicly traded

Bluebook   Citation manual providing rules for citing legal authorities

Boolean searching   Method of searching for legal authorities on the computer using numbers, symbols, and connectors rather than plain English language

Boutique firm   Law firm that handles specialized work or cases

Breach of contract   Failure to perform duties required by terms of contract

Brief   Document submitted to a court that includes legal argument (sometimes called a *trial brief*); short, written summary of a published case (sometimes called a *case brief*)

Bylaws   Rules governing a corporation's internal affairs

Canons of construction   Rules followed by courts in interpreting statutes

Capacity   Legal ability to take action, such as entering into a contract

Capper   See *Runner*

Caption   Heading in a court pleading that identifies the court, parties, title of action, and so forth

Case brief   See *Brief*

Case on all fours   See *On point*

Cause of action   A claim by a plaintiff against a defendant in a civil case

Certification   Referral of a question to the U.S. Supreme Court by a federal court of appeals; the process by which a nongovernmental entity identifies that an individual has met its standards

Certified Legal Assistant   The designation offered by NALA to those individuals who pass its examination testing paralegal competency

Certiorari   Latin for "to be informed of"; method of gaining a discretionary appeal

Challenge for cause   Request to eliminate a prospective juror for a valid reason, such as bias; unlimited in number

Charitable trust   Trust established for the benefit of some public, charitable, or like purpose

Child support   Payments to support a child of a dissolved marriage or relationship

Chinese wall   See *Ethical wall*

Chron file   A file of all documents prepared by employee in a law office, kept in chronological order

Circumstantial evidence   Evidence that creates an inference that a fact exists (also called *indirect evidence*)

Citation   Reference to a legal authority, such as a case

Civil action   Action brought by a private party to redress injury to the party

Civil law   A body of law depending more on legislative enactments than on case law, often seen in non-English-speaking countries

Civil litigation   Lawsuit between private parties

Civil union   Legal relationship between same-sex partners that affords some benefits of marriage; presently recognized only in Vermont

Client number   Number assigned by a lawyer or firm to a client

Closed-ended question   See *Closed question*

Closed question   A question that requires a yes-no or brief answer (sometimes called a *closed-ended question*)

Closing   Consummation of transaction (sometimes called *settlement*)

Closing binder   Binder including all documents relating to a transaction

Closing costs   Costs incurred in connection with purchase and sale of real property

Cloud on title   Defect that affects title to parcel of real property

Code of Ethics and Professional Responsibility   NALA's guide for paralegal ethical conduct

Codicil   Change to an existing will

Codification   Arrangement of statutes, bringing together all valid laws on the same subject with their amendments

Collective noun   Noun that stands for a group of items or people, such as *jury*

Commingling   Mixing of funds; specifically, mixing of attorney's own funds and those of clients

Common law   The body of law that develops and derives from judicial decisions as distinguished from statutes or constitutions

Common law marriage   Marriage formed by mutual consent and for which no marriage license is issued

Community property   Type of property ownership of married couples in which all property acquired during marriage is owned equally by husband and wife; recognized in nine states

Comparative negligence   Doctrine that determines fault of each party in a negligence action

Compensatory damages   Damages that compensate a party for losses incurred

Competent evidence Evidence that is legally sufficient (generally meaning that witness must understand obligation to tell the truth, must have personal knowledge of the event, and must be able to communicate)

Complaint Document setting forth a plaintiff's claims and that initiates litigation

Concurrent jurisdiction The shared power of two or more courts to hear a case

Concurring opinion Judge's opinion that agrees with result in a case but not its reasoning; persuasive only

Conflict check Method used by law firms and attorneys to determine if conflict of interest exists; often performed by paralegals using specialized software

Conflict of interest Situation that would involve competing duties to clients and breach the duty of undivided loyalty owed to clients

Consideration Bargained-for item of value, usually money, that induces another to enter into contract; element that must exist in all contracts

Constitution A document setting forth the fundamental law for a nation or state

Constitutional courts Federal courts created by Article III of U.S. Constitution—namely, district courts, intermediate circuit courts of appeals, and U.S. Supreme Court

Constructive eviction Impairment of basic rights of tenant—for example, impairing rights to water or heat, such that tenant is virtually evicted from leased premises

Contingencies In real property law, a condition that must be satisfied before title is transferred

Contingent fee agreement Agreement by client to pay legal fees only if attorney is successful in case; often used in personal injury cases

Contract Promise enforceable in court

Contract attorney Attorney who is not an employee of a firm but who works for the firm on a case-by-case basis

Contract paralegal See *Freelance paralegal*

Contributory negligence: Act by plaintiff that contributes to his or her injury and which precludes award to plaintiff

Conversion Taking and using another's property as one's own

Coordinating conjunction Words that join together words or groups of words—for example, *and, but,* and *or.*

Cornell Note-Taking System Method for taking notes, designed to assist users in remembering material; its six components are recording, reducing, reciting, reflecting, reviewing, and recapitulating

Corpus Money or items comprising trust (sometimes called the trust *principal*)

Count A plaintiff's statement of his or her cause of action

Counterclaim A claim by a defendant against a plaintiff

Courts of equity Courts that provide remedies and justice when monetary damages do not adequately compensate a party

Courts of law Courts that provide legal remedies—namely, monetary damages

Cover letter A letter that accompanies a document such as a resume and explains it; in litigation, a document that accompanies plaintiff's complaint and provides identifying information about the case

Cover sheet See *Cover letter*

CRAC Acronym for Conclusion, Rule, Analysis, Conclusion; method of analyzing cases by setting forth conclusion, rule, analysis, and conclusion

Crime An act against society committed in violation of a statute

Criminal litigation Action brought against a person by a governmental entity for an alleged criminal violation

Cross-claim A claim by one defendant against another

Dangling modifier Phrase that does not include a subject and does not modify any word or group of words in a sentence

Declaration of trust: Formal name of a document that establishes a trust

Declaratory relief A court order delineating the rights and duties of a party

Deed Document transferring title to real estate and showing its ownership

Defamation Publication of false information about another that harms the other's reputation

Default judgment Judgment entered against a defendant who fails to respond to a complaint

Delinquency matter Proceeding alleging criminal conduct by a juvenile

Demand letter Type of letter demanding some action, such as the payment of a debt

Demurrer See *Motion to dismiss*

Dependency matter Proceeding alleging abuse or neglect of a juvenile

Dependent clause Clause that cannot stand on its own

Deposition Out-of-court examination of party or witness under oath

Descriptive word approach Method of conducting research using alphabetically arranged indexes

Dictum Non-binding language in a case

Digests   Books or indexes that arrange one-sentence summaries or "digests"of cases by subject

Direct evidence   Information that proves or disproves a fact without relying on any other evidence

Direct examination   Questioning of a witness by the party who called him or her

Director   Manager of a corporation

Discovery   Investigation conducted by parties before trial to obtain information from each other

Dismissal with prejudice   Dismissal of a case such that it may not be reinstituted at a later date

Dismissal without prejudice   Dismissal of a case such that it may later be reinstituted by the plaintiff

Dissenting opinion   Opinion written by a judge in the minority; persuasive only

Dissolution   Termination of a relationship; in marital law, a term used interchangeably with *divorce*

Distinguishing   Method of analyzing cases by showing differences in cases

Diversity jurisdiction   A basis upon which federal courts take cases, due to the different or diverse citizenship of the parties in the case

Divorce   Court decree terminating a marriage

Docket   Law firm's calendar of its pending matters and related deadlines; a court's schedule of its cases

Docket number   Number assigned to a file or case by a court

Doctor-patient privilege   Evidentiary rule preventing doctors from testifying about confidential patient information

Documentary evidence   Evidence consisting of written records or documents

Domestic partner law   State law granting same-sex partners some of the rights of married heterosexuals

Due diligence   Careful review or investigation of documents and transactions

Earnest money   Money deposited by potential buyer of real property to show commitment to complete purchase

Easement   Right to use the property of another

Electronic discovery   Discovery in litigation of another party's electronic evidence, including e-mail, voice mail, electronic calendars, and so forth

Elegant variation   Practice of substituting one term for another in a document to avoid repetition of a term

Eminent domain   Power of governmental entity to seize real property for the public good

En banc   The hearing of a case by a full court

Engagement letter   Letter prepared by attorney or paralegal and signed by attorney and client that retains attorney to represent the client and sets forth fee arrangements

Equity partner   Partner who owns business assets

Escrow agent   Neutral party or company that acts for both buyer and seller of real property

Estate planning   Method by which a person plans to dispose of his or her property

Ethical wall   A means used by lawyers to isolate attorneys or paralegals who have a conflict of interest and thereby protect a client's confidential information; also called a *Chinese wall*

Evidence   Information that may prove or disprove a fact

Exclusive jurisdiction   The sole power of a court to hear a case

Executive summary   Short, concise written review provided before a full report

Executor   Person named in will to carry out instructions in will

Expert witness   Witness qualified by training or education to provide an opinion about a case or event

Extrajudicial   Proceeding that does not involve a court

Extranet   Computer network within an office that allows some limited access by those outside the office

Facsimile cover sheet   Top sheet that accompanies communications sent by facsimile with identifying information about the sender, recipient, and confidentiality

False imprisonment   Wrongful confinement or restraint of another

Federal question jurisdiction   The power of a federal court to hear a case based upon the fact the case arises under the U.S. Constitution or a U.S. law or treaty

Federal Rules of Evidence   Rules of evidence used in all federal courts and on which state rules of evidence are based

Federal Rules of Civil Procedure   Rules of civil procedure used in all federal courts for trial matters and on which state rules of civil procedure are based

Fee simple   Type of land ownership in which owner exercises absolute ownership rights over property

Field investigation   Investigation done outside of a law office

Fixed fee   See *Flat fee*

Flat fee   An agreed-on sum to be paid by a client to a law firm for performance of certain legal tasks, regardless of outcome of case; also called *fixed fee*

FOIA   See *Freedom of Information Act*

Foreclose   Reacquisition of real property, usually by bank that loaned funds for purchase of property and usually because of buyer's default in repaying loan

Foundation In a trial, requirement of providing background before evidence is introduced

Fraud Material misrepresentation or omission on which another justifiably relies to his or her detriment, causing damage

Freedom of Information Act Federal law allowing individuals to obtain records and information from government agencies (known as *FOIA*)

Freelance paralegal A self-employed paralegal who works on a case-by-case basis as an independent contractor; also called *contract paralegal*

Friendly witness Witness who is supportive of client's position

Functional résumé A résumé that focuses on skills and experience rather than individual listings of prior employers

Gay marriage A legal relationship between same-sex partners that would create a marriage relationship for all purposes

General counsel The most senior attorney on an in-house legal staff

General damages Damages intended to compensate for items such as pain and suffering, for which no precise amount can be determined

General jurisdiction The power of a court to hear almost any type of a case

General partnership Business structure with shared decision making and unlimited personal liability for its partners

General practice In law, a law firm that handles a variety of cases

Generic noun Noun that refers to either men or women, such as *athlete*

Googling Method of Internet research in which user types key terms or words into the search box provided on Google website at *www.google.com*

Grantor See *Trustor*

Guardian ad litem Literally, guardian for the suit; person appointed to represent the interests of another, often a minor or incompetent, in court

Headhunter A recruiter who places candidates for employment

Headnotes Brief, numbered paragraphs of points of law in a case

Health care proxy See *Advance Medical Directive*

Hearsay Out-of-court statement offered at trial to prove the truth of the matter asserted (sometimes called *secondhand information*)

Holographic will Will written entirely by hand

Home study Evaluation of environment of home into which an adopted child will be placed

Hostile witness Witness who is hostile to client's position

Hourly fee Fee paid by client for each hour of work performed on a matter

House arrest Order by a court that an individual be confined to his or her home pending court determination of guilt

Hung jury A jury that cannot reach a decision in a civil or criminal case

Hypothetical question Question that is based on speculation and asks the respondent to assume certain facts

Imputed conflict A conflict of interest involving one individual that affects others associated with the individual; a conflict that taints all attorneys in a firm when one is tainted; also called *imputed disqualification*

Imputed disqualification See *Imputed conflict*

Inactive file Client file for which work is completed

Indefinite pronoun Pronoun that does not refer to a specific person or thing

Independent adoption See *Private adoption*

Independent clause Clause in a sentence that can function as a complete sentence

Independent paralegal A paralegal who works directly for consumers without supervision by an attorney

Index In litigation, list of documents that have been Bates-stamped or numbered in some manner

Indirect evidence See *Circumstantial evidence*

Infinitive The word *to* plus a verb, as in *to plead*

Informed consent Consent provided by a party only after full disclosure of all information and risks

In-house counsel Attorney employed directly by a company to perform its legal work

In-house legal department Group within a company that performs legal work for the company

Injunctive relief A court order compelling one to take action or refrain from taking action

In personam jurisdiction See *Personal jurisdiction*

In rem jurisdiction Jurisdiction exercised by a court over a "thing" located in the court's jurisdiction

Intake memo Memo that describes a client meeting and the client's case

Intake sheet Form or checklist used by legal professionals to obtain information from clients

Intellectual property The fruits of creative endeavors, such as trademarks, copyrights, and patents

Intentional infliction of emotional distress   Intentional outrageous and extreme conduct that causes mental injury to another

Intentional tort   Civil wrong in which actor intended consequences of his or her action

Interference with contract   Wrongful act of interfering with another's contract so as to cause breach of the contract

International adoption   Adoption of a child from a foreign country

International Paralegal Management Association (IPMA)   An international organization for paralegal managers

Interrogatories   Written questions propounded by one party to another

Inter vivos trust   See *Living trust*

Intestate   Person who dies without a will

Intestate succession   Process of distributing property of a decedent who dies without a will

Intranet   Internal computer network within an office that allows workers to share documents

Invasion of privacy   Wrongful act that interferes with another's right of seclusion or privacy

Investigating   Locating information

Involuntary petition   In bankruptcy, a proceeding initiated against a debtor by creditors

IOLTA account   Interest on Lawyers' Trust Account; special accounts funded with nominal or short-term funds of clients, the interest on which is used to fund legal services for the needy or other similar projects

IRAC   Acronym for Issue, Rule, Analysis, and Conclusion; method of analyzing cases by setting forth case issue, rule, analysis, and conclusion

Irreconcilable differences   Common ground for divorce in which a party proves only that the marriage has irretrievably broken down

Job bank   Listing of available jobs maintained by an entity or school

Job hunting notebook   A binder containing all notes and materials relating to a job search

Joint and several liability   Liability for an entire debt

Joint custody   Court order that allows parents to share decision making about child and orders child to spend time residing with both parents

Joint tenancy   Type of land ownership in which multiple parties own land; on death of one, property belongs to the other(s)

Judicial notice   Concept that courts will admit some evidence without formal proof (generally, because it could be easily proven)

Jurisdiction   The power of a court to hear a case

Juvenile   A minor; generally, a person under 18 years of age

KeyCite   West Group's software program used to validate primary authorities to ensure they are still valid

Key Number   Number assigned by West Group to a topic of the law to enable researchers to find cases on similar topics

Key Number System   West Group's method of classifying the law to enable researchers to find cases on similar topics

Landlord   One who owns real property but rents it to another (sometimes called *lessor*)

Lateral hire   Attorney hired by one firm from another

Law clerk   Law student hired by attorney or law firm to perform research and other tasks

Law librarian   Individual specially trained in the law and in library science

Lay witness   Non-expert witness who has observed or experienced events testified about

Leading question   Question that suggests the desired response

Legal assistant   See *Paralegal*

Legal custody   Court order that allows a party to make decisions about all matters affecting a child

Legal document assistant   In California, a registered individual who provides legal document drafting services to members of the public

Legal memorandum   Research document that analyzes a legal problem in an objective manner; for interoffice use only; also called a *memo*

Legal nurse consultant   See *Nurse paralegal*

Legislative courts   Specialized federal courts not created by the U.S. Constitution

Legislative history   Background of a statute; may be examined by courts in interpreting statutes

Lessee   See *Tenant*

Lessor   See *Landlord*

Libel   Written defamation

Licensing   The process by which a governmental entity grants permission and issues a license to individuals to practice a profession, such as the paralegal profession

Life estate   Use of land during one's lifetime

Limited jurisdiction   Limitation on a court as to the types of cases it may hear

Limited liability company   New type of business entity that protects its members from unlimited personal liability

Limited liability partnership   New type of business entity that is governed by partnership law and protects partners from unlimited personal liability

Limiting word   Word that restricts the meaning of other words

Liquidated damage clause   Clause in contract imposing damages (intended as a penalty) in a specified amount in the event of breach

Liquidated damages   Damages agreed to in a contract as a penalty

Living trust   Trust established during its grantor's lifetime (also called an *inter vivos trust*)

Living will   See *Advance medical directive*

Long-arm statute   Statute that allows a state to exercise jurisdiction over nonresidents

Maintenance   See *Spousal support*

Majority opinion   Case opinion that is binding authority because it is written by a member of the majority of the court

Managing partner   Partner who directs or manages a partnership

Marital privilege   Evidentiary rule preventing spouses from being compelled to testify about their confidential communications

Mass mailing   Mailing of written material to numerous individuals or firms who have not requested the material

Matter number   Number assigned to each individual case or file handled by a firm for a client

Med-arb   Combination of mediation and arbitration in which arbitration is commenced after an unsuccessful mediation

Mediation   Process by which a neutral party attempts to help parties resolve their differences

Member   Participant in a limited liability company

Memorandum   See *Legal memorandum*

Mini-trial   Form of alternative dispute resolution in which parties present evidence to either a judge selected by them or a panel of their decision makers

Model Code of Ethics and Professional Responsibility   NFPA's standards for professional responsibility for paralegals

Model Guidelines for the Utilization of Legal Assistant Services   ABA guidelines directed to attorneys to assist attorneys who employ paralegals

Model Rules of Professional Conduct   ABA rules that govern attorney standards of professionalism and ethics; adopted in some form by almost all states

Model Standards and Guidelines for Utilization of Legal Assistants   NALA's guidelines to assist attorneys and others who employ paralegals

Modifier   Word that limits, describes, or qualifies another word or word group

Motion for judgment as a matter of law   Request that a court enter judgment for a party

Motion in limine   Request that a court exclude evidence or issues at trial

Motion to dismiss   Request that a court dismiss litigation (sometimes called a *demurrer*)

National Association of Legal Assistants (NALA)   A professional organization for individual paralegals

National Federation of Paralegal Associations, Inc. (NFPA)   A professional organization for state and local paralegal associations and individual members

National Reporter System   Sets of books published by West Group that report cases

Negligence   Failure to exercise the duty of due care that a reasonable person would exercise in like circumstances

Networking   Using personal contacts and relationships to further one's career

New matter memo   Memo prepared by attorney so a matter number will be assigned to a client's new transaction or case

No-fault divorce   Proceeding that does not require that one party prove the other committed an unsavory act to obtain a divorce

Nominal damages   Damages awarded when no actual damages are proved

Nominalization   Conversion of an adjective, verb, or adverb into a noun

Nonequity partner   See *Permanent associate.*

Nonrestrictive clause   Clause that is necessary to the meaning of a sentence

Nurse paralegal   A registered nurse who is trained as a paralegal; also called a *legal nurse consultant*

Of counsel   Term usually assigned to older, semi-retired attorneys, although it might refer to a senior attorney; see also *Permanent associate*

Offeree   Party receiving an offer

Offeror   Party making an offer

Official   Publication of law or case as mandated or directed by statute or court rule

Official report   Case book publishing cases as directed by statute or court rule

Online dispute resolution   New form of alternative dispute resolution in which all documents and evidence are submitted electronically and a decision is rendered electronically as well

On point   Case that serves as a precedent because it is factually similar and legally relevant; also called a *case on all fours*

Open adoption   Adoption in which adopting parents and birth parent(s) have contact with each other

Open question   A question that requires an explanation as a response; also called *open-ended question*

Open-ended question   See *Open question*

Opening statement   Introductory statement made at a trial by an attorney

Opinion letter   Letter that provides legal advice

Original jurisdiction   The power of a court to hear a trial

Paralegal   Generally defined as a person qualified by experience or education to perform substantive legal work and who is usually employed by an attorney or law firm; often synonymous with *legal assistant*

Paralegal Advanced Competency Exam (PACE)   A voluntary examination offered by NFPA; individuals who pass the exam are referred to as *certified paralegals*

Paralegal coordinator   See *Paralegal manager*

Paralegal manager   A paralegal who manages other paralegals; also called a *paralegal coordinator*

Parallel citations   Two or more references to a legal authority

Paraphrasing   Taking the ideas or expressions of another and putting them into one's own words

Parol evidence rule   Evidentiary rule that oral evidence may not be introduced to vary the terms of a written document

Parties   In litigation, plaintiffs and defendants

Partner   Owner of a firm or business that operates as a partnership

Partnership track   Firm's established course to become a partner

Per curiam opinion   Opinion of the whole court in which no author is identified

Peremptory challenge   Request to eliminate a prospective juror with no reason given; limited in number

Permanent associate   Attorney who will remain an employee of a firm rather than an owner (also called *senior attorney, of counsel,* or *nonequity partner*)

Personal jurisdiction   Authority of a court to exercise jurisdiction over the person of a defendant; also called *in personam* jurisdiction

Personal liability   Liability extending beyond what is invested in a business to one's personal assets

Personal property   Tangible items of property

Personal representative   Person appointed by court to carry out functions of executor if no executor is named in will (also called *administrator*)

Personal service   Hand-delivery of court documents

Petition   Document that initiates a court proceeding, such as a divorce petition

Petitioner   See *Appellant*

Physical custody   Court order that determines where a child will reside

Physical evidence   See *Real evidence*

Piercing the corporate veil   Process of imposing liability on corporate shareholders for corporate obligations, usually due to commingling of funds or lack of corporate formalities

Plagiarism   Taking another's ideas, thoughts, or expressions and representing them as one's own

Plain meaning rule   Rule followed by courts that words in a statute will be interpreted according to their ordinary meaning

Pleading   Document such as a complaint or answer filed by a party in a pending action

Pocket parts   Pamphlets inserted into back covers of legal books to provide current information

Prayer   Request for relief made in plaintiff's complaint

Precedent   A case or legal authority that governs a later case

Prejudicial error   An error that affects the outcome of a case; reversible error

Prenuptial agreement   Agreement entered into by couple before marriage, specifying how assets will be divided in event of death or divorce (also called *antenuptial agreement*)

Pre-trial conference   See *Scheduling conference*

Priest-penitent privilege   Evidentiary rule preventing clergy members from testifying about confidential communications by their penitents

Primary authority   Official pronouncement of the law by any of the three branches of federal or state governments; binding authority

Principal   See *Corpus*

Private adoption   Adoption arranged between birth parent(s) and adopting parents without agency involvement (also called *independent adoption*)

Private practice   Work environment in which individuals work for themselves or others rather than for a governmental entity or company

Privilege against self-incrimination   Constitutional provision protecting an individual from being compelled to testify against himself or herself

Privileged material   Matter that is inadmissible because of the relationship between parties in confidential discussions

Probate   Court-supervised process of ensuring a decedent's will is valid and administering decedent's estate

Pro bono publico   Latin for "for the public good"; representation of parties by attorneys or law firms at no cost to the party

Procedural law   Law that relates to the methods of enforcing substantive rights

Product liability   Responsibility of those in the stream of commerce when products are defective

Professional corporation   Corporation formed to provide professional services, such as a law firm

Project manager   Lead paralegal in a complex case, often a litigation case

Promissory note   Written promise to repay money borrowed

Prompting question   Question that motivates an interviewee to provide information

Pronoun   Word that replaces a noun

Proof of service   Verification that documents have been served

Protective order   Order issued by a court to protect a party from harassment or harm

Public policy   Societal reason for a rule or regulation

Punitive damages   Monetary award intended to punish wrongdoer when malice, intent, or gross negligence is shown

Ratio decidendi   Latin for "rule of decision"; the binding rule of a case

Real evidence   Evidence consisting of a tangible item (also called *physical evidence*)

Real property   Land

Redact   Striking out of material on a document, usually for confidentiality reasons

Redirect examination   Examination of a witness by plaintiff after defendant has cross-examined the witness

Reflexive pronoun   A *-self* pronoun, such as *myself*, which is used to refer back to a noun

Reformation   The revising of a contract to comply with the intentions of the parties

Registration   A method of regulation of paralegals by which paralegals' names are maintained on a register or list for consumer identification

Regulation   The process by which development of the paralegal profession is controlled; includes registration, licensing, and certification; also see *Rule*

Relevant evidence   Evidence that tends to prove that a fact is more or less probable

Relevant fact   Fact that contributes to a court's decision; if fact were different, court's result would be different

Relevant issue   Issue that contributes to a court's decision; if issue were different, court's result would be different

Rent-a-judge   Form of alternative dispute resolution in which parties engage the services of a retired judge to hear their dispute and render a decision or facilitate settlement

Reorganization   In bankruptcy, a restructuring of debtor's obligations rather than a liquidation of assets

Reports   See *Reporters*

Reporters   Books that compile cases

Request for admission   Written request that a party admit the truth of some matter or the genuineness of some document

Rescission   Remedy canceling a contract, usually due to fraud, and restoring parties to the positions they occupied prior to entering into the contract

Restrictive clause   Clause that is necessary to the meaning of a sentence

Retainer   Initial sum paid by a client to engage services of an attorney or a law firm

Retaliatory eviction   Eviction of tenant by landlord in retaliation for tenant's exercise of lawful rights

Right of quiet enjoyment   Right of tenant to use and enjoy property leased from landlord

Rules   Binding statements issued by agencies; also called *regulations*

Runner   An individual paid to procure business for an attorney; also called a *capper*

Run-on sentence   Sentence that combines two sentences into one

Sanction   Punishment imposed by a court

Scheduling conference   Conference held by court to determine disposition of a case (also called *pre-trial conference*)

Scheduling order   Order issued by court setting deadlines and dates related to trial

Secondary authorities   Any legal authority that is not a primary authority; non-binding authorities

Secondhand information   See *Hearsay*

Securities laws   Federal laws that regulate corporations whose stock is publicly traded

Security   Item pledged by promisor and that may be seized in the event of default in a promise by the promisor

Self-authenticated   Evidence that is presumed to be genuine with no further proof

Senior attorney   See *Permanent associate*

Sentence fragment   Incomplete sentence; a sentence lacking a subject or a verb

Serial comma   Final comma used to punctuate a series of three or more items

Service of process   Delivery of court documents

Session laws   Initial compilation of laws passed by state legislatures

Settlement   See *Closing*

Settlor   See *Trustor*

Shareholder   Owner of a corporation

Shepardizing   Process of validating primary authorities to ensure they are still valid

Slander   Spoken defamation

Slip form   Initial publication of cases and other materials on looseleaf paper

Slip law   Federal law initially published on looseleaf sheet(s) of paper

Sole practitioner   An individual who works for himself or herself; attorney who practices alone

Special damages   Monetary award intended to compensate for calculable and specific losses, such as lost wages

Specific performance   A court order requiring a party to comply with contractual obligations or to perform an act

Spendthrift trust   Trust established for a beneficiary who the grantor believes is incapable of handling the entire trust

Spousal support   Court order determining financial support for a spouse after a divorce (also called *alimony* or *maintenance*)

SQ3R method   A method of reading designed to improve comprehension; its five components are surveying the material, questioning the material, reading, reciting, and reviewing the material

Standing   The requirement that one have a personal stake in the outcome of a case

Stare decisis   Latin for "let the decision stand"; concept of relying on judge-made case law in similar cases

Start page   A reliable website used to begin research using the Internet

Statute   A law passed by a legislative body

Statute of frauds   Law in all states requiring some contracts, such as those for the sale of land, to be in writing

Stipulate   A voluntary agreement to take action or refrain from taking action

Stock certificate   Piece of paper that evidences one's ownership interest in a corporation

Strict liability   Imposition of liability on a party even when no fault is shown and party exercised reasonable care; usually imposed for inherently dangerous conditions and activities

Study group   A small group of students who work together to study class material

Subject matter jurisdiction   The power of a court to hear a certain kind of case

Sublease   Transfer of rented premises to another for less than the term of the original lease

Subpoena   Court order directing a person to appear at trial or deposition

Subpoena duces tecum   Court order directing a person to produce certain documents

Substantive law   Law that defines and regulates rights and obligations, such as real property law or contract law

Success fee   Excess fees paid by client to attorney or law firm for achieving certain preestablished goals

Summary dissolution   Form of divorce recognized by many states that expeditiously ends a marriage, usually one of short duration and with few assets

Summary judgment   Entry by court of pre-trial judgment for a party who shows there are no material triable issues of fact; eliminates need for trial

Summons   Document issued by court ordering a party to appear before the court

Supplement   Softcover book that updates a hardcover volume

Support staff   In a law firm, personnel other than attorneys and paralegals

Synthesizing   Method of analyzing cases by showing differences in cases

Temporary restraining order   Temporary order issued by court to prevent a person from taking certain action

Tenancy at will   Rental of property for no specific term or duration

Tenancy in common   Type of land ownership in which multiple parties own land; on death of one owner, his or her interest passes to heirs, not to other tenant(s) in common

Tenant   One who rents real property from landlord (sometimes called *lessee*)

Testamentary trust   Trust created by will

Testator   Male who makes a will

Testatrix   Female who makes a will

Testimonial evidence Evidence consisting of a witness's testimony under oath

Third-party beneficiary Party who receives some benefit from a contract or transaction although he or she is not a party to the contract or transaction

Third-party plaintiff A defendant who makes a claim against one not a party to pending litigation

Third-party practice A claim by a defendant against one not a party to pending litigation

Tickler system Method of providing reminders to individuals of tasks that need completion or action or that have pending deadlines

Timekeeping In law, practice of tracking and entering time spent on client and other work

Title examination Review of records pertaining to parcel of real property

Title insurance Insurance policy that guarantees that title to parcel of real property is clear

Titles Categories of statutes

Tort Civil wrong; may be intentional or based on negligence or strict liability

Toxic tort Wrongful act in which injury arises from harmful chemicals, pollutants, or the like

Traditional paralegal A paralegal who works under the supervision of an attorney, usually in a law firm, corporate law department, or governmental agency

Transaction fee Fee paid by client for work performed on an entire matter or transaction

Transactional document Document such as a contract used in a legal transaction

Transactional work In law, legal work related to business transactions rather than litigation-oriented work

Transcript Booklet providing testimony of witnesses at depositions or trial

Treatise Book or text on a legal topic that is written by expert author(s)

Trespass Wrongful entry on another's land

Trial brief Written argument submitted to a trial court (see *Brief*)

Trial notebook Binder prepared for trial with all information and documents needed at trial

Trust Document that provides for handling of property during person's lifetime or after death

Trust account Special, segregated interest-earning accounts for client funds

Trustee The person to whom legal title to trust assets is conveyed

Trustor The person who establishes a trust (sometimes called *grantor* or *settlor*)

Unauthorized practice of law Practicing of law by one without a license to do so; usually called *UPL*

Unconscionable contract Contract that is oppressive and unreasonable

Unfriendly witness Witness who is hostile to party's position

Uniform Commercial Code Uniform law adopted by all states except Louisiana governing contracts and the sale of goods

Unlawful detainer Name of action by which landlord evicts tenant from leased premises

Unofficial Private publication of law or case; publication not mandated by statute

Unofficial reporter Case book publishing cases without direction by statute or court rule

UPL See *Unauthorized practice of law*

Venue The appropriate locality for a trial

Verified Process of swearing under penalty of perjury that a pleading is true

Visitation rights Court order allowing a parent to see a child on a specified schedule

Voir dire The process of questioning prospective jurors

Voluntary petition In bankruptcy, a proceeding initiated by a debtor

War room In law firm, location for trial preparation, document production, and other trial-related activities

Will Document that declares how a person's property should be distributed on death

Witness statement Written record of a witness's interview, signed by witness

Work product Written mental impressions, conclusions, and opinions of attorneys and paralegals; need not be disclosed to others

INDEX